RUSSIAN POSTMODERNISM

RUSSIAN POSTMODERNISM

New Perspectives on Post-Soviet Culture

Mikhail Epstein, Alexander Genis,
and Slobodanka Vladiv-Glover

Translated by

Slobodanka Vladiv-Glover

First published in 1999
Revised edition published in 2016 by
Berghahn Books

Library of Congress Cataloging-in-Publication Data

Epstein, Mikhail, author.
Russian postmodernism : new perspectives on late Soviet and post-Soviet culture / Mikhail Epstein, Alexander Genis and Slobodanka Vladiv-Glover ; translated by Slobodanka Vladiv-Glover. — Second edition.
pages cm
Includes bibliographical references and index.
ISBN 978-1-78238-864-7 (pbk. : acid-free paper) —
ISBN 978-1-78238-865-4 (ebook)
1. Russian literature—20th century—History and criticism. 2. Postmodernism (Literature)—Soviet Union. 3. Postmodernism (Literature)—Russia (Federation) I. Genis, Aleksandr, 1953– author. II. Vladiv-Glover, Slobodanka, author. III. Title.
PG3026.P67E67 2015
891.709'0044—dc23
2015004789

British Library Cataloguing in Publication Data

A catalogue record for this book is available from the British Library.

ISBN 978-1-78238-864-7 paperback
ISBN 978-1-78238-865-4 ebook

CONTENTS

Preface to the First Edition

Thomas Epstein

Like its Western counterpart, Russian postmodernism and the discourse surrounding it have proven to be a vast, rich, and diverse storehouse of competing ideas and aesthetics. Alternately intriguing and maddening, insightful and bombastic, humble and totalitarian, Russian postmodernism and its discourse raise questions, some of them quite unpleasant, that are nevertheless fundamental to the cultural experience of the last third of the twentieth century.

The instructiveness of the Russian case is in part a result of its "unnaturalness": appearing with its all too familiar temporal lag (in this case, a result of decades of censorship and other forms of repression of the cultural process), Russian postmodernism presents a concentrated, intellectualized, and accelerated form of the phenomenon. Always taken with extremes, Russia has once again "caught up," and with a vengeance, producing a body of challenging, sophisticated, and sometimes extremely radical postmodern texts. This is no less true for the discourse *on* postmodernism, as the present volume demonstrates.

Given the deconstructionist underpinnings of much postmodern discourse, it is only natural that we begin with a question for which we do not claim to have a definitive answer: "Just what is Russian postmodernism?" Is it merely one cultural trend among others, foregrounding "play with the signifier," parody, de-centered discourse, and the absence of an organizing self? Or is postmodernism as such part of a larger cultural paradigm, the Postmodern, marked by a sense of fragmentation and historical breakdown or transition, to which artists of various stripes (Joseph Brodsky is but one telling example) have reacted, each in his or her own way? By this latter definition, we could talk about a Russian postmodern *period* in which the role of the avant-garde has been played by the postmodern*ists*, largely synonymous with Moscow conceptualism. Finally, from the outside, might we not speak of postmodern discourse as but another example of the tyranny of the theoretical, ideological, and reductionistic over the diversity of real phenomena?

One thing is certain: Russian literature of the period stretching from the late 1960s to the present has been remarkably productive. It includes such canonically Russian and Soviet-Russian authors as Alexander Solzhenitsyn and Joseph Brodsky, the neo-modernists Voznesensky and Evtushenko, the Romantic lyricism of Akhmadulina, the traditional avant-garde aesthetics of Sapgir, Aigi, and Vsevolod Nekrasov, the post-symbolism of the "metarealists" Zhdanov, Shvarts, Krivulin, and Sedakova, the various forms of polystylistics (including Iskrenko, Eremenko, Parshchikov, and Dragomoshchenko, some of which is akin to American "language poetry"), and the postmodern visual arts avant-garde itself, led by the conceptualists Kabakov and Bulatov on one side, and the *sots-artists*[1] Komar and Melamid on the other, which has found its most accomplished verbal embodiments in the poetry of Dmitri Prigov and Lev Rubinshtein, and in the uncompromisingly scatological prose of Vladimir Sorokin.[2]

Although some theorists of Russian postmodernism have argued in favor of identifying socialist realism as the first manifestation of the postmodern spirit in Soviet culture,[3] as a practical matter (that is, as a self-conscious movement) Russian verbal postmodernism was born in the early 1970s with the emergence of Moscow conceptualism, initially an art movement inspired by Joseph Kosuth's conceptualism[4] but which struck deep roots in the Soviet soil: using quotation, silence, and a parodic conformism as their tools, poets such as Prigov and Rubinshtein reached a "zero degree" of writing. Setting language against itself, they exposed the illusions of the self, the overdeterminations of ideology and monological discourse, thereby opening Soviet-Russian culture to the experience of *silence,* the something (or no-thing) that lies beyond. One of the central merits of the work here introduced is its highlighting of the spiritual and religious dimensions of this process; indeed the spiritualization of the postmodern aesthetic (or ethic) may be the most important distinction between Soviet-Russian and Western postmodernism.

Even more so than in the West, the 1970s and 1980s in Russia were a period of "post-history" (a period later to be called the era of "stagnation" by Soviet ideologues). Both officially and in theory, Soviet society had reached the paradise of communism, annulling history and time. However, while in practice the official culture continued to enforce a narrow, generally socialist-realist, aesthetic, in the underground a massive avant-garde flourished.[5] Marginalized from the centers of official culture (in sociological terms, this official culture can be construed as roughly equivalent, mutatis mutandis, to Western popular culture), the writers, artists, and poets of the underground were free to organize themselves into bands of like-minded brethren, living outside the march of time. Employed as laborers, night watchmen, or not at all, they in fact lived for and through literature (an already venerable tradition in a country notorious for difficult *living* conditions). Whether using this intense engagement with culture for purposes of parody (as was essentially the case with the conceptualists) or for reconnecting with Russian spiritual and avant-garde traditions, in particular with the not yet canonic Khlebnikov, Mandel'shtam, and Tsvetaeva, and the Oberiu poets Harms, Oleinikov, and Vvedensky (who themselves lived on the margins of official culture until their ultimate annihilation), these writers created a ready-made canon—or anti-canon—that burst into the mainstream during the latter half of *perestroika* (that is, after the exhaustion of the dissident culture that had taken center stage in the mid-to late 1980s). Not surprisingly, the results of this integration were paradoxical: while in a purely literary sense the aesthetic and spiritual values of the likes of Shvarts, Zhdanov, Rubinshtein, and Prigov clearly won the day, definitively reconnecting Russia with a variety of "lost" modernist traditions, this same emergence into the public eye, and the gaining of general public respectability that followed, turned into a kind of death-knell for the underground culture itself.

The situation was especially traumatic for the conceptualists: not only were they deprived of a subject matter as a result of the disappearance of a Soviet culture against which to set oneself, but the apophatic undercurrent of this "weak" and "impoverished" culture[6] was swallowed up in a several year orgy of postmodernism and the discourse on postmodernism. Played out in newspapers and on television, the term became an ideological bludgeon for a new wave of pseudo-Westernizers and Slavophiles who, depending on their point of view, saw it as a bearer of freedom or chaos, aestheticism or decadence, cultural rebirth or national death. In any case, the end of the Soviet era signaled (and is still signaling, for the process is ongoing) a redefinition, not only of the Soviet conceptualist avant-garde project but of Russian culture as a whole. Russia has entered, or is trying to enter, a new, confusing, and as yet unnamed period, dominated by material values.[7]

This, then, is a propitious moment to ask the question: "What *was* Russian postmodernism?" And: "What will come after it?" The selection of essays presented here, along with the "Who's Who in Russian Postmodernism" and a select bibliography, strives to begin this process. In her essays, Professor Slobodanka Vladiv-Glover applies the poststructuralist and post-Freudian insights of Jacques Lacan, Michel Foucault, and Jacques Derrida to the materials of Soviet postmodern culture, producing most interesting results. Alexander Genis, popular author, literary journalist and host of the radio broadcast "Above the Barriers" on Radio Liberty, incisively describes the immediate cultural context and deeper ramifications of the emergence of several of the leading Russian postmodern prose writers, especially Andrey Sinyavsky, Viktor Pelevin, and Vladimir Sorokin. Mikhail Epstein, who along with Boris Groys is the chief theoretician of Russian postmodernism, presents, under the rubrics *Literary Manifestos* and *Cultural Manifestos,* a contemporaneous description of the processes and attitudes associated with the creators and creations of Russian postmodern culture; in the longer essays he both holds a brief for Russian postmodernism and suggests a potential path of development for its future.

Unlike the Marxists and conservatives, Genis, Epstein, and Vladiv-Glover view postmodernism relatively optimistically, as the first stage in the emergence of a new kind of creativity. Having broken free of the monological, overdetermined world, we are now free either to see our nothingness as a positive foundation for future creativity (Genis), or to use quotationality and subsequent "disquotation" as a means of overcoming our own secondariness (Epstein). As Epstein writes in "The Age of Universalism":

> That is why contemporary art, literature, and philosophy are displaying a symbiosis of genres and methods, as well as translating one discourse into another. By contaminating images and concepts from various epochs and systems, contemporary culture strives to create a metalanguage of universal applicability. At the same time, at the point of collision between the various discourses, an awareness of their individuality and simultaneous transcending of their enclosed particularity emerges, producing elements of irony and parody without which no serious contemporary work of art can be created. However, it would be a grave mistake to take this by-product as its ground, that is, to regard the parodic as the ultimate horizon of contemporary art. This mistake is made by certain theoreticians of postmodernism and the trans-avant-garde in the West. The meaning of the process now being witnessed is not in the ridiculing of the pretentiousness and limitations of all existing mono-languages. It is in transcending these limitations and emerging onto the plane of a metalanguage which is that of a universalist creativity.[8]

As Epstein and others see it, the next stage in this rise of universalist creativity can be called the "new sincerity," which emerges on the other side of the parodic and the merely playful. Not a simple negation, this bracketing of the modernist and postmodernist projects creates the conditions for the emergence of a new, multidimensional discourse that promises a deeper form of *communication.* Only time will tell whether or not these speculations prove correct: what does seem certain is that Russian literature of the last third of the twentieth century has provided a vigorous and vital starting point for what is to come.

Notes

1. *Sots-art*: an art movement that conflates the principles of pop art and socialist realism.
2. This list is suggestive rather than exhaustive. It leaves out many of the authors taken up in the body of this book, including Venedikt Erofeev, Viktor Pelevin, Tatiana Tolstaia, Andrei Sinyavsky, Andrei Bitov, and Liudmila Petrushevskaia. See also the Appendix ("Who's Who in Russian Postmodernism") and the Select Bibliography at the end of this volume.
3. This is Mikhail Epstein's position (see, for example, "The Origins and Meaning of Russian Postmodernism," in Mikhail Epstein, *After the Future: The Paradoxes of Postmodernism and Contemporary Russian Culture*, trans. with Introduction by Anesa Miller-Pogacar (Amherst, Mass., 1995), pp. 188–210, and *The Slavic and Eastern European Journal* (Fall 1995), pp. 357–362. Boris Groys, by contrast, sees socialist realism as an extension of the "totalitarianism" of the historical avant-garde. On this subject, see *The Total Art of Stalinism: Avant-Garde, Aesthetic Dictatorship, and Beyond* (Princeton, 1992).
4. See Joseph Kosuth, *After Philosophy and After: Collected Writings 1966–1990* (Boston, 1991).
5. It should also be mentioned that a vigorous dissident culture, nurtured on ideological and social concerns, also flourished at this time, as well as a "quiet school" concerned with the individual and his or her private life.
6. See Mikhail Epstein's "Post-Atheism" and "The Charms of Entropy" in the present volume.
7. This is not to say that the authors studied in the present work are a dead letter for contemporary Russian culture. On the contrary: not only are many of them extremely active and sensitive to the new realities, but their works present a necessary starting point for what will come.
8. See chapter 13.

Preface to the Second Edition

Postmodernism and the Explosive Style of the Twenty-First Century

Mikhail Epstein

Now we can hardly doubt that the last third of the twentieth century will enter cultural history under the name of postmodernism. The beginning of the twenty first century reacted ambivalently to this heritage. Many concepts that postmodernism introduced into global culture are now undergoing revision in attempt to reappropriate what was lost or rejected during the previous thirty years. The practices of quotation, allusion, intertextuality, and the traits of irony and eclecticism are still current, as well as skepticism toward the universality of canons and hierarchies of all kinds. However, postmodernism, as it is perceived now, got stuck at the level of language games: it was obsessed with overcoding, subtexts, and metatextuality, and did not recognize anything outside this domain. By the early twenty-first century, this game continued by inertia alongside the new realities that challenged it: the Iraqi War, Chechnya, the dismemberment of Yugoslavia. … All these events took place far away from the United States, however, and major theoreticians such as Jean Baudrillard still were inclined to interpret them as postmodernist phenomena, including the mass media's control over the world scene and the information industry's games.

The limits of the game suddenly became starkly defined on September 11, 2001. The entire postmodernist era ended with deadly precision at 10:28 AM with the terrorist attack and collapse of the Twin Towers of the World Trade Center in New York City. Reality, authenticity, and uniqueness, the categories that postmodernism scorned, cruelly avenged themselves. The "ground zero" of 9/11 caused the present cultural cycle to hungrily absorb everything that the earlier epoch rejected: questions about life and death, the future, the eternal, love and suffering, hope and fear. Awareness of the vulnerability of the individual body and of humanity as a whole has grown more acute and, with it, so has the significance of the unique and the unrepeatable event which cannot be reduced to simulacra. The concept of "reality" no longer appears as ridiculously outmoded as it seemed twenty or thirty years ago.

The tonality and visuality of an explosion has become the archetypal and apocalyptic pattern of our time, and has entered its flesh and blood. Everything is exploding: planes, skyscrapers, cars, ships, trains, cities, banks, corporations, embassies, budgets, economies, states. Explosiveness is the core of contemporary sensibility. *Explositivism* (rhyming with "positivism" but constituting its opposite) is the dominant style of our times.

The explosion of 2001 became the "big bang" of the third millennium and determined the dynamics of today's civilization. This cataclysm was followed by another, no less intense and extensive—the economic crisis of 2008–10. Its waves spread outward from the tiny and humbly named "Wall Street," which is only a stone's throw from where the Twin Towers stood. The meaning of this explosion was the same as the one that shook New York seven years earlier. This new explosion represented the bursting of the bubbles of signs, the crash of the inflated world of simulacra created by the banks, of unsecured credits—signifiers whose signifieds were despised or forgotten. Thus the explosion of 2008, like the one of 2001, was a return to that neglected "reality," which in the not-too-distant past had looked like an obsolete word from the pre-postmodernist era. The history of the transformation of the "postmodern" style into the "explosivist" style is bounded by these two explosions at the beginning and end of the decade.

A century ago one of founders of Russian Futurism, Aleksei Kruchenykh, published a small homemade book called *Vzorval'* (1913), a manifesto of avant-garde poetry and visual art. The title, a neologism derived from the Russian verb meaning "to explode," can be rendered as "explozance." The opening lines of a similarly entitled poem from the manifesto run:

> the explozance of flames
> the sadness of the steed...

"Explozance" is an exact and expressive name for the avant-garde sensibility. It also conveyed a prophetic foreboding about the possible outbreak of a world war. The beginning of the twenty-first century obviously revives the provocative and explosive style of the early twentieth-century avant-garde. Paradoxically, this "explozance" arrives now *after* postmodernism and absorbs its weariness, detachment, and aestheticism.

One of the representatives of the new "explosivist" wave, the American composer John Adams, a key figure of musical postmodernism, composed a piece entitled "On the Transmigration of Souls" which was performed on the first anniversary of September 11. The genre of this Pulitzer Prize-winning composition for chorus and orchestra is defined by Adams as "the space of memory." A children's choir sings fragments from missing-persons signs posted at ground zero in the days after the attack: the names of the deceased and the notices hung up by relatives searching among the ruins for their loved ones. These texts are very simple: the descriptions of persons sought, and invocations such as, "Please, come back! We are waiting for you. We love you," or, "She looks alive in this photo."

Adams found inspiration for his composition when he saw footage of the burning skyscrapers, out of which millions of pieces of paper flew, covering the sky like a snowstorm: all the documents, faxes, graphics, circulars, letters, notes, the whole paper paraphernalia of civilization, slowly floating down to earth while the souls of their owners were soaring up to heaven. Adams's composition demonstrates the limits of postmodern "pantextualism" in its overcoming. Textuality itself is replete with existential tension that explodes the conventional borders of verbality and bursts beyond the confines of the signs to convey the absolute disaster and irrevocability of human loss together with the irresistible movement of human souls to other worlds.

Contemporary aesthetics, in the most general sense, combines stylistic enervation and the pluralism inherited from postmodernism with an inner tension, vulnerability and a low pain threshold: every vein in the gigantic organism of our well-maintained civilization can burst any minute. The possible causes are manifold: eco-catastrophe or techno-catastrophe, religious wars or information viruses. Or perhaps the main cause is fear elicited by all these causes, their self-fulfilling prophecies, resulting in a state of horror, a fear in the face of the possible, which exceeds the reality of the terror itself.

The premonition of total explosivity intensifies the feeling of life. The art of simulation and the technology of copying and cloning now form a strange symbiosis with the new vitalism and humanism. This facet of the sensibility of the twenty-first century could be described as "*techno-vitalism,*" a tragicomic blend of the two contrasting tendencies that underscore each other. On one hand, the Latin root *vit* (*vita,* meaning "life") is disappearing from language, more and more frequently replaced by roots *virt* ("virtual," imaginary, simulated) or *vitr* ("in vitro," in an artificial environment). Technology reigns supreme, the virtual realm is closing in, television and computer screens are constantly expanding in size, zones of wireless connections proliferate; communication is transparent and flows effortlessly from one channel into another, creating a techno-utopia in the spirit of Aldous Huxley. On the other hand, the human being appears naked and vulnerable in its pathetic mortal flesh, exposed to a piercing sense of finitude. The world is "undressed" in an existential sense, just as in Andrei Platonov's novels of the Stalin's era. Interestingly, *The Foundation Pit* and *Brave New World* were written at almost the same time, month to month, at the beginning of the 1930s, at the crest of the global modernist wave.

Now, in the mid–2010s, we witness the upsurge of the new modernist anxiety following decades of postmodernist playful relaxation. A new sense of the time, a new creative will, directed at something unheard of and unique are coming to displace postmodernism's recycling of the styles of earlier epochs. This forms the novelty of our "foundation pit," our "zero" cycle of the twenty-first century. Postmodernism was inclined to glide over the surfaces of things; it had a refined tactile sense and intentional superficiality. Techno-vitalism, on the contrary, is the art of touching the quick of things and turning them inside out: not to simulate them, but to stir them and shake them up. In the wake of all the matrixes, all semiotic systems, it is a new curiosity about real life that grips minds. Technology itself is perceived vitalistically, as something growing and living according to its own hidden laws.

Contemporary technologies are attempting to create artificial life and artificial intelligence, although these are distant possibilities at present. Closer at hand is our observation of a new, enigmatic form of life, technology itself, which multiplies by itself, absorbing all biological life which it also permeates through and through. Technology emerges as endowed with more vitality than many organisms that are ousted from our planet. Human beings, as a biological species, may find themselves among those organisms, as an object of a new nostalgia and sentimentality. At the beginning of the twenty-first century, we can witness a dramatic acceleration in the technization not only of the natural environment, but also of human beings.

* * *

The time has come for the humanities to reflect upon master this new style of "explozance." Many of the customary concepts of postmodernism are falling out of use. This is particularly true of "multiculturalism," which was the dominant regulating principle in the humanistic disciplines from the 1980s. It was thought that of the variety of cultures, each one is self-sufficient and self-reproductive, grounded in its own bio-psychological determinants. This conception of identities equal to themselves is no longer valid for the explosive development of civilization at the beginning of the twenty-first century.

We should recall that the "classical" postmodernism of the 1980s – 1990s had two main theoretical constituents: *multiculturalism* and *deconstruction.* As it turns out, the contradiction between these two major systems of thought is capable of exploding postmodernism from inside. In the past, their tension remained mostly unnoticed and did not reach the consciousness of either side from fear of weakening their unity in the face of a common enemy: the establishment, logocentrism, Eurocentrism, the cultural canon, and so forth.

What is this contradiction? Multiculturalism is an affirmation of an all-embracing determinism that reduces every cultural act to the constraints of its original nature, its racial, ethnic, and gender origins. Deconstruction, by contrast, rebels against any kind of determinism, erasing the very notion of origins, of authenticity, of genealogy. What is accorded primacy in the deterministic approach to culture is secondary from the deconstructionist viewpoint; what we consider to be our "origins," our "source," and our tradition is something that we determine ourselves. We shape our own identity. Race, ethnicity, even gender and sex—all of these are only social constructs, determined by our choices and our method of thinking.

One cannot deny the multicultural thesis that we differ from each other through our nature and identity, that each one of us is born either male or female, with our own skin color and psychological makeup. However, it is precisely deconstruction that points out the vector of evolution: we shed our nature and reinvent ourselves in the course of our cultural formation and self-expression. We resemble ourselves less and less as we spiritually mature. The greatest cultural breakthroughs occur at the boundaries between cultures, when a representative of one ethnic group ends up in the domain of another, or when a man finds himself in the realm of feminine culture, or vice versa. Crossing the borders between languages, ethnicities, and all sorts of other identities is the source of the most intense cultural creativity. It tends to weaken and become inertial or trivial as soon as it finds itself in the normative and homogeneous medium of its "own" culture, far from its boundaries.

Some examples of this intersection at the cultural border: Russo-French and Russo-English cultural bilingualism created the most brilliant specimens of Russian writing, from Pushkin and Lermontov to Nabokov and Brodsky. To various degrees, Dostoevsky, Turgenev and Tolstoy, Pasternak and Tsvetaeva were all bilingual and even multilingual. By contrast, while Russia remained monolingual and monocultural up to Peter's reforms, no cultural breakthroughs took place, and no literature of world significance was created.

Obviously, a natural identity has its own cultural value, but to be limited by it, to rivet oneself to it with chains of "belonging" and "representativeness," means to make a prison of it. In other words, I am willing to acknowledge my identity at the beginning of the way, but I refuse to remain bound to this identity to the end of my life, and to be determined by my race, nationality, and class. Culture is meaningful only as far as it transforms our nature, renders us "apostates" of our identities.

Why do I watch movies, go to museums, read books and ultimately write them? Is it in order to preserve my identity? No, I do all these things in order to find someone else within me, someone who is not me, and to partake of the experiences of other beings and existences, to undergo a series of historical and psychological metamorphoses. Culture is a metempsychosis, the *transmigration of souls* from one body into another, even while a person is still alive. It is true that we are born in separate natural and social cells, but we escape these by different ways in many directions. The encounters between the fugitives from various cells constitute culture. The figure of the renegade, the refugee, or the subversive who explodes his or her own culture is gaining in significance.

In this way the domain of cultural explosions grows: *transculture* replaces multiculturalism. Transculture is a new sphere of cultural evolution beyond the confines of established national, racial, gender, and even professional cultures. It is the space of "outsideness" or "not-being-found-there," which is the domain of freedom for every human being who wants to live at or beyond the limits of native culture. This invokes Hannah Arendt's notion of an "enlarged mentality" that frees us from the constraints of subjectivity through the encounter with the reality of otherness.

Let us recall that culture frees the human being from the dictates of nature. The culture of food or the culture of desire—expressed in ritual feasts and courtship etiquette—is the freedom from the inborn instincts of hunger and lust. Culture is the creative delay, the symbolic mastery of the instincts and their conscious gratification. However, if culture liberates the human being from the physical dependence and determination of nature, then transculture is the next level of liberation, freedom from the unconscious symbolic dependence on one's "native culture" and its predispositions and prejudices.

* * *

I am writing this preface to the second edition of *Russian Postmodernism* in a very difficult and fateful moment of Russian history. The first edition (1999) came out during the end of the Yeltsin epoch, which created an unprecedented openness in Russia toward world civilization, when all the curtains dividing it from the West appeared to be torn down for good. The second edition is being prepared at a historic moment, when humanity is commemorating the hundredth anniversary of World War I, fearful of the threat of a third world war which could be triggered by events in Ukraine. It is becoming clear that Russia, not having managed to solve the problems of its inner modernization, is again closing itself off from the world, preparing for a return to a pre-Petrine era, namely Old Muscovy.

In this context, postmodernism in Russia is placed under a question mark. If the country finds itself again thrown back to the premodern past, if all the attempts at modernization made since Peter the Great fail, what will be the fate of its postmodernist heritage? Will the postmodern phenomenon remain an exotic flower in the cultural history of Russia as a rogue state who could only for a short time, in the interval between the USSR and Putin's "New Muscovy," catch up with the civilized world, only to become hopelessly retarded again, and irrevocably? Or is postmodernism, as an experiment in overcoming the totalitarian consciousness, a salutary inoculation against the spiritual malaise of the new ideocracy, which is no longer Marxist but even more narrow and hopeless, based on imperialistic and chauvinist fervor?

Russia has always been a country with pronounced transcultural drives, dreaming of "the universal," "the panhuman," even in the Soviet epoch with its proclaimed "internationalism." In 2014–2015, the majority of the population chooses the "metanarrative" of Russianness or "Eurasianism," the self-propagating expansion of the "Russian world," the affirmation of its ethnic state identity. It would have been hard to imagine that, having cast off the Soviet system in a resolute and bloodless manner, Russia would seek to go back to the most dogmatic and repressive period of its history—manifested as a war on cosmopolitanism and the wish to erect a new iron curtain.

In the West, postmodernism is often perceived as a dead metaphor, a nostalgic memory of a "beautiful epoch" at the end of the twentieth century. In Russia, postmodernism as an experiment in deconstruction and the relativization of any totalitarian project is still looking toward the future, and it can turn out to be an effective weapon against the fundamentalist, parochial, and mythological monsters that are currently being forced from the depth of the national unconscious by the hysterical propaganda of the authorities.

Postmodernism in Russia has not yet accomplished its historical task. The more the country slides back into the premodern past, the more it is in need of the values of postmodernism: the stylistics of softness and plasticity, ethical tolerance and openness, and the ability to put the particular, the unique and the fragmentary above the totalitarian whole.

Paradoxical as it may sound, the destiny of Russia's modernization will depend on how well Russia can assimilate its own postmodern heritage, which draws it closer to the West than any other cultural trend.

* * *

The second edition contains several new sections: Mikhail Epstein's preface and chapters "Postmodernism, Communism, and Sots-Art" and "The Philosophical Implications of Russian Conceptualism";

Slobodanka Vladiv-Glover's introduction "'New Sectarianism' and the Pleasure Principle in Postmodern Russian Culture." The selected bibliography has been expanded and updated.

August 2014

INTRODUCTION

"New Sectarianism" and the Pleasure Principle in Postmodern Russian Culture

Slobodanka Vladiv-Glover

About three decades have elapsed since the Soviet cultural monolith dissolved into a myriad of heterogeneous parts, dispersing geographically into newly constituted national spaces and fast-forwarding in time to a post-postmodernism only sketchily anticipated in the first edition of this book in 1999.

While the origins of Russian postmodernism were well mapped in the first edition of *Russian Postmodernism: New Perspectives on Post-Soviet Culture,* and while this book was universally acknowledged as one of the first in the field,[1] the time seems ripe for a second edition. Recent events in the Russian cultural and political space appear to have taken Russia a step back in time, to a kind of retro- or reconstituted Soviet culture. Its representation can only be part of a negative dialectic if it is to be a truthful interpretation of Russian reality of the past decade and a half. In this introduction, two of the authors of the first edition will attempt to summarize the salient developments in Russian culture since 1999, or rather, the representation of these in the dominant forms in which they were manifested since *perestroika.*

The period of 1999 to 2014, with all its heterogeneity, can best be analyzed through the lens of popular or mass culture and the revaluation of value that the advent of post-*perestroika* mass culture in Russia entailed. This mass culture did not spring up overnight, as was the case of Russian postmodernism, which came out of the "underground" suddenly in the 1980s, revealing its 1960s roots.

This mass culture was in the making in the decades before *perestroika,* in the 1970s and 1980s, creating the conditions of possibility for a mass culture to appear and be represented as appearance in Russian culture (literature, cinema, music) after the fall of the USSR and the descent of Russia into consumerism and globalism.

One of the authors, Mikhail Epstein, has captured the phenomenon of mass culture value under the caption of "new sectarianism." This caption is used as an analytic tool by another author, Slobodanka Vladiv-Glover, to examine the value system of the "new Russia" and the "new Russians" as portrayed by Russians themselves in literature and film.

Epstein's "New Sectarianism"

In his 1985 tractate, *Novoe sektantstvo: tipy religiozno-filosofskikh umonastroenii v Rossii* (*New Sectarianism: Varieties of Religious-Philosophical Sentiment in Russia*),[2] Mikhail Epstein adopts an approach to the issue of value in the "new Russia" that is reminiscent of the treatment of religious sentiment in Tolstoy's aesthetic tractate *What Is Art?* (1899).[3] Just as Tolstoy uses the concept of "religious feeling" of an age to designate the value system of that age in terms of what is right and what is wrong, so Epstein uses the term *sektantstvo* as a code word for a system of "value" or "belief" with a slight parodic undertone, which points to his critique of the value system of the "new Russia." Epstein's "new sectarianism" is a metaphor and umbrella term, encompassing a whole range of shades of beliefs, from atheism to mysticism, allegedly manifested in Russia in the 1970s and 1980s. While Tolstoy's critique of value sets off from the revaluation of the value system ("religious feeling") of his own gentry class, Epstein's *Novoe sektantstvo* is a survey of the beliefs or "ideologies" of the Russian intelligentsia, notably its Moscow circles ("ottenki religioznykh umonastroenii, kotorye byli rasprostraneny v srede intelligentsia" ["shades of religious sentiments, which were widespread amongst the intelligentsia of the capital"])[4] in the 1970s and 1980s. This is how Epstein defines "new sectarianism":

> To, chto ia nazyvaiu novym sektantstvom—eto, po suti, vyrazhennaia v religioznykh poniatiiakh ideologiia nashei intelligentsii, tochnee, summa takikh ideologii, raskhodiashchikhsia po radiusam vo vse storony ot "tsentra" gosudarstvennoi ideologii.[5]

Epstein's book is a futuristic composition, in the sense of the Russian Futurists and the tradition of the literature of the absurd, which maps, in carnivalesque and parodic style, the proliferation of ideologies existing side by side with the central state ideology of scientific communism and the aesthetics of socialist realism. This mapping is allegedly based on questionnaires, administered during "three expeditions or field work stints, undertaken in 1975, 1979 and 1983."[6] During this "field work," the most varied evidence and testimonies were gathered, which the author claims to analyze in his book on "new sectarianism."

The author's own explanation of these "testimonies" is given in the postscript of the book. Here the author explains "why abstract conceptions have made such a decisive imprint on the history of the twentieth century. One possible aftermath of totalitarian ideology is the proliferation of multiple ideologies, which nevertheless remain totalitarian in their particular fields. Such is the situation in the former Soviet Union now [the book was written in the USA in 1992]: dozens of totalitarianisms cannot make up for a single pluralism."[7]

As can be seen from this "baring of the device" (as the Russian Formalists called the technique of disclosure of the principles of form in a work of art), Epstein's book is a culturological diagnosis of what Epstein calls the *Comedy of Ideas* (alluding to Dante's *Divine Comedy,* Balzac's *Human Comedy,* and Flaubert's "Dictionary of Received Ideas") which "plagued" Russian culture in the twentieth century. Thus Epstein discusses, under quasi-comical names, which are his own neologisms,[8] a series of sects that try to invest daily life with religious content. One such sect is called *pishchesviatsy*—"foodniks"[9] (as in published translation), "food saints," or "food gurus." All eating activities are linked by this sect to religious ritual and religious concepts. The very posture in which one eats is likened to humility (*smirenie*). The host of a dinner is said to represent a figure of respect since he is the likeness of the Father, "whose flesh created you." The dinner guest should also be respected as he is the image of the Son, "who nourishes himself on your flesh."[10] This view arises, one infers, as a reaction to the materialist view of history. A veiled swipe at the Marxist view of history as a process of production of food is rendered in sarcastic terms but from a new sectarian point of view, which can also not be taken without a grain of salt by the reader. Thus one sectarian (Marxist) view is replaced by an equally ("fundamentalist") sectarian ("fundamentalist") view, as can be seen from the following passage:

> Vsia istoriia stala rassmatryvatsia kak istoriia dobyvaniia pishchi, kak smena orudii i sposobov ee proizvodstva. Bylo skazano, chto prezhde chem myslit' i verit', chelovek dozlhen est' i pit', vosproizvodit' svoe telo. Eta teoriia vyshla iz pishchesviatskikh krugov, no postepenno priobrela kharakter iazycheskogo pishchepoklonstva.... Nam nuzhna filosofiia, kotoraia nachinala by s goloda, no prikhodila by ne k zrecheskomu pokloneniiu materii, a k zhertvennosti i shchedrosti samogo vselennogo materinstva, ot Otsa zachinaiushchego i kormiashchego grud'iu zemli chelovecheskoe ditia.[11]
>
> [History is regarded as a process of food manufacture, and of the evolution of tools and methods for its production. It was said that before thinking and believing, man had to eat and drink, manufacturing his own body. This theory emerged from the circles of "food saints" or "food gurus" but gradually acquired the dimensions of a pagan worship of food.... We need a philosophy which would start off from hunger, which would lead not to a pagan worship of matter but to sacrifice and generosity of the ecumenical Motherhood, from a Father who sires and feeds the human child with the sod of the earth.]

Another intellectual sect catalogued in Epstein's "theo-genealogy" bears the name of the Ark People (*kovchezhniki*), alluding to Noah's Ark as a symbol of survival after an apocalyptic event. This sect belongs, according to Epstein, to an eschatological religious stream in Russian and Western thought, whose followers believed in the salvation of a select few and who spent the best part of their lives building houses of shelter against the coming apocalypse. They were saved, according to Epstein, not because of their foresight but because humanity at large was wise enough to avert a nuclear holocaust.[12]

Epstein's witty, carnivalesque representation of ideologies circulating in the last two decades of the former Soviet Union is, as he says, a diagnosis of various forms of "fundamentalisms" which that had multiplied along the lines of the original totalitarian ideology of Marxism-Leninism. The inference which that can be drawn from Epstein's huge catalogue of ideologies—but which Epstein himself does not draw—is that in the face of so many competing value systems, none can be taken as the master narrative. In other words, "value" as a cultural construct in the Soviet Union of the 1970s and 1980s was already without essence and true obligation. Value was already, towards the end of the history of the Soviet system, value free, on a par with a fad or a fashion. This society, in which ideologies proliferated, was in fact emptied of ideological content. The very description given to the period of the 1970s and pre-*perestroika* 1980s as that of stagnation (*zastoi*) indicates that it was a "static" or empty time. Epstein draws the inference that the proliferation of ideologies, which we would call fads, did not constitute a "single pluralism." While dependent on one's definition of "pluralism," it is still not logical to posit "one pluralism" as a kind of receptacle or "block" that houses a mix of diverse values in free relations to one another. If pluralism is anything, it is the absence of "one" value or the "One." Without realizing or spelling out the implications of his culturological survey, Epstein has uncovered the true "religious feeling" of the age of late-Soviet culture, which prepared the coming of post-Soviet culture and served as its groundless ground. This new post-Soviet "religious feeling" was precisely the proliferation of individual sentiment as the ground of "private" value—a value that was as capricious and as bereft of essentialism as the individual unconscious which originates in the Freudian death drive.

That Epstein's "survey" of the "religious" ideas of the age leads to the above inference is strengthened by the fact that this survey refrains from promoting any one of the ideologies represented in it as the "right" or desirable one. All ideologies are treated as comical; all are parodies of beliefs which are recognizable as existing fads, not only in late-Soviet culture, but also in the mass culture of Western societies.

As the 1990s passed and Russian culture turned to postmodern forms of expression, Epstein's tractate on "new sectarianism" has acquired a new prophetic force. It has also become a fitting model for the analysis of the representation of post-Soviet ideologies in the Russian cultural space of the late 1990s and early twenty-first century. It is to Epstein's credit to have created a "genealogy of morals" that still has theoretical force in the twenty-first century. Representing a plethora of beliefs and ideologies in the style of a freak show at a country fare, Epstein's book serves to underline the trends in post-Soviet aesthetics, as manifested in the poetics of some recent works of postmodern Russian culture—both literary and popular (in particular, cinema)—in which belief systems of the late-Soviet period linger on in various permutations. The cross-pollination of aesthetics and ethics is nothing new: the good and the beautiful have been closely associated since Aristotle's *Nichomachean Ethics.* In Tolstoy's *What Is Art?* it is ethics that determines good form—aesthetics—of the authentic work of art in the modern age. In postmodern Russian culture, it is a new post-Soviet ethics that grounds a new post-Soviet literature, which resembles the literature of the Absurd Absurd. In turn, this new postmodern Russian Absurd Absurd serves as a tool of critique of postmodern Russian culture.

Artistic Representations of "New Sectarianism": Sorokin's Novel *Led* and Film Scenario *Chetyre,* Aleksei Varlamov's *Zatonuvshii kovcheg*

Several recent post-Soviet works have particular resonance with Epstein's theses on "new sectarianism": one is Vladimir Sorokin's novel *Led* (*Ice*) (2002);[13] a second is Sorokin's film scenario *Chetyre* (*Four*) (2004); a third is Aleksei Varlamov's novella *Zatonuvshii kovcheg* (*The Sunken Treasure*) (2002). All three works represent aberrant belief systems which are portrayed as the result or as coming in the wake of cataclysmic events: the Nazi invasion of the Soviet Union in the case of *Led*; the implosion of the Soviet social order and the onset of "late capitalism" in postmodern Russia in the case of *Chetyre*; and the event of Russian "modernity," seen as a telescoping of Russian history from Peter the Great's times to the Soviet 1950s and beyond, into an indeterminate static "present," in the case of Varlamov's *Zatonuvshii kovcheg.* All three works deal with the theme of *izbrannichestvo*—the phenomenon of the select, the chosen people. All three works represent messianism as a type of exclusionary belief system.

The construction of identity through the self-perception of exclusivity or apartness is common to all types of religious communities. In the three works, these communities are treated as parodies. One such community is represented by Marina's village and Marina's sisters in Sorokin's *Chetyre*; another is constituted by the "blond children" in Sorokin's *Led,* who are randomly segregated by the retreating Nazi army for membership of an exclusive sect whose initiates communicate directly with their hearts—a parody on the Nazi myth of a superior Aryan race and on all forms of sentimentality bred by totalitarian ideologies or utopias. Finally, the theme of *izbrannichestvo* is portrayed through Masha, the village *yurodivaya* (Fool-in-Christ character) in Aleksei Varlamov's novel, who is a different symbol to different believers—the rational utopians (represented by the teacher, Ilya Petrovich), the genuine Old Believers, and the apostate power-hungry impostors. However, the messianism of these various groups does not construct a future utopia. Their concern is strictly with a present in which the dominant force in the lives of the characters represented in all the named works is not thought (rational belief) but feeling and pleasure. In Sorokin's *Led,* the exclusivity of the select group is based on the ability of the heart to withstand the test of a blow with a mallet made of ice. The group of the select is united in rituals of communion in which direct communication of feeling is possible. While these aberrant rituals resemble sexual orgies, it is an ambivalent sexuality, if any, that comes to light in these practices. It is as if the "new religious" feeling of the "sentimental sect" (which resonates with several sects described in Epstein's catalogue) in Sorokin's *Led* were grounded in a sexuality without content, or a sexless sexuality. The emptiness that characterizes the ideologies of the 1980s in Epstein's catalogue is here replicated on the psychic level: the psyche of the heroine, Varka Samsikova (alias Khram), is dreamy (as was the psyche of the Modernist *femme fatale,* such as Alexander Blok's Stranger and other Modernist heroines), but this is a dreaminess without full-blooded sensuality, without contact with the libido. It is sensuality at one remove from the person whose experience it is meant to be, and it somehow resembles alienation. This is underlined by the dramatic monologue of the heroine who narrates her experiences in a reduced post-postwar Germany and back in Russia as a member of the sect of the heart. The substitution of sect names for the proper names of the characters involved determines the nature of experience that is constructed through their narrative: substitution is there as an end in itself, constructing a process of signification that is without substance or content. It is infinite semiosis without substance or value. It is pure metonymy which, according to Lacan, *is* desire.[14] Thus sensuality as a source of pleasure or desire is a force, emptied of content, a pure drive without value.

The confrontation of so-called rational belief and fanatical belief is represented in some detail in Varlamov's *Zatonuvshii kovcheg* (an allusion to the *Hort of the Nibelungen* saga and the role it played in the construction of German identity in the recent past—namely the Modernist 1930s and 1940s, with their Nazi affiliations). However, the divide between the atheistic physics teacher and school director, Ilya Petrovich, and the villagers of a quasi-mythological Bukhara, whose closed community of Old Believers has its roots in Peter the Great's time, is fluid. Ilya Petrovich's rationalism is undermined by his "desire" for Masha Tsiganova, one of his pupils. Masha is destined for sainthood by her Old Believers' community when she survives a direct hit by lightning, and the village of Bukhara celebrates the "miracle" by a mass "moral conversion": everyone starts to behave in a more loving way, and drunken orgies and violence recede in the community. Masha, as Ilya Petrovich's repressed desire, is a symbol of the people—*narod.* The idealization of the peasants has been a hallmark of the Russian intelligentsia since the beginning of the nineteenth century, reaching its apotheosis in Pushkin's revolutionizing of the Russian poetic language by turning to the Russian vernacular in High Culture (giving rise to the myth of the influence of his peasant nanny—his *nyanya*). *Narodnichestvo* (populism) characterized the poetics of the Russian major writers, notably Tolstoy and Dostoevsky, who found the Russian people to be carriers of a national and universal ethical and moral principle. While Aleksei Varlamov displays great tenderness toward and deep sympathetic knowledge of a backward, rural Russia, he does not fall into the trap of romanticizing the Russian village. His postmodern gaze is a clinical gaze that dissects the membrane of Russian village culture, in contact with Russian/Soviet atheistic civilization, and yet apart. What emerges from his forensic analysis (like that of a forensic pathologist) is the closeness of the rational-atheistic Soviet Russia and the Old Believers' sectarian Russia. Both have roots in myth. One is the naïve and pure historical myth of salvation based on the idea of divine intercession, manifested in signs and miracles, such as the *moshchi Evstolii*—the remains or relics of Evstolia, a village woman who was killed by the village butcher, symbolizing sacrifice at the inception of a community and forming a Russian version of the Oedipal myth. The other is the myth of rational, scientific knowledge, which masks a repressed desire for an elusive primordial national identity, embodied in Ilya Petrovich's repressed transgressive desire for the underage Masha (*otrokovitsa*). What Varlamov's drama, set in a Breugelesque fictional taiga village called Bukhara, illuminates is that the Soviet rational belief and the Old Believers' fundamentalist belief are indistinguishable in strength or force. Both are drivers of human action and both are grounded in unconscious drives. The Old Believers' age-old isolation and ritual secrecy adds the dimension of the uncanny to the ground of belief. The Enlightenment project, pursued by Ilya Petrovich during his "scientific communism" period, has the appearance of transparent rationalism. However, this transparency is shattered by the revelation of his "secret" and transgressive passion for his pupil, Masha. Thus both the old and the new beliefs are grounded in secret desire, whose ultimate ground is pleasure.

The content of the ideologies becomes immaterial in Varlamov's novella. The Old Believers' faith is subject to manipulation by false gurus, while the rational scientific belief can flip over into its opposite—fanaticism and fundamentalism. This is precisely the path traced by the life of the teacher, Ilya Petrovich. From "physicist and lyricist" (he is a science teacher in the Soviet 1950s who is also writing a novel), Ilya Petrovich degenerates into a convict, a drunk, and then a hardened fanatic driven by the desire to rescue his beloved Masha—and the world—from the abuses of History. His utopian vision is to rescue humanity by "correcting the mistake of the Enlightenment," by creating a new civilization based on the amalgamation of the moral purity of the Bukhara Old Believers community and the highest achievements of human intellectual thought. Thus in Ilya Petrovich's utopian vision, progress is to be reconciled with religious belief or faith (*vera*).[15]

This is not something that is achieved at the end of Varlamov's novella. In fact, all progress in Bukhara—a metaphor for Russia itself—stops with the reincarnation of Ilya Petrovich as the new and ultimate *starets* and leader of the Bukhara commune, now reduced to seven women. In this diminished and aberrant community, in which there is only one male, the values of progress and Enlightenment have passed out of living memory. The Bukhara values, based on exclusivity and *izbrannichestvo,* on the other hand, persist but are now revealed in their true origins: individual desire and pleasure. For the whole task of the old *skit* (monastery) is now reduced to procreation: the latest Bukhara *starets* (a reincarnation of the village teacher, Ivan Petrovich), impregnates all the women of the monastery, who flock to him of their own free will and whose ecstatic cries behind the monastery walls are the envy of the villagers at large. Thus the "religious feeling" of the "new" Bukhara (aka "new" Russia) is the feeling of pleasure, grounded in the freedom and indeterminacy of the sex drive.

The Pleasure Principle instead of the Myth of the People

Sorokin's film scenario *Chetyre* paints a picture of contemporary "new Russia" of "late capitalism" as a sphere from which belief is absent. All the characters of the film represent remnants of the late-

Soviet society and its defunct belief system. There is, first of all, a pianist turned piano tuner, who is what remains of the Soviet artistic intelligentsia. Next, there is a young would-be Kremlin *appratchik* (bureaucrat serving the State apparatus) who is a black marketeer, dealing in the sale of frozen meat and cloned pigs. Finally, there is the heroine Marina, a young prostitute, the "new Russian" woman, who is the reincarnation of a simple Russian girl of the people, the kind of girl portrayed by Andrei Bitov in Lyubasha or Faina in his novel 1960s novel *Pushkin House* (completed in 1971 but published in Soviet Russia only in 1987, serialized in *Novy mir*) Marina is of the same age as a *komsomol* or Metropol girl of the late-Soviet system. However, unlike her Soviet counterparts of the 1950s to the 1980s, Marina's professional activity is not ideologically motivated. She is not a prostitute in the services of the Soviet state (the Metropol girls having been used by the KGB to monitor foreigners staying at the Metropol Hotel in Moscow and other hotels for international visitors). Marina's prostitution is strictly business—it is part of the new post-Soviet economy of the open market and individual enterprise, where everything is for sale. Unlike Bitov's Soviet heroines Faina and Lyubasha, Marina is not opaque. She acts resolutely and makes bold individual choices (like calling off all clients in order to attend her sister's funeral). Marina is individualistic, self-reflexive and ethical: she acts as she thinks and feels. She lives in a heterogeneous society in which individual and consumer desire is everywhere on display. This is reflected in her city habitat: she occupies a flat in a new development on the outskirts of the city and while the infrastructure is primitive, everywhere there are signs of a developing economy. The entire city periphery appears to be a construction site. Marina's profession is thus a metaphor, at the root of which is the unconscious desire of the "new Russia": to partake in free enterprise as a means to individual freedom. This unconscious desire is revealed in Marina's self-conscious misrepresentation about what she does for a living when she meets the two male characters in the bar sequence at the beginning of the film. Marina claims to be in advertising and to be promoting a new device that regulates desire or moods. Lying is always, according to Freud, evidence of the unconscious at work.

The creation of a truly happy worker was on the agenda of the Soviet state but this had nothing to do with the promotion of individual desire. It was to be achieved through collective means and collective labor. Marina's fictitious invention is a device that is at the command of the individual and has the function of promoting the individual's pleasure as defined by the Freudian pleasure principle. Thus individual pleasure, which can be turned on through chemical means (like drugs), and freedom, which comes from free economic activity, constitute the belief system or "religious feeling" of the "new Russia" portrayed in Sorokin's film.

However, Marina's roots, like those of the majority of post-revolutionary Russia, are in the Russian village. Marina's journey into the past, back to her native village, near the provincial city of Saratov, for the funeral of one of her sisters, makes up the film's plot. What is apparent as the camera follows Marina's progress through the Russian countryside, in the train and on foot, is that the Russian village culture of the past is in a state of decay while the village populace (the people or *narod*) present a grotesque picture of gross hedonistic pleasure seeking—mainly in coarse eating and drinking. This is captured in the little cameo scene in Marina's train compartment, where she is constantly badgered—almost in a sexually aggressive manner—by the *prostonarodnyi* couple (a couple from the "people") to partake of their lavish snacking which never ceases throughout the long trip. A more extended version of this hedonism is displayed by the inhabitants of Marina's village.

Marina's village community is somewhat reminiscent of Old Bukhara at the end of Varlamov's novella in that it is self-contained, apart, and almost exclusively female. The one exception is the presence of the lover of Marina's deceased sister. This lone male living in the community of peasant women as the widowed boyfriend of Marina's sister is the symbolic remnant of the progressive Russian intelligentsia, who went "to the people" at the end of the nineteenth century, in order to bring education and enlightenment to them. However, Sorokin's belated *narodnik* does not know how to lead what remains of the village population and commits suicide after his girlfriend's funeral.

The village community of women is held together by a communal activity involving the chewing of bread, used as raw material for the making of giant carnival dolls. This cross between a Soviet *kolkhoz* and a traditional Russian community or *mir* is thus not engaged in peasant labor or in the manufacture of traditional artifacts but in an aberrant form of capitalist production, since the giant bread dolls appear to sustain the "new Russian" village economically. The village displays obvious signs of prosperity even if this prosperity is expressed in crude and basic material values: one of the peasant women has a new fur coat, all eat well and drink vodka in great quantities, all are housed well in the communal hut with adequate heating. The bread dolls are thus a metaphor of "new Russian" capitalism on the village level. As metaphor, the bread dolls are reminiscent of "dead souls"—an intertextual allusion that would escape very few Russian viewers. It was Gogol's vision of the nineteenth-century Russia as a land whose economy ran on the speculating spirit of a pseudo-gentry class of unproductive landowners. Gogol captured this pseudo-economy in the metaphor of buying and selling "dead souls"—deceased serfs whose existence on paper conferred status and power on the purchaser. Sorokin's "new Russia" is similarly a phantom economy that runs on its own version of "dead souls"—an invisible, grotesque system of exchange, powered by a "degenerate" populace reduced to the basic instinct of pleasure by an almost total blackout of cultural memory. The women in Marina's village can barely remember the traditional keening chants that custom obliges them to trot out at Marina's sister's funeral. Their "folksy" attributes are reduced to crude carousing (the drinking and revealing of tits by women who are long past their prime) while their traditional sense of community easily flips into a dogfight over a pig. The traditional Russian village turned capitalist is devoid of value and can no longer serve as the source of ethics for the postmodern Russian intelligentsia. Indeed, this intelligentsia is itself a defunct class: it exits the scene of capitalism like Marina's sister's boyfriend or it goes abroad to make its fortune in the West, like the saxophonist in Pavel Lungin's 1990 film, *Taxi Blues.* While Alexander Sokurov's film *Russian Ark* (2003) paints a positive picture of Russian culture as a museum—

one that is lovingly preserved through war and revolution by a caring intelligentsia—Sorokin's *Chetyre* paints a picture of a "new Russia" beyond the cultural museum, in a denuded landscape that resembles the surface of the moon or of a rubbish dump. This is made visible in the shots of industrial debris and building slosh on Marina's walk from the rural Saratov train station to the village funeral. This ugly post-postindustrial landscape alternates with images of neatly plowed fields, sown with lush green grass, indicating the potential of the vast Russian lands for growth and proper development. However, while the natural potential is there, the Russian "folk" or *narod* is represented as a race of degenerates, whose memory of their own national heritage—of an ancient *Rus'* glimpsed in fading memory of songs and funeral wails—has been erased.[16] The half-remembered, haphazardly performed funeral ritual and traditional funeral banquet degenerate into virtual cannibalism and lewd carousing by an unsightly group of older Russian peasant women. The unbridled release of the pleasure principle among the *narod* does not lead to cultural freedom but to another form of totalitarianism: that of formlessness and ethical ambivalence.

This ethical ambivalence of capitalism in the Russian countryside is mirrored by the absence of value in various forms of capitalist activity in the "new Russian" city.

What "new Russia" has to offer its younger generation by way of educational and economic opportunities are various forms of prostitution or bondage in a lawless environment, despite its outward structure of a free pluralist society. Thus the army seeks recruits among the prison population to run Russia's postcolonial wars, including the war with Chechnya. The pianist-turned-piano tuner is arrested on a trumped-up charge and press-ganged into the army. The arbitrary arrest of the piano tuner demonstrates the degree of violence that underpins the "new Russian" economy, while the selling of old frozen meat, dating back to Soviet times, testifies to the aberrations of a market that is underpinned by a black economy run from the "underground" by a mafia network. The ground for the economy of exchange of the "new Russia" is consumerism, whose ultimate aim is the creation and satisfaction of perverse desire. This is illustrated by the production of a new species of round pig, offered at great cost only to a select clientele. The principle of *izbrannichestvo* here sinks to a new depth: instead of messianic fervor, all that remains of its value as the "religious feeling" of the age is hedonism.

Paradoxically, Marina, who also represents this "new" Russian economy of exchange, where money, goods, and bodies circulate freely, is not unethical. Her ethical potential stems from her youth, physical beauty, and sexual freedom, and above all, her connection with her "dead" sister. It is the news of her sister's death that brings Marina's city life to a halt and moves her to undertake the journey to the village, into the community of her female relatives. As a member of this community, Marina is not portrayed as a pleasure seeker; instead her character represents a new constellation of desire grounded in the notion of the multiple and the anti-Oedipal.[17]

The symbolism of the "four" sisters, as opposed to three or a pair of siblings, points to the concept of the multiple as an organizing structure, as distinct from a ternary or binary principle. In postmodern cultural theory, the multiple[18] is identified as the organizing principle of the new post-hierarchic social formations. Thus the multiple, with its endless permutations and repetitions, grounds the heterogeneous structures of capitalist societies. As symbols of the multiple, Marina and her sisters carry the seed of a new community to come. This new community finds its ultimate bonding and ethical expression through the commemoration of a "dead" sister. This indicates a radical change in the ethics of new Russian society. Instead of observing the traditional values of a social hierarchy headed by a father (for example a leader like Stalin, who was popularly called *Batiushka* or "Father"), Russia's new civil society—at present still struggling against a rampant black economy and accompanying crude social mores—is prepared to honor "new gods" who are not gods at all. Marina's "dead" sister represents this new approach to value as an act of personal engagement and enterprise. Marina's dead sister remains the prime driver behind the village's bread-doll industry. Even in death, she directs the community's productive labor as an absent presence. As an entrepreneur with mythical proportions, the dead sister also elicits ethical action on the part of Marina, who cancels a lucrative appointment with a client in order to attend her sister's funeral. Thus the new myth of private entrepreneurship constitutes, according to Sorokin's analysis, the ethics of postmodern Russian society. The film posits this value as myth, but does not evaluate it in black and white, as either positive or negative. While leaving room for ambivalence in judging this postmodern Russian ethics of capitalism, Sorokin's representation of the construction of value in the present is testimony to a new approach to value which diverges from the traditional system of evaluation according to criteria external to the moment, say, from the perspective of a utopian future or a nostalgia for the past. The "new sectarianism" represented in Russian postmodern literature and film provides a picture of both the revaluation of value and dissolution of value in the current moment of Russian cultural history. The analysis of value through the code concepts of "religious feeling" or *sektantstvo* (sectarianism) is tantamount to a new method of cultural critique. This method was initiated by Nietzsche in his *Genealogy of Morals,* from which the concepts of "genealogy" of history and archaeology of knowledge have been derived by Michel Foucault and widely adopted in poststructural critical theory. Russian postmodern literature and film operate as genealogies of Russian history and construct a new way for Russians to look at themselves and their cultural identity, from a point of view in the present and without the mystifications of metaphysics.

Cultural Authenticity against Russia's Political "Inoperosity"

In rereading the works of Russian postmodernism through Epstein's model of "new Sectarianism," this author of the introduction was assisted by the work of the young Russian political scientist, Dr. Sergei Prozorov, Helsinki Collegium for Advanced Studies, University of Helsinki, in particular his article on "Russian Post-communism and the End of History"[19] What resonates in particular with our analysis of the absence of value in postmodern Russian ethics is Prozorov's finding about the nature of Russian politics in the Putin era:

> Thus, from October 1993 onwards the Russian political elite has, almost without exception, functioned in the inoperative mode exemplified by Rutskoi's vice-presidency, "relieved of all assignments." While in the 1990s this inoperative condition was partly concealed by the inconsequential politics of the diffuse spectacle, the Putin presidency makes this *inoperosity* its foundational principle precisely by suspending the very scene of messianic suspension, reducing Russian politics to the sphere of pure ritual.

The term "inoperosity" is a borrowing from Giogio Agamben's work.[20] Messianism is also theorized in terms of Agamben's theses in *The Time That Remains: A Commentary on the Letter to the Romans.*[21] Mirroring this ritual politics is the ritualization of pleasure as the "new sectarianism" or "religious feeling" of the age in post-Soviet Russian culture.

However, the fact that this "inoeprosity" of Russian politics and the "pleasure principle" as the ground of social ritual is a subject of representation in Russian art—in literature and cinema—has far-reaching effects. If we pose the question about the authenticity of Russian post-postmodern culture in terms of Tolstoy's "test"—namely that a work of art must be universally intelligible, infectious, and that it must reflect "the religious idea of the age"—what can we infer about Russian culture of the twenty-first century so far? Do the works briefly analyzed here pass Tolstoy's test of authenticity? Do they represent or portray popular mass culture in any other sense than that of seduction and consumption on the spot?

The answer is yes. While Sorokin's and Varlamov's analysis of post-Soviet "new sectarianism" conjures up the specter of rank consumerism and hedonism as the dominant forces in contemporary Russian society, the emptying of value also has a constructive social function. It wipes the slate clean of traditionalism and clears the space of discourse for the construction of new meaning. This new meaning is constituted, in the first instance, by the genealogical critique of "new" Russia which is embodied by the work of these authors and many other contemporary writers who constitute the post-postmodern Russian cultural canon: Ulitskaya, Petrushevskaya, Tolstaya and many others. The genealogical critique is not merely a cerebral activity but taps into the unconscious roots of modern, "new" Russian desire, which it models or mimics through form and content. The form is "popular" in that it relies on a modern, "new" Russian vernacular for the narrator's and characters' language (the first-person narrators in *Led* and *Zatonuvshii* kovcheg are constructed in *skaz* mode which is direct speech in the former and stream of consciousness or "experienced speech" in the latter). The content is relevant and reflects the form of knowledge "new" Russian society is able to construct through a close self-examination attained by means of the deconstruction of value (meaning re-examination down to the structural elements of value), bound to traditionalism, history and metaphysics. The *potlatch* (excess) embodied by this process of destroying old gods and revaluating all value means that the work of art in the "new" Russia is still performing its ritual function and that the "new" Russian avant-garde is still true to the ideals of art conjured up by the traditional avant-garde in the early twentieth century.

Notes

1. The first book on Russian postmodernism in English was Mikhail Epstein, *After the Future: The Paradoxes of Postmodernism and Contemporary Russian Culture* (University of Massachusetts Press, 1995), 392 pp.; in Russian, Вячеслав Курицын, Книга о постмодернизме. — Екатеринбург, 1992. — pp. Despite the title (which was already a fashionable term at that time), it did not say anything about postmodernism proper and offered some critical sketches on contemporary Ekaterinburg writers and artists. Mark Lipovetsky's first book *Russian Postmodernist Fiction: Dialogue with Chaos* (M.E. Sharpe, 1999), appeared simultaneously with our first edition of *Russian Postmodernism.* In 2000, two books were published in Russian: M. Epstein, *Postmodern v Rossii: Literatura i Teoria,* and, several months later, V. Kuritsyn, *Russkii literaturnyi postmodernizm.* An early appraisal of Russian postmodernism in the East European context was published by Slobodanka Vladiv-Glover in "Postmodernism in Eastern Europe after WWII: Yugoslav, Polish and Russian Literatures," *Australian Slavonic and East European Studies* 5, no. 2 (1991): pp. 123–44.
2. Mikhail Epstein, *Novoe sektantstvo: tipy religiozno-filosofskikh umonastroenii v Rossii (70—80 gody XX veka),* Pod redaktsiei Romana Levina (New Publishing House, 1993). All quotations are my translations. The pages given are those of the original Russian edition.

3. L. N. Tolstoy, "Chto takoe iskusstvo?" *Sobranie sochinenii v dvadtsati dvukh tomakh. Tom piatnadtsatyi: Stat"i ob iskusstve i literature* (Moscow: "Khudozhesvennaia literature," 1983), pp. 41–224. Also in English: L. Tolstoy, *What Is Art?* trans. Aylmer Maude, trans. (London and Felling-on-Tyne, New York, Melbourne: Walter Scott Publishing Co. Ltd., 1899?). Author's preface written in 1898; introduction by Aylmer Maude dated 1899.
4. Ibid., p. 6. ["That which I call 'new sectarianism'—is, in essence, the ideology of our intelligentsia expressed in religious concepts, more specifically, the sum of such ideologies, spreading out in a radius from the 'center' of state ideology."]
5. Ibid., p. 8. For a translation of the whole book, see Mikhail Epstein, *Cries in the New Wilderness: From the Files of the Moscow Institute of Atheism,* trans. and intr. by Eve Adler (Philadelphia: Paul Dry Books, 2002), 236 pp.
6. Ibid., p. 15.
7. Ibid., p. 177.
8. As Epstein says, none of the named sects, such as "*duriki,*" "*kovchezhniki,*" "*pustovertsi,*" can be found in Russian dictionaries. That is why these neologisms are also difficult to render into English.
9. Compare Mikhail Epstein, *Cries in the New Wilderness.*
10. Epstein, *Novoe sektantstvo: tipy religiozno-filosofskikh umonastroenii v Rossii,* p. 31.
11. Ibid., p. 32.
12. Ibid., p. 104.
13. Vladimir Sorokin, *Led* (Moscow: Ad Marginero, 2002).
14. Compare Jacques Lacan, "The Agency of the Letter in the Unconscious," *Écrits: A Selection,* trans. Alan Sheridan, trans. (New York, London: W. W. Norton, 1977), pp. 146–78. Lacan connects the two mechanisms of language, metaphor and metonymy, to the unconscious structure of meaning as it is constituted by means of the symptom (as a proto-sign or a trace) in combination with the agency of desire. "For the symptom is a metaphor whether one likes it or not, as desire is metonymy, however funny people may find the idea" (p. 175).
15. Aleksei Varlamov, *Zatonuvshyi kovcheg* (*The Sunken Treasure*) (Moscow: "Molodaia gvardiia," 2002). My paraphrase and translation of passages around pp. 385–86.
16. The erasure of the memory of local customs, manifested in songs and rituals, was documented in a recent academic study by the American Slavist, Laura J. Olson (University of Colorado, Boulder). Her monograph, entitled *Performing Russia: Folk Revival and Russian Identity* (New York and London: Routledge Curzon, 2004) finds repeated evidence of the absence of knowledge of folk customs and ritual songs, such as Christmas carols, among Russian village people in the late-Soviet and recent post-Soviet times. This lends support to Sorokin's representation of the Russian postmodern, post-*kolkhoz* village as a wasteland with a degree zero cultural heritage.
17. Compare the article by Slobodanka Vladiv-Glover, "The Russian Anti-Oedipus: Petrushevskaya's *Three Girls in Blue,*" *Australian Slavonic and East Euro-*

pean Studies 12, no. 2 (1998): pp. 31–56. The community of women and mothers in Petrushevskaya's drama is analyzed through Gilles Deleuze and Félix Guattari's concept of the multiple, which grounds a new model of perception and relation to the object, which is nonhierarchical and metonymic, consisting of endless connections and disconnections along a horizontal plane, proliferating in the manner of a rhizome.

18. Compare Gilles Deleuze and Félix Guattari, *A Thousand Plateaus: Capitalism and Schizophrenia,* trans. Brian Massumi, trans. (Minneapolis, London: University of Minnesota Press, 1987). Multiplicity underlies a sense formation that is distinct from metaphor. Deleuze and Guattari call this formation "the rhizome." "Unlike trees or their roots," they write, "the rhizome connects any point to any other point. It constitutes linear multiplicities with *n* dimensions having neither subject nor object, which can be laid out on a plane of consistency. The rhizome is an a-centred, non-hierarchical, non-signifying system, defined solely by a circulation of states" (ibid., p. 21). Multiplicity that engenders this atypical trope (the rhizome) underlies a free and multidimensional circulation of meanings. It provides an ideal model of the free market as a space of self-regulated exchange.
19. Sergei Prozorov, *Studies in European Thought,* 2008. See also: Sergei Prozorov, "Russian Postcommunism and the Politics of Pure Praxis," *Russia Forever: Towards Working Pragmatism in Finnish-Russian Relations,* ed. H. Rytovuori-Apunen ed. (Helsinki: Gummerus, 2008).
20. Giogio Agamben, *Means without End: Notes on Politics* (Minneapolis, University of Minnesota Press, 2000).
21. Agamben, *The Time That Remains: A Commentary on the Letter to the Romans* (Stanford, CA: Stanford University Press, 2005).

Part I

The Making of Russian Postmodernism

Chapter 1

The Dialectics of *Hyper*

From Modernism to Postmodernism

Mikhail Epstein

1. The Modernist Premises of Postmodernism

In contemporary discourse postmodernism is usually interpreted as a profoundly Western phenomenon whose appearance in non-Western cultures, such as the Japanese, is but part of an inevitable and growing process of Westernization. This chapter proposes to treat those laws of twentieth-century cultural development as shared by the West and Russia, in spite of the fact that Russia was isolated from the West and in fact set itself in vigorous opposition to it during this period. Indeed Russia's own "revolutionariness" is part of the global revolutionary paradigm of the twentieth century.

To a large extent, the first half of the twentieth century marched under the banner of numerous revolutions, whether "social," "cultural," or "sexual." There were also revolutionary changes in physics, psychology, biology, philosophy, literature, and the arts. Although the momentous changes that took place in Russia occurred in different spheres than in the West, both worlds were united by a common revolutionary model. This fact explains the typological similarities that have emerged by the end of the twentieth century between

Western postmodernism and contemporary Russian culture, itself evolving, as is its Western counterpart, under the sign of "post": as postcommunist or postutopian culture.

Revolutions are certainly part of the modernist project. In the broadest sense of the term "modern," this project is a quest for and (re)construction of an authentic, higher, essential reality to be found beyond the conventional, arbitrary sign systems of culture. The founding father of modernism in this sense was Jean-Jacques Rousseau, with his critique of contemporary civilization and the discovery of a primal, "unspoiled" existence of man in nature. Then Marx, Nietzsche, and Freud exposed the illusion of an ideological consciousness and discovered an "essential" reality in the self-motion of matter and material production, in the life instinct, in the will to power, in the sexual drive, and the power of the unconscious. These discoveries were all creations of modernism. As Lionel Trilling wrote in his work "On the Modern Element in Modern Literature": "I can identify [the modern element] by calling it the disenchantment of our culture with culture itself ... the bitter line of hostility to civilization that runs through [modern literature].... I venture to say that the idea of losing oneself to the point of self-destruction, of surrendering oneself to experience without regard to self-interest or conventional morality, of escaping wholly from societal bonds, is an 'element' somewhere in the mind of every modern person."[1]

James Joyce, with his discovery of the "stream of consciousness" and the "mythological prototypes" underlying the conventional forms of the "contemporary individual," was also modernist. The same can be said of Kazimir Malevich, who erased the multiplicity of colors of the visible world in order to uncover its geometric foundation, the "black square." As for Velimir Khlebnikov, he insisted on the essential reality of the "self-valued," "trans-sense" word (*samovitoe* and *zaumnoe slovo*), such as the shamanistic incantation of the type "bobeobi peli guby,"[2] rather than the conventional language of symbols. Although antagonistic to artistic modernism, the communist revolution was a manifestation of political modernism. It strove to bring to power the "true creators of reality" who "generated material well-being"—namely the working masses. These masses would bring down the "parasitic" classes, who distort and alienate reality, appropriating for themselves the fruits of the labor of others by means of ideological illusions and the bureaucratic apparatus.

On the whole, modernism can be defined as a revolution that strove to abolish the arbitrary character of culture and the relativity of signs in order to affirm the hidden absoluteness of being, regardless of how this essential, authentic being was defined: whether as "matter" and "economics" in Marxism, "life" in Nietzsche, "libido" and "the unconscious" in Freud, "creative élan" in Bergson, "stream of consciousness" in William James and James Joyce, "being" in Heidegger, the "self-valued word" in Futurism or "the power of workers and peasants" in Bolshevism. The list could go on.

Postmodernism, as is known, directs its sharpest criticism at modernism for the latter's adherence to the illusion of an "ultimate truth," an "absolute language," a "new style," all of which were supposed to lead to the "essential reality." The name itself points to the fact that postmodernism constituted itself as a new cultural paradigm in the very process of differentiating itself from modernism, as an experiment in the self-enclosure of sign systems, of language folding in upon itself. The very notion of a reality beyond that of signs is criticized by postmodernism as the "last" in a series of illusions, a survival of the old "metaphysics of presence." The world of secondariness, that is, of conventional and contingent presentations, proves to be more authentic and primary than the so-called "true reality." This critique of the "realistic fallacy" has nurtured diverse postmodern movements. One of these, Russian conceptualism, exposes the nature of Soviet reality as an ideological mirage and a system of "supersignificant" signs projected by the ruling mind onto the empty space of an imaginary "signified."

Our task here will be to explore the intricate relationship of modernism and postmodernism, seen as two complementary aspects of a single cultural paradigm subsumable under the general concept of "hyper." If Russian and Western postmodernism have common roots in their respective modernist heritage, then both share a parallel search for ways out of an analogous "revolutionary" past. For it was revolution, as a quest for, and affirmation of, a "pure" or "essential" reality, that led to the formation of those pseudo-realities or hollow, non-referential signs with which postmodern culture plays in both Russia and the West.

What follows is an attempt to analyze "the modernist premises of postmodernism in light of postmodern perspectives on modernism" or, put more simply, the interdependence of these two historical phenomena. My argument will focus on a variety of modernist approaches: in physics (quantum mechanics), in literary theory (new criticism), in philosophy (existentialism), across psychoanalytic theories and practices (sexual revolution), and across Soviet social and intellectual trends, such as "collectivism" and "materialism." All these trends manifest the phenomenon of "hyper" in its first stage, which is constituted by the revolutionary overthrow of the "classic" paradigm and an assertion of a "true, essential reality," or "super-reality." In the second stage, the same phenomena are realized and exposed as "pseudo-realities" thus marking the transformation of "hyper" itself, its inevitable transition from the modernist to the postmodernist stage, from "super" to "pseudo." I will argue that the development of the twentieth-century cultural paradigm depends on a necessary connection between these two stages of the "super" and the "pseudo." The concept of "hyper" highlights not only the lines of continuity between modernism and postmodernism, but also the parallel developments in Russian and Western postmodernisms as reactions to and revisions of a common "revolutionary" legacy.

2. "Hyper" in Science and Culture

A variety of phenomena in the arts, sciences, philosophy, and politics of the twentieth century can be united under the category "hyper." This prefix literally means "heightened" or "excessive." Its popularity in contemporary cultural theory reflects the fact that many tendencies of twentieth century life have been brought to the limit of their development, thereby revealing their own antithesis.

The concept of "hyperreality" has been advanced by the Italian cultural semiotician, Umberto Eco, and the French sociologist and philosopher, Jean Baudrillard, both of whom relate it to the disappearance of reality brought about by dominance of the mass media. Although mass communication technologies appear, on the surface, to capture reality in all its most minute details, on a deeper level the technical and visual means themselves construct a reality of another order, which has been called "hyperreality." Though this hyperreality is a phantasmic creation of mass communication, it emerges as a more authentic, exact, "real" reality than the one we perceive in the life around us.

An illustrative example is so-called hyperrealism, an influential art movement of the 1970s and early 1980s. Works produced by this movement included giant color photographs, framed to function as paintings. Details, such as the skin of a man's face, were rendered in such detail and on such a scale that it was possible to see every pore, every roughness of surface, and every protuberance not normally visible to the naked eye. This is the "hyper" effect, which allows reality to acquire an "excessively real" dimension thanks entirely to the effects of its technical reproduction.

According to Baudrillard, reality, which is firmly entwined in the web of mass communication, has disappeared completely from the contemporary Western world, ceding its place to a hyperreality produced by artificial means:

> Reality itself founders in hyperrealism, the meticulous reduplication of the real, preferably through another reproductive medium, such as photography. From medium to medium, the real is volatilised, becoming an allegory of death. But it is also, in a sense, reinforced through its own destruction. It becomes *reality for its own sake,* the fetishism of the lost object ...: the hyperreal.[3]

This paradox was discovered by scientists in quantum physics, long before the advent of the theoreticians of postmodernism: elementary particles, that is, the objects of observation, were largely determined by the instruments that measured them. The reality revealed to physicists from the late 1920s onwards came to be increasingly recognized as a hyperreality, since it was constituted by the parameters of the measuring equipment and the instruments of mathematical calculation. In the words of the American physicist Heinz Pagels,

> it is meaningless to talk about the physical properties of quantum objects without precisely specifying the experimental arrangement by which you intend to measure them. Quantum reality is in part an observer-created reality ... with the quantum theory, human intention influences the structure of the physical world.[4]

The most challenging methodological questions for present-day physics, engaged in the modeling of such speculative entities as "quarks" and "strings," are the following: What in fact is being investigated? What is the status of so-called physical objects and in what sense can they be called "physical" or even "objects" if they are called into existence by a series of mathematical operations?

Quantum mechanics became the first discipline to confess its hyperscientific character or, more precisely, the hyperphysical nature of its objects. In getting ever closer to the elementary foundations of matter, science has discovered the imaginary and purely rational character of that physical reality, which it allegedly describes but which in fact it invents. In the past, discoveries and inventions could be clearly distinguished: the former revealed something that really existed in nature, the latter created something that was possible and useful in technology. Today the categories of discovery and invention are not easily delimited, since all discoveries tend to become inventions. The difference between discovery and invention has become blurred, at least as far as the deepest, originary layers of reality are concerned. The more one penetrates into these layers, the more one finds oneself in the depths of one's own consciousness.

Similarly, the more perfect the instruments used for the observation of physical reality, the less reality itself can be detected in a proper sense, as something different from the conditions of its observation. This is precisely how "an observer-created reality" comes into existence, as expressed in Baudrillard's concept of hyperreality. This concept, in relation to cultural objects, was first introduced by Baudrillard in his book *Symbolic Exchange and Death* (1976), half a century after Niels Bohr laid the foundation for a new understanding of physical objects as "influenced" by human intention (1927). It is the improvement of instruments for the observation and reproduction of physical and cultural reality that obscured reality as such and made it interchangeable with its own representations. In his statement "From medium to medium, the real is volatilised," Baudrillard is referring to the most authentic and sensitive means for the reproduction of reality, such as photography, cinema, and television. Paradoxically, the more truthful the methods of representation, the more dubious becomes the category of truth. An object presented with the maximum authenticity no longer differs from its own copy. Hyperreality supplants reality as truthfulness makes truth unattainable.

This process is not limited to the field of hyperphysical objects but can be seen in literary criticism, philosophy, ideology, and in the theory and practice of the social and sexual revolutions. These spheres of "hyperization" are so diverse and at such a distance from one another that it is impossible to speak of a direct influence among these processes. Rather, they embody a new limit of cultural construction and "reality simulation," at which both Russia and the West simultaneously arrived.

3. Hypertextuality

Along with hyperphysical objects, what might be called hypertextuality has also emerged, altering the relationship between criticism and literature.[5] Modernist criticism of the 1920s and 1930s, as represented by its most influential schools, such as Russian formalism and Anglo-American New Criticism, and later structuralism, attempted to free itself of all historical, social, biographical, and psychological elements in order to isolate the phenomenon of "pure" literariness. This literariness of literature is analogous to the "elementary particles" of the texture of literature, its ultimate and irreducible essence. Criticism thus saw itself as engaged in a process of purifying literature by separating out all those "additional," "extraneous" layers introduced by earlier schools of criticism: the Enlightenment, romanticism, realism; biographical, psychological, and historical criticism; naturalism and symbolism, and all other critical fashions of the nineteenth and early twentieth centuries. Criticism now wanted to free literature from an imposed content in order to turn literature into pure form, to reduce it to the "device as such," to the text in itself. Everything that was formerly valued in literature—the reflection of historical reality, the author's world view, the influence of the intellectual trends of the times, the inferred higher reality of symbolic meanings—now seemed naive, old-fashioned, and extraneous to literature.

But as the process of purification of literature from all non-literary elements continued, reducing literature to the text itself, so the process of appropriation of that text by criticism developed alongside it, transforming the text into a thing wholly dependent on and even engendered by criticism. The literary work thus became a textual product, created in the modernist critical laboratory by means of the splitting of literature into "particles" or structural elements and by virtue of the separation of literature from admixtures of "historicity," "biographicality," "culturalness," "emotionalism," "philosophicalness," which were considered alien and detrimental to the text.

Just like textual criticism, quantum mechanics splits the physical object—the atom—into so many minimal component parts that its objective existence fades, becoming instead an ideal projection dependent on the methods of observation and the properties of the physical measuring apparatus. Pure textual signs, isolated in the literary text in the manner of the smallest irreducible particles or quants, are equivalent to ideal projections of the critical methodology. Since these signs are purified of all meanings, supposedly imposed by the author's subjectivity and extraneous historical circumstances, the critic is the only one empowered to read them as signs bearing potential meanings. Thus it is the critic, having initially purified it of all meanings, who determines the meanings of those signs.

The paradoxical result of such a purification of literature has been its increasing reliance on criticism and interpretive method. Both formalism and Anglo-American New Criticism make literature accessible to the reader through the intermediary action of criticism itself. Literature thus becomes a system of pure devices or signs, to which criticism assigns meaning according to one or another method of interpretation. In other words, criticism bans literature from its own territory, substituting itself for the power that the writer formerly exercised over the reader. As the critic George Steiner complained: "The true critic is servant to the poet; today he is acting as master, or being taken as such."[6] Or as the Nobel-prize winning novelist Saul Bellow put it: "criticism tries to control the approaches to literature. It confronts the reader with its barriers of interpretation. A docile public consents to this monopoly of the specialists—those 'without whom literature cannot be understood.' Critics, speaking for writers, succeeded eventually in replacing them."[7]

Certainly, these negative responses to the modernist revolution in criticism belong themselves to anti- rather than postmodernist consciousness; more precisely, they designate the limits of modernism but do not go beyond them. Postmodernism, by contrast, begins with the awareness of the inevitability of this situation: criticism, which itself gives rise to its object, understands the reality of the text as an illusionary projection of the critic's semiotic power or, more pluralistically, of any reader's interpretative power ("dissemination of meanings"). The critical revolution that began with Russian formalism in 1920s and continued with structuralism in the 1950s and 1960s ended with a brief reaction in the 1960s, when lamentations about "the critical situation" and the domination of critic over creator became popular. With the advent of postmodernism, both modernist enthusiasm for the "pure" reality of the text and antimodernist nostalgia for the "lost" reality of literature became things of the past.

4. Hyperexistentiality

Hypertextuality as a phenomenon of literary criticism parallels the phenomenon of the hyperobject created by physical science. Another form of "hyper" can be found in one of the leading Western philosophical trends of the twentieth century, existentialism, which sought to subject the "abstract," "rationalistic" consciousness of the idealistic systems from Plato to Descartes and Hegel to crushing criticism by turning its attention to the authentic reality of individual existence, to "being as such," which precedes any categorization or rational generalization. However, as early as Dostoevsky's *Notes from the Underground*, Russian literature pointed to the process of the production of being or "pure existence" from an "excessively developed" abstract consciousness that deprived being of all concrete form and reduced it to a completely empty, temporal presence. Existence thus became a product of consciousness, a pure abstraction deprived of all the characteristics that make for concrete being. In his concreteness, a man is either one entity or another: either lazy or diligent, a clerk or a peasant, etc. However, Dostoevsky's "underground man," who is one of the first existentialist (anti-)heroes in world literature, is not even capable of being a complete good-for-nothing, or an insect. His consciousness is infinite and even "sick" in its "excessiveness"; it destroys the definitiveness that enslaves the "dull," "limited" man of action, pushing toward that ultimate limit of existence, at which a human being is nothing concrete but merely *is*. He simply exists:

> Not only couldn't I make myself malevolent, I couldn't make myself anything: neither good nor bad, neither a scoundrel nor an honest man, neither a hero nor an insect.... [A] wise man can't seriously make himself anything ... [...] After all, the direct, immediate, legitimate fruit of heightened consciousness is inertia ... [...] I practise thinking, and consequently each of my primary causes pulls along another, even more primary, in its wake, and so on *ad infinitum*. That is really the essence of all thinking and self-awareness. [...] Soon we shall invent a method of being born from an idea.[8]

Thus the existentialist critique of routine forms of existence ("neither a hero nor an insect"), paradoxically brings forth an even more abstract kind of existence, "a method of being born from an idea." The quest for such absolute being, which precedes all rational definitions and general classifications (such as psychological traits or professional standing), is no less abstract and rational than the consciousness it critiques. Indeed it is even more abstract. It is the very limit of the abstraction of being, which is also an abstraction of singularity, resulting in a kind of "hypersingularity" which is only itself and alien to all forms of typicality. Such is the result of the existential quest. This "hypersingularity," based on the "in-and-for-itself" (to borrow a Hegelian term), is the highest possible abstraction, which clings to the "tip" of the self-conscious consciousness, dissolving all qualitative determinateness. It does so in the same way that quantum physics dissolves the determinateness of matter ("the principle of uncertainty") to obtain elementary particles as projections of mathematical description. Precisely because of its "elementariness," existence becomes the metaphysical "quant," the ultimate, indivisible particle of "matter," or existence-as-such: derived from the most speculative type of consciousness, it objectifies itself in the form of "being as such." The existentialist self-definition "I am" is much more abstract than "essentialist" definitions like "I am a reasonable being" or "I am a lazy man."

In Hegel, the Absolute Idea develops through its embodiment in increasingly concrete forms of being, according to the principle formulated as "the progression from the abstract to the concrete." In the existentialist tradition, being itself gradually becomes a form of abstraction. This is the abstraction of "the particular," the unique "this one here," which applies equally to any concrete form of existence, from insects to human beings, from the peasant to the artist, who are completely dissociated from any typical features of the *genus*, which Hegel still endows with the concreteness of the manifest idea. Contrary to conventional opinion, Kierkegaard can be regarded as a much more abstract thinker than Hegel. Hegel's thought proceeds from the abstract idea to its specific living manifestations, whereas Kierkegaard's thought proceeds from concrete idea to universal singularity. Hegel's Idea undergoes a process of concretization through being; the existentialists' being itself undergoes a process of abstraction through the ultimate generalization of the idea of "being." Thus being becomes "pure being," or an almost empty abstraction, a "hyperbeing," the form of Sartre's "nothingness."

Sartre's *La Nausée* demonstrates how the "unhappy" consciousness of Roquentin, not bound by anything and raised to the highest degree of abstraction, suddenly encounters the abstract texture of being, of the roots of a tree and of the earth itself, stubborn in their nausea-inducing absurdity. This absurdity, which the existentialist consciousness discovers everywhere as the revelation of a "true" reality, undistorted or non-generalized, and which precedes any act of rationalization, is in fact "hyperreality." It is the product of a rational generalization that singles out the "irrational" as the world's all-embracing trait.

Existentialism is not a negation of rationalism but rather its ultimate expansion, a method of rationalistic construction of the universal principle of irrationality, designated as "will" by Schopenhauer, "life" by Nietzsche, "existence" and "the individual" by Kierkegaard. This irrationality is eventually much more cerebral and abstract than all the forms of rationality that divide being into concrete types, essences, laws, and concepts. Rationality always contains at least a certain dose of concreteness because it is always in a determinate relation to "some thing"; it is "the sense of a concrete thing," the rationality of something that needs to be defined or specified from a rational point of view. "Irrationality" does not demand such concretization; it is "irrationality as such," "the absurdity of everything"; it represents "an all-embracing nonsense." It betrays its ultimate generality precisely through its totally and nauseatingly indiscriminate relationship to concrete things. The irrational world, which ostensibly eschews rational definition, is a product of the most schematizing rationality that negates all concrete definitions of things and finds its ultimate expression in abstractions such as "existence as such," "the particular as such," etc.

At this ultimate level of abstraction, being is only the opposite of non-being. As Sartre asserts in *Being and Nothingness*, consciousness, or being-for-itself, in its freedom from all ontological determinations, is pure nothingness emerging from itself and nullifying, or—to use a Sartrean term—"nihilating" the substantial definitions of the exterior world.

> The type of existence of the For-itself is a pure internal negation.... Thus determination is a *nothing* which does not belong as an internal structure either to the thing or to consciousness, but its being is *to-be-summoned* by the For-itself across a system of internal negations in which the in-itself [the world of objects] is revealed in its indifference to all that is not itself. [9]

As Hazel Barnes comments, in Sartre "consciousness exists as consciousness by making a nothingness arise between it and the object of which it is consciousness. Thus nihilation is that by which consciousness exists."[10] Therefore, the phenomenon of existence is determined by a series of "internal negations," proceeding from consciousness as pure nothingness. In this case, the absurdity of being, as it appears to the nullifying consciousness, can be understood as the derivative of this nothingness, of this abstraction that strips concrete things of their meaning. One would imagine that there could be nothing more abstract than "nothing," since it is deprived of all the peculiarities and specificities of being; but being, as it is posited in existential philosophy, is even more abstract than non-being, since it emerges as the second order projection of this nothingness. This is no longer that nothingness which has a reality in-and-for-itself, like the self-effacing nothingness of self-consciousness. This is a nothingness which has lost that intimate relationship to its for-itself and is turned toward the absurd Being that surrounds it, which is pure abstraction, deprived of even the concreteness of self-consciousness and of self-negation. This Being is simple nonentity—a being-for-no-one.

Behind the apparently authentic and self-evident "existence as such" postulated by existentialism, one can detect the hyperreality of reason abstracted from itself in the emptied form of ultimate irrationality. It is a conceptual abstraction to such a degree that it abstracts itself from its own rational foundation in order to affirm itself as its own opposite—as Being as such, ungraspable by reason, unconcretizable and untypifiable. There are two degrees of abstraction: a moderate abstraction, confined to the sphere of reason, and an extreme abstraction that goes beyond the limits of reason. This latter form of abstracting reason from itself is the one that gives rise to the notion of the "non-sense" of pure Being in opposition to reason.

5. Hypersexuality

In the twentieth century, the "hyper" phenomenon is also evident in the sphere of intimate personal relationships, in which experimentation with sex comes to the fore. War is declared on the Puritanism of the nineteenth century and the entire Christian ethics of "asceticism." The sexual instinct is set up as the primordial reality, underlying thought and culture. The Nietzschean celebration of the life of the body prepared European society, which had experienced the trauma of the First World War and the explosion of aggressive emotions, for the acceptance of psychoanalysis, which became the dominant intellectual trend of the 1920s. The scientific work of Sigmund Freud and Wilhelm Reich and their pupils, the artistic discoveries of the Surrealists, James Joyce, Thomas Mann, D. H. Lawrence and others, the new freedom of sexual mores characteristic of the jazz and cabaret culture—all of these things show the 1920s to have proceeded under the banner of the so-called "sexual revolution." "Basic instinct" is sought in theory and in art, and is extracted in pure form as the "libido."

But, as already noted by many critics, in this pure form, the "basic instinct," abstracted from all other human capabilities and driving forces, is nothing but an abstract scheme, the fruit of the analytic activity of reason. In the words of the English novelist and religious writer C. S. Lewis, "Lust is more abstract than logic; it seeks (hope triumphing over experience) for some purely sexual, hence purely imaginary conjunction of an impossible maleness with an impossible femaleness."[11] Moreover, the notion of an "abstract lust" emanates from a bookish, postlogical approach to *desire*, generated by the theorizing of the sexual revolution. The passionate Dionysian ecstasy of the "flesh as such" thus becomes like the burning fantasy of the "great Masturbator," who by pure mental effort separates the flesh from the diversity of individual spiritual and physical qualities of the desired "object." On an individual level, such exaggerated fantasies may lead to the exhaustion of physiological potency. On the scale of Western civilization, it brought the construction of still another level of hyperreality: the artificial reproduction of bodily images, more bright, tangible, concentrated, hypnotically effective than the physical reality of the body, and therefore evoking mental ecstasy while eroding the properly physical component of attraction. As T. S. Eliot noted about Lawrence's novels: "His struggle against over-intellectualised life is the history of his own over-intellectualised nature."[12] Similar to the case of existentialism, the struggle against rationalism is an expression of an overrational approach, an abstraction of "existence of such" or "flesh as such."

Critics often point to this internal contradiction of Lawrence's creativity: "... his world of love [is] more strangely and purely abstract than that of any other great author. The more intense and urgent it is the more it is a world inside the head ... the 'phallic consciousness' seems a hyper-intellectual, hyper-aesthetic affair, making *Lady Chatterly* one of the most inflexibly highbrow novels ever written."[13] It is interesting that Bayley still uses the prefix "hyper" to characterize the intellectual component of Lawrence's erotic images, while today we would call them "hypersexual." In the first case, "hyper" means "super," while in the second case it means "pseudo" or "quasi": the critic's implication is that Lawrence's images are *super*-intellectual, but *pseudo*-sexual. This evolution of meaning from "super" to "pseudo" constitutes the very core of the dialectics of "hyper" as will be discussed in the last section of this chapter.

Hypersexuality, as one might call this "rationally" abstracted and hyperbolized sexuality, emerges in the theories of Freud and in the novels of D. H. Lawrence, as well as, on a more basic level, in the upsurge of pornographic writing. Pornography is the very bastion of hypersexuality, presenting condensed simulacra of sexuality: glossy photographs and screen images of unthinkable sex, of unimaginably large breasts, powerful thighs, and violent orgasms.

Even the theory of psychoanalysis, for all its scientific caution and sophistication, reveals this hypersexual, and more broadly hyperreal, tendency. The world of the unconscious, proclaimed by Freud to be the primal human reality, was discovered or invented by consciousness, as its internal, in-depth "self-projection." This invention assumed the proportions of another reality, preceding and exceeding the reality of consciousness itself. True to its ultimate destiny in the twentieth century, consciousness thus creates something other than itself out of itself in order to surrender to this other as something primal and incontestably powerful. A more likely explanation of this phenomenon is that it is not at all a primary or "pre-existing" reality, opposed to consciousness from within, but that the unconscious is constructed by consciousness itself, as a form of self-alienation of consciousness, which then sets itself up as a "super-real" entity dominating the latter. Hyperreality is a mode of self-alienation of consciousness. The Freudian unconscious thus becomes one of the most pronounced and hypnotically convincing projections of consciousness "outside itself." According to V. N. Voloshinov (M. M. Bakhtin), "the Freudian unconscious does not fundamentally differ from consciousness; it is only another form of consciousness, only an ideologically different expression of it."[14] As Derrida later remarked, "the 'unconscious' is no more a 'thing' than it is a virtual or masked consciousness," the continuously delayed consciousness which can never come to terms with itself.[15]

Even Freud admitted that the discovery of the unconscious as a force dominating consciousness must serve the overall increase in the power of consciousness itself. Psychoanalysis is a process of decoding and illuminating the unconscious, which would allow consciousness to regain control over this "boiling cauldron of desires." In other words, consciousness discovers the unconscious in its "underground" in order to resume dominance over it. Thus psychoanalysis is a method of penetrating into those spheres of consciousness that consciousness itself had declared to be beyond its penetration; through the symbols of the unconscious, consciousness plays hide-and-seek with itself.

As distinct from quantum mechanics, which recognizes its physical object to be *prestructured* by consciousness *a priori*, psychoanalysis sets up the conscious structuring of its psychical object as its *final goal*. But in both cases the physical and psychic realities prove to be at least partial projections or functions of the intellect, which observes and analyzes them. Perhaps psychoanalysis would benefit methodologically if it followed the example of quantum mechanics, recognizing that the observed attributes of the unconscious are primarily determined by or even derived from the conditions of its observation and description.

The significance of the sexual revolution, theoretically dominated by psychoanalysis, did not lie in the fact that organic and sexual life went from being dominated by consciousness to dominating consciousness: this was but an ideological intention, the "wishful thinking" of the revolution. In the intimate sphere, in real-life sexual relations, instinct had always been dominant. The sexual revolution was in fact a revolution of a consciousness that had learned to produce lifelike simulations of a "pure" sexuality, which were all the more "ecstatic" the more abstract and rational they became. The result of the sexual revolution was not so much a triumph of "natural" sex as a triumph of the mental over the sexual.

This is especially true in the epoch of AIDS, with the growing fear of physical intimacy and propagation of its technical surrogates such as "telephone sex" and "computer sex." The "postmodern" also means the "postsexual." Sex becomes a spectacle, a psychological and technological commodity, reproduced in infinite fantasies of seduction, hypersexual power, hypermasculinity and hyperfemininity. This "hyper" that turns sexual images into mass products of popular culture is a quality absent in nature. It is a quality introduced by a consciousness with infinite powers of abstraction and simulation.[16]

6. Hypersociality

The four processes indicated so far, which led to the creation of hyperobjects—the hyperparticles of quantum mechanics, the hypersigns of literary criticism, the hyperbeing of existentialism, and the hyperinstincts of psychoanalysis and the sexual revolution—took place in the advanced Western societies of the twentieth century. Contemporaneously, particularly in the 1920s and 1930s, similar processes were taking place in the communist world, but these touched the entire social sphere. Communism itself, its theory and practice, can be viewed as a typically Eastern counterpart to the "hyper" phenomenon.

Soviet society was obsessed with the idea of communality, of the communalization of life. Individualism was castigated as the gravest sin and a "cursed remnant of the bourgeois past." Collectivism was proclaimed the highest moral principle. The economy was built on the communalization of private property, which came under the jurisdiction of the entire people. The communal was valued infinitely higher than the individual. Communal existence was considered to be prior and determinative in relation to individual consciousness, in full accordance with Marx's formula: "It is not the consciousness of men that determines existence, but social existence that determines consciousness."[17] In factories, *kolkhozes* (collective farms), at party meetings, in penal colonies, and urban communal apartments, a new man "of the communist future" was produced—a conscientious and effective cog in the gigantic wheel of the collectivist machine.

However, this new type of sociality, whose imperatives were infinitely more rigorous and demanding than the earlier (pre-revolutionary) ones, was in fact but another instance of hypersociality and a simulacrum of communality. In truth, the social bonds that unite people were rapidly being destroyed. By the mid-1930s, even people in familial relationships, husbands and wives, parents and children, could no longer fully trust one another; party loyalty and social obligations forced them to denounce and betray even their closest friends. Civil war and collectivization destroyed natural ties among members of the same ethnic, national, or professional community. "The most tightly knit society in the world" (a cliché of Soviet propaganda) was in fact an aggregate of frightened, alienated individuals and tiny, weak social units comprised of families and friends, each of which was trying to survive and withstand state pressure on its own.

Even the base of the entire state pyramid rested on the will of a single individual, who regulated the entire gigantic social mechanism. In a sense, it seems curious that it is precisely communism, with its will to *communality*, that always and everywhere gave rise to the *personality* cult: in Russia, China, North Korea, Romania, Albania, and Cuba. However, this is neither an accident nor a paradox: it is an expression of the hypersocial nature of the new society. Communism is not a natural, primary sociality, arising out of the biological and economic connections and needs that unite people. It is a sociality constructed consciously, according to a plan, emanating from the individual mind of the "founder" and enacted by the individual will of "the leader."

The "pure" sociality of the communist type is similar to the modernist models of "hyper" described earlier: the "pure" sexuality of psychoanalysis, the textuality of new criticism, and the elementariness of quantum mechanics. Communism thus represents a kind of hypnotic quintessence of the social body, which because of its abstractness excludes and destroys everything individual and concrete. Traditional sociality allowed for the entire gamut of individual diversity and forms of private property, just as traditional sexuality included the physical, emotional, social, and spiritual intimacy of two people, and the traditional work of art gave expression to the views of the author and the spirit of the age. But the "hyper," by virtue of its artificially constructed character, is the "extract," the "quintessence" as it were of one particular property to the exclusion of all others. Hypertextuality excludes all illusions of a separable, distinct content (opposed to form); hypersexuality excludes the notion of a "spiritual intimacy" or "sexual relation."[18] Similarly, hypersociality excludes the "illusion of independence and personal freedom." "Hyperization," the process enacted by modernism and realized by postmodernism, achieves this exclusion precisely because it represents the hypertrophy of an abstract property, its heightening to an absolute, "super" degree.

7. Hypermateriality

The same applies to very foundation of the Soviet *Weltanschauung*—"scientific materialism." From its point of view, physical matter comes first, is primary, while consciousness and spirit are secondary. Reality is thoroughly material; even thought, like physical, chemical, and biological processes, represents but one form of the "movement of matter." Thought and consciousness are only "the highest blossom of matter" (Friedrich Engels). Such is the postulate of "dialectical materialism," aspiring toward a completely sober, scientific approach to reality, verified by experience. According to authoritative Soviet dictionaries, "... The world is moving matter, and nothing exists which would not be a specific form of matter, its property or a form of its movement. This principle took shape on the basis of the achievements of scientific cognition and Man's practical mastery of Nature."[19] Matter is the ultimate and comprehensive reality, its very foundation. "Matter includes not only all immediately observable objects and natural bodies, but also all those that can be cognized in the future.... The entire surrounding world represents moving matter in all its infinitely diverse forms and manifestations...."[20]

Beginning from its very conception in Lenin's works, Soviet materialism absolutized the concept of "matter" while blatantly ignoring empirical data, materiality in its concrete and sensible manifestations. Lenin's book *Materialism and Empiriocriticism* (1908), which laid the foundation for Soviet materialism, was directed against the philosophy of "empiriocriticism" or "empiriomonism" of Ernst Mach, Richard Avenarius and their Russian followers, Alexander Bogdanov, Pavel Yushkevich, and others. Empiriomonism asserted the unity of sense-experience in which physical elements ("reality") cannot be separated from or opposed to psychic elements ("subjectivity"). Instead of this "principal coordination" of elements, Lenin advanced the general concept of "matter" abstracted from any specific sense-experience. According to Lenin, "matter" exists independently of any sensations, as a primordial reality that precedes and determines the contents of human experience.

In fact, it is conceptual thinking that allows us to bring together diverse elements of our perception, such as colors, sounds, weight, density, under the abstract category of "matter." We can then interpret this concept of matter as an ideal mental construction ("subjective idealism") or as a manifestation of some transcendental idea ("objective idealism"). Lenin attacks both versions of idealism, and hence traditional philosophy that recognizes the "ideal" nature of all philosophical constructions. Lenin also opposes the concept of "matter," deduced from an ideal generalization of sense-experience, to ideality itself, and proclaims matter to be the non-ideal and pre-ideal substance, the self-contained principle of existence—to the extent that matter itself allegedly generates and determines the life of ideas. What is secondary in the cognitive act of generalization is claimed to be the primary reality and the most universal ontological category. "Matter" in this materialist sense is nothing but *hyper-matter*, the most abstract of all ideas, endowed with the predicate of primordial and self-sufficient existence. Furthermore, to "matter" is attributed self-awareness, self-generated motion, dialectical contradiction, thesis and antithesis, assertion and negation, consent and dissent, i.e., all the qualities of an active, animated and even rational entity, although at the same time the "material" is posited as the antipode of the "spiritual" or "ideal."

Lenin's "dialectical materialism" is an extreme exaggeration of idealism and its simultaneous shift into the sphere of "hyper" such that the most abstract of all ideas claims to present itself as the most primary and authentic reality, the foundation of all experience and the substance of all existence. Thus, "matter" (*materiia*), as it is posited in Soviet materialism, is not just an abstract idea, but a simulacrum of matter, a copy which has no original and therefore substitutes for this absent original.

Lenin's philosophical hypermaterialism anticipates the practice of "communist construction" in the USSR, which developed from materialist assumptions but had a disastrous impact precisely on the material aspects of life: nutrition, housing, agriculture, trade, consumption, economical efficiency, and the physical security of citizens. As is well-known, in practice Soviet materialism never tried to conform to the laws of material reality but strove instead to refashion this reality. The material of nature was subjected to merciless exploitation, pollution, and destruction; the material life of the people was brought into decline, the economy subordinated not to the material laws of production but to entirely idealistic five-year plans and ideological edicts of successive party congresses. As Andrei Bely remarked at the beginning of the 1930s, the dominance of materialism in the USSR brought about the voiding of matter itself. Boris Pasternak's *Doctor Zhivago* also shows how "in the days of the triumph of materialism, matter turned into a concept and the questions of 'food supply' and 'fuel supply' came to substitute for food and fuel themselves."[21]

Materialism was, in essence, a purely ideological construct, which raised the primacy of material into a theoretical absolute but, in practice, annihilated the material. "Matter," thus elevated and separated from experience, from "bourgeois empiricism," becomes a simulacrum of matter, destructive of matter as such. Just as hypersociality served the cult of the singular personality, so hypermateriality became a means of legitimating abstract ideas in their scholastically enclosed finality. The materiality of this materialism was thus the same "hyper" phenomenon as "collectivism," "the libido," "the elementary particle," and "pure text."

8. From "Super" to "Pseudo"

It is significant that of the six spheres of hyperization, three are traditionally subsumed under the term "revolution": the social, sexual, and scientific. But the three others—hypertextuality, hyperexistentiality, and hypermateriality—can equally well be qualified by the term "revolution," since they too developed in a movement of complete revaluation of values: from essentialism to existentialism (the revolution in Western philosophy); from idealism to materialism (the revolution in Soviet philosophy); from "idea" and "content" to form, technique and text (the revolution in criticism). To this we can add the revolution of means of communication (the rise of mass media), which led to the birth of television, video, and computer technologies, producing a reality on the screen perceived as more real than the world itself.

The very nature of revolution appears in a new light—as the force productive of hyperphenomena. In its straightforward aims, the revolution is an "overturning"—it sets up one opposite in the place of another: matter in place of thought, the collective in place of the individual, text in place of content, instinct in place of intellect.... But paradoxically it is revolution itself that demonstrates the impossibility of this overturning: that which is victorious in a revolution gradually displays an even greater subordination to the very thing it was supposed to have vanquished. Materialism thus turns out to be much more detrimental to material reality and much more scholastic and abstract than any idealistic philosophy previous to it. Communism turns out to be more favorable to the absolute affirmation of a singular, omnipotent individuality than any kind of individualism preceding it. Literature reduced to "literariness," to text and a system of pure signs turns out to be much more dependent on the will of the critic than "traditional" literature, filled with historical, biographical, and ideological content. Matter, reduced to elementary particles, turns out to be a much more ideal entity, mathematically construed, than matter in the traditional sense of the term, which contains a certain inertial mass. Sexuality, reduced to pure drive, turns out to be much more cerebral and phantasmagorical than the ordinary sexual urge, which includes physical, emotional, and spiritual infatuation. It is this will to "purity," to "quintessentiality," that is the secret goal of all the above-named revolutions: pure sociality, pure materiality, pure sexuality and so on become perverted forms of the very things they seek to negate. Pure reality is thus a *simulacrum* of the property of "being real."

Let us return to the initial meaning of the prefix "hyper." Unlike the prefixes "over" and "su[pe]r," it designates not simply a heightened degree of the property it qualifies, but a superlative degree that exceeds a certain *limit.* (The same meaning is found in words like "hypertonia," "hypertrophy," "hyperinflation," "hyperbole.") This *excess* of the quality in question is so great that, in crossing the *limit,* it turns into its own antithesis, reveals its own illusionary nature. The meaning of "hyper," therefore, is a combination of two meanings: "super" and "pseudo." "Hyper" is the kind of "super" that through excess and transgression undermines its own reality and reveals itself as "pseudo." By negation of a thesis, the revolutionary antithesis grows into "super" but finally exposes its own derivative and simulative character. Certainly, this is neither the classic Hegelian dialectics of thesis and antithesis with subsequent reconciliation in synthesis, nor the modernist model of negative dialectics elaborated by the Frankfurt school (Theodor Adorno and Herbert Marcuse), in which a revolutionary antithesis is irreducibly opposed to a conservative thesis. *Postmodernist dialectics* (if it is still possible to combine such heterogeneous terms) *implies neither synthesis nor revolution but the internal tension of irony.* Antithesis, pushed to an extreme, finds thesis inside itself, and moreover proves to be an extension and intensification of this very thesis. Revolutionary negation proves to be an aggrandizement, a hyperbole of what is negated. Antithesis circles back on thesis, as its disguised and exaggerated projection.

In this way, materialism proves to be not a negation of idealism, but its most radical and militant form, ruthlessly destructive of materiality. Communism proves to be not a negation of individualism and voluntarism, but their most aggressive and despotic affirmation, ruthlessly destructive of communality. The "hyper" is the "other" of the initial quality ("thesis"), its "second order" reality, its virtual intensity. The excess of quality turns into the illusion of this quality whereas its opposite, which was intentionally negated, actually becomes heightened.

Thus hypersociality heightens the power of an individual over society. It is a sociality raised to a political and moral imperative, to an absolute degree of "oughtness" or "duty": no longer connected to any particular being (such as mother, father, child, one's neighbor), it instead destroys all such particulars in order to absolutize an all-powerful individuality (the "personality cult"). The meaning of "hyper" in this instance subdivides further into "super" and "pseudo." *Hyper*sociality is thus simultaneously a *super*-sociality and a *pseudo*-sociality. That is, the social factor is subject to such a degree of intensification that it exceeds and negates all the particularities that initially constituted the social.

Historically, intensity and illusion, the "super" and the "pseudo," evolve within the "hyper" only gradually, in two successive stages. Its first, "revolutionary" phase is represented by the "super." This is the phase of the enthusiastic discovery or construction of new realities: the socialist "supersociety," the emancipated "supersexuality," the elementary "superparticle," the self-referential "supertext," the self-propelled "supermatter." The first half of the twentieth century was mainly preoccupied with the revolutionary advancement of all these "super" phenomena. They germinated in the 1900s and 1910s in the theoretical soil of Marxism, Freudianism, and Nietzscheanism; in the 1920s and 1930s, these "super" theories took on practical form—as the social, sexual, scientific, philosophical, and critical revolutions.

This was followed in the second half of the twentieth century by a gradual realization of the simulative character of all these ubiquitous superlatives. On the other side of "hyper" we discovered "pseudo."

This transition from the "super" to the "pseudo," from the ecstatic illusions of pure reality to the ironic realization of this reality as pure illusion, accounts for the historical transformation of European and Russian culture in the twentieth century, and can be described as the movement from modernism to postmodernism.

From this standpoint, Gorbachev's *perestroika* (literally meaning "reconstruction") and Derrida's deconstruction can be seen as isomorphic stages in the development of Soviet hypersociality and Western hypertextuality.[22] Both exemplify a transition from the "super" stage, manifested in the rise of communism and formalism (New Criticism) in the 1920s and 1930s, to the "pseudo" stage of the 1970s and 1980s. Both demonstrate that "structuredness" (in the form of an ideally structured society or the structuralist conception of textuality), which was the goal proclaimed by communist and formalist-structuralist movements, manifests only the illusion of social integrity or logical coherence. In the same way that Gorbachev revealed the illusory character of socialism, which proved to be a utopian communality of alienated individuals, Derrida exposed the illusory character of structuralism, of the very notion of "structure," which proved to be a utopian communality of actually decentered, dispersed, disseminated signs.

The "pseudo" phase is the common denominator linking the crises that have overtaken the constructs of the early twentieth century: the social, scientific, philosophical, and other revolutions. Under the sign of "pseudo," there is the crisis of structuralism in the human sciences, the crisis of the concept of elementariness in physics, the crisis of leftist projects and Marxism in political ideology, the crisis of materialism, existentialism and positivism in philosophy, the demise of the Soviet ideocratic system and of communist society—such are the consequences of a world-wide metamorphosis of "hyper" from "super" to "pseudo." It is a crisis of utopian consciousness as such, followed by the construction of parodic pseudo-utopian discourses.

Only now, in its historical evolution from "super" to "pseudo," has the full significance of "hyper" been revealed, demonstrating the necessary connection and succession of its two phases, modernism and postmodernism. While modernism viewed its revolutionary accomplishments as a breakthrough into the metaphysically "pure" reality of the "super" (supersexuality, supermateriality, supersociality), postmodernism reveals the full range of the dialectics of hyperization, as an inevitable conversion of "super" to "pseudo." From a postmodernist perspective, socialist revolution, sexual revolution, existentialism, and materialism, far from being liberational insights into the highest and "truest" reality, are in fact intellectual machines designed for the production of pseudomateriality, pseudosexuality, pseudosociality, etc. Thus postmodernism finds in modernism not only a target of criticism, but also the historical ground for its own play with hyperphenomena. These hyperphenomena would be impossible if not for those revolutionary obsessions with the "super" that gave rise to the tangible "voids" and flamboyant simulacra of contemporary civilization, including totalitarianism's non-sensical, empty ideological forms that gave rise to Russian postmodernism.

In the final analysis, every "super" phenomenon sooner or later reveals its own reverse side, its "pseudo." Such is the peculiarly postmodern dialectics of "hyper," distinct from both Hegelian dialectics of comprehensive synthesis and leftist dialectics of pure negation. It is the ironic dialectics of intensification-simulation, of "super" turned into "pseudo."

Every revolution of the first half of the twentieth century is doubled and canceled out by its own "post" of the century's end. Contemporary society is postmodern, postcommunist, postutopian, postindustrial, postmaterialist, postexistential, and postsexual. At this point, the dialectics of "hyper" which shaped the ironic totality of twentieth century culture, comes to its complete self-realization.

Notes

1. Cited in *From Modernism to Postmodernism. An Anthology*, ed. by Lawrence E. Cahoone (Cambridge [MA], Oxford, 1996), p. 391.
2. "Lips were singing *bobeobi* " — an instance of futurist onomatopoeia.
3. Jean Baudrillard, *Selected Writings*, ed. by Mark Poster (Stanford, 1988), pp. 144–145.
4. Heinz R. Pagels, "Uncertainty an Complementarity," in *The World Treasury of Physics, Astronomy, and Mathematics*, ed. by Timothy Ferris (Boston, New York, Toronto, London, 1991), p.106.
5. The concept of "hypertextuality" as understood here has nothing to do with "hypertext" in the commonly accepted, "electronic" sense of the word. "Hyper"is used here in the sense of "super" and "pseudo," which relates it to the concepts of "hypersexuality," "hypersociality," etc.
6. George Steiner, "Human Literacy," in *The Critical Moment. Essays on the Nature of Literature* (London, 1964), p. 22.
7. Saul Bellow, "Skepticism and the Depth of Life," in *The Arts and the Public.*, ed. by James E. Miller Jr. and Paul D. Herring (Chicago, London, 1967), p. 23.
8. Fyodor Dostoevsky, *Notes from Underground/The Double*, trans. Jessie Coulson (London, New York, 1972), pp. 16, 26, 27, 123.
9. Jean-Paul Sartre, *Being and Nothingness*, trans. by Hazel E. Barnes (New York, 1966), pp. 256, 257.
10. Ibid., p. 804. This brief outline of existentialist thought does not allow us to go into the complicated question of the relationship between Dostoevsky's and his hero's voices, or, on another note, of Kierkegaard's and his pseudonyms' views.
11. C. S. Lewis, *The Allegory of Love* (New York, 1958), p. 196.
12. Cited in the book: *Lawrence D. H. A Critical Anthology*, ed. by H. Coombes. (Harmondsworth, 1973), p. 244.
13. John Bayley, *The Characters of Love* (New York, 1960), pp. 24, 25.
14. V. N. Voloshinov, *Freidizm. Kriticheskii ocherk* (1927), in *The Bakhtin Reader: Selected Writings of Bakhtin, Medvedev and Voloshinov*, ed. by Pam Morris (London et. al., 1994), p. 44. See a similar interpretation of the unconscious as a secondary cultural and semiotic projection in Yu. M. Lotman, *Kul'tura i vzryv* (Moscow, Gnozis, 1992), pp. 255–256.
15. Derrida, "Différance," in *A Derrida Reader. Between the Blinds* (New York, 1991), p. 73.
16. The phenomena of hypertextuality and hypersexuality, though in different terms, are considered in greater detail in my articles "*Kritika v konflikte s tvorchestvom*" (Criticism in Conflict with Creativity), *Voprosy literatury*, No. 2 (Moscow, 1975): 131–168, and "*V poiskakh estestvennogo cheloveka*" (In Search of a Natural Human Being), *Voprosy literatury* , No. 8 (1976): 111–145. Both articles are included in an expanded form in my book "*Paradoksy novizny. O literaturnom razvitii XIX–XX vekov* (The Paradoxes of Innovation. On the Development of Literature in the 19th and 20th Centuries) (Moscow, 1988), pp. 178–250.

17. K. Marx, Preface to *A Contribution to the Critique of Political Economy*, in *Marx, Engels, Lenin. On Dialectical Materialism.* (Moscow, 1977), p. 43.
18. See Lacan's "There is no sexual relation" in: *A Love Letter (Une Lettre D'Amour), Jacques Lacan & The Ecole Freudiènne: Feminine Sexuality*, ed. by J. Mitchell and J. Rose, trans. by J. Rose (London, 1983), pp. 149–161.
19. *A Dictionary for Believers and Nonbelievers*, trans. from Russian by Catherine Judelson (Moscow, 1989), p. 336.
20. *Filosofskii entsiklopedicheskii slovar'*, 2d ed. (Moscow, 1989), p. 349. Similar formulations can be found in all Soviet textbooks on dialectical materialism.
21. Boris Pasternak, *Doctor Zhivago*, in his *Sobranie sochinenii*, in 5 volumes (Moscow, 1990), vol. 3, p. 182.
22. Derrida's own comments on the relationship between the concepts of *perestroika* and "deconstruction" can be found in his small book describing his trip to Moscow in 1990, *Zhak Derrida v Moskve: dekonstruktsiia puteshestviia* (Jacque Derrida in Moscow: A Deconstruction of the Journey) (Moscow, 1993), p. 53.

Chapter 2

POSTMODERNISM, COMMUNISM, AND SOTS-ART

Mikhail Epstein

In 1991, the same year in which communism died, a reborn post-Soviet literature was immediately anointed with a new "ism." In the very beginning of the new decade (January 1991), my article "After the Future: On the New Consciousness in Literature" was published simultaneously in Russian and English journals.[1] Though the conventional Western term for the new cultural formation was "postmodernity," in Russia the same concept was designated as "postfuturicity" (*poslebudushchee*). One of the chapters in the article was titled "Our 'Postfuture' and Western Postmodernism." What was coming to an end in the Soviet Union was not merely "modernity," but the future as a communist utopia. Thus the shock of jumping into the "post" was even stronger in Russia than in the West, because communism was perceived as the ultimate future of all humankind. With *perestroika* this future quickly receded into the past.

After that, in the spring of 1991, a major conference on postmodernism was held at the Literary Institute. From then on the new "ism" began its triumphant march across the country: everything belonging to this movement was declared interesting and important, while everything else was immediately relegated to the archives. Already in early 1992, Viacheslav Kuritsyn noted in *Novyi mir* that postmodernism had become the sole living presence in the literary process.[2] And although the demise of communism and the arrival of postmodernism in Russia seemed to coincide only by chance, from the very beginning there appeared a "similarity of opposites," a kind of continuity in the very means of controlling public consciousness. Mark Lipovetsky points to the extent of Russian postmodernism's claim to ideological and aesthetic dominance: "Indeed, postmodernism does not claim to be just one more movement in a pluralistic landscape—it insists on its own dominance in all of culture."[3] While it is well known that the spirit of postmodernism is fully fledged pluralism—grounded in the dictates of minorities and the inherent value of diversity—postmodernism itself appears as an all-encompassing system that legitimizes this plurality.

Perhaps no other "ism" has arisen since the time of socialist realism that has so captured the attention and normative aims of the artistic community. The appearance of this new concept has spawned a multitude of tailor-made works and has brought about the belated recognition of earlier works as having foretold its appearance. The role of the "founder" of postmodernism—the role that Maxim Gorky filled for socialist realism with his novel *Mother* (*Mat'*)—is ascribed variously to Vladimir Nabokov with *The Gift* (*Dar*), Mikhail Bulgakov with *Master and Margarita* (*Master i Margarita*), Andrei Bitov with *Pushkin House* (*Pushkinskii dom*), and Veniamin Erofeev with his story *Moscow-Petushki* (*Moskva-Petushki*). Here pluralism is apparent—preoccupied, however, with the creation of a universal canon.

It seems to me that the similarity between postmodernism and communism as programmatic methods of influencing public consciousness is not at all coincidental. In Russia, it represents two phases in the realization of the same intellectual-aesthetic project. Whereas communism proclaimed the coming triumph of ideas that would transform reality, postmodernism reveals the absence of any reality other than the reality of ideas themselves (signs, images, names). Although postmodernism has been a topic of discussion in the West since the early 1970s and in Russia only since the early 1990s, it is in essence, like many such movements nominally adopted from the West, a deeply Russian phenomenon. One may even maintain that Russia is the birthplace of postmodernism, and that the time has finally come to acknowledge this surprising fact.

Nikolai Berdiaev's famous book *The Sources and Meaning of Russian Communism* (*Istoki i smysl russkogo kommunizma*) is very helpful in understanding the unusual nature of Russian ideological borrowings from the West. Communist doctrine came to Russia from Europe and seemed at first to be completely alien to this backward, half-Asian land. Yet the fact that Russia became the first and most powerful communist state in the world can be explained by the fact that the communal spirit was an active force in Russian history long before it became acquainted with the teachings of Marx and accomplished its mission through these.

Is not Russian postmodernism also such a phenomenon? Although postmodernist doctrines came to Russia from the West, primarily from France and the United States, the very readiness of Russian minds to immediately multiply and apply these doctrines to their native culture and make them a banner of spiritual renewal testifies to a certain innateness of postmodernism to Russian soil. If communist ideas existed in Russia before Marx, then is it not possible that postmodern ideas existed in Russia long before Derrida and Baudrillard?

The quick and easy change of the mainstream literature from the communist project to the postmodern project in itself indicates that they might have something in common. This is confirmed, on the one hand, by the predilection of the Russian practitioners of postmodernism—especially conceptualist writers and artists—for sots-art, for communist imagery and socialist realist ideological clichés. On the other hand, it is confirmed by the transparent left-wing political leanings of all the leading Western postmodernist theorists. Is not postmodernism, to use a vivid Leninesque expression, the highest and final stage of communism?

In fact, postmodernism has inherited much from the communist project, first and foremost that which relates to the end of modernity, to the exhaustion of such modern categories as truth, reality, individuality, authorship, time, and history. In the first part of this essay, I will examine the general features of postmodernism that make it comparable with Soviet communism. In the second part, I will examine the two basic stages in the development of communism into postmodernism: socialist realism and sots-art.

Part One. Postmodernism and Communism

Discussed below are a series of postmodern parameters of communism, which at the same time could be described as the communist elements of postmodernism, at least in the interpretation of postmodernism shared by the majority of those who write about it.

1. The Creation of Hyperreality

Among the most important characteristics of postmodernism is that which French philosopher Jean Baudrillard calls "simulation," or the production of reality. For Western civilization this is a novelty, having become possible only in the age of electronic mass communication. Television reproduces an event, which is specially produced in order to be reproduced by television. Such a counterfeit event, which supposedly reflects some sort of reality but instead replaces this missing reality, is called a simulacrum. Nationally televised American political party conventions, for example, are to a large degree simulacra, since the parties themselves, as specific collectives, reveal their existence only before the lens of the television camera. But the pseudo-event is surrounded by such pomp and is broadcast in such detail that for millions of people it appears more real than anything outside of the television screen.

Another important term here is "hyperreality." According to Baudrillard,

> reality itself founders in hyperrealism, the meticulous reduplication of the real, preferably through another, reproductive medium, such as photography. From medium to medium, the real is volatized, becoming an allegory of death. But it is also, in a sense, reinforced through its own destruction. It becomes reality for its own sake, the fetishism of

> the lost object: no longer the object of representation, but the ecstacy of denial and of its own ritual extermination: the hyperreal.[4]

Events specially staged to demonstrate the reality of that which doesn't exist stand out in the particular detail in which they are described. No one really knows, for example, whether the harvests reported in Stalin's or Brezhnev's Russia were ever actually reaped, but the fact that the number of tilled hectares or tons of milled grain was always reported down to the tenth of a percent gave these simulacra the character of hyperreality.

Baudrillard draws a sharp distinction between an imitation and a simulacrum that is especially helpful for understanding Russian postmodernism. An imitation presupposes the existence of some reality behind the image, and therefore the image can be false, can deviate from that reality. Behind a simulacrum there is no independent reality, since the simulacrum itself replaces the absent reality. There is nothing to compare it with. For example, the communist *subbotniki* introduced by Lenin were typical simulacra—events created purely for the sake of the event itself. Communist ideology cannot be accused of lying, since it creates the very world that it describes. Such typical Soviet ideologemes as "collective farm" ("kolkhoz") or the "party spirit of literature" ("partiinost' literatury") or the "unity of the party and the people" ("edinstvo partii i naroda") cannot be considered distortions of reality, since they do not reflect any reality, but rather create it themselves—and in this sense they correspond to it completely. All of Soviet ideology was like this. Between the ideology and the reality of the Stalin era there were almost no gaps—not because this ideology accurately reflected reality, but because in time there remained no reality in the country other than that of the ideology itself. Dneproges (the Dnieper hydroelectric plant), Magnitka, the pioneers, the apparatus of oppression—all of this was created by the ideology for the sake of confirming the correctness of the ideology itself. In this sense, the ideology was accurate—it was describing itself. And any reality that differed from the ideology simply ceased to exist—it was replaced by hyperreality, which trumpeted its existence by newspaper and loudspeaker and was much more tangible and reliable than anything else. In the

Soviet land, "fairy tale became fact," as in that American paragon of hyperreality, Disneyland, where reality itself is designed as a "land of imagination."

"Socialist realism" in this sense was a dual simulacrum, since it both created the image of hyperreality and was itself a component thereof—similar to the way a mirror enters into the interior and simultaneously reduplicates it. But all of socialist reality was socialist realism to the same degree, since it appeared as the image and model of itself. Factories were models of factories, collective farms models of collective farms—models of the same reality of which they were a part. Socialist realism is so important for understanding socialist reality because all of this reality represents socialist realism, i.e., that lofty, "literary" degree of "signness" ("znakovost") when the signifieds themselves disappear and the signifiers close in upon their own circle and become self-referential. Soviet ideology thus insisted on realism because it laid claim to the full semiotization of *all* reality, to its transformation into a text. Neither romanticism, nor surrealism, nor any other method was suited for this purpose, since they claimed to create some other kind of reality—ideal, visionary, spiritual, or subconscious—which by the very fact of its difference presupposed the preservation of "this" reality and coexistence with it. Only realism could merge with reality to such a degree that it could totally transform reality into itself, could swallow it up completely. Realism here can be understood not as an accurate reflection or copy coexisting with reality, but as the mechanism of its substitution, a recasting of reality into its sign and image, with the removal of the original itself. Realism turns into reality to the degree of its transformation—even reality itself becomes realism, i.e., a text about reality.

Another important Soviet ideologeme, "materialism," has the same function. The predominance of materialism, according to Andrei Bely, led to the disappearance of matter in the Soviet Union (the increase in shortages of all kinds, the lowering of the material standard of living, etc.). But the suffix "ism" itself in these conceptions should be understood not gnoseologically, but teleologically. Materialism and realism are those that aspire to become material, to become identical to reality, to replace every other reality and materiality. They are fundamental concepts, the historical function of which lay not in the useless doubling of reality, but in uniting with it and forming a single new reality. Factories and collective farms, canals and dirigibles, athletes and pioneers were the products of socialist realism no less than novels about factories and collective farms, since reality itself appeared as the means of the semiotic modeling of reality.

Here, of course, one may object: is not the creation of hyperreality the purpose and attribute of every ideology? And if so, how does postmodernism, whether in the West or in Russia, differ from previous systems of "totalizing beliefs," such as the ideology of the Middle Ages in Europe? The answer is that the ideologies of past centuries lacked the political and technological means to create hyperreality. The technosphere, ideosphere, and videosphere were not advanced enough to seize reality in all its manifestations and transform it into a system of signs. In earlier eras, ideologies did not so much construct hyperreality as strive toward a "higher" reality, a different, other-worldly reality. This other-reality contrasted with the existing reality, but did not claim to replace it. Social reforms and technological advances gradually made possible the ever more complete realization of ideology. The world of ideas and ideals was no longer projected onto the "other world" of reality, but became mixed with reality itself, "as it is"—the transcendental became imminent. In addition, the category of the "different," the "other-worldly" was replaced by the category of "simulation," and religious visionaries were replaced by video engineers. At this point, ideology no longer carried ideas beyond the limits of reality, since it was technologically and socially strong enough to fabricate reality itself.

The honor for this discovery of the postmodern age, when reality is simulated, fabricated, and pushed aside by an artificially created sign system, belongs to communism. True, communism was still not fully prepared technologically to create perfect simulacra and was therefore forced to resort to the physical annihilation of the "old" reality. Communism no longer strives toward the other-reality, that which is "beyond the limits," but it still believes in an ideal future for which the present must make sacrifices. It still cannot completely fabricate reality, and therefore actively works on its alteration and pushes it toward an ideology that partially simulates the new and partially, in fact, physically destroys the old. Mature postmodernism, coming to take the place of its communist precursors, is already the kind of ideology that has no need of ideology itself, having replaced it with video technology. There is no point in surgically altering reality—it is enough to visually fabricate it. While communism proclaimed the transformation of the world based on the recognition of its real laws, corresponding to the most advanced ideas and the willful efforts of the conscious part of the human race, postmodernism reveals the already complete "transformedness" of the world, the disappearance of reality per se, which is pushed aside by a system of artificial signs, by ideological and video simulations of reality.

2. Determinism and Reductionism

Postmodernism, like communism, is highly suspicious of any claims to free will, to the self-determination of human individuality. Communism established the dependence of humankind on unconscious mechanisms of economic production and accumulation, on the structure of social relations, and on the laws of the development of matter, and it reduced to nil the spiritual autonomy of the individual. Postmodernism establishes the dependence of individuality on an even greater number of unconscious mechanisms, including those that were formerly considered the most reliable guarantees of personal freedom and self-expression. Consciousness, desire, and language no longer liberate one from the fetters of matter, from the clutches of history. On the contrary, this is precisely where the main source of enslavement is located. Thus, a person is nothing more than a "tool of the unconscious," a "machine of desire," a "captive of language." And while communism still promised humanity an escape from the burdens of economic necessity, postmodernism promises no such escape from the dungeon of language, but rather asserts the joy of a frolicsome existence therein.

Communism proclaimed the construction of a classless society—and at the same time demanded a class-oriented approach in culture and ideology and was interested above all in the class origins of the individual. Postmodernism announces the end of all value hierarchies and prevailing canons (including the aesthetic one), and at the same time focuses attention on the ethnic, social, gender, and age identification of individuals, who are primarily judged as representatives of particular groups and minorities, on behalf of whom they speak. From this standpoint a woman writer is obliged to express feminist values and oppose male "chauvinism" in her work. Otherwise she is betraying her sisters in class, i.e., in gender. Furthermore, only a woman can adequately express feminist values—it is not only her duty, it is her exclusive right.

Although the theory of deconstruction denies the myth of the "beginning," of "originality," of "origins," considering all these categories unnatural constructs, the culture of postmodernism eagerly pursues the construction of these categories and their imposition on all the diversity of individuals. The category of individuality turns out to be illusory, representing the intersecting of various unconscious automatisms: desire, genes, social roles, etc. Thus, all behavior in culture and all textual strategies are assigned by a system of automatisms—above all the origins of the author. This applies to men and women, blacks and whites, homosexuals and heterosexuals—the representatives of any group. A white male who likes women turns out to be incapable of representing anything other than white male heterosexual chauvinism in his works, even if this man is Shakespeare or Tolstoy. Any discourse—even purely scientific, artistic, or philosophical—is interpreted as a discourse on power, as a conscious or unconscious attempt at a power grab by the author. As Lyotard writes, "There is no sign or thought of a sign that is not about power and of power."[5]

While communism insisted on the necessity of a class-oriented approach and in other respects allowed individuals to represent themselves—i.e., did not demand from women an exclusively feminist self-consciousness, nor from blacks an exclusively African self-consciousness—postmodernism, at least in some of its left-wing representatives, expands this genetic-group approach to all areas and all levels of identification. Furthermore, it is not the social characteristics that are most accentuated, but the most conservative, immutable, natural characteristics of the individual—and their detectability at the highest levels of cultural self-expression. Even in the sphere of artistic creation the individual turns out to be valuable not for his or her individuality, but for that which identifies him or her with a particular social group and almost automatically turns him or her into a spokesperson. Partly this resulted from the spread of popular culture in postmodernism rather than from the postmodern theory itself, which initially remained the domain of only the cultural elites. Thus, while communism used the method of reduction in a limited social-class sphere ("vulgar sociologism"), postmodernism grandiosely expands the range of application of this method and makes it universal. The process of looking for roots, the deterministic exegesis goes far beyond the framework of Marxism and spreads to all aspects of the behavior of the individual, who in any case is reduced to nothing but group membership and physical data.

3. *Antimodernism*

Postmodernism and communism display a similarity in their rejection of modernism (and all of its schools) as an obsolete, "chamber" movement in art. Antimodernism, anti-avant-gardism was the fundamental position of the Stalin era, and appeared, in relation to prerevolutionary modernist trends (and their echoes in Soviet art of the 1920s), like postmodernism, as the overcoming and outlasting of earlier "bourgeois" individualism, subjectivist exclusiveness, pure expressiveness, metaphysical and stylistic experimentation, elitism, complexity, etc. In his famous 1946 speech on Anna Akhmatova and Zoshchenko, Andrei Zhdanov, the leading Stalinist ideologue, said the following:

> Drifting out into the world came symbolists, imagists, decadents of all stripes, renouncing the people, proclaiming the thesis of "art for art's sake," preaching an ideology-free literature, covering up their ideological and moral dissolution in the pursuit of beautiful form without content.... The poets and ideologues of the ruling classes strove to escape from unpleasant reality in the clouds, in the fog of religious mysticism, in their petty personal problems and in plumbing the depths of their shallow little souls.[6]

These are almost the same reproaches that were, in somewhat more elegant form, aimed at modernism by postmodernist critics in the West in the 1970s and 1980s.

In particular, the famous literary manifesto of contemporary American writer Tom Wolfe, "Stalking the Billion-Footed Beast: A Literary Manifesto for the New Social Novel" (1989), is surprisingly reminiscent of Zhdanov's speech, although Wolfe could hardly have suspected such a similarity. Calling for the creation of a literature worthy of the great American reality (the "billion-footed beast"), Wolfe comes out against "an avant-garde position out beyond realism..., Absurdist novels, Magical Realist novels," and pities writers of the previous generation, such as Philip Roth and John Barth, who were "ruined" by modernism, which stifled their creative potential. Wolfe acknowledges that "many of these writers were brilliant. They were virtuosos." What else, one might ask, could a writer want? "But," Wolfe continues, "what was this lonely island they had moved to?... The action, if any, took place at no specific location.... The characters had no backgrounds. They came from nowhere. They didn't use realistic speech. Nothing they said, did, or possessed indicated any class or ethnic origin."[7]

Criticizing modernism for its insufficient attention to environment and origins, Wolfe pays tribute to the aforementioned obsession with every kind of reduction and identification—ethnic, gender, and social—that are so important for the theory and cultural practice of postmodernism. And further, entirely in the Stalin-Zhdanov aesthetic spirit, Wolfe compares the invention of realism in the eighteenth century to the "introduction of electricity into engineering" (recall that "writers are the engineers of the human soul"); he proposes creating "a battalion, a brigade" of writers like Zola and sending them out to study American reality[8] (recall the brigade method in Soviet literature of the 1930s). What is revealed here is not the direct influence of socialist realism on Wolfe, but the logic of postmodern rhetoric itself, which stands in opposition to the abstractness, experimentation, and individualism of modernist writing and therefore must resort to engineering and collectivist metaphors.[9]

4. Ideological Eclecticism

Postmodernism parts with the great ideologies—in Jean-François Lyotard's terms "metanarratives" (or "grand narratives") which appropriate a totalizing worldview that explains everything (such as Christianity, Marxism, Freudianism, traditional liberalism)—and brings culture into a state of ideological eclecticism and fragmentation. This would seem to have no connection whatsoever with the ideological predominance of Marxism in the USSR. Soviet Marxism, however, unlike the "pure" or "classical" Marxism that is still widespread in the West, is a highly eclectic mixture of various ideological elements. It incorporates elements of the enlightened populist ideology of Tolstoy with its idealization of the simple and deeply spiritual life of the working classes; Slavophile ideology with its faith in the superiority of the Russian (Soviet) people over the decadent civilization of the West; cosmic, Fedorovian ideology with its doctrine of the power of labor to transform the laws of nature and conquer the far reaches of the cosmos, etc. It is because Marxism formally became the ruling and only permissible ideology in the USSR that it, adapting to different circumstances and requirements in the fight for power, absorbed a multitude of other ideologies and mixed them in a "postmodern" manner—ideologies that in the West remained separate and independent, defending in a modernist manner their purity and exclusiveness.

Under Soviet conditions, the "right" and the "left," patriots and internationalists, conservatives and liberals, existentialists and structuralists, technocrats and "greens"—all of these found support and justification for their views in Marxism and themselves claimed to be the original Marxists. As a result, Soviet Marxism became the first and unsurpassed model of ideological pastiche, an eclectic mix of the most heterogeneous and garishly clashing elements, inside of which gradually developed the ironic awareness of their incompatibility, or, more precisely, their combinability in a new dimension of play.

A fully postmodern irony was already being played out even among the highly perceptive official ideologues who, with the allowable venom, criticized the internationalists for being insufficiently patriotic and the patriots for being insufficiently internationalist.

And furthermore, this irony over ideology—not only the ruling ideology, but ideology in general—was the most valid currency in the circles of the slightly dissident Soviet intelligentsia. In the 1970s and 1980s, when intellectuals in the West were still deadly serious in their left or right sympathies/antipathies, when they still defended the truth of their modernist heritage and fought for various projects for the rational reshaping of the world, in Russia a postmodern reevaluation of all values, a conceptualist game with all known ideological and cultural codes, was already in full swing. Marxism in the West, in spite of all the structuralist reexaminations, retained its modernist nature, it remained what it had been in the early 1920s—a project for remaking the world that challenged the Christian project and all other "metanarratives" that were allowed by the very freedom of the free world to retain their identity in open opposition to each other. Marxism in the USSR, owing to its omnipresence, became everything and nothing—a parody of ideological thought as such, a grandiose postmodern work in the genre of an "all-encompassing and all-conquering ideology."[10]

5. The Critique of Metaphysics: Dialectics and Deconstruction

The general enemy of communism and postmodernism is "metaphysics," which is understood as the assertion of supernatural and self-identical origins of existence, as the real embodiment of ideas or "logos" and the possibility of their cognition through pure logic. While in communist theory, metaphysics is critiqued by means of "dialectics," in postmodern theory (poststructuralism) it is critiqued by means of "deconstruction." Deconstruction may be defined as the revelation of the incompleteness and inadequacy of any rational judgment, the reduction of all signifieds (i.e., various realia, objects, and conceptual contents) into a plane of signifiers (i.e., words, nominations) and the free play with these signs. Postmodernism critiques the metaphysics of presence, according to which signs refer to something standing behind them, to so-called "reality." Postmodern theory claims that they refer only to other signs, and instead of reality it is better to conceive of the absence or unfulfilled expectation of reality, i.e., a realm of some sort of hiatus, an endless deferment of all signifieds, and consequently the untenability of the very concepts of "original," "origin," and "truth."

A similar unmasking of the "metaphysics of presence" was strangely enough also characteristic of so-called Soviet "dialectics," with its intuition of the void behind the swirling mass of signs and nominations. The dialectics of Soviet Marxism is by no means the same as what it claimed to be Hegelian dialectics, which posits historical process as both thesis and antithesis, which eventually unite in a synthesis (though Hegel himself didn't use the term "synthesis" but instead spoke of the "sublation" [*Aufhebung*] and "whole"). Soviet dialectics proceeded from some sort of slippery, elusive null point that was impossible to equate with any consistent position, but that allowed for the condemnation and rejection of any "other" position by declaring it "metaphysical," "nondialectical." Here lies the internal irony of militant Soviet dialectics, which was more or less recognized by the "dialecticians" themselves as complete relativity inherent in a totalitarian ideology.

Soviet ideology loved to argue with all theories from the West: philosophical, religious, social, historical, literary, and even cosmological. Soviet ideology labeled every one of them unilateral, "subjectivist" or "objectivist," "positivist" or "irrational," "individualist" or "dehumanizing," and towered over them with its own "dialectics." But this dialectical system was not a "sublation" of the theories being criticized, i.e., an overcoming which preserves what it overcomes, transcending their unilateral dimension and uniting them at a higher level. In Soviet Marxism, it was a pseudo-dialectics of the rejection of all positive theories, the revealing of their false, futile, and illusory nature—hence no positive adoption of these theories ever took place.

If we trace the movement of this dialectical whirlwind through Soviet history and outline the areas that suffered from it, we will find that for all practical purposes not one positive concept remained that by one name or another wasn't annihilated and disemboweled from the standpoint of a "higher dialectics." Even ideas that were sacred to classical Marxism were subjected to annihilation: materialism under the name of "mechanistic," "vulgar," "metaphysical" materialism; internationalism in the form of "ultraleft deviations" and "mindless cosmopolitanism"; the proletariat under the name of "workers' opposition" and the "cult of the proletariat"; collectivism under the name of "spontaneity," "egalitarianism," and "lack of personal responsibility"; and finally dialectics itself under the name of "minority idealism," "Hegelianism," "relativism," "eclecticism," etc. It goes without saying that opposing, "anti-Marxist" concepts—"idealism," "nationalism," the "bourgeoisie," "individualism," "metaphysics," etc.—were even more thoroughly annihilated.

Since the Soviet dialectical whirlwind pulled in and destroyed absolutely all concepts, one must assume that it came from some sort of vacuum and carried within itself an empty, madly spinning funnel. And, in fact, in the "dialectical" struggle against right- and left-leaning tendencies, against Trotskyism and Bukharinism, against Bukharinism and Deborinism, against voluntarism and revisionism, there remained no detectable part that could serve as a foundation for truth—everything was distributed either to the right or to the left, taking on the appearance of a sharpened blade, with which Andrei Platonov compares the general party line in *The Foundation Pit* (*Kotlovan*). A line is a geometric abstraction without physical dimensions in the real world. But even the image of a cutting line still has too great a straightening effect on the method of dialectical action, putting it in a positive light, as if it had its own path even though it lacks its own space. This path was also absent, since the dialectical blows were administered simultaneously from the right and the left, i.e., the presumed truth was located not in the center, but rather nowhere. The most devastating blow was the "double uppercut," the dialectical accusation of left/right leanings when, for example, the most inveterate left-revolutionaries who were spoiling for a fight for a world commune turned out to be the main abettors of the world bourgeoisie. Lenin's book *The Infantile Disease of Leftism in Communism* (*Detskaia bolezn' levizny v kommunizme*) served as the shining model of the tactics of this kind of dual fight. Since the blows were administered from two opposing sides, it was the center that turned out to be the chief victim. The center was attacked even more mercilessly than either of the extremes, since it was the center that could claim to be a dialectical synthesis of the two sides.

That is why Lenin, Stalin, Mao Tse-tung, and all other like-thinking communists unleashed their greatest fury on the centrists, the "double-dealers," who wanted to reach a compromise between the left and the right and voted with "both hands." The most heinous crime from the standpoint of this dialectical system was compromise, i.e., the attempt at a synthesis or mediation between opposites. Idealism and "metaphysical" materialism were condemned as ruinous extremes, but the tone of this judgment was relatively restrained, albeit still harsh and unforgiving: nothing at all can be adopted from such openly false theories—they themselves will expose their own shortcomings. The most severe criticism was reserved for the "pretense" of occupying a "third" position above the fray, of building bridges or finding a middle position between the two worldviews. Here, too, Lenin remains the unsurpassed teacher of the dual fight, since his main philosophical book, *Materialism and Empirio-Criticism* (*Materializm i empiriokrititsizm*) (1908), directs its sharpest attacks against philosophical centrism, against attempts to find a "principled coordination" between the physical and psychic, the materialistic and ideal elements of experience in a central, mediating concept of "experience" itself, "experiential unity," empiriomonism. The fight with the extremes did not produce as much dialectical enthusiasm as the fight with the center, in which all left and right elements of the totalitarian worldview were united specifically for the annihilation of the only thing that wanted to and could unite them.

Thus, communist dialectics did not merely annihilate all positive concepts and intellectual movements, which in its view were all unilateral, "nondialectical" and subject to elimination on account of their "determinateness" (after all, any determinate concept has its binary opposite and consequently falls into the category of the unilateral). Totalitarian dialectics also destroyed the very ground on which it was supposed to stand, if unilateral concepts were to be subject to some sort of positive removal. Along with the extremes, which were removed from the presumed center point, this dialectical system annihilated the center itself, its own starting point, thereby revealing itself as a technique of empty thinking, a kind of Marxist

"Tao." "Neither either/or, nor both/and, nor even neither/nor"—a boundless, gaping void that only needs determinate concepts in order to demonstrate their futility and illusory nature.

All that remained from the annihilation of these concepts, what became the "conquest" of dialectics, were oxymoronic phrases such as "materialistic idealism," "dialectical materialism," "revolutionary legitimacy," the "fight for peace," "optimistic tragedy," the "unity of theory and practice," "freedom as a conscious necessity," the "harmonious merging of the social and the personal," "international and patriotic education," etc. Furthermore, the concepts comprising these oxymorons were taken in such a ravaged form that they could only survive by propping each other up—they had no independent basis of their own. These concepts retained meaning only in their binary opposition to other concepts. Internationalism was significant in that it aided in the negation of patriotism by labeling it nationalism; patriotism in that it aided in the negation of internationalism as cosmopolitanism; materialism in that it negated idealism; idealism in that it negated material improvement, etc.

When such opposite negations are combined in an oxymoron, such as "material idealism" or "international-patriotic education," they form a zone of active emptiness of meaning. An oxymoron has a tension of meaning, since in itself it demonstrates the process of mutual destruction of opposite concepts. They unite in order to reveal the nothingness of each other, and thus the nothingness of that which unites them as well. This is not a static void, an absence, but rather an active, and even dual, self-referential, "self-emptying" void, which consumes not only the "alien," but also itself, its own basis.

It should be noted that this system of "destructive dialectics" has little in common with the negative dialectics that were disseminated in the West, primarily in the works of the German thinkers of the Frankfurt school, T. Adorno and H. Marcuse. The negative dialectics associated with the leftist, ultrarevolutionary interpretation of Hegelianism repudiates the category of synthesis, but emphasizes the category of antithesis as an irreconcilable contradiction in which the revolutionary antithesis, "The Great Rejection," stands in contrast to the conservative thesis and does not merge with it. Furthermore, both the thesis and the antithesis, because of their irreconcilability, do not erase or destroy each other, but, on the contrary, become even more determinate, acquire a more sharply defined bias, or unilaterality. What is represented in the West as a "negative" point of dialectics can from the Russian point of view only serve as an argument for its strengthened, "enraged" positivity, which avoids a "divine" synthesis in order to remain itself, in its own "demonic" arrogance. Negative dialectics do in fact present us with the demon of negation, a kind of Mephistophelian gesture of pure revolutionariness, but this is still a long way from totalitarian dialectics—the kingdom of the Destroyer itself, who demonstrates the infiniteness of its will by destroying its own basis. To avoid misunderstandings one should not label the dialectics of totalitarian thought "negative," i.e., apply a term to it that has become firmly associated with another, revolutionary consciousness. Dialectics of the Soviet type could be labeled a "destructive dialectics," since in it is produced not only a revolutionary negation of some positive concepts by others (the stage of antithesis), but the mutual destruction of all positive concepts. This is the stage of collapse of dialectics itself, which instead of developing concepts to full determinateness, reduces them to an initial, infinite nothing.

Dialectics—which, in the Hegelian method, functions as the ascent of concepts from nothing, from boundlessness, from aimless abstraction into the sphere of the concrete, positive, rationally real—in its communist variant began to function as the descent of concepts from the sphere of the concrete, of qualitative determinateness, into the depths of an indeterminate nothing. Of course, communist dialectics, unlike postmodern deconstruction, still uses the criterion of "truth," and even considers an approximation of absolute truth to be possible, although this absolute truth develops out of an aggregate of relative truths. Dialectics still proclaims its own cognitive infallibility, while deconstruction constantly deconstructs itself in the course of philosophical research.

6. Aesthetic Eclecticism

Postmodernism reduces to nil the avant-garde pretense of one particular artistic style to historical primacy, innovation, hermetic purity, and an absolutely true understanding of higher reality. Postmodernism reestablishes the connections between art and all the surrounding classical and archaic traditions and achieves its artistic effect by a conscious mixing of various historically incompatible styles. But the same ascent to a superstylistic level also took place in the aesthetics of socialist realism. Andrei Siniavsky, in his treatise "On Socialist Realism" (1959), already characterized this "creative method" as a union of the incompatible: realistic psychologism and socialist teleology, heroic enthusiasm and a predilection for lifelike details. Siniavsky did not so much condemn socialist realism for a lack of integrality as find in it a truly new quality, which required open acknowledgment and an aesthetic interpretation. While demonstrating the monstrous eclecticism of socialist realism, Siniavsky already at that time allowed for a bit of distanced aesthetic admiration of this eclecticism and called for making it creatively conscious, discovering a device for combining the incompatible, and enjoying its grotesque, ironic effect. Socialist realism, following Siniavsky's advice, has turned into sots-art, postmodernism. Siniavsky, for example, suggested that the aesthetics of Stalin should not have been dethroned after his death, but rather carried into a higher, sacred dimension: "If only the heirs of Stalin had thought to announce that he had ascended to heaven and that his remains had healing powers for the lame and possessed; if only children said their bedtime prayers to the cold, twinkling stars of the heavenly Kremlin, and Stalin himself, surrounded by all generations, watched over his people from above without saying a word through his mysterious moustache!"[11]

This aesthetic project of Siniavsky's was realized in a flash in the sots-art, postmodernist works of Vitaly Komar and Aleksandr Melamid, such as "Stalin and the Muses" ("Stalin i Muzy"), "The Origin of Socialist Realism" ("Proiskhozhdenie sotsialisticheskogo realizma"), and "As a Child I Once Saw Stalin" ("Odnazhdy v detstve ia videl Stalina") from the series "Nostalgic Socialist Realism" ("Nostal'gicheskii sotsialisticheskii realizm") (1981–83).

In fact, with its eclectic mix of elements from the classical, romantic, realist, and avant-garde (futurist) legacies, socialist realism paved the way for postmodernism and just missed sowing the seeds of self-irony itself, remaining absolutely serious, bombastic, and prophetic. Socialist realism is not some sort of separate, isolated artistic movement in the classical or avant-garde sense of the word. Socialist realism is metadiscursive in the same way that Soviet Marxism is meta-ideological. Socialist realism is a form of superstylistic aesthetics, an encyclopedia of all literary devices and clichés, and it is aware of this itself. The theoreticians of socialist realism always emphasized that the unity of socialist realism as an artistic method could only be achieved through a diversity of styles, and they presumed the necessity of such a diversity. The concept of "artistic method" itself, which was defended by both Stalinist and Brezhnevian theoreticians, is a metastylistic category. Already at the first meeting of Soviet writers, when the method of socialist realism was essentially proclaimed, Andrei Zhdanov demanded the "arming" of literature with all possible styles and devices: "Soviet literature has every opportunity to apply these kinds of weapons (the genres, styles, forms, and devices of literary creation) in all their richness and diversity, selecting the best that has been created in this area by all previous ages,"[12] The last literary encyclopedia of the Soviet era also insists on the superstylistic nature of socialist realism: "In contemporary discussions socialist realism is considered a new type of artistic creation that is not confined to one or even several means of representation."[13] Just as Soviet Marxism successfully simulated all ideologies, beginning with ancient polis democracy and the Catholic Middle Ages and ending with the tragic optimism of Nietzschianism and the Fedorovian project of transforming nature, socialist realism successfully simulated all literary styles and movements, beginning with the ancient epics and Old Russian byliny and ending with a refined Tolstoyan psychologism and the futurist poetics of posters and slogans.

7. Citational Mode

Postmodernism rejects naive and subjective strategies intended to demonstrate creative originality, to aid the self-expression of the authorial "I"—and opens up an era of the "death of the author" in which art becomes a game of citations, open imitations, borrowings, and variations on the themes of others. Postmodernism accepts as an axiom that citationality is the nature of all culture (though it was "discovered"—and expressed in the form of parody—by Flaubert, in his "Bouvard and Pécuchet" and his "Dictionary of Truisms"). The death of the author—not merely in the figurative, but also literal sense—was, however, one of the fundamental truths of the new socialist realist aesthetics and the topic of stressful meditations and "self-overcoming" even of such contemporaries as Mandel'shtam and Pasternak. "I am perfectly happy to come to naught in the revolutionary will" (Pasternak). Citation, the conscious act of being derivative, was in the blood of the socialist era, whose discourses were oriented toward the words of others, toward general truths that belonged to everyone—and no one in particular. The original subject of socialist realist culture was some sort of collective beginning—people or party—in the name of whom the artist comes forth, citing, as it were, that which he has been entrusted to say. These utterances, personal in form but "socialist" in content, were at times direct paraphrases of famous dicta from the classics (above all the classics of Marxism). Socialist realism was an aesthetics of diverse citations, so deeply implanted in the text that they became part of its very fabric. Simply to write "by decree of the party" was considered an insufficient level of both skill and party spirit: writers were supposed to write "by decree of their own hearts"; but their hearts belonged inseparably to their "beloved communist party" (Mikhail Sholokhov). Thus, in socialist realism an aesthetics of "heartfelt citation" is developed, which, unlike mature postmodernism, does not play itself up in its foreignness, but seemingly implants itself in the text, without, however, hiding its use of citation; on the contrary, it puts it on display as a badge of trustworthiness and reliability.

The most representative genre of the Soviet era is not the novel or poem, but the metadiscourse describing the codes of "cultural," "conscious" behavior and normative thought: encyclopedias, textbooks, readers, and collections of sayings that don't have authors, but only compilers—collectors and peddlers of citations. Properly speaking, even the novel and poem represented metadiscourses—they did not so much create artistic reality as describe the rules of its creation, the rules of the literary grammar in accordance with which the novel or poem had to be composed. Every artistic work was supposed to serve as a model of its genre, and in criticism the degree of its exemplariness was discussed, i.e., the degree to which it accurately modeled the rules of aesthetic discourse. While the avant-garde was an aesthetics of the primary, leading to the excitement of original discovery, socialist realism was openly derivative, based on citation, on the simulation of authorship and originality.

8. The Middle Ground Between Elite and Popular

Postmodernism erased the opposition between elite and popular culture.[14] While modernism is profoundly elitist and haughtily avoids the cults and stereotypes of mass society, postmodernism willingly adopts these stereotypes and patterns its own works after them. This adoption of the opposition of elite/popular was already systematically realized within the framework of the communist project, and not only by lowering the elite to the level of mass culture, but also by raising the level of the masses themselves. The policy of universal literacy and supervigilant censorship succeeded in accomplishing this dual task. On the one hand, the masses diligently studied reading and writing and were introduced to the treasures of classical culture, to the traditions of Pushkin, Tolstoy, Glinka, Tchaikovsky, Repin—while the crude, vulgar forms of mass culture, such as pulp fiction, carnival games, and barroom amusements were strictly forbidden and repressed. On the other hand, elitist movements in art and philosophy—and above all modernist "refinements" and avant-garde experiments designed for the comprehension of the chosen few, complex theoretical constructs, surrealism, abstractionism, existentialism, psychoanalysis, musical dodecaphony, etc.—were persecuted, mercilessly hounded out of society as symptoms of bourgeois "individualistic" decay, and an insurmountable barrier was erected against their penetration from the West.

Thus, Soviet society, finding itself in the double vice of a censorship/educational policy, was steadily pushed into a state of cultural homogeneity. A new culture of mediocrity was created, equally removed from the peaks and valleys that still remained quite polarized in the West. Soviet culture would not allow itself Stravinsky, nor Schoenberg, nor organ-grinders, nor burlesque cabaret. This artificial leveling of cultural contrasts paved the way for the postmodern effect of "leveled" value hierarchies and the simplification, the "stereotypification" of artistic language (unlike the extremely complicated language of modernist art, music, and literature).

9. Posthistoricism and Utopia

Postmodernism, as is apparent from the term itself, attempts to stop the course of historical time and construct a sort of posthistorical space, post-temporal world in which all discursive practices, styles, and strategies have an echo, an imitative gesture, and are included in an endless game of semiotic recodings. Fredric Jameson describes the purpose of the latest version of postmodernism as follows: "If history has become spatial, so also has its repression and the ideological mechanisms whereby we avoid thinking historically."[15] This escape into a post-temporal continuum was also a component of the communist project, largely achieved already in Soviet hyperreality. Soviet culture considered itself the last word in world culture and therefore, unlike avant-gardism, was not afraid of being derivative, willingly acknowledging its traditionality. It even claimed to be a synthesis and generalization of the best, "progressive" traditions of the past. In Lenin's famous saying: "You can only become a communist when you enrich your mind with the knowledge of all the riches that have been produced by humankind" (242). One could easily replace the word "communist" with "postmodernist." Soviet culture, like postmodern culture, did not in the least conceive of itself as a historically transient phenomenon, but rather as a collection of all the treasures of civilization, a meeting place of its giants. At this intersection of all historical pathways sit Shakespeare and Cervantes, Marx and Tolstoy, Hegel and Goethe, Pushkin and Byron, Gorky and Maiakovsky at a banquet of the human soul and raise a toast to the one happy place in the world that has united them for eternity. "Pushkin is here with us; Shakespeare is here with us; Tolstoy is here with us"—such was the favorite refrain of all the endless literary festivals and anniversary celebrations. The very predilection of Soviet culture—

especially in the later stages under Brezhnev—for celebrating anniversaries bespeaks the cyclical nature of the new experience of time, whose basic structure is repetition. More and more, time lost its unidirectionality and was enclosed in a circle of repetitive celebrations: the hundredth anniversary of the birth of ..., the fiftieth anniversary of the death of ..., etc. Practically every day was the anniversary of something, and the noise of the celebration never died out, with each gala evening passing into a festive matinée. It was but a short step to an official change of the historical strategy in the views on time, a change that was already partly anticipated by the introduction of the concepts "mature socialism" and "real socialism," which replaced the concept of communism with its orientation toward the future. "Mature" and "real" socialism was the completeness of the current times, the fulfillment of the age-old designs, the readiness to become one's own "descendants" and live in the present that our ancestors imagined as the distant future. The entire future, as the great Chernyshevsky stated, has already been transferred to the present, and therefore striving for a better future is now replaced by a love for the eternal present. The cry "now and always," appearing in communism when it was already in its death throes, had already been used by postmodernism, to which was also bequeathed the present holiday of post-temporality.

Postmodernism is usually perceived as an anti-utopian or post-utopian ideology, which places it in opposition to communist utopianism. To begin with, however, communism also fought with utopia, making quite an impression on this basis in the consciousness of millions of people who were enthralled with its "scientific nature" and "practicality." Postmodernism in this sense could only paraphrase the title of Engels's work *The Development of Socialism from Utopia to Science,* replacing the word "science" with "game." Cognitive criteria in postmodernism are replaced by the category of sign action, a linguistic game, the goal of which is found in the game itself. Second, the rejection of all utopias in postmodernism does not prevent it from being the last great utopia itself. Postmodernism rejects utopia in order to take its place. In this sense, postmodernism is more utopian than all previous utopias put together, since it establishes itself in post-time: not there, not later, but here and now. Earlier utopias, according to their own designs, were supposed to yield to the authentic reality of the future, whereas postmodernism cannot exhaust its utopian nature, because beyond its boundaries there is no reality more authentic than that which already exists within its boundaries. This reality is itself utopian and does not leave any thinking to be done in the future, in the further passage of time. In place of self-celebratory utopias of the future, there has arrived a utopia of the eternal present, a self-repeating game.

This last utopia, frozen at the end of everything, in an "infinite cul-de-sac," is postmodernism. Nothing can surpass it or turn it back, because it absorbs everything and encompasses everything. It consciously places itself after everything, at the end of time, no matter how long this end might last. Where earlier utopias, including communist, were oriented toward the future, paving their bloody way in battles with the past and present—it is in this very future that postmodernism settles in comfortably as an already realized utopia, which threatens no one and demands nothing of anyone. Communism and socialist realism still proclaimed their absolute novelty and for this reason alone should have acknowledged that they were historical in nature, that they belonged in time. Postmodernism overcomes this final weakness of previous utopias, which were too preoccupied with their own novelty and therefore inevitably built themselves into the historical order. Postmodernism acknowledges that it is a secondary, derivative, simulative formation, and consequently has a legitimate right to inherit everything and close the historical circle. The new must inevitably grow old, but the old never ages. Postmodernism is born derivative and lifeless, but that is precisely why it can never die. While losing at novelty, postmodernism ends up the winner as the final, irreplaceable phase of culture. This is what sets the postmodernist strategy apart from avant-gardism and socialist realism, which rushed to declare themselves the first word and knowingly deprived themselves of the chance to be the last word. While communism thought of itself as the culmination of all the past history of humankind, postmodernism proclaims the end of history itself.

* * *

Although the striking similarity between postmodernism and communism can be seen from the nine theses outlined above, it would be premature to consider them identical. Communist aesthetics still lack the carefree playfulness and ironic self-consciousness of mature postmodernism. Communism is postmodernism with a modernist face that still wears the expression of ominous seriousness.

Surveying the communist era now from the heights of postmodernism, one can conclude that communism was an immature and barbarous variant of postmodernism, an Eastern approach to it, as it were. Communism was still partly "modernist," maintaining continuity with the project of modernity, with an orientation toward the future, with faith in reason, progress, and objective laws of reality along with the possibility of apprehending them. Communism was such an early form of postmodernism that it was forced to establish itself by modernist means, i.e., by breaking with tradition, dashing into the future, using physical force on reality and ideological force on the consciousness of the populace—as the avant-garde, having leapt forward ahead of the bulk of the human race, is always forced to act.

In essence, Western postmodernism has merely ended the fight of its precursor, communism, with the spirit of modernity—and it has accomplished this by infinitely more effective and tolerant means. Postmodernism has finally rid itself of the "modernist birthmarks" of communism. It has stopped fighting with the past and working for the future, settling peacefully into the boundless spaces of post-temporality, the eternal present. Rather than fighting tradition, it has adopted all traditions, with the stipulation of ironic distancing; instead of citations from ideologically tested authors, it uses citations from aesthetically tested authors; instead of the destruction of elite culture in the name of popular culture, it gradually erases the distinction between the elite and the popular and creates a single middle-brow culture. In this sense, postmodernism has turned out to be the fulfillment of the designs that communism itself, because of its historical haste and immaturity, failed to accomplish. The famous Marxist division of the building of communism into two phases—the socialist and the truly communist—can now be reproduced as the doctrine of two phases in the coming of postmodernism: the communist and the truly postmodern.

Part Two. Socialist Realism and Sots-Art

In the second part of this chapter I will concentrate on two periods in the development of communist aesthetics in its transition from the modern to the postmodern: socialist realism and sots-art.

1. Socialist Realism between the Modern and the Postmodern

Historically, socialist realism, like the entire communist era in Russia, occurred between the periods of modernism (the early twentieth century) and postmodernism (the late twentieth century). The interim nature of socialist realism, a period with no apparent counterpart in the West, raises the questions of its relationship to modernism and postmodernism and of where exactly, under specifically Russian conditions, to draw a line between them. Should socialist realism be considered a late stage of modernism or an early stage of postmodernism? Or is it even possible in the evolution of this transitional socialist aesthetic system to distinguish the point where it escapes from the gravitational force of modernism and passes into the zone of incipient postmodernism?

Boris Groys, in his book *The Total Art of Stalinism* claims that socialist realism, and totalitarian art in general, is nothing other than the embodiment of the project of avant-garde (modernist) art with its ideal of subordinating all of reality to the experimentally audacious insight of the artist. In this sense, according to Groys, Stalin accomplished what Khlebnikov, Maiakovsky, Meyerhold, and Malevich dreamed of: transforming life into a work of art. At that point, artists themselves become superfluous and are subject to "removal": the greatest and essentially only artist of this period is Stalin himself.

> It is therefore no accident that the triumph of the avant-garde project in the early 1930s coincided with the final defeat of the avant-garde as an official artistic movement... In relation to the fundamental task of the avantgarde, namely the defeat of the museum, the escape of art

> directly into life, socialist realism was simultaneously both the completion of and a meditation on avantgarde demiurgism.[16]

One can argue with this conception, which has its weaknesses, especially in its exaggeration of the aesthetic experience and experimental boldness of the Stalin era. The avant-garde delight with which leftist Western artists of the 1930s embraced Stalinism, seeing in it a continuation of their own native futurist, constructivist, or surrealist experiment, is turned by Groys from a plus into a minus and, following this logic, can be transformed into a critique of avant-gardism based on the fact that it was continued and reached its crowning glory in the communist experiment.

But even if one agrees with Groys (however intently ironic his theory is) that the modernist project was realized by Stalin, one still must raise the question that the very fact of this realization brings about a new, postmodern consciousness—and therefore abolishes modernism, making it a "relic of the past." Hence the incredibly vicious attacks by Stalinist ideologues on any modernist tendencies, including futurism and surrealism, as hopelessly subjective and formalist flights from reality. Hence also the declaration of a new artistic method, socialist realism, which would fully and objectively reproduce a reality *already transformed* in light of progressive ideas.

One could construct a more balanced typology, presupposing that socialist realism is in one way a concluding stage of modernism and in another way an initial phase of postmodernism, but as a whole it is neither; instead, it is a *lengthy period of transition between the modern and the postmodern.* By the very fact that it was realized in the Stalinist period, the utopian project of the avant-garde ceased to be aggressively utopian and, becoming ever more deeply rooted in realism, irrealizing and hyperrealizing it, gradually turning into postmodernist irony and eclecticism. The messianic, transcendental impulses with which the avant-garde attempted to subordinate social reality to utopian visions were appropriated by socialist realism and turned into a triumphant characterization of an already transformed reality. Finally, postmodernism would discard the very idea of "reality" in favor of an ideological simulacrum, a chimera, the hyperreality of play.

Thus, the phenomenon of socialist realism itself, and totalitarian art as a whole, can be defined as a historical transition from an avant-garde purity of style to a postmodern playful eclecticism. The experimental purity of form in avant-gardism was deadly serious, militant, and goal-oriented, whereas the eclecticism of postmodernism appears in the form of play, recognizing its own conditionality and relativity. But why can't an eclecticism of style combine with an aggressive seriousness in a single cultural paradigm?

A *severe, intense, militant eclecticism* is the dominant in totalitarian art, which is thus positioned between the modern (avant-garde) and the postmodern as their connecting link. Totalitarianism, as is apparent from the name itself, attempts to embrace all diverse styles and forms and subordinate them to the single, integral, crucial task of transforming reality. The category that we propose of *serious eclecticism* enables us to explain, on the one hand, the connection between socialist realism and the serious goal-orientation and experimental purity of the avant-garde, and, on the other hand, between socialist realism and the playful eclecticism of postmodernism. While the East needed a special transitional period between the modern and the postmodern—the period of serious eclecticism—what was happening in the West?

In the West, of course, there was no violent break in the development of modernism. But here as well the difference between Russia and the West is not as great as it might seem, for even in the West the transition from the modern to the postmodern was not absolutely direct—there was a "buffer zone" between them at approximately the same time, 1930–50. We are not, of course, referring to socialist realism, which had a very brief run in the West and involved too few major artists. The Western counterpart of socialist realism, as a transitional period from the modern to the postmodern, was that which is customarily labeled "late" or "high" modernism. Thomas Mann, Hermann Hesse, François Mauriac, Ernest Hemingway, and William Faulkner can be considered the leading representatives of this artistic generation of the mid-twentieth century.

High modernism was wide open to various artistic and mythological traditions. It distanced itself from the purism of early modernism, the avant-garde, that had attempted to reduce its aesthetics to a single device or rigid system of devices. High modernism combines various techniques, including realistic psychologism, mythologism, parable-like forms, symbolism, stream-of-consciousness, defamiarization,, grotesque, and play of allusions and citations. But, in spite of the stylistic eclecticism, it nevertheless remained a serious and, in a certain sense, elite form of art, which set moral, psychological, ideological, and messianic goals for itself, and relied upon specially prepared readers who could handle the complex language.

Even with the incommensurable values of high modernism and socialist realism, both represent the aesthetics of serious eclecticism, which both in the USSR and in the West mediated the transition from early (avant-garde) modernism to postmodernism. Of course, this seriousness itself can appear in various registers: heroic-optimistic or tragic-pessimistic. The heroic spirit of socialist realism is based on the values of all-encompassing and militant collectivism, whereas the sublime and sometimes tragic spirit of high modernism—on the values of the individual, which in its attempts to join the universal (including the social) recognizes the inevitability of its profound existential alienation. But in spite of this enormous difference, there is a certain correspondence between the leading figures in Soviet and Western literature of the 1930s and 1940s: Mikhail Sholokhov and William Faulkner, Andrei Platonov and Ernest Hemingway, Maxim Gorky and Thomas Mann, Leonid Leonov and Hermann Hesse. One can't help noticing that the representatives of high modernism were much more warmly received by Soviet criticism than the early modernists—the expressionists, Dadaists, surrealists—who, even if they were leftists, were automatically placed in the camp of the formalists, antihumanists, enemies of social progress. What united Soviet writers with the late modernists, in spite of their enormous ideological differences, was the aesthetics of eclecticism combined with "serious," nonformal, nonartistic or superartistic goals, which contrasted with the early modernist "elitist, hermetic artistic constructions, laboratory form-creating."[17] Wanting to fill in the ranks of "progressive" literature with the greatest Western writers of the time, Soviet critics used such vague, "mushy" terms as "humanism," the "moral responsibility of the writer," etc. It was taken for granted that both Soviet and Western "progressive" writers, unlike the avant-garde, were concerned not so much with the purity of their stylistic devices as with the fate of humanity and the conditions of its survival in the age of social alienation and military threat.

The very concept of "high modernism" did not exist in Soviet criticism—not only because modernism, as a decadent bourgeois phenomenon, by definition could not be "high," except perhaps in the context of historical periods (for example, the term "high classicism" was applied to antiquity), but because all of the aforementioned writers were, the moment they were removed from the "pernicious" paradigm of modernism, placed in the camp of "critical realism." There appeared the ghost of a strange cyclical movement: Western literature, leaving the era of critical realism with Dickens and Flaubert and going astray for many decades in every sort of trendy decadent movement, by the 1930s had come full circle back to critical realism, which, of course, lay in the foothills of the peak of world art—socialist realism. In fact, all of these terminological games to equate Soviet writers with their Western counterparts were not entirely meaningless. Thus, the Russian scholar of American literature A. M. Zverev maintained that a "polemic with the conception of man and with the entire worldview expressed by modernism is the essence of such notable works of twentieth-century critical realism as Thomas Mann's *Doctor Faustus,* Hermann Hesse's *Bead Game,* and others."[18] In spite of the officiously rhetorical flavor of this statement, one could almost agree with it if one replaced the clearly inappropriate "critical realism" with "high modernism," which, in the person of Thomas Mann and Hermann Hesse, did indeed engage in a polemic with early modernism ("demonic," "aestheticist," etc.). Behind these magnanimous gestures on the part of Soviet critics toward the "progressive" writers of the West stood the genuine commonality of the two variants of serious eclecticism. This seriousness—heroic or tragic, political or aesthetic—connects socialist realism and high modernism to the avant-gardism that preceded it, while eclecticism connects it to the postmodernism that succeeded it.

Thus, we can trace three basic periods in the cultural development of the twentieth century:

1) Serious purism: avant-gardism, or early modernism—the first third of the twentieth century;
2) Serious eclecticism: socialist realism in the USSR, high modernism in the West—the middle third of the twentieth century;
3) Playful eclecticism: postmodernism—the last third of the twentieth century.

2. From Socialist Realism to Sots-Art

The stage in the transition from the modernism to postmodernism that followed socialist realism in Soviet aesthetics can be designated as sots-art. The movement from socialist realism to sots-art took place gradually from the mid-1950s to the mid-1970s, from the works of the Lianozovo Group (Evgeny Kropivnitsky, Igor Kholin, Genrikh Sapgir, Vsevolod Nekrasov) to the promotion of "programmatic" sots-art in the works of Vitaly Komar and Aleksandr Melamid, Ilya Kabakov, Erik Bulatov, and Dmitry Prigov. The term "sots-art" itself was coined in 1972 by Komar and Melamid and was first conceived as a Soviet counterpart to American pop art: while in Western popular consciousness it was the economic attributes of general concepts that predominated, in the Soviet Union it was ideological attributes. In both cases, art began to bring its perception of the surrounding world down to a lower, "popular" level: soup cans in pop art, street slogans in sots-art.[19]

For a long time, sots-art was perceived as the antithesis of official Soviet art, i.e., socialist realism. But this antithesis was significant only within the framework of the more important and inclusive community represented by the art of the communist era. It was sots-art more than any other movement in Soviet literature of the 1960s to 1980s—"village prose," "urban prose," "confessional" literature, "mythological" literature—that inherited the basic, "native" features of socialist aesthetics, such as the love of ideas, schemes, conceptual generalizations, and conscious derivativeness. Sots-art was forced into such a deep underground existence, pushed beyond the boundary of official Soviet art, precisely because in its aesthetics sots-art was much closer to it than all other movements in the arts of the 1960s to 1980s, whether traditional-realistic or avant-garde, whose aesthetics were developing on a completely different plane. It was possible to publish the works of Aleksandr Solzhenitsyn or Georgy Vladimov in *Novyi mir,* and the works of Andrei Voznesensky or Vasily Aksenov in *Iunost',* but sots-artists were not granted even the tiniest niche in socialist culture precisely because they were its most legitimate heirs—the children not of the "golden" (realistic) nineteenth century or the "silver" (modernist) early twentieth century, but "children of the iron gods" of the 1930s to 1950s. "Postmodernists," the "Men of the Seventies" (semidesiatniki) Ilya Kabakov and Erik Bulatov were much less "authorized" than the neomodernists (neo-avant-gardists), the "Men of the Sixties" (shestidesiatniki) like Dmitri Plavinsky or Vladimir Nemukhin, who were nonetheless permitted on occasion to hold exhibitions, thereby demonstrating the range of artistic tastes of "mature socialism."

There was no place for sots-art alongside mature socialism, because it was even more "mature" itself. Mythologizing romanticism, "stern" and "critical" realism, avant-gardism, even abstractionism were all methods and movements of the "presocialist past," which could be dutifully scorned as aesthetic "relics." And only sots-art carried with it the mystery of the coming carnival death and mock crowning of socialism itself, a perspective on its disintegration into sign components freed from any connection with signifiers. Just as Soviet socialism itself blithely mixed the signs of various ideologies (left and right, conservative and revolutionary) on its garish palette, creating the illusion of a "new reality," sots-art made use of the sign system of socialism to present it as a closed circle of signifiers. Sots-art is an artistic game using the signs of socialist realism, which are freed not only from the need to correspond to reality, but also from the need to create a realistic illusion of its transformation. This is a self-referential circle of ideas—signs that represent and express their own "signness." Socialist civilization became such a winning subject for sots-art because this civilization itself so exaggerated and displayed its own "signness," creating the unique semiocracy in history—the power of signs themselves, emphasizing with unprecedented zeal its break with reality and its intention of creating a new reality. The only thing left for sots-art to do was to take the artificiality and planned nature of socialist civilization and reveal it as a purely conditional sign system, a self-important artistic gesture, a signifier without a signified.

Of course, sots-art and postmodernism cannot be considered identical—these concepts differ in at least two areas. Postmodernism encompasses many different artistic movements, including conceptualism, which is especially significant and widespread in Russia. Within conceptualism, which works with the most diverse artistic languages and ideological systems, one can distinguish, among other things, sots-art, which concentrates on the sign system of socialist (communist) civilization. In terms of biological taxonomy, one could say that postmodernism is a "class" of aesthetic phenomena, while conceptualism is an "order" and sots-art a "family."

It is obvious, for example, that the novels of Umberto Eco or Andrei Bitov belong to other branches of postmodernism than the conceptualist texts of Dmitry Prigov, Lev Rubinshtein, or Vladimir Sorokin. But within conceptualism as well, even within the works of individual authors, one can distinguish among true sots-art (Sorokin's *The Norm* [*Norma*] or *Marina's Thirtieth Love* [*Tridtsataia liubov' Mariny*]; Prigov's poems about millionaires) and other "art" ("Russ-art," "psych-art," etc.) that work conceptually with the sign systems of the Russian psychological novel (Sorokin's *Novel* [*Roman*]) or the epistolary, idyllic, and elegiac genres (the poetry of Timur Kibirov). Within conceptualism, some authors are more sots-art than others, and, as we move ever further from the communist era, there is a noticeable trend toward eliminating sots-art even from the works of its founders, such as the artists Vitaly Komar and Aleksandr Melamid.

Nevertheless, even though it is growing more marginal and historically obsolete, sots-art maintains a special relationship with postmodernism as its "first love" or, more precisely, its umbilical cord, joining Russian postmodernism with communism, from whose womb it emerged into this world. Sots-art reveals the secret of communism as early postmodernism, and the secret of postmodernism as the legitimate, albeit bashful, heir of communism. Sots-art uncovers the aesthetic commonality of communism and postmodernism: their hyperreal nature, eclecticism, derivativeness, and cold passion for ideological allegories and the clichés of popular discourses.

While socialist realism is communism at the moment of its break with its modernist past, sots-art is communism at the moment of its recognition of its postmodern future. Sots-art disappears as communism transforms into postmodernism, as the "shadows recede at noon," remaining only a memory of, and partly a nostalgia for communism. While sots-art in the 1970s and 1980s was perceived as a battlefield of "progressive" postmodernism and "backward" Soviet art, in the 1990s it is identified more and more with the art of the Soviet period, as its highest, concluding phase: both a parrot's refrain and a swan song at the same time. Sots-art is the nostalgia of maturing postmodernism for its initial "radiant" and "pure" communist phase. In the 1990s sots-art is practiced by artists who are hopelessly stuck in the communist past, in the days of "great victories" and "glorious achievements": nostalgia in sots-art is starting to prevail over irony. Socialist realism has died, and sots-art is its sole legitimate heir. But it too is on its last legs—it surely cannot survive into the twenty-first century.

In O. V. Kholmogorova's book *Sots-Art,* the place of this movement in history is defined as "at the intersection of two … phenomena—indigenous Soviet socialist realism and world postmodernism of the late twentieth century."[20] The image of an intersection presupposes that Soviet socialist realism and world postmodernism have nothing in common, are moving in different directions, and meet only at sots-art. But, as has been argued above, socialist realism itself is a form and a phase in the development of the postmodernist artistic consciousness, the succeeding phase of which is represented by sots-art. The transition from socialist realism to sots-art took place according to the laws of the development of socialist aesthetics. This emerges from Andrei Sinyavsky's work on socialist realism mentioned earlier, in which he notes its transformation into sots-art, and the Lianozovo school of poetry with its alienated, naively ironic poetics of Soviet life and ideological clichés. These manifestations of postmodernism in Soviet culture in the mid-1950s partly preceded the analogous phenomena in the West, and in any case developed independently of them. Sots-art is not Western postmodernism belatedly hitched to the Soviet wagon, but rather the product of the organic growth and maturing of Russian postmodernism in its communist form.

Thus, it would be inaccurate to place Russian postmodernism solely within the confines the post-Soviet or the late Soviet period (1970s to 1990s). The postmodern development of Russian culture came to be unified in two of its hypostases—*socialist realism* and *sots-art.*[21] The period of socialist realism is characterized by the subordination of all reality to a system of ideas that transform it, the creation of an all-encompassing "hyperreality" where the real and the fictional are seamlessly blended together so that there is no clear distinction between where one ends and the other begins. The period of sots-art is characterized by the recognition of the conditional semiotic nature of this simulacrum and distancing from it according to the rules of play, irony, and parody.

Conclusion

It is no coincidence that the development of modernism, which in the West lasted into the 1960s, was in Russia forcibly interrupted earlier, in the 1920s, clearing the way for the development of immature postmodern, communist formations. The violent nature of the transition from the modern to the postmodern in Russia was obviously a reflection of the violent transition from the Middle Ages to the modern age in the time of Peter the Great. The modern age made a bloody entrance into Russia and a bloody exit; these bloody clashes of the past and future left no room for a peaceful life in the present, in "modernity." Not every act of force against the natural course of events is coincidental—it could be the manifestation of a more general pattern. In the East—including its western extreme, Russia—postmodernism began maturing earlier than in the West because modernity, with its cult of individualism, novelty, and historicism, with its Renaissance-Romantic blossoming of the individual, with its spirit of reformation, Protestantism, and criticism, with its strong objective/subjective divisions, was alien to the spirit of the East. Modernity began in Russia several centuries later than in the West, and therefore also ended several decades earlier.[22]

There is a well-known theoretical model according to which socioculturally backward countries, such as those of eastern Europe relative to western Europe, eventually progress through the same stages of development at an accelerated rate. Thus, Russian literature, having missed the Renaissance and Baroque periods of the sixteenth to eighteenth centuries, passed through them very rapidly in the nineteenth century in the works of Pushkin and Gogol. An alternative model posits not an accelerated repetition of the same stages of development, but rather an alternating sequence of deceleration in some stages and acceleration in others. In fact, every stage of development, while discarding the previous stage, repeats much of what preceded it. Thus, there occurs an alternation of basic historical paradigms, albeit with a multitude of variations and innovation. The Renaissance, in dispensing with the Middle Ages, harkened back to antiquity; Romanticism, in dispensing with the legacy of Classicism, harkened back to the Middle Ages, etc.

Thus, while Russia was very late entering the modern age and retained medieval features longer than the West, it entered the following period—postmodernity, or, in Berdiaev's terms, the "New Middle Ages"—ahead of the West. In Russian history, modernity coincides with the of Petrine epoch, i.e., it squeezes into a little more than two centuries, in contrast to the 600-year period in Western Europe from the fifteenth to the mid-twentieth century. And this Petrine epoch, like everything that begins too late and ends too early, began with a savage war with the Middle Ages and ended with an even more destructive war to construct a new Middle Ages. Thus, the model of the accelerated repetition of bypassed cycles can be supplemented with the following model: those countries that lag behind in one period of development enter the next period earlier.

Modernism in Russia yielded to the "postmodern" precisely because it became in a certain sense a restoration of the "premodern"—a "New Middle Ages" (in Berdiaev's words). Postmodernism reestablished the power over the individual of the superindividual mechanisms of government, ideology, language, and a collective "superego"; it made authorial originality subservient to citational mode (authoritative in communism, parodic in postmodernism); it savagely denounced modernist "cul-de-sacs"—"extreme individualism," "anarchism," "pointless cleverness and self-indulgent experimentation"; it halted the flow of historical time in a sort of universal continuum where there is nothing but a roll call of the leading minds of all eras and all peoples.

Thus, postmodernism is the state of culture that comes to replace modernity and throw into the past the "Faustian" project based on the value of objective knowledge, individual consciousness and rational action, and faith in the human power of conscious self-organization. That is why postmodern tendencies appeared earliest in those half-Western, half-Eastern countries where modernity arrived only belatedly and was unable to firmly establish its value system, allowing it to be prematurely ousted by the latest "postmodern" order with its unconscious mechanisms and its hallucinogenic dissolution of reality into hyperreality. One certainly may not speak of postmodernism in relation to the cultures of Asia and Africa, which completely missed modernity. But Russia is the country that managed to recognize the paradigm of modernity in the eighteenth and nineteenth centuries, consciously adopting and transforming it along with Western influences. But it also sensed its essential foreignness and attempted to achieve a historical "leap" beyond its boundaries. It was not by some miracle of cultural progressiveness, but by the very fact of its backwardness and alienation from the spirit of modernity that Russia turned out to be virtually the first country in the world to experience postmodernity. After all, "post" means "after," and Russia, having entered modernity after the West, ended up ahead of the West in its "postmodern" quality: first in the culture of conscious derivativeness, imitation, "simulation."[23]

The "production of reality," as the key postmodernist concept, appeared new for Western civilization, but it has been routinely accomplished throughout all of Russian history. Here, ideas have always tended to substitute for reality, beginning, perhaps, with Prince Vladimir, who adopted the idea of Christianity in 988 A.D., and proceeded to implant it in a vast country where it had, until that time, been virtually unknown.

Peter the Great ordered Russia to be educated and vigorously introduced such innovations as newspapers, universities, and academies. These institutions appeared in artificial forms, incapable of concealing their deliberateness, the forced nature of their origins. In essence, we are dealing with the simulative, or nominative, character of a civilization composed of plausible labels: this is a "newspaper," this—an "academy," this—a "constitution," none of which grew naturally from the national soil, but was implanted from above in the form of smoothly whittled twigs in hopes they might take root and germinate. Too much in this culture came from ideas, schemes, and conceptions, to which reality was subjugated.

In his book *Russia in 1839,* the Marquis de Custine described the simulative character of Russian civilization in which the plan, the preceding concept, is more real than the production brought forth by that plan.

> Russians have only names for everything, but nothing in reality. Russia is a country of facades. Read the labels—they have "society," "civilization," "literature," "art," "sciences"—but as a matter of fact, they don't even have doctors. If you happen to call a Russian doctor from your neighborhood, you can consider yourself a corpse in advance.... Russia is an Empire of catalogues: if one runs through the titles, everything seems beautiful. But ... open the book and you discover that there is nothing in it.... How many cities and roads exist only as projects! Well, the entire nation, in essence, is nothing but a placard stuck over Europe...."[24]

One can ascribe this negative reaction to a foreigner's prejudice, but Alexander Herzen, for one, believed that de Custine had produced a fascinating and intelligent book about Russia.[25] Moreover, no less a devotee of Russia's national roots than Ivan Aksakov, one of the most sincere and ardent Slavophiles of the nineteenth century, held a similar view on the "Empire of catalogues." He recognized the concepts of "intentionality" and "counterfeit" as fundamental to his native civilization:

> Everything in our country exists "as if," nothing seems to be serious, authentic; instead, everything has the appearance of something temporary, false, designed for show—from petty to large-scale phenomena. "As if" we have laws and even 15 volumes of the code of laws ... whereas half of these institutions do not exist in reality and the laws are not respected.[26]

Even the syntactical constructions of de Custine and Aksakov's comments seem to coincide: the former states that, "they have society ... but as a matter of fact," while the latter remarks, "we have laws ... whereas in reality...." Both of these authors, from diametrically opposite standpoints, indicate the "halved" and chimerical character of Russian civilization. For de Custine it is insufficiently European; for Aksakov, insufficiently Russian. But the result is the same: the ostentatious, fraudulent nature of the civilization begets external, superficial forms, devoid of both genuine European and intrinsic Russian contents, and remains a tsardom of names and outward appearances.

The most grandiose simulacrum, or "concept," that expressed the simulative nature of Russian civilization was, of course, Saint Petersburg: the city erected on a "Finnish swamp." "St. Petersburg, the most abstract and premeditated /*umyshlennyi*/ city in the whole world," according to Dostoevsky,[27] who sensed that the reality of the city was composed entirely of fabrications, designs, ravings, and visions, lifted up like a shadow above rotten soil, unfit for construction. Instability was laid into the very foundation of the imperial capital, which subsequently became the cradle of three revolutions. The realization of the city's intentionality and "ideality," the lack of firm soil to stand on, gave rise to one of the first, and most ingenious, literary simulacrums. In Dostoevsky's words:

> A hundred times, amidst this fog, I've been struck with a strange but importunate reverie: "And what if this fog were to scatter and leave for above, wouldn't this entire rotten, slimy city take off with it, wouldn't

it rise up with the fog and disappear like smoke, and the prior Finnish swamp would remain, and, in the middle of it, for beauty, I think, the bronze horseman on his hotly breathing, exhausted horse?"[28]

This vision might well have just come off the canvas of a conceptual artist, a postmodern master, such as Eric Bulatov, or Vitaly Komar and Alexander Melamid. This civilization, composed entirely of names,[29] reveals its nature in postmodern Russian art, which shows us a label removed from utter emptiness. Conceptualism is a set of such labels, a collection of facades lacking the other three sides.[30] Contemporary Russian conceptualism emerged, not from the imitation of Western postmodernism, but rather from the very same rotten Petersburg fog of Dostoevsky's "importunate reverie." For conceptualism, it is not enough to show that the "winter city," splendidly and proudly erected on the marsh, is a shadow and a phantom, concealing the authentic reality of the marsh itself: its densely congealed evaporation.

It is not surprising then, that the specter wandering through Europe, as Marx and Engels characterized communism in the first lines of *The Communist Manifesto,* settled down and acquired reality in Russia. This country proved to be especially susceptible to mistaking phantasms for real creatures. After the Bolshevik revolution, the simulative nature of reality became even more pronounced in Russia. All social and private life was subordinated to ideology, which became the only real force of historical development. Signs of a new reality, of which Soviet citizens were so proud in the thirties and fifties, from Stalin's massive hydroelectric plant on the Dnieper River to Khrushchev's decision to raise corn and Brezhnev's numerous autobiographies, were actually pure ideological simulations of reality. This artificial reality was intended to demonstrate the superiority of ideas over simple facts.

In its very adoption of European positivity as a system of symbols revealing the absence of signifieds, Russia constructed itself as a culture of modernity while simultaneously deconstructing modernity in its culture. Modernity in Russia was over practically as soon as it began, in the age of Peter, and further in the age of Catherine and Paul, with their rapidly ripening fruits of the European Enlightenment. This caused the head of the European Enlightenment, Denis Diderot, to comment in a letter to Catherine II that Russia was a "fruit that has spoiled before it was ripe" (*Materialy* 6). The fruits of modernity in Russia did indeed begin to spoil before they had ripened, but from this decay, which honed Russian rationalism, individualism, historicism, and other attributes of modernity, arose a new Russian culture that fully ripened and is in fact being harvested now—as Russian postmodern culture.

The fact that the term and the concept of "postmodernism" were borrowed from the West only at the turn of the 1980s does not mean that the postmodern was absent from Russian culture, but only that it was perceived as its normal inapprehensible state. This postmodern state was thus brought to light in Russia with the help of Western theory, because in Russia it was more organic than in the West, which had been rooted for centuries in the spirit and traditions of Modernity.[31]

Notes

Translated from Russian by John Meredig and Anesa Miller, revised by Slobodanka Vladiv-Glover.

1. Mikhail Epstein, "Posle budushchego. O novom soznanii v literature," *Znamia*, No. 1 (1991): 217–30. Mikhail Epstein, "After the Future: On the New Consciousness in Literature," *South Atlantic Quarterly* 90, no. 2 (Spring 1991): pp. 409–44. As a key note speaker, I first delivered this paper at the Fourth Wheatland International Conference on Literature, San Francisco, June 11–16, 1990.
2. Viacheslav Kuritsyn, "Postmodernizm: novaia pervobytnaia kul'tura," *Novyi mir* 2 (1992): pp. 225–32.
3. Mark Lipovetsky, "Spetsifika russkogo postmodernizma," *Znamia* 8 (1995): p. 193.
4. Jean Baudrillard, *Selected Writing*, ed. Mark Poster (Stanford: Stanford University Press, 1988), pp. 144–45.
5. Andrew Benjamin, ed., *The Lyotard Reader* (Cambridge, MA: Blackwell, 1992).
6. Doklad t. Zhdanova, o zhurnalakh "Zvezda" i "Leningrad" (Andrei Zhdanov,

speech on the journals *Zvezda* and *Leningrad*) (Ogiz, Gospolitizdat, 1946), S. 12.

7. Tom Wolfe, "Stalking the Billion-Footed Beast: A Literary Manifesto for the New Social Novel," *Harper's Magazine* (November 1989): pp. 49, 50.
8. Ibid., pp. 50–51, 55.
9. For a more detailed examination of the parallels between socialist realism and postmodern aesthetics, see Mikhail Epstein, "Tom Wolfe, and Social(ist) Realism," *Common Knowledge* 1, no. 2 (1992): 147–60.
10. For more on postmodern elements in Soviet Marxism, see Mikhail Epstein, *After the Future: The Paradoxes of Postmodernism and Contemporary Russian Culture* (Amherst: University of Massachusetts Press, 1995), pp. 101–63, esp. pp. 153–61.
11. Abram Tertz (Andrei Siniavskii), *On Socialist Realism* (New York: Pantheon, 1960), S. 92.
12. Andrei Zhdanov, "Sovetskaia literatura—samaia ideinaia, samaia peredovaia literatura v mire," speech at the First All-Union Conference of Soviet Writers (17 August 1934), Gospolitizdat, 1953; *Essays on Literature, Philosophy, and Music* (New York: International Publishers, 1950), p. 9.
13. *Literaturnyi entsiklopedicheskii slovar'*, Ed. V. M. Kozhevnikov and P. A. Nikolaev (Moscow: Sovetskaia entsiklopediia, 1987), S. 416.
14. Here is one of the many definitions: "Postmodernism is a period label generally given to cultural forms since the 1960s that display certain characteristics such as reflexivity, irony, and a mixing of popular and high art forms." Linda Hutcheon, "Postmodernism," *Encyclopedia of Contemporary Literary Theory: Approaches, Scholars, Terms*, ed. Irena R. Makaryk (Toronto: University of Toronto Press, 1993), 612.
15. Fredric Jameson, *Postmodernism or The Cultural Logic of Late Capitalism* (Durham: Duke University Press, 1993), p. 374.
16. Boris Grois, *Utopiia i obmen* (Moscow: Znak, 1993), pp. 37, 69.
17. *Literaturnyi entsiklopedicheskii slovar'*, ed. cit., p. 225.
18. Ibid.
19. The history of sots-art is described in the greatest detail in Zinovy Zinik, "Sots-art," *Tekstura: Russian Essays on Visual Culture*, trans. and ed. Alla Efimova and Lev Manovich (Chicago: University of Chicago Press, 1993), 70–88; Carter Ratcliff, *Komar and Melamid* (New York: Abbeville Press, 1988), pp. 14, 59–64, 118–19, 147; O.V. Kholmogorova, *Sots-Art* (Moscow: Galart, 1994).
20. Kholmogorova, *Sots-Art*, n.p. The passage cited is found under illustration 10 in the introduction.
21. In a number of my works, I have attempted to demonstrate that Russian postmodernism has a third, prerevolutionary hypostasis associated with the perception and adoption of modernity in Russia in the eighteenth and nineteenth centuries. See the chapter "Istoki i smysl russkogo postmodernizma" in Mikhail Epstein, *Postmodern v russkoi literature* (Moscow: Vysshaia shkola, 2005), S. 102–26; Mikhail Epstein, "The Origins and Meaning of Russian Postmodernism," in *After the Future*, pp. 188–212.

22. G. D. Gachev, *Uskorennoe razvitie literatury* (*The Accelerated Development of Literature*) (Moscow: Nauka, 1964).
23. The same derivativeness in the cultural stratum can be seen in the United States, which took its styles—architectural, literary, artistic—from the whole world, but primarily, of course, from western Europe. Here they are distanced from their historical place and time and become signs of the "postmodern," a derivative-ironic sense of the world. That is why Russia and America are organically more postmodern than truly European or Asiatic cultures, which are either too deeply rooted in modernity or passed it by completely.
24. Marquis de Custine, *Nikolaevskaia Rossiia* (Moscow: Izdatel'stvo politicheskoi literatury, 1990), 94, 155–56.
25. *Editor:* Alexander Ivanovich Herzen (1812–70) was a prominent writer and publicist who founded and edited the liberal socioliterary journal *The Pole Star* and its affiliated newspaper, *The Bell.* The latter was a leading organ in the debate over serfdom and land reform; it was printed abroad to avoid the tsarist censors and smuggled into Russia between 1857 and 1867.
26. K. Skal'kovsky, ed., *Materialy dlia fiziologii russkogo obshchestva. Malen'kaia khrestomatiia dlia vzroslykh. Mneniia russkikh o samikh sebe* (Saint Petersburg: A. S. Suvorin's Press, 1904), 106.
27. Emphasis added. Fyodor Dostoevsky, *Notes from Underground,* quoted from the translation by Michael Katz for the Norton Critical Edition (Norton: New York and London, 1989), 5.
28. Fyodor Dostoevsky, *A Raw Youth,* part 1, chapter 8. Dostoevsky has several variations on the theme of this vision, which affected him deeply, for example, in *A Weak Heart* (1848), in *Petersburg Dreams in Verse and in Prose* (1861), and in the sketches for *The Diary of a Writer* (1873).
29. Is it not this "nominativity," this pure concern with names, that gives rise to the sinister power of the *nomenklatura,* that is those people selected by no one and by no means meriting their stature, but who are named "secretary," "director," or "instructor" and have received power by virtue of these names?
30. On contemporary Russian conceptualism see chapter 1, "New Trends in Russian Poetry."
31. For more detailed analysis of historical and cultural premises of Russian postmodernism, see Mikhail Epstein, "Istoki i smysl russkogo postmodernizma," in his book: *Postmodern v russkoi literature* (Moscow: Vysshaia shkola, 2005), pp. 102–26.

Chapter 3

The 1960s and the Rediscovery of the Other in Russian Culture

Andrei Bitov

Slobodanka Vladiv-Glover

I. The Coming-Out of the Underground: *Pushkin House*

Until recently, the Soviet literature of the 1960s was regarded as a function of the post-Stalinist thaws, which initiated a more "honest"[1] treatment of Soviet reality, emancipated from the generalities and clichés of the socialist realist canon. The explosion of lyrical poetry by Andrei Voznesensky, Evgeny Evtushenko, Robert Rozhdestvensky, Bella Akhmadulina and others, as well as the advent of lyricism in the prose of Yury Kazakov, Vasily Aksyonov, Yuri Nagibin, Anatoli Gladilin—the so-called "young prose" writers of the mid-1950s and 1960s—have in the past been ascribed exclusively to the demise of Stalinism and socialist realism. Almost all the Western historians of Russian literature, from Marc Slonim to G. Hosking,[2] adopt this line of argument.

While there can be no doubt that the process of de-Stalinization of Russian society was responsible for an upsurge in Russian arts and literature, it is not a sufficient explanation for the kind of cultural production set in motion in the 1960s; for the Russian poetry, prose, and art of this period did not materialize out of nothing, even if Stalinism had created a vacuum in Russian culture between the 1930s and the 1950s. The cultural production of the 1960s in Russia had invisible connections not only to the Western popular culture of the 1950s, but also to antecedents in the preceding cultural era of modernism.

New ways of looking at the Russian culture of the past thirty years or so are needed, and they are emerging. One such approach is offered by Petr Vail' and Alexander Genis in their recent book about the 1960s. Vail' and Genis view the entire period as "the beginning of the end" of ideology, paving the way for *perestroika*. Their sociocultural reappraisal, which encompasses the realm of aesthetics, offers a model for new analyses and re-readings of the Russian cultural canon of the 1960s.[3]

Albeit in a romanticized form, the major new element that Vail' and Genis add to the analysis of the 1960s is an emphasis on Russia's "discovery" of America resulting from its reception of the life and works of Ernest Hemingway. In their discussion of the influence of the poetics of Hemingway's prose on Russian thaw culture and, even more importantly, of Hemingway's image of a free spirit in love with the "rough" and honest outdoor life of adventure, the two authors offer a plausible model for the analysis of many Russian prose works of the 1960s.[4]

What did, in fact, take place—whether through the reception of Hemingway, isolated and focused on by Vail' and Genis, or through a myriad of other receptions, such as Aksyonov's reading of J.D. Salinger's *The Catcher in the Rye* prior to the writing of his own *Oranges from Morocco*—was that Russia opened up to what had until then been its antagonistic "other." But even more important than the subsequent emulation of a lifestyle and imitation of a poetic practice, as pointed out by Vail' and Genis, the reception of Hemingway in Russian post-thaw culture allowed for a certain degree of assimilation and incorporation of this newly discovered other to enter into Russia's own cultural production. This incorporation took the form of representation . The other thus once again became representable in Russian culture. What is meant by "representation" is not merely the thematic reference to Americans in Russian literary texts,[5] or the emulation of an outdoor lifestyle that leads the hero to new insights,[6] but an abstracting of the concrete, cultural, and historic other (for example, America) into the other of discourse. For it is with the re-entry of this abstract other into Russian discourse that Russian culture comes out of "the underground" to resume, once again, a normal evolution along the trajectory of modernism/postmodernism, the same one traversed by Western European culture of the twentieth century.

Prior to the 1960s thaw, the other had found expression in the discourse of Russian modernism. One of the canonic examples of the representation of this other can be found in Andrei Bely's *Petersburg*, an archetypal modernist novel about the Russian nobility, the carriers of an "Apollonian" model of rational culture who face a dual abyss or split. On the one hand, Apollon Apollonovich Ableukhov is confronted by the abyss of popular culture, maintained by revolutionary ideologues who are associated with the dark forces of the Russian cultural unconscious and depicted as having a Mongolian face. On the other hand, this self-same cerebral high-ranking tzarist bureaucrat is alienated from his neurotic "Dyonisian" son, Nikolai Apollonovich, who is seduced into virtual parricide by a university friend with a split identity (Dudkin, Lippanchenko, Shishnarfne)—the cracked mirror refracting Nikolai's other as the limit of language.

In the transitional phase between the mid-1930s and the 1960s, representations of the other of discourse were unknown to official Russian literature. The absence of this other is given a masterly parodic treatment in Andrei Platonov's novel *The Foundation Pit* (*Kotlovan*), written in 1929/30. This ironic tribute to revolutionary popular culture in "monumental" (hyperbolic) style is narrated by a naive consciousness in the present. The naive narrating consciousness is identical to all the other consciousnesses with which it comes into contact. Platonov's novel has no other. That is, Platonov deliberately eschews the other of discourse because an unconscious has been banned from the life of the Soviet worker who has been reduced to an unthinking automatized cog in the state machine. Platonov's worker-cum-intellectual hero of the 1930s represents a consciousness that is as unitary as that of the little orphaned girl—

the "child of the revolution" or metaphor of the "young Soviet state"—who has been "adopted" by the pit workers and is under their protection. This "pit" in which the naive "popular hero" is toiling is a replica of his own inner void, which is like the universe before the Fall and the division into good and evil. The unitary psychic world of Platonov's proletarian is imbued with profound authorial irony. That is why Platonov's writing remains the single most potent and true representation of the Russian social and cultural homogeneity of the 1930s.[7]

Needless to say, there is no representation of the other of discourse in socialist-realist literature, in which polarities of any kind have only a surface (cosmetic) value. Village prose also does not feature representations of the other. Its excursions into the heroic or archaic national past, framed by narratives set in the Soviet present, create utopian and nostalgic myths that do not attain full-fledged expression of the other or the unconscious of contemporary Russian culture. For, in its proper function, this other must fulfill a heuristic, not a mythopoetic role. The representation of the other of discourse is ultimately a way to knowledge of a certain kind, a knowledge that is or leads to a *savoir*—a know-how, a competence, and a new discursive "practice." A culture that is able to reach its other through discourse is therefore a culture of practice and process, not one of production; for it is process, not production, that is liberating. Only through process can a culture accommodate heterogeneity and be home to a "philosophy of the act."[8]

There are at least two works of the 1960s—each at its own poetic level—that demonstrate the re-entry of the other into Russian literary discourse. One is Andrei Voznesensky's canonical poem-novella *Oza*, which we have analyzed elsewhere.[9] The other is Andrei Bitov's novel *Pushkin House*. Both works were created during the thaw period and provide textual evidence of the reinstatement of the unconscious as a legitimate object, if not the subject, of poetic exploration.

Like Bely's novel, to which it is genealogically related, *Pushkin House* is set in the cerebral city of St. Petersburg during its Leningrad period. As in Bely's novel and in Dostoevsky's fiction, there is not a single realistic scene in Bitov's phantasmagoria. Bitov's poetics—as the narrator A.B. suggests in a footnote regarding the "discarded" titles for the novel[10]—is grounded in an amalgam of Joycean and Proustian stream-of-consciousness narrative techniques. Or, more precisely, Bitov's prose (like Bely's) has its roots in the poetics of the novels of Dostoevsky (*The Double*, *The Adolescent*), which anticipate the stream-of-consciousness technique of European and Russian prose of the twentieth century.

Although it should have been the literary event of the decade, particularly the thaw decade, *Pushkin House* was conceived in the "underground"[11] of Russian literature in 1963. It was denied publication upon completion in 1971, despite an existing contract with the publisher Sovietskii pisatel.[12]

On one level, Bitov's novel purports to be a chronicle of Soviet life of the 1950s and 1960s. This period telescopes backwards, into the late 1930s and even earlier, to the beginning of the purges in 1929, the year the hero's grandfather is sentenced to twenty-five years of exile. Russian history is thus viewed via a portrait of the Odoyevtsev family. Their son, Lyova Odoyevtsev, is Bitov's contemporary, born, like the author, in 1937. The father, an academic of the Stalinist period, has survived the purges by renouncing his father and taking over his father's chair in Russian philology. The grandfather, Modest Odoyevtsev, is a philologist and mathematician of the 1920s who had established an entire school that is experiencing a revival in the 1960s through the critical work of Lyova, who is following in his grandfather's illustrious footsteps. This is the "historical" time-frame within which the novel's self-deconstructing plot is embedded. On this historical level, the novel can be read as a reconciliation of the 1960s generation with Russia's past, from which it was severed by the Revolution and Stalinism.

II. The Gap in Russian History and Lyova Odoyevtsev's Oedipal Repression

The "gap" in Russian culture created by the historical period of the 1930s to 1950s is nonetheless inscribed within the hero's psyche and as part of his individual development. It coincides with the gap which symbolizes Lyova's Oedipal repression, represented by Lyova's absent father—a father who is either not physically present because of his teaching commitments in the republics or who is not (consciously) registered by Lyova during childhood and early adolescence. After the war, in the late 1940s when Lyova is between ten and twelve years old, he "sees" (consciously registers) his father "at once and suddenly" [*odnazhdy i vdrug*], when he realizes that his father is his rival. Lyova thus discovers that he is jealous of his father in relation to his mother. At this point and until he meets his desire Faina at the end of high school, Lyova is antagonistic toward his father as he day-dreams about inheriting his *ermolka*—the skull-cap worn by the academic Odoyevtsev *père*—and his study, his father's inner sanctum.

It is in this period that Lyova also appropriates his father's library, which consists of the Russian classics. This period of Lyova's childhood (*detstvo*) symbolizes his entry into culture and identification with The-Name-of-the-Father. Metaphor as a signifying substitution is already at work here. For the son, who is prohibited from desiring the father's desire (the mother) on pain of castration, internalizes this transgressive desire, only to see it surface in its metonymic form: as identification with logos—the word of discourse and the position occupied by the Father's Name in the structure of discourse. One could say, speaking metaphorically, that little Lyova becomes or desires to become a little phallus and take the place of his father, the big phallus. The phallus in this context does not mean the anatomical organ, the penis, from which it only borrows its symbolic form.[13] In this context, the phallus is a metaphor for the Master Signifier as site of the subject's future identity and power. From now on—from the symbolic moment of the child-hero's entry into culture—the hero's desire will be directed toward nothing but the word of discourse. This, of course, is reflected both in little Lyova's predilection for literature and the adolescent Lyova's choice of tertiary studies. The pursuit of words will never leave Lyova and will be the substance—the sole substance—of his future existence. Lyova's successful passage through his Oedipus complex, which is described as "a drama in the field of the Other,"[14] is facilitated by two significant events: the reappearance of his parents' neighbor, Uncle Dickens, and the re-emergence from the "dead" of his grandfather, Modest Odoyevtsev.

Lyova's grandfather represents an absence in Lyova's childhood, one that frames Lyova's father's absence. The narrator says that Lyova, like all children, wanted to feel that "all were there" [*khotel choby vse byli*], present and correct as it were. This "all" has the effect of making the child feel at one with its primal object and enveloped in a totality. Such an imaginary totality, provided by the family, is the source of Lyova's first identification. By "not being there," grandfather causes Lyova to go through the experience of the "Not-All" or lack.[15] This lack puts Lyova into a (non-) relation[16] with the "real" of the "object," which is the cause of the subject's "split" or separateness from the totality, from the All. The experience of lack (or of the split) is the subject's originary experience in the field of the other. That is, by being confronted with the Not-All, the subject internalizes a lack, which turns into a permanent and enduring split or gap. This gap is the locus of the unconscious, in which the subject's desire is generated. Lyova tries to initially fill the gap that is created by his absent grandfather by fantasizing an other in his place: Uncle Dickens.

The meeting with his returned grandfather, like a hallucination, takes place in a phantasmagoric haze of inebriation and ends with Lyova vomiting in a taxi. This meeting with grandfather marks Lyova's confrontation with the real, which is not reality, but something opposed to the symbolic order of language while at the same time grounding it.[17] Confrontation with the real amounts to acceptance of symbolic castration (the subject's "division"), which brings on what is referred to as *secondary repression.*[18] Symbolic castration is experienced by Lyova as a cathartic spectacle—grandfather reaching for his fly in an unfinished obscene gesture, to flash his shrunken member. Lyova interprets this little masculine transgression as a symbolic reenactment of grandfather's failed life—his "castrated" manhood due to twenty years of exile. Testimony of this life elicits a "classic" response from Lyova: pity and fear (*"Lyova chut' ne plakal:chto sdelali s chelovekom !"*)[19] and terror at coming face to face with (t)his "real" (big) other (*"Gospodi!—uspel podumat' Lyova"*).[20]

This symbolic experience of castration (castration once removed, as it were, through identification with grandfather) causes Lyova to emerge into full "self-consciousness" (to use Hegel's term)[21] and establishes him as a subject of the unconscious, that is to say, a subject of language. But "self-consciousness" is not synonymous with "full self-knowledge." To say that a subject is a full-fledged subject of the unconscious is to say that the subject *knows* that he *knows.* It does not mean that the subject is *knowledgeable.* In fact, after Lyova leaves his grandfather who has proclaimed him "stupid," Lyova in effect does become a little opaque if not downright misguided. He evaluates his grandfather as "not at all clever" and goes away in a huff. Thereafter Lyova manages to repress the memory of the entire episode. Simultaneously, Lyova participates in establishing a "grandfather cult" and institutionalizing grandfather's *logos* (his scholarly and philosophical writings). On the moral plane, Lyova's behavior also testifies to a "split": like the other whose metonymy he has become, Lyova has nothing to "give," walking away from a colleague in need of moral support during a political crisis at the institute.

During the meeting with grandfather, Lyova "exchanges" his ideal (who belongs to the imaginary register) Grand-Father, Uncle Dickens, for his real Grand-Father, who represents the symbolic order or The Word (*slovo*). Grandfather Odoyevtsev is like a Grand Master of a secret sect, surrounded by enigmatic "servants," the somewhat crazy young poet Rudik, whose métier is words, and the even more schizophrenic Koptelov, previously a "master" of interrogation who made a career out of the yes/no binary structure of knowledge generated by human consciousness.[22] This Koptelov, who cannot stop *seeing all* (being conscious[23] without respite) did not kill grandfather "twice"—an allusion, perhaps, to grandfather's own double passage through Oedipus and the shedding of an ideal in favor of a real other. This Koptelov, whom Lyova dubs "Uncle Mitia," appears to be a silent double of Uncle Dickens. Koptelov is nothing but a pair of seemingly docile (passive) all-knowing eyes. According to grandfather, Koptelov can construct all human reactions before they are uttered in language or gesture. This alleged attribute of the former prison investigator and torturer, whose power is a matter of the past, transforms Koptelov into a symbol: he performs the function of the *gaze.*[24] Like the Grand Master of a chess-game, whose pawns are human captives of a totalitarian prison system, Koptelov was engaged in "facilitating" *confessions.* His presence at the scene of Lyova's meeting with grandfather provokes Modest Odoyevtsev's *grand confession.* In fact, Koptelov is the (silent) Master of the "prison-house of language"[25] in which "surveillance" (the gaze) is an agency of symbolization. Koptelov's silent gaze accompanies the entire scene between Lyova and grandfather. It is thus a secondary structural element in Lyova's Oedipus complex, in the sense that this gaze is instrumental in transforming Lyova into a secondary signifying system—the narrative of his own "life" which is synonymous with (his) *writing.*

After the confrontation with grandfather, Lyova's passage through Oedipal repression is complete. Vomiting is the externalization of disgust or nausea, which is a well-known effect of abjection and secondary repression.[26] Thanks to this process, Lyova becomes full-fledged, not as a character (although that as well) but as a subject of the unconscious, which is to say, as a subject of language and discourse. With this, Bitov's hero becomes a culture carrier in the modern sense. For, according to Lacan, the structures of culture "reveal an ordering of possible exchanges which, even if unconscious, is inconceivable outside the permutations authorized by language."[27] The rest of the novel, Parts II and III, are explorations of the unconscious, coextensive with Lyova's "knowledge" and his life and time, all of which are grounded in Lyova's language or relationship to *logos.* Thus the unconscious that is the subject of Bitov's discourse "is neither primordial nor instinctual; what it knows about the elementary is no more than the elements of the signifier."[28] The entire novel thus enacts not history, which it might reproduce mimetically and linearly, but something that takes place on that other stage (Freud's *other scene*), in the realm of the repressed—the realm that Derrida has called *writing.*[29] In this realm of general repression, the hero of the novel (the subject of the unconscious) constructs himself through and as inscription. That is, the hero of the novel—whose very existence as a singular and identifiable hero is questioned by the narrator—comes into existence not as a "historical type" but as a *memory trace.* In the Epilogue, where the narrator A.B. purports to visit the "historical" Lyova at the Pushkin Institute, the literary "hero" is "dead." Thus in his final narrative tour de force, A.B. (who is not the historical Bitov but his textual representative or the abstract author turned narrator) reveals the hero of his novel in his pure essence—that of a pure representation—a trace of a trace.

Above the bar of repression,[30] (that is, "above" Lyova's unconscious realm or the unconscious realm which is Lyova), on the plot level, Lyova leads a historical life, which is the effect of how others see him, including the narrator A.B. Bitov calls this historical life of his hero "*epokha.*" Lyova comes to resemble his father more and more. During his university studies, Lyova assumes the superior posture of the Master (Signifier), symbolized through his easy access to the institutionalized knowledge of the university, which gives him an advantage over the ordinary undergraduate of his generation. Lyova, in fact, becomes his father, or in a sense, takes his father's place, just as his father had once taken the place of his father, Modest Odoyevtsev. History thus repeats itself, even without Stalinist repression. The sons betray the fathers even while in the "seed," as Modest Odoyevtsev remarks in a frenzy following Lyova's attempt to sketch a portrait of his father's life, guided by a displaced sense of guilt and loyalty to the grandfather.

Repression, whether historical (Stalinist) or ahistorical (Oedipal, psychic), is overcome or sublated (*aufgehoben*) in the course of the hero's "educational journey" (*education sentimentale*), which constitutes the ostensible plot of the novel. In the confrontation with his desire (personified by Faina), the hero, Lyova, goes through a process of creative *alienation,* which is thematized as a self-doubling. Through this process of alienation, Lyova becomes identical with his (big) other. On the one hand, this other is represented by Mitishatyev, his equivocal childhood friend and rival. On the other hand, this other is enacted—as the hero's deed, what he does as opposed to what he *is.* This deed is his writing, represented by his deconstructive article on Pushkin, "Three Prophets," and the paraphrased article, "The Belated Genius." The hero's personal, psychic history thus grows into a *tableau vivant* of Russia's cultural history. On this historical level, the continuity between past and present is re-established literally through the growing up of the Russian post-Stalinist youth of the 1950s—Bitov's own generation.

The growing-up of the hero becomes an emblem of a general re-awakening of Russian society of the 1950s and 1960s. Lyova's stepping over the shadow of his father and shedding his ideal (imaginary) Father, Uncle Dickens, signals Lyova's coming of age as a man, shedding the Father's authority while assuming the Father's role and position in life.

At the same time, Lyova emerges from a two-dimensional linear narrative to find himself in a three-dimensional delinearized space (Parts II and III of the novel), in which he can "stand erect," as it were, and take over the phallic function in becoming the Master of the Word in his own and Bitov's discourse. Thus the hero, Lyova, emerges as a signifier and as a metonymy of himself—and hence as the split and alienated subject of consciousness *par excellence.* However, to achieve the status of the phallus (the "absent" signifier) in three-dimensional space and hence in a present continuum (Heidegger's "presence"), Lyova must first confront his imaginary ego ideal, Uncle Dickens, and participate in the little symbolic drama of separation and exchange, involving the banal (mundane domestic objects), which Uncle Dickens' appearance in Lyova's adolescence sets in process.

III. Uncle Dickens and the Singularity of Objects

Lyova's encounter with Uncle Dickens, his "first" and "small other," precedes the "encounter" with grandfather, Lyova's "big Other." But while the two events appear to be chronological—they are indeed narrated in chronological order—they are, in fact, interlooping, fitting into one another like a Borromean knot, bringing Bitov's narrative to a "consistency" analogous to that achieved by the psychoanalytic subject through the looping of the three psychic registers: the imaginary, the real, and the symbolic.[31]

Unlike grandfather, who constituted the first experience of *lack* in Lyova's childhood and who represented an *absence,* Uncle Dickens is very much a *presence* in Lyova's early years. However, Uncle Dickens is not there in person. He is represented—although Lyova does not *know* that he is dealing with a *representation*[32]—through the concrete *objects* (the false gifts) left with the Odoyevtsevs for safekeeping. These objects, which Lyova appropriates psychically as a child, are synonymous with or, more precisely, metonymies of *the thing*, the "original (primal) object" (the Mother, the breast), which is the source of the child's primary identification.[33] Uncle Dickens' furniture and *objets d'art* that populate Lyova's childhood symbolize the unity of subject/object, characteristic of the individual before his entry into self-awareness and, by extension, the symbolic order and culture. Uncle Dickens' "things" in Lyova's life symbolize the primary relationship of the subject to an object. The reclamation of these "goods" captures the moment of loss of the object for the subject. Thus Lyova experiences his first (originary) loss, simultaneously with the lack of grandfather, through the exodus of familiar childhood things, which had been a source of his earliest identity as a Self. These objects, which represent familiar things, turn out to belong to another, who feels no less defined by and through them. This other is Uncle Dickens. The furniture and *objets d'art* constitute a metonymy of this other; without them, this other—Uncle Dickens—has no identity.

Confrontation with this other enacts Lyova's initiation into discourse via a pantomimic display of the structure and logic of difference. Uncle Dickens performs this pantomime for Lyova by being himself quite different from anyone imaginable. This difference first becomes manifest in his "transgressive" language. "Difference" and "transgression" are two sides of the mechanism of metaphor, which involves repression. Both belong to the sphere of language. Both are originary to language. Uncle Dickens is a walking or actualized metaphor for the elementary structure of language, animated by the agency of difference (operating as metonymy or displacement) and repression (operating as metaphor, substitution and condensation). Uncle Dickens' nickname, with its allusion to the European literary canon, and his partiality to words, reiterate his metaphoric function.

Despite the concrete *presence* of this wiry, feisty "little man" (a "homonculus" or Lacan's *l'hommelette*[34]), "who could not, however, be called small,"[35] Uncle Dickens is in some ways quite unreal for he belongs to Lyova's imaginary, where he is a representation of the function of the "ungraspable" or "false" organ of the drive, the *lamella* or *objet a*. Hence Uncle Dickens' things are layered with symbolic meaning. They are not only a source of the hero's primary identification in childhood (before the "split"); they are also portents of the "small other"—the *objet petit a*, the unrepresentable "object"—which becomes the locus of lack in the subject, from which the subject's *desire* is infinitely generated.

As a fictional character, Uncle Dickens is a late Soviet reincarnation of the "Russian gentleman" of the *belle époque*—the turn-of-the-century and first two decades of the *Silver Age*. There are, in addition, allusions to the gentleman's pedigree, the "dandy" of the Pushkin era—the *Golden Age* of Russian culture—in the petty detail of Uncle Dickens' toilette articles and leisurely habit of "unproductive" reading in his gentleman's study. While such a character is hard to imagine in the Leningrad of 1956 (or the 1960s, when he reappears in one of the novel's "variants" of the hero's "life" to help Lyova repair the broken glass at the Pushkin Institute), it is not difficult to see how Uncle Dickens' stylishness is a stylization of a by-gone Russian and European cultural epoch, evoked as the immediate precursor and "lost cultural abode" of the Russian intelligentsia of the 1960s, "unhoused" by Stalinism. What makes Uncle Dickens especially attractive to this intelligentsia, represented by the Odoyevtsevs and Lyova in particular, is the fact that Uncle Dickens allegedly possesses a "home," which is fitted out with *art nouveau* bric-a-brac, with Puvis de Chavanne prints and books illustrated by the *decadent* Aubrey Beardsley. Lyova, who likes spending time in Uncle Dickens' tiny apartment,[36] also lives in a *Jugendstil* villa, designed by the famous Benois, associated with the modernist journal *Mir iskusstva* and the seaweed Liberty patterns found on the walls, cornices, and fabrics of the era of high modernism. This is state accommodation for the repressed but pampered and privileged academia of the Stalinist times of the Odoyevtsev *père* generation. Yet notwithstanding its concrete architectural presence, modernism as an aesthetics does not define Lyova's father, whose cultural role model for Lyova is confined to the representation of the (state) Law and its prohibitions, symbolized through father's strict adherence to state fashion expressed through the width of his trousers. Simultaneously, Father represents a "gap" in Lyova's childhood which is the locus of repressed desire. This desire manifests itself as the adolescent Lyova's admiration for Uncle Dickens—the belated and somewhat anachronistic culture carrier of the belle époque. The *fin de siècle* thus emerges as a cultural home to Lyova and, by extension, to Bitov, in whose novel Russian culture of the 1960s becomes synonymous with the reclamation and reappropriation of a repressed consciousness of Russian and European modernism.

In order for this consciousness of an earlier cultural era to surface, a general exodus from psychic repression is required. This coming out of repression is multi-framed. Lyova comes out of Oedipal repression at the same time as Uncle Dickens re-appears on the scene of Lyova's childhood (although chronologically this moment is located closer to the threshold between Lyova's adolescence and youth), to appropriate things—familiar objects—with which Lyova has had an intimate relationship. Lyova's parents come out of a mutual silence that shaped their conjugality, to demonstrate mutual love, made visible on their faces in the presence of Uncle Dickens. Various taboo topics emerge into social discourse—the proscribed topic of Lyova's grandfather and grandfather's critical project. All of these liberating transgressions have their emblem and their quasi-origin in Uncle Dickens' transgressive being, summed up in a verbal expletive: *Govno!* [Shit!]

Uncle Dickens brings the "forbidden" into the lives of the Odoyevtsevs: pornographic literature into Lyova's infantile innocence (although Lyova is between 16 and 18 years old at this point) and coarse language into the Odoyevtsev family kitchen. This infiltration of the "coarse" into the life of the restrained, aristocratic Odoyevtsev family has the force of an elemental rupture. Uncle Dickens' transgressive presence breaks all taboos. It has the strange effect of bringing into the open a pure, unadulterated "love" in the little family (Oedipal) triangle: Lyova-[Father-gap]-Mother. It is as if Uncle Dickens was the "middle term" or, rather, the "fourth term,"[37] required to bring this equation into "life" or at least into "love": "And much later Lyova understood that their love for the old man was so suddenly accessible and joyous for yet another reason, that given the purity of its selflessness it might be the means of love within the Odoyevtsev family, almost their sole means of love for one another."[38]

This "pure" and "selfless" love, which emanates from the Odoyevtsev parental couple and Lyova, is no ordinary "human" love-of-thy-neighbor. It is love of the "other."

The other, which is constitutive of the psychoanalytic subject—a poststructuralist version of the old-fashioned "human being"—is a *relation* within a structure, namely the structure of language. The other is, in fact, both a "position"—the locus of speech—and a void, a lack: "the want-to-be" (or *manque-à-être*). The other materializes out of a demand, addressed by the subject as he constitutes himself in the signifying chain. It is a demand that transcends need and can never be satisfied because it is a demand for a "complement," for a relationship of "transitivity" between subject and object. This relationship is as "interpersonal" as it is impersonal. The human being disappears or "fades" in this transitivity of language. What is left is a "metonymy" of the subject, formally expressed in signs—or names (words, nouns). Thus the subject ceases to exist as a separate entity from his language, which is his other, mediating his only possible relationship to the world. This relationship is a *demand* for love directed by the subject into the void which is the other:

> That which is thus given to the other to fill, and which is strictly that which it does not have, since it, too, lacks being, is what is called love....[39]

Uncle Dickens, who is a doubly laden symbol, points in the direction of this "big Other," represented by Lyova's "real" grandfather, with whose image Uncle Dickens frequently overlaps in Lyova's imaginings. Contrary to what might be expected in a novel-chronicle, the hero's "growing up" is not portrayed as a linear process but as a synchronic tableau. In the giant synchronicity of the novel, also reflected on the level of the circular plot, the hero's entry into the symbolic order as a subject of the unconscious is represented as a synchronous *rite of passage* from the "small other" to the "big Other." Uncle Dickens, who is in many ways a double of grandfather, is a representative of Lyova's "small other," which pre-empts the "big Other." As this generalized or transitional other/Other, Uncle Dickens has nothing to give (he takes back all his "gifts" to the Odoyevtsevs); he does not have a substantial existence (is a *manque-à-être*), and is thus not a "substance," and could be said to be "not of this world." "Alienation" (the reverse of which is perceived as "love"), which Uncle Dickens brings to bear on everything he touches—such as *War and Peace,* which he is reading, and which appears to Lyova to be different from the one that everyone else has read—is the natural habitat of this other/Other. And alienation, under the code name "disorientation" (*dezorientatsia*) is, according to Bitov, the main subject-matter of his novel *Pushkin House:* "And if you asked us at this moment what the whole novel was about, we would not, at that moment, feel bewildered but would confidently reply: Disorientation."[40]

But if Uncle Dickens represents the originary alienation of the subject through (metonymic) identification with objects, he is also a function of the subject's "clean and proper body,"[41] which separates itself from the "filth" of nature in an attempt at imaginary unity and autonomy of the self. Uncle Dickens' fastidiousness—complementing his parsimoniousness and lack of generosity—serves to establish the boundaries between the self's clean and proper body, which is a guarantee of identity (in the sense of the subject's individuality) and difference (in the sense of the individual's distinctiveness from all others). The "improper" and the "unclean" belong to the "natural" sphere: they are not separate from nature.[42] The "proper" (one's own) and "clean" belong to the symbolic order, which is an "un-natural" reality of the second order. This aspect of Uncle Dickens' "portrait" is evoked in the absolute absence of smell in his home and on his body. He was a "kind of standard for the absence of stink."[43] This unnatural little man, who is all verbal posturing or verbal game, is Lyova's bridge into the symbolic. Uncle Dickens' "gentlemanliness"—the mask that conceals his "lack-of-being"—goes together with his "minimalism" of expression (what is the shortest definition of a *lorgnette*?[44]) and the terseness with which he "curses." Taken together with his petty-bourgeois origins (he is the son of a Kazan innkeeper), Uncle Dickens—whose very nickname is a verbal mask, behind which lurks his relationship to *texts* or *writing*[45]—is reminiscent of Ivan Karamzov's petty-bourgeois, anachronistic, gentleman-devil—a representation of the unconscious sanctioned by literary tradition.

IV. Aristocratism as a Metaphor of Identity and Difference

As a representation of the other, which is synonymous with the unconscious, Uncle Dickens is, in fact, a representation of the *unrepresentable,* of that which cannot be represented. For the unconscious is not a thing, an object, an organ or something visible. The unconscious is a gap, which manifests itself only as a *symptom.* The symptom, in turn, belongs to the structure of the *sign.* The symptom is thus a kind of proto-sign. Consequently, the unconscious is a "space" or a "spacing," in which the signifying chain is constituted. Lacan said that the unconscious operates "like a language," that is, it is the space in which the signifying process takes on form through condensation into discrete signs. As such, it is the locus of the subject, who is constituted in and by language. Language is a differential system of signs. That is, meaning in language is derived from the operation of *difference* (one sign is *not* another) and not from the fact that each sign is a "substance" or "essence." In order for one sign to be differentiated from another, it is first necessary that the sign be itself, and not be like any other sign. A sign thus operates in the system of language by being a unique "particular" and by having a one-of-a-kind character.[46]

This "uniqueness" of the sign is embodied by Uncle Dickens as a character of the novel and is expressed through the metaphor of *aristocratism.* Lyova, who is equipped with a quasi-historical aristocratic pedigree (demonstrated in *name* alone—"the Odoyevtsevs"—and not dwelt on in any genealogical detail[47]), also shares in this uniqueness. We can safely assume that aristocratism, as portrayed in Bitov's novel, is not a true class distinction; firstly because Uncle

Dickens is of plebeian origin (his sister, who comes to collect his effects, shares none of his aristocratic features); secondly because Lyova is a "typical" man of "his (Soviet) time," which we have on Bitov's authority: "That is why even our Lyova is a type, despite his belonging to an extinct breed."[48] The portrait of Lyova also testifies to his historical affiliation with the *homo sovieticus,* evoked by grandfather in his grand and drunken confession before Lyova.

In typical Soviet social style, Lyova manages to drink his way through the entire fake (phantasmagoric) plot of the novel. He is seen spitting into the Neva (or having just spat) after the sightseeing tour with the American guests. Nikolai Apollonovich Ableukhov, for instance, on whom Leva's stream-of-consciousness plot is modeled, is never depicted through this kind of banal gesture, although he indulges in absurd grimacing and gesturing. Inasmuch as Lyova is ever glimpsed in a "naturalistic" setting—and such moments are rare in Bitov's novel—Lyova is never seen visiting the theatre or the Bolshoi Ballet, only restaurants. When he attends dances, it is at Soviet-style parties in a communal flat or a crowded sitting-room, not in a ballroom or the like. Lyova's "naturalistic" portrait is at all times overshadowed by literary allusion (as when he leans on the parapet Onegin-style) or through the haze of his visceral, inside-out portrait obtained through a *vivisection* of his psyche. (His *desire,* Faina, who causes Lyova's "doubling," is actually called a "vivisector.") But when the naturalistic portrait of the mature Lyova does protrude from the background darkness, what we get is something closer to an image of that 1950s idol of French New Cinema, Jean-Paul Belmondo—the *gamin*-like nonchalant posture, a cigarette hanging out of the corner of his mouth, spitting casually and pulling his neck into the collar of his coat—than the cliché pose of a "gentleman" or "aristocrat."

The category of *identity* (or uniqueness) is first elaborated in the novel through Uncle Dickens. Uniqueness originates in transgression and transgression is the *raison d'être* of Uncle Dickens as a character. He is "transgressive" and hence "atypical" by virtue of being completely "unique" and "exemplary." There are no two Uncle Dickenses. Uncle Dickens is a single exemplum, not even one of a kind, but a particular, a singularity and hence unrepeatable. In order to give this "uniqueness" form, Uncle Dickens is represented as an "eccentric," an oddity. But not an oddity of the kind evoked in the petrified stylist of the 1950s, the lonely aging *stilyaga,*[49] who is an anachronism at the end of the 1960s—the purported "narrative time" of the novel. For Lyova (and the narrating Bitov) Uncle Dickens is not anachronistic but "aristocratic" and "elegant." His attire, which would have raised eyebrows on the streets of Leningrad in the fifties (and which the narrator "Bitov" offers without the slightest irony), seems to fit the turn-of-the-century interior of the Hotel European, where he dines every evening in the style of an Edwardian gentleman (on his returned servicemen's pension ..., an ironic detail that is "blurted out" almost as a Freudian slip, betraying its incongruousness). Uncle Dickens' portrait is thus a nostalgic reminiscence of a lifestyle and of a social type which have long gone out of existence in Russian and European society. His "eccentricity" and "anachronism"—which the narrator emphasizes are different from the sad anachronism of the *stilyaga*—underline his "uniqueness." As a character, Uncle Dickens thus represents something that is, paradoxically, at the same time "unique" and *non-existent.*

Uniqueness is a category that designates the subject of consciousness. Even if this subject has fluid boundaries, and even if his only support is fantasy (or the *imaginary*), the subject still retains a sense of selfhood (the "soul" or "personality" endures, i.e., remains the same[50]), not as "essence" but as a *desiring* one-ness, a particular that cannot be destroyed by any historical or cultural circumstances. This axiom is illustrated by the case of Lyova's grandfather—a man entirely broken by the march of history, whom Lyova fails to recognize—who nevertheless retains a *sameness* (the same "soul" or ego) throughout his life's vicissitudes. Only the "rehabilitation" deprives grandfather of his uniqueness—and this is when he goes mad, according to the first variant of his life-story.

The uniqueness of the self, its unrepeatability and its unity, which is equal to that of the numeral "one," is represented in Bitov's novel by the metaphor of *aristocratism.* This metaphoric aristocracy has, according to Mitishatyev's astute analysis, no guiding transcendental idea and no ideology. It is, like Lyova's parents, totally apolitical. It is a "class" and it is only this sense that guarantees its survival. But this class affiliation is ahistorical, because "class" here means the same as "classification." To belong to a class means to be a singular unit among many singular units of the same class. In retaining one's singularity, one is thus "different" from all others, both of the same class or of another class. The metaphor of aristocratism thus encompasses the concept of *difference.* To be aristocratic in Bitov's novel means to be an "in-and-for-oneself" and "different" from others. As such aristocratism stands for the Hegelian dialectic of *identity* and *difference,* the same dialectic expressed through the Master/Slave relationship and enacted in the rivalry between Lyova and his "childhood friend" Mitishatyev. Without *difference,* there is no singularity. Hence, when grandfather is deprived of his *difference*—the life he constructed for himself as *his* own in the gulags, fashioned and willed by him and no one else but him—grandfather collapses as a singularity and that is the end of "the man."

Uncle Dickens' "oddity" is not the same, then, as that of the petrified social type of the Soviet *stilyaga* of the 1950s. His stylistic peculiarities are evaluated quite positively by the narrator and by all the characters in the novel. They are taken as a given. They are not perceived as anachronistic or peculiar or funny by anyone, although they should be perceived as all three if one were to look at them through the lens of a realist and mimetic poetics. This is so because they have a symbolic and not a mimetic function. Uncle Dickens' "oddity" is that of the singular *fact,* the givenness of the singular *object* or the irreducibility of the *thing named.* Ludwig Wittgenstein's model of language is refracted through the structure of this fictional portrait. According to Wittgenstein, "the world divides into facts" (1.2), and "what is the case—a fact—is the existence of states of affairs" (2). This non-essential and non-determined *givenness* of a totality of facts produces a relational model of reality, in which "[A] state of affairs (a state of things) is a combination of objects (things)" (2.01). "Things" or "facts" cannot exist on their own. They are innately relational and combinable with other things:

> Just as we are quite unable to imagine spatial objects outside space or temporal objects outside time, so too there is no object that we can imagine excluded from the possibility of combining with others (2.0121).

Thus, as it is stated in Wittgenstein's *Tractatus Logico-Philosophicus,* in itself a project of European modernism, "[O]bjects make up the substance of the world ..." (2.021). As "substance" (and "substance is what subsists independently of what is the case" [2.024]), objects are irreducible, that is: "Objects are simple" (2.02). Objects are represented *metonymically* in propositions, that is, in language:

> "In a proposition a name is the representative of an object" (3.22). And finally, "names," which are signs, are irreducible entities, singularities: "A name cannot be dissected any further by means of a definition: it is a primitive sign" (3.26).[51]

Uncle Dickens is the unconscious carrier of this philosophy of language. As a character of the novel, he does not apply this attitude consciously to words or in his own *writing.* What he does is *act out* this philosophy in his capacity as a Wittgensteinian primitive sign. This is why Uncle Dickens is evoked as a character amidst a plethora of concrete *things.* His *medium*—the means by which he comes to life as a character—is that of material objects, petty objects, occupying a prescribed space. The novelistic logic dictates that a psychological motivation for his partiality to furniture, and to all the other material objects that delineate the limits of his enclosed existence, must be offered. Hence the reference to his "egoism," which seems quite natural in a bachelor and aged veteran of two world wars and a revolution. But an egotistical old man would be of no interest to anyone—and indeed he is initially "irrelevant" or *ni k chemu,* "of no consequence" at all to the novel or to its hero. However, by the logic of discourse (and not of the genre nor the plot of the novel), this formula is turned around and this *ni k chemu* is turned into *k chemu*—a positive form that does not exist in standard Russian but is derived from a double negation—both meaningful and deprived of (standard) meaning, and hence reduced to a mere *play* on meaning. This is the substance of Uncle Dickens; he has no other "profile," no other "essence." He is surface, style, and transgression. Apart from his cursing and his shibboleth *govno,* he does not say much, except to define words. His favorite reading is a dictionary—*Dal's* Russian dictionary. Uncle Dickens and words seem to enjoy a special relationship. His body and his actions seem to underwrite the concreteness of words, their plasticity or materiality, their irreducibility and their "truth," which is coeval with their presence, their "being there." Uncle Dickens, his *things* and *words* are in a symbiotic relationship. They are analogous to each other, synonymous with each other. They are metonymies of each other. But by being anchored to the irreducible material object—his furniture, his stove, his (transgressive) toilet and all his other "things"—Uncle Dickens also gains in authenticity, and in turn authenticates everything he comes in contact with: the Odoyevtsevs, the Russian classics he reads, and the Russian history of the 1930s through the 1960s, which he "portrays."

Uncle Dickens is credited with all these good deeds in the service of truth and freedom not because of anything he says or does. Indeed he performs no heroic feats (his own wounding in the war is glossed over in less than a sentence); nor does he offer a new moral philosophy. In fact, he refuses to get involved with, be committed to or accept responsibility for others. He is simply not there for people who "need" him. He transcends "need," because he belongs to the dialectic of demand, desire and the other.

But his "not being there" is precisely the point of his existence in the novel. He is the *ni k chemu,* which is the starting point for discourse and for the subject. The *ni k chemu* which, in an ironic and catachrestic inversion (breaking the rules of syntax to generate a trope), becomes only *k chemu.* Uncle Dickens is that gap, that nothingness that is the precursor of the other in the structure of discourse. For although he appears to be an ordinary historical character in a "chronicle" novel, he is, in fact, totally ahistorical. It is in transgression that Uncle Dickens takes shape as a character, not in history or mimesis. This removes him from Lyova's "time," which itself materializes only as a "gap" instituted by Uncle Dickens' transgressive presence.

Such a gap is graphically marked by multiple full stops or dashes in the text of the novel, positioned at the end of Part One, in the chapter entitled "Naslednik (*Dezhurnyi*)" [The Heir (On Duty)].[52] This chapter picks up the plot in the "present," namely on the "eve of the November holiday," when Lyova falls asleep at the table in the Director's office and is awakened by a telephone call from Mitishatyev. The rest of the plot (Parts II and III of the novel) takes place in the present and is literally situated within this graphic gap. But this plot, far from taking the story forward, keeps returning to the beginning and resketching the already narrated part of Lyova's youth, which becomes coeval with Lyova's "life" and Lyova's "time." Thus the *sujet*, which takes shape through the remaining two parts of the novel, represents the hero's journey not through history or "his time" in the sense of the Lermontovian "hero of his time," but through *desire* and *writing*. At center stage of the hero's drama of *desire* are two characters who are inextricably linked: Faina and Mitishatyev. Together they embody another version of Lyova's symbolic other. What Lyova experiences in confrontation with this "collective" other will constitute the "real," a psychic state that can be assimilated to the experience of one who "fell into the hands of the living God."[53]

V. *Pushkin House* as Archeology

The plot of *Pushkin House* is thus not a chronology but a temporality and a synchronicity. The three parts of the novel: *Part One—Fathers and Sons*; *Part Two—The Hero of Our Time*, and *Part Three—The Humble Horseman*, fit together like the threads of a skein of wool, which is being wound into a knot or a ball. Another image suggested by the plot is a spiral, which is open-ended and hence points in the direction of infinity. But since the plot also appears to return perpetually to a point which had already been passed, it could also be likened to a Moebius strip[54] or the reverse eight,[55] which has neither beginning nor end. Lyova, the hero and subject of this novel, constitutes himself not in chronological time, but as a position in space. This space is defined by Lyova's various imaginary and symbolic "doubles." Thus, Uncle Dickens materializes into an image of the ideal Father (or Grandfather) to constitute Lyova's "small other" (Lacan's *objet petit a*) of the *imaginary*. Grandfather Odoyevtsev, who appears when Lyova is at the threshold of adulthood, forms Lyova's "big Other" in the symbolic register. Together with Mitishatyev, into whose image Lyova eventually doubles (in Part III of the novel), Lyova becomes the other of "time" (*vremia*). This other is Russian history's unconscious of the 1960s.

The investigation of the unconscious of an era (Bitov's *epokha*) has acquired a name in recent Western theory. Through Michel Foucault, this methodology of historical research has been called "archeology."[56] Such an archeology seeks to uncover not totalizing unities and teleologies, but discontinuities, difference(s) and dispersions. The failure of traditional historical research to perceive discontinuities is attributed to the tendency in Western culture to want to "preserve, against all decenterings, the sovereignty of the subject, and the twin figures of anthropology and humanism."[57] The perceived failure of Western nineteenth-century historicism to uncover "the whole interplay of differences," or to see "discontinuities," "transformations," the function of "levels" (dare we say, with Deleuze and Guattari, "plateaus"), "limits," and "specific series," is diagnosed by Foucault as issuing from a general fear of the other as a category by which our own thought defines itself: "As if we were afraid to conceive of the *Other* in the time of our own thought."[58] While it may be true that historical discourse has eschewed the category of the other in its methodology, the representation of the other has been a fact of European aesthetics at least since the times of modernism. However, it is only through postmodern discourse that an imperative has been established to extend this representation to the entire epistemological field. Hence Foucault's call for a new "archeological" methodology of history and the human sciences. In his own way, Bitov answers this call.

With *Pushkin House*, Bitov undertakes a complex task. His novel, which combines features of a work of fiction and an essay on art,[59] must serve, in the context of Russian culture of the 1960s, both as a recuperation of a lost Russian cultural past—that of the Russian avant-garde and modernism of the beginning of the twentieth century—and as a "scientific" project, aimed at a radical re-evaluation of Russian history of the first half of the twentieth century and the dissemination of a new epistemology that would uproot the transcendentalism of socialist realism.

That is why Lyova, Bitov's hero, is engaged in an "archeological" project on the Russian culture of the nineteenth century. This he does through his study of Pushkin, Tyutchev and Lermontov, which results in various articles appearing as titles or in paraphrase only ("The Belated Genius," or "The Median of Contrast," which addresses *The Bronze Horseman*). The exception is an article entitled "Three Prophets," part of which appears in the text of the novel, at the end of Part Two. Here, while apparently going over old themes of Russian literature, Lyova manages to offer a new, individual re-evaluation of old material: this novelty results from the introduction of a single new element—namely, Lyova's own experience. Lyova's article on "The Three Prophets" is not, the narrator alleges, about Pushkin, or Lermontov, or Tyutchev, but about Lyova himself. This imparts to Lyova's critical work, which the narrator evaluates as even somewhat naive and unscientific, the quality of "inner freedom."[60] It is this unabashedly subjective study of the past that becomes a kind of "monument" at Lyova's institute, circulating in a well-worn and slightly tarnished samizdat-like copy: it is something "without precedent," unique and "different."

However, it is not just that Lyova's archeological project is different and without precedent; it is that such a project is a project on difference, discontinuities, and series which do not form totalities. Thus, instead of looking for the continuity of Pushkin's poetic tradition in Tyutchev's poetry, Lyova looks for and uncovers a "secret" duel going on across the generations, a duel between Tyutchev and his predecessor. This duel is one-sided, since Pushkin is not aware of his poetic adversary. In fact, Pushkin is not a "real" opponent for Tyutchev, but Tyutchev's other—a phantasmic being, constructed by Tyutchev in a relationship of *jealousy* or *envy.* According to Lyova's study, it is this other that enables Tyutchev to define himself in the history of Russian poetry, as a *vtorostepennyi* ("second tier") poet in relation to the "Pushkin tradition" or "Pushkin line" in

Russian literature. Bitov's reader knows that this is a monstrously unfair judgment of Tyutchev, which cannot possibly be taken at face value. The point of Lyova's study of Tyutchev, Pushkin, and Lermontov (the latter figuring only nominally) is not in its truth value: its value lies in its relation to Lyova's own experience. And Lyova's experience consists of his total identification with Pushkin and his subjective reading of Tyutchev as Pushkin's envious and presumptive heir in Russian poetry. It is not that Lyova rejects or denies Tyutchev's genius as a poet. On the contrary, Lyova gives Tyutchev his historical due, his place in Russian poetry as the "master of *concrete* poetry."[61] Lyova even asserts, in his drunken polemic speeches during his night on duty at the institute (which resemble grandfather's drunken confession to Lyova), that there is no such thing as the "Pushkin line" in modern Russian literature. This is because modern Russian literature is closer to the poetics of Tyutchev than it is to Pushkin.

What Lyova uncovers in his study—and this is the actual novelty of it—is that Pushkin was Tyutchev's *desire* ("first love")[62], and that this desire shaped Tyutchev's subsequent destiny as a poet. This desire took on the form of a desire for recognition by the Master (Pushkin) that was never granted. What Lyova does not say but what his study "re-enacts" (not as a "historical" re-enactment but as an *intertextual* replay of the theme of desire in Bitov's novel) is the fact that desire is by definition unsatisfiable. As such, it is the agency of something called infinity. This infinity is not something transcendental or beyond the human subject. It is part of the constitution of the subject and the subject's relationship to language. It is in the *jouissance* of language—the *jouissance* beyond the phallus—that man experiences the infinite and the sublime. However, Lyova's study does not take us that far. As a typical *homo sovieticus,* Lyova is still below the level of appreciation of the sublime, even if he can intuitively grasp the category of the other of discourse. This is not so for Bitov. The author of *Pushkin House* (or the abstract level in the structure of the text representing his discourse) is no longer a *homo sovieticus* and can therefore show, using his hero, the excess that is productive of discourse. This he does in Lyova's final orgy of writing (albeit for only a brief spell) during his night of duty at the institute, when Lyova discovers his "old" manuscript on "The Median of Contrast," which he relives ecstatically for a moment as both reader and writer (archeologist) in an attempt to complete the unfinished work. This *jouissance* of writing is accompanied by a blaze of light-music [*svetomuzyka*],[63] which is the synesthetic effect of Lyova's inebriated state in which he orgiastically switches on all the chandeliers at the institute.

It is in fact Tyutchev with whom Lyova identifies more than with Pushkin, even if, unlike the reader, he does not realize it. Lyova understands Tyutchev because Lyova has come to understand the dialectic of desire through his own experience of desire. Desire is not just one of Lyova's experiences: it is his self-defining experience.

Just as he was for Tyutchev, Pushkin is also Lyova's desire. As Lyova's desire, Pushkin, for all his historical concreteness (his poetry, letters, his documented historical personality), shares the elusiveness of Lyova's beloved, Faina. Pushkin was unattainable for Tyutchev, his contemporary. Pushkin is even less attainable for Lyova, who is his "belated" contemporary.[64] For Lyova imagines, vainly, that he would have reacted differently to Pushkin, had he been in Tyutchev's place: he would have embraced Alexander Sergeeevich . Here, the narrator Bitov shows skepticism. Did we not, he asks, see Lyova's reaction to grandfather, who, it is implied, was Lyova's contemporary and carrier of a cultural (critical) tradition that Lyova aspired to inherit? The encounter with grandfather—Lyova's other—resulted not in a loving rapprochement, but in total alienation. However, this alienation was not nihilistic for this "encounter" with grandfather transformed Lyova into a "mature" unconscious and his "life" into *logos.* For it is after the encounter with grandfather and during Faina's habitual absence, that Lyova's work on his postgraduate dissertation gets off the ground (to Mama's satisfaction), eventually leading to the study "Three Prophets." The archeological project, which is the form Lyova's *logos* assumes, is in itself not unproductive. It enables Lyova to look into the past and see his own image reflected in it. This is Tyutchev's "guilt" before Lyova: "He [Tyutchev] was to blame for Lyova's recognition, the recognition of himself in the ugly face of his own experience."[65] This is what Lyova held personally against Tyutchev even if, in the same breath, Lyova recognized that it was

Tyutchev's poetics (not Pushkin's classicism) that formed the bridge to Russian twentieth-century literature ("Tyutchev *vanquished* him [Pushkin] in poetry.... Pushkin's line has no supremacy."[66]). Identifying the relationship of the poetic discourse of an era (Bitov's *epokha*) with a cultural other (the Tyutchev/Pushkin relationship) is what gave Lyova's "archeological" project on Russian literature such a unique experiential quality. In fact, what Lyova did was question the authority of the past. He dared profane the sacred monuments of Russian culture and use them to further or assimilate knowledge about himself and his own time. Thus Tyutchev became Lyova's mirror. In this sense, Lyova utilized the past in a constructive way. He brought the past out of its "museum" and turned it into an analytic tool of the present moment. This constituted Lyova's "archeological" methodology.

But it is also Bitov's methodology. With his novel, Bitov, too, is offering an archeology, not of the past, but of the 1960s—his own "time" or contemporeneity (*vremia*), which is the time of the writing of his novel. Bitov's archeological project overlaps with Lyova's. For it is Bitov's original and deconstructive reading of the past which reanimates the (historical?) relationship between Tyutchev and Pushkin. The question of whether Bitov's analysis of that relationship is factually correct or critically plausible is irrelevant. In a work of fiction, the author is allowed to use everything as metaphor. The only constraint he faces is that his metaphor be relevant to his project, the main concern of his fiction. Bitov's metaphor, built on the Tyutchev/Pushkin historico-poetic dichotomy, ends with a parallel reading of two poems on madness. Both Russian poets had visions of madness, which they expressed in poetry. Each of them depicted madness as either a flame with a shadow or a shadow surrounded by a flame. Which poet's vision was which remains unclear and, ultimately, irrelevant. The point is made that each poet's *logos* was like a light illuminating dark space and that either this light or this surrounding darkness corresponded to the concept of madness or non-meaning, which is the same thing. But this madness or non-meaning is not the end-point of their poetry. On the contrary, it is the precondition of *logos*, its reverse or underside, the concealed portion that corresponds to the concealed intersection of the Moebius strip. This generative or originary madness, symbolized by light and its shadow, is a metaphor. Light is the image of metaphor, a metaphor of metaphor. A similar image occurs at the end of grandfather's writing. The madness Tyutchev and Pushkin described but which only Pushkin "feared" (Pushkin, the classicist, would have balked at the futurists' *trans-sense* language or the *literature of the absurd*) is the same madness embodied in grandfather's life and written word. It is a madness coeval with non-sense or with *silence*, both of which are on the other side—beyond the *limit*—of language. Silence is opposed to *mnogogovorenie*[67] (babbling), both in Bitov's "critique of critiquing" (his attack on "negation" and "nihilism") and in grandfather's attack on "mediocrity" (*poshlost'*) and "consumerism" (*poterbitel'stvo*). But if both Bitov's and grandfather's critiques of the "production" of words (criticism, critical thought) were to prevail as the sole principle of discourse, then discourse itself would become an impossibility. This reductio ad absurdum can only be overcome through archeological criticism. And it is as an archeological project that Bitov's discourse ultimately functions.

The two "archeologies"—Lyova's and Bitov's—form a unified whole. They frame each other in a combined function, namely as cultural *memory* and as the contemporary unconscious. And while memory is always of something already past, memory as archeology is brought into the present and becomes the "chronotope" (Bakhtin) that supports the culture of the present. Memory as chronotope or as archeology, or as the unconscious of "time" (*vremia*) is not subject to *museification*. It does not turn into a dead monument. And while Bitov's novel appears to be littered with monuments of the Russian past—the very setting of *Pushkin House* embodies such a notion—Bitov's archeological method of evoking this past is radically subversive. All the concretized "monuments" of the past—Pushkin's pistols (a "proven" historical artifact), Grigorovich's inkwell (an "unproven" artifact, which has the flavor of yet another double literary allusion, namely to Ivan Karamazov's inkwell, which is a "graft" onto Luther's inkwell), *The Bronze Horseman*, Pushkin's death mask—are subjected to laughter and parody. Pushkin's pistol, used by Lyova in the symbolic duel with Mitishatyev, is left smoldering not from gun powder but from Mitishatyev's semi-extinguished cigarette butt, which the latter stuffs into the barrel of the gun before disappearing from the institute and from Lyova's life. Pushkin's death mask, which is broken in the scuffle, turns out to have been only one of hundreds of copies held in the basement of the museum. Grigorovich's inkwell is retrieved, unbroken. Lyova straddles the bronze lion in front of the Admiralty Building, scratching the monument with a coin, to prove that this was not the "marble beast" [285/E] straddled by Pushkin's hero Yevgeniy in *The Bronze Horseman*. Historical artifacts, which belong to the museum of Russian culture, are played with *transgressively* and exploded as "relics"—objects of worship and quasi-religious admiration. History as *factual* museum of dead exhibits and decontextualized artifacts is subverted in favor of history as *archeology* or the lived unconscious of time (*vremia*). Since a historical fact can never be reinstated in its fullness outside of its past context, all factual history is of necessity distortion of the facts.[68] Bitov's entire novel, with its quasi-historical title and its monumental network of literary allusions, is hence an exercise in transgression and in sacrilegious treatment of traditional cultural authority. When Bitov says that he is offering a "museum novel" (*roman-muzei*), he does not mean it literally. Quite the opposite. Or rather, he does mean it, only he is not telling the whole story. The other side of his story is that by allocating the past its place in the museum, his "museum narrative" becomes a deconstruction of the museum of the past. The museum of culture can be deconstructed through the methodology of "archeological research" into the national cultural tradition. This past manifests itself as the intertextual other of the present cultural and historical moment. This other, constituted out of the material of the past as a living *logos* or *present* (*presence*), is embodied by the hero, Lyova, whose identity as "hero of his time" is established through and by his writing.

Lyova's portrait appears at several points in the narrative. He is "seen" as a chubby infant, running into loving outstretched adult hands. Then as a young man "in 1955," in his first tailor-made suit, cut according to the fashion magazines of the time. Then with an elongated, iconlike face, resembling a photo of grandfather Odoyevtsev taken in adolescence. Finally, even that iconlike quality of the face is replaced by the illumination of a light shaft, falling elliptically on Lyova's ear and an "obtuse" angle of his head (its lower portion, his chin). Thus Lyova's portrait is progressively erased: it metamorphoses from representing a "body" (that of the child and of the young man) and a "face" (an icon, a sign—the "image" of a young and ideal(ized) grandfather Odoyevtsev), into an emptiness or a gap. In the italicized text of the narrator "A.B.," Lyova is represented through a "crack" (gap), to be perceived as a partial object—an ear and a voice—on the other side of a wall:

> And Lyova himself ... only by a slanting ray through a random crack—the rim of an ear, a deep shadow under the chin—we've made do without a portrait. His voice is barely audible on the other side of the wall....[69]

Through this transformation from a body and a face to a partial object, a voice, and a function of speech and listening, Lyova becomes identical with a pure unconscious. For the ear, as the only bodily "orifice that cannot be closed,"[70] is the only of the five senses directly related to the unconscious in both Freud's and Lacan's models of the psyche.[71] Lyova thus represents the unconscious of Bitov's text, which in turn is a representation of the unconscious of Bitov's "time" (*vremia*). Lyova is thus a representation of a representation and not of an assumed (historical) reality. As an effect of the auditory sense (listening), Lyova becomes the other of the text—not only of Bitov's text, but of the text[ure] of Russian culture of the 1960s. As this other, he literally becomes the place or the "field" in which this culture comes to be constituted. Lyova is thus not a traditional "hero of his time," who can "represent" Russian reality outside the individual, as a separate totality. Lyova is the totality called Russian culture, which consists both of visible signs and their invisible, unconscious, archeological, historical determinants that "supplement" it. Since these determinants are never pre-given—they occur at a given moment as the effects of the "game" of *absence/presence* played out between those who make up a cultural epoch and that epoch's other

—culture is not a static totality but a dynamic process of self-generating cultural texts and cultural practices.

The cultural texts of a certain "time," which are subject to archeological investigation in the Foucauldian sense, constitute what has been called an *episteme.* In his function as the unconscious of discourse, Lyova represents the new episteme of Russian culture of the 1960s. This is the same episteme as the one evoked by Jacques Derrida, among others, in an experimental text entitled *Glas*,[72] which privileges *signifiance* (signification as *meaning* and *interpretation* as opposed to "communication") as a deconstructive process of delinearizing history and culture.

Bitov's novel represents a project similar to Derrida's *Glas*. The circularity of the plot of *Pushkin House*, the repetitions in lieu of linear progression, and the grafting of citations from foreign texts as a principle of construction—all of these elements produce a novel that is about semiosis as *the* textual and cultural process, the first Russian semiotic novel to mark the advent of postmodernism in Russian culture in the 1960s. *Pushkin House* even contains a hint at the "parallel texts" method that structures *Glas*. This can be seen in the many quotations that appear side-by-side as epigraphs to the chapters of Bitov's novel, in the graphic and visual grafting of a newspaper fragment onto the page of the fictional text (in Part One) and, above all, in Lyova's research project "Three Prophets," which is a study of three parallel texts—Pushkin's, Tyutchev's and Lermontov's—that literally appear side-by-side on a page to presumably be read simultaneously, in the manner of the parallel texts (of Hegel, Genet, Derrida) in *Glas*.

The postmodern archeological relationship to cultural texts—to culture as text—is grounded in a new perception of reality and a new understanding of representation. Unlike the positivist project loosely associated with nineteenth-century realism, the modern episteme culminating in twentieth-century modernism is not determined by a reality to be sought outside the textual or virtual reality. This reality is embodied in and by the process of signification or the construction of meaning, which is essentially a process of inscription of the subject of consciousness (or the subject of the unconscious) by language and the symbolic order. This process Derrida calls *writing*.

VI. Bitov's Novel as a Supplement to Russian Culture

Writing in this sense does not refer only to the written word. Writing refers to everything within culture that produces texts—that is, totalities consisting of signs placed in a meaningful or "signifying" relationship with one another. This kind of writing is not self-sufficient. It requires the complementary process of reading in order to "signify." In other words, writing is a combined process of *inscription* and *interpretation.* Writing is thus grounded in a signifying chain which is simultaneously an interpretive chain, what Derrida calls a *supplement.* This supplement is an order of "the regulated substitution of signs for things."[73] As a substitution, it stands in place of nature: "The supplement is the image and the representation of Nature. The image is neither in nor out of Nature. The supplement is therefore equally dangerous for Reason, the natural health of Reason."[74] The "dangerous supplement" is a concept Derrida extrapolates from Jean-Jacques Rousseau's *Confessions*—a text credited with instituting the episteme of modernity in Western culture and serving Derrida as a model of writing as a process of inscription, interpretation and erasure (of the inscribed). The supplement is dangerous because it simultaneously "dispossesses" and "constitutes" the subject of language through the law of language. Speech, which is the subject's experience of language, appears to the subject as something "immediate" and "present." But this immediacy is a "mirage." Speech always contains a "concealment," something which cannot be said or which cannot be known by the subject. Speech is *opaque* and lacks "transparency." The signifier can never fully reveal the concealment or exhaust the "excess" that constitutes the signified. This is because the signified is not the *thing* named, but the gap in which the process of naming takes place. The *signified* is the Freudian unconscious.

Bitov's novel is structured like a supplement. This is the rationale for all those commentaries "from the author," or "from A.B." or the part-chapters entitled "My Italics" (*Kursiv moi*). These are mini- or micro-supplements, instructions on "how to read" Bitov's "text." The representation of the hero's life is a monumental *tableau vivant* of the unconscious, or of writing in Derrida's sense. The novel is simultaneously a representation of the structure of the subject of consciousness and this subject's relation to time (*vremia*) and history (*epokha*). The novel is thus a supplement to Russian history, if that history is taken to derive its meaning from discourse or texts, to be history as text and interpretation rather than as factography.

According to Derrida's model of writing or the supplement, the "mirage of immediacy" of speech dispossesses us "of the longed-for presence in the gesture of language by which we attempt to seize it."[75] We as speaking subjects, or subjects of language and consciousness, are subjected to the experience of "the robber robbed" (evoked by Jean Starobinski). This experience is instituted in the "mirror stage" when the (child) subject first experiences himself as an other in the mirror image. This mirror image, which "'captures his reflection and exposes his presence,' lies in wait for us from the first word. The specular dispossession, which at the same time institutes and deconstitutes me, is also a law of language. It operates as a power of death in the heart of living speech: a power all the more redoubtable because it opens as much as it threatens the possibility of the spoken word."[76] A dispossession or "robbery" of the kind described by Derrida occurs at the start of Lyova's relationship to his *desire,* Faina. She who robs him of his identity and self-esteem is in turn robbed by him, who steals and substitutes her ring. The other (Faina), on whose account the subject is radically decentered, "teaches" the subject to play its (the other's) game: the game of substitution. For substitution is at the heart of metaphor (the originary signifying substitution), which is the core of speech or discourse.

In the reference to "death in the heart of living speech," we perceive an allegorical analogy to M. C. Escher's famous *Eye* (1946), with a skull peering out of the pupil at the spectator. This symbolic "power of death" constitutes the "danger" of the supplement. For while it "inaugurates speech," it also "dislocates the subject that it constructs, prevents it from being present to its sign."[77]

The symbolic "death in the heart of living speech" (symbolic because it is part of the virtual process of signification and not of the real biological process of dying) is equivalent to absence. Absence is "death" and "death" is absence. It is when someone is not there, when someone has gone away. And in as much as the subject of speech is always absent to his sign (which makes the subject, like Lyova, *opaque* or *unknowing*), so the subject is coeval with *absence* or symbolic "death." This explains why Lyova, the subject of Bitov's novel, appears as a corpse in the opening pages. It is through this symbolic "death of the subject" that the novel—symbolizing discourse in general—can constitute itself as a "game" of *absence* and *presence* or a concatenation of signifiers (coils of rings or *kol'tsa,* which the narrator privileges as the instituting structure of his plot, emanating from "the history of the ring"), whose signifieds are represented by *absence, silence* or *madness.* The "power of death" or of absence that underlies this "game," is reflected, parodically, in the staged death of the hero. It is only at the end of the novel that the reader is supposed to realize that the corpse found in the opening pages of the novel is a symbol: a symbol of the real, which is unrepresentable and which provides writing with a kind of underside or negativity. The corpse, if taken at face value and literally, implies that the hero is "dead" at the outset of the novel, that is, at the instituting moment of writing. This makes death a kind of precondition or suturing (the zero point) of writing which "anchors" its meaning like a *point de capiton.*[78] "To fix the ultimate meaning of any discourse is to determine the signifiers that have been repressed by that discourse."[79] In other words, the anchoring point of discourse, that which gives discourse relative stability and solidity, is the *repressed* portion of discourse. The image of a corpse, which evokes absence and material presence (in the domain of the real) simultaneously, is the image of the repressed whose palpable effect of non-existence and unrepresentability is Freud's *uncanny.* To reveal the repressed content of discourse is the task of deconstructive or archeological analysis of discourse. Such archeological analysis is the "stuff" of Bitov's novel. While the precondition or anchoring point of its discourse is "death" (the death of pre-Revolutionary Russian culture, of the past, of Lyova's *epokha* and, metaphorically, of Lyova), its condition of possibility or mode of existence is the *supplement,* which is quotation, framing, masking, *mise en abîme* and infinite signifying substitution or—metaphor.

The entire structure of Bitov's novel is supported by the symbolic death of the hero. Lyova is decentered (alienated) through his death in the symbolic, which is replayed in a cameo variant in the Epilogue, where "Lyova, the literary hero" [*Lyova—literaturnyi geroi*] "dies" in order to give way to "Lyova, the man" [*Lyova-chelovek*]. The series of supplements ends here, for *Lyova-chelovek* is literally a "closed book" at the end of Bitov's novel. To the narrator A.B., who "visits" him at the Pushkin Institute, and to the reader, he is already a new and unknown quantity. In order to get any closer to Lyova than he does during this visit, the narrator A.B. would have to undertake another archeological project, similar to the one just completed. For the reader, the Lyova of the Epilogue is a representative of a new "time" (*vremia*), which has not been investigated through an exploration of its unconscious—its cultural other. Neither Bitov nor the reader can get anything out of this distant relative of Lyova the literary hero (*Lyova-literaturnyi geroi*), with whom they have just parted. It is in fact this *Lyova-chelovek* who does not exist. He is not even a cipher—he simply *is not*. The historical Lyova can thus not exist outside the frame of reference of the cultural supplement, which is formed by the unconscious or other of a cultural epoch.

Supplementarity is thus both a principle of the structure of Bitov's novel and a model of perception constituted in and by the novel. In accordance with this poetics of supplementarity, the subject of the novel is, in Bitov's own words, alienation. This alienation is not so much that of Sartre's existential philosophy, although the latter can be subsumed in it quite comfortably; it is alienation in the sense of the semiotic (poststructuralist) model of the psyche, which renders the subject of consciousness "not present" to the sign that he/she produces in constituting him/herself. Lyova is thus "not present" to his sign. That is, he is neither aware of everything about himself, at any given moment of his psychic development (the narrator A.B. stresses this in his disquisition on how to portray Lyova in a mode less limiting than Realism), nor is he "knowledgeable" about language and the other. Lyova's "blindness" is particularly obvious in relation to his love, Faina. Lyova never "sees" Faina as she really is or as others (including the reader) see her. He is similarly not impartial with respect to Albina, whom he misjudges completely. But neither does he "see" his grandfather except as an antagonist who had pronounced him "stupid." Faina is an obvious "unreality" and "absence" in Lyova's life. The text is explicit on this point: Faina is the "Stranger," she is *podmennaia*—a "substitution." And she cannot be known by Lyova "as she really is": "*Fainu real'nuiu—on ne videl ni razu.*"[80] Not only that, she is a "masquerade." The fact that Faina is portrayed spending an inordinate amount of time "fixing" her face, making up, before going out with Lyova, describes her "essence," which is related to camouflage or mimicry: an essential "doubling" or specularization of the animal, a first relation to space, an empty, aesthetic play that is an end in itself and a precondition for signification or meaning.[81] As absence, Faina is Lyova's desire. Lyova spends his entire life—his "life" within the novel—chasing Faina. And although he does not possess her, she is, as Bitov points out, *his* and does not go away from him. That is, Faina does not occupy another space. When she does (on her frequent mysterious and "adulterous" trips away from Lyova), she is invisible and simply true to her essence as absence. Faina is thus not only Lyova's *desire* but Lyova's *supplement,* the elusive and unreal object that "supplants" his "first love"—Mama, who as Name is in turn a *supplement* to nature.

Derrida explains, using Rousseau's model case as the exemplum, the relationship of the subject's desire to the original object of desire, which is not nature or the mother, but the word Mama. And according to Bitov's novel, it is to such a name, "Mama," that all the women in Lyova's life can be reduced. It is Mama-as-Name (as supplement) that sets off the metonymic chain—a chain of supplements, revealing the possibility of endless "signifying substitutions" or metaphors, covering over the originary split or gap in the subject of language.[82] Through the sequence of supplements (the doubling and even tripling of Lyova's women in the surface plot—Faina, Albina, Lyubasha), the mode of *differance* (Derrida's combination of "deferral" and "difference") as a model of language and as the "new" attitude to the Word, advocated by grandfather, is formulated. *Differance*—or the combined effect of *difference* and *deferral* by which a sign is constituted in a signifying chain—belongs to the dialectic of *presence/absence* and the decentered subject. This dialectic eliminates all essentialism, all teleology and correspondence between sign and thing, making discourse a virtual mode of mediated perception with immediate effects. This revolution of the "spirit" (Hegel's "Geist") in European culture, intimately bound up with the discovery of the supplementarity of the symbolic order, is what the European mind finds difficult to grasp, even in the second half of the twentieth century:

> Through the sequence of supplements, a necessity is announced: that of an infinite chain, ineluctably multiplying the supplementary mediations that produce the sense of the very thing they defer: the mirage of the thing itself, of immediate presence, of originary perception. Immediacy is derived. That all begins through the intermediary is what is indeed "inconceivable [to reason]."[83]

Bitov's novel is an attempt to remedy this misconception, which is general to Western culture but of more immediate concern in the Russian-Soviet cultural situation beginning in the 1960s. With his self-reflexive and self-deconstructing novel, whose poetics of representation is grounded in the poststructuralist principle of the supplementarity (citationality) of all discourse, Bitov not only reclaims the aesthetics of a lost or interrupted Russian modernism and the avant-garde of the 1920s, but furnishes the material from which the bridge to Russian postmodernism is constructed.

The dialectic of *absence/presence* of the sign is, however, not the ultimate truth about the supplementarity of the signifying process or the poetics of the supplement of Bitov's novel. In the first place, the indeterminacy of the absence/presence dialectic does not amount to relativity or arbitrariness of meaning. The supplement is determined not by arbitrariness but by *surprise*: the surprise that the "presumed subject of the sentence might always say, through using the 'supplement,' more, less, or something other than what he *would mean* [*voudrait dire*]."[84] Surprise is a state of affairs of *being held within* [*prise*]—within a system of language and logic, which the writer uses but cannot dominate. The supplement thus suggests a method of reading which is not relative but fully determined by, and immanent to, the text:

> He [the writer] uses them [language and logic] only by letting himself, after a fashion and up to a point, be governed by the system. And the reading must always aim at a certain relationship, unperceived by the writer, between what he commands and what he does not command of the patterns of language that he uses. This relationship is not a certain quantitative distribution of shadow and light, of weakness or of force, but a signifying structure that critical reading should *produce*.[85]

Accordingly, Bitov's reader is as much implicated in Bitov's text as Bitov's hero. The reader is part of the supplement; the reader is the supplement of the supplement. As such, the reader is drawn into the text as an integral element of the process of *signifiance* or discourse.

VII. Writing As Process: Grandfather Odoyevtsev's Prayer

The model of critical reading, described as the supplement, is suggested both by grandfather Odoyevtsev, in his "writings" and his "drunken" speeches, and the deconstructive experiments that the narrator A.B. carries out with the text of the novel. In the fragments *Boga net etc.* [God Does Not Exist etc.], Modest Odoyevtsev despairs of the practice of *potrebitel'stvo*—the usurping of both the realm of Nature and the realm of Words. Usurpation is the arbitrary reclamation (*recoupment*) of existing words and the invention of new words in a generative system whose logic is based on recoupable production. "Production" within a "system" breeds "certainty" and certainty kills "God" (the unconscious) or infinity. Certainty thus represents the inability to be "surprised." Certainty takes the subject of language outside language, into the realm of metaphysical essences, ideal assumptions, and Platonic "truths." Modest Odoyevtsev, like some kind of Job of the free realm of the unfettered Word, sends his prayer of despair to God to save the world from the over-production of words, from the materialization of concepts into "false coins" of essences and absolutes, and from the comforts of systemic thinking, which "they" (the communist masters of Russia), he says, have instituted during his thirty-year absence from the scene of Russian culture—in the "false" gap ("pit") that was Stalinism. Contempt for "the system"—any system and not just the Soviet totalitarian system—is expressed by grandfather in his ironic throw-away comments, like : "*oni potriasiaiushche ustroilis*"![86]

The conscious manipulation of the meaning of words, so that they acquire ready-made meanings prescribed by or derived from some system, is as contrary to the logic of the supplement as is the notion of the author's "intentionality." The act of reading, which is contained in the logic of the supplement, "cannot consist of reproducing, by the effaced and respectful doubling of commentary, the conscious, voluntary, intentional relationship that the writer institutes in his exchanges with the history to which he belongs thanks to the element of language." Reading is "bound" by a given text, so that there can be nothing arbitrary about a reading even in the broad band of interpretive possibilities accorded by different readers.[87] Each reader must remain true to the text and not seek a reality outside it: "Yet if reading must not be content with doubling the text, it cannot legitimately transgress the text toward something other than it, toward a referent (a reality that is metaphysical, historical, psychobiographical, etc.) or toward a signified outside the text whose content could take place, could have taken place outside of language, that is to say, in the sense that we give here to that word, outside of writing in general. (…) *There is nothing outside of the text; there is no outside-text* [*il n'y a pas de hors-text*]."[88]

The axioms that reading (interpretation) is not a reproduction of the text and that "there is nothing outside of the text" are implicit in the poetics of Bitov's novel and come to light through Lyova's archeological project—his *writing* on the three Russian poets of the nineteenth century. Lyova's innovativeness appears to be constituted precisely by his excursion into the "biographical," into the intersubjective relationships of Tyutchev to Pushkin and Pushkin to Tyutchev. But this is deceptive, because the evidence for this psychobiographical relationship is purely and exclusively textual: it is literally based on Lyova's "reading" of Pushkin's and Tyutchev's poems, which are united through a theme and alleged intertextual dialogue. Similarly, and by extension, Bitov's novel is also a "reading" of a "reality," based exclusively on the tautology of language—which is to say, on textual evidence. Bitov constructs

Russian cultural history (*epokha*) through reading (actually quoting) Russian literary texts, and in turn offers a history of his own time, the 1960s, in the form of interpretation and contemporary reception of these texts. His chronicle is thus a reading of a time (*vremia*—a contemporeneity, a present which was and has thus become *epokha*) through another time, which by the novel's Epilogue has also become *epokha*. As a reading *in time*, Bitov's text is called into *presence* while at the same time erasing itself through numerous self-reflexive interventions by the narrator who deconstructs while he constructs. The text of the novel thus becomes a *trace* of an always already accomplished past (*epokha*). The "real life," or the "real existences" of Pushkin and Tyutchev, which are of interest to us no less than the Russian literature of the past, are inaccessible to us except through texts. And, as Derrida warns, "we have neither any means of altering this, nor any right to neglect this limitation."[89] Thus what one might call "real life," or "the flesh and bone" of the existences of Pushkin and Tyutchev (to transpose Derrida's comment on Rousseau and to take the two Russian poets as paradigmatic), cannot be reached except through an interpretive activity (which itself has something of the character of "automatic" *inscription* that characterizes the unconscious) called *writing*. For, as Derrida tells us, "beyond and behind what one believes can be circumscribed as Rousseau's text,[90] there has never been anything but writing; there have never been anything but supplements, substitutive significations which could only come forth in a chain of differential references, the 'real' supervening, and being added only while taking on meaning from a trace and from an invocation of the supplement, etc. And thus to infinity, for we have read, *in the text,* that the absolute present, nature, that which words like 'real mother' name, have always already escaped, have never existed; that what opens meaning and language is writing as the disappearance of natural presence."[91]

True to its supplementarity, Bitov's novel, while being a quest for *presence* in its attempt to capture the life of the "hero of his time," ends up by transforming *presence* into a trace of the past. This transformation is the stuff of archeology in Foucault's phenomenological sense of the term. It is a "discontinuity," which does not fit into any preconceived system and is not subject to recuperation. It is *process,* and not production. Bitov's novel aspires to become process in the archeological project of rememoration and reclamation of the "lost" Russian past. But as process, it escapes monumentalization. Hence the "author's" (A.B.'s) ironic and auto-parodic "apologia" about his novel being a "museum" novel. *Pushkin House* is *not* a museum novel, it does not belong to the "museum of Russian culture." Rather than reproduce the Russian cultural past, it deconstructs it. *Pushkin House* is discourse in and as process. As such, Bitov's novel is not easy reading. It resists interpretation and hence assimilation to the very end. Even after the book has been put down, the reader is still grappling with it. The reader's difficulties are practically insurmountable if he wishes to interpret in the traditional mode, by assimilating "what happens" in the plot with "Russian reality" outside the text. In part this difficulty stems from the fact that such an interpretation is already encoded in the text of the novel itself, in its supplementarity, which combines writing and reading. There is therefore no space for the reader in which to manipulate the text. Instead, the reader is drawn into the text as process and is manipulated himself into becoming a supplement of the text.

Discourse as process is what we have already called writing. The latter consists of "substitutive significations," also known by another name: metaphor. Writing is thus a *process* of "substitutive significations" or the generating of *metaphors.* This process is underpinned by the privileged use of quotations in Bitov's novel. The gloss or the quotation is, in fact, the structuring principle of the novel. The declared museum character of the novel is, as we have already said, parodic. The narrator A.B. is not attempting to reproduce the Russian culture of the past in its "museified" form, but uses the form of the "cultural museum" as a metaphor masking the structural principle of his narrative, which is that of the gloss and of writing. But if writing is a self-deconstructing presence and a sliding into a memory trace, then Bitov's novel about Russian culture is also a metaphor of culture—*all* of culture—as a museum.

There are two possible attitudes to the "museum of culture." One is displayed by Bitov through the poetics of his novel; the other is explicitly parodied in the text. The parodic attitude to the preservation of the museum of culture is entrusted to grandfather. It is grandfather Odoyevtsev who castigates the preservation of culture by turning on his "liberal" contemporaries, who berate the Russian Revolution for having allegedly "put an end" to Russian culture. According to grandfather, the Revolution did not put an "end" to, but actually "created" Russian culture by—it is implied—drawing a line under the "past" and turning this "past" into a "sphinx," an object of worship and an "oracle" of ready-made truths. Worshipping this "sphinx" which he does not understand (or understands literally and not deconstructively) is the "lecturer Il'ev" [*dotsent Il'ev*—a parodic foil of Lyova perhaps, with a play on the hero's name: "i Lev" versus "i Lyova"?], sketched in a miniature portrait in grandfather's chapter-fragment "God exists." This anonymous little *apparatchik* of language runs after Modest Odoyevtsev following the faculty meeting at which Modest was allegedly the architect of his own undoing. Il'ev's gesture is that of a "disciple" in search of a cultural "guru" (by implication a demagogue), who can interpret the sphinx of culture and guide him. Grandfather could have been such a guru—just as Stavrogin could have been Peter Verkhovensky's *Ivan Tsarevich*—had grandfather stooped to assimilate to the "politically correct" discourse of the post-revolutionary 1920s. Instead, grandfather engineered his self-destruction—in the interest of absolute freedom of the word—by refusing, it is implied, to have a historical text, considered subversive, namely the Book of Ecclesiastes of the Old Testament, appropriated for the political discourse of the day. Grandfather shows respect for the text and its open-endedness, while Il'ev, who speaks for the political establishment of the 1930s, looks at the text functionally, as would a *potrebitel'* (consumer), who can extract whatever he needs from it whenever the occasion requires.

Il'ev, a cultural "worker" in the worst sense of the term, is a time-server, who believes that words have "substance" and that the needs of the present moment (*vremia*) are absolute. Il'ev demonstrates this in his interpretation of Blok's poem *To Pushkin House*, which he fundamentally "misunderstands," according to grandfather. Il'ev reacts to Blok's poem with the affect of *enthusiasm*, instilled by a false sense of identification or "solidarity" with the *word content* of Blok's poem. Il'ev thinks, according to grandfather's sneering analysis, that Blok and Pushkin can be co-opted as "cultural dissidents" in the cause of the "preservation" of Russian culture in the face of a hostile regime. But this reductionist reading mistakes the nature of freedom revealed in Blok's poem to Pushkin. The freedom which Pushkin symbolizes for Blok is not political but metaphysical—it is freedom from all signifieds, ideological as well as cultural. It is the freedom of the *tabula rasa*, which is the "archeological" space, cleared out of the ruins of culture, in order to pronounce a WORD ANEW. This is what Blok's poem in its attitude to Pushkin points to, according to grandfather's reading: freedom from the past as the "open road" of infinite signification and supplementarity, without usurpation of the discourse of the past that turns "heritage" into a monument or a signified. To create culture anew necessitates a break with the past. For it is only in empty space or in silence or nothingness that a new *logos* can come into existence, according to grandfather: "… behind is the abyss, ahead is non-existence, on the left and right they've got you by the elbows…."[92]

The elliptical "they've got you by the elbows" alludes to the final scene of Kafka's *The Trial*, in which Joseph K. is being marched off to his "sacrificial death" by two anonymous agents of the Law. The freedom of the "open road" thus has its own necessity that comes across as "sacrifice" and "destiny." This destiny is the Law of *logos*, resting on the twin pillars of "lack" ("the abyss") and *irreality* ("non-existence"). For "irreality" is a "condition of life."[93] And practically repeating Lacan's formulaic definition (of the Law) of language, grandfather adds: "Everything is shifted and exists a step away with a purpose other than it was named for."[94] In other words, everything (all meaning) is "displaced" in language, whose basic structure is that of the *supplement;* so that language always expresses "more, less or something other" than it wanted to say (*voudrait dire*). To try to infuse the discourse of the past with "reality" is to attempt the impossible. What exists on the plane of "reality"—in the sense of the "real," which is impossible and unrepresentable—is God. What exists outside the real is always that which has separated off from it and is "divided, multiplied, canceled out, and the canceled out is annihilated."[95] So there are no pure, "authentic grounds" of "existence"(*sushchestvovanie na chestnosti podlinnykh prichin*).[96] There is only *supplementarity.*

As a model of indeterminacy and freedom of the Word (not to be confused with "freedom of speech"), supplementarity is tied to one precondition only: *silence.* This silence is what characterizes discourse *before* it comes into being, *before* it becomes discourse. At first, discourse is a gap ("an abyss"), occupying a total space which is as yet not a totality or identity. It is the gap of a continuous present, which as such does not exist *in time.* This is the silence of the "night," into which grandfather has been plunged by his God (in the fragment "God Exists"). This silence is raised into a "prayer"—not a "silent" prayer, but silence as prayer. Prayer is an attitude of expectation, an opening up to something that may come (in the future). Prayer is thus an opening up to the future out of a silent present. This is what constitutes grandfather's prayer in the fragment "God Exists." In his prayer, grandfather becomes a "virtual" word: that is, he feels "blinded" by the originary silence of language; "castrated" would fit even better, in anticipation of the symbolism of the "blinding" of Oedipus. Thus in his prayer grandfather stands on the threshold of transformation: from a "heart" which is "empty" and "silent" like the "sky," into a "gaze," blinded by the sun. Grandfather, masking his own "split" into subject and object under a "lament," thus comes "face to face" with a faceless God, who is his silent other. Grandfather's prayer is thus a *demand,* sent by the subject to his other, which is the subject's "real." Confrontation with the real produces pain—hence grandfather's anxiety in the "face" of the "silence" (total space) of the other. But this "pain" is also the "open road" referred to in Blok's poem, which grandfather's "commentary" turned into a "supplement" of his "prayer." Pain is "interrogation," the unanswered "question" and the open-endedness of "the road" to the other. This other is not a "model" to be copied, not a sphere of production (of words), but a silence in which speech can constitute itself, not as "presence" (edict, teaching) or as "babbling," but as what has always already been said. Hence speech as supplement, which is coextensive with the other as absence.

Pushkin House—an embodiment of Bitov's speech—is precisely such a supplement, "dangerous" not only for the repressed Russian post-Stalinist reading public of the 1960s, but no less threatening for the reader of the 1990s. For it confronts him with a horrific past not as "literariness" and cathartic spectacle, from which he could distance himself, but as supplement, which "castrates" through the "real" of language in order to perpetuate his place in the signifying chain of culture and the order of infinity. And while there may be protection (through temporal distancing) from the "reality" of the past (Stalinism, the gulags, the disappearances, the lost generations), there is no escape from the real of the supplement. And this is why *Pushkin House* was—and still is—dangerous reading.

Notes

1. Thus sincerity in Russian literature was demanded in V. Pomerantsev's famous article "Ob iskrennosti v literature," which caused a literary scandal, and which Tvardovsky, who published it in *Novy mir,* no. 12 (1953), considered an epoch-making article of the thaw.
2. Marc Slonim, *Russian Soviet Literature: Writers and Problems 1917–1967* (OUP, 1969); Geoffrey Hosking, *Beyond Socialist Realism: Soviet Fiction Since Ivan Denisovich* (Granada Publishing, 1980).
3. It was the pioneering analysis of Vail' and Genis that lead me to posit an even broader philosophical context in which to re-examine Russian literature and culture of the 1956 thaw.
4. Compare S. M. Vladiv, "Post-Modernism in Eastern Europe After World War II: Yugoslav, Polish and Russian Literature," *Australian Slavonic and East European Journal,* vol. 5, no. 2 (1991: 123–143.
5. For instance, the American passenger on the internal Aeroflot flight from Khabarovsk to Moscow in Aksyonov's story "Half-way to the Moon" (*Na polputi k lune*), *Novy mir,* no. 7 (1962): 86–98.
6. See my analysis of Nagibin's story, "Chetunov, the son of Chetunov" (*Chetunov, syn Chetunova*), published in *Yuri Nagibin, Rannei vesnoi: Rasskazy* (Moskva, 1961): pp. 168–97, in S. M. Vladiv, "Post-Modernism in Eastern Europe After World War II," p. 128.

7. Anticipating our analysis of *Pushkin House*, it is interesting to note the extended allusion to Platonov's *Foundation Pit* made by grandfather in his speech to Lyova about the effect of the Soviet system on the production of words. In this passage, grandfather literally duplicates Platonov's use of the metaphor of the pit, to symbolize a groundless abyss at the edge of which the Soviet people are building their "house" of state. Compare Andrei Bitov, *Pushkinskii dom* (Ardis, 1978), p. 85: " Ia tut idu nedavno, smotriu, riadom s odnim iz zdeshnikh domov bol'shoi kotlovan vyrili ..." [I was walking along here recently, I looked and they'd excavated a big cellar hole beside one of these apartment buildings ... (Andrei Bitov, *Pushkin House*, trans. Susan Brownsberger [London, 1987], p. 69).
8. Compare M. M. Bakhtin, *Towards a Philosophy of the Act* (*K filosofii postupka*), trans. Vladimir Liapunov, ed. M. Holquist and V. Liapunov (Austin, Texas, 1993). This early essay, which was first published in a full version in Russia in 1986, connects Bakhtin's thought with Western phenomenology and Husserl in particular. Bakhtin's philosophy of the act is based on the concept of "lived experienced" (life as "postuplenie," "a single, continuous performing of individually answerable acts or deeds and, therefore, analogous to the single act or deed"), p. 81, note 10. Like the other of discourse, phenomenological thought was completely repressed during the Soviet period. Bakhtin's work was allowed publication briefly in 1963 and then only during perestroika. Thus the re-entry of the other into Russian discourse twenty years earlier, in the 1960s, signaled a return to phenomenology in Russian theoretical thought, but it was only an early manifestation, which was quickly repressed by the *zastoi* [stagnation] mentality of the 1970s. Andrei Bitov's *Pushkin House* is probably the most comprehensive reclamation of phenomenology through the poetics of the novel and as such a milestone in Russian phenomenological discourse. It anticipates in many ways the genealogical/archeological projects of Foucault and French poststructuralism.
9. See "Literarische Avantgarde: Festschrift für Rudolf Neuhäuser," ed. Horst-Jürgen Gerigk, *Contributions to Theory and Practice of Interpretation,* vol. 7 (Dresden, 1998).
10. "The novel changed its title several times, in keeping with successive authorial interventions. *A la recherche du destin perdu, or Hooligan's Wake.*" Andrei Bitov, *Pushkinskii dom* (Ann Arbor, Mich., 1978), p. 402 (my translation).
11. "Underground" is used in English by Potapov in order to free the term from the specific meaning that the Russian equivalent term, *podpolie,* might evoke.
12. See the interview with Andrei Bitov, published in the Belgrade literary bimonthly *Književna reč,* no. 367–368 (January 1991): 13–14. *Pushkin House* was first published in Russian by Ardis, Michigan, in 1978. It appeared in an English translation by Susan Brownsberger, published by Weidenfeld and Nicolson (London, 1988). It first appeared as a complete novel in Russia in *Novy mir,* no. 10, 11 and 12 (1987). For a meticulous cataloguing of Bitov's works, see Ellen Chances, *Andrei Bitov: The Ecology of Inspiration* (Cambridge, 1993).
13. Lacan goes beyond Freud in separating the symbolic function of the phallus as signifier from the anatomical organ, the penis. See Jonathan Scott Lee, *Jacques Lacan* (University of Massachusetts Press, 1991), p. 66.

14. Jacques Lacan, *Four Fundamental Concepts of Psychoanalysis,* ed. Jacques-Alain Miller, trans. Alan Sheridan (W.W. Norton & Company, 1981), p. 204.
15. The opposition of "All/Not-All" forms a very complex dialectic in Lacan's theory of the subject. The "Not-All" can be roughly equated with the particular, whereas the "All" represents the general. The relationship between the general and the particular is an "impossible" relationship and as such the metaphor for "absolute difference."
16. Since the "real" is non-relational, to confront it is to experience paradox as a structure and thus to be initiated into the "limit" of language.
17. The "real" in Lacanian theory is not "reality," but, put somewhat simplistically, the uncanny "object" or the uncanny (the unrepresentable limit of language) as object. Jonathan Scott Lee summarizes it thus, quoting Lacan: "The real is that which is 'prohibited' [*interdit*], but also that which 'is said between the words, between the lines' ... Lacan regularly describes the real as 'that which prevents one from saying the whole truth about it'" (p. 172). See also p. 136, where, among other thing, it is stated: "The real, the grimace of which is reality, is, as we have already noted, the unconscious." Lacan also relates the unconscious (*das Unbewusste*) to the Freudian *Unbegriff*—"non-concept" (Jacques Lacan, *The Four Fundamental Concepts of Psychoanalysis,* p. 26). Bitov's novel contains at least one indirect metaphoric allusion to the Lacanian formula of the real. During his night on duty at the institute, Lyova is visited by Mitishatyev, whose face appears in the window, distorted, like a grimace of time or reality: "*Kogda on podoshel k dveri, perebiraia kliuchi—k steklu uzhe pripalo, raspliushchiv nos, tolstoe litso Mitishat'eva,*" [When he approached the door, fumbling with the keys, Mitishatyev's fat face, with nose flattened, was already glued to the glass] *Pushkinski dom* (Ardis), p. 298 (my translation). With his elusiveness and *nedogovorennost'* [speaking through allusions and innuendo], Mitishatyev represents the real for Lyova, whose face is literally a grimace of (Soviet historical) reality.
18. "Secondary repression" is a metaphor for the subject's entry into the symbolic order of language. It encompasses both a "doubling" and a "censoring" operation, which allows the subject to perceive objects of the external world and to structure them through the operations of condensation and displacement—or the linguistic mechanisms of metaphor and metonymy—into images or representations.
19. "Lyova almost cried: look what they've done with the man!" Andrei Bitov, *Pushkinskii dom* (Ann Arbor, Mich., 1978), p. 87 (my translation).
20. "My God!—flashed through Lyova's mind." Ibid., p. 67 (my translation). The "small other"/"big Other" forms the complex dialectic of primary and secondary identifications of the subject with its object and is dramatized by Bitov with amazing psychoanalytic accuracy in the overlapping portraits of Uncle Dickens and grandfather.
21. Psychoanalytic theory avoids the Hegelian term "self-consciousness." "[T]here is no self-consciousness of ourselves—we are obliged to know ourselves via others," says Eric Laurent commenting on Lacan in "Alienation and Separation," *Reading Seminar XI: Lacan's Four Fundamental Concepts of Psychoanalysis,* ed. Richard Feldstein et al. (State University of New York Press, 1995), p. 22. However,

Hegel's idea of "self-consciousness" does touch on the category of the psychoanalytic subject of the unconscious. For a non-metaphysical reading of Hegel's thought, see Frank B. Farrell, *Subjectivity, Realism and Postmodernism: The Recovery of the World in Recent Philosophy* (Cambridge University Press, 1996), pp. 15–20, and elsewhere. In our usage of the term "self-consciousness," we imply (as does Hegel some of the time) a consciousness of the self who "knows that he knows." In other words, "pure" self-consciousness is "abstract" self-consciousness, and this is close to the Lacanian subject of language as tautology or doubling.

22. An "interrogative text" forms part of the topology of postmodern fiction. See, for instance, the "interrogation" of the "father" in Danilo Kiš's novel *Hourglass* or the self-interrogation of the hero Venichka in Venedikt Erofeev's *Moscow Circles* [*Moscow to the End of the Line*] (*Moskva-Petushki*), which structures and propels Erofeev's narrative.
23. Just as the Hegelian term "self-consciousness" does not presuppose a unitary self, so the psychoanalytic (Lacanian) terms conscious/unconscious do not belong to a system of binary oppositions. The Freudian dialectic of preconscious-conscious-unconscious is transposed by Lacan onto a continuum of the unconscious, which is structured as a relational field, in which the subject of the unconscious is constituted as a (geometric) quaternary structure of relations and non-relations to his "others": the "small other" (*objet petit a*), the "big Other," the phallus, and the signifier. This psychoanalytic model of the subject is alluded to indirectly in the narrator's play with parallelograms, in the subchapter entitled "Version and Variant," in Part Two of *Pushkin House.*
24. The gaze in psychoanalytic and phenomenological theory is an agency of symbolization which is quite distinct from the organ of the eye and of the action of ordinary vision. The gaze is "revelational," in that it transforms the world it perceives into discrete and meaningful signs or images. It can thus be said to structure reality as a construct of imagination and memory.

    See, for example, Maurice Merleau-Ponty's essay "Cézanne's Doubt," in Maurice Merleau-Ponty, *Sense and Non-Sense,* translated, with preface, by Hubert L. Dreyfus and Patricia Allen Dreyfus (Evanston, 1964), pp. 9–25. See also Jacques Lacan, "The Split between the Eye and the Gaze," in Jacques Lacan, *The Four Fundamental Concepts of Psychoanalysis,* ed. Jacques-Alain Miller, trans. Alan Sheridan (New York, London, 1981), pp. 67–78. See also Maurice Merleau-Ponty, "Eye and Mind," in Maurice Merleau-Ponty, *The Primacy of Perception and Other Essays on Phenomenological Psychology, the Philosophy of Art, History and Politics*, edited, with an introduction, by James M Edie (Evanston, 1964), pp. 159–189.
25. Frederic Jameson's famous critique of the dominance of language over the human being (see *The Prison House of Language: A Critical Account of Structuralism and Russian Formalism* [Princeton, N.J., 1972]) offers a convenient catch-phrase to use as short-hand for the relationship of the psychoanalytic subject to language and discourse.
26. Kristeva describes nausea as an effect of abjection, which in turn she defines as "a twisted braid of affects" which do not have a "definable object." "The abject

has only one quality of the object—that of being opposed to the I. If the object, however, through its opposition, settles me within the fragile texture of a desire for meaning, which ... makes me ceaselessly and infinitely homologous to it, what is abject, on the contrary, the jettisoned object, is radically excluded and draws me toward the place where meaning collapses. (...) ... it is a brutish suffering that "I" put up with, sublime and devastated ... A massive and sudden emergence of uncanniness, which, familiar as it might have been in an opaque and forgotten life, now harries me as radically separate, loathsome. Not me. Not that. But not nothing, either. A "something" that I do not recognize as a thing. A weight of meaninglessness, about which there is nothing insignificant, and which crushes me. On the edge of non-existence and hallucination, of a reality that, if I acknowledge it, annihilates me. There, abject and abjection are my safeguards. The primers of my culture. Loathing an item of food, a piece of filth, waste, or dung. The spasms and vomiting that protect me." Julia Kristeva, *Powers of Horror: An Essay on Abjection* (New York, 1982), pp. 1–2.

27. Jacques Lacan, *Ecrits: A Selection,* p. 148.
28. Ibid., p. 170.
29. See Jacques Derrida, who, in taking Freud's definition of the unconscious as his point of departure, says in "Freud and the Scene of Writing": "... for the main thread of the article on 'The Unconscious,' its example, as we have emphasized, is the fate of a representation after it is first registered. When perception—the apparatus which originally enregisters and inscribes—is described, the 'perceptual apparatus' can be nothing but a writing machine. The 'Note on the Mystic Writing Pad,' twelve years later, will describe the perceptual apparatus and the origin of memory." (Jacques Derrida, *Writing and Difference,* trans. Alan Bass [Routledge, London & Henley, 1978], p. 221). *Writing* is thus *inscription,* which, however, can only take place in conjunction with the simultaneous *erasure* of what is inscribed. This erasure of the "trace" (Freud's *Bahnung*) constitutes the process of repression, which is "not only an accident that can occur here or there, nor is it even the necessary structure of a determined censorship threatening a given presence; it is the very structure which makes possible, as the movement of temporalization and pure auto-affection, something that can be called repression in general, the original synthesis of original repression and secondary repression, repression 'itself.'" (ibid., p. 230).
30. In adopting Saussure's structure of the sign, Lacan inverts the position of signifier and signified, making the signifier sit "on top" of the signified, from which it is separated by a line or "bar." This line represents, in Lacan's algorithm, the "bar of repression," since the signified is always the absent or repressed part of the sign. This positioning implies, for Lacan, that the signifier and the signified are "distinct orders separated initially by a barrier resisting signification." Jacques Lacan, *Ecrits: A Selection,* p. 149.
31. The three psychic registers—the "real," the "imaginary," and the "symbolic"—form three interlooping rings, represented by Lacan with a diagram of the Borromean knot. This knot is, according to Philippe Julien's reading, a "hole" or a "knot-hole" "that comes to be substituted for the Other," in which is situated

the "cause, not of love, but of desire: the *objet petit a.*" Phillipe Julien, *Lacan's Return to Freud: The Real, the Symbolic, and the Imaginary*, trans. Devra Beck Simiu (New York and London, 1994), p. 183. The three psychic registers are also envisaged as a "braiding," which brings about the "consistency" of discourse. This consistency is the only "substance" of discourse, which otherwise lacks "essence" or "support" and is grounded in (Hegelian) negativity or its equivalent—the Borromean "*one* knot-hole engendering a space." Ibid.

32. Lyova does not "know" because he is an "opaque" subject of the unconscious; the latter's processes remain beyond the subject's horizon.
33. See S. Freud, "The Ego and the Id," in *The Freud Reader,* ed. Peter Gay (Norton, 1989), pp. 638–40.
34. See Jacques Lacan, *The Four Fundamental Concepts of Psychoanalysis,* pp. 147 and 196–197. Lacan describes the lamella as an imaginary "organ" of the libido, which separates off from the subject during the subject's primary division. "This lamella, this organ, whose characteristic it is not to exist, but which is nevertheless an organ ... is the libido. It is the libido, qua pure life instinct, that is to say, immortal life, or irrepressible life, life that has need of no organ, simplified, indestructible life ... . And it is of this that all the forms of the *objet a* that can be enumerated are the representatives, the equivalents. The *objets a* are merely its representatives, its figures. The breast ... the placenta for example—certainly represents that part of himself that the individual loses at birth, and which may serve to symbolize the most profound lost object." The metaphor of *l'hommelette* is a pun, built on the notion of the "false" organ, the lamella, whose movement (of separation from the unitary subject) is described by Lacan to be analogous to the "spilling" movement of a raw egg on a flat surface, which also resembles the movement of an ameba. *L'hommelette* designates a kind of substitute for the "primal man" or "the primal" in man. Goethe, with the Romantics and the medieval alchemists, used the image of the homonculus—a virtual man who could be derived out of a substance in nature through a man-made process, yet not a robot.
35. "To this pile of a portrait we should add that Uncle Dickens' person was withered and miniature, yet he could not be called small." Andrei Bitov, *Pushkin House*, p. 25.
36. Dickens' claustrophobic little apartment, crammed with incongruous objects, is reminiscent of Sophia Likhutina's bedroom and sitting-room, which are tiny boxes resembling a doll's house. It is in this miniature space that Andrei Bely plants the sumptuous figure of his heroine. The inversion of proportions between the space and the object (subject) it frames in turn evokes surrealist representations of objects in space, such as Rene Magritte's *The Wrestlers' Tomb* [*Le tombeau des Lutteurs*] 1961, or *The Listening Room* [*La chambre d'écoute*] 1958. These representations also resonate with the Wittgensteinian proposition that an object is unimaginable without the space (absence or nothingness) from which it is carved out.
37. Lacan's psychoanalytic subject is a quaternary structure, like metaphor, and involves the subject's relationship to the "small other," the "big Other," and the phallus, which stands for the Signifier produced through the subject's split,

constituted by his separation from the (M)other and identification with the Name-of-the-Father/(other) or the Law (discourse as social structure). Lacan's algorithms representing this structure of the subject often resemble parallelograms like the ones Bitov plays with in the subchapter "Version and Variant" in Part Two of *Pushkin House.*

38. Andrei Bitov, *Pushkin House,* p. 24.
39. Jacques Lacan, *Ecrits: A Selection,* p. 263.
40. Andrei Bitov, *Pushkin House,* p. 92.
41. See Julia Kristeva, *Powers of Horror: An Essay on Abjection,* trans. Leon S. Roudiez (New York, 1982), p. 102: "The body must bear no trace of its debt to nature: it must be clean and proper in order to be fully symbolic." Thus Uncle Dickens' cleanliness is a function of his role as an agent of the symbolic order who must promote the hero's passage into language and culture or the field of the "big Other."
42. The "unclean" is not the reverse of the "clean" and hence does not have the negative connotation which it usually assumes in bourgeois culture, which is Oedipal and hence totally in the sphere of the symbolic. The "unclean" is etymologically related to the "sacred" (*sacer* in Latin). Filth, dirt, excrement and other extruded substances become metonymies of the process of separation (of the subject from the primal object) and as such are portents of a mysterious (unconscious) and necessary (sacred, categorical) rite of passage of the individual human being from the imaginary to the symbolic.
43. Andrei Bitov, *Pushkin House,* p. 30. It is interesting to note that in a postmodern narrative, such as Patrick Süskind's novel *Perfume,* the anti-hero, Grenouille, a serial killer, is distinguished from all other human beings by his absence of smell. Grenouille is a pure representation of the unconscious or of the other.
44. "Tell me, but as concisely as you can, what is a lorgnette?" Andrei Bitov, *Pushkin House,* p. 41.
45. On the definition of *writing* as *inscription* and *erasure,* see note 29 above.
46. In language, the *particular* manifests itself first and foremost as an *articulation* —that is, as something which is "qualitatively once-occurent" or "*einmalig.*"
47. The narrator gives this away when he expostulates on how little his own "aristocratic pedigree" meant to Lyova, who considered himself to be "*skoree 'odnofamilets,' chem potomok*" [more a "namesake" than a descendant]. A. Bitov, *Pushkinskii dom* (Ardis), p. 110. Lyova is, the narrator declares, "*kak by vpolne sovremennyi molodoi chelovek*" [he seems to be a completely modern young man] (my translation).
48. Andrei Bitov, *Pushkin House,* p. 92.
49. A *stilyaga* is a young (teenage and early twenties) cultural "dissident" of the first post-Stalinist thaw, representing a mild Soviet equivalent to the Western hippie.
50. In looking through grandfather's unfinished manuscript, entitled "Journey to Israel (Notes of Goy)," Lyova comes to the conclusion that grandfather was a unique "historical" entity, irrespective of the changes which life and history wrought on him: the ego ("individuality" or "*lichnost'*") remains one and the same through any duration of time. See Andrei Bitov, *Pushkin House,* p. 124

and *Pushkinskii dom* (Ardis), p. 147. The dialectic of "sameness" (of the individual) and "difference" (of the one individual relative to all others) impinges also on the symbolic connotation of the word "Goy." The name "Goy" is given to a non-Jew by one who is a Jew. To speak from the point of view of a non-Jew is to seek to identify with some sort of otherness and to implicate an other's perspective or be complicitous with the discourse of an other. Grandfather's "Journey to Isreal (Notes of Goy)" represents grandfather's discourse as "discourse of the other."

51. Ludwig Wittgenstein, *Tractatus Logico-Philosophicus,* trans. D. F. Pears and B. F. McGuinness, with an introduction by Bertrand Russell (Routledge, 1989). First German edition in *Annalen der Naturphilosophie* (1921). First English edition, with a translation (1922). Numbering in parentheses indicates the paragraph of the *Tractatus.*
52. Lacan pointed out the connection that exists between the multiple dots as a punctuation mark and the symptom: "Not long ago, someone I listen to in my practice (…) someone articulated something for me, by linking the symptom to the dotted line. The important thing is the reference to writing as a means of situating the repetition of the symptom …" Jacques Lacan, "Seminar of 21 January 1975," *Feminine Sexuality: Jacques Lacan and the Ecole Freudienne,* ed. J. Mitchell and J. Rose (London, 1983), p. 166. Later in the same essay, Lacan explains: "The dotted lines of the symptom are in fact question marks, so to speak, in the non-relation. This is what justifies my giving you this definition: that what constitutes the symptom—that something which dallies with the unconscious (see Figure 1)—is that one believes in it" (p. 168).
53. This line, from Paul's *Epistle to the Hebrews* (10:31), is uttered in Dostoevsky's *The Brothers Karamazov* by Father Zosima's night visitor, a Russian "gentleman" known only as Mikhail, who murdered his mistress fourteen years earlier, confessed, and then died. As elsewhere in Dostoevsky's oeuvre, murder becomes a metaphor for entry into symbolic exchange, while its effect (speech or writing) is represented by the deferred "confession." Lyova's passage through the symbolic is experienced in a similar fashion as "trauma." See F. M. Dostoevsky, *Polnoe sobranie sochinenii v 30-ti tt.,* vol. 14 (Nauka, 1976), p. 281, and Fyodor Dostoevsky, *The Brothers Karamazov,* trans. David Magarshack (Penguin, 1985), p. 364.
54. See *The Infinite World of M.C. Escher,* with texts by M. C. Escher and J. L. Locher (New York, 1984), Plate 8: "Moebius Strip II. 1963."
55. The "reverse eight" figures as a diagrammatic representation of Lacan's topology of the subject (his "interior 8"), in Jacques Lacan, *Four Fundamental Concepts of Psychoanalysis,* ed. Jacques-Alan Miller, trans. Alan Sheridan (New York, London, 1981), pp. 155–6. The "interior 8" looks like "two intersecting fields," with a continuous edge, which, however, is "hidden" at one point by "the surface that has previously unfolded itself" (p. 155). Lacan first situates the libido and desire at this intersection. However, he then goes on to point out that what is created by this intersection is not two surfaces but a hole, a void. It is thus this void that becomes the locus of desire and the "support" of the subject. See also François Regnault, "The Name-of-the-Father," in *Reading Seminar XI: Lacan's*

Four Fundamental Concepts of Psychoanalysis, ed. Richard Feldstein, Bruce Fink, Marie Janus (State University of New York, 1995), pp. 71–72.

56. In his book *The Archeology of Knowledge and Discourse on Language* (first published as *L'Archeologie du Savoir,* Paris, 1969), Michel Foucault defines this new methodology of the social sciences as something like the old history of ideas and yet quite different from it. The difference is in the fact that "archeology" takes discourse itself as its object of research. It treats the past as discourse or as numerous discourses and it regards these past discourses as "monuments." "Archeology" is thus not "an interpretive discipline. It does not seek another, better-hidden discourse. It refuses to be 'allegorical.'" *The Archeology of Knowledge* (New York, 1972), p. 139. In *The Order of Things*—a book that preceded *The Archeology of Knowledge,* and whose methodology Foucault undertakes to "explain" in the latter—the method of investigation described as "archeology" is defined as a desire "to reveal a positive unconscious of knowledge." Michel Foucault, *The Order of Things: An Archeology of the Human Sciences* (*Les Mots et les choses,* Paris, 1966) (London, 1992), p. xi (from the Foreword by Michel Foucault, 1970, not published in the original French edition).
57. Michel Foucault, *The Archeology of Knowledge,* p. 12.
58. Ibid.
59. Thus Susan Brownsberger writes, in her "Translator's Afterword": "At least one academic bookstore, deceived by appearances, has shelved this novel under criticism instead of fiction." Andrei Bitov, *Pushkin House,* p. 360.
60. Ibid., p. 125.
61. Andrei Bitov, *Pushkinskii dom,* p. 275.
62. Ibid., p. 278.
63. Ibid., p. 338
64. Ibid., p. 283: "opozdavshii Lyova" [Lyova, the belated arrival].
65. Ibid.
66. Ibid., p. 281.
67. Ibid., p. 283.
68. Ibid., pp. 281–2.
69. Andrei Bitov, *Pushkin House,* p. 110.
70. Jacques Lacan, *Four Fundamental Concepts of Psychoanalysis,* p. 195.
71. See Freud's topographical model of the psyche in "The Ego and the Id," (1923), and especially his diagram of the psyche in the shape of a "bulb" with a "listening cap." See "Das Ich und das Es, " in *Sigmund Freud, Studienausgabe Band III* (Frankfurt-am-Main, 1975), p. 293.
72. Jacques Derrida, *Glas,* English translation by John P. Leavey Jr. and Richard Rand (Lincoln and London, 1990), first published in France, in 1974.
73. Jacques Derrida, *Of Grammatology* (Baltimore and London, 1976), p. 149.
74. Ibid.
75. Ibid., p. 141.
76. Ibid.
77. Ibid.
78. Jacques Lacan, "Subversion of the Subject and the Dialectic of Desire," in *Ecrits: A Selection,* p. 303. See also Jonathan Scott Lee, *Jacques Lacan,* p. 61:

"The *points de capiton,* then, serve as the signifieds for the signifying chains of a subject's discourse, and Lacan maintains that 'the schema of the points de capiton' is essential in human experience." It is possible to connect the idea of these repressed *points de capiton* with Jacques-Alain Miller's concept of suturing as a structural principle of discourse, based on Frege's question of how (the concept of) a number evolves from the zero. The occulted passage of meaning from non-meaning (zero) to a sign (the number one) can also be linked with death as a metaphoric expression of the twin phenomena of *absence* (the dead man who is no longer a man, who has "gone away") and *presence* of the sign (the corpse in its materiality). The revulsion triggered by the sight of a corpse or death in general adds the dimension of *repression* (with disgust as its symptom) to the metaphor, which thus comes to embody the three dimensions of discourse: *absence/presence/repression.*

79. Jonathan Scott Lee, *Jacques Lacan,* p. 61
80. Andrei Bitov, *Pushkinskii dom,* p. 176 and p. 177 "The real-life Faina he failed to perceive even once" (my translation).
81. See Roger Caillois, "Mimicry and Legendary Psychasthenia," *October 31*: 17–33. There is a cryptic footnote on moths, attached by the narrator to the word "Disorientation" (Andrei Bitov, *Pushkin House*, p. 92), which allegedly pinpoints the major theme of the novel. The connection between an actually published "scientific study" on insects (moths) by the zoologist Niko Tinbergen and "disorientation" ("alienation") becomes clear only in the context of an anthropological study such as that of Caillois, which makes the point that an initial relationship to space, manifested as a primitive "doubling"—"mimicking" or "imitating" of the environment—inheres in even the lowest forms of animate life, such as mantises and leaf insects. This animal "mimicry," which, as Caillois stresses, is not primarily in the interests of camouflage and survival, is thus on the same paradigm as "alienation" in human subjects, the effect of which is language as a form of human mimicry or camouflage.
82. Jacques Derrida, "… That Dangerous Supplement …", in *Of Grammatology,* pp. 56–57.
83. Ibid., p. 157.
84. Ibid., pp. 157–8.
85. Ibid., p. 158.
86. Andrei Bitov, *Pushkinskii dom,* p. 84: "'They have a marvelous set-up!'" (my translation).
87. See the article by the Australian Biblical scholar David Routledge, "Faithful Reading: Poststructuralism and the Sacred," *Biblical Interpretation* 4, 3: 270–287, in which the author reaffirms the Derridean phenomenological position (to cite from his Abstract to the article) that "[w]hat poststructuralism demands, in the final analysis, is not the abandonment of meaning but its reconfiguration: notions of faithful reading and respect for the text which embrace difference, ambiguity and an understanding of the sacred as the site not of uncontestable command, but of enquiry and interpretation." In other words, the absence of closure in a text is a guarantee of its infinite interpretability.

88. Jacques Derrida, *Of Grammatology*, p. 158.
89. Ibid.
90. In our case, Pushkin's and Tyutchev's (S.V.-G.).
91. Jacques Derrida, *Of Grammatology*, p. 159.
92. Andrei Bitov, *Pushkin House*, p. 354.
93. Ibid.: "Unreality is a condition of life."
94. Ibid. Compare also with Derrida's (Lacan's) *voudrait dire.*
95. Ibid. [Modified translation]
96. Andrei Bitov, *Pushkinskii dom*, p. 411.

Chapter 4

PERESTROIKA AS A SHIFT IN LITERARY PARADIGM

Alexander Genis

A Lost Generation

During the unsettling period associated with *perestroika*, Russian literature was engaged in a struggle for survival in which it sought a compromise between the past and the future. Even so it actually stood still, afraid to turn back and equally unable to trust in future perspectives. In this transitional condition, Soviet-Russian literature lost both of its distinguishing features, ceasing to be either Russian or Soviet.

All of its genres degenerated into journalism. The life of a literary work came to be measured not in terms of generations, but in terms of months, weeks, and even days. The kings of literary perestroika reigned but for an hour: *The Sad Detective* by Victor Astafeev, *Fire* by Valentin Rasputin, *The Execution Block* by Chingiz Aitmatov, *The Children of the Arbat* by Anatoli Rybakov. The most distinguishing common feature of these works is their date of publication (the late 1980s).

The literature of *glasnost* could not have had any other complexion, since glasnost itself was an artificial extension of the thaw of the 1960s, which had allowed the half-said to come to full expression. The ontogeneric relationship of perestroika to the thaw is as incontestable as it is unnatural; for the sense of purpose that marked the 1960s was patently absent from perestroika. The 1960s creativity emanated from a teleological perception of reality. The authors of the thaw—from Ehrenburg to early Aksyonov—drew their energy from a cosmic happy ending, giving their works an optimistic if infantile character.

The force that had moved Soviet literature in its heyday—socialist realism—was largely inoperative by the late 1970s and early 1980s. Only the ruins of words were left behind, and they served as building blocks for a temple of Truth. For Truth is the God of the enslaved man. Truth assumes that the world has meaning and purpose. Thus the overall subject matter of Soviet literature was always reducible to a revelation, that is, to a proclamation of Truth: about leaders, about the government, about the rural economy or heavy industry. This reductionism was always embodied in the linear structure of the Soviet novel; its plot motivated by a progression from error or deviation to the correct path, and from falsehood to Truth. The hero of such a literature was always an adolescent and its content was inevitably a rite of passage: a partaking in the sacral knowledge that revealed the true state of affairs.

Having voiced the Truth, the author would recede into a (previously) joyful or (later) distracted silence. The way out of this impasse was provided by communism, which was the justification for everything on another, non-literary plane. Only in the metaphysical sphere of communism could the Soviet writer achieve relative victories. Like the exegetist in medieval scholasticism, the Soviet author was allocated the role of commentator of a general Truth.

But this entire edifice of Soviet literature collapsed under the weight of perestroika. The writers of the 1960s, seizing power of the arts after it had became practically de-institutionalized under perestroika, were left to finish saying in the 1980s what they had started saying in the 1960s, though their words were now lacking the legitimizing power of the general Truth.

Having thus come face to face with their own dream of freedom under perestroika, the generation of the 1960s finally acquired the status with which it had always flirted—that of a lost generation.

Operatic Peasants

Under perestroika, liberal literature only succeeded in creating a stronghold for itself in the periodical press, which had been abandoned after the departure of the *village prose* writers.[1] These populists had betrayed the native literature, leaving it without its "innards" and national specificity. Moreover, the village prose writers ultimately betrayed themselves.

Battling with phantoms of their own making—*Russophobia* being their chief bugaboo—important authors such as Vasilii Belov and Valentin Rasputin turned to writing simplistic political tracts. The artistic failure of the village prose writers can be explained by their inability to translate the national content of their prose into the language of universal culture. Such artistic synthesis had brought the great Latin-American prose of the mid-twentieth century into existence, but a Russian "magic realism" failed to materialize.

Moreover, the village prose writers did not even master their own narrower task, which was the description of Russian peasant life. The nineteenth-century populist writers, *narodniki* as they were called, such as A. Engelgardt, N. Zlatotvatsky, V. Selivanov, Sergei Maksimov, and G. Uspensky, started out from empirical fact. Today's populists start out from the literary tradition. As a result, what they created was an impossible literary hybrid: Nekrasov's old woman Nenila and Dostoevsky's peasant Marei settling in a Soviet collective farm. Paradoxically, too, the contemporary populists made use of ideas from the nineteenth-century revolutionary democrats who bequeathed to them a hatred for private property, an aversion toward bourgeois values and a deification of the collective.

The mutant hero of the village prose writers was born of two types of utopianism: Westernizer and Slavophile. From the new utopian amalgam of the village prose writers, the new skein of isolationism and messianism unwound, leading to a fantastic model of a future Russia. This new Russia was to be a fortress of morality amidst a spiritual desert. Thus Russia found herself once more in the hands of enemies, this time represented by American dollars. Moreover, moral purity was seen as the antithesis of material well-being.

Again the thesis "poverty as a symbol of spirituality" reigned supreme, born of an acute inferiority complex.

However, while defending the economic innocence of the Russian people, today's village prose writers could not fall back on the positions of their predecessors. The original populists were at least preoccupied with the problem of bringing progress to the village. For example, A. Engelgardt, a remarkable writer and very successful farmer, dreamt about villages populated by the intelligentsia. Today's populists, on the other hand, dream of reforming the city intelligentsia by cleansing it with village purity and wisdom.

The heroes of village prose of the 1980s became operatic villagers, while village prose itself became stylization. Its authors had indeed moved far from the people. Yet, having occupied a place not their own, the village prose writers did not wish to turn this place over to those who might be in a position to introduce an authentic populist current into contemporary literature. Without such a current, however, Russian literature is just as unimaginable as North American literature without Faulkner or Latin American literature without García Márquez.

Soviet reactionary writers, poets, critics, and literary officials gathered on the pages of the ultranationalistic literary magazines *Nash sovremennik* and *Molodaya gvardia*. In this forum, those forms of Russian culture that did not resemble the dull and didactic literature of Belov and Rasputin—who, incidentally, had become their own epigones by the late 1980s—were proclaimed evil, dangerous, and anti-Russian, *russofobskimi*. Ironically, the Russian village prose writers were desperately fighting against their own potential allies. They failed to recognize their own man in Vladimir Vysotsky—the most Russian of the postwar poets. They attacked Vladimir Voinovich's comic populist and very Russian novel about the adventures of the soldier Chonkin. And they continue to display hysterical rage in the face of Russian rock-and-roll, failing to recognize that in the *bylina* mode of poet-singer Alexander Bashlachev there are echoes of their own idol, Sergei Esenin. Instead of applying their craft to enrich and multiply Russian culture, the populists were paralyzed, petrified with fear that they might be losing their power-base in popular culture.

Physiological Sketches, Second Edition

Also running out of steam very quickly was the most popular genre of perestroika—*chernukha* or the "black genre," a kind of writing based on horrifying descriptions of everyday Soviet life. The problem with this "black prose" was not just its authors' passionate predilection for kitchen realism and love of dirt. What was worse was that none of this was new: it had been seen one hundred and fifty years earlier, in the physiological sketch.

The Russian "natural school's" physiological sketch, with its daguerreotype realism, had focused on the "lower depths" of the nineteenth-century Russian city, its organ grinders, doormen, and apartment janitors. The physiological sketch irritated the critics of the day, but its readers were just as fascinated by the genre as the readers of our century.

One merit of the *chernukha* genre, just like the physiological sketch of the previous century, was its opposition to oppose the ideologically driven writing contained in the avalanche of journals associated with glasnost. The writer who depicted a raw slice of life did not moralize or teach: he or she was but an invisible mediator between the reader and real life.

The laws of the daguerreotype also put a certain constraint on the writer. This genre did not tolerate a "happy ending," a moral rebirth or the eradication of evil by the authorities.

With its best examples, like Sergei Kaledin's novel about Moscow gravediggers called *The Quiet Cemetery*, the contemporary physiological sketch returned to its sources in nineteenth-century literature. Perhaps the physiological sketch, with its exact ethnographic detail, its interest in life on the margins of society, and its fanatical adherence to the descriptive power of the word, could have served as the foundation of a major mainstream literature. Unfortunately, Russian *chernukha*, while drawing on the tradition of the "natural school," lost all sense of proportion in the way it treated the subject-matter of the contemporary "lower depths."

A good illustration is Leonid Gabyshev's hair-raising narrative about adolescent reform schools, *Odlyan, or the Air of Freedom*. This work is a document, a chronicle, a testimony. The truth of this life, which is nauseating to retell, is even more horrible to read. But even more horrible still is the fact that such works are classified as *belles lettres.* Since everyone is already familiar with the jargon of the *gulag*, since everyone has assimilated the hecatombs of Soviet history, it is now necessary to escalate the horror and nightmarish atmosphere in order to satisfy the reader's expectation. In this kind of writing the arsenal of horrors is ransacked pell-mell; atrocities are heaped one on top of another with great attention to detail. Reality—for Gabyshev's is a description of something that really happened—conquers the world of imagination, making fiction superfluous. The reader's co-experience of this reality thus becomes a physiological act.

Thomas Mann noted that his compatriots who had lived through the Nazi era developed a self-satisfied air born of suffering. Such a negative messianism is also a Russian hallmark. What can we in Russia learn from people who cannot decode the acronym GULAG? The tyranny of suffering leads to an impotence of the spirit. Literature that evolves in its shadow degenerates into a funeral lament, a martyrology, a list of complaints to the Maker about the imperfection of the universe.

The evil that has outgrown the aesthetic dimension deprives literature not of hope but of poetry.

The Literature of Silence

During the perestroika years the hour of the Russian avant-garde finally arrived as well. The pity is that its hour was so long in coming.

Every culture builds its own aesthetic hierarchy, its canon and icons. Each canon has a corresponding anti-canon. All idolaters have corresponding iconoclasts. The building of a culture is unthinkable without its own destruction. Similarly, literature cannot be written on a single side of the page. For there is no tragedy without comedy, no lofty style without a vulgar style, no sacred without the profane.

The avant-garde, constituted by the underground and counterculture, was a natural reaction to the attempt by official literature to only exist on one side of the page. However, the late 1980s and early

1990s witnessed the collapse of the entire system that dutifully nurtured the Union of Soviet Writers. This collapse of tradition also carried in its wake the collapse of the anti-tradition.

The avant-garde functions only within a well-defined sign system. As soon as that sign system becomes meaningless, the avant-garde itself is thrown into crisis. Thus *sots-art* becomes a mechanical copying of old symbols, for it is also a natural law that proscribes the writing of literature only on the reverse side of the page.

The apologists of the avant-garde, in an attempt to rescue it from this crisis, speak about the ideological debriefing of literature. Their aim is to free the avant-garde from the power of the sacramental adjective "Soviet."

It is at this point that the ghost of the literature of anti-texts and anti-meanings makes its appearance. A literature soiled by both untruth and truth comes to reclaim itself.

An avant-garde achieving such a breakthrough can leave the confines of Soviet literature and enter the vast, grown-up world of the cold and silent classics of contemporary literature, those who have already reached a "zero degree" of writing by exhausting not only literature but meaning itself. The chief prophet of this anti-literature was Samuel Beckett, in whose plays pauses are more meaningful than replies. What is important is not so much what Beckett's characters have to say, but what they do not have to say, their silences. The avant-garde world experience, combined with the Russian tradition, would be and is capable of being productive but only on the strength of innovativeness.

The path of the absurd has not been trodden to its end, though it has been well worn, both in life and in literature. The absurdist playwright Václav Havel has lived a no less absurd plot in his transformation from political prisoner to president of Czechoslovakia and then Czech Republic than have the characters in his plays.

In the final analysis, the absurdist trend leads to the impasse of silence, which can manifest itself in various ways: through eloquence or babbling, allusions to profound meaning or simply as non-sense. Whatever the specific character of this "silent" literature, it serves as testimony to the following fact: literature has ended; it has exhausted itself. It has done all it could and now has to bow out, scraping the floor.

The solemnity of this melancholy scene is disturbed only by the fact that we have bidden farewell to and buried literature so many times in the past. Belinsky began his career with a cry of desperation: "And so, we do not have a literature!" Whereupon he proceeded to write thirteen volumes of critical articles about this non-existent object. Saltykov-Shchedrin, who was Dostoevsky's and Tolstoy's contemporary and publisher, ranted and raved because of the disintegration of literature. Mayakovsky announced the death of art by throwing the Russian classics overboard.

Such a protracted process of literary eschatology and burial, extending over centuries, cannot but serve as a cautionary tale about the true nature of these lamentations. The question we must ask is this: are we not perhaps confusing the death of our model of culture with the Last Judgment?

Time in Flux

In Andrei Platonov's diary there is an incredibly arrogant entry, written in fact at the very height of the Great Terror.[2] Who, he wrote, was it who said that Pushkin and Gogol will remain unsurpassed?

We would be hard put to find such faith amongst our contemporaries, none of whom would dare repeat Platonov's words. For the age of revolution has passed and we may even have arrived at the end of History, as prophesied by some philosophers in Western Europe and America. We have thus entered the final loop, inside of which—for better or worse—we are destined to march in a never-ending circle.

Perestroika spelled the end of utopia. Neither the classless society nor the kingdom of the Holy Ghost are casting their utopian rays on the world any longer: indeed they no longer give off any warmth at all. It is as if the world now prefers that which is to that which will be. The power of the present has finally conquered all.

Russia, which put its trust in the future more than any other nation on earth, has found it particularly difficult to part with the idea of utopia. This perhaps explains in part why many Russians did not even notice that the utopian idea had died; for in post-Soviet society there can of course be neither a Soviet nor an anti-Soviet literature. There is no place left even for perestroika—the term having been compromised by its own temporality and its transitional content.

To live in a world which has shrunk into an extensionless point is not very comfortable. However, every point in turn becomes a seed, which swells up by feeding on endless perspectives. The chance of a lifetime was thus offered to Russian culture, a chance that usually comes to a society only after crushing defeat in war: the chance to start from scratch.

The current generation, which will live without communism, will be free to merge with the present, past, and future generations. The elimination of geographical and temporal boundaries has placed Russian culture in a strange position: different cultural epochs can now mingle with each other. But the remedial action of perestroika —the reclamation and revelation of the forgotten and repressed past—is not a sufficient condition for the future development of Russian culture.

Having opened a window onto Europe, Russia, like Peter the Great, has obtained a magic mirror, through which it can now look not only at its neighbors but also at its own and their past. It is now a matter of looking through this window without running away in fright. Russia, which has merged with the surrounding world, must also engage in solving the world's problems. This means that no matter how the past might tempt Russia, she can only go in one direction—forward, and together with everyone else. But where exactly is she heading?

In Search of Emptiness

The phantoms of the future are disquieting and cause constant anxiety. The still indefinite forms of a future literature cause us to gaze anxiously from side to side—insecurely yes, but with hope too.

The first question that must be answered is: what did Russian literature lack in the past?

Taking a panoramic view of Russian literature from the vantage point of today's extreme situation, we will immediately note a gaping hole: a severe shortage in the entertainment and adventure genres, a lack of action. Heinrich Boll, who reproached German literature for the same shortcoming, accused it of being responsible for the catastrophes of German history. Russian parents very well know that the heroes of their children's favorite stories have foreign names, taken from the novels of Dumas or Fenimore Cooper. Is this, therefore, not the source of one of Russian literature's major vices: the lack of action in many Russian classics?

One of the eternal themes of the masterpieces of Russian literature is the theme of inaction. The classical Russian hero renounces action: Onegin does not marry Tatiana; Chichikov does not finish his business; Raskolnikov does not put the spoils of his double murder to any use; Dmitry Karamazov does not kill his father, Oblomov does not leave his couch. The climax of this tradition of negated action comes in the works of Chekhov, who portrays a thoroughly modern existential world in which action is an impossibility, in which all activity is illusory, in which the plot always brings the characters back to the point of departure, and in which even death changes nothing of the original equation.

The passivity of the nineteenth century has been avenged by the hyperactivity of the twentieth. Beginning with Gorky's works, new heroes appear in Russian literature, men and women unable to find a place for themselves. However, unlike their nineteenth-century counterparts—the *superfluous men*, for whom there were not enough places—the Soviet protagonists of passivity find that there are too many prospective places. They fight without respite: against enemies or shortages, combating the bourgeoisie or chaos, struggling with love or duty and finally with themselves.

The apotheosis of this thirst for activity is Pavka Korchagin, the hero of Nikolai Ostrovsky's programmatic communist novel *How the Steel Was Tempered* (1934). He cannot be stopped, either by a bullet, love, or paralysis. He can act in any situation. In the novel he is like a steam engine with cream poured into its gear box. Pavka is always rushing forward.

This enraged yearning for action is the theme of one of the best Soviet narratives, Alexander Fadeev's novella *The Rout (Razgrom)*

(1927). The author's theme is not victory but action, not a result but the process itself. Fadeev's Levinson, like Kopenkin of Andrei Platonov's novel *Chevengur* (late 1920s), is a knight of pure action. His heroism does not require a reward; the elemental sphere of activity is reward enough. (It is also worth noting that the most successful children's books, such as the enormously popular novellas *School* [1930], *A Military Secret* [1935], *Timur and his Team* [1940] by Arkady Gaidar, appeared in the era of early socialist realism.)

The heroes of labor and combat who populated early Soviet literature rushed along the earth as if possessed. The energy by which they were consumed was so powerful that they ceased to care about the purpose of their activity. All that mattered was that they be doing *something*: excavating a pit, tearing down churches, routing the bourgeoisie, executing counter-revolutionaries, destroying the *kulaks* as a class. These heroes paradigmatically lack self-interest. They need nothing and claim nothing for themselves. Instead, they sacrifice themselves in song at the altar of Action.

This kind of hyperactivity, typical of the Soviet hero, is quite different from the purposeful activity of the action hero in, say, a European adventure novel. Although the latter is as much driven by a thirst for action as his Soviet counterpart, the hero of the Western adventure novel is entirely focused on his personal aim, whether it be defending his dignity, paying back a debt of honor, or satisfying his love for adventure or simply his love of profit. Even when the goal of the adventure-novel hero is governed by caprice or chance, it is nevertheless always presented as a completely pragmatic aim.

On the other hand, while classical Russian literature preached the renunciation of a purposeful aim—and Soviet literature the pursuit of such an aim at any and all cost—the aim itself nevertheless always remained diffuse, suspiciously close to an empty justification of the hero's activity. The actions of these heroes in fact led nowhere.

While the hero of the classic Russian novel always remained standing in place, the authors used this opportunity to get to know him better. Hence the richness of psychological detail that became the hallmark of the Russian nineteenth-century novel. And it was the very psychological complexity of this hero, the inevitable contradictions that polarized his psyche, that thwarted plot development.

In the 1920s, the Serapion Brotherhood—comprised of M. Zoshcenko, V. Kaverin, K. Fedin and several other Leningrad writers who united to form this literary group named after E.T.A. Hoffmann's famous work—found itself in a situation analogous to that of contemporary Russian literature. They too tried to invest Russian prose with energetic plots. However, their experiment was interrupted by the triumph of socialist realism, with its stylistic simplifications and suppression of hyperbole in all its possible manifestations—in subject matter, plot, and psychological detail.

Soviet literature, with its artificial isolation from world trends, remained in this trough the longest. (Incidentally, this "trough" also explains why such a phenomenon as Solzhenitsyn's monumental yet nevertheless mundane realism could appear in the 1950s and dominate the scene until the 1970s.) At present, Russia is heading toward that extreme limit, beyond which psychological, social, and historical realities are crumbling. This process is reflected in the works of the Russian conceptualists. In this race—which is a race toward emptiness—Russia is quickly catching up with the West.

The general nostalgia for purposeful action now goes hand in hand with a mistrust of action. Hence structures are becoming circular, subjects virtual, and authors—not literary characters—suddenly appear on the scene in the role of superfluous characters, listlessly hallucinating in circles.

A Glimpse of the Future

In order to change the course of post-Soviet literature it is crucial to master Western mass culture and create a homemade one. New literary forms can be conceived only within the structure of popular art. One of the most important problems in contemporary Russian literature is how to overcome a seventy-year span of isolation, merge into the cosmopolitan modern world of mass culture, and use the situation for a fruitful exploration of potentialities.

The popular literature of the twentieth century brought two genres to prominence: mystery and science fiction. In both the West and Russia, these genres have conquered mass public taste. During the last years of perestroika, at Moscow's black market, it was possible to trade three copies of the anti-Stalin novel *Life and Fate* by Vasilii Grossman for one copy of the collection *Nigerian Detective Stories.* Instead of turning away from such books in disgust, should we perhaps not investigate them? Indeed, is the interest in them not part of the process described by the formalist critic Viktor Shklovsky in which low genres are raised into high genres and gradually take their place?

In actual fact, the *rapprochement* between elite and mass art is taking place on a soil well fertilized by the detective genre and science fiction. One of the most prominent examples of this *rapprochement* is the international best-seller *The Name of the Rose*. Its author, the Italian semiotician Umberto Eco, successfully combined the science of semiotics with the methods of Sherlock Holmes.

The obvious inferiority complex suffered by the standard detective novel is connected with the fact that it does not aim at psychological authenticity. Its mystery is pure intellectual play, an extremely provisional mental abstraction, which neither can nor wishes to support the illusion of believability.

The detective novel is an artificial creation. It is a product of technocratic thought. It is structured like a puzzle and solved like one. It does not have that polyvalent subtext that guarantees the richness and longevity of "high" literature. The detective novel is, moreover, a strictly limited genre. It focuses only on facts that are directly relevant to the case at hand: the puzzle. It appears that the causal chain is even more constraining in the detective novel than elsewhere: the gun in *this* genre is always fired. The detective novel has one special characteristic relevant to our paradigm of action: the detective novel always contains action.

In place of history, which encumbers the subject of a novel, and in place of contemplation, which destroys the plot, the detective novel offers an alternative: crime. The action of a detective novel is its sole *raison d'être.* The essence of this action—a crime—is a very individualistic motif. Social evil is the precinct of the historical or political novel. That is why the detective novel is in a better position to preserve its own autonomy. It is folded in upon itself and can survive amidst ideological ruins.

The other virtue of a detective novel is its poverty. Because its plot unfolds in a "laboratory" universe, it can cut its ties with the real world. More precisely, the historical and social reality penetrate the detective novel only as backdrops, imparting a kind of enchantment to the stories of Conan-Doyle, for instance.

The crisis of artistic realism does not affect the authors of detective novels, because the latter never contained realism. The detective novel has to do only with a fictitious, invented reality. Thus, the detective genre does not mirror an existing reality but invents new realities; it does not examine the everyday world but investigates the world created by the poet's fantasy. The greatest defect of the mystery novel is that it is structured not around a secret but a puzzle; hence it does not differ much from a schoolbook drill.

Stanislaw Lem, who wrote a treatise on the future of literature, overcomes this paucity or defect inherent in the detective novel. He does so in practice, by writing detective novels that lack a *denouement,* that is, that are written without a resolution. In his novel, *Investigation*, there is a crime, but there are no criminals. However, this does not reduce his novel to a variation on Kafka's absurd. Rather Lem offers the reader many answers instead of just one correct one—and, as it happens, none of the answers he offers is the correct one. It is at this point that the mystery novel begins to resemble a philosophical construct, in which natural chaos opposes all attempts at introducing an artificial clarity and definition into the world. Lem's detective novels at the same time create and undermine the foundations of the genre.

The same results are achieved, via another route, the genre of science fiction—which is another invention of scientific progress. This genre presents the author with the same task as the detective novel, namely that of creating multiple realities. Like the detective novel, science fiction offers a reduced model of reality, from which the superfluous element of psychological analysis has been expunged.

Thus a space is opened up for free action, which drives the plot of the fiction in an arbitrary direction.

However, the genre of science fiction also has—or had—a cardinal disadvantage: its atavistic relationship to science. For as long as the genre was willing to tolerate this senseless symbiosis, science fiction was slavishly dependent on the method of classical science—to simplify the world by reducing it to repeatable phenomena. Science, at least in its old positivist version, did not concern itself with the investigation of phenomena: art's sole interest was in phenomena.

Now, having freed itself from the burden of science and technology, science fiction has become the source of a new mythology. In its best exemplars, such as Lem's *Solaris,* or the stories of Borges, science fiction becomes an artistic theology and a form of literary religious ritual.

Ignoring the question of verisimilitude, science fiction opens up new worlds. However, it is crucial that these worlds not be taken too literally, as was done by the classical science fiction writers—from Wells and Alexi Tolstoy to Bradbery and the early Strugatskys—who merely transposed the earth's problems onto other planets. The real "alterity" of science fiction is connected with adventures of the spirit and not the flesh. True science fiction constructs models of other consciousness, not other societies.

The third possible source of future literature is generated by a humanist rebellion: art about art.

According to the model of literature generated by this rebellion, the secondary or "culture-bred" reality replaces the primary, empirical reality. Disengaged from the soil, thought is freed from earth's gravity and enters the field of theoretical fantasy, the realm of the imaginary. One of the theoreticians and exponents of this new kind of "humanistic literature," Mikhail Epstein, whose thought appears elsewhere in this study, describes his own literary genre as a development of literature through its own self-consciousness.

While upholding the right to intellectual game playing and experiment, which may even encompass mad hypotheses, we have nevertheless become accustomed to thinking of humanists as the servants of culture, as its exegetists. What we are not so well aware of is that humanist thought can also be creative.

Some of the more obvious examples are Bakhtin's philosophical adventures in Rabelais' and Dostoevsky's worlds, the courtly lyrical "novel of Sinyavsky about Pushkin," the linguistic fantasies of Brodsky the essayist, the historico-religious studies of Averintsev, and the brazen philological half-prose and half-poetry of Dmitry Gachev. All these phenomena carry the promise of regeneration and a new, fascinating dawn for a literature exhausted by struggles.

In a solution now saturated with culture, a new and individual literature is crystallizing. Nurtured in a hot-house and torn away from earthly roots, this new literature transposes the sphere of action into the field of highly differentiated thought.

At the intersection of these unrelated genres—the detective novel, science fiction, and humanistic *belles lettres*—we encounter a common orientation: representation of reality is abandoned in favor of the modeling of reality.

The twentieth century, which created the movies, television, computer games and Disneyland, has experimented with artificial reality so much that the time has come for literature, which has forgotten the roots of its craft, to reap some of the benefits of this virtual revolution.

What indeed is left for humanity to do, now that its history has been taken away from it? Is it now time to play?

Notes

1. Village or country prose is a genre of post-thaw literature "which deals in a sympathetic way with rural life and with the people who are not in the mainstream of organized, Party-controlled, production-oriented literature" (Victor Terras, *Handbook of Russian Literature*, p. 91).
2. Stalin's purges, which occurred at the end of the 1930s.

Part II

Manifestos of Russian Postmodernism

Chapter 5

THESES ON METAREALISM AND CONCEPTUALISM

Mikhail Epstein

The "Theses on Metarealism and Conceptualism" were read on 8 June 1983, at the Moscow Central House for Arts Workers (Tsentral'nyi Dom Rabotnikov Iskusstv) during an Evening of Poetry devoted to "Debates on Metarealism and Conceptualism."[1] This was probably the first public event in the USSR in half a century—since the Communist leadership's banishment of the relatively free competition of the literary groups of the 1920s and its instatement of socialist realism as the only officially sanctioned method of Soviet literature (1932)—in which creative "isms" were openly proclaimed as theoretical grounds for new, nonconformist artistic movements.[2]

1. The opposition between metarealists and conceptualists is of a kind possible only between strict contemporaries. It is this polarization that allows an epoch to reach the limits of its possibilities.

2. In every epoch, poetry is the battleground of convention [*uslovnost'*] and freedom [*bezuslovnost'*], playfulness and seriousness, analysis and synthesis. In the 1960s and the first half of the 1970s, the struggle was between realism, based on *vraisemblance* or the lifelike, and metaphorism, which celebrated contingency and play (the works of

Alexander Tvardovsky and Andrei Voznesensky are exemplars of these two poles). This opposition, from which poetry derived its dynamics and its tension, acquired new forms from the middle of the 1970s onward—namely, in metarealism and conceptualism. Though the old battles still continue, they have lost their relevance.

3. Metarealism is a new poetic form which, freed from conventionality, opens up onto the "other" side of metaphor, not preceding it like a literal, lifelike image, but embracing and transcending its figurative meaning. "Meta," the common prefix for words such as "metaphor," "metamorphosis," "metaphysics," conjures up a reality that opens up beyond the metaphor, to a region where metaphor carries over or transfers its sense, beyond that empirical dimension from whence it took off. While metaphorism plays with the reality of the actual world, metarealism earnestly tries to capture an alternative reality. Metarealism represents the realism of metaphor, the entire scope of metamorphosis, which embraces reality in the whole range of its actual and possible transformations. Metaphor is but a fragment or remnant of myth, whereas a metarealistic image (a unit of metareal poetry) attempts to re-establish mythic unity; it is an individual image that tries to converge with myth to the extent possible in contemporary poetry.

4. Conceptualism is a new form of conventionality that denies mythic unity as something inauthentic and inorganic. A concept is an idea attached to a reality to which it can never correspond, giving rise, through this intentional incongruity, to alienating, ironic or grotesque effects. Conceptualism plays with perverted ideas that have lost their real-life content, or with vulgar *realia*, whose idea has been lost or distorted. A concept (Russian *kontsept* as a unit of conceptualist art) is an abstract notion, which is attached to an object like a label, not in order to become one with the object (as in myth) but in order to demonstrate the impossibility and the disintegration of such unity. Conceptualism is a poetics of denuded notions and self-sufficient signs that has been deliberately detached from the reality it is supposed to designate. It is a poetics of schemas and stereotypes, in which form falls away from substance, and meanings become detached from objects. In conceptualism, the naive mass consciousness serves as the object of self-reflexive and playful representation.

5. Within one and the same culture, metarealism and conceptualism fulfill two necessary and mutually compensating functions. They peel off the layers of conventional, false and ossified meanings that words have acquired (conceptualism) and restore to them a new polyvalence and fullness of meaning (metarealism). The verbal texture of conceptualism is untidy, rough, shredded, artistically not fully fledged. All of this is in keeping with the initial aims of the movement, namely, to show the shabbiness and doddering old-age impotence of the lyrical-ideological vocabulary with which we make sense of the world. Vsevolod Nekrasov, for instance, uses mostly interjections, subordinate and connective words, like "eh!" "that," "who," and "yet," which have not yet lost the ring of truth, as distinct from elevated, nominative words, such as "thought," "love," "faith," and "country," which have suffered from ideological corruption. Metarealism, on the contrary, constructs a lofty and sturdy verbal edifice, striving for fullness of meaning through the complete spiritual transfiguration of objects and their reunification with universal meanings. Metarealism seeks out true value by turning to eternal themes or the arch-images of contemporary themes, such as love, death, *logos*, light, earth, wind, night, garden. Its material is nature, history, art, and "high" culture. Conceptualism, by contrast, shows up the contingent and illusory nature of all designated value, which is why its themes are demonstratively linked to the present moment, to everyday life, political and colloquial clichés, to the "low" forms of mass culture and mass consciousness (such as the image of the "militia-man" in Dmitry Prigov's verse).

The middle ground between "high" and "low" is occupied by the world of technology and science. This technical lexicon has influenced Alexander Eremenko, who stands half-way between the metarealists and the conceptualists.

6. In its fundamental logic, the debate between the metarealists and the conceptualists is reminiscent of the debate between medieval realism and nominalism. It was no accident that the moderate branch of nominalism, which was called "conceptualism," provided the contemporary conceptualists with their name. The question for medieval philosophy was: are general ideas, such as "truth," "love," and "beauty" endowed with reality in its fullness, or is their existence limited to the sphere of words (nominalism) and notions (concepts)? This scholastic debate, which was so difficult to resolve through logic, has found a resolution in contemporary poetic practice. Reality and ideas are both united and dissociated, depending on which side of reality one looks at. Metarealism consistently aspires toward unity, while conceptualism is directed toward disunity and the separation of signs from their signifieds. The former manifests the creative potential of reality to fuse with an idea, the latter the corruption and falsity of ideas that have been separated from reality through a reductionist schematization. Contemporary culture would be incomplete if either one of these two principles were removed from it—the analytico-rational or the synthetico-mythological.

7. Metarealism and conceptualism are not so much self-contained literary groups as poles between which contemporary poetry moves. There are regions in between, and there are as many transitional phases as there are new poetic individuals who have jettisoned the framework of the earlier opposition of realism and metaphorism. The differences between the new poets are defined by the degree to which ideas and *realia* in their poetry are either unified (seriously, unconditionally, mythologically) or separated (in an ironic, grotesque or self-reflexive mode). *Metarealia* belong to the sphere of unity, while concepts belong to that of separation.

8. An example of the most consistent and extreme metarealism is the poetry of Olga Sedakova, whose images are pure religious archetypes and as such form almost transparent signs. The poetry of Ivan Zhdanov is more concerned with contemporary *realia*, and this gives dynamism to his images and dislocates their archetypal meanings. In the transitional space between metarealism and conceptualism we can further situate the systems of presentism of Alexei Parshchikov and Ilya Kutik (see thesis 9 below). Alexander Eremenko is close to the presentist group, but he combines the poles of metarealism and conceptualism by means of the grotesque rather than through a smooth mediation between them. He accentuates the very rupture between the two systems: using "serious" words to create a new, tangible reality for objects, he simultaneously deconstructs them through irony and grotesque use of technological jargon in landscape descriptions.

The shift to conceptualism is embodied in the poetry of Dmitry Prigov, for whom reality is exclusively a playing-field for a conceptual game, even if this game is conducted according to the rules of traditional prosody. Vsevolod Nekrasov has moved even closer to the limits of conceptualism, mainly using auxiliaries and parentheses, interjections, and other abstract elements of language. Finally, there is Lev Rubinshtein, who represents the most extreme and logically consistent form of conceptualism. He no longer uses words, but ready-made verbal blocks, or constructions of the type found in catalogue entries, instructions in official memorandums, or commands of computer systems.

Thus contemporary poetry's entire field of representational possibilities is covered by the movement from archetype to stereotype, which passes through the subtlest shifts in the relationship between ideas and objects.

9. A special designation should be reserved for Alexei Parshchikov and Ilya Kutik, who are located at the center of the contemporary poetic scale, equidistant from both poles. This tendency can be called presentism, or "the poetry of presence," "the poetry of the present moment." Although based in the futurist tradition, with its predilection for urbanism and the technical plasticity of objects, the poetry of presence is devoid of futurist socio-aesthetic militancy and utopianism. Presentism is oriented not toward a future but toward an eternal present and the given fact as such. Here, between the extremes of poetic monism (the merging of object and meaning in metarealism) and dualism (the separation of object and meaning in conceptualism), a phenomenological approach to reality prevails. The poetry of presentism affirms the very presence of the object, its visibility and tangibility as the necessary and sufficient condition of its signifying. The structural principle of the poetic work is based both on the succession of diverse perspectives on the object, and the methods of perceiving and describing it, which in their totality manifest the object's own "essence." The object is thus the appearance of the object, as postulated by phenomenology. The object is neither united with the idea nor opposed to it, but is itself "idea," or *eidos,* in the primordial sense of this word—a "visibility," something that represents or "presents" itself.

10. The problem of resemblance to life [*vraisemblance*], that is, of the correspondence of the image to external reality—treated in different ways by realism and metaphorism in the 1960s and 1970s — is sublated in contemporary poetry, for which the structuring and differentiating principle is the correlation of *realia* with ideas within the image itself. Such poetry is *ideational* in the most literal and lofty sense of the term—whether the idea be taken as a "concept" in the sense of its ironic withdrawal from reality, or as *metarealia*, mythically consubstantial with reality, or as *presentalia* phenomenologically equated with reality.

Thus a contemporary poetic style declares itself not by is adherence to one or another group or trend, but to the degree it partakes in the multiple oppositions that determine the dialectic of self-division, self-transcendence, or self-coincidence of the artistic image, designated as conceptualism, metarealism, and presentism. These three designations outline the major concentrations or constellations of contemporary poetic culture, between which there remains sufficient free space to give rise to new gifted poets and influential styles.[3]

1983

Notes

1. All Epstein's manifestos were written in Moscow (the author moved from Russia to the U.S. in 1990).
2. The following publications in the USSR offer the earliest introduction to the work of metarealist and conceptualist poets: *Den' poezii-1988* (Moscow: Sovetskii pisatel', 1988), pp. 159–165; *Poeziia, almanac,* 50 and 52 (Moscow, Molodaia gvardiia, 1988 and 1989); *Molodaia poeziia-89. Stikhi. Stat'i. Teksty* (Moscow: Sovetskii pisatel', 1989); *Zerkala, almanac 1989,* vol. 1, compiled by Alexander Lavrin (Moscow: Moskovskii rabochii, 1989). See also Select Bibliography.
3. M. Epstein developd these theses across several extensive studies of metarealist and conceptualist movements. See the following books: *Paradoksy novizny. O literaturnom razvitii XIX–XX vekov* (The Paradoxes of Innovation: On the Development of Literature in the 19th and 20th Centuries) (Moscow, 1988), pp. 151–175; *Vera i obraz. Religioznoe bessoznatel'noe v russkoi kul'ture XX veka* (Faith and Image: The Religious Unconscious in Twentieth Century Russian Culture) (Tenafly, N.J., 1994), pp. 56–85, 90–95, 143–146; *After the Future: The Paradoxes of Postmodernism and Contemporary Russian Culture,* trans. with an introduction by Anesa Miller-Pogacar (Amherst, Mass., 1995), pp. 30–43, 46–49, 60–70, 76–78, 193–195, 200–203.

   See the following articles and essays: "Kliuchevoe slovo—kul'tura. O novoi moskovskoi poezii" (The Key Word—"Culture." On the New Moscow Poetry). *Moskovskii komsomolets,* August 3, 1984, p. 4; "Pokolenie, nashedshee sebia. O novoi poezii vos'midesiatykh godov" (The Generation Who Found Itself. On the New Poetry of the 1980s). *Voprosy Literatury,* 1986, No. 5, pp. 40–72; "Kontsepty ... Metaboly ... O novykh techeniiakh v poezii" (Concepts ... Metaboles ... On New Trends in Poetry). *Oktiabr'* (Moscow), 1988, No. 4, pp. 194–203 [also in *Vzgliad. Kritika, polemika, publikatsii.* Moscow: Sovetskii pisatel', 1988, pp. 171–196]; "Exposing the Quagmire." *Times Literary Supplement,* London, April 7–13, 1989; "Iskusstvo avangarda i religioznoe soznanie" (Art of the Avant-Garde and Religious Consciousness). *Novyi Mir* (Moscow), 1989, No. 12, pp. 222–235; "Chto takoe metabola? O tret'em trope" (What is Metabole? On the Third Trope). *Stilistika i poetika: Tezisy vsesoiuznoi nauchnoi konferentsii,* vypusk 2. Moscow: Institut russkogo iazyka AN SSSR, 1989, pp. 75–80; "Zerkalo-shchit" (The Mirror-Shield), *Poeziia,* almanakh, 52, Moscow: Molodaia gvardiia, 1989, pp. 86–88; "Like a Corpse I Lay In the Desert ...," in *Mapping Codes: A Collection of New Writing from Moscow to San Francisco* (special issue of *Five Fingers Review*), San Francisco, 1990, No. 8/9, pp. 162–167; "Katalog novykh poezii/Ein Katalog neuer Lyriken" (in Russian and German), in *Moderne russische Poesie seit 1966.* Eine Anthologie. Herausgegeben von Walter Thümler.

Berlin: Oberbaum Verlag, 1990, S. 359–369; "Posle budushchego. O novom soznanii v literature. (After the Future: About the New Consciousness in Poetry). *Znamia* (Moscow), 1991, No. 1, pp. 217–230; "After the Future: On the New Consciousness in Literature." *The South Atlantic Quarterly*, Spring 1991, Vol. 90, No. 2, pp. 409–444; "Avant-Garde Art and Religious Consciousness." *Vanishing Points: Spirituality and the Avant-Garde* (special issue of *Five Fingers Review*). San Francisco, 1991, No. 10, pp. 165–180; "Afterword: Metamorphosis," in *Third Wave: The New Russian Poetry*, ed. Kent Johnson and Stephen M. Ashby. Ann Arbor: University of Michigan Press, 1992, pp. 271–286.

Chapter 6

On Olga Sedakova and Lev Rubinshtein

Mikhail Epstein

The 1980s generation, though opposed to the aesthetics of the 1960s, has aesthetic divisions of its own, which are not very perceptible to the broad reading public because these divisions are devoid of moral-political coloration.

Two poles or extremes stand out, toward which, in one way or another, the writers of the "new wave" tend to gravitate. One of these is metarealism: an art of metaphysical revelations, striving for realities of the highest order, which demand spiritual ascents and the mystical intuition of the artist. This movement may be related to neoromanticism or neosymbolism, with the notable difference that it is devoid of the haughty pretensions of the romantic personality and the abstract [*uslovnye*] codes of symbolic doubleness [*dvoemiriie*]. Metarealism is a poetics of the homogeneous, indivisible unfolding of a multifaceted reality, where the lyrical "I" gives way to a lyrical "It."

> You will unfold in the broadened heart of suffering,
> wild dog rose,
> o,
> the wounding garden of the universe!

The wild dog rose is white, whiter than any other.
The one who will name you would out-argue Job.
While I remain silent, disappearing in mind from
the beloved glance,
not taking my eyes
and not taking my hands off the fence.
The wild dog rose moves along like a stern gardener,
knowing no fear,
with the crimson rose,
with the hidden wound of compassion under the wild shirt.

[Ty razverneshsia v rasshirennom serdtse stradan'ia,
dikii shipovnik,
o,
raniashchii sad mirozdan'ia.
Dikii shipovnik i belyi, belee liubogo.
Tot, kto tebia nazovet, peresporit Iova.
Ia zhe molchu, ischezaia v ume iz liubimogo vzgliada,
glaz ne spuskaia
i ruk ne snimaia s ogrady.
Dikii shipovnik idet, kak sadovnik surovyi,
ne znaiushchii strakha,
s rozoi puntsovoi,
so spriatannoi ranoi uchast'ia pod dikoi rubakhoi.]

Olga Sedakova's poem "The Wild Dog Rose" is one of the emblems of the new poetry, which is religious not so much in signs of the creed that is being expressed, but in the intensity of the act of belief itself, whose every manifestation reveals the limit of oversignification and the miracle of transfiguration. The "wild dog rose" is the image of an intensified and cruel universe [*mirozdaniie*], where innocence is what is most deeply wounded: yet it is in fact its thorny path that leads to the sacred garden, and its suffering to salvation. The only one who could "out-argue Job" is someone who is more innocent and more tormented. Thus, a wild bush reveals the nature of an overgrown, neglected universal garden, which represents simultaneously the Gardener—the Savior, whose suffering cultivates this garden and transforms "a hidden wound" into a "crimson rose." Its ceremonial name already resonates within the poem before becoming its meaning: "*razverneshsia* ," "*rasshirennom* ," "*mirozdan'ia.*"[1]

Such is the poetry of spiritual structures of the universe, which now shows through the thinning fabric of history. No longer is it necessary—as in the era of the symbolists—to relentlessly stress the meanings of certain select words and to elevate them to the status of otherworldly symbols: the bountifulness of earthly existence and of available vocabulary is such that it allows one to refer to other worlds without distancing this one, without thinning it out, but concentrating it in colors and assonances. Or is this the maturity of time itself, which has come to the harvest of meanings in earnest, when God, as prophesied, would become All in everything—no longer demanding seclusion in the temple and separate prayer?

The other movement, or the other extreme of contemporary movements, is commonly called conceptualism. Here, linguistic signs do not strive for fullness of meaning, but on the contrary reveal the vacuousness of their essence, their freedom from the signified. Conceptualism, which emerged as an artistic movement in the West at the end of the 1960s, acquired a second homeland in the Soviet Russia of the 1970s and 1980s. By this time ideological consciousness had decomposed into a rich collection of empty fictions and hollowed-out structures.

Despite the fact that conceptualism disavows any kind of signification or "content" in art, it also marks its last, eschatological meaning. The world has become so mute and clean that signs cease to signify anything at all: they are to be swept out like trash from an emptied art vault. The deliberate misarticulation and linguistic alienation of the conceptualists—as if they were erasing the meaning of the words pronounced or were putting them in quotation marks—is *the negative manifestation of the same "beyond" that the metarealists seek to represent in a positive form.* The conceptual treatment of language leaves us in a zone of tense silence, of the decay and decrepitude of all uttered or possible words—in a kind of nirvana of discarded sign systems.

Here, for example, is a fragment from Lev Rubinshtein's "On and On" (*Vse dal'she i dal'she*), which is presented as a kind of "catalogue" in which all the entries are written on separate index cards. This is one of the key genres of conceptualism, marking the enumerability of images, their schematic disengagement into "first," "second," "third," etc.: the abstraction of quantity deliberately triumphs over the plasticity of quality:

> 1. It all begins here.
> Here is the beginning of everything.
> However let us go on.
> 2. You won't be asked here, who you are, and where you're from.
> There's no need to—it's clear.
> Here is the place where you are spared a multitude of tiresome inquiries.
> But let us go on.
> ...
> 12. Here it is written: "Pedestrian. Stop. Think."
> 13. The next sign reads: "Pedestrian. Stop. Try to think of something different, better than this."
> 14. Here we read: "Pedestrian. Sooner or later—you yourself understand . . . Thus—you understand yourself . . ."
> 15. Here it is written: "Pedestrian. Beware—you may not understand anything anyway."
> 16. Here: "Pedestrian. We didn't even know each other. What's there to talk about?"
> 17. And here: "Pedestrian. Don't stop. Keep going."
> 18. Let us go on. [. . .]

If one thinks about it, these passages depict the same "final" reality as in Sedakova's poem: a kind of absolute space, which in one approach is designated as a "garden," and in another as "here." For Rubinshtein, all the descriptions of this place either say nothing or are deliberately misleading: the passerby is invited to stop and think, and at the same time not to stop and to keep going. All of this is "here." The movement "on and on" also occurs in one place, which turns out to be infinitely expandable. One could say one thing or something completely opposite about it. This place is expandable not only spatially, but also logically. In rendering each of the definitions meaningless, Rubinshtein creates an image of the limitless, the unnameable, the unrepresentable [*vneobraznoe*]. This is a kind of a metaphysics of negative terms, which point toward the Absolute by erasing all of its particular definitions.

If metarealism is a poetry of a positive *beyond*, which may be seen as an Eden, then conceptualism is a poetry of a negative *beyond*, which may be called a nirvana. But the common trait of *both* movements is precisely this directedness toward a *beyond*, which sharply distinguishes them from all the most recent trends in our literature, which have been devoted to the historically flowing "current" reality.

1984

Note

1. The Moscow critic Vladimir Saitanov's observation.

Chapter 7

WHAT IS METAREALISM?

Facts and Hypotheses

Mikhail Epstein

This manifesto was read on 5 December 1986 and hung on the wall in the Central Exhibition Hall, Kuznetsky Most (Moscow), at an evening devoted to "Metarealism in Poetry and Painting."

1. Metarealism is a stylistic trend in Russian literature and art, which was born in the 1970s but became widely known only in the 1980s. The Moscow poets who best represent metarealism are: Ivan Zhdanov, Olga Sedakova, Vladimir Aristov, Alexei Parshchikov, Ilya Kutik, and Alexander Eremenko. The painters who represent the trend are: Evgeny Dybsky, Igor Ganikovsky, Vladimir Suliagin, Zakhar Sherman, Evgeny Gor, V. Markovnikov, A. Tsedlik.

2. The term "metarealism" was coined in December 1982, following the Exhibition of Hyperrealists and the ensuing debate at the House of Artists. It became clear that in order to overcome the traditional realism of "the typical," at least two ways presented themselves. One group of artists sought to consolidate and enlarge the external, illusionist layer of reality, while another group was trying to tear down that layer. One group was *hyper*-trophying the visible surface of objects, while another was exposing their *meta*-physical depth. One group was partial to *hyperbole*, or to an exaggeration of the given; the other group adhered to *metabole*, or its displacement into otherness, "trajecting" into the possible ("metabole" literally means "to cross over," "to throw over," "change of place," "change of direction.")[1]

3. The concept of *metarealism* can be read in two ways. On the philosophical plane, it is a *meta-physical* realism, which is a realism not of the physical given but of the multidimensional nature of objects. On the stylistic plane, it is a *meta-phorical* realism, which has substituted a real consubstantiality and intercommunion of objects for conventional resemblance or similarity, that is, which has turned from metaphor to metabole. The prototype of metabole in ancient mythological art is metamorphosis.[2]

4. If, at the syncretic stage in art, objects are transformed into one another (*metamorphosis*), and at the stage of differentiation they are compared to one another in a purely conventional sense (*metaphor*), then at the synthetic stage they partake of one another or share in each other's presence, that is, they are convertible while retaining their particularity, or integrate on the basis of difference (*metabole*).

5. Following the path of metaphor, art comes to the semantic limit of conventionality, beyond which lies the region of contemporary metamorphoses (*metaboles*).

The difference between the metarealists of the 1980s and the metaphorists of the 1960s (Andrei Voznesensky, Bulat Okudzhava, Bella Akhmadulina, Novella Matveeva, Robert Rozhdestvensky and others) is the following: the quest for similarities and resemblances gives way to the process of penetration into a true, mutually interdependent presence, which is revealed in metabole.

The following is an example of metaphor:

Like gilt-glimmering cupolas
in the light scaffolds of construction—
the orange-groved mountain
stands in the deserted forests.

Andrei Voznesensky

An example of metabole is as follows:

> In the dense metallurgical forests,
> where the process of creating chlorophyll was under way,
> a leaf came off. Autumn had set in already
> in the dense metallurgical forests.
>
> *Alexander Eremenko*

Metaphor divides the world distinctly into the compared and the comparing, into literal and figurative meanings, into represented reality and the means of its representation. In Voznesensky, the autumnal forest of the Dilizhan mountain[3] is compared to the timber scaffolding around a church. Metabole stands for a unified and authentic world, indivisible but revealing many dimensions within itself. In Eremenko, nature and factory metamorphose into one another by means of the timberlike constructions, which are growing and "creating chlorophyll" by their own mysterious laws—the organics of technology at work. Together they form one reality, in which metallurgical and arboreal properties intertwine recognizably and poignantly.

Metabole opens up on the other side of metaphor, as the reality of the "other," which is only alluded to by metaphor's conventional sign. Instead of similarity there is a co-presence and reversibility of different worlds, which are all equally real and true. The sphere of literal meaning is extended—by virtue of the fact that even the "figurative," "apparent" meanings become "literal":

> The sea, clasped in the beaks of birds—rain.
> The sky, encompassed by a star—night.
> The unfinished gesture of a tree—whirlwind.
>
> *Ivan Zhdanov*

The sea does not resemble the rain, nor does the sky resemble the night; here one thing does not serve as the point of reference for the other. The one *becomes* the other, comprising a part of an enlarged reality.[4]

Metaphor is a readiness to believe in miracle, metabole the method of making the miracle palpable.

6. What is called "realism" is the realism of a single reality. Metarealism is a realism of multiple realities, interconnected through the continuity of metabolic displacements. There is a reality open to the vision of the ant, and there is another accessible to the scanning of the electron; there is yet another reality expressed in a mathematical formula, and still another about which the poet wrote that it was constituted by "the flight of the angels in the heights."[5] The metabolic image represents a method of interconnecting all those realities, of affirming their growing unity.

The prefix "meta" only adds to realism that which traditional realism subtracts from the all-embracing Reality when reducing it to one of its forms.

7. Metarealism should not be seen as another version of symbolism, which divided reality into "higher" and "lower," thereby preparing the rebellion of that "lower" reality and the subsequent victory of a flat realism. Metabole is distinguished from the symbol precisely by virtue of its presumption of a non-hierarchical interpenetration of realities and not of reference of the one (the auxiliary or surface reality) to the other (the true, essential reality). Such privileges are abolished. In metarealist art every phenomenon is perceived as the archetype or prototype of itself, as an end in itself, and never as a means to an end. The Kantian categorical imperative, intended for a human subject alone, is extended to the entire world of objects.

8. Metarealism has very little in common with surrealism, inasmuch as it does not address itself to the unconscious, but to the superconscious. It does not intoxicate but sobers up creative reason. "The surrealist image is the same as the image conjured up under the influence of opium." (André Breton, *Surrealist Manifesto*). The surrealists' starting point is the rejection of an exceedingly sober and dry "bourgeois" reality that surrounds them. Metarealism however starts by rejecting the drunken haze and quagmire of "communist" reality that envelops the historical horizon. It sends out a call for an awakening and the abandoning of the hypnotic fascination with the one and only—"this" reality—in favor of a multidimensional perception of the world.

9. The premise and source of metarealism is the entire history of world art, in its condensed cultural codes, encyclopedic summaries and extracts. Metabole is in essence a dictionary entry, a *microencyclopedia* of culture, compressed with all its genres and its levels, and translating itself from one language into another. Hence the absence of a clearly defined lyrical hero, who is substituted—for better or worse—by the *sum of perceptions*, the geometrical space constituted by points of view, equidistant to the "I," or—which is the same thing—extending this "I" into a "Meta-I," constituted by a multiplicity of *eyes*: polystylistics, stereoscopy, metalyricism.

In essence, metarealism has always existed—but a long deviation from it was required in order for it to become visible as a particular trend in contemporary art.

10. Metarealism was originally identified as a particular stylistic trend and a theoretical concept at an evening of poetry held on 8 June 1983, when it was first distinguished from conceptualism. Hence the title of that evening: "Stylistic Experiments in Contemporary Poetry: The Debate on Metarealism and Conceptualism."[6]

Along with the differentiation of styles within one and the same art form, priority must be given to the interaction of various art forms within a single style. This task of stylistic consolidation of the various arts media was addressed at the evening of "Metarealism in Poetry and Painting" held on 7 December 1986.

11. Differences in individual methods aside, the metarealist poets and artists are united in their profound sense of spatial continuity, which reveals the meta-physical dimension of things. It is through space that each thing borders something else, extends into otherness and transcends its own limits. In metarealism, phenomena are not presented as separate "objects" or "symbols"—discrete quality is overcome by presenting objects as image-continuities, lines of force and energy fields, all of which distinguishes metarealism from both mimetic and abstract art.

In painting, metarealism emerges as a sublation of the binary opposition abstract/concrete. Instead, the structure of things is represented as the "thingness" of structure itself, manifesting its own tangible substance and visible extension. Midway between a conventionally geometric abstraction and a realistically painted object is space itself. Space is an abstraction from individual objects, but at the same time presents the physical continuity and substantiality of the abstraction itself. With its multiple levels, its elasticity, resilience, and expandability, its ability to extend *out* of itself and *beyond* itself, in its visible meta-physicality, space is the major player in metarealist art.

What has been removed in a metarealistic painting is the external layer of space, the "skin" which is the object of hyperrealist investigations. But this removal does not expose the geometrical schema, the anatomical "skeleton," formerly the subject of abstract art. Metarealistic painting cuts through the body tissue between the skin and skeleton—the layers of muscle, the concatenation of fiber, the lymphatic knots and arteries, the soft organic tissue—conducting flows through which the material exchange of the body takes place, that is, the *metabolism* of the spatial continuum.

12. Perhaps metarealism is not just art, but also a world view. And a way of life. To be a metarealist means to experience oneself as a link in a chain of many realities, and as responsible for the integrity of that chain, consolidating it through word, thought, and action.

The metarealist, therefore, does not belong wholly to any one reality. Not because for him these realities are a game, in which he constantly changes masks, but because he takes reality seriously in all its dimensions.

1986

Notes

1. From the Greek *metabole*, meaning "change," "turn," "shift."
2. For details compare with the chapter "From Metaphor to Metamorphosis," in M. Epstein, *The Generation Which Has Found Itself,* in *Voprosy literatury* , No. 5 (1986): 64-72.
3. A famous national park in Armenia (a Trans-Caucasian State).
4. Albena Lyutskanova, a graduate student in comparative literature at Emory University, has drawn my attention to the fact that my description of

metabole, as distinct from metaphor, parallels the notion of rhizome in Deleuze and Guattari: "... Unlike trees or their roots, the rhizome connects any point to any other point. (...) It constitutes linear multiplicities with *n* dimensions having neither subject nor object, which can be laid out on a plane of consistency.... (...) Unlike a structure, which is defined by a set of points and positions, with binary relations between the points and univocal relationships between the positions [cf. metaphor—M. Epstein], the rhizome is made only of lines: lines of segmentarity and stratification as its dimensions, and the line of flight or deterritorialization as the maximum dimension after which the multiplicity undergoes metamorphosis, changes in nature. (...)... The rhizome is an acentered, nonhierarchical, nonsignifying system ..., defined solely by a circulation of states" (Gilles Deleuze and Felix Guattari, *A Thousand Plateaus: Capitalism and Schizophrenia*, trans. by Brian Massumi [Minneapolis, London, 1987], p. 21). Thus, metabole can be defined as a rhizomatic trope whose constituents are not subordinated to the treelike hierarchy of literal, figurative, and symbolic meanings but present a free, multidimensional circulation of meanings.

5. Alexander Pushkin in his poem *The Prophet* (1826).
6. See chapter 4 of this book, "Theses on Metarealism and Conceptualism."

Chapter 8

What Is a Metabole?

(On the Third Trope)

Mikhail Epstein

Metabole is a relatively new term in literary theory. It is used by the authors of *General Rhetoric*, in the broadest sense, as a rhetorical figure, as "all manner of transformations relating to any aspect of language."[1]

What we propose to do here is to give the term "metabole" a narrower and more rigorous meaning by finding a place for it in the already existing system of tropes, in the gray area separating metaphor from metonymy. "Metabole," translated from the original ancient Greek, literally means to "throw over." Its commonly accepted meaning is "turning-point," "a crossing-over," "transfer of place," "change." In chemistry and biology, the term "metabolism" designates the exchange of matter in living organisms, while in architecture it indicates the use of dynamic construction models with substitutable elements (as in "a floating city," for instance).

In stylistics and poetics, the type of trope that should be called "metabole" is one capable of revealing the very process of

Originally published in Russian as "Chto takoe metabola? (o 'tret'iem' trope)," in *Stilistika i poetika. Tezisy vsesoiuznoi nauchnoi konferentsii*, vol. 2 (Moscow: Academy of Sciences of the USSR, The Institute of Russian Language, 1989), pp. 75–80.

transfer, or transfiguration of meaning [Russian *perenos*, whose derivative *perenosnyi* means "figurative"], the intermediate link in the semantic shift from literal to figurative meaning, and the hidden ground on which objects are linked and likened. The difference between metabole and metaphor in this respect can been demonstrated on the basis of the definition of metaphor as found in the *General Rhetoric*:

> We can describe the metaphoric process in the following manner:
>
> $$I \rightarrow /M/ \rightarrow R$$
>
> where I = Initial Word, R = Resulting Word, and M = the *middle* term designating the transition from the first word to the second, *which is never present in discourse* ...[2]

To provide an elementary example, the metaphor presenting eyes as stars has an initial word "eyes" and the resulting word "stars" while the *brightness* or *shining* which is the probable "middle term M," the ground for similarity, is not present in metaphoric discourse.

If metaphor always omits the middle term M, then metabole raises this middle term to the level of discourse, where it becomes central, connecting distant images, or figurative objects, and creating a continuous transition between them. "The sky, encompassed by a star—night" (Ivan Zhdanov[3]): here, sky and night are in a metabolic, as distinct from a metaphoric, relationship to each other, by dint of the M—"the star"—which belongs in equal measure to both spheres—to sky and night. In this metabole, the middle term, "star," that connects "sky" and "night" and brings them into one complex image, emerges on the level of discourse. By means of this M, an "exchange of matter," or, to be more precise, an exchange of meanings takes place in the image-metabole. In themselves, "sky" and "night" are not connected either through metaphoric "similarity" or through metonymic "contiguity." They recognize each other only in the "star" as a unifying link between two realities, by virtue of which they can achieve mutual transformation.

Hence the origin of these poetic "equations," which impart exact syntactic form or even the rigor of a formula to the following images-metaboles:

The sea, clasped in the beaks of birds—rain.
The sky, encompassed by a star—night.
The unfinished gesture of a tree—whirlwind.
Ivan Zhdanov

"The beaks of birds" is the middle term between the sea and the rain, an algorithm of transformation of one into the other. The rain is not *like* the sea, it *is* the sea, splashed by the "beaks of birds," which mediate between the two images.

Previously[4] we have described this type of image as a "metamorphosis," in deference to the fact that this term had already been used by scholars trying to extend the traditional classification of tropes.[5] However, the term "metamorphosis," while accurate in designating the "transformation" of the components of the image, is not entirely apt in that it presupposes the extension of this process in time. It also has too direct a link with the type of transformations described in the *Metamorphoses* of Ovid, associated with the naive mythological belief in the universal "transmutability" of all objects. In the case of contemporary poetry, what is essential is not the process of mutual transmutability of objects, but the moment of their communion or conjoining [*vzaimoprichastnost'*] outside the dimension of time while retaining their separate identity and meaning.

The metabole is just such an instantaneous "shuttling" of meaning, thanks to which objects are connected atemporally, in a multidimensional space, where one thing can be identical with another and yet retain its separateness. The terms at either extremity of the metabole, which are "rain" and "the sea," "the sky" and "night," "the tree" and "whirlwind" in the given example, could be called *metabolites*. There is no transfer of meaning between these terms according to the principle of metaphorical similarity or metonymical contiguity, and there is no "metamorphical" transformation in time. There is only an atemporal belonging via the middle terms, which can be called *mediators:* "the beaks of birds," spraying the sea, turning it into rain; "the star," condensing darkness around light and thereby revealing night through sky; "the unfinished gesture of the tree," which in its movement to break its own bonds becomes the storm.

The metabole thus represents a new phase of wholeness established among disparate phenomena, a kind of trope-synthesis, equipped with some characteristics of the ancient syncretic trope, the metamorphosis, but arising out of the latter's disintegration in the later dualistic tropes, namely metaphor and metonymy. If, at the syncretic stage (metamorphosis), phenomena turn into each other, becoming completely identical, and at the stage of difference (metaphor and metonymy) they are conditionally and provisionally assimilated by an "as if," then in the synthetic phase (metabole), they are appropriated by each other, integrated on the basis of difference.

Objects in the metabole are thus separated by a middle term and simultaneously connected with each other through it. The metabolites do not turn into one another (as elements of metamorphosis do, such as Narcissus becoming a flower). By the same token, objects are not assimilated to each other as in metaphor. For instance, in the metaphor "*berezovyi sitets*" [calico—literally birch chintz], there is no real connection between the birch and the chintz, no real mediator or middle term. What is implied in this metaphoric vision of Russia as "the country of chintz-like birches"[6] is that in its black-and-white bark the birch tree is similar to chintz. Chintz, however, is only a conditional, "resulting" image which has no place in the reality of the Russian landscape and relates to it only figuratively, through the visual resemblance of birches.

As for the structure of metabole, the metabolites "sky" and "night" both coincide with, and remain apart from, the mediator "star." There is no actual resemblance between "sky" and "night," but they belong to one another through the star that represents a segment of their intersection, the "skyness" of the night and the "nightness" of the sky.

The introduction of this third, mediating member into the structure of the image endows it with a quality of authenticity stronger than the one present in metaphor. Objects manifest not only a similarity but a convergence at a third point, which expands the capacity of the integrated image. It is not just a case of M being inserted between I and R. It is thanks to this mediation that I looses its one-sided "originary" quality and R its "resultative" quality. In a binary structured metaphor, these two members are sharply distinguished according to their function, such as literal or figurative, real or illustrative. For example, the metaphor "the heart burns" contains I ("heart"), used in its literal meaning, as well as R ("burns"), used in a figurative sense. The literal meaning of the word "burns" and the figurative meaning of the word "heart" are here excluded from the contextual semantic field. One is only I, the other is only R.

If a third, intermediary member is introduced, the two binary members, located at opposite poles, become reversible in their "originary"/"resultative" functions; the image is poised in equilibrium between the two. An example of this is to be found in Ivan Zhdanov's poem, "The heart burns softly, like autumn. . . ." Here "burning" is the intermediate member between "the heart" and "autumn," the M that reveals their shared, hidden reality. In the subsequent development of the image, it is no longer possible to affix a single role to either term, whether it be I or R, literal or figurative, since "burning" takes place in both worlds, that of the autumn forest and the enchanted heart. Each is both a primary reality and the representation of a second, fictional realm. The heart may be treated as an image of autumn, or autumn as an image of the heart. Literal and figurative meanings can exchange places because a third element has been found and verbally manifested—the reality of "burning," in which the first two converge. *The image thus becomes reversible.* Metabolites are transformed into each other, without specifying "primary" or "secondary" meaning. While reading Zhdanov's poem, we cannot be certain whether it is about the heart (in which case autumn is involved only in a figurative sense), or about autumn (in which case the heart is used only metaphorically).

In the suggested scheme of the metabole, the middle term M is no longer bracketed (as it is in the *General Rhetoric*'s description of metaphor), since it participates in the discourse. At the same time, the links are designated by two-way arrows, since the relationship between I and R is reversible. Each binary member at the opposite pole may be perceived as both initial and resultative:

The metaphor:
I → /M/ → R Eyes → /Shining/→ Stars

The metabole:
I/R ↔ M ↔ R/I Sky ↔ Star ↔ Night

The roots of metabolic poetics, which burgeoned into an independent system in the works of some of the poets of the 1980s—the so-called metarealists[7]— go back to the classic poets of the twentieth century—Rainer Maria Rilke, Paul Valery, Osip Mandel'shtam. For example, one of the most hermetic of Mandel'shtam's poems, *Sisters—heaviness and tenderness, your signs are the same …*,[8] reveals its most transparent meaning on the plane of metabolic imagery, by selecting "intermediary concepts," through which the properties of heaviness and lightness, gravity and tenderness, enter into a mediated relationship.

The imagery of this poem is constituted in a zone M, in relation to which I and R are completely reversible: it is impossible to affix to one set of words literal meanings and an originary status, and to another figurative meanings and a resultative status.

Sisters—heaviness and tenderness—your signs are the same.
Bees and wasps suck a heavy rose.
Man dies. Warmed sand goes cold,
And yesterday's sun is carried on a black stretcher.

Ah, heavy honeycombs and tender nets!
A stone is easier to lift than your name to repeat!
My one remaining care on earth:
A golden care, how to live out the burden of time.

What these different images—honeycombs and nets, a stone and a name—have in common is the transformation of heaviness into tenderness and vice versa, the metabolical exchange of these properties between poetic objects. The lightest insects tenderly swoop down on heavy buds. The lightest of all entities—"a name"—turns out to be heavier than "a stone," while to repeat is more difficult than to lift. The most burdensome problem of all turns out to be the lightness of being, the excess of time. The equivalence of "care" [*zabota*] with "live out" [*izbyt'*] is established by phonetic structure (the repetition of *zbt* in the roots of both words), despite the usual identification of "care" with lack or deficiency. "Honeycombs" [*soty*] and "nets" [*seti*] is a mediation of softness and hardness, which emerges through the phonetic texture of the two words, composed respectively of hard and soft consonants, not to mention the heaviness of filled honeycombs and the lightness of the meshed nets. Further on, the air becomes heavy and murky, displaying the properties of muddy water.... Fleeting, ephemeral time manifests the heaviness of earth turned by the plow, while roses manifest the heaviness of the soil from which they spring:

> Like dark water I drink the turbid air.
> Time is turned by the plough, and once the rose was soil.
> In a slow vortex, the heavy tender roses,
> Heaviness and tenderness have entwined roses in double wreaths.
>
> [Slovno temnuiu vodu ia p'iu pomutivshiisia vozdukh.
> Vremia vspakhano plugom, i roza zemleiu byla.
> V medlennom vodovorote tiazhelye nezhnye rozy,
> Rozy tiazhest' i nezhnost' v dvoinye venki zaplela.]

The roses are at the center of the poem's system of metabolic imagery: in their buds "heaviness" is graphically portrayed, while their petals carry the sign of "tenderness." The roses also serve as a mediator between the elements; formerly "earth" itself, they now float on moving waters. It is through roses that heaviness and tenderness become entwined like sisters, to make "a double wreath."

In essence, the metabole is just such a "double wreath," entwined in the slowly rotating whirlpool of a multidimensional reality that folds back on itself and develops from itself like a Moebius strip: impossible to fix a limit or rupture in it; impossible to determine where inner becomes outer, literal becomes figurative and vice versa. The metabole presents an undulating picture of the world, not a corpuscular one. In this "wave" artistry, the similarities and likenesses of separate objects are transformed into fluid congruencies, while separate particles are drawn into the field of energy generated by universal and mutual participation. Here there is no division into an "assimilated" real foreground and a provisional and illusory "assimilating" background, as in the case of comparison or metaphor. There is no division of words into "originary" and "resultative" or of meanings into "literal" and "figurative." But there is a mediation and interval, within which metabolic process takes a place: between heaviness and tenderness, between sea and rain, night and sky, tree and storm ...

The metonymic method of connection by contiguity is partly incorporated into the metabolic image: in the cited poems, wasps are contiguous with the rose, the rose with earth, the rain with sea, tree with storm. The essential difference between metabole and metonymy, however, is to be found precisely in what distinguishes metabole from metaphor: binary structure is transcended by, and resolved in, an irreducible third or middle term, which makes possible the organic and polyvalent growth of the image.

In metonymy, a resultative member substitutes itself for an originary member, assuming the latter's literal meaning as its own figurative meaning. For example, in the classical Pushkin metonymy "all the flags will hurry to our shores,"[9] the "flags" have the meaning of "foreign nations." Here the originary word is "nations," the resulting word is "flags"; thus "nations" becomes the "figurative" meaning of the metonymy "flags."

In metabole, one member is not substituted for another; rather, a third is sought, capable of revealing the one *through* the other, as night and sky exchange their meanings through a star; rain and the sea, through birds' beaks; heaviness and tenderness, through the bees and wasps that suck a heavy rose ...

Thus, the components of the metabole are not substituted for one another or assimilated to one another, but manifest themselves in one another, forming a third, synthetic, non-dualistic type of imagery. Neither similarity nor contiguity, but communion, mutual participation among diverse parts of reality, so that one becomes a hypostasis of the other—such is the higher degree of wholeness in metabolic imagery. It is a semantic totality leading from the two types of binary images (metaphor and metonymy) to a third, triadic image, which initiates us into the very mystery of the trinity, its internal structure of dissimilarity-indivisibility.

1986

Notes

1. Group [Mu], J. Dubois et al., *A General Rhetoric*, trans. Paul B. Burrell and Edgar M. Slotkin (Baltimore, 1981). Cited in Russian translation: J. Dubois, F. Edeline et al., *General Rhetoric* (Moscow, 1986), p. 56.
2. Ibid., p. 197. Italics are mine.
3. Ivan Zhdanov (born 1948) is a leading representative of metarealism in contemporary Russian poetry.
4. Mikhail Epshtein, "Pokolenie, nashedshee sebia. O novoi poezii 80-ikh godov." (The generation, which found itself. On the new poetry of the 80s.) *Voprosy literatury,* No 5 (1986): 64–72.
5. For example, the academician Victor Vinogradov suggested calling "metamorphoses" the images like "Ia k nemu vletaiu tol'ko pesnei i laskaius' utrennim luchom" (I fly into his room only as a song, and I snuggle up to him like a sunbeam) (Anna Akhamatova). V. V. Vinogradov. "O poezii Anny Axmatovoj", in his book: *Poetika russkoi literatury* (Moscow, 1976), pp. 411–412. A woman "metamorphoses" into a song or a sunbeam. However, this type of image presents a conventional comparison, slightly modified by the use of the instrumental case in Russian.
6. This image is from the poem *Ne zhaleiu, ne zovu, ne plachu …* (1922) by the Russian poet Sergei Esenin (1895–1925). Sergei Esenin, *Sobranie sochinenii,* in 5 volumes, vol. 2 (Moscow, 1966), p. 111.
7. See the manifesto "What Is Metarealism?" See also the chapters "On Metarealism" and "From Metaphor to Metabole" in the following: Mikhail Epstein, *Paradoksy novizny. O literaturnom razvitii XIX–XX vekov* (The Paradoxes of Innovation. On the Development of Literature in the 19th–20th Centuries) (Moscow, 1988), pp. 159–169.
8. *Sistry—tiazhest' i nezhnost'—odinakovy vashi primety …* (1920), in Osip Mandel'shtam, *Sobranie sochinenii* in 3 volumes, 2d ed. (Washington, 1967), vol. 1, pp. 76–77.
9. "*Vse flagy v gosti budut k nam*"—this is a line from the prologue to Pushkin's long poem *The Bronze Horseman* and is part of a speech given to Peter the Great.

Chapter 9

LIKE A CORPSE IN THE DESERT

Dehumanization in the New Moscow Poetry

Mikhail Epstein

1. The new Moscow poetry has a disquieting effect on those readers who feel in it a fuzziness of aesthetic orientation points. There are complaints about its hermetic quality, its excessive complexity.... It is not a question of complexity of language only, but of the absence of a stable center, which used to be identified with the lyrical hero. All complexities were clarified once they were correlated with a centralized system of self-reference: "I am so-and-so ... I see the world as such ...." Whether or not such a hero was demonically horrible or cynically depraved, fanatically cruel or naively obtuse (as in the poetry of the decadents, futurists, members of Proletkult or the Oberiuts[1]), he would nevertheless provide the reader with the pleasant possibility of aesthetic empathy, of expanding the reader's self by assimilation of the author's or the lyrical hero's.

Now there is no one with whom to identify. Poetry ceases to be the mirror of the narcissistic Ego. All that remains of this Ego's last lyrical sighs on the surface of the poetical mirror is a murky little stain of banalities. Instead of multiple mirror images, there is the crystalline structure of stone, which does not return the gaze back upon itself. The poetry of Structure displaces the poetry of Ego. At a decisive historical moment, the "I" exposed its own insubstantiality and inauthenticity. Like a traitor, it relinquished its responsibility. The latter was subsequently picked up and carried by structures: the social, semiotic, atomic, and genetic structures.... It is not the human being who speaks through the discourses of these structures, but an "other," who persistently addresses the human being. It is up to us to understand this speech.

The new lyric poetry is an experiment in assimilating these alienating, im-personal or supra-personal structures, behind which one feels the presence of an entirely different subject, who does not nearly measure up to the accustomed yardstick of subjectivity, like the one conjured up in Protagoras's saying "man is the measure of all things." Rather, it is the object that becomes the measure of all that is human, since in its objectness it mediates this recalcitrant other, which the human subject experiences as originary to the self. The new poetry is thus not *self*-expression, but rather *other*-expression. It is a journey through worlds in which humanness has left no trace, but into which the human subject has been allowed to peer through the strangely structured crystalline lens of the poetic eye.

The proliferation of "extreme cruelty" and "primordial tenderness" as the forms of animal and plant life in man, which Alexander Blok once identified as the "crisis of humanism," has now reached its maturity.[2] In our present day and age, the locus of the former individual is occupied by a multiplicity of self-animated forms of being, bonding through a kind of "musical" pressure: "the civilization of humanism" has been vanquished by the "spirit of music." Osip Mandel'shtam left a similar testimony, expressed in almost the same words: "The synthetic poet, our contemporary ... In him the voice of ideas, of scientific systems, of political theories is singing in just the same way as nightingales and roses sang in his predecessors."[3] The movement of lyric poetry beyond the sphere of the lyrical "I" reveals the depths of a new experience, which is more primordial, more originary, and hence more holistic. Its structuredness and trans-subjectivity defy definition and are best described in religious terms, even if this description has no immediate connection to any concrete religious tradition. The essential thing is not the object of representation, but the subject of enunciation, which in the new poetry is located beyond the auctorial persona. This elusive subject, as a consequence of all the processes of dis-embodiment and "de-personalisation," cannot help manifesting the characteristics of a transcendental subjectivity.[4]

2. The structures that have replaced the absent center—the "lyrical hero"—differ in kind. The conceptualist poets (Dmitry Prigov, Lev Rubinshtein, Timur Kibirov, Mikhail Sukhotin) investigate the mechanisms of mass consciousness and colloquial speech, which appear to function automatically in by-passing the will and consciousness of the human subject. They speak "through" him. What is exposed are the empty schemas of commonplace ideas, the exhausted dummies of contemporary world views—"concepts" [*kontsepty*] in general. "Life is given to man for the rest of his life ..." (Lev Rubinshtein); "The outstanding hero, he marches on without fear ..." (Dmitry Prigov); "Stalin's falcons are proudly soaring ..." (Timur Kibirov); "Sing me a song of anything you like, a swan song, oh my bright red cotton flag ..." (Kibirov).[5]

Conceptualism is the poetry of crossed-out words, words that cancel themselves out at the moment of utterance, as if devoid of meaning. Their presence stands out precisely because of the absence or erasure of sense. They present a riddle of self-manifest emptiness. Each time "the absolutely correct" or "the absolutely banal" word is uttered, an uneasy pause follows, a strained silence, betraying the actual presence of the Absolute. Only this Absolute is that of negativity, of nothingness. It is as if no one speaks like this—except that this comrade No One continues to speak like this, and even claims to occupy a leading role in literature and life. As a result of this, many conceptualist poems have been written in the name of this No One, providing the reader with a striking opportunity to identify with *no one*. But the main point lies elsewhere. Deliberate banality conceals its own opposite sense, widening the zone of the unsaid. If conceptualist poetry is not met with sheer laughter, taken as a parody of stereotypes of mass consciousness, then it is possible to perceive something else through it: the authentic lyricism of the silent Super-Subjectivity standing behind the speaking No One. For it is only in relation to Its super-abundant silence that all words ring hollow, flat, trivial, and disharmonious—just as they are made to ring, deliberately, in conceptualist poetry.

The sentimental self-appellation of this literary group is "Soulful Conversation" (or "Heart-to-Heart Talk"—*Zadushevnaia beseda*). This title in itself is, it seems, a deliberate play on someone else's tarnished words, deprived of their sense, which is a hallmark of the conceptualist *procédé*. For this group's poetry is neither "soulful" nor reminiscent of a "conversation." Rather it is intentionally superficial and replete with "borrowings" or quotations. It is reminiscent of a dictionary or catalogue.

Nevertheless, a keen ear will catch in these "near-verses" a certain echo of Chekhovian intonation, for example, when Chebutykin in "Three Sisters" is reading aloud from the newspapers: "Tsitsikar. An epidemic of small-pox is ravaging the district ...," or when he is trying to convince his interlocutor: "But I am telling you, *chekhartma* is mutton." Behind this banal text is a subtext of nonsense, loneliness, and mutual unintelligibility. Compare this with Prigov: "The President has been chopped again, this time in Bangladesh ...," or with Rubinshtein: "Oh, come, do not talk such nonsense! What does this have to do with *Woe from Wit,* when these are *Dead Souls.*" All of these are instances of emptied signs in a discourse of "useful" information or "content-filled" communication. The subtext itself as the "other meaning" dissolves in conceptualist texts to give way to "non-sense." The twentieth century has spewed out such a flood of words that it annihilated all underlying psychological foundations, opening up a gaping abyss of metaphysical emptiness. These dead words, "like bees in an empty hive,"[6] are swept out by the conceptualists, allowing silence itself to be heard at the limit of our disappointed auditory sense.

3. Other poets—like Olga Sedakova, Faina Grimberg, Ivan Zhdanov, Alexei Parshchikov, Ilya Kutik, and Vladimir Aristov—have incorporated into their poetic vocabulary, as if into a red book[7] of speech, all the words that still have life left in them. They have placed the sense of these words under high tension, even excessive tension, in order to reveal the structure of a multidimensional reality. This ultimate reality is not reducible to a lyrical "I" either, but, unlike in conceptualism, it is revealed in positive terms, "cataphatically," not as an erasure, but as an excess of meaning. Metarealism—the name applicable to this poetic movement—reveals multiple realities, ranging from the one perceived by an ordinary human eye to the one that is open to the compound eye of insects and the otherworldly insights of prophets. The challenge to traditional realism can come from the *devastation of reality* (conceptualism), or, on the contrary, from *multiplication of realities* (metarealism).

The metarealistic image does not simply reflect one of these realities (as in mimetic realism), nor is it simple comparison or simile (as in metaphorism), nor does it refer one reality to another by means of allusion and allegory (as in symbolism). The metarealistic image discloses an excess of realities, their simultaneous presence and mutual transformability, testifying to the credibility and inevitability of miracle. "... I know a thing or two about miracles: they are like sentries on duty" (Olga Sedakova). Each reality is manifest in another through a transgression of that reality's laws of being, and as an exit into another dimension. That is why the metarealistic image becomes a succession of metamorphoses that capture reality in its entirety, in its dreaming and its waking, in its bonding and dissociating linkages.

The words used in these images are not crumpled up and discarded; they are not thrown out as if they were "no one's," as happens in conceptualism. Instead, they gravitate toward a limit of all-pervasive resonance and polyvalence, where they take root in the depth of the memory of language. The more the various layers—such as the temporal and ethnic—of the cultural soil intermingle, the more fecund the germination and the more abundant the shoots. Metarealism is a poetry of semantically overloaded and underlined words, which exceed their customary meanings.

The following lines by Ivan Zhdanov could be a self-characterization of this poetry:

> Either the letters cannot be understood, or
> their grand scale is unbearable to the eye—
> what remains is the red wind in the field,
> with the name of the rose on its lips.[8]

Meaning acquires such intensity that the difference between the signifier and the signified disappears. Of the letters, which designate the name of the rose, only the wind remains, spreading the color and smell of the rose to become "red," thus acquiring the quality of the designated flower. To "name" is thus to acquire the distinguishing features of that which is named. In the metareality explored by the metarealist poets, the humanly constructed, arbitrary opposition between object and word has been abandoned. Objects exchange distinctive features with words so that the world is read like a book written in letters of incomprehensible proportions.

The poets who went through the experience of stagnation, of frozen time [*bezvremen'e*], understand the grandeur of condensed and saturated cultural space. By contrast with the poets of the 1960s who saw the world in terms of its divisions into epochs and periods, countries and continents, the poets who started to write in the 1970s and to publish in the 1980s have their spiritual existence in a multidimensional continuum, in which all times and all consciousnesses, from the neolithic period to the neo-avant-garde, converge. The flow of history has forfeited that linearity of direction called progress. Having slowed down and broadened out, time has formed a delta: this is a descent into an ocean, where times do not follow one another in sequence, but where waves roll in all directions in an infinite space.

The new poets are catchers of the oscillations of meaning, which traverse all epochs simultaneously: an "ooh!" emitted in the Middle Ages is echoed in the middle of the twentieth century.[9] All of these poets have experienced not only the negative effects of historical stagnation, which has transformed them into a belated, "stagnant" generation, but also the positive discovery of supra-historical foundations, rising out of the shallows of recent decades.

Stagnation is a parodic monument to eternity. Thus, the group of metarealist poets is addressing itself to this eternity; another, the conceptualist group, is exposing its parodic nature; while a third is commemorating it as a monument.

4. The poetry of the *Moskovskoe vremia* [Moscow Time] group and of the group of poets who are close to it (Sergei Gandlevsky, Alexander Soprovsky, Evgeny Bunimovich, Bakhyt Kenzheev, Victor Korkiia and others) contains a multitude of signs betokening contemporaneity. But this present emerges as a meticulously preserved layer of the past in a region of future archeological excavations. "... We recognize the years of our lives in the concentric circles of Moscow" (Evgeny Bunimovich). The poets of this circle rarely lapse into the distant past or into metaphysical inquiry. They are closer to the crowded and phantasmic milieu of Moscow's antiquity of the 1970s and 1980s. For antiquity it is, by virtue of the fact that it has been viewed, by accident or design, from a new post-historic perspective, in which it appears as one of the curious cast-offs of a bygone era, even if this era is still our lived present. This contemporaneity as antiquity is the last remnant of temporality itself, the bitter-sweet, nostalgic experience of parting.[10]

It is significant that the poets of this group retain a lyrical hero in their verse. But this hero is not so much experiencing life as hoarding lived experience—sad and honest testimonies with which he fills the precious archives of the disappearing "personality of the twentieth century," the museum of the Last Man.

> Was I here or not on occasion,
> Rhyming verse on a live thread?
> To this day I am torturing my heart,
> All is grist to the die-hard.
>
> *Sergei Gandlevsky*

As distinct from the grassroots poets, the *archaists*,[11] who endeavor to defeat the present by the past and who seriously adopt literary styles prevalent some one hundred years ago and more, the poets of *Moscow Time* exhibit the tastes and sensibilities of *archeologists*, who do not substitute one time for another, knowing the fragility and friability of the half-decomposed material of which the "lyrical I" is made. With this "I," the *Moscow Time* poets are carrying on their painstaking restoration work, knowing how quickly it may crumble if exposed directly to the here and now. In their poems, this "lyrical I" is illuminated as a distinctly outlined but frozen silhouette, seen as if inside a transparent fossil. In the dense associative texture of their writing, time coagulates in the form of clear ingots that have cooled down and been tossed ashore by an ancient surf. What name will posterity give to this epoch, this generation? Perhaps it will be called the "Amber Age" of Russian poetry.

5. For readers brought up on the poetry of preceding generations, this metapoetry—conceptualism, metarealism, archeologism ("lyrical archive")—seems deathlike owing to the fact that it is not engaged in the "battles" of contemporaneity. Where are the passions, the enthusiasm, the call to action? Gone is the lyrical hero, emotionally open, bursting with eagerness or indignation, having traversed the world from Canberra to Calcutta, or, contrariwise, having stayed ascetically moored to the shores of his native land.[12] In the place of this affective "I" or a thoughtfully reserved and self-assured "We," there is now a strange lyrical "It."

This "It" is impersonal and cannot be visualized in concrete human form. Even love no longer represents an emotion, a force of attraction, but the outline of a tightly enclosed, self-enveloping space, whose curvature is ruptured now and again by an earthquake, which separates the lovers, or whose shattered mirror breaks in order to unite them again. *The Earthquake in the Bay of Tse*, a poem by Alexei Parshchikov, and *The Distance Between You and Me is You ...*, a poem by Ivan Zhdanov, are both about love. But love is treated in them from the perspective of topology and geophysics rather than of psychology and the "human sciences."[13]

The new poetry is thus not like a child of Modernity, with its focus on Man as the center of the universe. It is rather like the memory of past ages or the foreboding of future times, in which Humanity may cease to be a necessary starting-point and will instead become the point of ultimate arrival.

In any case, what makes us think that poetry must be "cut to size" to fit the human subject, or that the poetic hero must be fashioned in the image of his historical contemporary? That he must have the same burning heart, the same eyes dimmed with daydreams or passion, and the same language fit for communicating with fellow citizens? By contrast, the prototypical image of the lyrical "It" is embodied in wheels, one inside the other, which were moved by the Spirit of the holy cherubim.[14] "The spirit of the living creatures was in the wheels," not in the human face or figure. And this "projection that had the power of sight" did not emanate from two human eyes but from the myriads of eyes around the wheels, reminiscent of Parshchikov's representation of the superhuman expansion of sight in the aftermath of an earthquake:

The paths of vision have opened up,
tangled like mycelia,
I have achieved transformation,
as much as I could be transformed.
...
... My self throws together objects,
I have become the environment
of the whole planet's vision.
Tremors, tremors....

[Otkrylis' dorogi zreniia,
zaputannye, kak gribnitsy,
i ia dostig izmenenia,
naskol'ko mog izmenit'sia.
...
... Smykaia soboi predmety,
ia stal sredoi obitaniia
zreniia vsei planety.
Trepetanie, trepetanie....][15]

Is it not then in the Book of Ezekiel nor in the Book of Isaiah that we find the origins of the poet-prophet, such as was first foreshadowed in biblical poetry and subsequently bequeathed to Russian poetry by Pushkin? We may recall Pushkin's *The Prophet* (1826)—a truly prophetic poem in regard to this new way of trans-subjective thinking: after the lyrical hero meets a seraph in a desert, his weapons of subjectivity—the sensitive heart and the idle tongue—are to be torn out. The flaming coal and the snake's stinger that replace them are signs of the dehumanization of the poet's being, allowing him to rise above sentimental self-expression and to attest to a spirit that is not reducible to an anthropomorphic image.[16] All that is human dies in him:

"Like a corpse I lay in the desert ..."

What sort of a creature was the monster that lay in the desert with a coal in its breast and a sting in its mouth? A corpse that was yet a prophet, ready to arise at the call of the Lord.

Contemporary Russian poetry also has a corpselike aspect at times, since it has lost all the distinguishing features of the living, the human. What juts out are forked tongues, membranes, charcoallike objects. But we feel it: this entire unimaginable aggregate is ready to arise and proclaim the truth at the first word from above—it is made to palpitate. The seraph has already completed his laborious task: the new superhuman organism is ready for life. And those who see in it only a subhuman monster and a conglomerate of mechanical devices do not suspect that it is from It that they can receive the Word containing God's will and thought. To transmit this message to humanity, the prophet has to kill all that is human in him. To set hearts on fire, the prophet has to have a burning coal in the place of a heart.

We are living in an uncertain time interval of perhaps a very short duration.

... And the voice of God called out to me ...

Nothing else is left now but to listen and anticipate so as not to miss this voice in the desert, a desert surrounding the solitude of the prophet who, at least for the moment, resembles a corpse.

1987

Notes

1. Movements in Russian poetry covering the first third of the twentieth century.
2. "Man is an animal; man is a plant, a flower; he reveals features of extreme cruelty, as if not human, but bestial, and features of primordial tenderness, also as if not human, but vegetable." Alexander Blok, "Krizis gumanizma," in A. Blok, *Sobranie sochinenii*, in 6 vols. (Leningrad, 1982), vol. 4, p. 346.
3. Osip Mandel'shtam, "Slovo i kul'tura," in O. Mandel'shtam, *Sobranie sochinenii* in 3 vol. (New York, 1991), vol. 2, p. 227.
4. See the notion of religious alienation and theomorphism in the chapter "Post-Atheism: From Apophatic Theology to Minimal Religion."
5. In the original, "Spoi mne pesniu pro vse, chto ugodno, lebedinuiu pesniu, kumach," Timur Kibirov plays with the surname of the poet Vasily Lebedev-Kumach (1898–1949), an official bard of Stalin's era, who wrote many poems and songs glorifying the Soviet regime. "Lebedev-Kumach" literally means "Swan-Red Calico" (the cloth with which Soviet flags were produced).

6. "And like bees in an empty hive, dead words smell bad" — from Nikolai Gumilev's poem *Slovo* (1921).
7. This is the book of the endangered, threatened forms of life, disappearing animals and plants.
8. "Oblast' nerazmennogo vladen'ia …", in Ivan Zhdanov, *Nerazmennoe nebo* (Moscow, 1990), p. 63.
9. See Nikolai Berdiaev's concept of the "new Middle Ages" and its interpretation in the chapter "Post-Atheism: from Apophatic Theology to Minimal Religion."
10. See the manifesto "The Paradox of Acceleration" herein.
11. What is alluded to here is a group of traditionalist poets, populists, and neo-Slavophiles, who are emitting nostalgic sighs about the archaic Russian past and using Pushkin's meters to do so. They believe themselves to be the legitimate heirs of the classical Russian literary tradition. The critic Vadim Kozhinov has tried to create an aesthetic and theoretical platform for this group, which includes members of both the older generation, such as Nikolai Rubtsov, Nikolai Triapkin, and Anatoly Peredreev, and the younger generation, such as Nikolai Dmitriev, Viktor Lapshin, Vladimir Karpets, and Mikhail Shelekhov. This group is introduced by the critic Larisa Baranova-Gonchenko, in the literary miscellany *Den' poezii – 1988* (Moscow, 1988), pp. 165–171.
12. The groups alluded to here are those of the previous two generations of poets, known as the "confessional'" or "variety" poets of the 1950s and 1960s (Evgeny Evtushenko, Andrei Voznesensky) and the "quietistic poets of the soil," who came to prominence in the 1970s (Vladimir Sokolov, Nikolai Rubtsov).
13. For a more detailed analysis of these poems, see Mikhail Epstein, *Vera i obraz. Religioznoe bessoznatel'noe v russkoi kul'ture XX veka* (Faith and Image: The Religious Unconscious in Twentieth Century Russian Culture) (Tenafly, N.J., 1994), pp. 50–53.
14. "As I looked at the living creatures, I saw wheels on the ground, one beside each of the four … [I]n form and working they were like a wheel inside a wheel … All four had hubs and each hub had a projection which had the power of sight, and the rims of the wheels were full of eyes all around. When the living creatures moved, the wheels moved beside them; they moved in whatever direction the spirit would go; and the wheels rose together with them, for the spirit of the living creatures was in the wheels." The Book of the Prophet Ezekiel, 1:15–20, in *The New English Bible with the Apocrypha.* (Oxford, Cambridge, 1970), p. 1005.
15. *The Earthquake in the Bay of Tse,* in Alexei Parshchikov's collection of poems *Figury intuitsii* (Moscow, 1989), pp. 22, 23.
16. "And a six-winged seraph appeared to me at the crossing of the ways.… With his right hand steeped in blood he inserted the forked tongue of a wise serpent into my benumbed mouth.… He clove my breast with a sword, and plucked out my quivering heart, and thrust a coal of live fire into my gaping breast." *The Heritage of Russian Verse,* introd. and ed. Dimitri Obolenski (Bloomington, London, 1976), pp. 92–93.

Chapter 10

A Catalogue of New Poetries

Mikhail Epstein

While contemporary Russian prose (Alexander Solzhenitsyn, Anatoly Rybakov, Georgy Vladimov) is mostly trying to settle accounts with history, the new Russian poetry is paving the way for a new aesthetics. Poetry is thus an experimental model of the future Russian democracy—opening up possibilities of speaking in different languages, not mutually intelligible perhaps, but nevertheless allowed to be spoken without interruption. Thus out of the ruins of social utopia, a utopia of language is being born. It is the Tower of Babel of the Word, in which multiple cultural codes mingle with diverse professional jargons, including that of Soviet ideology. The ideal of mystical communism is at last being realized in the sphere of speech practices, as an expropriation of semiotic systems of all epochs and styles, and as a dismantling of their hierarchies of value. Supra-personal levels of consciousness are thus assuming priority, while lyricism is devalued as a remnant of ego-ideology and anthropocentrism.

Never before has Russia produced such a multitude of similar poets and such a quantity of varied *poetries*.[1]

This once normative concept, like that of culture itself, can now be used legitimately in the plural. In this new form, the noun "poetries" indicates the heterogeneity of the contemporary poetic household, where various stylistic epochs coexist comfortably: the intonations of the patriarchal popular *chastushka*[2] are heard alongside the deconstructionist procedure of a deliberate desemantization of the text. I shall take the liberty of compiling a list of these new poetries, which distinguish the poetic scene of the 1980s from all preceding decades.

1. Conceptualism is a system of linguistic gestures, drawing on the material of Soviet ideology and the mass consciousness of socialist society. Official slogans and clichés are reduced or augmented *ad absurdum*, revealing the split between the signifier and the signified. The sign is whittled down to a naked concept, which is separated from its real content—the signified. This poetry of devastated *ideologemes* is close to what is called *sots-art* in painting. Its chief exponents in poetry are Dmitry Prigov, Lev Rubinshtein[3], and Vilen Barsky.

2. Postconceptualism, or the New Sincerity, is an experiment in resuscitating "fallen," dead languages with a renewed pathos of love, sentimentality, and enthusiasm, as if to overcome alienation. If the absurd dominates conceptualism, postconceptualism moves in the direction of nostalgia: a lyrical intonation absorbs anti-lyrical material, comprised of the wastes from the ideological kitchen, errant conversational clichés and foreign loan-words (Timur Kibirov and Mikhail Sukhotin).

3. Zero style, or the "Great Defeat," is the reproduction of ready-made language models, such as, for example, those of the Russian classics of the nineteenth century or the avant-garde of the early twentieth century, through a verbal medium of maximum transparency. This textual practice lacks any distinguishing features which might identify the author's individuality and appears as an unacknowledged quotation from someone else's text. The author recognizes his "great defeat" in the face of the overabundance of preceding cultures (Andrei Monastyrsky and Pavel Peppershtein).

4. Neoprimitivism uses a childish and philistine consciousness for its games with the most stable, familiar, and surface layers of reality.

All the other layers are metaphysically unknowable, and hence prone to ideological falsification. "A little knife" (*nozhik*), "table," "lolly-pop" are non-substitutable words, and hence cannot be exchanged for the counterfeit signs of general ideas (Irina Pivovarova and Andrei Turkin).

5. Ironic and grotesque poetry hovers around the stereotypes of everyday life, the oddities of the life of the "typical" citizen of a "model society." Unlike conceptualism, which works with language models, ironic poetry works with reality itself at the level of concrete utterances and ideolects, not at the more abstract level of their grammatical description. It is designed to provoke laughter rather than the feeling of metaphysical absurdity and emptiness. Hence the authorial position, which is absent in conceptualism, is explicitly present in this poetry: irony, sarcasm, humor, caricature (Victor Korkiia, Igor Irteniev, and Vladimir Salimon).

The five categories above represent the *left* faction of contemporary, and in a broader sense conceptualist, poetries, which gravitate toward *anti-art* and the *subversion of language*. Now let us look at the *right* and, in a broad sense, metarealist faction, which aspires toward a *super-art* and a *linguistic utopia.*[4]

6. Metarealism is a poetry embracing the higher levels of reality, the universal images of the European cultural heritage. The emphasis is on a system of gestures of reception and authorization, enacted in relation to the "high" culture and cult poetry of past ages, from Biblical times to symbolism. Archetypal images such as "garden," "wind," "water," "mirror," and "book" tend toward the absoluteness and atemporality of mythologems. There is an abundance of echoes from classical poets and variations on "eternal themes" (Olga Sedakova, Ivan Zhdanov,[5] Victor Krivulin, Elena Shvarts, and Olga Denisova).

7. Presentism is correlated with futurism but without being directed toward the future. Instead, it is a "technical aesthetics" of objects, focused on the present, on the magic of the object's visual and material *presence* in human life. It is based on a phenomenological approach: the world of phenomena is captured in its appearance, as a given, without any reference to "another," "transcendental" essence. The gaze is consistently de-humanized, emanating straight from the eye's retina and is anterior to any psychological, emotional refraction. Presentism is oriented toward systems of signs, which are the currency of exchange in contemporary science and the technological environment. It presupposes the metaphoric usage of special terminology and of professional jargons. Even nature is described in terms of contemporary civilization, as a totality of artifacts; for instance, the sea is a "dumping ground for handlebars"[6] (Alexei Parshchikov and Ilya Kutik).

8. Polystylistics is multicoded poetry, uniting various discourses using the principle of *collage*. The "low" discourse of everyday life, the heroic-solemn ideological discourse, the language of traditional landscape painting and technological instruction manuals—these collages play with a multiplicity of intermingled discourses (for example, the "metallurgical scaffolding" that breeds "chlorophyll"[7]). Unlike presentism, which achieves a unity of different codes through a total, "encyclopedic" description of objects, Polystylistics plays with the incongruity of objects in its collages and the resultant catastrophic disintegration of reality (Alexander Eremenko and Nina Iskrenko).

9. Continualism is the poetry of fuzzy semantic fields, *voiding* the meaning of individual words. This poetry is designed to make meaning dissolve and disappear. Deconstruction—the methodology used in contemporary (poststructuralist) literary criticism to de-semanticize the text under investigation—is raised here to the status of an artistic method. The word is placed in a context that ensures its maximum indeterminacy of meaning, its "free associativeness." The word ceases to be a discrete unit of sense, but is stretched out in an uninterrupted set forming a continuum with the meanings of all other words (semantic waves rather than atoms). The yoke of meaning is removed, making way for an epiphany of indiscriminate, unsegmented signification (Arkady Dragomoshchenko and Vladimir Aristov).

10. The lyrical archive, or the poetry of the disappearing "I," is the most traditional of all the new poetries, having retained a psychological center in the form of a lyrical "I." But this lyrical "I" is unstable; its objectness is elusive. It appears in the mode of the impossible, an elegiac yearning for the individual self in a world of reified and impersonal structures. There is realism in the descriptions of the contemporary milieu, but not as an active and living presence. Instead, this milieu is revealed as a stratum in a zone of future archeological excavations, to be labeled "Moscow culture of the twentieth century." Emotionally nostalgic, this realism is archeological in subject matter (Sergei Gandlevsky, Bakhyt Kenzheev, and Alexandr Soprovsky).

A dozen or more new poetries could be added to this list. Some of them coexist happily in the work of a single poet. A case in point is Vsevolod Nekrasov, whose poetic work fits both the categories conceptualism and neoprimitivism. Or better still, one could create a new category for him, since ultimately each poet and even each work constitutes a new poetry.

Even the list itself presented here can be regarded as an integral part of the new poetries, since it belongs to the currently productive genre of the *poetic catalogue*. The present work would thus represent category No. 11 of our list, the category of *paradigm poetry*, enumerating and systematizing the remaining categories.

This symbiosis of poetry and criticism demonstrates the extent to which contemporary poetry and contemporary critical theory cross-pollinate each other. The point is that contemporary theory converges with poetry to the same degree that poetry embraces theoretical procedures. Both share a common distinguishing feature, namely the paradigmatic structure of the text, which in these theoretical "stanzas" "projects the principle of equivalence from the axis of selection into the axis of combination," to use Roman Jakobson's famous definition of "the poetic function."[8] This structure does not produce a message in a language already known to the audience, but formulates the rules of a still unknown language, setting out the declension and conjugation tables of new poetic forms. The old-fashioned reader is soon bored by this material because he is like a pupil who has been presented with a foreign language textbook instead of experiences to be shared in his own native language.

To paraphrase the Russian revolutionary writer, Nikolai Chernyshevsky,[9] who proclaimed that literature is "a manual of life," contemporary poetry can be declared to be "a manual of language," generating models of possible syntactic and semantic worlds. Russian literature, which had been engaged for such a long time in restructuring life and in teaching its readers how to live, is ready at last to restrict itself to the domain of language and to embrace language as its *limit*.

This *limitation* not only breathes new life into contemporary poetry, it also allows Russian life to breathe more freely.

1987

Notes

1. Translator's note: I have used the English plural *poetries* to render the timbre of aesthetic innovativeness conveyed by the use of the Russian noun *poeziia* in the plural in Epstein's original.
2. A short rhymed folk lyric, mostly of humorous nature.
3. For a detailed analysis of Prigov's and Rubinshtein's poems, see Mikhail Epstein, *Paradoksy novizny*, pp. 153–158; *After the Future*, pp. 31–36.
4. In the previous manifestos, conceptualism and metarealism were discussed as broad stylistic zones or poles of contemporary poetry. In the course of time, with the growth of stylistic diversity, it has become possible to demarcate specific trends and categories within these two zones. Thus, conceptualism, in a narrow sense, may be classified as only one specific trend in a broader conceptualist zone (subversion of language), which also includes "postconceptualism," "zero-writing," "neoprimitivism," etc. In the same way, metarealism, as a specific trend, is a segment of a broader metarealist zone (utopia of language), along with "presentism," "polystylistics," "continualism," etc.
5. For a detailed analysis of Sedakova's and Zhdanov's poems, see Mikhail Epshtein, *Paradoksy novizny*, pp. 145–147, 161–166, 168; *After the Future*, pp. 25–26, 38–43, 45.
6. Alexei Parshchikov. For a more detailed analysis of presentism and Parshchikov's poetry, see Mikhail Epshtein, *Paradoksy novizny*, pp. 142–143, 147–148, 172–174; *After the Future*, pp. 23, 27, 48–49, 84–85.
7. This poem of Alexander Eremenko is treated more extensively in "What Is Metarealism?" For a more detailed analysis of Eremenko's poetry, see Mikhail

Epshtein, *Paradoksy novizny*, pp. 143–145, 173–174; *After the Future*, pp. 24–25, 44.

8. Roman Jakobson, *Language in Literature*, ed. Krystyna Pomorsky and Stephen Rudy (Cambridge, Mass., London, 1987), p. 71.
9. The author of the famous novel *What Is to Be Done?* (1863) and numerous critical pieces proclaiming realism and didacticism as the chief functions of progressive art.

Chapter 11

ESSAYISM

An Essay on the Essay

Mikhail Epstein

The essay is part confession, part discursive argument, and part narrative—it is like a diary, a scholarly article, and a story all in one. It is a genre legitimated by its existence outside any genre. If it treats the reader as a confidant to sincere outpourings of the heart, it becomes a confession or a diary. If it fascinates the reader with logical arguments and dialectical controversies, or if it thematizes the process of generation of meaning, then it becomes scholarly discourse or a learned treatise. If it lapses into a narrative mode and organizes events into a plot, it inadvertently turns into a novella, a short story or a tale.

The essay retains its character only when it constantly intersects with other genres. It is driven by a spirit of adventure and motivated by the desire to attempt everything without yielding to anything. As soon as the essayist tries to take a breath, to come to a stop, the nomadic and transmigratory essence of the essay crumbles to dust. If sincerity threatens to cross a limit, the essayist intervenes with abstractions. If abstract reflection threatens to grow into a metaphysical system, the essayist unexpectedly throws in a peripheral detail or an anecdote in order to undermine its systematicity. The essay is held together by the mutual friction of incongruous parts that obstruct one other. At the heart of the essay is an uneven and discontinuous intonation that can be identified as the hallmark of the genre. Its typical voice is that of the sad exile or the brazen vagabond, combining a lack of self-confidence with an extremely casual demeanor. Not knowing from moment to moment what he will do next, the essayist can do most anything. He is in a permanent state of need or lack, but he releases, in a single line or page, enough riches to potentially fill an entire novel or treatise.

A good essayist is neither a completely sincere man, nor a very consistent thinker, nor an extraordinary and imaginative story-teller. The writer who cannot successfully construct his *sujet* or argument, and who consequently loses out as a novelist or author of a treatise, gains as an essay writer. This is because in the essay only the digressions matter. The essay is thus an art of compromises, of surrenders. In the essay, the weaker side wins. The founder of the genre, Michel Montaigne, declares his creative and intellectual weakness on almost every page of his *Essais* (1571). In the essay *On Books* he complains to the reader about his inability to create something striking, polished, and generally useful due to his lack of philosophical and artistic talent. "If someone exposes my ignorance, he will not insult me because I do not take the responsibility for what I am saying even before my own conscience, let alone before others. Any form of self-complaisance is alien to me ... Even if I am able to learn a few things occasionally, I am definitely incapable of committing it firmly to memory. (...) I borrow from others what I cannot express well myself, either because my language is poor or my mind is weak."[1]

The essay is the product of a convergence of poor unsystematic philosophy, bad and fragmentary literature, and an inferior and insincere diary. However, it is just this sort of hybrid and bad pedigree that has given the essay its flexibility and its beauty. Like a plebeian who is not burdened by traditions of nobility, the essay easily adapts to the eternal flow of everyday life, the vagaries of thought, and the personal idiosyncrasies of the writer. The essay, as a conglomeration of various deficiencies and incompletions, unexpectedly reveals the sphere of a totality normally hidden from the more defined genres (such as the poem, the tragedy, the novel, etc.); determined by their own model of perfection, these genres exclude everything that cannot be encompassed by their aesthetic model.

We can now clearly see that the essay did not originate in a void. Rather, it came to fill the space of that form of unified knowledge and representation that once belonged to myth. Because its roots run so deep into antiquity, the essay's second birth in the sixteenth century, in Montaigne, appears to be without origins and without tradition. In fact, the essay is directed toward that unity of life, thought, and image, which in its early syncretic form was at the origin of myth. Only at a later stage did this original unity of myth divide into three major and ever proliferating branches: the sphere of facts and historical events, the sphere of the image or representation, and the sphere of concepts and generalizations. These three spheres correspond to three broad categories of genre—the documentary-descriptive, the artistic-imaginary, and the theoretical-speculative.

Essay writing, like a weak and somewhat sickly growth, found a place for itself in the gap created by the branching out of myth into those three major directions. From there, this thin branch grew vigorously to become the main offshoot of the great tree of myth. The essay thus became the central trunk of that totality of life, image, and thought, which split into the various branches of knowledge that have become further specialized over time.

In our own times, which have seen a renaissance of mythological thinking, the experience of spiritual totality finds expression more and more frequently in the essay. With Nietzsche and Heidegger, it is *philosophy* that becomes essayistic; with Thomas Mann and Robert Musil it is *literature*; with Vasily Rozanov and Gabriel Marcel it is the *diary*. Henceforth it is no longer only peripheral cultural phenomena that acquire qualities of the essay but mainstream ones as well. The pressure of mythological totality can be felt from all directions. In the essay, however, this totality is not experienced as a given, as accomplished, but as a possibility and an intent, in its spontaneity, immediacy, and incompletion.

Almost all the mythologems of the twentieth century have their origins in the essayistic mode: Camus' Sisyphus, Marcuse's Orpheus,

Miguel de Unamuno's Don Quixote, Thomas Mann's Doctor Faustus and "magic mountain," Kafka's "castle" and "trial," Saint-Exupéry's "flight" and "citadel." This kind of essayistic writing is in part reflexive, in part representational, in part confessional and didactic. It attempts to deduce thought from being and to lead it back to Being. All the major trends of literature, philosophy, and even the scientific disciplines of the twentieth century have acted as tributaries to this mainstream of *essayism*. Among its exemplars are Carl Jung, Theodor Adorno, Albert Schweitzer, Konrad Lorenz, André Breton, Albert Camus, Paul Valéry, T. S. Eliot, Jorge Luis Borges, Octavio Paz, Yasunari Kawabata, Kobo Abe, Henry Miller, Norman Mailer, and Susan Sontag. In Russia too, outstanding poetry and fiction writers, philosophers, and literary scholars expressed themselves as essayists: Lev Shestov, Dmitry Merezhkovsky, Marina Tsvetaeva, Osip Mandel'shtam, Victor Shklovsky, Ilya Ehrenburg, Joseph Brodsky, Andrei Bitov, Andrei Sinyavsky, Georgy Gachev, and Sergei Averintsev.

Essayism is a considerably broader and more powerful trend than any single artistic or philosophical movement; broader than surrealism or expressionism, phenomenology or existentialism. It is of such interdisciplinary scope precisely because essaysim is not a trend arising out of one of the branches of culture or a method of one of the disciplines, but a distinctive feature of contemporary culture in its entirety. Essayism tends toward a neomythological wholeness, a merging of image and concept inside culture itself, but also a merging of culture with Being itself and with the sphere of raw facts and daily occurrences that are usually considered beyond the limits of culture.

Essayism is thus, like its earlier counterpart, mythology, an all-encompassing mode of creative consciousness. Essayism functions as a metadiscourse in relation to all the artistic, philosophical, and documentary modes of representation that feed into it and that originated in mythological consciousness.

However, there is also a profound difference between mythology, which was born before cultural differentiation, and essayism, which arose out of these differentiations themselves. Although essayism unites the disparate—fact, image, and concept, or the sensible, the imaginary, and the rational—it does so without destroying their autonomy. This is how essayism differs from the syncretic mythology of earlier epochs as well as from the totalitarian mythologies of the twentieth century. The latter tend to unite by force what was naturally not subject to differentiation in antiquity. Thus totalitarian mythology requires the ideal to be treated as factual; possibility or even impossibility to be treated as real; an abstract idea to be treated as material force, the prime-mover of the masses; and one individual to be treated as a model for all other individuals. Essayism, too, unites fragmented portions of culture. But in so doing, essayism leaves enough space between them for play, irony, reflection, alienation, and defamiliarization. These are definitely antagonistic to the dogmatic rigidity of all mythologies based on *authority*.

Essayism is a mythology based on *authorship*. The self-consciousness of a single individual tests the limits of its freedom and plays with all possible conceptual connections in the unity of the world. In an essay, individual freedom is not negated in the name of a myth, with its tendency for depersonalization, but flourishes in the right to individual myth. This authorial, mythopoetic freedom, which includes freedom from the impersonal logic of myth itself, constitutes the foundation of the genre. The essay thus constantly vacillates between myth and non-myth, between unity and difference. Consequently, the particular coincides with the universal, image with concept, being with meaning. However, these correspondences are not complete, edges protrude, creating uneven surfaces, disruptions, and discrepancies. This is the only way in which the contemporary perception of the world can come to realization: aiming for totality, it at the same time does not claim to overcome difference in its constituent parts.

The literal meaning of "essay" is an "attempt," an "experiment." This is its indispensable quality. The essay is *experimental mythology*, the truth of a gradual and unfinalizable approximation to myth, not the lie of a totalizing coincidence with it. Essayism is thus an attempt at preventing the fragmentation of culture on the one hand, and the introduction of a coercive unity on the other. Essayism is directed against the plurality of fragmented particulars as well as against the centripetal tendencies of a dictatorial totality. Essayism is an attempt at stemming the tide of narrow disciplinary particularization at work in contemporary culture. But it is also a bulwark against the petrification of culture into cult and ritual, which becomes all the more fanatical the greater the discrepancy grows between the extremes of fantasy and reality (which makes it all the more difficult to force them into the immutable dogmatic unity of faith).

Essayism is an attempt at unification without violence, an attempt at projecting compatibility without compulsory communality. It is an attempt at leaving intact, in the heart of a new, non-totalitarian totality, the experience of insecurity and the sphere of possibility, the sacred Montaignesque "I cannot" and "I do not know how," which is all that remains of the sacred in the face of the pseudo-sacralizations of mass mythology. "I speak my mind freely on all things, even on those which perhaps exceed my capacity ... and so the opinion I give of them is to declare the measure of my sight, not the measure of things."[2] Two conditions must be met: audacity of vision and awesome respect for things themselves. Or, to put it differently, *boldness of propositions and meekness of conclusions.* Only by fulfilling these two conditions, inherent in the essay, can something of true worth be created in our age: namely, a universe of unfinalizable totality.

The present essay has transcended the confines of its topic—"the essay"—and entered the wider sphere of "essayism," which carries a new hope for contemporary culture. But it is only by transcending its topic that the essay remains true to its genre.

1982

Notes

1. *The Complete Works of Montaigne,* trans. Donald M. Frame (Stanford, 1957), p. 298.
2. Ibid.

Chapter 12

THE ECOLOGY OF THINKING

Mikhail Epstein

The phrase "ecological approach" is frequently used today in a broad, even figurative sense. The principles of "ecological thinking" extend far beyond environmental issues in their application to society and culture. What is usually meant by the expression "the ecology of culture," as used in the articles and public statements of the academician Dmitry Likhachev, the poet Andrei Voznesensky, and other respected and renowned authors, is the preservation of books, paintings, icons, buildings, and other cultural monuments of the past. This is an urgent and noble task, especially with a view to the long neglect and suppression of Russia's cultural heritage under the Soviet regime.

Culture, however, is not constituted by works already completed and by ancient monuments, the preservation of which is certainly our responsibility. Culture is constituted also by thought and by intellectual activity.[1] Has the time come to extend the principles of "ecological thinking" to the sphere of thinking itself? The world that we inhabit is not constituted solely by a living but also by a thinking environment. The noosphere (the sphere of reason),[2] however, is just as polluted by the waste of intellectual production and ideological activity as is the biosphere by industrial waste. What then is this ecology of thinking?

The ecological approach is opposed to the instrumental approach with its indifference to the fate of the object and its willingness to sacrifice it in the name of external, utilitarian aims. For centuries, nature was perceived as but a means for the development of industry, enrichment of society, and the self-aggrandizement of man. But as we can now see, these very aims are inscribed into nature as a whole and are attainable as such only at the expense of its destruction, which would almost automatically entail the self-destruction of human life on earth. Similarly, we have been accustomed to evaluate intellectual processes in relation to their practical goal and result. "Where does this lead?" "What conclusion have we come to?" "Where can we go from here?" These are commonly accepted criteria for the evaluation of thought. Thinking is not treated as valuable in itself but as an auxiliary form of action, which of necessity has to be assimilated to something useful if extraneous. Hence the habit of coming to "conclusions," making "inferences" and "generalizations," abstracted from the very movement of thought in the form of its final product.

Inside systems of thought, the principle of homogeneity has reigned supreme. The enormous variety of phenomena is deduced from a single postulate, from the primacy of the "idea" or "matter," from the "senses" or "reason," the "will" or "knowledge," the "individual" or the "collective." One of the elements always plays the leading role, as the "basis," "the first cause," while another is subordinated, ravaged, deprived of meaning, turned into a "superstructure" or a prop, without an independent place in the constructed universe. Thought is viewed as instrumental and, turned into "ideas," becomes a tool for enslavement and mastery. Perhaps the twentieth century will be remembered as the century of "ideas," since their inexorable logic reigned over all spheres of life, caught up in the network of causal relationships and held in check by the steel chains of premises and inferences. The ideas and the people who became their tools are responsible for the greatest tragedies of the twentieth century: world and civil wars, death camps, atomic explosions, ecological catastrophes, political terror. This was the principle of subordination of one side of being to another or its annihilation by the other.

Gradually, however, as the end of the century approaches, the power of "ideas" is decreasing. Humankind is coming to the realization that there are values even more important for humanity's self-preservation and development: love, life, nature, the fascination of the particular, the unrepeatable. Idio-syncrasies are taking the place of Ideo-logies.[3] A new spiritual sphere is forming, a sphere of wisdom and love, of understanding and harmony among all living beings on Earth: it is the sphere of White Spirituality, encompassing all the colors of the spectrum in its purity (sophiosphere).[4]

"Ideas" are thus bound to return to the milieu of natural thinking and to dissolve in its organicity. The type of thought we have called "essayism" reasserts its value here. It is ideologically "non-polluting" and "waste-free" because it pursues no aims outside itself. There is a kind of thinking, similar to walking or dashing, which embodies a locomotive or gripping reflex and is of necessity directed toward a goal. Such thinking moves assiduously toward a conclusion, and a "result" is its ultimate goal. But a "goal" (*tsel'*) is merely a degenerate kind of a "whole" (*tseloe*), as its one separate part assumes mastery over all others. Essayistic thinking is not purposeful, it does not aim at a certain target; it is, rather, *holistic.*

Essayistic thinking can be compared to breathing: thought breathes the Ego out into the world and breathes the world back into the Ego. One is revealed within the other, not deduced from the other as in a causal relationship. Each phenomenon is autonomous and significant in its own right and, at the same time, is the image or representation of other phenomena. No relationship of mastery is established between them, but a relationship of correspondence and mutual belonging.[5] The essay shows how the object exists in the world and how the world exists in the object. This quality of reversibility and of dual direction, which is innate to breathing, is engraved in the very noun "essay": it is a word that in Russian (*esse*) reads the same backwards and forwards.

Proof and refutation are alien to essayistic thought, which regards them as tendentious and intellectually self-interested. Where thought is exploited in the name of an "idea," where it yields a "surplus value" in the form of a rigid priority of one concept or referent over another, essayistic thought is absent.[6] Like breathing, the essay cannot be unidirectional. If it stops at the entrance or the exit with a "Hurray for...!" or a "Down with...!" death ensues. Lao-tse said that "truthful words resemble their opposites," while Borges remarked that every significant book also contains an "anti-book." These remarks apply to the essay, in which thought develops along opposite pathways, covering the entire field of possibilities.

The time has therefore come to admit that an instrumental attitude toward thought, as well as toward nature, is a threat to the existence of man as a thinking being, as *homo sapiens.* The *ecologoy of thinking* is a new humanistic discipline, born in an epoch of a maturing of the mind, in which the latter can no longer be satisfied with an instrumental role in the construction of life but manifests itself as an autonomous whole. The purpose of thinking is the progress of thinking itself. Not long ago, this would have sounded like heresy. But the bitter lesson of using nature "instrumentally" has taught us differently. What is the goal of this forest, this river, this blade of grass? Its goal is the same as that of a human being—it is the end in and of itself. Thought itself becomes manifest as a self-valuable need and pure joy of the human mind, as innate as breathing. Marcus Aurelius aptly remarked: "No longer let thy breathing only act in concert with the air that surrounds thee, but let thy intelligence also now be in harmony with the intelligence which embraces all things. For the intelligent power is no less diffused in all parts and pervades all things for him who is willing to draw it to him than the aerial power for him who is able to respire it."[7]

Who, then, should be better qualified than we, citizens of the ideocratic State, who have suffered the disruptive power of mutated, "conscripted" forms of consciousness, to become the pioneer-ecologists of the noosphere and guardians of its purity?[8]

1982

Notes

1. In fact, this was the primary meaning of the word "culture" after it extended beyond "tending of natural growth" to become a process of human development. Thus Thomas More: "to the culture and profit of their minds"; Bacon: "the culture and manurance of minds" (1605); Hobbes: "a culture of their minds" (1651). See Raymond Williams, *Keywords: A Vocabulary of Culture and Society* (New York, 1976), p. 77.
2. "Noosphere" is a term coined by the French Catholic thinker Pierre Teilhard de Chardin (1881–1955) and used in contemporary thought to designate the totality of artificial constructions and accommodations on the Earth, manifesting the capacity of human reason to work as a new geological factor in the transformation of our planet. The noosphere includes human reason in the diversity of all its spiritual and material dimensions and productions.
3. The Greek adjective *idios* means "one's own" or "private."
4. If "noosphere" refers to Earth's reason, then "sophiosphere," to Earth's wisdom.
5. Compare with metabole as a poetic trope, described in the section "Literary Manifestos."
6. For a detailed description of the economy of ideological discourse, see the chapter "Relativistic Patterns in Totalitarian Thinking: The Linguistic Games of Soviet Ideology," in Mikhail Epstein, *After the Future: The Paradoxes of Postmodernism and Contemporary Russian Culture* (Amherst, Mass., 1995), pp. 101–163 (especially pp. 157–163).
7. "The Meditations of Marcus Aurelius "(VIII, 54), trans. George Long, in *The Harvard Classics*, ed. Charles W. Eliot, 55th pr. (New York, 1963), vol. 2, p. 263.
8. This manifesto, as well as "The Age of Universalism" and "The Paradox of Acceleartion" in this section, was first published in Russian in Epshtein, *Paradoksy novizny* (Moscow, 1988), pp. 382–388, 402–405.

Chapter 13

Minimal Religion

Mikhail Epstein

"Minimal religion"[1] is a phenomenon of post-atheist religiosity, which is perhaps the most unusual outcome of the seventy-year history of Soviet atheism. At first it looked as if the so-called "religious renaissance" of the 1970s in Russia was a return to traditional religions and the ancient covenants. The prodigal son, it seemed, had returned to his father's house. All of this has been observed and described many times.[2] It looked as if the religious "returnees" were distinct from traditional believers not by virtue of the essence of their faith, but by the intensity of their religious consciousness, which is typical for neophytes, whose involvement and participation is always more enthusiastic. It thus seemed to be a psychological distinction, not a dogmatic or ritualistic one. And in fact it required enormous effort just to return to religion at all, to overcome the inertia of the preceding atheistic decades.

But the process of spiritual revival could not be frozen at this merely "reconstructive" stage. Like the European Renaissance of the fourteenth to sixteenth centuries, which brought something completely new to European civilization while appearing to be a return to antiquity, the Russian post-atheist renaissance revealed new aspects irreducible to the restoration of prerevolutionary religious traditions. This development did not take place inside the churches, in the cradle of tradition, but in "mundane" spiritual life and in contemporary thought.

The evolution of post-atheist Russian spirituality in the 1970s brought into relief the phenomenon of the religious avant-garde, which in some respects corresponded to the Western phenomenon of "radical theology." The "death of God," announced by Nietzsche, remains the last word in this radical or "atheistic" theology. The latter tries valiantly to teach humans to live in God's absence and in a secular world. It is a lesson for orphaned children, who have been left to their own devices, with precepts of order and discipline with which to cope. Thus the Protestant theology of the "death of God" (Thomas Altizer, William Hamilton and their precursor, Dietrich Bonhoeffer) reflects the secularization of a faith that has to survive in "a world without God."[3] What I call "minimal religion," by contrast, has already crossed this border: it is not the last link in the chain of secularization but, perhaps, the beginning of a new cycle of religious history. God, who is already dead, is being resurrected in the very country that was the first to crucify Him most relentlessly. A new and potentially powerful faith is *in status nascendi,* whose prerequisite and fountainhead was the unique historical phenomenon of mass atheism.

The new theology—not the Protestant but the post-atheist one —is a theology of *resurrection,* of the new life of God beyond the confines of the church, which was His historical body. The theology of resurrection is not the same as the traditional theology of the life of God in the historical church. Nor is it the same as the radical theology of the death of God in an atheist or agnostic world. The zero, or even minus degree of faith (agnosticism and godlessness), has been left behind. Resurrection is more than just a life in its usual course of degradation, an inevitable decline-toward-death. Resurrection is life after death, not before death. The new type of spirituality is born from the demise of mass atheism and was impossible before it. The theology of resurrection presupposes an intensification of faith, a theistic explication and assimilation of atheism, not just a return to a pre-atheist position.

Minimal religion is a "poor religion." Its name conjures up a state of religiosity that elicits pity or sympathy or the expression of condolences. It begins from zero and has apparently no tradition. Its "goD" is one of (be)coming, of the second or the last coming, which will pass ultimate judgment on the world. The atheistic spelling of the word "goD" with a small initial letter is preserved, but the last letter of the word is, written in uppercase. GoD is perceived as not the "alpha" but the "omega" of the historical process.

This "poor" religion has the same relationship to traditional religions as the avant-garde has to realism in art: by going beyond the limits of the representable, faith brings a crisis to the representation of a reality. "And their eyes were opened, and they knew Him; and He vanished out of their sight" (Luke, 24:31). This is how the resurrected Christ appeared to the apostles. He disappears from sight at the very moment He is recognized. The theology of resurrection puts an end to representational theology.

Minimal religion addresses itself to the ironies and paradoxes of Revelation, in which everything that is revealed is at the same time concealed. This is evident even in the early prophecy of Isaiah on the future appearance of the Messiah: "He shall not cry, nor lift up, nor cause his voice to be heard in the street" (Isaiah, 42:2). "...[H]e hath no form nor comeliness; and when we shall see him, there is no beauty that we should desire him ... [A]nd we hid as it were our faces from him ..." (Isaiah, 53:2–3). Thus from the very beginning, the atheistic stage, the "hiding [of] our faces from him," is (pre)inscribed in our perception of the Messiah. Post-atheism accepts this "disappearance" of God but interprets it as a sign of His authenticity rather than evidence of His absence. God presents Himself as the crisis of (re)presentation, as the refutation of the realistic fallacy in theology. Atheism thus prepares a way for minimal religion, which addresses God in the *poverty* of His manifestation.

The new religiosity is "poor" because it has no worldly possessions: neither temples, nor rituals, nor doctrines. All it has is a relationship with God—which is in the here and now. This "poor religion" is not like a prolific forest growth or an elegantly thriving garden. This "poor religion" emerged in an atheistic state like a crooked, pitiful shoot pushing up like a blade of grass through concrete. And yet, what can compare with the force of growth of these single blades of grass? The strength and the weakness of this "poor religion" is in the adverb *almost.* It has *almost* no concrete forms of expression, but it participates in *almost* everything, providing a meaningful tension to our weakened, ignominious lives. For in the face of the general demise of all meaning—pragmatic, aesthetic and ethical—it is this barely radiating religious meaning that can justify the most elementary acts of existence.

In 1921, Osip Mandel'shtam wrote that under post-revolutionary conditions, almost everyone was unintentionally becoming Christian. The impoverishment of material life was such that the only way to live was by equating life with spirit. Thus even a mundane family meal could became the ingestion of the holy sacraments: "Culture has become our church.... The worldly life no longer touches us; we do not consume food, we have ritual meals, we do not live in rooms but in monastery cells, we do not wear clothes but are clothed.... Apples, bread, potatoes do not satisfy our physical needs alone but also our spiritual hunger."[4]

Mandel'shtam's diagnosis is correct and penetrating. However, poverty is not only a question of material scarcity, but of a deficit in meaning. Every object taken from mundane Soviet reality was so hackneyed, and its meaning impoverished to such a degree of transparency, that it appeared to radiate with transcendence. Due to the fact that life had lost its self-sufficient cultural and pragmatic validity, religion did not have to divorce itself from life. Simply to live was already an act of faith. Such a faith could not be eradicated since its temple was in almost every home. And it could be practiced both by those attending the old houses of worship and those who came directly to "minimal faith."

In this we can see the Protestant idea as if going beyond its own limits; not a protest against the church as a dwelling of faith, it is rather an attempt to find faith in the midst of worldly life. There is a well-known poem by Fyodor Tyutchev, entitled *I love the liturgy of the Lutherans ...*,[5] which describes faith as it ("she") crosses the threshold of an empty and unadorned Lutheran church:

> She had not crossed the threshold yet,
> The door was not yet closed behind her ...

> But the hour has struck, has come ... Pray to God,
> This is your last prayer now.

After faith crosses beyond the threshold of the church, her service begins outside the church, in the depth of the world, in the everyday need to correlate life with absolute meaning.

* * *

In ethics, this transition from pre-atheistic Protestantism to post-atheistic minimalism presupposes a spiritual concentration on one's immediate surroundings. This can be called "neighborhood-thinking" and "neighborhood-feeling" (*blizhnemyslie* and *blizhnechuvstvie*), meaning that one's thoughts and feelings should be dedicated in the first instance to one's own "neighbors," to those who are nearest and closest to oneself. The ideals of universal brotherhood and equality, which have inspired modern thought since the Enlightenment, were usurped and compromised by abstract atheistic humanism. From the atheistic point of view, the universal goals of humanity could ultimately be achieved through the sacrifice of particular individuals or even classes (tzars, capitalists, landowners, priests, conservatives, etc.) that were regarded as obstacles to the common good. Atheism introduced the ethical imperative of love for the "distant one." In practice, this meant, for example, that a Soviet citizen should feel more compassion for the suffering nations of Africa than for his own neighbors incarcerated in a concentration camp. This distancing from one's neighbors, certainly, has nothing to do with the Christian commandments. Even when Christ prescribed that one should "love one's enemies," he did not mean "distant ones," but the enemies among one's neighbors.

Consequently, in the spirit of religious minimalism, no human being claims to be universal in his/her ethical responsiveness and responsibility. Instead, each individual is dedicated to the sanctification of his immediate vicinity, which he then attempts to widen. The space of the minimalist church grows out of that point, occupied by each individual in the center of his neighborhood, until it reaches its maximum, which is coextensive with "communality." Hence personal and familial relations are the focus of religious life, expressed as love and brotherhood. As difficult as it is to be a brother to one's own brother, it is far more difficult to be a brother to all people, although, as Dostoyevsky noted in *The Brothers Karamazov*, it is much easier to love all humanity than to love one human being.

As minimal religion spreads into the theological field, the specific object of theology becomes *the particular.* Each individual and each thing, in its singularity and particularity, become a kind of revelation about God. What we know about Him better than anything else is that He is One, or, perhaps, oneness itself. Hence theology becomes an investigation of the unique, the unrepeatable, which is manifested in every thing as "the image and likeness" of God.

Certainly, this kind of theology runs the risk of becoming a pantheism that borders on atheism: if God is in everything, then He is in nothing. Minimalist theology, however, eschews pantheist assumptions. God is not in everything but in each thing, in the *eachness* of every thing. He is in that which distinguishes one thing from another. God is not in the continuity of things but their discontinuity. It is in separating one thing from another, in grasping its uniqueness in the universe, that we reveal its theological aspect, its likeness to God. In ancient Hebrew, the very word that bears the concept of the holy, "kadesh," literally means "separation" and "distinction."

All entities in the world, with one exception, exist in multitudes: galaxies, planets, nations, individuals, animals, atoms.... If not for the singularity of God we would find ourselves drowning amidst sheer numbers, quantities, multitudes. God is the source and force of individuation, and the Godlikeness of any entity is equal to its singularity, its irreducibility to any general principle or abstract quality. All sciences, including the human sciences, study the general qualities of their respective subjects: particles, atoms, literary works, historical epochs. There is only one discipline devoted to the Singular, to the source of all other singularities: theology. The true subject of theology is the world of singularities, the uniqueness of all things as created in the image of the single Creator.

God is the Creator of all things, inasmuch as He is the Creator of the differences among them. Genesis is the history of creation through the division of light and darkness, heaven and earth, water and dry land, and so forth. It is in this uniqueness of each thing that its sacred dimension is revealed. Each thing is unique only by virtue of the fact that God Himself is unique, and vice versa. Each thing is theomorphic (identical with God in form) by virtue of being singular, "this."

Maximalist theology strove for generalizations, interpreting God as the First Principle, the Absolute, the most universal of universals, etc. Minimalist theology, having survived the death of God and the atheistic experience of "the universal without the Unique," has arrived at a simple conclusion: God is not All in everything but the Single One in each singularity. In each entity God constitutes this minimal quality (or "gift") that makes it different from all other entities. The task of theology thus becomes to speak about the infinite multiplicity of things and phenomena in their unique mode of existence, which means in their likeness to God.

There is almost nothing defined or formulated in minimal religion. It manifests itself above all in the mundane, everyday reality of an immense number of individuals who know very little about one another. Minimal religion is without ecclesiastical or denominational forms of organization; it exists without prophets or augurs and is not based on any single Revelation, written or oral.

* * *

It is not the Word which is holy now, but rather Listening and Hearing. God has been silent for many centuries, and because no new verbal revelations appeared, rumors were generated about His absence or death, providing a foundation for atheism. In the post-atheist era, we have begun to understand that God's silence is a way of His listening to us, His attention to our words. Such *active silence* is necessary for the continuation of dialogue where one speaker alternatively gives the floor to another. After God had uttered His word in the Old and New Testaments, in Scripture and in Flesh, what else could He say? It is time for human beings to reply to God, to respond to His word.

This is what constitutes the uniqueness of the current situation. Having lost contact with the word of God for a long period of time, many people now find themselves in the presence of Divine Listening; not loud-voiced prophets speaking in the name of God, but many ordinary people who feel as if Someone were listening to their words, as if they were speaking "into His ears" (to use an expression from *The Book of Psalms*).[6]

Hearing is the last realm that cannot be colonized by the reifying force of atheism. God's word, no matter how inspirational and mysterious, can still be reified, retold, reinterpreted, ridiculed, rejected. But God's hearing extends beyond the sphere of objectification. God's hearing is unsurpassable, it surrounds and encloses our voices like the horizon. While all existing churches still serve as vehicles and mouthpieces for God's word and try to maximize its effect on believers, minimal religion has nothing to say on behalf of God but it is open to and aware of God's hearing. In the face of this hearing, one does not speak *about* God, one speaks *to* God. Thus, hearing prepares people for judgment day, when the speaking and answering will be done by them, and the listening and deciding by the Judge. In the beginning, God's word was spoken to human beings in order to guide and lead them on their way to God. In the end, a human being himself speaks and answers to God, giving account of this way.

Thus, post-atheist spirituality is neither the religion of God's *voice*, as it was and continues to be in traditional churches and denominations; neither is it agnostic indifference, existential despair or atheistic challenge in the face of God's *silence*. Rather it is a feeling of responsibility arising from the belief that God is silent because He is *listening* to us. God's hearing is what gives to our "human, all too human" words their "minimal" religious dimension. It is minimal, because the contents of our words are purely human, articulating the profanity and dullness of everyday life. What imparts a religious meaning to them is not their source and contents, the personality of the communicator, but the personality of the Addressee of this communication. Not who but to Whom. God's capacity and willingness to hear us before the judgment is made is what gives "human" meaning to God's silence and religious meaning to our ordinary utterances.

1982

Notes

1. For a more detailed interpretation of the phenomenon of "minimal religion" in the context of Christian apophaticism and the theological innovations of the twentieth century, see the chapter "Post-Atheism: From Apophatic Theology to Minimal Religion" in this volume.
2. See, for example, Vladimir Zelinsky, *Prikhodiashchie v tserkov'* (Paris, 1982); Tatiana Goricheva, *Talking About God Is Dangerous: The Diary of a Russian Dissident* (New York, 1987).
3. See Thomas J. J. Altizer, comp., *Toward a New Christianity: Readings in the Death of God Theology* (New York, 1967); Thomas J. J. Altizer, *The Gospel of Christian Atheism* (London, 1967).
4. Osip Mandel'shtam, "Slovo i kul'tura" [Word and Culture], in Osip Mandel'shtam, *Sobranie sochinenii,* in 3 vol. (New York, 1971), vol. 2, p. 223.
5. "*Ia liuteran liubliu bogosluzhen'e …*" (1834), in F. I. Tiutchev, *Polnoe sobranie stikhotvorenii* (Leningrad, 1987), p. 122.
6. "In my distress I called upon the Lord, and cried unto my God: he heard my voice out of his temple, and my cry came before him, *even* into his ears" (Psalm 18:6).

Chapter 14

THE AGE OF UNIVERSALISM

Mikhail Epstein

The last decades of the twentieth century will perhaps go down in the history of culture as the age of new universalism. All artistic styles and trends, all philosophical schools have come to the point of exhaustion in their competition for the best presentation of and mastery over reality.

Hence the characterization of the new era by means of prefixes, such as "post" and "trans": postmodernism, trans-avant-garde, poststructuralism. But it is evident that things characterized in this way betray their dependence on the very states of affairs which they strive to transcend.

The key point here is that the avant-garde and structuralism were chronologically the last schools to develop individual artistic and philosophical languages that were presented as "other" and "more authentic" in relation to the preceding ones. The situation has now changed. No mono-language nor single methodology can lay claim to a complete conquest of the real or the ousting of earlier methods. All the languages and codes used by humankind to communicate with itself, all the philosophical schools and artistic trends, have now become signs of a cultural metalanguage. They are like piano keys on which new, polyphonic symphonies of the human spirit are played out. No one would think of claiming that one piano key is better ("more progressive," "more true") than another: they are all equally necessary in order to make music.

This is the essence of a universalism that is no longer the utopia enacted in Hermann Hesse's *Glassperlenspiel* (The Glass Bead Game), but the reality of the contemporary artistic and philosophical quest. Just as an alphabet cannot consist of one letter, so the alphabet of the cultural metalanguage encompasses all those languages that evolved earlier, in the context of separate, historically determined national schools, styles, canons, and methods. Without this ascent to the level of a universal human self-consciousness, no further evolution in the separate professional disciplines would be possible.

That is why contemporary art, literature, and philosophy are displaying a symbiosis of genres and methods, as well as translating one discourse into another. By contaminating images and concepts from various epochs and systems, contemporary culture strives to create a metalanguage of universal applicability. At the same time, at the point of collision between the various discourses, an awareness of their individuality and simultaneous transcending of their enclosed particularity emerges, producing elements of irony and parody without which no serious contemporary work of art can be created.[1] However, it would be a grave mistake to take this byproduct as its ground, that is to regard the parodic as the ultimate horizon of contemporary art. This mistake is made by certain theoreticians of postmodernism and the trans-avant-garde in the West. The meaning of the process now being witnessed is not in the ridiculing of the pretentiousness and limitations of all existing mono-languages. It is in transcending these limitations and emerging onto the plane of a metalanguage which is that of a universalist creativity. This new universalism implies mutual translation and "hybridization" of all existing and possible languages of culture, not the supremacy of one of them.

Measured in historical terms, this process is advancing very rapidly and has become a clear part of the general acceleration of humanity's movement toward an "x" or "omega" point. It is a well-known fact that a person in mortal danger can experience a moment of illumination, in which all the pictures of his life rush past his inner eye, accurate to the smallest detail and yet mutually overlapping and united into a whole. Something similar is taking place at present, but for all humanity. On the brink of extinction, the whole of history is experienced anew, in a reduced and fatally compressed form, into which are packed scores of historical epochs and cultures, hundreds of ideas and styles, in order to be illuminated by an ultimately transparent meaning. This extreme moment, projected onto the scale of historical time, may take several decades, the time humankind needs to square its existential account with life. The very End itself, which is organizing our consciousness so forcefully on a new plane, may not come at all; it may be preempted by our inner work, which could turn a deserved retribution into a successfully withstood temptation.

In the past, the universal consciousness that transcends national, professional, and confessional limitations was experienced by a select few representatives of humanity. At present, this universalism is becoming the air all humans breathe, as if it were the last gulp of earthly life and spiritual freedom. In the words of the great Russian twentieth-century thinker, Daniil Andreev, author of the treatise *The Rose of the World* (1950–1958), "universalism, in ceasing to be an abstract idea, has become a global necessity."[2]

Only after having equipped itself with nuclear weapons did humanity enter its adult phase, becoming a fully fledged ethical subject, entrusted with the right to choose between life and death. In the past, it did not have the means for self-extermination and, like a child, perceived life as a gift, which could not be declined. Now it is technically possible to exterminate humankind as a whole, and so life itself has for the first time been placed into question, demanding a commensurate and binding answer. If life is preserved, it will acquire a new spiritual perspective, since it will have been chosen by humankind as totally meaningful thanks to the conscious renunciation of death.

It is not unlikely that the state of gnawing uncertainty—with the apocalyptic weapons of mass destruction, but without world war—will last for a long time, perhaps allowing humanity to get used to holding onto life with determination and, after overcoming its suicidal tendencies, to mature into the free and conscious creation of life.[3]

Humankind will then have to develop a new ethics and a new metaphysics, which will allow it to save itself from itself. If it survives, it will do so not thanks to the superior and nurturing forces of nature but by virtue of its own free will and reason, by virtue of its cultural strength, not its technological weakness, as in previous centuries.

From the moment humanity acquired the means of self-destruction, a new historical era began. This is the era of universalism. Everyone *lives* according to his own dictates, but the *death* of humanity will be one for everybody; all will perish alike. Hence all are obliged to survive together. The catastrophe, which looms inexorably ahead, is a factor working in favor of humanity's reeducation and unification. It is no longer possible to throw one's opponent into the abyss without falling into it with him. Such is the new irony of universal *brotherhood,* which binds us now with the force of *chains.* It is no longer possible to perpetrate violence without oneself succumbing to its destructive consequences. The universalism of this ethics of "measure for measure" has become a political imperative.

Thus universalism is the fullness of humankind communing with itself, as a united and perhaps unique creator of culture in the universe. Having acquired power over its own life, and that freedom which was once the domain of only separate grown-up individuals, *humankind now turns into an integral human being, a self-conscious individual,* for the first time humanized in its *wholeness.* Humankind becomes an auto-communicator now capable of addressing itself directly in its entirety, speaking in all the languages ever devised by different epochs and peoples, arts and crafts, sciences and faiths. Universalism is neither a mingling or intellectual melding of various languages, nor a cultural esperanto, but a momentary illumination revealing in the depths of humanity its total and indivisible self.

1983

Notes

1. "Irony, metalinguistic play, double-coded re-telling"—this is how the Italian semiotician Umberto Eco defines postmodernism. See Umberto Eco, Post-script to *The Name of the Rose* (New York, 1984).
2. Daniil Andreev, *Roza Mira: Metafilosofiia istorii* (Moscow, 1991), p. 9.
3. This essay was written in the period of Yuri Andropov's rule (1982–1984), when the Soviet Union was again dangerously close to global military confrontation with the United States.

Chapter 15

THE PARADOX OF ACCELERATION

Mikhail Epstein

"What's new?" This impatient and superficial question harbors the potential for a profound answer, which is normally ignored by us. "What is new inside me" or "in the world" are concise formulaic expressions for the things about which one ought to be thinking and about which it is worthwhile to talk. This does not mean discussing the news. Many things can constitute "news," but newness itself is always unique. It is the focus of constant mental vigilance, for it contains the condensed image of times past and an abridged message of future times. Newness is an ever growing degree of completion, acquired by things. It is a maturing of time, which is followed by a harvest. And since the time of the End is not determinable, newness is its nearest approximation, addressing itself to us and demanding permanent attention and spiritual concentration.

There is nothing more mysterious than newness. How clear and simple is the world of Platonic ideas, the eternal *eidoi*! The great revolution, which was accomplished at the beginning of the Christian era, made the world more mysterious than it had been, endowing every moment between "before" and "after" with essential and unique meaning. We find ourselves in a kind of adventure-novel plot, in which the tension of mystery and breathtaking uncertainty accumulates with each moment. The action develops along an ascending trajectory. Let us reflect: we are living in "a new era," in "the new times" of the new era, in the "latest period" of the new times of the new era.[1] Even the newest has been renewed within the "newest period" of history several times. Language does not have a supra-superlative degree of comparison to designate this multiplication of "extra-new" historical periods of the last few decades. Every year is so replete with newness that it almost rivals former centuries.

If the laws of plot progression are approximately similar in all narratives including history, does not such an acceleration of tempo signify the approach of the climax and dénouement? In each unit of time more and more events are taking place, until what will have taken place is *Everything*....

It should be pointed out, however, that acceleration is a contradictory process. It is divided between newness and oldness, both of which grow at the same mutually interdependent rate. The faster cultural renewal takes place, the faster the process of archaization within it. The speed of development overtakes itself and transforms itself into inertia or stasis. Articles published two or three years ago are more dated than Sumerian cuneiform inscriptions and are covered with a thicker dust of oblivion. At the instant of its appearance, almost any contemporary novel or monograph becomes a monument to its own just passed era, reminiscent of those recent samples bricked into the granite of a Chicago building or buried in the distant desert sands,[2] the sole aim of which is to present a record for future civilizations. *The idea of progress turns into the reality of the archive.* Culture cannot but strive toward the greatest productivity and extreme acceleration. But this also means an accumulation of a gigantic mass of material in treasuries, museums, archives, and catalogues, the transformation of the edifice of culture into an ever-expanding burial crypt. At the top level of this crypt a kind of life still seethes. But when tomorrow comes, it too will descend into the sphere of silence and deadness.

This phenomenon is felt with particular acuity in the West. Artistic tendencies and lifestyles, which only a few years earlier had their heyday, retreat into the sphere of archeological interest. The new, which comes as a replacement, is fitted out in advance with attributes of its coming fame and future memory: it packages its own content into cardboard, or a collection, or a catalogue, or an archive, or an encyclopedia. Hence the totality of devices that can be characterized as *archeo-art*—an art that employs the methods of archeology and archeography, mimicking ancient, petrified forms of culture. There is hardly any time left for a living relationship with the present. Life seethes only in the antechamber of the future, in immediate proximity to it. The present, meanwhile, is already a walled niche, which will one day perhaps become of interest for the curious historian. Culture appears to be "contemporary" only on the surface. Below the surface, culture is *a museum* and *an archive* sagging under the weight of its own previously worked layers. It is the twentieth century on the outside and ancient Egypt on the inside. It is an eternity of stone over which time has settled in a microthin layer, like dust.

Hence, the further development of this process is not a mere abstract hypothesis. Each singular fact becomes history the moment it appears, preserved in audio, visual, and textual images. It is recorded on tape, photographed, stored in the memory of a computer. It would be more accurate to say that each fact is generated in the form of history. It does not have an infancy, it is old from birth, endowed with a memory of its own past. Ultimately, inscription of the fact precedes the occurrence of the fact, prescribing the forms in which it will be recorded, represented, and reflected. History halts its march because everything becomes history. The flow of time can move between solid banks, in the midst of stability and tradition, but when everything becomes time and innovation, then the flow ceases to be flow and is instead the rhythmically swaying ocean of eternity.

Thanks to video recordings and personal computers, it is technically possible to transform every individual life into an archive, which can be easily accommodated by the growing volume of electronic memory. A painting by Leonardo or a symphony by Mozart, a telephone conversation or playing with a child, the odor of a flower or a skyscape at dusk—all of this can be inscribed in a stack of punched cards or a digital disc; it can be represented in symbolic, coded form. Reality, consisting of a series of successive moments, is now represented on a single plane and synchronously, a totality of informational units stored in the memory of the machine. *Succession* gives way to *selection.* With what do you wish to start off the day: sunset or sunrise, Renaissance music or Surrealist paintings?

As the memory of the machine increases in volume, the whole of history—the history of everything—can be held in the palm of the hand. History, therefore, cancels itself out through its own historicity. Each person is surrounded by the eternity of the archive, through which he or she can comb the files at will. In this museum, the present is epistemologically indistinguishable from the past, and represents an equally accessible object of selection, depending on which key is pressed and which channel of information is switched on. Museum curators and archeologists are the prophets of this future world, which will be transformed wholly into a mode of the past in the form of an inscription, image or collection.

This is what one possible variant of "the end of time" looks like. Our task, however, is not to generate predictions, but to grasp the nature of the universal process of acceleration, whose maelstrom is consuming ever larger chunks of history. "Acceleration" is not just a topical political concept[3] but a philosophical category, referring to the global problems of history and eschatology (if the latter is understood as the doctrine of the end of time and the ultimate destiny of the world). We must repeat once more: the march of history from epoch to epoch has accelerated as a whole and has reached, at the end of the twentieth century, unprecedented speed. One year in politics, science, and culture contains as many events as would have taken up a century in the past. It would appear that such acceleration gives the lie to the ancient prophecies, according to which the world would come to rest in "eternity and peace," and "there should be time no longer" (*Revelation*, 10:6).

However, history strikes us with its paradox: the immutable, eternal content of culture increases with the rate of acceleration of all changes. While heading in the direction of the future, culture transforms itself into its own past. The new and the old, which accelerate at the same rate, seem to meet and neutralize each other, creating an inert zone in the midst of the acceleration, approaching a zero point in time—the kingdom of the eternal present. The world, which attains extreme speeds, comes to a standstill in mid-flight. If "rest is the essence of movement" (Lao-tse), then with more movement there abides more rest.

As the general theory of relativity has shown, in systems whose speed approaches the speed of light, time ceases to flow. Perhaps the same law is applicable to historical time, at least in the phase of its maximum acceleration. In that case, eschatology, with its anticipation of "the eternal kingdom," does not so much negate or suspend history as elevate it to a higher register of historicity—a *standstill-in-acceleration.* Eschatology is thus history moving close to the speed of light. It is the luminescence of reality itself, the disembodiment of matter into light. History can be overcome only from within history, as a paradox of its increasing intensity, as a revelation of the meaning of eternity in each moment, as the con-temporaneity of all times.

1985

Notes

1. In Russian, the term for the epoch of modernity is "the new time(s)," and for the period after World War II—"the newest time."
2. Ten or fifteen years ago there was a project to preserve the greatest achievements of human civilization for future generations by burying capsules with memorable cultural objects in the foundations of the Tribune Tower in Chicago and in the desert sands of the Arizona wilderness.
3. Soon after coming to power in 1985, Mikhail Gorbachev announced the need for Russia to engage in a socio-economic process of "acceleration."

Part III

Socialist Realism and Postmodernism

Chapter 16

Archaic Postmodernism
The Aesthetics of Andrei Sinyavsky

Alexander Genis

The prophetic character of Andrei Sinyavsky's essay on socialist realism—*What Is Socialist Realism*—has become apparent only now, after the end of Soviet civilization. Before then, the question mark that the author consciously omitted from the title rang out as an affront to the regime. Now however, when people have stopped expecting an answer to the implied question, it has become possible to introduce some poetic license into the problem and ask in the conditional perfect: *What could socialist realism have become?*

The change of mood from the indicative to the conditional endows this text, written long ago, at the end of the 1950s, with a constructive dimension relevant to the present. Indeed, because history has deprived the author of his antagonist, we are entitled to seek in Sinyavsky's text not only an aesthetic summary of a past era of Russian culture, but sign posts pointing to a new art.

What gave this essay its innovative character was not so much its content as its method of investigation. While purporting to analyze socialist realism, the essay in fact framed the whole of Soviet civilization. While performing this exercise the author of necessity stood apart from his subject, for he had to be in a position to gaze at the complete picture. Having described socialist realism as a historical phenomenon, the author identified its content and temporal and formal boundaries. In so doing, he went beyond the scope of the phenomenon itself.

Having constructed a teleological model of Soviet culture, Sinyavsky proceeded to demonstrate the lack of consistency with which the model was applied in actual practice. According to him, socialist realism was destroyed by eclecticism, which was incompatible with its classicist, canonical, and strictly hierarchical structure. However, this inference did not imply that socialist realism was inherently inauthentic. On the contrary, Sinyavsky defended it on theoretical grounds. The justification itself, however, contained its ultimate condemnation. From the vantage point of the present, we can give this paradoxical methodological conception a widely accepted name: *sots-art.*

Jumping at least one generation ahead of his time, Sinyavsky abandoned contemporary artistic trends in order to formulate the principles of a new aesthetics. Writing about the socialist-realist model of culture from the outside, he depicted it as exhausted and fully developed, that is to say dead.

Sinyavsky was the first to reveal that socialist realism's place was not in books and literary journals, nor in the garbage heap of history, but in the museum. The relationship to a theory-turned-museum-exhibit changed with it. The question of choice—of whether to accept it or to reject it, whether to fight against it or to defend it, whether to develop it or to reject it—became obsolete. Instead of the former perspective, which characterized the 1960s, Sinyavsky pointed to a new context: that of aesthetization. Having established the death of socialist realism, he could place this artistic method in the context of other methods, thereby initiating the play of dead aesthetic systems. At a time when rumors about the death of socialist realism appeared highly exaggerated, Sinyavsky was giving clear-cut recommendations on how to treat the corpse. It was not an accident that Sinyavsky used the future tense when he said: "If socialist realism really wants to rise to the level of the great world cultures and produce its *Communiad*, there is only one way to do it. It must give up realism, renounce the sorry and fruitless attempts at writing a socialist *Anna Karenina* or a socialist *Cherry Orchard*. When it abandons its effort to achieve verisimilitude, it will be able to express the grand and implausible sense of our era."[1]

This task was carried out by *sots-art*, albeit with a long delay. The theoretical *Communiad* of Sinyavsky's essay became embodied in the art of Vitaly Komar and Alexander Melamid, Vagrich Bakhchanian, Eric Bulatov, Igor Kholin, Vsevolod Nekrasov and many other artists, writers, and poets, who reconstructed and deconstructed the ideal of socialist realism, thereby bringing it to its logical conclusion.

An entire cultural epoch passed between the appearance of Sinyavsky's essay and the practice of *sots-art*. As a general rule, the authors associated with Khrushchev's "thaw," Brezhnev's "stagnation" and Gorbachev's *perestroika*, exploited the principles of *eclectic* aesthetics, about whose aridity Sinyasvky had warned. Seen from the present, all of Soviet art that appeared after Sinyavsky's essay can be evaluated as a misunderstanding if not a mistake. The grafting of "critical" realism onto socialist realism did not take. Eclecticism took revenge on art by generating an idiosyncratic hybrid of thaw literature, which had its epigones amongst all the bestseller authors of perestroika.

Digging in the virgin soil of formerly forbidden topics, Soviet literature followed the path of expansion dangerous to both its own and the general ecology. It was only natural that its confrontation with the free word would result in the bankruptcy of Soviet literature. Having lost their former authority with their readers, the idols of the thaw as well as of perestroika dropped out of sight. No new *Anna Kareninas* or *Cherry Orchards* appeared. Communism and socialist realism with a human face failed to materialize.

The very fact that Sinyavsky could predict this crisis thirty years before it occurred should cause us to pay respectful attention to his aesthetic conception. As he wrote: "We do not know which way to go, but having understood that there is nothing to be done, we begin to envisage the construction of intuitions and the making of assumptions. Perhaps we may even create something amazing."[2]

This amazing thing was his aesthetics, which he developed, polished, and refined in essays written over the next decades. It should be kept in mind that the opening salvo of this creativity was *What Is Socialist Realism.*

Andrei Sinyavsky's magnum opus is Abram Tertz.[3] Rather than investigate the biographical, social, and political circumstances that gave birth to him, I propose here to explain the Tertz phenomenon as a purely artistic necessity.

The device of attributing a work of literature to an invented author is not new. Russian writers often used a fictitious persona in order to distance the text from its author. Such a need always arises when new artistic structures and a new style and language are being introduced into literature. A programmatic example is Pushkin's *The Tales of Belkin* or Gogol's *Evenings on a Farm Near Dikanka.*

However, as distinct from Ivan Petrovich Belkin or the beekeeper Rudy Panko, Sinyavsky's Tertz is not merely a character created by the author, but an author in his own right. He is not a mask, but a person. The author's person is thus split into two, but neither of the hypostases can substitute for the other.

Both Sinyavsky and Tertz led independent lives. Indeed they were so successful at it—if "successful" is the word to use here—that the Soviet justice system could not disentangle their identities, sentencing them both to prison. At any rate, while Andrei Sinyavsky was in prison camp, Abram Tertz wrote books.

The symbiosis of Sinyavsky with Tertz renders their books both autobiographical and biographical. Each author quotes the other in brackets, as it were.

Sinyavsky needs Tertz in order to avoid straightforward utterance. By belonging to another author, the text becomes consciously other and, as such, can be considered a gigantic, book-length quotation. Sinyavsky, freeing himself from the responsibility of having to answer for his double, can thereby allow himself the space for reflection about Tertz's oeuvre and personality.

The most lucid and confessional of their jointly authored books—*Good Night*—is devoted to this complex relationship. One of the two authors is the creator of an autobiographical novel or *bildungsroman.* It tells the story of Andrei Sinyavsky, who was first a schoolboy, then a university student, a clandestine writer, a political prisoner, and who finally becomes an émigré. Each chapter reveals a particular aspect of Sinyavsky's personality—the hero and the government, the hero and love, the hero and his genealogy, and the hero and his epoch.

However, in order to read *Good Night* as a truly traditional novel, it would be necessary to cross out all the passages written by Sinyavsky's co-author, Abram Tertz; for at the center of the novel is a metamorphosis—that of the real person into a fictitious character. It is the story of the transformation of Andrei Sinyavsky into Abram Tertz. Thus the book is structured by the stylistic and compositional contrasts between the fragments of realistic prose belonging to Sinyavsky's pen, and the surreal stream of discourse created by his co-author.

In this way, Sinyavsky is writing a novel that is constantly being undone. It is in this bipartite process that the aim of Sinyavsky's aesthetics becomes clear: to frame the text so as to draw a sharp line between art and life.

It can be said that Sinyavsky approaches his own text as if it were someone else's. He is thus simultaneously its author and reader. This position, consciously taken and profoundly developed, produces a new artistic, poetic, creative, and authorial model. It is this model that Sinyavsky and Tertz explore over the course of their novels.

Sinyavsky's entire oeuvre has in essence but one object of investigation: the self-perception of literature from inside literature. Tertz's best books, such as *Strolls with Pushkin* and *In the Shadow of Gogol*, are devoted to this theme. This is equally true of Sinyavsky's major essays and monographs, including his last chronological work, *Ivan the Fool.*

Who then is the poet according to Sinyavsky? How can he be defined? Here we encounter the paradox of Sinyavsky: the poet does not exist.

Sinyavsky continuously tries to diminish the author's active role and to translate his creative activity into a passive mode. To describe the poet Sinyavsky requires the use of epithets from the semantic field of debased words: fool, thief, idler, jester, clown, holy fool (Russian *yurodivy*).

It was precisely these kinds of epithets that outraged many readers of *Strolls with Pushkin.* But the point was not in the denigrating epithets, which could appear insulting if taken out of context. What was more important was the fact that the poet's customary place in the hierarchy of culture was taken from him. Insisting that "emptiness is Pushkin's signified,"[4] Sinyavsky refused to acknowledge the poet's most important claim—that he was the author of his own verse. Indeed Sinyavsky tried, at all costs, to avoid stating straightforwardly "Pushkin wrote poems." Instead he resorted to the passive voice: the verses were written or wrote themselves.[5] Thus Sinyavsky substitutes the tension of the authorial will with the elemental freedom of verse: "Pushkin untied his hands, he let the reigns go, and he started to fly."[6] The artist merely surrenders to the muses and allows them to create through him. The poet is thus a medium in a spiritistic seance of art. All that is required of him is that he remain worthy of his ambivalent position. In Pushkin's case, for example, all that was required was that he not get out of bed. Sinyavsky is endlessly fascinated by Pushkin's lack of seriousness, his superficiality, his lackadaisical and idle lifestyle. Along with Socrates, he could say: "Idleness is the sister of freedom."

But it must be remembered that according to Sinyavsky, freedom always means freedom of the word, its independence from every and any contingent circumstance or social pressure. It is a freedom that has its source in chance, in destiny, and in contingency; in the play of the mysterious forces that transform the human being into poet.

In his monograph *Ivan the Fool,* Sinyavsky gives a detailed description of the main character's "philosophy," which bears a close resemblance to the figure of the ideal poet depicted in *Strolls with Pushkin.* Sinyavsky tries to explain why the fairy-tale's preferred protagonist is the silly and lazy man: "The fool's function is to prove—or rather not to prove, since the Fool proves nothing: rather he overturns all proof, hence to make manifest—that nothing depends on man's reason, knowledge, effort and will...." And later: "The essence of these views consists in the rejection of the ubiquitousness and omnipotence of reason, which interferes with the attainment of a higher truth. This truth (or reality) appears to man and makes itself manifest to him of its own accord, in a happy instant when consciousness as it were switches itself off and the soul emerges into an idiosyncratic state—that of receptive passivity."[7]

This state of soul, identified by Sinyavsky as "receptive passivity," and reminiscent of Taoism, according to him, explains that quality of "intuitive receptiveness" toward every idea and culture so characteristic of Pushkin.[8] The poet's universal receptivity, his infinite openness, his humility and saintliness, thus appear to be directly correlated with the cultivation of idleness and a deliberately casual, free, and easy approach to life.

This is also the source of Pushkin's pan-eroticism, an attitude that disposed the poet to embrace the world and abandon himself joyously to life. Eroticism is for Sinyavsky yet another proof of the presence of an unconscious, non-individualized, intuitive, instinctual, and even "animal" nature within the work of art. Thus the poet who immerses himself in the work of art goes "under" and sheds his human face. The guarantee of poetic success is the renunciation of the self in favor of the text. This proposition is formulated by Sinyavsky in *Good Night* as follows:

> When one writes one can't think. One needs to switch oneself off. When one writes, one loses oneself, one is floating and, above all, one forgets oneself and lives without thinking about anything. Finally, one no longer exists, one dies.... One has disappeared into the text.[9]

All of Sinyavsky's favorite literary figures accomplish this process of "disappearing into the text": Pushkin, Gogol, Rozanov, and the nameless story-tellers who dissolve in the anonymous universe of folklore. This is the price all of them have had to pay for the metamorphosis of poet into text. Pushkin accomplished it too, managing to "overcome his base human nature and the split between man and genius."[10]

The theme of the double in the above-defined sense—i.e., that of the author and his double—is central to Sinyavsky's work. Not only does it figure prominently in his early prose, such as *Pkhents*, but receives even more extensive treatment in his later works. By separating the man from the poet, namely Sinyavsky from Tertz, Sinyavsky managed to invert traditional literary structures and to create a special literary space for Tertz. Sinyavsky is continually engaged in the destruction of the canonical forms of the novel, short story, and literary analysis in general. He does this by introducing elements of self-reflexivity and authorial self-consciousness into traditional forms. All his works can be summed up by the following sentence in *Good Night:* "This will be a book about how this book was written. A book about a book."[11]

Such deliberate self-reflexivity destroys the work of art's essential prerequisite: its self-evidently conventional character. Sinyavsky is not writing novels but drafts of novels. He turns the pyramid upside down by transforming the book into a manuscript and moving it backwards to the stage of the sketch, the jotting, the variant. It is therefore not by accident that his most successful works have the structure of diary entries or letters from the labor camp.

With a superficial glance it may appear that Sinyavsky is relinquishing strict formal discipline in favor of the authorial person(a). That is, the intimate and private nature of the text appears to blur the generic boundaries of his texts. However, the exact opposite actually takes place: the authorial person(a) surrenders to the power of the genre, which should simply be called "the book."

Sinyavsky's concept of the ideal book, as his image of the ideal poet, is bound up with the "philosophy of the fool" and the principle of inactivity. The ideal book is thus a book of total indeterminacy, a "book that goes backwards and forwards, advances and retreats, approaches the reader only to run away from him, all the while flowing like a river."[12] Such a book becomes a stream of pure literature or literariness, which the writer understands in the sense of a collection of words endowed with a magical and mysterious unity. Following the author, the reader plunges into this river of words and abandons him- or herself to its powerful current, a current that will wash both reader and author up wherever it chooses. This form of reading, which constitutes a form of co-authorship, involves an act of renunciation of the self in favor of not the author of the book, but the book, art, or the word itself.

Sinyavsky deprives his texts of structure so as to leave them more room for air, more space for chaos, chance, unpredictability. He wants the book to return to its primeval form, which is that of the scroll. For, as he says in *Good Night,* the scroll had "continuity and extensive development, unintentionally resembling the flow of a river."[13] This method of riverlike, flowing text construction is reminiscent of folklore, which always served as his point of "aesthetic orientation."[14] What fascinated him most about the folktale, the anecdote, and the criminal song—all of which he has written about—was that self-sufficiency of a literary work that lacked an author; for the work of folk art, so to speak, narrates itself.

Word weaving, the play of self-sufficient forms, ritual dance, ornamental drawing, and the smooth flow of the text: these are the prototypes of Sinyavsky's prose. His aesthetic universe is constructed out of these prototypes. This is not to say that in this universe, art takes primacy over life. Rather, art and life are not correlated with one another—as entities they cannot be compared, for they are incongruous. It would be more correct to say that in Sinyavsky's cosmogony, art is a source of life. It is that primary impulse of energy that generates the world.

Art is not a teleology for Sinyavsky. It is a reverse genesis, a return to the source. Art is not the construction of something new but a reconstruction of something old. The meaning of art is in "remembering—and recognizing—the world through its image residing in a distant past and flickering as image in memory."[15] Viewed from this perspective, questions of traditional aesthetics, such as the relationship of form and content, or the problem of "art for art's sake," become meaningless. According to Sinyavsky, such questions are tautologies: since form is content, art cannot be anything else but art. Everything is mere obstruction on the path leading from the past to the present, shoals in the river into which the writer plunges his reader.

Sinyavsky's world literally opens with the Gospel statement: "In the beginning was the word." And this word has a calling: not to write art but to remember it.

When we try to correlate Sinyavsky's aesthetic views with the contemporary literary process, we discover that contemporary Russian literature is forging ahead along the very path that Abram Tertz mapped for it. Although the word "postmodernism" was not in use at the time Tertz was writing, it was he—his writing—that prepared the ground for Russian postmodernism.

Sinyavsky thus stands at the source of Russian postmodernism. It was he who first rejected the modernist conception of socialist realism. He questioned the modernist project of connecting literature to life and of demanding the reconstruction of the world according to a literary model. Instead of the world, Sinyavsky reconstructed himself. He showed the path of transformation from man into writer by setting a personal example. Having placed himself inside the text, he established a seductive precedent for other modes of conquering artistic reality. Abram Tertz is a man-quotation and, as such, a popular model for postmodern Russian writers. The man-quotation is almost a writer who is not a writer. For Sinyavsky, the text is in principle always someone else's text.

Nonetheless, the key point about Sinyavsky's aesthetics is not its similarity to contemporary theories of postmodernism: it is his creation of a new perceptual model for art.

Sinyavsky led an "archaic" rebellion against the present. If postmodernism's symbol of faith is the quotation mark and the quotation, he can be said to have quoted not the content and form of past works of art, but the very texture and ground of literature. He leads the reader against the flow of the river, back toward its source. His aesthetic opposition to the neo-Slavophiles[16]—including the ultranationalistic literary magazines "Nash sovremennik" and "Molodaya gvardia"—can also be explained by this "archaic" rebellion. The neo-Slavophiles are conservatives who stylize the past in an attempt to return to some idealized historical epoch, distilled through an ennobling literary imagination. Sinyavsky, on the other hand, sharply turns the corner toward the very source of art, to its primeval state located not in history or temporality, but in eternity.

What characterizes Sinyavsky's "archaic postmodernism" is a backwards movement, a never-ending attempt to eliminate the structures of art and to uncover the unique and universal *arch*-text, which the writer endeavors to recover from memory in order to merge with and become one with it. On this journey of recovery and remembrance of the forgotten, the artist confronts that residue in the work of art that is called the mystery of art. This residue represents the limits of interpretation. Having reached this limit, both reader and writer have to resign themselves to this mysterious residue, which Sinyavsky calls "a magic or incantatory verbal formula" that is passed on from generation to generation, "as the greatest mystery and the holiest of holies."[17] While we cannot understand these ruins, we cannot at the same time help being struck by their grandeur. "Archaic postmodernism" is an archeological or paleontological artistic method. It is the reconstruction of a whole on the evidence of the fragments that have survived down to our times.

This activity of reconstructing the primal wholeness of art purifies it of all those alien elements that time has added to it. Logic, psychology, society, and utility—all of these categories are, according to Sinyavsky, alien to art. Like an alchemist, the artist is engaged in producing an unalloyed, pure art. This pure art has a magical quality: it is capable of obliterating the boundaries between the material and the spiritual worlds, between word and deed. According to Sinyavsky, the "Word has its own materiality. The Word is itself an object.... The magical incantation is naming—knowing the exact name, thanks to which the object comes into being."[18]

The poet, who is a magician, since "a magic or conjuring power is at the root of all creativity,"[19] is the one who finds the proper names for things. When he succeeds in doing this, he calls things up from non-being. Sinyavsky himself was able—as a result of writing or naming—to evoke his own destiny, which he described in detail, including his arrest before it actually took place in life. There is nothing strange in this, since art precedes life and is older than life. Indeed, "[w]e are destroyed not by art but by the connection of art to life."[20]

In conclusion, we can say that what is most peculiar to Sinyavsky's aesthetics is the definitive disconnection of art from progress. By turning art around to face the past, Sinyavsky ceases to offer it the vista of a future utopia of reason. Instead he confronts it with that "divine truth, which does not lie near to or alongside art in the form of a real-life milieu, but rather lies on the other side of art, in the past, at the very source of the artistic image."[21]

Notes

1. Abram Tertz, *Chto takoe sotsialisticheskii realism,* in *The Fantastic World of Abram Tertz* (London, 1967), p. 444. English translation by George Dennis, *On Socialist Realism* (New York, 1960).
2. Ibid., p. 446.
3. This is the name under which Sinyavsky signed several of his works, including *What Is Socialist Realism.*
4. Abram Tertz, *Progulki s Pushkinym* (London, 1975), p. 64. English translation by C. Nepomnyashchy and S. Yastremski, *Strolls with Pushkin* (New Haven, Conn., 1993).
5. Translator's note: in Russian, the passive voice *pisalis'* covers both actions.
6. Abram Tertz, *Progulki s Pushkinym,* p. 84.
7. Andrei Sinyavsky, *Ivan-durak* (Paris, 1991), p. 39.
8. See Abram Tertz, *Progulki s Pushkinym* [Strolls with Pushkin], p. 9.
9. Abram Tertz, *Spokoinoi nochi* [Good Night] (Paris, 1984), p. 263. English translation by R. Lourie, *Goodnight!* (New York, 1989).
10. See Abram Tertz, *Progulki s Pushkinym,* p. 140.
11. Abram Tertz, *Spokoinoi nochi,* p. 86.
12. Abram Tertz, *Golos iz khora* (London, 1973), p. 7. English translation by K. Fitz-Lyon and M. Hayward, *A Voice from the Chorus* (New Haven, Conn., 1995).
13. Abram Tertz, *Spokoinoi nochi,* p. 373.
14. A. Sinyavsky, *Ivan-durak,* p. 8.
15. Abram Tertz, *Progulki s Pushkinym,* p. 103.
16. A contemporary movement in the arts and thought that calls for a return to an idealized, purely "Slavic" way of life and culture.
17. A. Sinyavsky, *Ivan-durak,* p. 71.
18. Ibid., p. 150.
19. Ibid., p. 58.
20. Abram Tertz, *Spokoinoi noch,* p. 347.
21. A. Sinyavsky, *Ivan-durak,* p. 71.

Chapter 17

POSTMODERNISM AND *SOTS-REALISM*

From Andrei Sinyavsky to Vladimir Sorokin

Alexander Genis

1.

The development of contemporary Russian literature can be likened to a classic love triangle, comprised of the avant-garde, socialist realism, and postmodernism. At the same time, the relationship between the postmodernists and the previous generation of Russian writers is reminiscent of the nineteenth-century struggle between "fathers" and "sons." A striking example of the current tension was the speech delivered by Alexander Solzhenitsyn, in the winter of 1993, on the occasion of his being awarded the honorary medal of the National Arts Club in New York. In this speech, Solzhenitsyn virulently attacked the postmodernists and linked them directly to the avant-garde. According to him, Russian postmodernism represents a contemporary variant of the old anti-cultural phenomenon that rejected all cultural traditions and values. The earlier version of this scourge was called futurism: the contemporary version is postmodernism.[1]

Another example of this same struggle is an article written by yet another leading figure of the 1960s, Vasily Aksyonov. In an essay entitled "Dystrophy of the Thick Journals and the In(de)finite Space of the Thin Ones," Aksyonov expounds a line of thought similar to Solzhenitsyn's, namely that postmodernism is a continuation of modernism. Unlike Solzhenitsyn, however, Aksyonov has a positive attitude toward the avant-garde. Indeed, for him, the avant-garde is synonymous with a renaissance in literature. The aim of this avant-garde—of which he considers the Russian literature of the 1960s a part—was to "liven up" literature, as Aksyonov puts it, or to "defamiliarize" it, as Shklovsky would have put it.[2]

Aksyonov and Solzhenitsyn come to a similar conclusion in their articles. Both see contemporary Russian literature as in a transitional state and postmodernism as a futile attempt to fill the gap. Solzhenitsyn cherishes the hope that Russian literature will return to the tradition interrupted by the avant-garde. Aksyonov, on the other hand, hopes for a rebirth of the avant-garde "carnival and jazz of the 1960s."[3]

The postmodernists themselves, curiously enough, see no great discrepancy between the views of these two *maîtres* of the 1960s. As the young prose writer, Igor Irkevich, writes:

> Solzhenitsyn and Aksyonov, despite their apparent esthetic differences, are in fact remarkably similar in their poetics. This is because communism looms large in the poetics of both writers. Everything that is anticommunist is evaluated as good, whether it be jazz, the church, sexual and alcoholic neurasthenia, the populist spirit, rebellion in the gulags.... Such a poetics does not allow for the individual "I." Dialogue is carried on solely in the name of the masses or of entire generations.[4]

Irkevich's statement demonstrates a symptomatic distancing of the "sons" from the "fathers." While the older generation remains tied to the old aesthetic, the younger generation has freed itself from the eschatological anticipations that communism imposed on both Soviet and anti-Soviet literature. For the same reason, the writers of a-Soviet literature (a term coined by Viktor Erofeev[5]) refuse to subscribe to avant-garde poetics. As the Russian philosopher and postmodern theoretician Boris Groys sees it, the new art finds it impossible simply to resume the evolution of the violently interrupted Russian avant-garde. For Igor Smirnov, this return is impossible because of the fundamental difference in the way the two movements approach being: "The avant-garde is an ontology without semantics, while postmodernism is a semantics without ontology."[6] This definition is in turn inverted by the critic Viacheslav Kuritsyn, who considers the avant-garde work of art, such as Malevich's black square, to be "a cold being of signs, indifferent to a castrated content."[7] Kuritsyn's inversion does not bring the two poetics into greater proximity. This opposition between the avant-garde and postmodernism that emerges from Kuritsyn's conception is also the foundation of Mikhail Epstein's model, according to which the avant-garde represents the art of an era that strove to reveal "true reality." On the other hand, postmodernism, which constructs phenomena of hyper-realism or simulacra, which are copies without originals, is itself a producer of reality.[8] As final proof of the distance between the two movements there is the phenomenon of *sots-art,* created by Vitaly Komar and Alexander Melamid, whose works are programmatically oriented against the avant-garde aesthetics.

The relationship between postmodernism and the avant-garde depends, to some extent, on the perspective of the spectator, that is, whether the phenomenon is viewed from inside or outside the cultural context. The theoreticians and practitioners of postmodernism in Russia refuse to acknowledge the genetic link to the historic avant-garde that the writers who came of age in the 1960s have tried to impose on them. This does not mean that a dialogue between postmodernism and the avant-garde is inappropriate; in order to carry on such a dialogue, the Russian postmodernists prefer to turn to the third member of the triangle, namely to socialist realism.

2.

In order to properly evaluate the relationship of Russian postmodernism both to the avant-garde and to socialist realism, it will be necessary to transpose the debate into the context of Western aesthetics. This is because postmodern discourse became the order of the day in the West long before it was articulated in Soviet culture, which was preoccupied with its own specific problems. In the West, postmodernism is usually discussed in terms of a crisis of modernism. This crisis is usually associated with the 1960s. Octavio Paz, whom Habermas called the last "partisan of modernism," maintained: "The avant-garde of the year 1967 is mimicking the acts and gestures of the avant-garde of 1917. We are witnessing the end of the art of Modernism."[9]

In an article devoted to the relationship of postmodernism to the avant-garde, Andreas Huyssen also connects the birth of postmodernism to the "eruption of the 1960s," which represents an era capable of neither constructing a functional social model nor a productive counter-culture. After the student protests of May 1968, the avant-garde, which had lost its "feel for the future, came to an end.[10] Having said this, it should be noted that Western postmodernists never strove for a radical break with the avant-garde tradition. As Jean-François Lyotard, one of the fathers of postmodern philosophy, wrote, "Post-modernism was already covertly contained in Modernism."[11]

Nonetheless, in order for postmodern aesthetics to take its rightful place, a devaluation of the avant-garde had to take place. Again, according to Huyssman, "taking on board the precious heritage, postmodernism simultaneously deprived the avant-garde of its most dangerous traits—its aspirations toward universality and normativeness."[12] As a result, postmodernism took on the form of a meek avant-garde, freed of the latter's utopian ambitions and displaying a tendency toward compromise.

Thanks to this quality of postmodernism, a truce was reached in the relentless struggle between high art and popular culture. Suddenly there was a hope that this tragic rift, which appeared to be a hallmark of mass culture, could be overcome. The history of Western postmodernism begins with a disillusionment with abstract expressionism and the appearance of Andy Warhol and pop art.

It should be pointed out that this aspect of the Western cultural situation, namely the "attempt at a truce," has been ignored by both the apologists and detractors of Russian postmodernism. In all likelihood, this is an expression of an aristocratic conception of culture, which is detached from the marketplace, unaccustomed to paying attention to the voice of the masses or taking into account its views. It is telling on this score that all the Russian theoreticians of postmodernism so far mentioned are either indifferent to mass culture or openly hostile to it.

Postmodern aesthetics owes much to the American literary critic Leslie Fiedler and his manifestolike piece, "Cross the Borders—Close the Gap." This article, which was published in *Playboy* magazine in 1969, offered an entire postmodern program. Fiedler begins his article by announcing the death of high modernism, with its focus on recherché art accessible only to an elite public: "The age of Proust, Mann and Joyce is over, and this should be openly stated.... Because no one has even the hope of being reborn unless he knows first that he is dead." For the resurrection to take place, Fiedler believes it necessary for culture to fill in the gap between critics and readers and to obliterate the boundary between art and mass culture. This gap will be overcome by a literature that learns to make use of the low genres of popular art in the search for a new aesthetics of "entertainment."

Here, at the root of postmodernism, is the recycled aesthetics of the Russian formalists, with Shklovsky's theses on low genres clearly echoed in Fiedler's manifesto.[13]

Analyzing the literary scene at the end of the 1960s, Fiedler with uncanny foresight pointed to those genres with the greatest productive potential. The first he mentions is the Western, with Ken Kesey's *One Flew Over the Cuckoo's Nest* as an example. To this we can add the "cowboys-and-Indians" Western, such as the Oscar-winning *Dances with Wolves.* Next he turns to science fiction, using Kurt Vonnegut as an example. His final genre is the erotic, of which *Lolita* is Fiedler's model. In a special aside he even states that Nabokov consciously abandoned the poetics of high modernism for the sake of *Lolita.*

Fiedler regards pop culture as innately infantile and religious, based on fairy-tale-like miracles and magical transformations. This is why postmodernism finds with in it the source of a new mythology. Pop art thus becomes a form of the folkloric universe, since "the 'folk songs' of an electronic age are made not in rural loneliness or in sylvan retreats, but in high-tech studios by boys singing into the sensitive ear of machines."[14]

The postmodern writer is thus a "double agent," Fiedler concludes. His literary product is polyphonic, predestined for both connoisseurs and an uncritical mass readership.

The presumption of the double coding of a postmodern work of art, which embodies a symbiosis of high and low art, has found its application in the arts of the 1980s in various aesthetic forms. Among the phenomena to be included here is the burgeoning of music television (MTV), which combines the most daring formal experiments of avant-garde cinema with pop and rock music. Another example of the symbiosis of high and low art is Umberto Eco's bestseller *The Name of the Rose,* which first brought intellectual "semiotic prose" to a mass reading public. Analogous phenomena can be observed in painting, in the cinema, and even in the "high" art of ballet with the appearance of Sally Banes' emblematic book *Terpsichore in Sneakers: Postmodern Dance.*[15]

Given the very important role of architecture in postmodern aesthetics, it is apt to quote the prominent critic, Charles Jencks, who wrote that the avant-garde architecture of the so-called international style suffered from elitism. This was overcome by postmodernism, "not by means of a simplification, but by means of extending the language of architecture in the direction of assimilating and absorbing the local peculiarities of a place, of tradition and of the commercial slang of the streets. Hence the double coding of architecture, which addresses both the elite and the man in the street."[16]

As early as 1962, Stanislaw Lem spoke about such a double coding. Lem, who is not only a first-rate writer, but also an original theoretician, offers an analysis of Nabokov's *Lolita* in which he declares that contemporary literature has a special frontier that it must conquer. In Nabokov's case, according to Lem, "this frontier is without clear definition, located somewhere between the thriller and psychological drama. Such border areas can be found more easily by straddling the line between a psychopathological study and the detective novel, between science fiction and literature, or between mass and elite culture … [N]o matter how crazy such a cross-breeding of genres so incongruous may seem[…] I would nevertheless venture to bet on such hybrids."[17]

3.

The task of defining the situation of contemporary Russian literature can be facilitated by borrowing a concept from Western aesthetics that we have just encountered in our brief overview. The borrowed formula is the follows:

postmodernism = avant-garde + pop culture

It will be shown that this formula provides a fitting description for Russian literature of the Soviet and post-Soviet cultural period, although certain peculiarities of that culture may require us to slightly modify the formula.

Frederick Jameson sees the emergence of postmodernism in terms of a canonization of the avant-garde, which was already complete in the West by the 1960s. As soon as the erstwhile revolutionary and innovative art found itself in museums and in academies, the art of such creators was promoted to the status of "classics" thereby becoming indistinguishable from the classics that they, in their own day, had tried to overthrow. [18]

This process of the avant-garde's "museumification"—to use Boris Groys' term—has still not been completed in Russia. Constant official intervention in the natural evolutionary process of twentieth-century Russian culture meant the creation of an extremely chaotic situation. Thus while Mayakovsky's poetry was read in schools, the major works of Victor Shklovsky were only republished in 1990. The same absurd situation pertained to the embrace of Western culture. While Kafka became accessible in the 1960s, the Russian translation of *Ulysses* was delayed another quarter of a century. As a result, Russian culture was obliged to master the unknown or forgotten avant-garde while at the same time having to oppose and reject it.

The generation of the 1960s did not have to face this problem. They either accepted the avant-garde wholesale or rejected it unconditionally. The postmodernists, however, elaborated a more nuanced position toward the avant-garde: before making use of it, they deconstructed it. In fact, they divided the avant-garde into form and content. The theurgical aspirations of avant-garde art were cast aside, but avant-garde forms—such as textual devices—were retained. The postmodernists put into practice Shklovsky's dictum about studying "the methods of old literature, not its themes."[19] Also useful for them was the definition of "content as one of the manifestations of form," and the principle, mentioned earlier, that states that "new forms in art [are created] by way of the canonization of the forms of popular culture."[20] The allusion to the fundamental double coding of postmodern art is also to be found in Shklovsky's works. This is contained in his "concept of 'irony' not as 'ridicule,' but as a device for the simultaneous reception of diverse speech phenomena, or as the simultaneous reference of the same speech phenomenon to two different semantic sets."[21]

The question of how Russian postmodernism absorbed the avant-garde has now been answered. What remains open to question is how the second term of the equation—namely mass or popular culture—was absorbed.

The most appropriate way to deal with this question is by way of a substitution. If we substitute the term *sots-realism* with the term "popular culture," appropriate to Western societies, we obtain the correct transformation of the proposed equation, which yields a formula appropriate to Soviet and post-Soviet society.

In order to make such a substitution possible, Russian postmodernism had to process *sots-realism* in the same way that Western postmodernism had processed popular culture. In the first instance this involved a re-evaluation of the basic concepts of *sots-realism*—Shklovsky's injunction of "studying the method and not the theme" was followed.

The process of alienation of form from content began in the late 1950s, with the appearance of Sinyavsky's article *What Is Socialist Realism.*[22] This seminal text, which could be considered the first manifesto of Russian postmodernism, appeared at the same time as Western theoretical works on the subject. But neither Soviet nor dissident

Soviet culture paid due attention to this problematic, as the inertia of *sots-realism* continues to exert pressure on Russian literature, even if now only unconsciously.

The process of alienation of form from content in the literature of the 1960s was not fully registered for another reason. Although the themes of Russian literature changed in the 1960s, its method remained the same. This question has been explicitly posed by Ivan Kavelin (Mikhail Berg) in his article "The Name of Non-Freedom" [Imia nesvobody]. Here the author asserts that "Soviet man is a child," while "Soviet life is the life of children. Not realizing that they are children, they believe they are just like grown-ups because they do not know how grown-ups differ from them." Kavelin concludes, correctly, that "Soviet literature is children's literature."

As a children's literature, Soviet literature's dominant theme in the 1950s and 1960s was "enlightenment" or "education." This kind of literature expressed but one typology of the hero: he is "honest in his own way, but has not yet thought things through or in a profound manner. Finding himself in a novel existential situation, he sees for the first time things he had ignored until then. Afterwards, having been enlightened, nothing more happens. The author has no idea what to do with an enlightened hero. Having reached adulthood, the hero loses his attractiveness. This is because the author is interested only in the crucial moment of the hero's loss of his socio-ideological innocence." This is the structure of the plot [*sujet*] of "all the works of Soviet literature without exception," according to Kavelin. It does not matter who the author or what the subject is—whether "Ehrenburg and his *Thaw,* Kazakevich's *Star,* Nekrasov's *In the Trenches of Stalingrad,* even Solzhenitsyn in *Ivan Denisovich* and *The Cancer Ward.*"[23]

It is revealing that the generation of Russian writers and artists of the 1960s, who were chronologically close to *sots-realism,* did not perceive *sots-realism* as an aesthetic challenge. Solzhenitsyn, for instance, considered it to be beyond the boundaries of art. For him, *sots-realism* as a cultural phenomenon never in fact existed.[24]

Solzhenitsyn's verdict on socialist realism is diametrically opposed to the position taken by the Western Slavist Katerina Clark, author of the well-known monograph on socialist realism, *The Soviet Novel: History as Ritual.* In the preface to her book, Clark speaks about the difficulties experienced by the Western scholar trying to come to terms with the concept of socialist realism: "It is easy for us to compare works of Melville, Flaubert and Dickens because their novels perform a fairly homogeneous esthetic function in the literary systems of America, France and England.... The Soviet novel performs a totally different function ... and this difference has given rise to a different kind of text." Next, Clark formulates three methodological approaches to the study of socialist realism.

First, the socialist-realist novel was conceived as a variant of mass literature, which is why it is exhaustively formalized. As such, "it thus lends itself to a comparison with other varieties of popular formulaic literature, such as detective stories and serial novels."

Second, the strong didactic tendency of socialist realism allows it to be compared with medieval culture, and in particular the hagiographic canon.

Third, the socialist-realist novel has served as "the official repository of state myths," which allows the application to socialist realism of analytical methods reserved for the analysis of mythological structures.[25]

These above-mentioned approaches have since been put into practice by the Russian postmodernists. Perceived in this manner, socialist realism became for them a source of literary devices and clichés. Its firm and exhaustively formalized canon allowed its structures to be taken as given facts. Finally, its essentially anonymous folkloric universe allowed it to become the source of rich mythological material.

In Russian postmodern culture, socialist realism has acquired the same function that popular culture once held for Western postmodernism, as pointed out by Leslie Fiedler. If his formula of Western postmodern aesthetics is transposed onto Russian aesthetics, then the new version of the formula is:

Russian postmodernism = avant-garde + *sots-realism*

4.

The productivity of the above model can be verified through the example of the most typical genre of Soviet literature—the production or shock-worker novel. Katerina Clark notes that the main conflict in the *sots-realist* metasubject is "between the forces of 'spontaneity' and the forces of 'consciousness.'"[26] This conflict is essentially a variant of the classic nature/culture dichotomy of Western literature. In the Soviet version of this dichotomy, communism plays the role of culture. Its hero is the vanquisher of chaos, the subduer of chthonic forces, the organizer of amorphous matter. This amorphous matter is the locus of all the heroes of the novel who are still ideologically "unconscious." The subject matter of the book is constituted by the organizational process—the process of transformation of "raw" material into a finished product, a finished object. All socialist-realist texts have this structure and are in effect production novels.

However, this genre was in fact inherited from the avant-garde, for which the mechanical object was of central aesthetic concern. Much of the avant-garde poetics was based on ideas of functionalism, simplicity, unity, and integrality. That is why it sought its ideal, not in the world of biological nature, but in the sphere of mechanical life.

The avant-garde utopia is created for identically operating, perfectly substitutable, machinelike people. In Khlebnikov's *The Swan Song of the Future* (Lebediia Budushchego), "all the children were reading the same book at once."[27] His "street-creators" pay particular attention to the creation of cities consisting of "tents—all of the self-same design,"[28] into which standardized, glass-box apartments will be fitted. The journey in this novel is not undertaken by a man, but by a glass container with a man inside. This container is loaded onto a train and then onto a ship. Khlebnikov's fascination with glass is characteristic of the avant-garde, and is shared by Sergei Eisenstein. The latter, while on a trip to the United States, conceived of making a film that would be set in a glass skyscraper. He even carried out negotiations with a glass factory in Pittsburgh about the construction of the set.[29] The transparent wall material would render human life completely accessible to the gaze and thus "purify" it from biology. Khlebnikov's glass city is as beautiful as a clock without its housing.

Avant-garde cinema is also replete with such poetization of industry. In Dziga Vertov's films, for instance, the camera focuses admiringly on the uniform mechanical movements of the hand of a female telephonist, or the fingers of female workers packing cigarettes, or the pumping legs of athletes. Human being is beautiful only in motion and only when emulating a machine. For the avant-garde, the machine is a metaphor for human being.

Thus the production novel of the avant-garde could have become the new Divine Comedy, if it were not for the *anti*-avant-garde paradigm created by socialist realism that gave the production novel a new turn, as has been convincingly demonstrated by Vladimir Papernyi.[30] Rather than machine as metaphor for human being, human being became a metaphor for the machine. The subject matter of this restructured anti-avant-garde novel was constituted by the humanization of technology and its transposition into private life. The workshop thus became a continuation of domestic life, the brigade an extension of the family, production relationships a variant of love relationships. It is no accident that the shock-worker is a winner not only in socialist but also in sexual competition.

Although such a production novel is replete with technical information (on the basis of which Clark compared it to the novels of Arthur Hailey), here the countless technological descriptions serve metonymy alone. The production process represents a higher ontological reality—the victory over the enemy, the fulfillment of the production plan, the construction of communism. Thus each finely etched *realium* of the text, every fuse, every meter of piping, has a double coding, a "lower" and a "higher" one: it is at the same time a real object and a step in the direction of the final goal.

The persistence of such a "metaphysical" model of the production novel was so great that it proved a suitable vehicle for any kind of ideological content, from Ehrenburg's *Thaw* to Dudintsev's *Not By Bread Alone,* as well as numerous novels of later vintage. One of the most recent—and profoundly postmodern—production novels is Vladimir Sorokin's *Four Stout Hearts.* In this novel, Sorokin deconstructs the opposition between Man and Machine, which is fundamental to the production novel genre. In so doing, he demonstrates the falsity of both the avant-garde and the socialist realist interpretations of the genre. In Sorokin's universe there is no difference whatsoever between animate and inanimate matter. The plot of his novel features intensive production processes involving objects that could be either human or mechanical. The text can therefore be interpreted as sadistic if read as populated by living beings, or comical if the characters are interpreted as inanimate. Sorokin's characters are thus "non-machines" and "non-people."

In deconstructing the categories of animate/inanimate, Sorokin challenges our preconceived conceptions of the ontological status of people and machines. By extension, he also subverts the avant-garde notion of the perfect machine, as well as its antithesis: the vulnerable human being.

Moreover, Sorokin's deconstructive method also cancels out the socialist-realist opposition between the productive process as signifier and the result of that process—communism—as signified. In fact, Sorokin's text never gains access to the signified, which for socialist realism is the justification for the text. Sorokin's text instead brims with feverish but unmotivated activity. Seemingly, the characters' actions are devoid of sense or cause, positioned as they are at the border between sense and non-sense. Thus Sorokin's text follows the convention, originating in European modernism, of writing at the limit, a convention that includes the tradition of the *absurd* as well as the whole heritage of postmodernism.

Sorokin's deconstructive method simultaneously preserves and destroys the socialist-realist structure of the production novel. At the same time *Four Stout Hearts* satisfies the criterion of "double coding": the novel can be read as a metaphysical parody of man and a semiotic comedy of masks. The book can also be read as a "black" novel. It could—if a prediction is allowed—be transformed into a film script and produced as a block-buster thriller.

Sorokin's experiment is the most graphic, if not the only, example of the postmodern deconstructive strategy. A most original reappropriation of socialist-realist themes is to be found in the prose works of the young writer Viktor Pelevin. He is the topic of the following chapter.

Notes

1. Alexander Solzhenitsyn, "The Relentless Cult of Novelty and How It Wrecked the Century," *The New York Times Book Review,* February 7, 1993. See also the Russian original in *Novy mir* 4 (1993).
2. Valery Aksyonov, "Dystrophy of the 'Thick' and *Bespredel* of the 'Thin,'" *World Literature Today* (Winter, 1993), p. 20. From here on, the terms "avant-garde" and "modernism" will be used interchangeably since both are anti-traditionalist to the same degree.
3. Ibid., p. 23.
4. Igor Irkevich, "Literatura, svoboda, estetika, and Other Interesting Things" [Literature, Freedom, Aesthetics, and Other Interesting Things] *Ogonek, 2* January 1993.
5. Viktor Erofeev, "Russkie tsvety zla" [Russian *fleurs du mal*] *Panorama,* 632, 19–25 May 1993.
6. Igor Smirnov, *Bytie i tvorchestvo* [Being and Art] (Marburg, 1990), p. 28.
7. Vyacheslav Kuritsyn, *Kniga o postmodernizme* [A Book About Postmodernism] (Ekaterinburg, 1992), p. 25.
8. Mikhail Epstein, "The Origins and Meaning of Russian Postmodernism" in *After the Future: The Paradoxes of Postmodernism and Contemporary Russian Culture* (Amherst, Mass., 1995), pp. 188-212.
9. Quoted in Jurgen Habermas, "Modernism—An Unfinished Product," *Voprosy filosofii* 2 (1993): 42. This text is a speech given by Habermas in 1980 on the occasion of his being awarded an honorary prize named after Adorno. Published in *Wege aus der Moderne: Schlusseltexte der Postmoderne-Diskussion.* H. von W. Welsch (Weinheim, 1988), pp. 177–192.
10. Andreas Huyssen, "The Search for Tradition: Avant-Garde and Postmodernism in the 1970s," in *Postmodernism,* ed. T. Doherty (New York, 1993), p. 225.
11. J. F. Lyotard, *The Postmodern Condition: A Report on Knowledge,* trans. G. Bennington and B. Massumi (Manchester, 1984).
12. Andreas Huyssen, "The Search for Tradition ...," p. 231.
13. According to Shklovsky, high culture grows from low culture. For example, Pushkin's work came out of the (low) album poetry of his time; Chekhov's mature prose grew out of his own early humorous sketches, signed by his alter ego Chekhonte; Blok's poems grew out of urban folk songs, etc.
14. Leslie Fiedler, "Cross the Border—Close the Gap," in *The Collected Essays of Leslie Fiedler,* vol. 2 (New York, 1971), pp. 461–485.

15. Sally Banes, *Terpsichore in Sneakers: Postmodern Dance* (Wesleyan, Conn., 1987).
16. Charles Jencks, *The Language of Postmodern Architecture* (Moscow, 1985 [London, 1977]), p. 12.
17. Stanislaw Lem, "Lolita, or Stavrogin and Beatrice," *Literaturnoe obozrenie* 9 (1991): 85.
18. Frederick Jameson, "Postmodernism, or The Cultural Logic of Late Capitalism," *New Left Review* 146 (1984): 56.
19. Victor Shklovsky, *Gamburgskii schet* [The Hamburg Rating] (Moscow, 1990), p. 371.
20. Victor Shklovsky, *Sentimental'noe puteshestvie* [Sentimental Journey] (Moscow, 1990), p. 235.
21. Ibid., p. 242.
22. Abram Tertz, "Chto takoe sotsialisticheskii realizm," in *Fantasticheskii mir Abrama Tertsa* (London, 1967).
23. Ivan Kavelin, "Imia nesvobody" [The Name of Non-Freedom], *Vestnik novoi literatury* 1 (Moscow, 1990): 176–196.
24. Alexander Solzhenitsyn, "The Relentless Cult of Novelty and How It Wrecked the Century," *The New York Times Book Review,* February 7, 1993. See also the Russian original in *Novy mir* 4 (1993).
25. Katerina Clark, *The Soviet Novel: History as Ritual.*, 2d ed. (Chicago and London, 1985), pp. xi–xiii.
26. Ibid., p. 16.
27. Velimir Khlebnikov, *Sobranie proizvedenii v piati tomakh* [Collected Works in Five Volumes], vol. 4 (Leningrad, 1930), p. 289.
28. Velimir Khlebnikov, *Sobranie sochinenii,* p. 280.
29. N. Kleiman, "Neosushchestvlennye zamysly Eisensteina" [Eisenstein's Unrealized Projects], *Iskusstvo kino* 6 (1992): 11.
30. See Vladimir Paperny, *Kul'tura 'Dva'* [Culture 'Two'] (Ann-Arbor, Mich., 1985).

Chapter 18

BORDERS AND METAMORPHOSES

Viktor Pelevin in the Context of Post-Soviet Literature

Alexander Genis

Perhaps the most remarkable thing about post-Soviet literature is that it has yet to find a name for itself. The memory of the immediate past has allowed this literature to maintain a continuity with the preceding period—a period with which it apparently does not want to break. Moving neither forward nor back, it seems to be standing in place, poised on the edge of the abyss of the future.

The most obvious, if not the only reason for this state of affairs, is the unexpectedly easy fall of the Soviet regime. Its stability proved illusory; nonetheless, its ghosts have endured. The regime's power over reality has become manifest only after the death of the regime itself. Under the spell of these necroeffects, contemporary culture is striving to assimilate the mechanisms with which the regime created—and much more successfully than was previously thought—its own reality. The question is how to utilize this experience in a world that is becoming more and more conscious of its own "constructed" or virtual nature. This explains why the traditional polemic between the generations in Russian literature today quite often takes on the form of a struggle over the Soviet heritage. A divide has already been established: the "fathers" of the 1960s are the heirs to the rational side of the Soviet past, their "sons" to the irrational. Or to put it colloquially, the former embody the conscious part of "Soviet man," the latter personify his unconscious.

Only by resolving this conflict can many of today's aesthetic, as well as social, problems be solved. Up until now, the political changes affecting post-Soviet society have been addressed only to the rational and conscious part of the individual, leaving unconscious structures untouched. However, the USSR, defined as the immortal unconscious of Soviet man—to borrow an expression from the Russian philosopher Mikhail Ryklin[1]—occasionally surfaces, ghostlike, in the political arena. The Zhirinovsky phenomenon, for instance, can be explained in terms of the neglect of this unconscious side of the post-Soviet psyche. It is its revenge for the attempt to solve all problems solely on the conscious level and in the rational sphere of politics.

The new culture, which defines Soviet power as a national form of the collective unconscious, is performing a prophylactic task for Russian society. The diagnosis is itself already a form of therapy.

On the other hand, the discovery and illumination of the national unconscious is, as Jung said, the task of art. It should therefore come as no surprise that many of the initial successes of post-Soviet Russian literature have been concerned with this very task; that is, the authors of this literature are working, for the most part, with socialist-realist material. What interests them is the sphere of the Soviet unconscious, the source of myth-making forces. For these post-Soviet writers, the legacy of socialist realism is of paramount importance. Indeed, for them, socialist realism has the same function as do dreams for Jung. What is important is not what is said intentionally but what is said accidentally: it is the "slips" that reveal the content of the collective unconscious of Soviet society. And it is these slips that are of interest to *sots-art,*[2] but that also reveal it to be a transitional phenomenon, the final phase of Soviet art and the beginning of a new era. *Sots-art* exploits the material of socialist realism: post-Soviet culture deconstructs its methods.

A representative example of post-Soviet culture is the prose of Viktor Pelevin, winner of the 1993 smaller Booker Prize for his collection of short stories *The Blue Light* (Sinii fonar'). He is also the author of the novels *Omon Ra, The Yellow Arrow, The Life of Insects,* and *Chapaev and Emptiness.*[3]

The features specific to the new poetics of post-Soviet prose emerge more fully in a comparative analysis of the works of Pelevin with those of Vladimir Sorokin. Each of them has his own strategy, which complements that of the other writer. Read together, they demonstrate how post-Soviet literature is dealing with its Soviet heritage.

Sorokin is an impressionist, offering the reader an objective portrait of psychic reality: a portrait of the soul without the retouching effects or corrective displacements wrought by mind, morality, and custom. Pelevin, on the other hand, is an expressionist, consciously distorting his representation, subordinating it to his didactic purpose.

Sorokin demonstrates the disintegration of the rational, purposeful, teleological universe of Soviet man. His primary theme is the Fall of Soviet man, who, after his loss of innocence, is cast from the *sots-realist* (socialist realist) Garden of Eden into the senseless chaos of a world that does not fit into a general plan. Sorokin's heroes, who founder at each stylistic level, crash into the linguistic Hell of a language beyond meaning. The journey from the kingdom of necessity into the world of freedom ends in a fatal neurosis—the pathology of a language that chokes on its own non-sense.

Pelevin does not destroy: he builds. Using the same fragments of the Soviet myth as Sorokin, he constructs both subject matter and concepts. While Sorokin reconstructs the dreams and nightmares of Soviet man, Pelevin depicts prophetic dreams—the dreams of a clairvoyant. If Sorokin's dreams are incomprehensible, Pelevin's are not (yet) understood.

Plunging into the unconscious, Sorokin finds symptoms of illness. This illness becomes the topic of his artistic investigations. Pelevin, by contrast, is interested in the symptoms themselves. He is envious of the "mystical" ability of the totalitarian regime to "generate dreams."

In the story "The Weapons of Retribution," there is a detailed description of the mental attitude of a group of people who work at a socialist think-tank, blindly

> immersed in their own mystical visions [to the point where] the very existence of mysticism becomes for them a state secret. But the negation of the mysticism which threads through life and history is itself a very subtle and dangerous form of mysticism. Subtle because it makes invisible the corner-stone of the social structure, causing government institutions and ideologies to take on cosmic proportions. Dangerous because even a minute threat, which is declared non-existent, can prove fateful.[4]

For Pelevin, the Soviet government's power is not a function of its sinister military-industrial complex, which he holds up to vicious ridicule in the novella *Omon Ra*. Rather, the basis of Soviet power is in its ability to impart materiality to its phantoms. Although these techniques are not the sole possession of totalitarian regimes, it is they who most successfully create a mystical "field of miracles," a zone, inside of which anything can happen.

The voluntarism of power in relation to reality, its unwillingness to tolerate a natural evolution of things, led to a confusion of culture and nature in Soviet society. The mature Soviet myth passed off the artificial as the natural. Socialism, merging with the landscape of surrounding life, created an organic, if uncomely, whole. Post-Soviet culture has been created by the final Soviet generation, which was accustomed to this landscape. Unlike its predecessor of the 1960s, this generation did not strive to improve the regime: it took it as a given. Soviet power was not perceived as an artifact, imposed by external forces or historical circumstances, but as a natural sphere of being. The new literature could thus not accept the idea, so dear to the previous generation, that there existed a "normal" world that had been subjected to artificial deterioration through the violence of state power.

For the post-Soviet authors, the world around them represents a sequence of artificial constructs, in which man is forever doomed to search for a "pure," "archetypal" reality. Although these parallel worlds are not "true" in any absolute sense, they are not "false" either, at least as long as someone believes in them. Each version of the world exists only in each individual soul. Psychic reality, as Jung pointed out, knows no lie.

This is the postulate upon which the novella *Omon Ra* is built. Emphases are changed in the story: fiction becomes the instrument for the construction of reality instead of the violation of reality. This credo is formulated by the agent of power, the Commissar of the cosmic city:

> As long as there is just one soul, in which our cause is alive and victorious, this cause will not die. It will make for a whole universe.... One pure and honest soul is enough for our country to become the first in the world in the race for the conquest of the cosmos. One such soul is enough to raise the red flag of victorious socialism on the distant Moon. But one such single soul is necessary, if only for a moment, because it is in that soul that the flag will be unfurled.[5]

By negating the surrounding space and reducing it to the psychic space of the individual, the new literature has extended its narrative possibilities. The extensionless point of the soul remaining in isolation can be traversed by innumerable lines, each of which will unite the subject with the fruits of his imagination.

This multiplicity of worlds is related to a special "theology of doubt," based on the obliteration of boundaries between actual reality and invented, virtual reality. Unusual rules apply here: to reveal a lie is not to come closer to the truth, while to multiply lies is not to distance oneself from the truth either. Addition and subtraction participate equally in the process of creation of invented worlds. The recipe for the construction of these phantoms consists of the writer's variation of the scope and constitution of the "lens," namely the window frame from which his hero observes the world. Here is an example of how such a view from a "window" is portrayed in the story "The Ontology of Childhood":

> To take just the two squares of sky on the wall (the sky seen from the lower bunk versus the upper bunk, when the tips of the distant wide funnels are still visible). At night stars appear in them, and during the day clouds, eliciting many questions. The clouds accompany you from childhood on, so many of them have been generated through the windows that you are amazed every time you come across something new. Here, for instance, in the window to the right, hangs an open pink fan (it is almost dusk) made up of a multiplicity of downy stripes—as if it

> had been produced by the entire world of aviation (incidentally, it is interesting to contemplate how the world is perceived by those who do their time in the skies), while the window to the left of the sky is just a slanting thin line.[6]

In Pelevin's stories everything takes place on the "windowsill," the boundary between different worlds. Every boundary underlines as well as creates difference. But a boundary not only divides, it also unites. The more numerous the boundaries, the more border zones proliferate. Along these limits or border areas, the features of one's own culture and those of the other, neighboring culture, are not erased but emerge more boldly. The boundary thus generates a special type of relationship, in which difference, expressed even in terms of irreconcilable antagonisms, serves as bonding material. Animosity strengthens ties more than friendship, as can be demonstrated by a glance at the world map or a current newspaper.

The author of the new post-Soviet literature is a poet, a philosopher, and a physiologist of these border areas. He dwells in the zone where realities collide. The site of this contact generates expressive artistic effects: one picture of the world succeeds another, creating a third that is distinct from the first two.

In order to elucidate the mechanism by which art is created at a boundary, let us recall the art of the surrealists, and of René Magritte in particular. Plunging the viewer into the absurd, Magritte balances between norm and anomaly, investigating the limit that separates one from the other. His canvases as if embody the invisible line separating phenomena: the animate from the inanimate, waking from dreaming, art from nature, the living from the dead, the possible from the impossible. In *Discovery* (1927), for instance, Magritte portrays a naked woman. However, the viewer can see that a portion of her skin has the texture of polished veneer, which leads to the question: is this living nature or *nature-morte?* All of Magritte's pictures include this inherent mechanism, which negates the possibility of giving an unambiguous answer to the question. Fried eggs wink like a real eye, a pair of curtains becomes a fragment of sky, a bird becomes a cloud, shoes grow nails, a nightie is equipped with a female bust. Magritte is a student of that minimal shift that transforms the real into the surreal.

The writer living at the boundary of two eras must perform a similar task. Pelevin can thus be seen populating his texts with heroes who inhabit two worlds simultaneously. Soviet officials in the story "The Prince of the Gosplan" live simultaneously in one or another computer video game. The *Lumpenproletarier* (prole) in the story "The Day of the Bulldozer Driver" turns out to be an American spy, the Chinese peasant Chzhuan is a Kremlin leader, and a Soviet student turns out to be a wolf.

The most inventive use of the limit or boundary theme is evident in the story "Mittelspiel." Its heroines—the foreign currency prostitutes Liusia and Nelly—were Party workers in the Soviet period. In order to adjust to the social transformations, they later underwent not only a change of profession but of gender. Nelly confesses to Liusia that she once served as the secretary of the *raikom* (the regional committee) of the *komsomol* (Communist youth organization) and that her name was Vasily Tsiriuk. Liusia, in turn, confesses that in her past life, she, too, had been a man and had similarly served as a subordinate to this same Tsiriuk, who fails to recognize her:

> "You had a mustache, then," said Liusia, shaking back her hair from her face. "And, do you remember maybe, that you had a deputy director of management? Andron Pavlov? They called him 'nit.'"
> "I remember," Nelly said, looking amazed.
> "He fetched your beer? You reprimanded him for failure in graphic propaganda, that time they drew Lenin on the wall newspaper in gloves and Dzherzinsky without a shadow?"[7]

Critics often try to reduce the plot twists of this kind of narrative to the level of anecdote. But such skepticism, from which many post-Soviet critics suffer, does not take into account the second, allegorical level of post-Soviet texts. The episode with the Communist transvestites is a particular case of a more general motif of transformation. What is important in *Mittelspiel* is not who the heroes once were, and not what they have become, but the fact of the transformation itself. The boundary between the two worlds is inaccessible, it is impossible to cross, since both worlds are projections of consciousness. The only way of crossing over from one reality into another is to transform oneself, to go through a metamorphosis. The ability to transform oneself becomes the means of survival in a breathtakingly rapid and arbitrary succession of phantom realities.

The limit is in fact a provocation, eliciting a metamorphosis, which in turn propels the hero in the direction the author wants him to go. Pelevin has his own "message," his symbol of faith, which is revealed in his texts and to which he seeks to lead his reader. Despite the popular view that the new wave literature lacks spirituality, Pelevin tends toward spiritualism, proselytism, and hence didacticism. Most critics consider him a satirist: in truth, he is closer to being a fabulist.

One such fable is *The Life of Insects*, a novel that takes the reader into the animal kingdom, the fable's customary topos. This peculiar "biophilism" is characteristic of much of the new culture. Prominent examples of it are Anatoly Kim's parable *The City of the Centaurs,*[8] Vladimir Makanin's *Manhole,*[9] and the paintings of the *Mitki* group.

The beast who appears in post-Soviet culture is associated with fantastic and mystical qualities. At the risk of making a bad pun, one could say that post-Soviet authors are seeking symmetry in the world of beasts: while in the Soviet era, *sots-realism* portrayed men as half-god and half-man, in the post-Soviet era they are portrayed as half-man and half-beast.

The beast fits the agenda of the post-Soviet author with its primal otherness or alterity. This is because its complementary alterity allows the author to reverse the usual direction of metaphysical quest—not up but down the evolutionary ladder. The animal is also an "other," possessing a separate consciousness and sharing with us not only living space but also the mystery of our being in it.

Pelevin frequently turns to animals because they also enable him to explore yet another limit: that between species. In the story "The Hermit and the Six-Fingered One," two chickens are engaged in metaphysical experiments at a "chicken farm named after Lunacharsky."[10] In the story "The Problem of the Werewolf in the Middle Region," the transformation of a man into an animal fills the soul of a werewolf with sublime meaning. This "animal" theme is treated in extended form in Pelevin's novel about insects.

Although insects are not the only creatures who go through metamorphosis, their chain of transformation (egg-larva-pupa-adult individual) is very long and varied. With regard to people, insects play a double role: they least resemble humans but live with them more often than other creatures. Their vast numbers also echoes of the human species. Hence it is not surprising that insects have often been cast as literary protagonists. *The Life of Insects* was in fact written as a polemic against some works in which insects figure prominently.

Foremost amongst them is the play by the brothers Karel and Josef Chapek, entitled *From the Life of Insects* (1921). The title of the Chapek play is quoted virtually verbatim in the title of Pelevin's novel. The entomological collection of *dramatis personae* is also intertextual: the dung-beetles, ants, and moths. In the Chapek brothers' play, comic hyperbole structures character portrayal. The names of insects serve as masks, permitting the reduction of human character. This entomological masquerade is a function of the process of abstraction. In their preface to the play, the brothers write:

> We intended to write not a drama but a mystery play in an archaic, naive manner. Just as Avarice, Egoism or Virtue appeared personified in medieval mystery plays, in our play certain moral categories are embodied in insects for the purpose of being made more visible.... We did not write about people or about insects but about vices.[11]

Insects and people are one and the same in Pelevin's novel. What they represent in each separate episode is not decided by the author, but by the reader. This is reminiscent of those popular optical illusions in which, with the help of perspective, two different figures are depicted in the same drawing, although only one can be seen at a time, depending on the focus of the viewer. Such effects, well known to quantum mechanics, are common in contemporary art. The Oscar-winning film *Forrest Gump* is structured along this principle of reception: whether the protagonist is perceived as "a fool or a saint" depends not on the author, but on the way the audience perceives him.

Thus Pelevin's prose can be read as a contemporary novel of manners if the reader concentrates on the descriptions of thoughts and feelings. However, if the reader is conscious only of the physical shape of the heroes, then he is plunged into the promised "life of insects." This device of multiple reception can be observed in the love scene between the Western entrepreneur and his Russian sweetheart:

> He leaned back against the stone and for a time felt nothing, as if he had become part of the rock made hot by the sun. Natasha squeezed the palm of his hand. Half-opening his eyes, he saw directly in front of him two large facet-grained hemispheres. They glistened in the sun like broken glass, and between them, around a fluffy proboscis serving as a mouth, taut little mustaches-feelers moved.[12]

The juxtaposition of scientific naturalism and psychological realism produces hybrid heroes. All these characters who think like people and look like insects go back to the most famous of all entomological heroes, Kafka's Gregor Samsa of *The Metamorphosis*, whose theme is the tragedy of missed happiness. By his metamorphosis Gregor has a chance of escaping the cruel kingdom of necessity and freeing himself from the responsibility that violates his soul. Having become an insect, he breaks out of the chains that bind him to his home and hated job. At the very beginning, before Gregor himself believes in his metamorphosis, he reasons in the following manner: if his relatives are frightened at seeing his new shape, then "he is no longer responsible and can calm down." The metamorphosis thus opens a way to freedom for Gregor. The tragedy is not in his having been turned into an insect; it is rather in the fact that he did not know how to use the opportunity given to him by the metamorphosis.

This situation, in reverse, is treated by Kafka in the short story "A Report to the Academy," in which an ape is turned into a man. This happens because the beast, locked up in its cage, has no other choice. Once it becomes a man, he begins to reason thus: "I did not ask for freedom. I only wanted a way out—to the right, to the left, in any direction." Gregor Samsa did not find a way out despite the fact that the text alludes to the possibility of there being one, through the open window in whose vicinity the protagonist feels a "liberating sensation." He could simply have flown to freedom because his metamorphosis afforded him that ability.

The subject of metamorphosis and freedom is one of the topics addressed by Nabokov in his Cornell lectures on literature.[13] Here he rejects the traditional interpretation according to which Gregor is transformed into a common cockroach. In trying to reconstruct the shape of Kafka's insect (Nabokov's drawings of him have even been preserved), Nabokov comes to the conclusion that Gregor becomes a beetle, similar in fact to a dung-beetle although without being one in the technical sense. What is of more importance, however, is its hard round back, pointing to the fact that wings are hidden inside it. But the beetle Gregor, so says Nabokov, never clarifies the fact that he has wings under this hard carapace. The beetle into which Gregor was transformed could simply have flown out the window. Such a happy ending to the metamorphic process is offered in a book written by the entomologist Jean-Henri Fabre, itself entitled *The Life of Insects* (both Kafka and the brothers Chapek made use of it in their own work). Of the dung-beetle, Fabre has the following enthusiastic comment: "Oh, happy creature! ... you know your craft. It assures you peace and food, which for humans are obtained only through hard and painful labor."[14] Was it perhaps this paragraph that gave Kafka the idea of freeing his hero from the burdens of being a man by turning him into an insect? At any rate, Gregor the beetle had the possibility of becoming happier than Gregor the man.

A metamorphosis consists of a series of changes, by means of which a fully grown being is distinguished from an immature one. It is thus not only a transformation but a centripetal movement, directed toward a goal. Metamorphosis gives transformation a teleological character. It leads the subject toward a "moral." This hidden but insistent didacticism, diffused throughout Pelevin's book, points to the proximity of genre between his novel and its direct literary source, namely Ivan Krylov's fable *The Dragon-Fly and the Ant.*

What Pelevin does, in fact, is translate the story of the "ant" who wanted to become a "dragon-fly" into the language of the soap opera. The heroine of the novel, Natasha, who does not wish for a repetition of the impoverished and boring "life of labor" of her parents, breaks with her native ant customs and goes off with the flies, to the horror of her honest mother Marina:

> She had already torn the little wall of the cocoon and saw, instead of the modest little ant-body with four long wings, a typical young fly dressed in a green, whore-like mini-skirt decked with metal spangles.[15]

This metamorphosis from one winged creature to another does not, however, bring happiness to the heroine. Instead, after a brief affair with an American mosquito, Natasha perishes on a sheet of flypaper.

Pelevin, in making use of this classic Russian fable for his novel, does not simply paraphrase or parody it. Rather he deconstructs it, adding his own "moral" to the old fable and reintroducing its heroes in the epilogue of the novel. One of them is "a fat red ant in a sailor's suit, with the words *Ivan Krylov* embroidered in gold letters on his sailor's hat, with decorations of merit glistening on his chest, fertilizing his sash with the dung of a protracted and senseless life." The other is a dragon-fly who performs on television. "The dragon-fly skipped several times on the screen, spread out her transparent wings and began to sing … 'Tomorrow I'll fly away/Into the sunny summer/Buddy, I'll do whatever I like.'"[16]

The word "Buddy," which is a phonetic reminiscence of the word "Buddha,"[17] serves as an interpretive key to the novel. It transposes Pelevin's sarcastic prose into a metaphysical register. The parallel plot of the novel unfolds on this allegorical level and is embodied in the spiritual evolution of the moth Mitia and his *alter ego* Dima. Like the others, they too go through metamorphoses; however, unlike them, the metamorphoses of Mitia/Dima lead not to emptiness and death, but to spiritual enlightenment.

The hero's metamorphosis thus has a twofold appearance. It can be read as physical or metaphysical, depending on the reader's point of view:

> … He [Mitia] opened his eyes and saw that he was standing in a spot of bright blue light, as if several light projectors were directing their beams on that one point. But there were no light projectors anywhere—the source of the light was he himself.[18]

Thus the little moth Mitia has turned into a glow-worm.

Such spiritual metamorphoses bring the novel back to the theme of boundaries. The ultimate boundary is that limit separating the virtual world of mundane reality from authentic, "pure" existence or being. The mystic Pelevin locates this pure being inside the individual soul. Inviting post-Soviet Russian literature to cross the ultimate—transcendental—boundary, Pelevin simultaneously tries to show this literature how to cultivate a metaphysical reality, which does not exist, but can be created.

Notes

1. Mikhail Ryklin, *Terreorologiki* (Tartu-Moscow: Eidos, 1992), p. 202.
2. A term denoting a movement in art and literature that combines elements of socialist realism with pop art.
3. Viktor Pelevin, *The Blue Lantern* (Moscow, 1991); *Omon Ra, Znamia* no. 5 (1992); *The Yellow Arrow, Novy mir,* no. 7 (1993), *Zhizn' nasekomykh* [The Life of Insects], *Znamia,* no. 4 (1993).
4. V. Pelevin, *The Blue Lantern.*, p. 287.
5. V. Pelevin, *Omon Ra, Znamia* 5 (1992): 62.
6. V. Pelevin, *The Blue Lantern,* p. 211.
7. Ibid., p. 236.
8. Anatoly Kim, *Poselok Kentavrov* [The City of the Centaurs], *Novy Mir,* no. 7, p. 92.
9. Vladimir Makanin, *Laz* [Manhole], *Novy mir,* no. 3, p. 91.
10. V. Pelevin, *The Blue Lantern,* p. 22.
11. Karel Chapek, *Iz zhizni nasekomykh* [From the Life of Insects], in *Sobranie sochinenii* (Collected Works in 7 vols.), vol. 4 (Moscow, 1976), p. 206.
12. V. Pelevin, *Zhizn' nasekomykh,* p. 26.
13. Vladimir Nabokov, *Lectures on Literature* (New York, 1980), pp. 258–9.
14. Zh. Fabre, *Zhizn' nasekomykh* (Moscow, 1963), p. 287; *Souvenirs entomologiques* (Paris, 1946–51).
15. V. Pelevin, *Zhizn' nasekomykh,* p. 62.
16. Ibid., p. 65.
17. Translator's note: in the Russian original, the word "Buddha" is brought into the dragonfly's song by way of a spelling error in the verb "to be" (*buddu',* meaning "I shall"). I have taken liberties with the original text in order to transmit the phonetic play on words.
18. V. Pelevin, *Zhizn' nasekomykh,* p. 32.

Part IV

Conceptualism

Chapter 19

The New Model of Discourse in Post-Soviet Russian Fiction

Liudmila Petrushevskaia and Tatiana Tolstaia

Slobodanka Vladiv-Glover

Of the Russian literature published during and since *perestroika* a new poetics has come into force, one hard to describe with the tools of traditional Russian criticism. The "new" Russian prose of the 1980s and 1990s has been variously identified as the "new wave literature" (*novaia volna*), "other prose," and "alternative prose."[1] One of the first critics to describe the new movement was Vladimir Potapov,[2] writing in *Novy mir* in 1989. Potapov identifies the "alternative prose" writers as Tatiana Tolstaia (born in 1951), Evgeny Popov (born in 1946), and Viacheslav Pietsukh (born in 1946), the young Afghanistan war veteran Oleg Ermakov (born in 1961), Viktor Erofeev (born in 1947), author of the soft-porn novel *A Russian Beauty* (Russkaia krasavitsa), as well as the older and renowned Venedikt Erofeev (1938–1990) of the *Moscow Circles*. To Potapov's list must be added Liudmila Petrushevskaia (born in 1939), whom Potapov mentions only in passing. Potapov leaves out a whole host of lesser-known younger writers, who are included in the most representative collection of contemporary Russian fiction to date, edited by the poet Oleg Chukhontsev.[3]

Chukhontsev's anthology in turn omits Vladimir Sorokin (born in 1955), considered by some to be the foremost Russian post-avant-garde writer, and also leaves out the winner of the 1992 Booker Prize, Mark Kharitonov.[4] What all these omissions indicate is that the field of the new Russian "post-Soviet" literature is only just being mapped out in Russian criticism. The process of mapping is ongoing. It is barely in step with the continuous literary production belonging to the new Russian aesthetics and the cultural paradigm of Russian postmodernism.

"Alternative prose" is seen by Potapov as "coming out of the underground," where it was born as unpublishable literature: "We find that alternative writers share a common genesis, or more precisely, ontogenesis. This is the prose of yesterday's 'outsiders'; it is 'self-seeded' literature (*Eto proza vcherashnikh neformalov ... literaturnyi samosev).* It grew and made its mark outside the officially approved literary process under conditions which ruled out any movement toward socialisation."[5]

In using the English word "underground" to describe the ontogenesis of this "alternative prose," Potapov is anxious to free the word from the purely political connotations of the Russian word *podpol'e*. For, according to Potapov, it was not only the censor who would have rejected Russian "alternative prose," but also the Russian readers, who were unprepared for the "otherness" (*inakost'*)—or "alterity" (to use a Bakhtinian term)—of this "new prose." "This is why (alternative prose) behaves like the delinquent of our literary culture and why it constantly has difficulties in talking to a reader brought up on other paradigms...."[6]

It is in its otherness or alterity, and the attendant poor reception of this new prose by the Russian reading public, that Potapov finds the common denominators of the emerging Russian postmodern literature. He does not, however, call it by its name.[7] In all other respects, Potapov sees "alternative prose" as "a conglomerate of heterogeneous literary events belonging to quite different trends rather than to what is conventionally understood by a movement or a school."[8]

While stylistic heterogeneity is the hallmark of Russian "alternative prose," works belonging to it are related not only ontogenetically, like the prose of "yesterday's outsiders." They can and should be viewed in the context of a new cultural paradigm and a new model of discourse, which has been in the making in both Eastern Europe and the West since the mid-1950s. The roots of this paradigm go back to the avant-garde movements of the early twentieth century,[9] in which modern art turned to the study of the object as a substitute for the universal Renaissance humanist subject.[10] The new Russian postmodern prose is thus in part a reclamation of the lost or repressed impulses of Russian and European modernism and in part a deconstructive verbal game with the cultural icons and master discourses of the twentieth century.

In Western critical theory, the debate over postmodernism began in the late 1970s in American academic circles.[11] In France, where the continuity between modernist and postmodern aesthetics is best preserved,[12] the new cultural paradigm emerged as early as the 1950s-1960s, heralded by the *nouveau roman*, the literary structuralism of Roland Barthes, the "new" Freudian psychoanalytic school of Jacques Lacan, the psychoanalytic criticism of Maurice Blanchot, the "grammatology" of Jacques Derrida, and the "archeological" (later "genealogical") criticism of Michel Foucault. In Russian critical appraisals of the new literature of the 1980s, which began to emerge tentatively in the late 1980s, the term "postmodernism" occurred only sporadically and initially without theoretical backing. This is probably due to the fact that until recently, Soviet literary criticism lived in total isolation from Western critical theory. Its own native-grown structuralism and semiotics, pioneered in the late 1950s-early 1960s by the Moscow-Tartu School (Y. Lotman, B. A. Uspensky, A. K. Zholkovsky, Y. Shcheglov, V. V. Ivanov, B. M. Gasparov), had a restricted reception, mainly among German Slavists. Thus, in the words of A. K. Zholkovsky, writing from the position of a Soviet immigrant scholar in the United States, the poststructuralist paradigm of the 1970s and 1980s "had a fairly negative resonance in Slavic scholarship—in that it essentially by-passed it."[13] The exception to this is the highly productive reception of M. M. Bakhtin,[14] which formed the basis for the only theoretically oriented branch in Russian literary criticism in the 1970s and 1980s.[15]

The new postmodern model of discourse, in both Russian and Western literatures, displaced the "classical" nineteenth-century mimetic and solipsistic modes of representation.[16] After World War II, most national literatures of the Western world (and even some of the Eastern block, like those of Yugoslavia)[17] entered a postmodern phase of "schizo-aesthetics."[18] This because they could more or less continue along the tracks of high modernism, modulating into a new but related key of representation. Russian literature, on the other hand, developed differently. First of all, its high modernism, which is now referred to as the "first Russian avant-garde,"[19] was interrupted in 1934. Up until the thaw of 1954, Russian literature was "underground," in both a political and psychological sense. What emerged in the 1950s and 1960s was a sudden irruption of "Soviet" postmodernism—in the new lyrical prose of Kazakov, Nagibin, Aksyonov, Gladilin, and the wave of lyric poetry of Evtushenko, Voznesensky, Rozhdestvensky, Akhmadulina, and others—but only the tip of the iceberg was revealed. The major works of Bitov, Erofeev, Bazunov, to name only a few, remained inaccessible to the Russian reading public. Russian art was also "underground," but generating its own new aesthetics: a still repressed conceptualism in the late 1960s (Ilya Kabakov's *Uslovnye oboznacheniia* [Conventional Signs] in 1968),[20] a deconstructionist historicism in the 1970s (Tatiana Nazarenko's early work *Utro. Babushka v Nikolke*),[21] and an unabashed reclamation of the avant-garde in the 1980s (see, for instance, Olga Bulgakova's quotation of Max Ernst in *The Painter and His Picture*, 1989).[22]

With the liberalization of the Russian literary scene in the mid-1980s (through perestroika), the traditional Soviet Russian literary journals became a new home for Russia's reclaimed and rehabilitated avant-garde as well as the new "alternative" prose, poetry, and drama. Overnight, so to speak, Russia had postmodernism.

The new postmodern literature immediately meant the end of the official genres of the 1970s—village prose and socialist-realist prose in various guises.[23] However, the new model of discourse in which Russian postmodernism was grounded did not really spring into existence with the formal dissolution of the Soviet Union in

1991. In my nomenclature, in fact, the term "post-Soviet" encompasses works written at various (often unspecified) times since the 1960s. Like Potapov's "alternative prose," which refers to the literature of "yesterday's outsiders," I use the term "post-Soviet" to encompass the works of the 1960s, the 1970s, and 1980s, which could not have been published under normal conditions in the former Soviet Union. The term "post-Soviet" is therefore not a strictly chronological or historical concept. It is an ahistorical tag that subverts the idea of history and historical progression, coinciding with a phenomenology (or "archeology"[24]) of discourse in the age of *post-histoire*.[25] The unifying principle of the works belonging to this post-Soviet model of discourse is in the fact that their structure depends on and is determined by a semiotic model of perception in the broadest sense.[26] This semiotic model has to do not with structuralist semiotics in the narrow linguistic sense, but with the structure of the sign as it relates to the constitution of discourse (the process of meaning and semiosis) and the subject of discourse (the psychoanalytic subject of the unconscious). It is thus not "semiotics" but "the semiotic"[27]—a heterogeneous space with undefinable boundaries that belongs to the imaginary (pre-symbolic) and symbolic registers of language—which is modeled by the new Russian prose and which it in turn models. What "the semiotic" is about, then, is the construction of the world (of meaning and signification) as subjective experience and not about how the world looks from an assumed point of view outside the subject of perception.

This phenomenological semiotic model of perception emerged in Russian literature in the mid-1960s, miraculously keeping step with Western literary developments of the time, but without being granted due recognition. Voznesensky's *Oza* and Bitov's *Pushkin House*, both works of the 1960s, are grounded in such a model of perception.[28] The Russian writers of the post-Soviet era continue to explore and exploit the same model. While it is many-sided, all of its diverse facets converge on the relationship of the human subject, not to other human subjects, but to language as humanity's ultimate object. It is to the writers of the "new" post-Soviet, postmodern prose—the "other" prose of the 1980s and 1990s—that we shall now turn for a closer look.

Liudmila Petrushevskaia's New Russians and the Scene of Writing

Belonging to the same generation as Andrei Bitov, Liudmila Petrushevskaia (born in 1938 and a member of what was at one stage known as the generation of the "forty-year-olds"[29]) began writing short stories in the 1960s. She became known as a screen writer in the late 1970s and a playwright in the early 1980s. Her story "A Modern Family Robinson" is a paradigmatic example of the new postmodern model of discourse and as such lends itself to a semiotic or deconstructive reading.

In "The New Robinsons,"[30] as the title of the Russian original goes, Petrushevskaia apparently undertakes to write a first-person family chronicle of the 1930s. The heroine, who is also the first-person narrator, remains unnamed. Similarly, members of her family are referred to only by their name in the family relation: "father," "mother," "my younger sister." This heroine describes, in the most minute detail, her family's retreat to a remote northern region of Russia and the day-to-day struggle for survival amidst diminishing resources, such as food supplies. The narrator betrays no emotion as she tells her story of hardships. In fact, the narrative displays the zero degree of affectivity, which Jameson has identified as the hallmark of postmodern forms of representation.[31]

However, despite its depressing story-line, this modern Robinsonade recalls Daniel Defoe's adventure through its lightness of tone. This lightness emanates partly from the lack of pathos in the narrating voice, but may also be ascribed to the childish temperament of the adolescent heroine whose perspective on events is retained by the grown-up memoirist looking back on her childhood experiences. In constructing her narrative, Petrushevskaia is thus using a double frame, reminiscent of the device employed by Andrei Bely in his novel *Kotik Letaev*—a work of Russian high modernism. The voice of the child is inside the voice of the grown-up narrator, separate from the grown-up who nevertheless manipulates it in sovereign fashion as the voice of memory.

Although the heroine's family appears to be hiding from a real threat, which could be assumed to be the Stalinist purges, concrete historical detail remains practically banned from the narrative. Referents to actual historical time are non-existent. From the sparse references to space, the reader infers that the family is retreating ever deeper into the harsh Siberian forest regions "beyond the river Mora." But while some real geographic markers are used, the space in which the story is located is so generalized that it can be identified only as a primeval, almost mythological region, beyond the pale of civilization. Unlike Defoe's eighteenth-century story, in which the primitive peoples are excluded from the world of European culture, in Petrushevskaia's story it is the family of a member of the Russian twentieth-century intelligentsia who represent the "excluded." The Siberian natives, the peasant women, who are the only other protagonists in the story, and who would be the equivalent of Robinson's Man Friday, are treated as people who are in their "proper place." These characters are granted proper names.

The plot consists of various unconnected and seemingly unmotivated events, such as an abandoned baby being found on the doorstep of the Robinson family home, or the father leaving the family to go and live separately, in his new hide-out, when the abandoned baby "arrives." The narrative itself consists of a network of singular and trivial acts, connected with the daily hunt for food and shelter. All the events take place and are related in the historic present. Allusions to the past are few. There are no memories about the life left behind and reminiscences are abruptly dismissed (such as the narrator's reference to her grandparents in the city: "to hell with them both"[32]). The entire action of the story takes place in a generalized present that seems to have no beginning and no end. The plot, if any, can be reduced to a limited motion in space: from one hide-out to another, going ever deeper into the forest. The story ends with the prospect of the next move. Instead of closure there is the open-ended perspective of an infinite repetition of the same movement.

The ostensible motivation of this movement deeper into space is the family's attempt to escape an invisible and unnamed enemy. The story is literally propelled by the tension created by what is not named, the minimal actions of the unnamed family members and the unnamed danger threatening them. The unnamed, almost a parody of the modernist unnamable or ineffable, is augmented by the mystery of the family's "banishment," for which no explanation is given either explicitly or through allusion. Hence what might have been described as ordinary political exile is reduced in the story to a generalized concept of exclusion and absence. Being a part of the family Robinson, which is multiply-framed, becomes a metaphor of pure difference. The family members are represented as different—as the excluded outsiders—in relation to the "native" peasant women, who populate the story. The family members are also the excluded in relation to a distant and past society, in which they might have had their origin, but which now takes on the appearance of an absent and unnamed threat, which communicates itself to the emotions as a kind of uncanny *presence*. It is this absent *presence* that comes across as a threat to the family. But it is also this threat or absence that keeps the family together, in one place, allowing its members to identify themselves precisely as family members. The absent—fantasized or actual—threat from outside the family thus becomes the unnamed other for the story-teller and for her story. The story therefore moves on, literally, by constantly eschewing its other. This movement, which subverts the notion of linear progression or plot development, is dramatized by the family's retreating deeper into the forest, from one hide-out to another. The other of the story thus assumes *representational form* as a primary structure (hence the apparent primeval diegetic space in which the story unfolds), which is the abstracted ground or condition of possibility of the story as staged metaphor, constituting itself simultaneously as a metonymic chain (of associative links) grounded in an absence that is synonymous with the lack which constitutes desire. The latter manifests itself as primal, non-verbal rhythm—repetition and silence—which exist as states of affairs that defy the linear movement of cause and effect and chronology or history as progress in time. Hence the irony of the subtitle of Petrushevskaia's narrative, which is in point of fact an anti-chronicle and an anti-history.

In the multiple exclusions that structure Petrushevskaia's story, the close family members, who are cocooned in their hide-out, create the impression of forming an inside. However, the family as an inside becomes an outside in relation to the reality of the peasant women in the village and that of the distant, absent world of "other people." Hence the borders between inside and outside are obliterated in the story, just as they are in the surrealist paintings of Giorgio de Chirico (for example, *The Seer*, 1915),[33] forming a virtual space or the non-Euclidean topos of the unconscious. In this inside-out space, the family forms an isolated *totality*: at one point the family feels entirely "alone in the world," a world that remains silent even on their little radio receiver. This totality which is "the family" is thus carved out of another, more originary, primeval totality: silence and absence. The totality of the family is self-sufficient; no voices from the outside intrude into this world; no other "people" enter the family's space: it is, we could say with Hegel, "in-itself" and "for-itself" (*an-sich* and *für-sich*). Linearized as a story of survival in the wilderness—the family grow their own food in the small vegetable garden—the self-constituting, self-sufficient totality which is the family becomes synonymous with the place of (agri)culture and the symbolic order, literally carved out of the primeval space of the imaginary (primary unconscious) that grounds it.

In nineteenth-century Russian culture, the concept of the *imaginary* found an "unscientific" popular equivalent in the attitude of *sozertsanie*, which is portrayed in Ivan Kramskoy's painting of a peasant "frozen in thought," entitled *Sozertsatel'*. This painting captured Dostoevsky's imagination and compelled him to use it in his novel *The Brothers Karamazov* to elucidate the portrait of the epileptic (agent of the unconscious) Smerdyakov. Dostoevsky's commentary on Kramsksoy's *Sozertsatel'* provides a cogent description of how the process of psychic *inscription*, which remains repressed, creates a repository of accumulated sensations, which amount to *memory traces* constituting the imaginary and serving as the ground of future radical "conscious" or intentional acts:

> And yet [Smerdyakov] used sometimes to stop dead in the house, or the yard, or on the street and ponder, and he would stand still like that for as long as ten minutes. A physiognomist, looking closely at him, would have said that he did not think of anything in particular, but was just vaguely contemplating. The painter Kramskoy has a remarkable picture

> called *The Contemplator.* It depicts a forest in winter, and on the roadway in the forest a little peasant stands quite alone in a torn coat and bast-shoes. He seems to have wandered there by chance and seems to be standing there thinking, but he is not really thinking but only "contemplating" something. If you were to nudge him, he would give a start and look at you as though he had just woken up, but without understanding. He would, it is true, have come to life at once, but if you asked him what he was thinking of while standing there, he would most certainly not remember anything. But he would most certainly never forget the sensation he had experienced during the time of his contemplation, but would always keep it hidden away inside him. Those sensations are dear to him, and he is doubtlessly accumulating them imperceptibly and without being aware of it—why and for what purpose, he does not know either: perhaps, having accumulated such impressions in the course of many years, he will suddenly give up everything and go on a pilgrimage to Jerusalem in search of salvation, or perhaps, too, he will suddenly set fire to his village....[34]

As such, it is clear that the principles of characterization in Petrushevskaia's story do not obey the norms of typization (*tipichnost'*) of literary realism. The characters in the story do not, in fact, mirror life. The minimalistic setting, reduced to a primordial natural landscape, the narrating voice stripped of pathos, the characters reduced to signifiers in a relational field, structured by formal or pure difference ("mother" is not "sister," "father" is not "mother")—all of this points in the direction of metaphoric and not mimetic representation. It is, in point of fact, the very structure of metaphor, operating as a substitutive signification, that the story models and takes as its subject of representation. That is why the story leaves no room for an allegorical reading, even if such a reading is alluded to through the minimalized *realia* and spatio-temporal references that have been deliberately de-historicized. The "family Robinson" is thus not a simulacrum of an "allegorical" or "typical" family of the repressed Russian intelligentsia during the purges, although it *could be* construed as such. It is also not an Oedipal family, although it could become one if it were to change contexts (migrating from the imaginary to the symbolic register). The family Robinson, rather, is comparable to Ludwig Wittgenstein's "family" metaphor. Arguing that concepts have fluid and not fixed boundaries, Wittgenstein sees language as constituted of general terms (concepts) whose disparate entities are not reducible to a single common denominator. When we take the general term "game," for instance, we "are inclined to think that there must be something in common to all games, say, and that this common property is the justification for applying the general term 'game' to the various games; whereas games form a family the members of which have family likenesses. Some of them have the same nose, others the same eyebrows and others again the same way of walking; and these likenesses overlap."[35]

What this analogy between "general concepts" and "family resemblances" implies is that, in language, there are no boundaries between concepts that can be predetermined outside a context. All concepts exist in a fluid synchronicity, which is segmented and linearized by the operation of difference—a discontinuity expressed through plus/minus features activated through contexture (condensation or metaphor).

Wittgenstein's attack on generalizations (the "craving for generality") is an attempt to dismantle the preconceptions that burden our ordinary use of language and lead to the false assumption about the identity of concepts (signifiers) with the things they designate (signifieds). Instead of being "generalized" images of things, concepts or words are, according to Wittgenstein, signs whose function is to "refer" or "point" to things. The most elementary sign is a proper name. Names are "tags," which do not have meaning by themselves. Names mean only in propositions, that is, in relation to other names.

The family members of Petrushevskaia's "Robinsons" represent signs that signify through radical but minimal difference with respect to other signs. These "new Robinsons" (*novye Robinzony*) are the "new Russians," whose national characteristics have undergone a "phenomenological reduction" (Husserl) rendering them into a function of the virtual field of discourse and representation. That is why they remain without proper names, appearing only as metonymies of objects in a relation. Consequently, the "new Russian" Robinsons represent a metaphor of the structure of language and not of the structure of Soviet society of the 1930s. It is in this way that they are called "new" and figure in a "chronicle of the end of the twentieth century," which is to say, a chronicle about "the end of time," the end of the world as chronology, as History, and Progress. The "family" of the "new Russians" has thus been thrust into the relational field of language—a playing field in which each player's significance (meaning) is determined solely through *difference*, which has neither substance nor essence, but is itself a limit dividing sense from non-sense, presence (or speech) from absence (the unconscious). Petrushevskaia's story is situated at this limit—represented as a region which is at the periphery or boundary of known European settlement and civilization. Difference structures the meaning of the story—not a particular meaning, which could be disclosed through a socio-historic content—but meaning as *form*, as possibility, and as *future*. Meaning as form is represented by the structure of metaphor, which is one of the two fundamental mechanisms of language.[36] The "family Robinson" is an embodied or actualized metaphor that comes into presence or (re-)presents itself. As metaphor, the family doubles: it is what it is—a family— but equally a representation of the concept "family." In either sense it is always already a representation. It does not point beyond itself, into another space, say, that of the Russian socio-historic reality of the 1930s. If evoked at all between the lines, such a historic reality emerges only as symbol (symptom) of the "real," intruding as threat or absence into the imaginary order in which metaphor is engendered. As a representation, constituted as metaphor against a "real" manifested as absence, the "family" refers back to itself as a tautological image—a representation of a representation: it mirrors nothing but itself.

By contrast with the "family," whose members do not have proper names and hence form part of the dialectic of pure difference, the women peasant characters of the story have archetypal Russian names: Anisia, Marfa, Tania, Vera. They are a foil for the family and embody the other half of the Wittgensteinian definition of a concept. They are primitive signs—irreducible components of meaning—which are expressed in language as proper names. For, according to Wittgenstein, "(T)he simple signs employed in propositions are called names" (3.202).[37] And, concomitantly: "A name cannot be dissected any further by means of a definition: it is a primitive sign" (3.26). A proper name is thus the ultimate identity of an object which, in turn, is the ultimate perceived reality for any subject. That is why the peasant women with proper names appear endowed with a concreteness and a materiality that allows no questioning, no analysis. They just are—for the story's narrator and for the reader. Moreover, because signs that occur in propositions are in a "determinate relation to one another" (3.14), the peasant women act as if by a preordained necessity, dictated at the plot level by the sheer instinct of survival, and on the metaphoric level by the preexistence of the system of language, which they literally embody.

The same necessity appears to govern the behavior of the family Robinson, whose entire existence is, in addition, determined by an invisible and unnamed anxiety. This anxiety does not spoil the family's life, however. The narrator, who is recalling the events of the story as something belonging to a distant childhood, still manages to evoke an atmosphere of lightness and even enchantment. The anxiety, generated by the unnamed threat from somewhere "outside" the primordial space of the village hide-out, is thus a metaphor subordinated to the structure of the story.

Since Petrushevskaia's story is told from the point of view of one of the excluded, it can be said to constitute itself structurally in opposition to something from which the narrator feels excluded. This something is the story's unnamed other. The story does not seem to be otherwise motivated than as a movement against or heterogeneous to this other, which is perceived as an abstract threat. The other of the story at the same time defines the main narrating character as a "self-consciousness."[38] It is only in relation to this other that she—the narrator—constitutes herself as a speaking or narrating subject. Without the unnamed threat, which is the cause of a generalized anxiety or "lack," there would be no chronicle, no story and no story-teller. Neither subject of speech (narrating consciousness) nor object of speech (narrated story) would exist without the absent, unnamed other, whose *representational form* is an abstracted affect: fear. But this affect remains flat and two-dimensional, as it were. It does not communicate itself to the reader. It does not "infect," as

Tolstoy demanded in his *What Is Art*?[39] The narrating subject, who remains a *voice* and an unnamed simple *moi* (me), defined only in a familial relational field, remains *invisible*. This *voice*, who is identified as feminine only through the constraints of grammatical gender (which is revealed through Russian morphology but lost in English), does not even *say* "I." What the narrator's "I" does is disappear in the folds of the narrative. The "I" thus *fades* almost programmatically in order to re-emerge as text or discourse.

As discourse, the narrative has a linearized form: it is a *chronicle* of day-to-day, particular events. But these events are ahistorical—they constitute the signifying chain pure and simple, and not a causal chain. Hence the apparent disconnectedness of the separate events. This signifying chain seems to unfold almost independently of the submerged "I" of the narrating voice. It is the chain that seems to determine the "I" and not vice versa. The subject of the "I" is thus driven by the laws of language, which are its "destiny," not the laws of the land (Stalinism). This is how the "I" constitutes itself in the symbolic order of language out of its "exile" in the primeval region of the imaginary (primal repression): as a temporal, linearized manque-à-être (being that lacks being) and as discourse of the other.

This framing of the subject in a tautological relationship with its other (its object, its language) reflects the tautological structure of logical propositions. According to the phenomenology of language of the modernist philosopher Wittgenstein, emerging from his *Tractatus*, tautologies and contradictions delimit logical space and thus set a limit to what can be thought. "Tautologies and contradictions lack sense" (4.46). They are not "pictures of reality;" they "do not represent any possible situations. For the former (tautologies) admit all possible situations and the latter (contradictions) none" (4.462). Consequently, a tautology "does not stand in any representational relation to reality" (4.462).

The story-teller and her story are in a tautological relationship. They are like a self-enclosed and self-propagating totality. The story-teller and her story form the logical space, in which states of affairs or propositions come into existence within a virtual, decentered, and—speaking with Husserl—"transcendental consciousness." Or, more precisely, the story-teller and her story represent the primal scene of the repressed—site of the memory trace and unconscious inscription.

Although the chronology of events in the story is not pegged to any real or historical time (the story is thus in no representational relation to "reality"), the simple fact of a sequential order of narrative is nevertheless inescapably established. This linearized sequence of otherwise unconnected events creates the impression that the story generates itself. It is as if the story were pouring out of an unspecified imaginary. This imaginary[40] is more generalized than the imagination of a solipsistic subject because the subject of this imaginary is decentered in two ways: once as memory and once as discourse of the other. Hence the double frame of the "chronicle" as a record(ing) of memory of a child in an adult. It is as a doubly-framed, decentered subject that a member of the family of the "new Robinsons"—a "new Russian" Robinson—is reborn as subject of the unconscious. Hence the "new Russian" Robinsons reinvent themselves in a primeval space, which is the vacuum of Russian culture created by the fall of the Soviet Union and the old order of Soviet metaphysics. The space of the "new Russia" is thus coeval with the space of the unconscious—an infinite totality that transcends all borders and all national boundaries. In this "country without borders"—the space of the New Europe or the "new" European culture of postmodernism—there are no more "Russians," only "Robinsons": universal subjects reduced to primitive signs in a level playing field—the virtual landscape of discourse (Husserl's "transcendental consciousness") grounded in a universe of silence, emptiness, and absence. The postmodern world of the Internet and the global Web site.

Petrushevskaia's story has no traditional moral to offer, no philosophy of life and no obvious message. This is because its medium is its message and its form is its content. The story is an exercise in the construction of meaning out of the material of language. It is thus a semiotic exercise. The family Robinson and the peasant women are a complex metaphor for the semiotic process, which frames Petrushevskaia's narrative as a "text within the text" or as metatext. But as an exercise in metatextuality, the story puts an entirely new order of reality square before the reader. This is the virtual order of language—of the imaginary and the symbolic. It literally abounds in meaning, is *all* meaning, not as "truth" or "essence," but as an open-ended, infinite field of "possible meanings" or of meaning as possibility. This is "what is the case" for the story, the story-teller and the "new Russian" readers in an ideal (hoped-for) reception. It is the new given and the new truth for the "new Russian Robinsons," who must make a clean sweep of their recent history (which haunts the story between the lines like the uncanny), their state ideology, and their socialist realist metaphysics in order to go back to the "primal" way of looking at the world of phenomena—as children or primitives, or the Adamists of Russian Acmeism. The "new Russian Robinsons" find themselves at the end of the twentieth century, like the European Robinson of the eighteenth century, on an uninhabited island, where they must create their civilization anew, out of absence and silence and the sheer force of thought. The experience of thought as memory and inscription constitutes the "real" order of the "new Russians." This new "world order" is that of virtual reality, in which truth has no identity beyond that of creative play or of a cerebral game—a game of chess, for instance.[41]

Tatiana Tolstaia's Transitional Russia and the *Presymbolic Imaginary*

The postmodern (semiotic) model of perception is also thematized in the structure and content of Tatiana Tolstaia's oeuvre. The grand-daughter of A. N. Tolstoy and a distant relation of L. N. Tolstoy, Tatiana Tolstaia began writing in 1983. She published short stories in Russian in various journals. Her first collection, *On the Golden Porch* (Na zolotom kryl'tse sideli, Moscow, 1987), was brought out in English in 1989. Her second collection has also appeared in English translation, under the title *Sleepwalker in a Fog* (New York, 1993).

In the story "Loves Me, Loves Me Not," the heroine's name is Maryvanna. It is the fusion of a name and patronymic: Maria Ivanovna. Maryvanna is actually the anti-heroine of the story. For the story is experienced and narrated as memory and from the point of view of yet another adolescent narrator: a girl who is not yet seven and who also remains unnamed. Maryvanna is the governess-cum-French-teacher of the child narrator and her sibling. The story is set in post-revolutionary Leningrad, in which pre-revolutionary cultural values linger on in families of the Russian intelligentsia, like the family of the child narrator.

But as in the paintings of Tatiana Nazarenko, history is evoked in Tolstaia's story only through scraps of memory, which are captured in old photographs. The story sacrifices history for the present moment, which is constructed with vehemence through the aggressive self-centeredness (ego) of the subject of the story, the child narrator. The seven-year-old girl's likes, dislikes, fears, and fantasies are carved out of a durable present and stand out in relation to the surrounding emptiness or space in the form of fragmentary and fantastic images, that is, images of the subject's fantasy or imagination. However, just as in the earlier story by Petrushevskaia, this heroine's imagination is not cast as the solipsistic imagination of a particular individual. This imagination is, instead, a generalized semiotic space, which psychoanalytic discourse calls the pre-symbolic imaginary. The imaginary is the locus of discontinuous dreamlike images and the store-house of memory traces, which constitute language and the symbolic order.[42] There is something infantile about these fantasies of the child heroine, something naive and close to the nature of dreams, where concept and image have not yet been separated.

The unity of image and concept is reflected in the lack of distance between the grown-up, whose mind evokes the memories of the seven-year-old narrator of the story, and the child she once was and still is in the shape of her own memory of childhood. Thus narrated event and the event of narration are brought together, obliterating any notion of development, or progress in time. The entire story can be seen as a single speech act or a dream consisting of several synchronous sequences. The immediacy of the dream or the speech act, as an instantaneous and particular (*once-off*)[43] articulation (like that of a bullet fired from a pistol), is reinforced by the spontaneity and youthful caprice of the pre-adolescent consciousness, through whose prism the world is refracted.

The reflected world, however, is not the world outside. It is the world of subjective childhood memory, of childhood fantasy, and even of delirium, induced by childhood sicknesses and fevers. Thus scraps of memory, like the visit to the flea-market with "father," are fused with bed-time stories or poems, which come to life as the child's imagination invests objects in the nursery and in the read poems or stories with phantasmic reality. This process of giving names to unnamable fantasies is reflected in the childish practice of anthropomorphizing the nursery world with creatures like The Snake, The Dry One, The Nameless One, Indrik and Hindrik. These invisible phantasms, which grow into "word concepts," mingle with fragments of the Russian literary tradition—stories, poems and fairy-tales heard or read (such as those of Pushkin, Lermontov, or other Russian classics)—as well as with scraps of poetry attributed to the Uncle, Maryvanna's mysterious love, which abound with themes of violence, death and desire. These narratives coalesce into discourse —or into the texture of the story that comes to embody it—to form the child's world. It is through this world of discourse that the child defines herself as an ego, which is to say, a sensibility—a bundle of fears, fevers, deliriums, and affects (likes and dislikes).

The family is, once again, the site of discourse or the scene of writing. Just as self-referentiality (in the imaginary) is the safe "home" of "childhood"—and the child, returning from a walk around strange streets when the park is closed, is relieved—so meaning is constituted within the self-referential (tautological) structure of the "familial" grid, marked by difference in relation to the unmapped "wild" and uncanny (unfamiliar) world "outside."

Maryvanna, the governess, is perceived by the child-narrator as a part of this "outside." Maryvanna, says the child narrator, "is not family." Maryvanna is the unloved Stranger, the "other" who appears to make the child feel excluded and unloved, but who also is the means by which the child narrator defines herself as a totality, as an ego. The governess, who is refracted through the child's consciousness as an evil intruder, is not perceived as evil by the reader or, indeed, by other children in the story, to whom she was once governess. Maryvanna's name has a magic sound quality for the reader, and it is this mellifluous quality of the governess's name that foregrounds her function as a Saussurean sound image. Within the structure of the narrative—and hence in relation to the child's imaginary—she represents a signifier pure and simple.[44] But Maryvanna is also a subject of her own narrative-reminiscence, which is propelled by desire generated around the figure of the elusive and faintly transgressive (incestuous) Uncle, who is the love of her youth and to whom all her memories return. This Uncle, invoked by the child-narrator in a fantasy induced by poems attributed to him, becomes the "other" of the narrative, once as the source of sexual desire (Maryvanna's) in the symbolic, and once as the origin of the child's ecstatic dread (in the experience of night fears) that prefigures it in the imaginary. Thus, like Petrushevskaia's story, Tolstaia's also owes its existence to a phantasmic or fantasized other. Its origin—like that of discourse—is situated in the pre-adolescent, narcissistic imaginary, whose production is analogous to hallucinations or day-dreaming.[45]

The end of the child's reminiscences, with Maryvanna's permanent exit from the life of the narrator, completes the utterance that the story represents. Maryvanna, who as governess floats in and out of the lives of children, helping them define themselves as egos in relation to an other, thus accomplishes her role in the language game, which represents both the form and the content of Tolstaia's story.

In this game, Maryvanna is an agent of alienation. The child feels alienated ("unloved") by Maryvanna, who comes into her life following the departure of a much-loved nanny. The difference between the two nannies is that the earlier one understood the child's feelings "without words." Maryvanna, on the other hand, brings words (poems) and picture-stories (old photographs with memories attached to them) into the child's world. Maryvanna—whose name is half a sign in Saussure's definition[46]—thus introduces "word concepts" into the unitary, self-sufficient world of the child's imaginary, in order to lead the child out of this world into that of culture and the symbolic order, which impinges on the production of signifiers originating as memory traces ("old photographs"). Maryvanna is the muse of this world of exchange of signs and memory. It is no accident that Maryvanna's entry into the child's world (and the reader's entry into the realm of the child's imaginary) is greeted with dialogue or direct speech and that the opening dialogue of the story is about the children "going out" with Maryvanna: "The other children are allowed out by themselves, but we have to go with Maryvanna!"[47] This "going out" with Maryvanna—the agent of alienation—represents, in the child's development, the going out of the register of the imaginary into the register of the symbolic. This is the register of language and speech, in which the child ultimately has to constitute herself as a human subject of discourse.

There is an interesting though still linear reading of "Loves Me, Loves Me Not" in Helena Goscilo's recent monograph.[48] Although Goscilo recognizes the significance of the linguistic profile of Maryvanna, she evaluates the older nanny, Grusha, as more positive in the context of the story because "her mode of communication is bodily, tactile—that of the domestic microcosm, a domain in which individualized, immediate experience plays a more prominent part." This seems to imply that what the child experiences through language (brought into her orbit by Maryvanna, as Goscilo agrees) is not "individualized, immediate experience." The point of the child's intense experiencing of the "poems" of "Uncle George," whose function in the story Goscilo identifies correctly as a spoof on decadence but incorrectly as unreflexive bona fide and "realistically" portrayed bed-time reading in the nursery, is to dramatize the imaginary as the locus of the production of metaphor. It is not a mimetic exercise in the representation of an actual child and its actual governess, or the solipsistic imagination of an individual infantile sensibility. Goscilo also identifies the problematic of the "limits of language" as a central issue of Tolstaia's story, but locates this limit in "human communication," that is, in dialogue. The "limit" in Goscilo's reading becomes the dividing line between the success or failure of communication between two people (Maryvanna and the child) instead of a phenomenological (virtual) limit located in subjectivity. The subject comes up against this limit even if he or she is stranded on a desert island. Every writer is such an "island" because language or discourse (as opposed to communication in dialogue), which is modeled by the story's structure, is grounded in the "wilderness" of the imaginary and has as its only support what is on the other side of the limit (of sense): non-sense, *le néant* (nothing) or silence. Rather than failing "to acknowledge the human other in the child," Maryvanna leads the child successfully through a rite of passage into the symbolic order representing the discourse of the other. If the child were to remain with her "beloved nanny" Grusha and never "experience" the break or split in the imaginary, she would be locked in her autistic (pre-verbal) phase of development. The point about love, which the story makes, is the one made by Lacan, when he said of the subject's other: "That which is thus given to the other to fill, and which is strictly that which it does not have, since it, too, lacks being, is what is called love...."[49] Maryvanna is not a mimetic portrait of a governess but this other that "lacks being," and as such exists only as a play of shadows, constituted as negativity and the uncanny.

"Loves Me, Loves Me Not" carries a theme that is submerged under the general scaffolding of the structure of the metanarrative. It is related to the theme of *desire*, made explicit in Maryvanna's references to the Uncle and in Uncle's poems. Desire emerges in those interpolated texts (poems attributed to the Uncle or to an imaginary Pushkin) as a second order reality, perverse and violent, which inspires dread but also *negative pleasure* (a potential or repressed *jouissance*) in the pre-adolescent child. This generalized dread is the precursor of the child's sexual identity, which is a matter of the future, namely her future in the symbolic order of cultural relations. By contrast with the grown-up world of desire, sexual desire for the child is a "polymorphous perversion" only in potentiality. It appears in anticipatory form as nocturnal fears, caused by terrifying and perverse bed-time stories about or by the Uncle. This perverse *jouissance*, complemented by the child's negative desire for Maryvanna, conceals the pleasure principle as the mainspring of the child's development as an ego and a sensibility. For what the child dislikes—does not want—dominates the *sujet*. What she dislikes most of all is her governess. There are no explicit reasons stated for the child's antipathy for Maryvanna; it is simply there, as a given grounding the heroine's identity, constituted as negativity and desire —will, caprice, and judgment of taste.

These, manifest in the child's whining insubordination, generate the story as memory in the concrete form of inner speech. The child's memory, which unfolds like an interior monologue emanating from a decentered subject of unspecified age, represents the phenomenological reality of speech. It is this reality which the reader is drawn into in the course of the act of reading. This act itself is a multilayered dramatic inner monologue of many voices, which includes the voice of the story mingling with the voices or associations that they trigger in the reader's memory. The story is thus both an act and a re-enactment. It is a speech-act that is re-enacted in the process of reading, which is itself structured as the speech of an other. The process has no beginning—in that the narrative will always precede any reader who takes it up to re-enact it—and no end. For the reader can always re-enact the speech-act of the child's narrative by simply taking up the story again to reread it. It is this game of discourse as re-enactment of repressed memory, manifested as inner speech, which is modeled by Tolstaia's story. Discourse as reenactment of memory corresponds to the modernists' technique of stream-of-consciousness in that it is always already repetition, a "re" without an "original" zero point of consciousness. The re-enactment is always already a performance and a scene—a virtual production of a "transcendental consciousness" (Husserl) which stages itself as memory, not that of the subject, but that of the subject's other. That is why memory as modeled in postmodern texts invariably has a double frame: it is a refraction of "two" subjects, set within each other in the manner of a Matryoshka or a Silenus. This "encapsulated" memory that doubles up on itself encompasses desire and repression: the miser's casket hidden between the folds of discourse and the invisible side of the fold that constitutes the unsaid or the excess of the signified. This double frame of memory is portrayed by both Petrushevskaia and Tolstaia with the aid of the device of a split narrator: a narrator who is both an adult and a child, a present and a past self, a subject who is simultaneously knowledgeable and opaque (naive).

In "Hunting the Woolly Mammoth," the heroine, Zoya, also has a name that attracts attention: "Zoya's a beautiful name, isn't it? Like bees buzzing by."[50] Like Maryvanna, Zoya as character is represented as a sound-image. This immediately situates the narrative about her in the field of semiotic discourse. The narrative is told by a third-person narrator but from Zoya's perspective, rendering Zoya both subject and object of her story. However, as subject, she is not fully fledged, remaining throughout the story too close to the object. Indeed, she is focused on objects—petty consumer objects of the command economies of Eastern Europe: "a wall unit with a colour television," "a light and graceful robe (full of ruffles, made in East Germany)," "pink light coming from the Yugoslav lamp."[51] Zoya also perceives herself as an object, that is, she wants to be an object of "universal" aesthetic appreciation. She is constantly imagining how other people are evaluating her beauty, upon which she sets a high value. She lives in the expectation of the admiring gaze of others, which fails to materialize. She wants to be greeted by the ecstatic sighs of "Oh!" She wants to render speechless through her appearance, which in her eyes is something close to an absolute. Zoya's articulated desire is to be reified, to annihilate the distance between subject and object, and to figure as a "transcendental" signified, thereby becoming the object of a universal quasi-religious worship.

What stands in the way of Zoya's self-realization as a transcendental object (signified) is her location in a world of language, which is delimited by what this language makes possible and impossible. From the very beginning of "her" story, Zoya is defined as a name—a primitive sign—and accorded the status of an agent of language. Except for her own self-centered gaze, turned in upon herself, Zoya is insignificant. That is to say, she does not signify, is not a signified, but rather is a sign among other signs, engaged in an ongoing struggle for recognition and coming into meaning within the open-ended system of the symbolic order of language.

As a sign or signifier, Zoya is opaque. Although the story is told from her perspective, she does not know as much about herself and her world as the reader and the abstract author know. She literally serves the story to point to certain realities. But as pointing stick or signifier, she has no overview of the total picture presented by her narrative. For instance, she does not know very much about Vladimir, the man she is obsessed with marrying. Altogether, her point of view is that of the *ingénue*, who blurts out truths without knowing their true worth. Zoya never overcomes this limitation and is thus left in limbo at the end of the story. She does not progress, does not learn, and never comes into subjecthood, although her unconscious desire is to achieve the latter. This is what gives "her" story a certain tragicomic pathos even if such affectivity is only parodic mimicry, behind which lurks the narrator's superior knowledge of the true multifaceted state of affairs.

What Zoya seeks consciously and with determination is certainty. For her, certainty is represented by various closed systems: the hierarchy of a technocratic world, in which surgeons have more prestige than engineers; the cozy perks of a state system, such as a small flat in Moscow; a cushy job in hospital administration, with petty bribes from patients and affordable, balmy holidays in the Caucasus. Ultimate certainty for Zoya can be found in an institutionalized system, represented in the story by the metaphor of marriage. Zoya's story is the story of a "hunt," motivated by her quest for certainty and prestige. Because Zoya is scheming and stalking a quarry, she is, in her own eyes, in a position of mastery. However, in the eyes of the reader, she is no more than a parody of the Hegelian Master who hunts but does not work, and who is engaged in a prestige fight to the death with her adversary, Vladimir. The fight itself is parodied by Zoya's tacit but categorical demand: "marry me or else." The tables are turned on poor Zoya even before her story starts, the moment she introduces herself by name. For even then, the closed system of certainties that she yearns for is, like the former Soviet Union, mere history and nostalgia.

What Zoya misjudges in her quest for recognition as an absolute (metaphysical) object is the nature of the "other," namely her adversary, Vladimir. Objectively, from the reader's perspective, Vladimir has been tamed and domesticated by Zoya. His love for Zoya is established between the lines, in the subtext of Zoya's naive and subjective story. If Tolstaia's narrative were about the relationship between "this man Vladimir" and "this woman Zoya," there would not be much of a story. The theme of a love story is executed in the subtext of the actual narrative: Vladimir loves Zoya, tries to please her and never alludes to leaving her. End of story. The nature of Vladimir, and not Vladimir's relationship to Zoya, is thus the key to Tolstaia's narrative.

This man, whom Zoya neither "wants" nor "loves" but wishes to subjugate into "service," does not fit into her preconceived system of certainty. This is because Vladimir belongs to an elemental sphere, pulsating with irrepressible life and joy, and is as close to the concrete "real" as Zoya is to the stasis of a metaphysical "unreal." This "unreal," which is tantamount to primal repression in the pre-symbolic imaginary, puts her out of touch with her own language and prevents it from coming into articulation. That is why "her" story is told by an invisible third person narrator—a technique identified by Dostoevsky as that of a stenographer able to listen in on the stream of thought of an inarticulate (uneducated, mad, infantile, impaired) fictional character. Her inability to "come into language"—her own language—finds expression in her constant anxiety about being dispossessed of her ideal beauty. Vladimir is active, he is forever in motion, doing something, tinkering with a kayak, going canoeing, inspecting "underground" conceptualist art, engaging in intellectual debate. He loves the outdoors, loves nature, the elements, hands-on sports. All of these traits amount to a new sense of freedom and concreteness of being. Vladimir's body reflects this concreteness and materiality, which is not to be confused with materialism. He is stout and hardy; he has, like the woolly mammoth—who becomes his metaphoric double in the story—a lot of obstinate red hair, which grows on his face in the form of two mustaches, one on his lips and one on his chin. Both the woolly mammoth and Vladimir are, in turn, metaphors for the Master Signifier, which is the thematic and structural axis upon which the narrative turns. Both belong to the exotic and/or archaic (repressed) "real," which is erupting in Soviet History as a heterogeneous force, theorized by George Bataille as a cultural antithesis to homogeneity:

> Homogeneous reality presents itself with the abstract and neutral aspect of strictly defined and identified objects (basically, it is the specific reality of solid objects). Heterogeneous reality is that of a force or a shock. It presents itself as a charge, as a value, passing from one object to another in a more or less abstract fashion, almost as if the

> change were taking place not in the world of objects but only in the judgment of the subject.[52]

Vladimir represents this "force" or "shock." He stands for the new field of force of heterogeneity, embodied in the landscape of the northern Russian rivers—the habitat of a new "community" of Russian friends who have an annihilating effect on Zoya's self-esteem, triggering a crisis in Zoya, the effect of which could be said to give birth to Zoya's unconscious. Both the woolly mammoth and the unloved Vladimir are part of Zoya's "bad dream," which constitutes her nightmarish "hunt" for certainty. For Zoya is at the same stage of development as the six-year-old child in *Loves Me, Loves Me Not.* That is, she, like pre-perestroika Soviet society, is immature, that is, pre-Oedipal. She has not yet entered the symbolic order of discourse and post-history, grounded in the heterogeneous "real" that is represented in the pictures of the conceptualist artist, or by Vladimir and the kayak he brings into Zoya's cramped flat. The kayak—a visible object carved out of (an invisible) space[53]—is a metonymy of the phallic, restless Vladimir: a signifier without a signified, brought down from metaphysical heights into the concrete space of the post-Soviet citizeness, filling her with emptiness and malaise, but producing an effect that could be called the birth of unconscious *desire.*

Zoya's unconscious desire is alluded to in her tentative wish for a surgeon husband of unorthodox (*uncanny*) profile. While this wish remains unrealized (repressed), Zoya's unconscious, which is born simultaneously with and from this wish, is presented as a metaphor erupting within the manifest plot of the story in the form of Zoya's memory of the three pictures of the "underground" Russian artist. The cellar studio of the conceptualist painter whom Zoya and Vladimir visit is situated literally "below ground"—in the region of the repressed imaginary—the locus of latent dreams and the site of production of dream thoughts condensed into pictures or metaphors. This is the sphere of the unconscious—a second order reality of potential meanings that is synonymous with the heterogeneous, the "spiritual" ("underground") home of the forces of perestroika, which swept across Russia in the 1980s. Vladimir, his kayaking friends and their frolicking dirty-faced women who embody this heterogeneous force are taking Russia with them, into a new exuberant freedom. Even the conservative Zoya is swept along, unwilling though she may be, following Vladimir dutifully, motivated by her overt agenda, and unaware of being driven by a hidden agenda of her own unconscious.

The artist, whose paintings are accurately reproduced by Zoya from memory (amazingly, since she does not like the paintings and hardly seems to notice them), has views on reality that are totally antithetical to Zoya's own. The conceptualist artist rejects "concepts" with vehemence. "Concepts" smack of the old ideological order, of abstractions and generalizations imposed on life. Like Wittgenstein, one suspects, the underground artist feels that "concepts" are generalizations about the concrete and the particular. They are at variance with the heterogeneous elements of life because "concepts" can never subsume the multiplicity of particular "facts" that make up life's diversity. Hence, "concepts" (like Zoya's autoerotic concept of beauty) idealize and distort reality. The heterogeneous does not lend itself to conceptualization or abstraction. According to Bataille, with whom Vladimir's painter friend might side, "(K)nowledge" of the heterogeneous reality "is to be found in the mystical thinking of primitives and in dreams: it is identical to the structure of the unconscious."[54]

This unconscious, which is coeval with the heterogeneous, is represented by the three pictures viewed by Zoya and Vladimir at the artist's studio. These three pictures frame Zoya's "story" like the latent content of a manifest dream—her "bad dream" about the frustrated "hunt" for a husband.

The three pictures at the artist's studio are all deconstructionist representations of the homogeneous world of concepts. As such, they have much in common with the American pop art of the 1970s.[55] On the structural level of the narrative, the three pictures may also be viewed as three separate dream sequences, through which Zoya's unconscious is making a single statement.

The first one, entitled *Concordance*, is a deconstruction of ideological clichés: "a large egg, with lots of tiny people coming out of it, Mao Tse-tung in canvas boots and an embroidered jacket floating in the sky with a teapot in his hand."[56] The ideological icon of communism is here represented irreverently as a two-dimensional carnival float divested of its power and reduced to the level of the banal, evoked by the domestic slippers and the folksy embroidered jacket. This is a pictographic comment on the process of transformation of socialist realism into popular culture. The masses, who used to serve as fodder for Mao's political power, are now seen as a self-generating heterogeneous force, oozing out like a bodily fluid from a place whose origins are as imprecise as the answer to the question: what came first, the chicken or the egg? The title of this picture—*Concordance*—is at first glance not obviously related to this picture itself. In fact, it is not, for it relates to the larger picture of Tolstaia's story, which is structured like a metaphor, of which the prime mover is the mechanism of substitution. "Concordance" might mean "correspondence," in which case the title would be an ironic allusion to the correspondence of signifier and signified assumed in all transcendental aesthetics, including Zoya's own homespun one. However, "concordance" extends its associative field to "resemblance," which in turn belongs to the structure of the signifier. For it is through the mode of substitution of the similar ("like") that difference ("not like") is established, to constitute metaphor.[57] *Concordance* is therefore an ironic title, pointing to the mis-representation (lie) carried by all cultural icons (signifieds), which also embodies the aesthetic principle of representation operating in Tolstaia's story as a whole. This principle is the same as that employed by Petrushevskaia and has to do with representation as a function of language, which always says more or less than it wants to say (*voudrait dire*). Hence all representation is mis-representation (lying), and to ignore this in the case of cultural icons that are taken seriously is to give up freedom of thought for doctrinal truth.

The second picture is a comment on scientific knowledge, which is, according to Bataille, of the order of the "homogeneous."[58] The picture represents "an apple with a worm crawling out of it wearing glasses and carrying a briefcase."[59] The apple is an allusion to Newton's apple. But the apple of modern science (Newtonian physics) has a "bureaucratic worm" in it: that is, science, which relies on positivistic knowledge, is like a bureaucrat, serving only his own ends and those of the apparatus.

The third picture features the "woolly mammoth," from which the story derives its title. This is a canvas featuring

> a wild craggy cliff, growth of cattails, and from the cattails comes a woolly mammoth in slippers. Someone tiny is aiming at it with bow and arrow. On one side you can see the little cave: it has a light bulb hanging from a cord, a glowing television screen, and a gas burner. Even the pressure cooker is drawn in detail, and there's a bouquet of cattails on the table. It's called *Hunting the Woolly Mammoth.*[60]

This surrealist picture, whose precision of realistic details and their incongruent juxtaposition recalls the paintings of Max Ernst (in particular, his 1921 *Elephant of Celebes*),[61] is like a graphic dream version or a rebus of Zoya's own "story." All the symbols of domesticity in the cave recall similar symbols of modern consumerism populating Zoya's imagined or desired life in her tiny one-room apartment. The cave itself symbolizes a primordial reality—the primary unconscious of Zoya's unitary Soviet psyche and the retrograde state of consciousness of homogeneous and repressed society. Itself endowed with the comforts of technological progress, such a society is on the same level of "historical evolution" as that of the stone age man, following the discovery of basic tools. In this regressive homogeneous social order, man is still trying to capture a primordial and allegedly extinct animal—the woolly mammoth—using primordial tools: a bow and arrow. The hunt is as pointless as Zoya's hunt for certainty. Both hunts are tautological, both symbolize one thing: the impossibility of capturing or taming the primordial object, that "extinct" *thing* (Freud's Ding,[62] which Zoya confuses with the *signified*)—the "real" or *objet petit a*, which is "archaic" in the sense that it goes to the very foundations of the unconscious as the absent and unrepresentable "cause of desire"[63]—source of heterogeneous reality and of discourse.

The conceptualist "landscape of the unconscious" in this picture is coextensive with Zoya's unconscious. It is the scene of primary repression (hence its "primordial" character), from which the signifier can emerge as metaphor or meaning through the process of "secondary" repression. But in order to come into secondary repression, the subject of language has to go through another unconscious process—namely that of symbolic castration,[64] which signifies the subject's separation from the imaginary primal object and entry into the symbolic order—the order of the signifier, of language, of speech and of *writing*.[65]

This process is represented by Zoya's ostensibly conscious wish for a prestige marriage to a surgeon. However, the kind of surgeon she evokes in her "wishful thinking"—in and of itself at least potentially an unconscious process—is not an ordinary doctor, whom the reader would normally associate with any modern civilized medical system. The surgeon of Zoya's desire is not one to be found in a Moscow general hospital or, for that matter, in any modern hospital. He is more like a symbolic castrator, a *kolich* going through the motions of a ritual act, who "perform(s) the highest judgment," who comes down "to chop off, to punish and to save, and with his glowing sword give life." This give-away formulation (a Freudian slip perhaps) means that the pre-Oedipal ("retarded") Zoya, is unconsciously yearning to go through the process of symbolic castration, to be split by the castrator's "glowing sword" (a kitsch symbol of the phallus) and to be "given life" as a new "split" subject, "crossed" by language. In the course of her manifest narrative, Zoya's wish is not granted. She is not propelled into the symbolic order of heterogeneous discourse. However, the parallel existence of a latent content, which frames her plot (her "marriage project") like a latent dream or repressed memory trace (or her stream-of-consciousness albeit assigned to the narrator's text), signals a crisis and a transformation in the making. On the level of her unconscious wishes, Zoya would love to go through her Oedipal phase and emerge into "life," just as Russia of the mid-1980s would love to enter the life of pluralist discourses and the heterogeneous systems of the Western democracies. This time of change notwithstanding, Russia, like Zoya, is still adulating the transcendental signified—the Party, Lenin, and a reality literally beyond this world. But in this time of change, Russia, like Zoya, is grappling with the "primordial animal"—the larger-than-life object that is no object at all: the "concrete" ("real") but elusive, forever absent signified, always "sliding" under the signifier to form the "gap" or space that constitutes the unconscious or non-meaning—a heterogeneous reality without boundary or fence. Zoya's mistake is to confuse the signifier (which bears Vladimir's features) with the signified (the woolly mammoth of her "dream" memory) and to project the elusiveness of the latter onto the former. Zoya, in fact, is not familiar with the structure of language as a signifying substitution and hence does not appreciate the dialectic that grounds the story's metaphor of the woolly mammoth, which she experiences unreflexively as a "picture." This is not so for her maker, Tatiana Tolstaia, or the reader. To them, Vladimir, whom Zoya wants and rejects at the same time, is a metonymy of the repressed signified (the "primordial animal" of Zoya's "picture") and as such forms part of the "logic of the signifier."[66] The signifier, which has its origins in the unconscious that is tautologous with the signified, is laboriously sought by Zoya, who represents a passing order through whose perspective the story is narrated. The reader can feel Zoya's pain, the anxiety which the transformation is generating in her "soul." Zoya's plight elicits the reader's sympathy while Zoya's tragicomic lament—enclosed in itself like a bubble of affectivity—pours forth in a simulation of a stream-of-consciousness that appears to carry her circular story forward. In her self-enclosed righteous indignation, Zoya is a sensibility as yet unborn as a free subject of language. But the pain and frustration which she experiences, and which are the only things she can articulate concretely (apart from her accurate reproduction of the conceptualist paintings as a memory trace or dream thought), are portents of a birth or a rebirth of Zoya in a future that is open on all sides, like the pan into which she fails to "corral" her quarry (Vladimir as her other). However, this development belongs to another, future story.

Zoya's "case history" thus contains a "lesson" for the Soviet reader who might be going through a similar social transformation. It tells that the hunter and self-styled "master," Zoya, must ultimately experience frustration in her quest for supremacy and absolutization. The future is with her "slave," Vladimir, the man who loves her and wants to give her pleasure. Supremacy in the new post-transformation society belongs not to the Master, but to the Master Signifier, whose pedigree is in "slavery," "service" and "work." Like Vladimir who embodies it in the story, the signifier belongs to the field of the heterogeneous, which has its concrete being in conscious mental action, expressed as the will to freedom.

Zoya misunderstands the nature of the new force of transformation, embodied by Vladimir. But even her misconception belongs to the process of change that has already colonized her unconscious in the form of the misrecognized wish for a surgeon-husband alias symbolic castrator. Thus Zoya's conscious wish for certainty (for unity and sameness) is simultaneously subverted by her unconscious wish to enter a new order—the symbolic order of language, whose subject is by definition a split subject. Through this unconscious wish, Zoya is already marked by the story as a potentially de-centered heroine even if she cannot, by definition, "know" this. She experiences alienation but only in the form of a malaise which she thinks she can explain in terms of her desire for a formality—a prestigious marriage, which is eluding her. What she mis-recognizes is the fact that this is already a desire for *oformlenie*, that is, for a coming into form. Her quest for certainty thus has an aspect which is the opposite of her avowed desire: namely, a wish for symbolization, expressed in three "pictorial" dream sequences, which are anagrams of the structure of metaphor and the logic of the signifier.

The representation of the cave in the picture entitled *Hunting the Woolly Mammoth* alludes to Plato's famous metaphor. In Tolstaia's "cave," the human subject has no identity beyond that of powerlessness and archaism: it is shrunk to minuscule proportions ("someone tiny"), who is taking aim with an antiquated bow and arrow. This subject appears overwhelmed by the enormity of the space represented by "the scene." The scene itself is the scene of signification[67] and the space is the virtual space of discourse. The subject, shrunk to an "extensionless point" in that space, is decentered and almost insignificant (not signifying anything). Tolstaia's cave is inhabited by *banal objects*, which are self-sufficient signs, pointing to nothing beyond the "real" of the objects themselves. It is in the banal that the object can be captured in its essence. Hence the trivia of objects in conceptualist art—both in the domesticated details of the three paintings represented in the story and in Ilya Kabakov's conceptualist installations, analyzed elsewhere. The banality of the object is shared by Zoya and Mao Tse-tung, both of whom are stripped of any metaphysical "conceptual" value, which might refract a "higher truth" situated outside the "cave." Both the post-Soviet citizen and the icon of communism are brought down to the level of the object, which is the subject's banal ("real") other and ultimate "truth."

It is thus Zoya's potential split through the "real" of the object that generates Zoya's tortured inner monologue, whose tension is maintained by the unanswered question: "will he marry me?" The entire narrative appears to generate itself through the structure of this interrogation. Both the questions and answers appear to be supplied by Zoya, since hers is the only consciousness through which the world of the narrative is refracted. However, the interrogative text has an autonomy—derived from the unconscious which, as the Dadaists demonstrated, was "automatic" *writing*—that constitutes a quasi-conversation between Zoya and her other. This is what renders even the old-fashioned, homogenous and Soviet Zoya into not one but two characters: herself and an other. Unknown to her opaque self, Zoya is thus as decentered as the "someone tiny" in the dream-picture of the woolly mammoth.

For this reason, it is difficult to situate Zoya's actions in the sphere of intentionality. Her conscious self-interrogation, which is apparently controlled by her will, is at the same time a function of the unconscious structure of language. In other words, her obsessive interrogative text is the very language of the unconscious, pouring forth without origins or closure, constituting itself as discourse as if without the will or intention of the subject. For Zoya's intention, if any, is replaced by wishful thinking (desire for a surgeon husband), or negative yearning (she did not love Vladimir yet the less she loved him the more intensely she wished to marry him). In her private emotional "underground," Zoya subverts her assumed and overt value system as much as the "underground" artist, whom she rejects on the conscious level. On the unconscious level Zoya is thus a new conceptualist subject in the making. She has appropriated—or has herself been appropriated by—conceptualist images, which take shape in her unconscious as memory. These images, grounded in the banal, are an integral part of the new heterogeneous reality, represented by the voluptuous Vladimir—the object of Zoya's ambivalent desire. The transition signaled by the heroine's crisis and alienation from her desire points in the direction of freedom as a new form of being in a heterogeneous reality. Events since the mid-1980s have shown that Russia has gone in the direction in which Tolstaia's heroine first dared to look in her negative day-dreams.

* * *

The readings of the stories of Petrushevskaia and Tolstaia offered here demonstrate the richness of texture of Russian postmodern prose. This prose is grounded in the semiotic or signifying structures of language, which render every text simultaneously as a metatext—that is, a text reflecting its own laws of production. These laws are subsumed under the two basic mechanisms of language, metaphor and metonymy, which bring signs into signification or meaning. Rather than pointing beyond themselves, to possible allegorical or mythological meanings, these texts recapture the gaze of the reader and redirect it into their interiority—or into what has elsewhere been described as the "unconscious structure" of the text, which operates like a language. Presented in a formally concentrated prosaic genre, reminiscent of the Chekhovian short story at the beginning of the twentieth century, these texts are structurally layered and thus vertically significant. This places novel exigencies on the interpreter. Instead of reading the stories in linear fashion and commenting on their content (by asking "What happens?"), one must ask, as in all post-absurd literature, "Who is speaking?" To answer this question, the texts must be read vertically or in cross-section, following Foucault's "archeological" method of "vivisection."

Poststructural critical theory offers an eclectic array of models, ranging from phenomenology to semiotics and psychoanalysis, which provide a critical instrumentarium that is adequate to such archeological analysis. Ultimately, such tools allow for a critical reading of texts that form the postmodern discourse of post-Soviet Russian literature. This new discourse allows the middle and younger generation of Russian writers (the forty-year-olds of the 1980s and the thirty-year-olds or younger generation of writers of the 1990s) to refract "Russian" reality more accurately than was possible through the epigonal mimetic modes of late Soviet aesthetics. This new reality is that of thought, out of which a new Russian *socius* and a new Russian post-Soviet *sociality* have begun to constitute themselves. The postmodern model of discourse, whose genesis in Russian literature has yet to be analyzed in detail, has brought post-Soviet Russian literature abreast with the mainstream representational modes of the contemporary Western cultural paradigm. This represents a giant paradigmatic leap into the world of the heterogeneous, following seven decades of systematic repression of thought and cultural homogenization.

Notes

1. Among the Russian critics, the following have recognized and commented on the new paradigm: Mikhail Epstein, "Iskusstvo avangarda i religioznoe soznanie," *Novy mir* 12 (1989): 222–35, writes on the "post-avant-garde;" Andrei Zorin, "Prigorodnyi poezd dal'nego sledovania," *Novy mir* 5 (1989): 256–8, writes on Venedikt Erofeev's *Moskva-Petushki;* Petr Vail' and Alexander Genis, "Novaia proza: ta zhe ili 'drugaia'? Printsip matreshki," *Novy mir* 10 (1989): 247–50. The authors have jointly published a book analyzing the paradigm shift in Russian culture since the 1960s, Petr Vail' and Alexander Genis, *60–e: Mir sovietskogo cheloveka* (Michigan, 1988). See also Vladimir Potapov, "Na vykhode iz 'andergraunda,'" *Novy mir* 10 (1989): 251–7; the same article appeared in English, under the title "Coming out of the 'Underground,'" in *Soviet Literature* 5 (1990): 157–64; Naum Leiderman and Mark Lipovetskii are joint authors of an article entitled "Mezhdu khaosom i kosmosom," *Novy mir* 7 (1991): 240–57; and Natalia Ivanova maps the paradigm shift in "Smena iazyka," *Znamia* 11 (November 1989): 221–31. In Australia and New Zealand, the following articles have attempted to define the new Russian literary paradigm: Collin Dowsett, "Allegory in Contemporary Soviet Literature: Vladimir Makanin's Utrata," *Australian Slavonic and East European Studies*, vol. 4, no. 1–2 (1990): 21–35; Slobodanka Vladiv-Glover, "Post-Modernism in Eastern Europe after World War II: Yugoslav, Polish and Russian Literatures," *Australian Slavonic and East European Studies*, vol. 5, no. 2 (1991): 123–44.

2. See his article in *Novy mir* 10 (1989).
3. Oleg Chukhontsev, ed., *Dissonant Voices: The New Russian Fiction* (Harvill, 1991).
4. Kharitonov's entry, *Lines of Fate or Milashevich's Casket* [Linii sud'by ili sunduchok Milashevicha] first appeared in *Druzhba narodov* 1 (1992).
5. Vladimir Potapov, *Soviet Literature* 5 (1990): 158 and *Novy mir* 10 (1989): 251.
6. Potapov, *Soviet Literature* 5 (1990): 158.
7. On the other hand, Ivor Severin, in his article "Novaia literatura 70–80–kh," *Vestnik novoi literatury*, no. 1 (1990), uses the term "postmodernism" but only in the restricted sense of a "literature without tendentiousness."
8. Potapov, *Soviet Literature* 5 (1990): 157.
9. See Slobodanka Vladiv-Glover, "Postmodernism in Eastern Europe After WWII: Yugoslav, Polish and Russian Literatures": 123–44. See also the recent "dictionary" of postmodernism by Deborah L. Madsen, *Postmodernism: A Bibliography, 1926–1994* (Amsterdam/Atlanta, 1995), in which the compiler has identified the first occurrence of the term "postmodernism" in 1926. Such a finding emphasizes the continuity of modernism/postmodernism as a European cultural paradigm of the twentieth century.
10. An analysis of the modernist genesis of the representation of the object in postmodernism is given in my deconstructive reading of Voznesenksy's *Oza*, forthcoming in *Literarische Avantgarde: Festschrift für Rudolf Neuhäuser*, ed. Horst-Jürgen Gerigk, *Contributions to Theory and Practice of Interpretation*, vol. 7 (Dresden, 1998). In the genre of "object (thing) poetry," articulated most vigorously around the time of the World War II by the Polish poets Herbert, Biaoszewski, and Milosz, the study of the object was testimony to a quest for the "real" which is still ongoing in the arts of the late twentieth century. See Hal Foster, *The Return of the Real: The Avant-Garde at the End of the Century, An October Book* (Cambridge, Mass., 1996).
11. For an overview of the history of the postmodern debate see, Andreas Huyssen, "Mapping the Postmodern," *New German Critique* 33 (Fall 1984):5–53.
12. The American Marxist critic, Frederic Jameson, postulates a radical break between the modernism of the early twentieth century and postmodernism, which he, together with many others, situates in the 1950s and early 1960s. See Frederic Jameson, "Postmodernism, or The Cultural Logic of Late Capitalism," *New Left Review* 146 (July–August 1984): 53–93. The thesis about the continuity of French (and by extension European or Western) thought in the twentieth century is developed in the analysis of vision in Martin Jay's monograph *Downcast Eyes: The Denigration of Vision in Twentieth Century French Thought* (Berkeley, Los Angeles, London, 1994). Modernism/postmodernism thus become modulations of the same essential aesthetic and perceptual paradigm. Another way of looking at the relationship of modernism to postmodernism is to see the latter as accomplishing or bringing to a logical conclusion the impulses of the former.
13. A. K. Zholkovsky, "Zh/Z: Zametki byvshego post-strukturalista," *Literaturnoe obozrenie* 10 (1991): 31–35. In this article, Zholkovsky takes a retrospective

look at Soviet criticism and literary theory based on the insights he gained as a Soviet émigré scholar living in the United States since 1979.

14. See the works on Bakhtin by the American Slavist scholars Michael Holquist, Katerina Clark, Caryl Emerson, and Gary Saul Morson.
15. The present author situates her own early critical work within the context of the structuralist/poststructuralist reception of Bakhtin, which began with the Bakhtin criticism of German Slavists (notably Wolf Schmid and Horst-Jürgen Gerigk). Compare the monograph by Slobodanka Vladiv, *Narrative Principles in Dostoevskij's Besy: A Structural Analysis* (Berne, 1979).
16. Once again, most of the theoretical work on the paradigm shift in European poststructuralist thought has come from France. For example, Michel Foucault, in *The Order of Things: An Archeology of the Human Sciences* (Les Mots et les choses) (London, 1992; Paris, 1966), locates a radical break between what he calls "classical" thought and "modernity" at the end of the eighteenth century. However, Foucault's "modernity," which produces a new mode of representation, structured through the agency of the "clinical gaze," is a process that takes over a century to evolve from a "scientific" method into an aesthetics. It is thus at the end of the nineteenth century that "modernity" becomes a fully fledged new cultural paradigm, privileging language as a new philosophical domain: "Language did not return into the field of thought directly and in its own right until the end of the nineteenth century. We might even have said the twentieth, had not Nietzsche the philologist ... been the first to connect the philosophical task with a radical reflection upon language." Michel Foucault, *The Order of Things*, p. 305. On the application of Foucault's paradigm to Russian literature, see Vladiv-Glover, "What Does Ivan Karamazov Know? A Reading Through Foucault's Analytic of the 'Clinical Gaze,'" *New Zealand Slavonic Journal* (1995): 23–44.
17. On the question of Yugoslav postmodernism, see Vladiv-Glover, "[*Danilo Kiš*] Hourglass as the Scene of Writing," *Review of Contemporary Fiction*, vol. 14, no. 1 (Spring 1994): 147–60; "Postmodernism in Eastern Europe after WWII: Yugoslav, Polish and Russian Literatures," *Australian Slavonic and East European Studies*, vol. 5, no. 2 (1991): 123–144; and "New Paradigms in Contemporary Yugoslav Literature: 'That' Literature and 'Other' Prose," *Melbourne Slavonic Studies*, vol. 16 (1982): 22–42.
18. The term "schizo-aesthetics" is my adaptation of Arthur Koestler's term "schizo-psychology," used by him to describe the post-Auschwitz European reality which he, among others, felt called upon to represent in literature. The original context, in which this new mode of representation was first alluded to critically, was Theodor Adorno's famous declaration that no more poetry could be written after Auschwitz. See Karol Sauerland, *Einfuhrung in die Ästhetik Adornos* (de Gruyter, 1979), p. 65, note 2, as well as Adorno's reiteration of his famous statement in *Noten zur Literatur III*, in Theodor Adorno, *Gesammelte Schriften*, vol. II, 2d ed. (Suhrkamp, 1984), p. 422.
19. See Mikhail Epstein, "Iskusstvo avangarda i religioznoe soznanie," *Novy mir* 12 (1989): 222–35.
20. See Ilya Kabakov and Boris Groys, *Zhizn' mukh. Das Leben der Fliegen* (Cologne, 1992), p. 13.

21. V. E. Lebedeva, *Tatiana Nazarenko* (Moscow, 1991), illustrated monograph.
22. *Vernisazh v Moskve. Kunstausstellung in Moskau. Exposicion de artes plasticas en Moscu. Exposicao em Moscovo*, ed. Viktor Jegorytschew (Moscow, 1989), plate 25.
23. Thus a novel like Chingiz Aitmatov's *The Day Lasts More Than One Hundred Years*, published in *Novy mir* 11 (1980), and hailed as a challenge to the official Soviet canon, is steeped in a revised socialist-realist poetics with a quasi-metaphysical dimension, valorizing a new Soviet hero with a "diligent soul" (*chelovek trudoliubivoi dushi*). See Aitmatov's Preface to his novel in *Novy mir* 11 (1980). Similarly, Anatoly Rybakov's 1960s novel, *The Children of the Arbat*, first published in 1987, and hailed as a perestroika work attempting to re-evaluate recent Soviet history, is an amalgam of the young prose (which took Russian teenagers of the 1960s as its subject: Aksyonov's *Oranges* from Morocco is a good example) and socialist realist prose, with its optimistic faith in the infallibility of Lenin and the Party. As for village prose, despite its oppositional attitude toward bureaucratic neglect and abuse of rural Russia, the basic features of optimism and didacticism are retained by writers as diverse as Solzhenitsyn (*Matryona's Home*) and Valentin Rasputin (*Money for Maria*).
24. The term "archeology" in the sense used by Michel Foucault is explained in the footnotes of the chapter on Bitov.
25. The "end of history" and the "disappearance of Man" is, strictly speaking, "located" in the time of Hegel's writing of his *Phenomenology of Spirit*, in 1804, during the Battle of Jena. See Alexandre Kojève, *Introduction to the Reading of Hegel: Lectures on the Phenomenology of Spirit*, assembled by Raymond Queneau, ed. Allan Bloom, trans. James H. Nichols, Jr. (Ithaca and London, 1993), first published Paris, 1947. Postmodernism adopts Hegel's "end of History" and the "disappearance of Man" as an axiom. See Francis Fukuyama's *The End of History and the Last Man* (London, 1992).
26. Vladimir Potapov also partly recognizes this, in that he sees "alternative prose" as a "phenomenon of language." See Vladimir Potapov, *Soviet Literature* 5 (1990): 160.
27. On the content of "the semiotic," see Julia Kristeva, *Revolution in Poetic Language*, trans. Leon S. Roudiez (New York, 1984), pp. 19–90.
28. A reading of Bitov's work is offered in Chapter 2 of the present volume.
29. Willi Beitz, ed., *Vom 'Tauwetter' zur Perestroika: russische Literatur zwischen den fünfziger und neunziger Jahren* (Bern, 1994), p. 330. Beitz gives Petrushevskaia's date of birth as 1938, while Chukhontsev gives it as 1939. Like Bitov, Petrushevskaia represented "today's forty-year-olds" in the heyday of perestroika in the mid-eighties. See also the interview with A. Bitov in the Belgrade bi-monthly *Knjizevna rec*, no. 367–368 (January, 1991), pp. 13–14.
30. First published in *Novy mir* 8 (1989).
31. Frederic Jameson, "Postmodernism, or The Cultural Logic of Late Capitalism," *New Left Review*, no. 146 (July–August 1984): 64.
32. Liudmila Petrushevskaia, "A Modern Family Robinson," in Oleg Chukhontsev, ed., *Dissonant Voices: The New Russian Fiction* (London, 1991), p. 420.

33. *Surrealism: Revolution by Night.* Exhibition organized by National Gallery of Australia, curated by Michael Lloyd, Ted Gott, and Christopher Chapman (Sydney, 1993), p. 79, cat. no. 31.
34. Fyodor Dostoevsky, *The Brothers Karamazov*, trans. David Magarshack (Harmondsworth, 1985), p. 147. Refer also to F. M. Dostoevsky, *Sobranie Sochinenii v 10 tomakh*, v. 9 (Moscow, 1958), p. 161.
35. Ludwig Wittgenstein, *Preliminary Studies for the Philosophical Investigations*, generally known as *The Blue and the Brown Books* [First English edition 1958] (Oxford, 1969), p. 17. *The Blue Book* contains his Cambridge notes from 1933/34.
36. Compare Roman Jakobson and Morris Halle, *Fundamentals of Language* (Mouton, 1971; First Printing, 1956), pp. 91–96.
37. Wittgenstein, *Tractatus Logico-Philosophicus*, trans. D. F. Pears and B. F. McGuinness, with an introd. by Bertrand Russell (London, 1989; First German edition 1921, first English edition 1922). Unless otherwise indicated, all quotations from the *Tractatus* will be from this edition and will be followed by the paragraph number in parentheses in the body of the text.
38. "Self-consciousness" is used here in the sense of an "ego" or a (Lacanian) "*moi*," and not a solipsistic Cartesian subject who "is" because he "thinks."
39. Leo Tolstoy, *Chto takoe iskusstvo?* in L. N. Tolstoi, *Sobranie sochinenii v dvadsati dvukh tomakh*, vol. 15 (Moscow, 1983), pp. 41–222. See also the English versions, *What Is Art?* trans. Aylmer Maude (London, 1899), and trans. Richard Peaver and Larissa Volokhonsky (New York, 1995).
40. Lacan's concept of the "imaginary" designates the pre-symbolic psychic register, which corresponds roughly to the Freudian unconscious of the primary processes. It is a zone of "silent" and repressed inscription, in which "writing" has not yet been transformed into logos or speech. Although the relationship of the three registers proposed by Lacan (the real, the symbolic, and the imaginary) is a complex one, and although it takes all three registers to produce the subject of language, the imaginary is seen as a site where metaphor rather than metonymy reigns. It is thus comparable to the site of dreams, where the signifier still has not separated from the signified (the image from word concept). See Jean Laplanche and Serge Leclaire, "The Unconscious: A Psychoanalytic Study," and "Postscript" by Jean Laplanche, and "Symbolic," by Jean Laplanche and J.-B. Pontalis, *Yale French Studies*, no. 48 (1972): 118–202.
41. It was Saussure who first compared language to a game of chess: "But of all the comparisons that might be imagined, the most fruitful is the one that might be drawn between the functioning of language and a game of chess. In both instances we are confronted with a system of values and their observable modifications. A game of chess is like an artificial realization of what language offers in a natural form.(...)The respective value of the pieces depends on their position on the chessboard just as each linguistic term derives its value from its opposition to all other forms." Ferdinand de Saussure, *Course in General Linguistics,* ed. Charles Bally and Albert Sechehaye, in collaboration with Albert Reidlinger, trans. Wade Baskin (New York, 1959), p. 88.

42. See Elizabeth Grosz, *Jacques Lacan: A Feminist Introduction* (Sydney, 1990), pp. 24–47.
43. Compare, for instance, Bakhtin's use of the term *edinstvennyi* (German *einmalig*), which is analogous to Heinrich Rickert's concept of "the historical as that which is individual (in the sense of that which is qualitatively once-occurrent) ...," in M. M. Bakhtin, *Towards a Philosophy of the Act*, trans. Vadim Liapunov, ed. Vadim Liapunov and Michael Holquist (Texas, 1993), p. 79, note 2. When shooting from a pistol, one can repeat the "articulation" (the shot) but only with another bullet ("utterance"). The metaphor of "shooting" representing speech as a violent act is used extensively in Vladimir Sorokin's novel *Four Stout Hearts* [Serdsta chetyrekh]. As if to underscore the function of speech in the genre of the novel, the main heroine's occupation is that of an Olympic champion "sharp-shooter."
44. According to Saussure, a sign consists of a "sound image" and a "concept." The "sound image" corresponds to the signifier, while the "concept" is Saussure's "signified." See Ferdinand de Saussure, *Course in General Linguistics*, pp. 12, 66. In Lacanian theory, the signified is always absent or repressed and as such is coeval with the unconscious.
45. Freud pointed out the similarity between the structure of "conscious" and "unconscious" thought or between dreams as wish-fulfillments and thoughts as hallucinatory wishes: "Thought is after all nothing but a substitute for a hallucinatory wish; and it is self-evident that dreams must be wish-fulfillments, since nothing but a wish can set our mental apparatus at work." Sigmund Freud, *The Interpretation of Dreams*, trans. James Strachey, ed. James Strachey and assisted by Alan Tyson. The present edition is edited by Angela Richards (New York, 1975), p. 721.
46. "The linguistic sign unites, not a thing and a name, but a concept and a sound image." Saussure, *Course in General Linguistics*, p. 66.
47. Tatiana Tolstaia, *On the Golden Porch* (New York, 1989), p. 7.
48. Helena Goscilo, *The Explosive World of Tatyana N. Tolstaya's Fiction* (1997), pp. 29–37.
49. Jacques Lacan, *Ecrits: A Selection*, p. 263.
50. Tatiana Tolstaia, *On the Golden Porch*, p. 55.
51. Ibid., pp. 58–59.
52. The opposition of heterogeneous/homogeneous is used by Georges Bataille to theorize about archaic cultural practices, such as sacrifice and ritual violence, which have organized human behavior since the beginning of time. Any organized system, such as a state or a primitive community, a religious system and even the system of language, belongs to homogeneous reality. "The heterogeneous world includes everything resulting from unproductive expenditure." Georges Bataille, "The Psychological Structure of Fascism," in Georges Bataille, *Visions of Excess: Selected Writings 1927–1939*, Fourth Printing, ed. Allan Stekl. *Theory and History of Literature*, vol. 14 (Minnesota, 1991), p. 142.
53. One is reminded here of René Magritte's surrealist picture of a disproportionate red rose filling a room in *The Wrestler's Tomb* [1961] or the giant egg filling the entire space of a birdcage in *Elective Affinities* [1933].

54. Bataille, *Visions of Excess*, p. 143.
55. Tolstaia's Mao Tse-tung is like a quotation (perhaps intended) of Andy Warhol's installation of *Mao Wallpaper* (Paris, 1974). There is something "domesticated" about the Warhol image of Mao. It is "bovine" but "alien, one might even say 'un-American.'" Carter Ratcliff, *Andy Warhol* (New York, 1983), p. 67. What Warhol achieves with his installation is the deconstruction of an icon (implying an image with a signified, a fixed meaning attached to it) into a mass consumer image (one that must be "consumed on the spot"). But while banalizing the image, he also makes it "strange," elevates it to the status of the "unfamiliar" and hence of the "other." Thus it is the image—or representation—which becomes the uncanny other of mass culture. Tolstaia is chasing a similar effect with her deconstruction of Mao.
56. Tatiana Tolstaia, *On the Golden Porch*, p. 62
57. See Juliet Flower MacCannell, *Figuring Lacan: Criticism and the Cultural Unconscious* (London and Sydney, 1986), pp. 96–97.
58. "... the structure of knowledge for a homogeneous reality is that of science ..." Bataille, *Visions of Excess*, p. 143.
59. Tatiana Tolstaia, *On the Golden Porch*, p. 62.
60. Ibid., p. 63.
61. See Simon Wilson, *Surrealist Painting* (London, 1975), plate 1.
62. Lacan's concept of the *objet petit a* is a distant relative of Freud's concept of *das Ding*—seen by Freud as early as the *Project (Entwurf einer Psychologie*, 1895; first published 1950) in terms of "the nucleus of the ego and the constant perceptual component," which he opposed to "the inconstant component" or "*predicate*" of *the thing*, which is language. Freud, *The Standard Edition of the Complete Psychological Works*, trans. and ed. James Strachey, in collaboration with Anna Freud, vol. 1 (1886–1899) (1966), p. 328.
63. The *objet petit a*, which is unrepresentable and always absent, is said by Lacan to be "the cause of desire."
64. For an overview of the significance of symbolic castration for the formation of the subject of language, see Jonathan Scott Lee, *Jacques Lacan* (Amherst, Mass., 1990). Generally speaking, it is the (phantasmic) threat of (symbolic) castration which forces the subject to give up his/her desire for the Mother (qua primal object) and to replace this "incestuous" desire with an imaginary identification with the phantasmic "other"—the Master Signifier or discourse that gives the subject (the illusion of) mastery.
65. *Writing* does not mean "the written word," but corresponds roughly to "stream-of-consciousness," which is a self-generated flow of memory traces emerging from the imaginary register and inscribing itself in the symbolic register. See Jacques Derrida's definition of writing, derived in the main from Freud's theses in *Note on the Mystic Writing Pad*, according to which "writing" is a process of inscription of the memory trace activated by the psychic apparatus, which is "nothing but a writing machine." This machine produces "representations." Similarly, "speech," says Derrida, quoting Freud, "must be understood not merely to mean the expression of thought in words, but to include the speech of gesture and every other method, such, for instance, as

writing, by which mental activity can be expressed." Jacques Derrida, *Writing and Difference*, trans. Alan Bass (1978), pp. 221 and 220. Thus "speech" and "writing" become synonymous in the Freudian/Derridean sense of the terms. It is in this sense that both terms are used in the present essay.

66. On the structure of the signifier, compare Jacques-Alain Miller, "Suture (Elements of the Logic of the Signifier)," *Screen*, vol. xviii, no. 4 (Winter 1977/78): 24–34.
67. Derrida has called this "the scene of writing." Jacques Derrida, "Freud and the Scene of Writing," in Jacques Derrida, *Writing and Difference*, pp. 196–2.

Chapter 20

HETEROGENEITY AND THE RUSSIAN POST-AVANT-GARDE

The Excremental Poetics of Vladimir Sorokin

Slobodanka Vladiv-Glover

Postmodernism and Russian Underground Art

For nearly five decades, from the 1920s to the 1970s, Soviet Russian literature labored under the constrictions of a homogeneous social and cultural system. During this time, the literary scene was not entirely static, but its concerns were of a regional rather than of a universal nature. Isolated international literary phenomena, such as Pasternak or Solzhenitsyn, were either celebrations of by-gone literary eras (the case of Pasternak), or voyeuristic gazing, by a mainly Western reading public, into an other, hitherto undisclosed part of world history, of itself unproductive of new literary forms (the case of Solzhenitsyn). Of course, there was the thaw in the mid-1950s. This brought to the fore the Hemingwayan "young prose" of Aksyonov, Nagibin, Kazakov, Gladilin, and signaled a return to the early twentieth-century Russian poetic models, in new Soviet thematic simulations of the monumental or catachrestic poetry of Russian futurism. Evtushenko, Voznesensky and Rozhdestvensky declaimed their verses, in histrionic

Mayakovskian style, to mass audiences in the Soviet Union and around Western capitals, demonstrating the new, but strictly monitored "openness" of their homogeneous society. There were also, in the 1960s and 1970s, the village prose writers, with their criticism of Soviet bureaucracy (but not Soviet ideology), and this bureaucracy's policies of neglect toward the Russian countryside. There were attempts at cultural mainstreaming of the writers of the Soviet republics. Of these, Aitmatov was the most successful showpiece of Soviet multi-ethnic social policy.

Still, the distinction between those Russian or Soviet writers, writing in Russian, who had their works published abroad, and those who did not, was insignificant. They were all, to a greater or lesser extent, creating within the confines of the dominant Soviet canon of socialist realism. This was as true for the *derevenshchiki* (village prose writers) as it was for Aitmatov and Solzhenitsyn.

A partially successful attempt at breaking away from the canon was made in Soviet literary criticism by Andrei Sinyavsky and in Soviet prose by the so-called "jeans prose"[1] writers—the Hemingwayans.[2] But despite the return of young prose to concreteness and lyricism, these efforts were stifled in the embryonic stage by an exodus of talent (Gladilin, Aksyonov, Nekrasov) and the onset of the period of stagnation of the Brezhnev years in the 1970s and early 1980s. Sinyavsky's theoretical assault on official Soviet aesthetics ended in 1965, as is well known, with nearly seven years of labor camp, followed by emigration in 1973. But while the official canon of socialist realism held center stage, and while village prose remained the only tolerated and hence productive genre in Soviet *belles lettres* throughout the 1970s and early 1980s, backstage a new Russian literary and cultural paradigm was in the making.

The big break with the official canon was being prepared by the writers of the underground: a loosely linked group (or groups) which, amidst official persecution, published in almanacs of restricted editions (up to five copies permitted by law), such as *Glagol* (Word) and *Metropol'* (the latter in 1979). The *Metropol'* writers included, among others, Andrei Bitov, Viktor Erofeev, and Evgeny Popov. These writers pointed in a new direction that has been revealed in full, in the wake of perestroika, as that of Russian postmodernism.[3]

This new Russian writing has been identified in contemporary Russian criticism as "new wave literature" or "other prose"[4] and even as the "post-avant-garde." It is seen by Vladimir Potapov, writing in *Novy mir* (10, 1989) and *Soviet Literature* (5, 1990), as a literature that has emerged from the underground. Potapov's list of underground writers is much larger than the *Metropol'* list, which includes Evgeny Popov and Viktor Erofeev, Viacheslav Pietsukh, Venedikt Erofeev (1938–1990), Tatiana Tolstaia, and Vladimir Sorokin. To Potapov's list must be added the new prose writers whose works appear in the recent anthology edited by the poet Oleg Chukhontsev.[5] These include the 1992 Booker Prize finalist, Vladimir Makanin, born the same year as Andrei Bitov (who is also included in Chukhontsev's anthology), Liudmila Petrushevskaia, and Oleg Ermakov.

The above list of writers is far from complete; most have emerged in print, both in Russia and in some cases abroad, since the late 1980s. In the case of the so-called "middle generation" writers (born around World War II), publication came twenty years after the creation of their work. Bitov's *Pushkin House*, conceived in the 1960s, came out in full in Russia in 1987. Venedikt Erofeev's *Moscow Circles* (Moskva-Petushki), also a creation of the 1960s, was published in the Soviet Union in 1988.[6]

While it is true that the above writers do not form anything resembling a movement or a school, it is possible to identify their works with features of a new cultural paradigm, which, when reduced to the simplest possible definition, represents the "cultural logic of late-capitalism," to use Frederic Jameson's formula,[7] and an aesthetics of the heterogeneous.[8] This aesthetics is connected with the ongoing Western European modernist/postmodern project of mapping the realm of the unconscious as the source of identity of both the subject of discourse and that subject's relationship to the object of perception. As such, heterogeneous aesthetics can be traced back to the rise of psychoanalysis and the surrealist movement in its various permutations (futurism, expressionism, the absurd), and the poetic philosophy of Georges Bataille. The dissenting French surrealist and artistic pornographer began his literary career in 1928, with the publication of a long poem entitled *The Story of the Eye.* [9] As the modern source of what has been called "excremental culture,"[10] Bataille's aesthetics of negativity encompassing the ugly and the perverse still holds the key to the poetics of "contemporary" (that is, ongoing since the 1950s) Western European postmodernism in literature, art, and film. The paradigm of "excremental culture" has emerged in the works of the Russian post-avant-garde, represented by both the middle and younger generation of Russian writers, artists and filmmakers. *Sots-art,* a popular movement in Russian visual art,[11] contains strong elements of excrementalism. The work of Valery Belenikin (who is in his late thirties),[12] emphasizes, in banal form, the ugly and the carnal as metaphors of the pleasure principle and sensuality which ground desire and subjectivity. But elements of *sots-art* are also discernible in the middle generation of Russian painters, like Tatiana Nazarenko (b. 1944), whose transgressive self-parody in *The Acrobat* (Tsirkachka) (1984)[13] is an obvious subversion of beautiful form. Dengiz Abuladze's *Repentance,* a film of 1984–86, is a prominent example of excremental postmodernism in Soviet-Russian-Georgian cinema, relying heavily as it does on the grotesque effects of the ugly and the perverse. Post-perestroika films that echo the perverse violence of excremental poetics include Vitaly Kanevsky's *Freeze, Die, Revive* (1989) and *Luna Park.* Unmotivated and unmitigated violence, which is inherent to excremental poetics, also structures Russian prose works, such as Leonid Gabyshev's *Odlyan, or the Air of Freedom* (Odlyan, ili vozdukh svobody) and Venedikt Erofeev's *Moscow Circles.*

Excremental poetics is by no means an invention of the twentieth century. In the picaresque German tradition of the thirty-years-war period, there are works that emulate spitting through the accumulation of expletives and swear words, while excrementa are a constant backdrop to H. J. C. von Grimmelshausen's *Simplicissimus* novel. Even Jonathan Swift's political satire *Gulliver* is replete with references to the hero's excremental bodily functions, which are in "excess" of the mode of Enlightenment satire in which the novel is cast. It is, however, in this historical period that Foucault and Simone de Beauvoir situate an ontological break in European discourse, marked by the emergence of the excremental writings of the Marquis de Sade. Michel Foucault, writing on one of Bataille's contemporaries, Maurice Blanchot, relates Sade's poetics to Blanchot's (surrealist) prose and Hölderlin's poetry of the limit, in which language becomes the main character, represented in its virtual dimension as something existing as an "outside":

> Can it be said without stretching things that Sade and Hölderlin simultaneously introduced into our thinking, for the coming century, but in some way cryptically, the experience of the outside—the former by laying desire bare in the infinite murmur of discourse, the latter by discovering that the gods had wandered off through a rift in language as it was in the process of losing its bearing?[14]

Simone de Beauvoir ascribes similar importance to the phenomenon of Sade's excremental and pornographic prose. In her 1951/52 article "Must We Burn Sade?" Beauvoir attributes to Sade the fundamental break with the world of appearances, by which she means "concepts," which had dominated aesthetics and epistemology until his time.

> Sade's immense merit lies in his taking a stand against these abstractions and alienations which are merely flights from the truth about man. No one was more passionately attached to the concrete than he.(...) He adhered only to the truths which were derived from the evidence of his own actual experience. Thus he went beyond the sensualism of his age and transformed it into an ethic of authenticity.[15]

The "ethic of authenticity," ascribed by Beauvoir to Sade's "excrementalism," underwrites the ongoing experiment with language and its limits represented by the prose of Vladimir Sorokin, who has been called the "Russian de Sade." The opposition between appearance and experience discerned by Beauvoir in Sade's prose is no less apparent in Sorokin's literary project. This consists of dismantling the numerous social and cultural discourses that mask or obstruct concrete, bodily experience and the pulsing of desire that seeks its outlet beyond language and discursivity, in the immediacy of the present moment in which it consumes itself without residue, in sacrifice as a gesture of excess.

It is because Sorokin's work focuses on the status of language and its relation to desire, which is a denizen of both the unconscious and discourse, and because it does this through the negative form of the excremental, the pornographic, the perverse, and the ugly that it is attracting such attention, particularly outside Russia. It is as if Sorokin's excremental prose was giving new adrenalin to a somewhat tired and aging European tradition by returning to its surrealist source and invigorating an once dominant heterogeneous poetics by adding new and hitherto unexplored cultural ("ethnographic") material, in the form of various Russian social discourses, to its "college of sociology" documents.[16] Like the College of Sociology group, whose members sought a rapprochement between art and sociology or ethnography in the pursuit of the "real" as a lived object, "consumed on the spot," Sorokin's prose simulates cultural production which has a "use-value" as opposed to an "exchange value." It is through Sorokin's excremental prose that one can gauge the extent of the road already traveled by the Russian post-avant-garde since it surfaced in post-Soviet culture in the last decade. The relative unpopularity of Sorokin among his native reading public of all age groups and this readership's reluctance to engage with his discourse is, on the other hand, an alarming *indicium* of the distance that exists between the Russian literature of the post-avant-garde and the "new Russia."[17]

Sorokin's Deconstruction of the Russian and Soviet Canon

Born in Moscow in 1955, Sorokin[18] is a graphic artist by profession. He came to literature, as he himself declares in an interview with the journalist Tatyana Rasskazova,[19] in the mid-1970s, via the conceptualists who were part of the Russian "underground" art scene. Apart from Ilya Kabakov, Sorokin mentions Erik Bulatov and Andrei Monastyrsky as artists who exercised an influence on his own poetics. Sorokin declares, in the same interview, that prior to his entry into literature, he had traversed the road of re-assimilating the Russian and European avant-garde of the 1920s: the futurists, the dadaists, and the *Oberiuty.* Sorokin also admits to the influence of Kafka, Nabokov, and Orwell. Sorokin has thus undergone a development similar to that of Bitov and Petrushevskaia, as well as their younger contemporaries, who emerged as fully fledged postmodern writers in the 1980s via a rememoration of the traditional avant-garde of European and Russian modernism.[20]

What the conceptualists gave Sorokin was, according to his own testimony, a "distancing from one's own work of art and from culture in general."[21] This distancing manifests itself, according to Sorokin, with an absence of a particular personal prose style. Instead, his artistic method consists of a playful relationship with the styles of other writers. His style is, by his own definition, the use of various manners of writing.[22] In other words, his style is the stylization or the parodying of many styles, many voices, many social and individual speech registers.

Sorokin's interest in linguistic phenomena as thematic material for his writing turns his writing into a kind of scientific investigation of different types of texts. Sorokin does not discriminate between texts: for him, there is no hierarchy of literary and non-literary, of "high" and "low" texts; everything is suitable for appropriation:

> For me, there is no difference between Joyce and Shevtsov,[23] between Nabokov and some sort of railway advertisement. I can be fascinated by any kind of text. The most attractive areas are those that have not been "enculturated": the bureaucratic, officialese language, the language of the mentally ill—their letters. I am an avid reader of the literature of the Soviet period—I read everything, from the ideological literature, like the *Short History of the Communist Party,* to artistic texts. The presentation of the post-war Stalinist novel, for example, strikes me as stupendous.[24]

Sorokin's idiosyncratic conception of literature leads him to a radical deconstruction not only of the socialist-realist canon, but of the grand narrative of Russian nineteenth-century discourse. His prose works represent zero writing par excellence since they are emptied of both ideological and literary codes. Their content follows the logic of *Witz* (Freud's "joke"), which is etymologically related to wit—a creative intrusion of the imagination into the presence of speech. His prose is thus a dramatization of pure nonsense, which is a relative of the futurists' trans-sense or *zaum*: it is non-mimetic and portrays nothing but recycled clichés of earlier literary genres—be it those of socialist realism or Turgenev's idylls. In other words, Sorokin recycles "rubbish," like Ilya Kabakov in his *Rubbish Novel.* Perhaps it is the deeply felt need of the Russian writer to reclaim lost ground in the sphere of aesthetics that leads Sorokin to eschew avowed social, political, and ethical concerns in his literary practice. Thus he says that in writing his novel *The Queue* (Ochered'), which has been translated in the West, he was not inspired by the Russian sociological phenomenon of queuing up for consumer goods. What interested him was the "queue as the bearer of specific speech characteristics, as a non-literary polyphonic monster."[25] Sorokin's *The Queue* is thus the contemporary Russian manifestation of what Foucault has called "language from outside" or the "experience of the outside." In this experience, one is not seeking to uncover "the truth" behind the phenomenon of speech; instead, the phenomenon (of speech) is the truth—it is all that there is, all that is given to sense perception. It is language as an exteriority on which sense in its determinate (predetermined) form has lost its bearings. Like Holderlin's poetry and Nietzsche's impossible, non-systemic philosophy, Sorokin's prose bears witness to the disorientation of sense following the ousting of God (the transcendental *signified* and the Platonic "concept" or "essence") from man's phenomenological field.

Sorokin openly disavows any interest in the politics of contemporary Russia. "I have no social interests," he says in the cited interview. "To me it is a matter of total indifference, whether it is the period of stagnation or perestroika, totalitarianism or democracy."[26]

This is also why he is not attracted to the idea of living in the West. He is repelled by the masses, he declares. And in the West, he says, he experiences the same sort of "ontological alienation" from the masses as at home. The masses arouse in him only "a feeling of anxiety and the desire to retreat into privacy." "Social life" does not interest him, he says, because "it does not have the power to transform human nature." And he is not willing to settle for less.[27]

However, despite his declared aversion to being read as a sociologist of post-Soviet life—hence his apparent rejection of the social and, by extension, the ethical in favor of the aesthetic—Sorokin is not a thoughtless writer.

Indeed, pure thought, one might say, is the very essence of his prose. He himself gives a clue to his essentially philosophical preoccupations, which if anything sound more pious than unethical or amoral. Thus he says that he has an empathy with Heidegger who "devoted many pages to the working out of the problem of man being thrown"[28] into the world of phenomena. "Each morning, on opening my eyes," says Sorokin, "I experience the most extreme surprise at being squeezed into this body and at waking up once again into this world." This surprise then gradually turns into "a state of consternation (*sostoianie udruchennosti*)."[29]

Sorokin's laconic description of his development as a writer indicates the general outline of his poetics which is, like that of Bataille, a poetics of the body. Sorokin thematizes the body as the surface of inscription. As such, the body represented in his prose has a dual function: it is, on the one hand, a metonymy of the subject and hence (paradoxically) a kind of "disincarnate"[30] symbolic self and, on the other, a fetishized and eroticized "partial object" of the unconscious, implicated in the "authentic experience" of desire and *jouissance*. Thus by reconstituting the body in concrete experience and sensation, Sorokin rediscovers sensibility—feeling as sensory judgment—as the ground not only of postmodern aesthetics, but of perception and meaning as such, thereby restoring Russian prose to the post-Kantian phenomenological project disrupted by the socialist-realist episode in Russian culture.

The key to Sorokin's poetics can be sought, in part, through the poetics of the Russian conceptualists,[31] but in part also through George Bataille's cosmology of the heterogeneous and the sacred that continues to ground both critical and textual practices in Western postmodernism.

Russian Conceptualists and Bataille's Heterogeneous

According to Mikhail Epstein, Russian conceptualism is at the core of the poetics of the Russian post-avant-garde. By looking at the installations of Ilya Kabakov, Epstein arrives at a model that is similar to Bataille's excremental poetics, but he comes to this via an excursion into Byzantine medieval culture and apophatic theology.

The conceptualists of the 1960s and 1970s are identified by Epstein as the avant-garde of the second call (*avangard vtorogo prizyva*). What distinguishes them from the Russian avant-garde of the 1910s through the 1920s, according to Epstein, is their anti-utopianism. The first Russian avant-garde—Andrei Bely, Velimir Khlebnikov, Wassily Kandinsky, Kasimir Malevich, and Vladimir Mayakovsky—subscribed to an "ethics and an ontology of mystical communism," which, when subsequently put into practice by the Russian historical reality, turned into a seventy-year-long nightmare of totalitarian abstractionism.[32] The second Russian avant-garde or post-avant-garde (a term coined by Epstein) turned, in the 1960s and 1970s, to "completely non-ideological, purely commercial objects (pop art) or to objects which had no substance and represented pure ideological signs (*sots-art*)."[33]

Out of *sots-art* or with it emerged the movement of conceptualism, which Epstein evaluates as the most important trend of the contemporary Russian avant-garde. While Epstein admits that it is difficult to define the precise relationship of *sots-art* and conceptualism, he ventures to suggest that conceptualism "liberates both objects and signs from their mutual co-responsiveness" (*ot vzaimnoi otvetsvennosti*), and introduces both into a sphere of "non-corresponsive correspondence" (*bezotvetstvennogo sootvetsviia*).[34] Epstein's analysis of the poetics of Ilya Kabakov's art works and installations offers a succinct model of Russian conceptualism and, by extension, a mini-model of the contemporary Russian postmodern paradigm.

Used first of all as a term belonging to the underground culture and almost as a euphemism for *sots-art*, conceptualism, with its privileging of the terms "concept" and "conception," is, according to Epstein, analogous to the medieval philosophical nominalism that stood in opposition to philosophical realism. Conceptualism is also attached to the whole ideological consciousness of Soviet society and is not merely the expression of one of its constitutive layers. Conceptualism is, although Epstein does not say it explicitly, a radical critique of ideology as "class consciousness." Leaving aside Western critical models, such as those of Hegel, Heidegger or Bataille, Epstein develops an analogy between conceptualism and Zen-Buddhism to arrive at the philosophical core of the Russian post-avant-garde movement. He locates this core, which is essentially analogous to Hegel's concept of negativity, in Russian apophatic theology.

Thus conceptualism is "emptied form" and "formed emptiness" (*opustoshennaia forma i oformlennaia pustota*).[35] It is "some sort of reality that reveals its illusory ghostlike character, and gives way to the perception of pure nothingness" (*nekaia real'nost' obnaruzhivaet svoiu illyuzornost', prizrachnost' i ustupaet put' vospriiatiu samoi pustoty*).[36] This is illustrated through Ilya Kabakov's *Rubbish Novel* (*Musorochny roman*) "in 16 volumes" and his *Man of Rubbish* (*Musorochny chelovek*). The *Novel* is, according to Epstein, a series of albums, into which are sewn and glued old documents, papers yellowed with age—receipts, tickets, coupons, pictures from cardboard boxes and all sorts of other junk (*chepukha*). The *Man* is made up of scraps of everyday trash attached to a massive wooden stand: detritus that is usually found on the floor and underneath the sofa or deep inside a drawer, such as bits of fluff, thread, and cloth. Glancing at one trivial detail after another, one wonders why all this stuff has been gathered together and what artistic idea it generates.

> Meanwhile, a label is attached to each object, identifying when and in what connection the object was bought, selected, used, and discarded, as well as other relevant information. All these elements of the rubbish are strictly documented and woven into the canvas of the author's own life. In the assembly of these objects there is no chaos, no debauchery, no eructations resembling those seen on a rubbish heap; on the contrary, the objects are carefully assembled, laid out in straight vertical and horizontal rows along the stand, and carefully glued into the album. This ideal orderliness, appropriate for a government archive or a museum, together with the solemn tone of the descriptions, stands in obvious contradiction

> to the triviality of the objects themselves. Here is some piece of rope and there an apple core—and all of it is furnished with a dry and detailed running commentary, normally reserved for historical objects.[37]

One infers from the above passage that the incongruity established by Kabakov's representation of rubbish in a historical and documentary frame has the effect of foregrounding the banal at the expense of the traditional notion of history as a series of significant events in linear progression. The banalization of history is not a negation of history but the sublation (*Aufhebung*) of history by the trivia of the "real" which must be consumed on the spot. As Epstein points out, conceptualism does not "affirm negation" (as did Nihilism); it "negates affirmation."[38] Epstein may have claimed with equal validity that conceptualism affirms negativity (which is more than simple negation) as a grounding of the historical process, making the latter analogous to the process of signification. What history needs in order to establish itself as history is, paradoxically, the notion of non-history or of the unconscious of history. In the same way, what the "I" needs according to Hegel's phenomenology in order to come into self-consciousness is the "Not-I" or "other." The banalization of existing reality in Russian conceptualism is thus a movement of alienation that is more than defamiliarization. The function of the banal and trivial is, according to Epstein, to draw attention to the existence of another reality for which "there are no words," no adequate means of expression. This is the reality which apophatic theology—concentrated in the teachings of the fifth-century (anonymous) author known as Pseudo-Dionysus the Areopagite—identifies as "God," who is "utterly unknowable" but "present in all creation in his energies. The energies are God and can be experienced."[39]

Conceptualism thus opens up a sphere that does not entirely coincide with that of discursivity and that redefines ultimate reality in terms of an unknown and unspeakable "other world." Boris Groys, in discussing Kabakov's installations, reinscribes the dichotomy established by conceptualism as the phenomenological opposition between the "visible" and the "invisible."[40] Humanity's self-defining experience in confrontation with this (invisible) reality—which is the "real"—is, according to Bataille's heterogeneous aesthetics, that of terror. But this terror is a creative experience, constituting the rite of passage of the self from the sphere of the profane into the sphere of the sacred.

The sacred is a primary (primal) conceptual category that appears to be opposed to the profane when, in fact, it encompasses it. For profanation and transgression lead from the profane to the sacred whose asymmetrical polarity thus constitutes pure difference. The sacred is inherently anti-systemic, polymorphous, and non-hierarchic, and cuts across all binary oppositions, such as good/evil, high/low, holy/cursed. The sacred has the power to transform the self from a profane into a religious being. What it means to become a religious being in the context of Bataille's notion of the sacred is that the self opens up to the experience of the heterogeneous, which in ordinary life comprises things that are "hidden, obscured, subject to prohibition or censorship—objects of revulsion, excluded from quotidian contact or touch, abstracted from use."[41]

Paradoxically, these sacred things "abstracted from use" have a "use-value." But Bataille's "use-value" has nothing to do with utilitarianism[42] or usefulness. On the contrary, it encompasses unmotivated expenditure, excess, and consumption on the spot. Sacrifice is Bataille's favorite metaphor of the practice of such consumption.

Bataille's sacred is thus a sphere grounded in pure negativity, which represents the new ontological relation of the part to the whole or of the general to the particular, a relation which is inscribed on the body and played out as the subject's experience of the "real" which resists representation. The part and the whole (Hegel's self-consciousness and freedom of the universal will) therefore form an incongruous correspondence (Epstein's "non-corresponsive correspondence"), which coincides with the structure of paradox.

This non-relational relation (paradox) finds its ideal metaphor or model in the human body, with its flows and scissions, its multipurpose systemic connections and disconnections, and its temporalized teleology whose end is death as autoerasure of the system. This heterogeneous body, which despite its concreteness possesses a phantasmic rather than material reality for the subject, comes into existence through and as transgression, to form a boundary or limit by virtue of being constantly crossed and re-crossed.[43] This same body is also a producer of flows (of energy, affect, excrementa, tears, sperm, saliva, and blood), which are subject to rupture and resumption of flow. Such discontinuity of its systems is essentially violent and is thus experienced (unconsciously) as shock, rupture, or trauma. In all of this the body models discourse, which is lived as a break from the totality of the natural state of the animal or the human infant or as a relation of non-corresponsive correspondence with the real of the object (world).

The Heterogeneous and Excremental Poetics

The heterogeneous, which privileges bodily processes and with them violence, is at the core of the excremental poetics of Sorokin's prose and that of other Russian postmodernists, such as Viktor Erofeev, Leonid Gabyshev, and Alexander Kabakov. For these writers, obscene violence and pornographic spectacle are stylistic means of representing rupture and shock.[44] The heterogeneous is also the sphere of consciousness (or, more precisely, the unconscious where desire is situated), in which the drama of dismemberment of the total into the particular and singular, the momentary and unique, is played out. In this drama, Bataille, reading Hegel, describes the primary and sole player as the "monstrous energy of thought, of the 'pure abstract I,' which is essentially opposed to fusion and which must lead to man's—the subject's—disappearance and death. The energy, or the violence, of Understanding—the Negativity of the Understanding." Thus Bataille, reading Hegel, is opposed to the "pure beauty of the dream, which cannot act, which is impotent."[45] This is because the essence of human "objective reality," says Bataille in quoting Kojève's reading of Hegel, is "the Nothingness which manifests itself as negative or creative Action, free and self-conscious."[46] Pure beauty, by contrast, is "not susceptible to acting." Beauty has no "consciousness of itself"; it suffers "from feeling the break-up of the profoundly indissoluble Totality of what is (of the concrete-real)." This beauty would like to

> remain the sign of an accord of the real with itself. It cannot become conscious Negativity, awakened in dismemberment, and the lucid gaze, absorbed in Negativity. This latter attitude presupposes the violent and laborious struggle of Man against Nature and is its end. That is the historic struggle where Man constitutes himself as "Subject" or as "abstract I" of the "Understanding," as a separated and named being.[47]

According to Bataille's model of negativity, derived from his insights into Kojève's and Hegel's thought, Beauty has no part to play in modern aesthetics and epistemology. Just as absolute beauty cannot act, according to Hegel, so the "beautiful soul" (*die schöne Seele*), in its absolute desire to remain identical to itself, is poised on the threshold between rejection of consciousness, which is action and actual existence, and awareness of the need "to externalize itself and change itself into an actual existence." Because it fails to resolve this contradiction, the "beautiful soul" (Hegel's derivation of the classical moral and aesthetic Beauty, which formed the basis of German romanticism) is "disordered to the point of madness, wastes itself in yearning and pines away in consumption. Thereby it does in fact surrender the being-for-itself to which it so stubbornly clings; but what it brings forth is only the non-spiritual unity of [mere] being."[48]

Hegel's critique of absolutized concepts, like that of pure beauty, and its moral representative, the "beautiful soul," both of which fail to arrive at self-consciousness because they lack "otherness," is the cornerstone of the poetics of negativity—the poetics of "emptied form" and "formed emptiness" that finds expression in the obscene and the pornographic. The assimilation of this poetics by the European avant-garde of the 1910s and 1920s and, post factum, by the Russian post-avant-garde of the 1970s through the 1990s, has seen the transformation of beautiful forms into the ugly and the deviant. Sorokin's ugly reality is not only actual because it reflects alleged practices in contemporary post-Soviet society.[49] It is also actual, because the ugly is concrete and active. It generates energy emanating from (negative) feelings: disgust, fear, awe, abjection. The ugly is thus opposed to the static abstractness and passivity of so-called "pure concepts" (such as "pure beauty"), which fail to come into a non-corresponsive correspondence with the "real" through the operation of the negativity of desire as free, negative, and creative action.

The ugly as negativity and freedom finds expression in the pornographic and the obscene. The boundaries of the pornographic have been extended in recent theorizing to include "scandal, violence, humiliation, repression."[50] The obscene is generic to the negative affects (fear, awe, disgust) and as such is defined as "ill-omened, abominable, disgusting, indecent."[51] But the obscene was originally "a term of augury," and augury, in turn, belongs to "divination" and its rituals. Through augury, the obscene is thus generically related to presentiment, anticipation, and presage. It is turned toward the future as promise. Rather than pointing to some kind of moral degeneracy in the traditionally accepted sense, the obscene in the context of heterogeneous aesthetics is equivalent to "a significant token of any kind."[52] The obscene, like the pornographic, is thus pure transparent sign ("formed emptiness"), divorced from all transcendental signifieds and predetermined sense, pointing to nothing but the Nothingness and absence that are its ground.

The pornographic and the obscene are inalienably linked to the perverse which circumscribes the sphere of the negativity of desire. That is, what the "I" desires is to be the desire of the "other," which is the desire to become an (impossible) object, the cause of desire or *objet petit a*. Desire, which always hinges on the destruction of the object (Hegel), finds its expression in the mutilation of the desired object or, as Lacan puts it: "I love you, but, because, inexplicably I love in you something more than you—the *objet petit a*—I mutilate you."[53] Sacrifice is the theater of this drama of the desire of the other. It is in ritual sacrifice that "we try to find evidence for the presence of the desire of this Other," which Lacan calls "the dark God" of discourse.[54] Thus the theater of the pornographic—ontologically connected with Artaud's "theatre of cruelty"—reaches its climax in sacrifice which represents, in Bataille's cosmology of the sacred, the highest expression of sovereignty, emanating from the negativity of desire.

This model of sovereignty, whose source is in Hegel's negativity, is a model of action, expressed in terms of the absolute freedom of human self-consciousness, will or desire. This absolutely free self-consciousness (the subject's particularity) is, according to Hegel, "the supreme reality" and, paradoxically, the antithesis but also the sole object of a "universal freedom." This "universal freedom" is an abstract Totality—a universality, which "does not let itself advance to the reality of an organic articulation, and whose aim is to maintain itself in an unbroken continuity."[55] What does not come into articulation is the impossible "real"—the "unknowable" God of apophaticism and Lacan's "other" or "dark God" of discourse.

The Heterogeneous, Ritual Sacrifice, and the Sacred in Sorokin

The "real," which is beyond metaphor, is at the core of Sorokin's poetics and textual practices. Although unrepresentable in language, it is mediated by the body and has effects that are articulated through sensibility. As a totality (universality) that strives ("desires") to objectify itself as a particular freedom, it turns itself into a "cause of desire," and through its representatives, the *objets petit a*, inscribes itself on the body as fetish, partial object, gaze, and drive (oral, anal, scopic, and so on).

Sorokin's prose works, like those of his role model Sade, offer a panorama, if not an orgy, of graphic representations of the body, in particular of bodily functions, such as excretions of all kinds, and bodily mutilations. Sorokin's language, concomitantly, is replete with Russian expletives and swear and curse words, which in the Slavonic languages almost all derive from excremental and erotic bodily processes. Sorokin's poetics is a poetics of the body, in which body parts function as corporeal or incorporated representations of signs caught up in the drama of desire and signification (*signifiance*). The body is thus a producer of signs and as such a transgressive "limit," offering access to experience and allowing discourse to be lived by both the speaking and reading subject.

In Sorokin's prose negativity and the heterogeneous come to expression in both the theme and structure of his works. In *Four Stout Hearts* (Serdtsa chetyrekh), the plot consists of the inverted and pathologized "spiritual quest" of the four major characters, who seek sacrifice in the form of death by self-mutilation. The characters form a kind of "family group"—a descendant of Dostoevsky's celebrated "accidental family" (*sluchainoe semeistvo*). Like the latter, this family group is in fact a group of signifiers in a relational field rather than a dysfunctional post-Soviet family. As such, these heterogeneous and "false" family members model the relationship between the particular and the general in a manner that is reminiscent of Wittgenstein's famous analogy between "family likenesses" and the structure of difference as a shifting boundary or limit between concepts. Wittgenstein's example involves various games which are subsumed under the general term "game."[56] Sorokin's four major characters form a group—a totality—which is constituted through difference both in relation to the members of the group and to other groups, like the military or the Ukrainian mafia; these are not distinguishable from the "four hearts" through their actions or their minimal personal characteristics, but only through the fact that they are "other." The "four hearts" are thus a model of metonymy (meaning as negativity or non-corresponsive contiguity), which is coeval with the structure of desire as lack or difference. And desire is "the Freudian *cogito.*"[57]

Through its four negative protagonists, who can be counted as one, two, three, four only by virtue of the fact that each is, as a particularity, a part (partial object) of a whole body, and as such an organ of desire ("the heart"), Sorokin's novel models *cogito* or consciousness and is an allegory of the production of meaning. It thus performs the same task as Russian conceptualism, which, according to Iosif Bakshtein, "has perpetuated such traditions of Western conceptualism as a 'post-philosophical activity,' which, as a practice, constitutes an investigation into the production of meaning in culture."[58] Since pornography has the effect of emptying the fictional characters of social, historical, and ideological content, the dramatis personae of the novel become pure signifiers or "transgressive" particulars in a relational field (a "family relation"), caught up, through the negativity of desire, in a teleology whose ultimate end is their own incorporation of (or as) the "real."

The members of this "false" family, representing a heterogeneous totality, consist of Seryozha, a boy aged about thirteen; Staube, a World War II amputee with a wooden leg, who is the boy's mentor and seducer as well as a kind of pathological superego of the group; Rebrov, an entrepreneurial group manager in his thirties with connections to the military and the Ukrainian mafia; and Olga Vladimirovna, a young former Soviet champion sportswoman (sharpshooter), mistress to the "group manager" as well as incestuous surrogate mother to Seryozha. Seryozha's own mother and father are ritually killed by the group, with Seryozha's active participation, enacting a perverse exteriorization of the Oedipal transgression. His mother's mouth is cut out of the dead body and ritually stored in a jar, while the foreskin of his father's penis is cut off and passed around the group for ritual (repetitive) chewing and spitting out. Rebrov's mother is also ritually killed, liquefied, and carried around in a suitcase which, like the miser's casket or Venichka Erofeev's *chemodanchik* (suitcase), becomes the concretized repository of the desire of the "four hearts." The substance in the suitcase—called the Liquid Mother and representing a parodic variant of Kant's "primal matter"[59]—is used in the final suicide-pact ritual, in which the "four hearts" are compacted by a preconstrued giant machinery (like a meat press), which crushes them, liquefies their remains, freezes them into four cubes, stamps them with random numbers, and drops them onto the frozen Liquid Mother. Thus the giant mechanical apparatus of the symbolic order (of language) literally commodifies the "four hearts," transforming them, as actualized metaphor, into the *petit a*—the object of desire of the other, which is to say, the "invisible," "dark God" of discourse and of the symbolic apparatus of culture. However, the end of the "spiritual quest" of the "four hearts" is not the journey's end; for the journey through language has no end. Its closure is, instead, an eternal return of the same; for out of the fusion with the "real"—the primal matter of the Liquid Mother or the repressed primal unconscious—the ground (or condition of possibility) of a new discourse is ideally established.

But Sorokin's novel is parody, which is related to paradox. By actualizing the Lacanian metaphor of desire (the *petit a*), Sorokin's novel turns into a comic play on the process of repression through which meaning emerges from the nothingness of the "real" ("formed emptiness") as the "emptied from" of the signifier. It thus stages itself as pure nothingness, erasing sense through the non-sense of parodic play, redoubling the desire of the other as a comic negativity—namely, as the "desire of desire."

Because they represent concepts in status nascendi whose birth can come about only through the repeated crossing of a limit (transgression and repetition), the members of the group are in constant motion. They purposefully go on errands and perform ritual acts whose ultimate motivation remains a mystery to the reader. This ceaseless and mostly negative activity of the "four hearts" resembles the constantly shifting spatial positions of pawns in a chess game—itself a Saussurian metaphor for the process of meaning. But the reader, who must read the narrative as a linear and temporal sequence, does not perceive this activity as metaphor during the act of reading. He is thus placed in the position of eavesdropping or peeping in on a scene where a private and secret ritual is taking place. The transgressive rites witnessed by the reader border on the dire and the repulsive, and hence inspire the "negative pleasure"—"awe and respect"—of the Kantian sublime, which is homologous with that "other scene" Freud called "the unconscious" and Bataille renamed "the sacred." According to Bataille, the sphere of the sacred is mediated through laughter, sacrifice, and unknowing (non-meaning), while its defining experience is that of terror. The sacred is "the opening of the self to terror shared." Terror and transgression define the self and constitute the self's rite of passage from a "profane world" of homogeneous objects to a "sacred world" of heterogeneity structured by pure difference.[60] The affect accompanying transgression and the passage from the profane to the sacred (a more radical division than that of good and evil, according to Durkheim, as pointed out by Michelson), is fear, defined by Freud as a mixture of awe and disgust. Pain, a primary affect, also forms part of the affective groundwork of the passage into the sacred.

Primary affects, ambivalence, ritual transgressive acts, terror, awe, and disgust—all of these are present in Sorokin's work, whose fictional universe thus "circumscribes" the sphere of the sacred. The characters in Sorokin's novel all perform ritual acts of sodomy or sadism or are subjected to such acts. Olga, for instance, is required to sit in a dentist's chair, receiving the dentist's feces into her open mouth. Although she needs some friendly coaxing from Rebrov to perform this negative rite, she nevertheless agrees to it freely. This excremental rite becomes an exercise in abjection, which prepares the self for a radical (self-)annihilation or "fading" (aphanisis) beneath the signifying chain,[61] which is tautologous with "the monstrous energy of thought," "the energy, or the violence, of Understanding" and "Negativity."

Abjection is an affect of the "underground" or repression. The ego's self-effacement in abjection is represented in the form of parody or *Witz* in the Vorontsov episode on the hidden suburban dacha inhabited by the "four hearts," whose "true proprietor" is absent (is absence). Here, the family group hold a prisoner in a cellarlike hole. Vorontsov is a secret agent (*syshchik*), attached to the military, and is an "undercover" colleague of Olga. Hence, like the latter, he is a memory trace or a proto-sign. Kidnapped by the "four hearts," he lives chained to the floor of the electrically heated concrete hole, operating a machine. Vorontsov's excrement covers the concrete floor of his prison. The hole thus resembles a cesspool, reminiscent of the "cistern" in which John the Baptist of the decadent Oscar Wilde is held before decapitation (symbolic castration). This Vorontsov is made to perform a ritual of memorizing and reciting what he has memorized, responding, like Pavlov's dog, to a trigger word from Rebrov. Part of what he has memorized is a medical textbook-type definition of the act of defecation. All the various texts which he is made to recite resemble a dialogue/monologue from the absurd theater of Artaud or Beckett. At the end of this ritual repetition of memorized absurdist texts, pressure is put on the man to agree to a fourth ritual amputation as proof of a renunciation of demand and acceptance of sacrifice through negative free desire.

Vorontsov is thus an absurd (both comical and disgusting) actualized metaphor of the zone of psychic repression—the field below the Lacanian "bar," which divides the "four hearts" (who are four signifiers) above ground from the signified below the bar. In this field, which is analogous to Freud's primal scene, language is a matter of automatic writing and the production of the memory trace—a process of which the subject of language can never have a memory. The recall of a trace is a matter for the ego (Rebrov), who has apparent mastery in the process of *cogito*. But this will to mastery, which transcends need, only leads the ego (the Master) to freely desire subjugation and self-annihilation, through which he is distinguished from the slave Vorontsov, who needs to be coaxed into another voluntary amputation.

Desire that is "inarticulable"[62] is represented in Sorokin's novel as a perverse negativity which comes into articulation literally through a "fantastic" incorporation: the transformation of the bodies of the "four hearts" into four cubes of frozen liquid or four *objets petit a*. These four ice cubes are the parodic non-residue of their "quest" for total "consumption on the spot," staged as a perverse ritual "consummation" and identification with the sacred or the impossible "real." In other words, staged as paradox, the iced surface of the Liquid Mother, which is the site of this sacred, is both the "slippery" ground of their desire and the "transparent" and ephemeral support of their discourse, literally re-enacted by them as a self-erasing ritual that models discourse (representation) as the desire of the other.

The orgy of sacrifice by means of a giant meat press is the novel's ultimate parodic symbol of castration and excess. Thus the "four hearts" who are one "soul" (one unconscious, though not a unitary one), seek death as the teleological end of their desire, which is to become desire incarnate. This impossible demand for absolute mastery articulates itself as a categorical imperative, whose teleology is pursued by the "four" in the face of insurmountable obstacles and personal hardships. But since the teleology of their quest is a pure teleology or a "purposiveness without a purpose," it is, like Kant's sublime, a negativity that comes into form as free and creative action and belongs to the sphere of aesthetic judgment. Because desire is not directed toward a need and does not answer a demand (is not self-serving in a materialist sense), it is also ethical.[63]

However, like conceptualist art, Sorokin's novel recycles everything it appropriates. Thus both Kantian aesthetics and Lacanian ethics are parodic quotations constituting an extended comic metaphor of negativity that mimics itself. The pornographic and excremental subject-matter of Sorokin's novel, which appears to cancel out any notion of morality such as could be identified with a traditional concept ("patriotism," "Christian virtue," or "fear of God," etc.), is in fact a tour de force which reinstates the unconscious as ethical discourse of desire, whose phenomenological form is that of *Witz*—a transgressive black humor (negativity) that mediates the sacred.

Sorokin's narrative is literally woven out of a myriad of mundane, trivial acts, rendered through a matter-of-fact protocol narrative. However, this mundane narrative is never sustained for long without a rupture or a violent shock propelling the reader out of the mundane (profane) into the pathological and transgressive (the sacred). This technique of rupture is illustrated at every turn in *Four Stout Hearts*, so much so that the reader accepts, albeit with heavy heart (and a feeling of *udruchennost'*—consternation), the pathology of these deviant, non-sensical, and seemingly self-generating outpourings of discourse, reminiscent of Sade's eroticized texts.

The trivia assume the same importance in the subjective universe of the "four hearts" as the *melochi* ("insignificant details") in Dostoevsky's "detective" novels. It is the trivia which, like the Freudian slips, betray that the unconscious is at work here. The trivia constitute a universe of the banal in Sorokin's novel, reminiscent of Ilya Kabakov's banal world of objects and pedantic commentary. The banal is, like dirt, beyond comparison. Like excrement, it is formless and indeterminate and thus lends itself as a substitution for the unrepresentable "real." But as metaphor (signifying substitution or representation) of the unrepresentable, the banal defies its own representation. That is why Sorokin's entire poetic project must of necessity display an anti-representational thrust. Almost all his prose works—*Norma, Roman, A Month in Dachau*—appear to destroy the very condition of possibility of representation. This is only an apparent gesture. Sorokin's excremental poetics constitutes the Russian writer's attempt to clear the space of discourse like one "clears the land." This allows him to free himself from the demands of tradition (the classic nineteenth-century novel as well as socialist-realist prose) in order to scale the immeasurable magnitude of the "real," which is postmodernism's version of the romantic sublime and Kant's "absolutely great" in nature.

A similar quest of the "real" has driven artistic production in Western European culture since the beginning of the twentieth century.[64] But while in Western Europe this quest took its natural course, manifesting itself in the poetic platforms of the numerous artistic "isms" spawned by modernism, in Russia its early manifestation was interrupted in the 1920s and any possibility of further development foreclosed on ideological grounds. Sorokin's achievement as a Russian postmodern writer lies precisely in the fact that his prose fills this lacuna in Russian culture. He dismantles various traditional Russian discourses, among them the nineteenth-century Turgenevian novel and socialist realism, and strips discourse down to its bare bones, transforming it into a bleached "outside" which is opaque and reflects nothing—no society, no history, and no inner life of the individual. The skeletal structure of this prose is a self-supporting "minimalist" grid of pure metonymies (signifying chains), whose teleological end is not to reflect a reality but to construct or simulate a "real" that will act as a snare and implicate the reader in the process of the desire in language and the seduction of the text.

Notes

1. The term "jeans prose" was suggested by Alexander Flaker in his seminal study of the young prose of the 1950s, which emerged throughout Eastern and Western European literatures in the wake of J. D. Salinger's prototypical *Catcher in the Rye*. A. Flaker, *Proza u trapericama* (Zagreb, second, enlarged edition, 1983; first edition, Zagreb, 1976).
2. The term "Hemingwayans" suggested itself to me after I had read the excellent and ground-breaking analysis of Soviet culture in the 1960s, presented by Alexander Genis and Petr Vail' in their book, *60-e. Mir sovetskogo cheloveka* (Ann Arbor, Mich., 1988).

3. To the above underground groups and individual writers must be added: the Leningrad underground writers Krivulin, Shvarts, Dragomoshchenko, and Berg (1970s and 1980s), and their magazines *Chasy*, *Obvodnyi kanal*, and *Krug*. In Moscow, the conceptualist poets Prigov, Rubinshtein, Zhdanov and others were active in the 1970s and 1980s. In the early 1960s, there was also the underground group *smog* (Gubanov, Aleinikov, Kublanovsky), as well as the earlier group of non-Soviet writers like Daniel Andreyev, Yury Mamleyev, and Genrikh Sapgir.
4. P. Vail' and A. Genis, "*Novaia proza: ta zhe ili drugaia?*" *Novy mir* (No. 10, 1989): 252.
5. It is published in English as *Dissonant Voices: The New Russian Fiction* (Harvill, 1991).
6. See Venedikt Erofeev, *Moscow Circles*, trans. J. R. Dorrell (London, 1981). Erofeev's novella came out in Russia for the first time in *Trezvost' i kul'tura*, No. 12 (1988). A. Bitov's *Pushkin House* was published by Ardis (Ann Arbor, Mich.), in Russian, in 1978. It came out in full in Russia only in 1987 (in *Novy mir* 10, 11 and 12). On the genesis of his novel, see Bitov's interview in the Belgrade literary newspaper, *Književna reč* (No. 367–8, January 1991): 13–14.
7. Frederic Jameson, "Postmodernism, or the Cultural Logic of Late Capitalism," *New Left Review* 146 (July–August 1984): 53–93. Boris Groys theorizes about the differences between Russian modernism and Soviet/Russian postmodernism in his ground-breaking monograph *Die Erfindung Russlands (*The Invention of Russia) (Munich, Vienna, 1995), in a chapter entitled "Die postsowjetische Postmoderne," pp. 187– 204. Groys establishes that the term "postmodernism" in Russian criticism has come to signify, in the first instance, a stylistic pluralism (p. 187). However, Groys's claim that "the only formal device of postmodern culture is the technique of appropriation, that is, the transposition of elements of low, commercial mass culture into the sphere of high art" (p. 193, my translation) is true only in part. The opposition of "low"/"high" culture was posited by the Russian formalists as the dialectic of literary evolution, but they illustrated this thesis on the basis of nineteenth-century literature (Gogol, Dostoevsky, the adventure novel, *Sterne*). Modernism sublated the boundary between "low" and "high" culture through the idea of the "ready-made" artistic object and the mass reproduction of the work of art. Thus the appropriation of "low" culture by "high" culture is not the "only" formal device of either modernism or postmodernism. Everything is appropriated in postmodern culture: it is citationality or "supplementarity" (Derrida) that is postmodernism's artistic "dominant," and in this Groys's thesis is correct.
8. The "cosmology" (or non-systemic system) of the heterogeneous was first introduced into European modernism by Georges Bataille. See Julian Pefanis, *Heterology and the Postmodern: Bataille, Baudrillard, and Lyotard* (Sydney and Duke, 1991). See also Annette Michelson, "Heterology and the Critique of Instrumental Reason," *October* 36: 11–127.

9. Boris Groys also locates the source of postmodern artistic practices in the works of the modernists Marcel Duchamp and Francis Picabia, and that of postmodern criticism in Bataille's and Lacan's opus. See Boris Groys, *Die Erfindung Russlands*, p. 249.
10. See Arthur Kroker and David Cook, *The Postmodern Scene: Excremental Culture and Hyper-Aesthetics* (Montreal, 1986).
11. See Elisabeth Sussman, "The Third Zone: Soviet 'Postmodern,'" *Between Spring and Summer: Soviet Conceptual Art in the Era of Late Communism*, ed. David A. Ross (Cambridge, Mass., 1990), p. 64, where Sussman says: "Sots art, which was definitely born with the work of Komar and Melamid and other Soviet underground artists involved in unofficial 'Aptart' or apartment exhibitions of the early seventies, was linked, generally, to American pop art. Sots art was an avant-garde which inscribed itself in a reflection of the banal, the quotidian, as signifiers of the social."
12. Belenikin's work was recently shown at the Victorian Artists Society Gallery in Melbourne (Australia).
13. See V. E. Lebedeva, *Tatiana Nazarenko* ("Sovietskii khudozhnik," Moscow, 1991), plate 58.
14. Michel Foucault, *Maurice Blanchot: The Thought From Outside*, trans. Brian Massumi (New York, 1987), p. 17.
15. Simone de Beauvoir, "Must We Burn Sade?," in *The Marquis de Sade: The 120 Days of Sodom and Other Writings*, compiled and trans. A. Wainhouse and R. Seaver, introductions by Simone de Beauvoir and Pierre Klossowski (London, 1990), p. 61–62.
16. The College of Sociology was an influential philosophical, artistic, and literary forum between 1937 and 1939, whose founding members included Bataille, Roger Caillois, and Michel Leiris. Their glossy review, entitled *Documents*, came out between 1929 and 1930, but in that short time established a counter-aesthetic or anti-aesthetic movement that privileged the heterogeneous as a "science of the sacred" (see Georges Bataille, *Visions of Excess: Selected Writings*, 1927–1939, ed. and with and introduction by Allan Stoekl, trans. Allan Stoekl [Minnesota, 1991], p. xx). The program of *Documents* was reflected in the journal's title: "A document is, by its very definition, an object devoid of artistic value." Denis Hollier, "The Use-Value of the Impossible," *October* 60 (Spring 1992): 5.
17. In October 1997, a conference dedicated exclusively to Sorokin's work was held in Mannheim, organized by Dagmar Burkhart, professor of Slavic Literatures at Mannheim University, and attended by younger and middle-generation Slavists from Germany, Austria, France, the United Kingdom and Australia, as well as by a number of young Russian art and culture critics. Sorokin's best reading public is in Germany, where his works are being vigorously translated. On a lecture tour in St. Petersburg following the Mannheim conference, I encountered an unenthusiastic response bordering on animosity toward Sorokin's work.
18. Sorokin was one of the four finalists for the 1992 Booker Prize. His entry *Serdtsa chetyrekh*, the title of which is translated by Judith Armstrong (a

reviewer for the *Sydney Morning Herald*) as *Four Stout Hearts*, has been published in Russia and Germany and is due to be published in English in *Glas*. Sorokin's first novella, *The Queue* (Ochered'), translated by Sally Laird, was published by Readers International (New York, London, 1985). It was first published in Russian, in Paris, by Syntaxis in 1985. His novel *Marina's Thirtieth Love* (Tridtsataia liubov' Mariny) has been published in German as *Marinas dreissigste Liebe* (Zurich, 1991). Sorokin's prose piece *A Month in Dachau*, which simulates the genre of "film script," was published in Russian in Germany in 1997, and in English in *Grand Street*, vol. 12, no. 4 ("Oblivion" 48): 233–253. His two latest novels, *Norma* and *Roman*, have been published by Obscuri Viri (Moscow, 1994). Since then Sorokin has turned to film scripts because he thinks film is the genre of mass culture relevant to Russia's current reality. He believes that literature as *belles lettres* is a thing of the past that has no consumer appeal for the "new Russians."

19. The interview is published under the title *Autoportrait*in Vladimir Sorokin, *Sbornik rasskazov. Predislovie D. Prigova* [Collected Stories. Introduction by D. Prigov] (Moscow, 1992). I am grateful to Viacheslav L. Nepomnyashchy for sending me a copy of this text from New York.
20. It is because a process of reappropriation of the Russian and European modernism was ongoing throughout the 1960s and 1970s, albeit as an "underground" process, that Russian culture could conjure up its postmodernism within the minute span of the perestroika decade and the post-Soviet 1990s. A similar thesis in relation to the visual arts is propounded in Elisabeth Sussman's excellent analysis, "The Third Zone: Soviet 'Postmodern,'" *Between Spring and Summer: Soviet Conceptual Art in the Era of Late Communism* (Cambridge, Mass., 1990), p. 64, where Sussman quotes Boris Groys, who has written: "… since the beginning of the fifties, since the time of the thaw that occurred after Stalin's death, Western art magazines, books and catalogues have arrived at somewhat regular intervals, if not to the general public, at least to circles directly involved in the production and evaluation of art." Elizabeth Sussman also dismisses the myth of the absolute cultural polarization between East and West during the "Cold War" by insisting that in cultural matters "there can be no complete and emphatic separation—indeed … one has not existed in an essentialist form for many years." Ibid, p. 62. A sophisticated model of the exchange relationship between Western and Soviet art is proposed by Victor Tupitsyn in "East-West Exchange: Ecstasy of (Mis)Communication," *Between Spring and Summer: Soviet Conceptual Art in the Era of Late Communism*, pp. 83–107.
21. Sorokin, *Autoportrait*, p. 120.
22. "Moi stil' sostoit v ispol'zovanii toi ili inoi manery pis'ma," says Sorokin in his *Autoportrait*, p. 120.
23. I. Shevtsov, a socialist realist writer, is mostly remembered for his attacks on realism and the left-wing intelligentsia of the 1960s in his novel *The Louse,* which provoked a polemic with Andrei Sinyavsky in *Novy mir* 12 (1964). See Boris Kagarlitsky, *The Thinking Reed: Intellectuals and the Soviet State from 1917 to the Present*, trans. Brian Pearce (Verso, London, New York, 1989), p. 168.

24. Ibid. (My translation).
25. Ibid. (My translation).
26. Ibid. (My translation).
27. Ibid. (My translation).
28. Sorokin uses the Russian *zabroshennost'* to translate Heidegger's German term *Geworfenheit.*
29. Ibid. (My translation).
30. Annette Michelson uses the term "disincarnate self" when she speaks of the process of thought in Bataille's subject as a "ritual" and an "undressing." Annette Michelson, "Heterology and the Critique of Instrumental Reason," *October* 36 (1986): 111.
31. See Mikhail Epstein, "Iskusstvo avangarda i religioznoe soznanie," *Novy mir* 12 (1989).
32. Epstein's selection of artists who demarcate the first avant-garde is reminiscent of Peter Bürger's thesis in *Theory of the Avant-Garde* (trans. Michael Shaw, foreword by Jochen Schulte-Sasse [Minneapolis, 1984]), which sets up the "traditional" avant-garde as an oppositional aesthetics based almost exclusively on ideological concepts. Burger's thesis is echoed in other current theorizing about Russian postmodernism. Elizabeth Sussman also holds that there was a utopian modernist agenda that collapsed in postmodernism. See Elizabeth Sussman, "The Third Zone: Soviet 'Postmodern,'" *Between Spring and Summer: Soviet Conceptual Art in the Era of Late Communism,* pp. 61–73.
33. Mikhail Epstein, "Iskusstvo avangarda i religioznoe soznaie," p. 227. It is noteworthy that Giorgio de Chirico produced what looks like an early version of Andy Warhol's Campbell's soup cans in his 1916 or 1917 painting entitled *The Faithful Servitor.* See *Four Modern Masters: De Chirico, Ernst, Magritte, and Miro* (New York, 1981), p. 30, plate 9. Although de Chirico's painting represents a series of six near-identical yet different packets of biscuits and not soup cans, this early appearance of an alimentary commodity in an otherwise abstract painting (representing de Chirico's frames and transparent easels) seems to be a prescience of pop art. The commentary on de Chirico's picture supplied in this catalogue is significantly off the mark. It ascribes the significance of the banal objects, namely the "biscuits in their glittering wrappings," to de Chirico's physical deprivation in the military hospital in Ferrara during World War I. The commentary is quoted from James Thrall Soby, *The James Thrall Soby Collection* (New York, 1961), p. 38. A parallel example of a modernist banal object, stripped of any ideological significance and given, instead, as a metaphor of the banal and of transgression, is Marcel Duchamp's famous urinal. The development of the photograph and film (art in the age of technical reproduction) during modernism was also already "postmodern."
34. It seems appropriate to take the word "*otvetstvennost*" not in its ethical connotation of "responsibility," but to read it instead—as Epstein most probably means it to be read—as a structurally descriptive notion, bespeaking a morphological rather than a semantic relationship between object and sign.

This reading is reinforced by Epstein's subsequent elucidation of the work of Ilya Kabakov.

35. Epstein, ibid. (My translation). A programmatic text, which is the basis of much of Epstein's theorizing about conceptualism, is Ilya Kabakov's manifesto "On Emptiness," trans. Clark Troy, in *Between Spring and Summer: Soviet Conceptual Art in the Era of Late Communism*, p. 53–61.
36. Epstein, ibid. (My translation).
37. Ibid. (My translation). A similar text appears in Mikhail Epstein, *After the Future: The Paradoxes of Postmodernism and Contemporary Russian Culture*, trans. Anesa Miller-Pogacar (Amherst, Mass., 1995), p. 60. My understanding of Epstein's Russian text differs significantly from that of Miller-Pogacar, particularly with regard to the point raised in footnote 34 above.
38. Ibid. (My translation).
39. *Penguin Dictionary of Religions*, ed. John R. Hinnells (New York, 1986), pp. 242–3.
40. Boris Groys, *Die Erfindung Russlands*, p. 199. For the grounding of the complementarity of the visible/invisible diad in phenomenological theory, see Maurice Merleau-Ponty, *The Visible and the Invisible* (Evanston, Ill., 1968).
41. Annette Michelson, "Heterology and the Critique of Instrumental Reason," p. 115.
42. Most of the Russian constructivist experiments with simple objects in the 1920s, such as Tatlin's "proletarian" coats or stoves, also fall within the domain of the object's "use-value." But because "use-value" is easily conflated with "utilitarian" (utopian) value, modernism is credited with a utopian project by which it is distinguished from postmodernism.
43. The dialectic of the "outside" finds its complement in Foucault's essay on the "limit," entitled "A Preface to Transgression," in *Language, Counter-Memory, Practice: Selected Essays and Interviews*, ed. Donald F. Bouchard (Ithaca, 1977), pp. 29–52.
44. Thus Sorokin explains, in the previously cited interview, that he does not understand the indignation to which his pornographic or hard-core subjects give rise. To him, all of that represents only "letters on paper" (*eto lish' bukvy na bumage*). See his *Autoportrait*, p. 121. One has exactly the same impression when reading Sade's prose: the excremental subject-matter has more to do with style than with titillation, although who is to say where style ends and "seduction" (of the text, in Lyotard's sense) begins.
45. Georges Bataille, "Hegel, Death and Sacrifice," in *On Bataille*, ed. Allan Stoekl, *Yale French Studies* 78 (1990): 16. This essay, first published in *Deucalion* 5 (1955), is part of Bataille's study of the (Hegelian) thought of Alexander Kojève.
46. Georges Bataille, "Hegel, Death and Sacrifice," p. 10.
47. Ibid., p. 17.
48. G. W. F. Hegel, *Phenomenology of Spirit*, trans. A. V. Miller, Analysis and Foreword by J. N. Findlay (Oxford, 1977), pp. 406–7, paragraph 668.
49. A recent article (which has since been rumored to have been a journalistic hoax), with accompanying pictures, in *Time* (Australia), vol. 8, no. 25 (June

21, 1993): 30 ff., shows two Moscow boys aged nine and their pimp Sasha, who plies his trade with the boys around the Bolshoi Theatre area. The domestic scenes, showing Sasha serving dinner to "his boys" and dressing them, in almost paternal fashion, for their daily prostitution duties, could have been taken out of Sorokin's novel *Four Stout Hearts*.

50. Susan Griffin's model of pornography is extensively quoted in Janine Lanagan's excellent article, "Icon vs Myth: Dostoevsky, Feminism and Pornography," *Religion and Literature* 18, 1 (Spring 1986): 63–72.
51. *The Shorter Oxford English Dictionary*, 3d ed., vol. 2 (Oxford, 1973).
52. Ibid., vol. 1, p. 132: the entry for "augury."
53. Jacques Lacan, *The Four Fundamental Concepts of Psychoanalysis*, ed. Jacques-Alain Miller, trans. Alan Sheridan (New York, 1981), p. 268.
54. Ibid., p. 275.
55. G. W. F. Hegel, *Phenomenology of Spirit*, trans. A. V. Miller (Oxford, 1977), p. 359, paragraph 590.
56. Ludwig Wittgenstein, *The Blue Book*, in Preliminary Studies for the "Philosophical Investigations," generally known as *The Blue and Brown Books* by Ludwig Wittgenstein (Oxford, 1969), p. 17.
57. Jacques Lacan, *The Four Fundamental Concepts of Psychoanalysis*, p. 154.
58. Iosif Bakshtein, "On Conceptual Art in Russia," in *Between Spring and Summer: Soviet Conceptual Art in the Era of Late Communism*, p. 77.
59. The genesis of the beautiful in nature is, according to Kant, in "primary matter"—"a fluid substance (the oldest state of matter), one part of which separates and evaporates while the rest rapidly solidifies (cf. the formation of crystals)." Gilles Deleuze, *Kant's Critical Philosophy: The Doctrine of the Faculties*, trans. Hugh Tomlinson and Barbara Habberjam (Minneapolis, Mich., Fourth Printing, 1993), p. 53.
60. See Annette Michelson, "Heterology and the Critique of Instrumental Reason," *October* 36 (1986): 115.
61. See Jacques Lacan, "The Subject and the Other: Aphanisis," in *The Four Fundamental Concepts of Psycho-Analysis*, pp. 216–29.
62. Jacques Lacan, *Ecrits: A Selection*, p. 302.
63. Ibid.
64. See Hal Foster, *The Return of the Real: The Avant-Garde at the End of the Century* (Cambridge, Mass., 1996).

Chapter 21

Emptiness as a Technique

Word and Image in Ilya Kabakov

Mikhail Epstein

1. A Mysterious Attic and the Ritual of Looking-as-Reading

In the late 1970s and early 1980s, Ilya Kabakov's studio on Sretensky Boulevard became a kind of sanctuary for the new, conceptualist art.[1] The studio, which had housed the shareholders company "Russia" before the revolution, was located in a garret in one of Moscow's older houses. To get to it, one had to climb a narrow side staircase, onto which the tenants of the surrounding apartments would put out their garbage bins. After negotiating these six floors of garbage, emerging at the top of what was once "Russia," the visitor crept along wobbly, squeaky floor planks that led to the hallowed doors. Once inside, he found himself amidst an intimate fraternity, limbering up with jokes and chatter before beginning its deadly earnest, spiritual seance.

Ultimately the visitors found themselves seated around a special pedestal, on which the artist's portfolio was spread out. Kabakov would leaf slowly through it, allowing the spectators sufficient time to look at each picture separately and to read the text that usually accompanied it. For example, one might be looking at the album entitled "The Window-Gazing Arkhipov" (*Voknogliadiashchii Arkhipov*), from the series "Ten Characters" (1972–75).[2] This album tells the story of a hospital patient who spends his time gazing out the window of his room and simultaneously depicts what he sees. It begins with little scenes of life beyond the window, out on the street; next come fragments of memories, as if reflected on the inner panes of the window; then the space of the window begins to fill with giant wings, leaving only a narrow slit between them. Gradually, the wings disappear, leaving behind a score of empty white pages (Figure 1). Further still, on separate sheets of paper, are comments from the patient's doctor and his acquaintances, from which it becomes clear that Arkhipov has died and that on the clean pages we were viewing his death.

This album leaves a mystical rather than an aesthetic impression on the spectator: one has the feeling of having been through a ritual of initiation. The slow, rhythmic turning of the album's pages is in itself hypnotic, as if human life were marked off in advance minute by minute, moving inexorably toward its end. The correlation of image and text has an equally mystical effect, the former conveying the point of view of the sick man, while the latter depicting the sick man himself. The representation of what the sick man sees becomes, in essence, an indirect narrative about him. The text at the beginning and at the end of the album transforms the little pictures into links of the narrative chain, investing them with the characteristics of a text. On the other hand, the text itself comprises part of the pictorial space: once Ankhipov's vision failed, words about him replaced images, as if at this point they only reached him through hearing. We had the feeling that the soul of the deceased was among us, continuing to perceive what we were perceiving about him.

This double effect was created through the correlation of word and image: above each of the views from the window, the word "Window" was inscribed; below each view, the word "Windowsill" (in the same standard, long-hand writing that was used throughout the text). Without the word "Window," the spectator would not have been differentiated from the represented character; it would hence have been a one-dimensional representation of a soldier, a girl, a train station etc., as in an ordinary picture. Thanks to the word "Window," however, it becomes the picture of the "window-gazing" Arkhipov; and since we, the spectators, see the same scene as he does, the impression is created that he also knows about our presence, though he does not see us, as we do not see him. The dispersion of focus, caused by the interaction of word and image, enables the spectator and the represented character to be aware of each other; it enables us to know about the death of Arkhipov, and Arkhipov to know that we know about his death. Thus new points of reference are created and perception is multiplied, alternating between character and spectator.[3]

We shall explore one aspect of this aesthetic mysticism—namely the artistic space that arises between text and visual image. At precisely the point at which text and image begin to echo one other, a mythical space is created, and it is this space that deserves our attention.

2. The Borders between Literature and Painting

The borders between literature and painting have always been considered clearly drawn, at least since the appearance of Lessing's influential treatise *Laocoon* (1766). Lessing's starting point was the obvious fact that poetry and painting use different materials: painting uses colors, which are laid out side by side in space, while poetry uses words, which are arranged in sequence one after another. Consequently, these two forms of art have two different forms of appropriation of reality: painting represents objects in space while poetry represents their transformation in time. Of course, the poet may also evoke a static scene, but without "painting it" (in Russian, *zhivopis',* "painting," literally means to "writing out live"). Instead, he uses words to reveal the process of perception. For example, in the *Iliad*, Homer does not describe Helen's exterior: he describes how the old men saw her. All attempts to "paint" in words lead to failure. According to Lessing, this claim to visual effects characterizes the poetry of German and French classicism, which is weakest in its attempt to capture "picturesqueness" in its portraits and landscapes.

Conversely, time is alien to painting. Painting is therefore doomed to failure when it attempts to portray different events in time in the same picture, that is, when it tries to develop a scene into a *sujet.* Narrative painting is just as much a traitor to its *genre* as descriptive poetry is to its predestined poetics. The good landscape painter or sculptor concentrates on representing a single moment, packing into it all that preceded it and all that may issue from it. Such a perfect execution Lessing found in the sculpted group of "Laocoon," which gave his treatise its title.

Lessing's distinctions were ideal for his epoch (the middle of the eighteenth century), when the centrifugal tendency of maximum differentiation of the art genres reached its peak. As paradoxical as it may sound, Lessing's criticism of classicistic practices (the contamination of criteria of painting and poetry) is the most lucid expression of the classicistic theory itself, with its demand for the strict segregation of the arts into separate genres. Lessing's view is correct to the extent that the theory of differentiation of the arts is justifiable. However, what neither Lessing nor eighteenth-century aesthetic theory took into account is the fact that each artistic genre evolves by means of a struggle against its own "innate" limitations and through the overcoming of its specificity.

One of the most important trends in European painting after Lessing was the move toward temporalization of the visual arts: the spatial contours of objects were dissolved under the pressure of time passing through them. This form of art culminated in Picasso's paintings, in which the representation of a figure is not focused into a single point in time but diffused along its entire axis, with past and future equal partners with the plane of the present, thereby depriving it of the privileged status it had held in traditional painting. Another variant of the same kind of temporalization of the represented object is offered by Chagall. In his work the outlines of objects are multiplied and disintegrated in the flow of time, as if sucked into the vertigo of memory. These objects, gathered in a single painting, form multiple layers of associations and temporal references, becoming a tight spatial knot that links all the different poetic-narrative strands.

Modernist literature, too, evolved in opposition to Lessing's poetics of narrative. In the twentieth century, literature became spatial in the same way that art became temporal. In his well-known study, "Spatial Form in Modern Literature,"[4] Joseph Frank showed that the mythologization, parabolization, and archetypization of literature was prompted by an attempt to bring literature out of the confines of narrative time and into the sphere of permanence and repetition, in which images are arranged in a spatial order. From this standpoint, the works of Joyce and Kafka are static visual structures ("paintings"), situated in a kind of mythical space. They are forms of verbal sculpture, in which time has stopped.

However, all of these anti-Lessingian developments remained confined to their given art form and therefore did not destroy the sovereignty of each separate genre. The fact that Picasso introduced temporality into his paintings did not make him cease to be a painter; nor did Kafka's parables, constructed according to spatial laws, make him any less recognizable as a writer. The move into spatiality took place within the medium of words themselves, while the move into temporality was accomplished within the medium of color itself. These different media remained the boundary-marks of the different art forms. The centripetal tendency, emerging in the culture of the twentieth century, set various forms of art on a course of convergence without destroying the dividing-line between them. The various streams became proximate without merging with each other.

Conceptualism went beyond this point. It attempted to change the status of both visual and verbal art by merging them into one. The artistic strategy of Ilya Kabakov represents this point of convergence. The essence of the experiment consists in placing word and object side by side in order to make them reflect one another, thereby foregrounding the phenomenon of culture itself; for culture is what is hidden behind the difference in art forms. The generating model of these forms is exposed only at the moment of translation from the language of one art into another. When a drawing is translated into a sentence, and a sentence into a drawing, it becomes clear: what is essential is not what is being said by the sentence or the drawing, but by culture itself, speaking through the various discourses. Culture is the very process of translation. The different art forms are mutually translatable because they are component parts of a meta-artistic cultural code. In this sense, visual art and literature are merely two discourses of culture, in which culture dialogizes with itself.

Conceptualism is thus not just an artistic trend, but a movement of art beyond the limit of art, into the sphere of culture itself. Conceptualism follows not so much the complex lines of development of the separate art forms as the equalizing (and at times simplifying) lines of culture itself. The more sophisticated and rarefied the diverse artistic discourses, the greater must be the universality of the code which allows them to be translated into another form. Conceptualism is thus no longer the self-expression of the artist, but the self-reflexivity of culture, its dialogue with itself. The *ideational* and *visual* aspects of culture, both of which issued from a concept with an identical Greek root—*eidos*—but which have grown apart during their centuries-long development, are attempting to come together again. In conceptualism, the *idea*, which reaches its full expression in the word, and *vision* (Russian *vid*), which achieves clarity in the visual representation, are focused on each other, exploring the possibilities of a future synthesis.

3. The Neutral Style and the Cliché

Such an experiment, if it is extreme, demands that all specialized artistic projects, entrenched in artistic untranslatability, be sacrificed to it. The case of the avant-garde speaks loudest in favor of such a sacrifice. For it is impossible to find a conceptual equivalent for Picasso's visual discourse, just as it is impossible to translate Joyce's refined verbalism into pictorial images. It may be that eventually even these extreme forms of artistic specializations will find a place in an all-embracing future synthesis. But the foundation of such a synthesis is in a neutral point: in culture as such, in the mass reception and mass acceptance of its discourse.

Since in conceptualism the entire field of meaning has shifted into the relationship between the visual and verbal signifying chains, these signifying chains themselves are structured by Kabakov in the most traditional manner, almost unprofessionally, in a deliberately mediocre "non-style." The artist must be given credit for his sacrifice to culture on behalf of both art forms—a sacrifice that initially threatened to lower his professional status among artists as well as writers. It is not the visual innovations themselves, nor the literary experiments of modernism and the avant-garde of the twentieth century (such as stream of consciousness, catachrestic imagery and so on) that attract Kabakov's attention. His innovativeness goes further: into the sphere of culture as such, into the region of the neutral and synthesizing principles of its structuration.

This is why Kabakov's expressive manner, which is organic to him and easily recognizable, is not in any way reminiscent of the great painters of the twentieth century. Rather it is most similar to magazine and book illustrations, forms of visual mass-production, whose typical feature, however indistinct it may be, has been picked out and slightly exaggerated, to obtain exact, sharp but not very carefully drawn lines, in bold blues and even in coarse, tasteless colors. A young woman in fancy boots, striding against a background of tall buildings, could easily have found her way into Kabakov's album ("The Window-Gazing Arkhipov") from the pages of a teen magazine, in which such a picture would have been accompanied by an article about the daily life of a *komsomol* youth and the social and cultural problems in a contemporary workers' settlement.

From a dilettante's point of view it would be easy to dismiss Kabakov as a "dauber," a typical Soviet hack, a jack-of-all-trades, who simply paints a picture, embellishes it with all sorts of verbal convolutions, fits it out with a "profound" expert artistic commentary—and executes it all in a mediocre, unoriginal style. It is almost as if Kabakov himself measured his art by the yardstick of this mass-oriented, workshop like professionalism of "the trade." It is as if his paintings were forms of this conscious and deliberate dilettantism, this artistic "all-ness" (*vsemstvo*), eclecticism and *bricolage*.

Kabakov's texts, which accompany the visual representations, are also remarkably devoid of style. They represent a cross-section of everyday consciousness, such as exclamations from the crowd, various banal remarks, kitchen chit-chat, and mass psychologemes of the type " May I be seated?"—"Yes, please make yourself comfortable,"

"Ivan Ivanovich is a very good chap," "I think he loved his wife but could not express it," and so on. For example, the text from the Arkhipov album offers the following characterization of the hero by his colleague Fomina: "When I saw him, he looked well and was in a good mood. The doctors told him he was getting better. He himself feels much better than at home. He says that he will finish the calculations himself after he gets out of the hospital, and not to touch them." Here the most ordinary words are used, lacking any psychological subtlety, any dialectological timbre, any crudity of jargon; in fact, they are free of all authorial self-consciousness or artistic originality. These words are emphatically neutral, as if they had been taken from a textbook on Russian grammar.

The hallmark of Kabakov's style is this artistic neutrality. His language looks as if it came from a grammar book, his images as if from a manual on painting or clichéd magazine illustrations. This prosaic style, which we come across in magazines and textbooks without taking notice of its uniqueness, is transformed into a special object of demonstration in the work of Kabakov, into a mysticism of the prosaic or, more accurately, and in his own words, into "the metaphysics of the commonplace."[5] It is precisely because style here is deprived of all artistic virtue, of all modernist complexity and refinement, gravitating instead toward "a pure zero, greyness, facelessness," that the aesthetics of style gives way to the metaphysics of the cliché. Everything is presented in artless form in order to demonstrate how far all this is from any artistry, any artifice. It is in this aesthetically empty space that a new criterion of artistic precision allows us to outline the "geometric space" of culture, which is equidistant from all specific cultural divisions and manifestations. This is an attempt to construct culture in the forms of culture itself, within the parameters of its unspent elementary wholeness, which was once fragmented by the various art forms but is now once again being collected into a whole.

4. The Merging of Word and Image

In general, the correlation of word and image does not represent the exception but the rule in traditional art. In this correlation, however, word and image are more often than not treated unequally. Either the word is pushed to the margins of the image or the image is ousted to the periphery of the word. Either the word is demoted to a *caption*, serving the self-valuable work of art, or the picture functions as a mere *illustration* to the self-valuable work of literature. Caption and illustration represent the ultimate degradation of the verbal and representational principles in their mutual correlation. The caption is a pitiful fragment of the verbal signifying chain, while the illustration is an auxiliary fragment of the representational chain. Both word and image are inserted into heterogeneous chains of signification—they are poor guests at someone else's feast.

These marginal, dependent forms, which appear to be especially adapted to alien contexts, are the forms with which Kabakov works, directing them toward a synthesis. As the artist himself explains, "a caption is not a work of art, but a caption taken in the context of a classical picture has the potential for gigantic dramatic collisions."[6] It is precisely the part that is "not a work of art" that Kabakov draws into a new, trans-artistic synthesis. The vast majority of Kabakov's pictures are executed in the form of illustrations to texts, while the majority of his texts are in the genre of enlarged captions to pictures. The marginal forms of earlier culture and fragments of traditional art forms become central to the new culture, whose point of departure is the moment at which word and image declare their mutual incompleteness. It is out of this incompleteness that a new form of artistic *supplement* grows.

As Kabakov's texts and pictures are created for one another, it is often difficult to decide which are originary and which auxiliary. The drawings confirm the writing and vice versa. Repetition thus becomes a conscious tendency in conceptualism: repetition on the textual and visual level. The entire Russian conceptualist movement can be said to be based on an aesthetics of repetition. Elsewhere I have discussed the automatization of the image in conceptualist art,[7] which operates by fatiguing the reader's attention, thereby creating a space for emptiness and dissipated boredom. The automatization of the image occurs not only through its transformation into cliché, the utilization of ready-made verbal or visual idioms, but also through the doubling of the artistic codes themselves. It is expected that if a picture depicts a beetle, the inscription under the picture should be a story or poem about that beetle. Kabakov in fact has such a picture: children's verses about a beetle accompanied by a gigantic wood panel, several meters long, representing an anatomically correct, greenish-blue beetle. Thus we have a combination of two clichés, superimposed upon each other: commonplace verses, evidently taken from a children's anthology, and a picture that looks like an enlargement from a school zoology textbook. The combination of these two clichés produces another, of greater magnitude: namely, a flawless universal cultural cliché.

Kabakov's texts and pictures borrow each other's aesthetic devices. The text is structured paradigmatically, as a static list, register or enumeration of items that are represented or absent from the picture, or of the reactions that spectators might have to the picture. This does not constitute a syntagmatically developed utterance, but a collection of all appropriate or possible utterances or speech acts relevant to the picture and ascribed to potential characters or spectators. Such a text can be presented as a graphic, a list, a time-table, an announcement, a public notice, a dictionary. What is important is the enumerative and registering intonation, from which the category of time and becoming has been excised. For example, Kabakov has one picture representing an ordinary crowd and queue in a grocery shop. The entire assortment of goods—the kind sold everywhere in such shops—is written right across the shelves and just below the scowling face of a middle-aged female shopper: "Selling today and every day, in great variety, in groceries and shops of Lengostorg. . . ." (Figure 2).[8] This is followed by columns, classified according to departments—meat, milk products, fish, groceries:

Cracow Sausage	Fresh River Carp
Moscow Sausage	Fresh Lake Perch
Connoisseur Sausage	Fresh River Caviar
. . .	. . .

In many instances Kabakov dispenses with the representation, the image, substituting it with a graphic, a schedule, or some other text inscribed into strict spatial coordinates. To this type belongs the stand that reads "In Favor of Cleanliness. Roster for the removal of carnage tins in house No 24, entrance No 6, V. Bardin's Street, ZhEK No 8, District of Bauman."[9] The stand is inscribed with the surnames and apartment numbers of the tenants, from which the garbage tins will be carried out according to a strict schedule over the next five years, from 1979 to 1984. Another stand, "Coat-hanger," is comprised of a coat-hanger, a walking stick and a toy steam train, directly alongside of which is the following text, entitled "Answers of the Experimental Group at Pavlov. RSKS":[10]

> *Nikolai Pavlovich Malyshev:* Here I shall hang up my new raincoat.
>
> *Nikolai Arkad'evich Krivov:* I bought this steam train for my son Volodya.
>
> *Aleksandr Alekseevich Koss:* The nail was driven in by my wife, Briukhanova Anna Alekseevna.
>
> *Anna Borisovna Gorodovina:* I don't understand anything …

The rejoinders concerning the objects form a kind of completed and static expanse of ZhEK[11] experimental thought. One way or another, Kabakov's text, which has landed in the pictorial space, begins to function as an image; that is, the text no longer narrates, it represents a verbal happening in static form.

Conversely, Kabakov's images, which fill up entire albums, collections, and series, coherently succeed one another in time. Such a dynamic sequence is appropriate to book illustrations, which are usually accompanied by a narrative text. The difference lies in the fact that illustrations are normally divided and fragmented by the text and have no connection outside of the text. Kabakov's images, on the contrary, form a closely knit, inseparable chain of representational self-motion in time. In the album "The Window-Gazing Arkhipov" the images—views from the window—tell a story about the patient and create the history of his illness.

Kabakov's texts are frozen in space, like pictures, while his images move in time, like texts.

5. *Lubok* and Myth

The only cultural precedent that is in any way reminiscent of the Kabakov phenomenon is the *lubok.*[13] It is a syncretic genre that was wide-spread in the folk art of European countries during the seventeenth and eighteenth centuries. Antiquity knew a similar literary genre: the description of pictures or sculptures—*ecphrasis.*[12] But such descriptions existed separately from the pictures themselves and were not intended for simultaneous reception. Ecphrasis was considered an independent work of verbal art. The artistic consciousness of antiquity made an attempt to shape words in plastic fashion. This was a mark of the statuary and sculptural nature of the entire world view of antiquity, which Alexei Losev (in his multivolume *A History of Ancient Aesthetics*) identifies as the fundamental distinguishing feature of the epoch. With a powerful injection of medieval logocentrism, the text ceased to be determined by the picture; the picture, instead, came to be defined by the text, as the visible supplement and exegesis of the Holy Scriptures.

It was after the Renaissance, in an era of dynamic equilibrium between picture and word, classical and biblical legacy, that the art of the lubok, a popular print illustration, burgeoned, reaching its peak in the seventeenth through the nineteenth centuries. In this way, an "undercurrent" of popular syncretism compensated for the sharp differentiation of genres in the "high" culture of classicism. It was with the lubok that image and word met as equal participants in a cultural event. Of course, emphasis sometimes varies in luboks. Some are illustrations of well-known biblical or folkloric subjects: faithful to the details of the narrative in all respects, they use the text as their point of reference. Others represent a collection of striking and interesting pictures, to which appropriate captions are appended—for instance, various beasts with accompanying sayings, expressing their allegorical traits. With these luboks, visual perception has the upper hand. On the whole, however, the dominant principle of the lubok is a naive, spontaneous placing together of text and picture, while the primacy of the one or the other element is not strictly predetermined, depending instead on the attitude of the spectator-reader and the degree of his/her literacy. A lubok is a picture reduced to an illustration, or a caption grown into a description. With all its vacillations, the lubok retains an equilibrium between word and picture, giving the genre its syncretic nature.

It was the naive coincidence of picture and narrative that gave pleasure to the spectator-reader of the lubok. Word and image not only met as equals but affirmed each other. The clever cat with dyed whiskers, killing mice that appeared as non-Christian Orientals, was described in a caption exactly as "the clever cat killing mice appearing as non-Christian Orientals (*myshi-busurmane*)." Or an inscription above the picture of two swaggering heroes: "These courageous young men are good fighters, but if ever one overcomes the other in a wrestling fight, he will get two poached eggs." In fact, a cap with two eggs is lying at the feet of the young men. Another picture portrayed a woman putting *bliny* into an oven, while a gentleman with explicitly carnal intentions is seen creeping up on her. Accordingly, the inscription above the picture reads: "Please leave me alone, I'll have nothing to do with you, you've come grabbing for my bum, spoiling the baking."[14]

The effect of the lubok is very much compatible with the "aesthetics of identity," as defined by Yury Lotman in *The Structure of the Artistic Text.*[15] Folklore, and similar genres of art, do not challenge (as was later prescribed by the criterion of originality) but correspond to the reader's expectations. The reader experiences a childlike pleasure in hearing time and again what he already knows. "However," Lotman adds, "in order for identity to exist, difference must also exist."[16] Difference is created in the lubok by the doubling of narrative and visual sequences. The spectator-reader enjoys the different codes conveying an identical message.

The same doubling or even tripling is particular to contemporary conceptualism, where identical objects can be rendered in words, images and in their physical presence. For example, the American artist Joseph Kosuth (b. 1945) presented three incarnations of a single object in his *One and Three Chairs* (1965): a real chair, its photograph, and a dictionary definition of the word "chair." As Sandro Sproccati has noted, in conceptualism "[t]he work itself coincides in a tautological sense with the 'reflection about the work.'"[17] This tautology restores the "aesthetics of identity" found in lubok.

It may be conjectured that lubok, as a genre of popular culture, served as a repository of mythological sensibility. A myth presupposes the unsegmented identity of a concrete object with the abstract concept of that object. The elements of the lubok, consisting of the concreteness and plasticity of the object, and the caption (text), which represented a concept, history, allegory, moral, etc., created the conditions for a mythological perception—a perception that had not yet dissociated the visual from the verbal aspects of the work of art. The spectator-reader was engrossed in reading the picture and in visualizing the text. The conceptual and the perceptual were indivisible. These unsegmented "eidoi" or "idea-visions" acquired an integrity in the environment of popular culture. This unity was lost in the sphere of high culture, where word and representation (image) were insistently separated, as in Lessing's aesthetics.

The question that must be asked is why the creativity of a contemporary artist such as Ilya Kabakov comes so close to lubok syncretism, which was archaic even in the nineteenth century. The answer is: because the twentieth century has breathed a new and terrifying breath of life into this old art form, transferring it from the popular periphery into the very center of culture and into the avant-garde of social life. Are not the modern advertisement, the placard, poster, and propaganda stand resurgences of verbal-pictorial syncretism, increasing their value as they offer their services to the latest mythologies? One of the innate features of totalitarianism was the resurrection of ancient semi-folkloric genres, such as the heroic epic or the ode, as well as of the syncretic forms of folk art, close to the unity of ritual. In such syncretic, ritual forms of art, representation, dance, word, and music are knit into one whole. This helps to explain why the synthetic music drama [*Totalkunstwerk*] of Richard Wagner was so popular in Nazi Germany.

In Russia, the synthesis of word and image also served mythological ends. What the party and the government proclaimed by word was immediately graphically incarnated in the works and destinies of the people. A typical propaganda stand represents a catch-all or slogan, underneath which are visible testimonies to its successful application in life. For example, fattened cows in green meadows are used to illustrate the concept of accelerated development in the cattle and dairy industry. Sun-tanned, smiling children at the seaside, surrounded by palm trees, illustrate the importance of child care in the Soviet state.[18] In conjunction with visual representations, the word demonstrates the identity of idea and reality.

Visual mass propaganda is the most recognizable feature of the Soviet regime, its universal signaling system triggering in every citizen a feeling of his or her ineradicable "Sovietness." This citizen is surrounded by portrait-slogans, poster-images, stand-poems—all of them political luboks, telling him what they show him, in order to subject him to a double control, a doubly reinforced signifying chain, from which he can no longer free himself. Meanwhile, the controllers control each other. The picture verifies the correctness of the slogan, while the slogan verifies the suggestiveness of the picture. Thus literature and the visual arts carry out a constant policing of each other. Both are agents of the regime—and that means they must be vigilant and prepared to denounce each other.

6. Neo-Lubok and the Profanation of Myth

Against such a social backdrop, Kabakov's artistic activity receives added meaning. On the one hand, the growing specialization and fragmentation of high-brow art motivated Kabakov to seek a new cultural synthesis, uniting image and word. On the other hand, this process of unification was already taking place outside culture, on a mass scale. Culture was subordinated to the dictates of political myth and propagandistic ritual. The problem of the separation and polarization of word and image thus became critical.

This is what constitutes the spirit of the neo-lubok artistic creation of Kabakov. On the one hand, this art stands on the opposite end of intra-cultural, "modernist" specialization, on the other it also stands apart from extra-cultural, "totalitarian" integration. Thus it takes up the position of culture itself. In other words, Kabakov is trying to bring into realization *a simultaneous synthesis of fragmented artistic forms and an explosion of the totalitarian myth by ironic analysis.* The result is the *neo-lubok*, a domestic, auctorial myth, ironic in relation to the official government myth.

This displacement of official myth by kitchen myth produces what Kabakov describes as Soviet "lumpenized culture," which is absurd and dreamlike.[19] The mystical content of the originary myth is sublated and transformed but is not suspended. The major Kabakovian myth—as the artist has often stressed himself—is the communal apartment and the ZhEK *(zhilishchno-ekspluatatsionnaia kontora)*, "the office for the management of neighborhood housing." These two Soviet institutions constitute the archetypal space of the Kabakovian myth. The ZhEK, with its "red corners," citizens' tribunals formed to air apartment squabbles and gossip publicly, exemplifies the communality of the apartment culture on a larger scale. As if through a dark glass, the old religious idea of *sobornost'* (togetherness, communal spirit) begins to be glimpsed here. The idea of *sobornost'*, which has been the standard for many ideological and philosophical movements, beginning with Khomiakov and other Slavophiles, is deeply entrenched in Russian culture. In the Soviet instance, a double substitution takes place. First, the Soviet state transforms the idea of *sobornost'* into declared communism and, in practice, totalitarianism.[20] Communism is thus a compulsory and profane form of *sobornost'*, consciously rejecting religiosity on the rational level but unconsciously permeated by religiosity and covertly marked by *sobornost'* itself. When Kabakov turns this myth inside out a second time, domesticating it and transforming its site into a communal apartment, the religious dimension recedes even further; yet it necessarily retains its connection with the *arche*-myth, thus becoming a pseudo-*sobornost'*. All the paradoxes of Kabakov's *kommunalka* are situated in this doubly profaned structure of *sobornost'*, where individuals exist both indivisibly and separately. Although all the tenants have their own rooms, their own private lives, they live under constant mutual surveillance, under the threat of intrusion in bathroom or toilet, obliged to share a small, narrow kitchen and gas stove: it is as if the entire apartment labors under a cloud of the "collective unconscious," enclosed within four walls.

In one of Kabakov's stands we see a fly and above it, in opposite upper corners, a verbal exchange:

> *Anna Borisovna Stoeva:* Whose fly is this?
> *Nikolai Markovich Kotov:* This is Olga Leshko's fly.

This is the mundane "*sobornost'* consciousness" of the communal apartment. On the one hand, we have, as it were, angelic voices, emanating from beings who are unrepresentable. If the authors and the addressees of those voices were to appear in the picture, its mystical effect would be entirely destroyed, transforming it into a caricature. On the other hand, this *sobornost'* consciousness is focused on a visible object, the fly, which must also be "somebody's," like a teapot or a box of cookies. The voices of the characters who are absent permeate every object. The representation of the fly is only a point of contact for this polyphony, constituting the very being of the *kommunalka.* Something is spoken out aloud, something is retained in the soul, but the tenants of the *kommunalka* are persistent interlocutors; their lives are a sequence of verbal exchanges, separating, uniting, rearranging each unit of the communal household. Herein lies the source of the impression of the mysticism of those voices, flying from corner to corner in Kabakov's pictures: the structure of *sobornost'* is being revealed to us, although turned inside out two times; first in the "heroic" manner, as "communism"; then parodically, as "communality." Kabakov's stand is thus something of a mystical parody, which obtains its effect through a "forked language" (double code) : voices from another world and the representation of a fly.

As Kabakov himself stresses, the communal apartment is for him first and foremost a cultural phenomenon, even if a debased one. It is precisely because of its profane character that it retains its wholeness. High culture, by contrast, tends toward differentiation: spiritual layers are distinct from material ones, sociality is distinct from morality, art distinct from science, drawing from writing. Only on its mass or popular folkloric levels, which are correlated with the concept of the lubok, does culture retain its wholeness.

In ancient times, the space between word and representation was filled by ritual. In our era totalitarianism has filled that gap. In

Kabakov's work, the synthesis of different art forms expresses the mystical phenomenon of culture itself as a newly perceived totality, different from its primitive (mythological) and totalitarian (ideological) forms.

Despite its own claims to rationality, culture as a whole is mystical. For culture is the heritage of the primordial totality of cult or the all-encompassing ritual. Ordinarily we do not perceive culture as a totality. This is because in modernity, culture always confronts us in its diverse manifestations, its genres and subdivisions, in relation to which we have already constructed our strategies of distancing, relativization, and one-sided reflexivity, engendered by the rational reception of the artistic illusion. When the folds of culture are drawn again, we feel once more caught in a kind of mythological trap. Hence the comparable mystical impression created by Wagner's synthetic musical dramas and the Soviet visual propaganda of the *Agitprop* of the 1920s and 1930s (despite the discrepancy in the respective aesthetic levels of the two cultural forms). When one art form, transgressing its limits, begins to interact with another, it reveals its primordial ritual meaning. Culture as a totality represents just such a ritual, arising in the gaps between the various forms of art.

7. Discrepancy between Word and Image: The Synthesis of the Arts and the Disintegration of Myth

This mystical phenomenon is refracted in Kabakov's work through the lens of the reflexivity that characterizes "high culture." Couched in the form of an official poster or a propaganda stand, Kabakov's picture (or graphic) appears synchronous with the text. However, this synchronicity is produced in such a manner that, on the one hand, the unity of the "eidos" (idea-vision) is partially retained, while, on the other, this unity is dissolved in order to allow the artist's irony and self-reflection to be expressed in the picture. Kabakov is the creator of minor myths, kitchen myths, apartment myths, table myths, myths about teapots, rubbish bins, or flies. These small myths contain a drop of the gigantic, oceanic official state myth. In this way, colossal myths are parodied by small myths. Displaced into a context of private self-reflection, the vast mechanisms of the large myths grind to a squeaky, noisy halt under the stress of their reduction in scale. The falsehood of the social mythology is thus exposed. Its tragic lack of substance, its elegiac helplessness, and heroic self-delusion are shattered not by means of abstract intellectual criticism, but through an intense process of transposition into a reduced, parodic scale.

In so doing, the myth is deconstructed in the same way it was constructed. That is, an unfillable gap, a partial incongruence emerges between the idea and its appearance. For instance, since an artistically executed schedule or time-table is characteristic of the planning mentality of Soviet rationality, Kabakov goes to great lengths to reconstruct this model of rationality in all its details and aspects: however, instead of using it to outline a five-year plan for industry, he applies the plan to a lofty five-year project for rubbish collection in a communal apartment building. In another case, Kabakov makes use of a schedule that might have been produced in the administrative office of a construction plant: in its well-divided columns he inscribes the carefully conceived life plans of some diligent dreamer, including fishing holidays and siesta hours to be spent on the divan. This trivial text, inscribed within the monumental schedule, parodies the latter's form, which is intended for recording "historical" events.

Not only history but geography took on sacred-symbolic status in the Soviet epoch. Geography was allied to the notion of closed zones, mysterious troop movements around the country, concentration camps and secret missions. Kabakov makes use of this sacralized geography through a system of coded circles and squares that appear in his work, "The History of Anna Petrovna" and "Olga Markovna and Brunova Go Visiting" (Figure 3).[21] Circle No 1 designates Olga Markovna, circle No 2, which is next to circle No 1, belongs to Brunova. In front of them stands ellipsis No 3, a tram. In the distance, there are further circles delineating Karp Davidovich and Boriskina, who are evidently about to meet along the way and sit down in circle No 5, a taxi. This will take them to the farthest circle, No 7, which delineates Nikodimov, possibly the same person whom they all intended to visit originally. Such topographically precise imagery, resembling general staff charts, is in harmony with the consciousness of the Soviet people, even if parodied by Kabakov. For a journey into another part of town represents, for *Homo Soveticus*, an act of strategic importance, consisting of the following elements: perseverance and skill in finding an exact location for mounting the tram, a plan of operation for catching a scarce taxi, a rational distribution of participants along the taxi's entire anticipated route, and so on.

The forms of discrepancy between Kabakov's text and image are manifold. Often something will surface in the text that is absent from the image. For example, a huge whitewashed stand has a barely noticeable yellow dot in the middle. It becomes clear from the text, situated on the right-hand side of the stand, that a soccer game is being represented (Figure 4). However, in it, all the players have become invisible for some reason, while the ball is hardly visible in the middle of the field. This is the yellow dot. Another example deals with reproductions of subjects neatly inscribed on a lithograph: Ivan Semenovich is asking Peter Nikolaevich for permission to sit down on the stool in the corner, to which Peter Nikolaevich replies "Please, do!" A stool is portrayed alongside the dialogue; however, there is no one sitting on it.

Most often it is Kabakov's text that has an excess of meaning in relation to the image. Sometimes the text expels and even does away with the image, although a certain space is left vacant for it. For example, a large brown stand is divided into two halves. The left side is taken up with a description of a picture entitled "The Guilty Woman," which tells us that the woman is standing at the window, with gaze lowered in front of her, sad forebodings crowding her mind. She is depressed and guilt-ridden in relation to someone she loves. This is, in other words, a typical *sujet* for a psychological portrait. However, the right side of the stand, which should be a representation or image of the "guilty woman" just evoked in the textual commentary, is empty. In place of the image there is only the plain brown texture of the canvas's surface. The verbal description of the subject of the portrait is so exhaustive that it makes its representation superfluous. Yet, since the space for the image is left intact, the work remains bi-lingual. At the same time, the messages coded in the two languages are presumed to be so identical that one can substitute for and cancel the other. A contradiction is thereby introduced into the picture, since something that is not there is being spoken about. Kabakov masterfully handles this kind of repetition that creates a contradiction and explodes the lubok from inside. The verbal sequence coincides with the visual sequence, forcing the latter to disappear altogether. Through the focus on the identity of the two codes, a contradiction and an absurdity emerge. The text destroys precisely that image it announces and to which it corresponds in intention.

A shift takes place in Kabakov's image: it is not adequate to the word, even though the genre would appear to offer the possibility for a perfect concordance of word and image. In the traditional lubok, image and word supplement each other. This constitutes its felicitous totality of meaning. Kabakov's totality, however, is no longer completely felicitous, because there can be no real totality in a world in which centrifugal artistic forces split this totality into parts, while centripetal political forces violently unite the separated parts. By inserting bindings and links into the torn work of art Kabakov simultaneously demonstrates the fragility of forced connections. It is a twofold task that constantly complicates itself in the course of its own execution. Kabakov moves along a border, on the one side of which is the diversity of art and on the other the totality of myth. He avoids both artistic specialization and the totalizing power of myth. Kabakov's space is that of pure culture, which is neither fragmented in its depths nor petrified on its surface. Kabakov thus moves *between barbarism, which aspires toward unity, and professionalism, which gravitates toward specialization.* The standard adopted here is *to create nothing less than culture, transcending the limits of art, and nothing more than culture, rejecting the pretensions of myth. Culture is a self-synthesizing multiplicity of artistic forms and a self-analyzing mythical totality.* The art of Kabakov is a cultural phenomenon in the narrow and finite sense of the term "culture," according to which culture is distinct from both myth and art.

8. Artistic Bilingualism and the Articulation of Emptiness

But what does "culture" mean in the specific case of Kabakov? In one interview, he stated that becoming a student at the Dnepropetrovsk School of Art was an event of great significance for him. It represented a transition from a zone of non-culture, which surrounded him at home and in his neighborhood, into the world of culture. "But," he added, "one should keep in mind the following: the culture which greeted me was already destroyed. My generation did not inherit an authentic culture, but one that was mixed with mystification and almost totally processed by ideology. To love such a culture, to be interested in it, to wish to live within it was impossible. There was a paradox in the fact that the child's non-cultural consciousness fell into this zone of a destroyed culture."[22]

This paradox of his childhood experience is preserved in Kabakov's mature art. The cultural space which he discovers in-between the literary and visual orders is left unoccupied and empty. Culture is present here as a gaping hole, a place where one has an appointment with culture but to which culture never shows up. This is why one can say that emptiness is the salient constructive principle of Kabakov's artistic works. Even those works boasting a dense materiality and visual fullness, such as the albums in the series "Ten Characters," always end with blank sheets of paper. Ultimately, life always leads his characters to emptiness. Or, as Kabakov himself puts it, "the individual at the end of his journey always comes face to face with a white emptiness, with nothingness."[23] The same emptiness is encountered in Kabakov's stands, in which the presence of the text forces us to a more profound perception of the empty space of the image. This space is reserved for figures and colors, but remains unfilled. A chair remains empty even though one of the invisible characters is asking for permission to sit down, while another invites him to sit on the chair. A soccer field remains empty, populated by invisible players, while only a yellow spot—indicating the soccer ball—alludes to the possible organization of this emptiness, allowing us to experience its magnitude. Similarly, the place where the "guilty woman" should appear on the stand remains empty. Or again: Kabakov presents us with five vertical columns of equal width (Figure 5). The first column on the left is filled with scores of names, patronymics, and surnames, accompanied by the same sacramental question: "Where are they?"

> Where is Efim Borisovich Teodorovsky?
> Where is Innokentii Borisovich Raisky?
> Where is Sofia Alekseevna Kostorzhevskaia?
> ...
> Where is Vladimir Aleksandrovich Fedotov?
> Where is Anatolii Veniaminovich Letin?
> Where is Elizaveta Mikhailovna Korobova?

The remaining four columns on this giant stand are empty, reinforcing the impression that these people are no longer among the living or that nothing is known about them. The question "Where?", repeated many times, without eliciting an answer, acquires a mystical significance. One is not sure whether it is an incantation about people who disappeared suddenly and without trace in the recent past, or an address to the world beyond the grave in an attempt to trace its topology and determine the placement of the dead souls. The emptiness in a place reserved for an expected answer cries out with its silence. It becomes an answering emptiness, whose meaning is equivalent to that of the repeated questions. Such a conception could not have been executed on a smaller scale; say, within the confines of a small sheet of paper, where the same questions could have been placed. This is because the non-answer that these questions elicit requires a huge expanse of emptiness, greatly in excess of the height of the artist himself; it requires enormous labor to arrange the studio and white-wash a giant panel; nor is it a small task to find a fitting application for such a monumental panel, that is to say, to ultimately find nothing more fitting than to leave the panel four-fifths empty. Thus the emptiness of the stand had to be carved out and separated from the surrounding emptiness, and framed as cultural emptiness, as the place of emptiness in culture itself.

Kabakov's need for cultural bilingualism and a constant overlaying of verbal sequences over visual sequences thus becomes understandable. This bilingual procedure is analogous to a pair of scissors, cutting out emptiness from the artist's surrounding world. What emerges between text and image is a culturally shaped emptiness. The discrepancies between text and image form silhouettes of emptiness, which are manifest beyond the text in the absence of the image, or beyond the image in the absence of the text. Kabakov's neo-lubok perverts the logic of the lubok genre by inverting or suspending the correspondence between word and image.

If Kabakov were working with one language and a single material medium, the representation of *absence* would be impossible. The material of a representation dictates that everything representable be represented. Only language, which penetrates the space of the picture, traces the field of the unrepresentable. Until we are told about the invisible soccer players by the text, they simply do not exist, and the yellow dot (marking the place of the soccer ball) is simply a yellow dot. The representation is equal to the represented. But as soon as the text appears, the represented is catapulted from the field of representation. Through their entry into language, the invisible players and the soccer field inscribe their absence on the picture itself. Absence enters the picture, and cultural sequences take shape in the zone of the non-correspondence between the visual and the verbal sequences. To paraphrase Kabakov, it is possible to say that it is not the caption by itself, but the relationship between the caption and the representation that contains "the potential for gigantic dramatic collisions." The collision is not produced by the fact that text and image enter into a mutual struggle, but because both surrender so easily, annihilating each other in the process and revealing vast zones of emptiness, silence, and invisibility.

Here is another of Kabakov's compositions, with a typical conglomeration of elements (Figure 6). At the top of the stand are the following verbal rejoinders:

> Where is Alyona Mikhailovna?
> Where is Sofia Musievich-Belova?

And at the bottom of the stand, the answer:

> They have been absent for a long time …

At the bottom of the stand, an ordinary fly is painted in oils. What is this work of art about? It is about the unrepresentable expressed in words and the unnamable painted in colors. The fly has been painted, but nothing can be said about it. Questions have been asked about Alyona and Sofia, but these persons cannot be represented. By being superimposed upon one another, words and images create zones of silence and invisibility within each other. Kabakov's works use visible outlines to inscribe emptiness.

This combination of text and representation functions as an unfailing device. When text and image deviate from one another, they cause shadows of non-being to converge upon each other. But even when text and image converge, when they coincide absolutely, the very meaning produced by such a concordance falls within the zone of nothingness. For example, Kabakov sketches the conventional rough outlines of a mountain chain and above the mountains a rhomboid frame with the inscription "Caucasian Mountains" (which is the title of this 1971 work, executed in ink and colored pencil on paper).[24] The correspondence of inscription and sketch cancels their meanings, shifting them to a zero point of tautology and repetition. If, in actual fact, we had before us a Caucasian landscape—in romantic, realist or impressionist style—the concrete wealth of the representation would add to the inscription. However, the standard undulating outline of the mountains, which could be the Himalayas or the Pyrénées, hills on the outskirts of Moscow or mounds in a children's sand-pit, adds nothing to the inscription. The inscription is thus pure repetition; it is nothingness revealed through doubling.

It is thus possible to distinguish between two types of emptiness. One is the emptiness created by the difference arising from two codes. It is a seductive emptiness. The other type of emptiness is created through repetition, which arises from the tautologous message of the two codes. This is a nauseating emptiness. Some of Kabakov's works are therefore difficult to view, eliciting boredom or nausea in their refusal to supply the movement and informative variation that perception demands. Thus the series "Ten Characters" (1972–1975) is an exemplar of seductive emptiness. Another of Kabakov's series, consisting of twenty albums entitled "On Grey and White Paper" (1977–1980), creates an impression of boring emptiness. What is represented in this series is one and the same object, such as, for example, a vase, with minuscule elements of change from page to page (such as a different handle or a slight variation in ornament pattern), which actually reinforces the effect of tautologous repetition. The aesthetic value of such tautologies can be questioned but, in my view, an artist has the right to distill emptiness for me in such a way as to allow it to migrate inside me and be experienced as my own inner emptiness, as an oppressive boredom, a numbness of the soul brought about by the experience of a nauseating infinity.

Kabakov's artistic bilingualism is thus not a formal device but a method of cultural articulation of emptiness. It is a means of extracting emptiness from the world so that the muteness of language can be seen in the form of representation, and the invisibility of the represented made evident in the form of the text. It is also a method of manifesting non-sense through the correspondence of text and image and their tautologous repetition.

9. Negative Emptiness

What is the significance of emptiness for Kabakov? Why does he seek to impart cultural forms to it and imprison it in the clutches of words and images? In trying to answer these questions, we shall turn to Kabakov's own contradictory stance on the subject, with his two opposing views about the nature of emptiness.

One of these views has been expounded by Kabakov in his theoretical piece entitled "On Emptiness." "First we must say something of the psychic constitution, the psychological condition of the people who were born in the void and live there."[25] This is how Kabakov describes the essence of his native Soviet-Russian world as he experienced it against the backdrop of his first trip abroad, to Czechoslovakia in 1981. The Soviet world appeared to him as a giant reservoir of emptiness, which could not be filled by any imaginable human effort. In Europe, emptiness is still a vacant space, not yet cultivated, waiting to be conquered and husbanded, requiring active human intervention, care and work. In Russia, emptiness itself is an active principle, a frenzied vacuum that sucks all human initiative and endeavor into nothingness, all history, tradition and culture into its whirlpool-like sieve. It is a commonplace that "nature does not tolerate a vacuum," but it is equally true that a vacuum "does not tolerate nature."[26] Instead, it swallows nature, devastates forests and fields, devours and dissolves all positive value and every constructive principle. Such a vampirelike emptiness cannot remain alive for a single instant without drawing the living blood out of its inhabitants, without implanting in them a gnawing feeling of nausea and mortal self-destruction: "... things are begotten of nothing, nothing is connected with nothing else, nothing signifies anything, everything is suspended in and disappears into the void blown away on the icy wind of the void."[27] Kabakov's perception of Russia as a "negative lesson" to the world is similar to Chaadaev's.[28] But it is tinged with even deeper despair because, over the century and a half since Chaadaev, this void that was then perceived only by a few refined minds has managed to grow into a terrible Eurasian abyss, whose edges are rimmed by a widening landslide. The adjacent European and Asian countries could all be sucked into it, without hope of ever extricating themselves. Russia has thus become the black hole of humanity. If emptiness in Europe were represented by a table-top, awaiting the serving of dishes on its surface, then in Russia someone is sitting under the table, constantly pulling off the table cloth, so that everything on the table is immediately thrown off and disappears into the void. Such is Kabakov's nightmarish and panic-stricken vision of his homeland: a metaphysical abyss.

What can an artist accomplish in such conditions? Following Kabakov's logic, it is patently clear that there is no possibility of filling this emptiness or covering it up with cultural constructions. This kind of emptiness is not susceptible to order, structure or hierarchization. Under such circumstances, one could imagine the following model of collaboration between artist and emptiness: since emptiness cannot be overcome or vanquished, the artist can only adopt it and transform it into a stylistic device. Since art cannot fill this emptiness, it itself comes to be filled by it. The artist, absorbing the emptiness around him, has but one alternative: allow emptiness to become part of the structure of his own works. By turning its flanks the artist delineates the boundaries of emptiness, although in itself it remains limitless. Art thus becomes a rite of circumnavigating emptiness, of slow, cautious, and deliberate capitulation. It is Kutuzov's,[29] not Napoleon's, tactics of encountering emptiness: instead of attacking it with militant cultural projects, one retreats, ceding a place to it where emptiness least expects to find a place—at the heart of the artist's creation. In order to prevent emptiness from swallowing up this creation, depriving it of meaning from the outside, it is made to curl up inside it, like a quiet, well-fed, docile wild animal in a cage.

These are the tactics chosen by Kabakov to combat emptiness. Unlike many of his contemporaries, Kabakov does not attempt to apply a super-charged weapon of rationality or create a superabundant structure of meaning in the texture of his canvases. On the contrary, he cuts through the texture, manufacturing a kind of trap which is able to capture an *en-O-rmous* emptiness. To catch this emptiness, speaking metaphorically, two nets are used. Both can be sprung with the same string. One is a net of words, the other a net of images. What has flown into one net can not fly out the other. What has slipped through the invisible net of images is captured in words. What has disappeared through the transparent net of words is reclaimed through lines and colors. Thus a concept demonstrates the emptiness of reality, while reality shows up the emptiness of the concept.

Casting such nets into the "ocean of emptiness," as Kabakov calls the Russian world, he is able to catch the larger emptiness in its smaller image, which, although encompassing only the several-meters width of the artist's canvas, is virtually equivalent to the whole of Russia. Kabakov skimps neither on material nor on the labor required for the preparatory work—and then he leaves the work unfinished, just as God did with Russia, endowing her with a huge territory and natural resources, only to leave all this material unprocessed.

Kabakov's studio contains huge stands, displaying a minimum of artifacts, white-washed like the map of an uncharted continent or the ice-clad Antarctic, to which he compares Russia in his essay, "On

Emptiness." Elsewhere in the studio are piles of rubbish, distributed among a host of boxes and files that are labeled and classified. There are albums made up of useless receipts, tickets, and scraps of paper, all with captions and explanations. Rubbish is another form of emptiness, its static material manifestation. When emptiness penetrates the very structure of objects, eroding them from the inside, when it thrusts inner spaces onto the surface, when it reveals the wretched side of things, their futility and neglect, then out of emptiness *rubbish* emerges into the light of day, becoming Kabakov's second most favored object of contemplation and artistic device.

At a cursory glance, this may appear to be nothing more than a form of artistic laziness. Instead of mastering chaos, the artist lets it overwhelm him, filling his folios and albums with all sorts of trivia and garbage, leaving yards and yards of unused, blank space on his giant billboards and stands. However, Kutuzov was also a "lazy" general, but even Napoleon recognized in him "an old Russian fox," suspecting cunning at work in Kutuzov's compliant tactics. Similarly, Kabakov plays a cunning fox's game with emptiness, covering the tracks of his artistic intention, adopting a posture of weakness, absence of resolve, a yearning for rest. He appears to say: "I've drawn five columns and I've filled one with writing—that's enough...." Emptiness, for its part, which is always lurking somewhere nearby, ready to attack and devour any kind of superstructure or rationally drawn plan, settles down peacefully in the remaining four empty columns, enclosed in boundaries, caught in the frame of the empty-looking stand. Emptiness caught by such cunning means has been turned into a device.

Certainly, one still feels uncomfortable looking at an ice-clad continent, at an expanse covered by unanswered questions like "Where is Yefim Borisovich?", at the transparent and disappearing wings beyond the window of Arkhipov's hospital. Nevertheless, the artist has succeeded in transporting this emptiness onto paper: one can look at it even if one cannot see it. Kabakov's entire universe is just such a porous body, whose function is to allow emptiness in and then enclose it within the limits of a work of art.

10. Positive Emptiness

The question is, what happens to this emptiness once it has been captured, arranged on a board, canvas or paper? Is it the same malicious, wild, envious, and negative emptiness it was before? Or does the artistic canvas bring out a new quality in it, like a positive out of a negative?

An answer can be obtained from Kabakov's other interpretation of emptiness, which is seemingly diametrically opposed to the preceding catastrophic and disconsolate one. This second interpretation is to be found in his sketch "The Seventies" and several other works, devoted to the Moscow artistic scene and principally to his own works produced in the course of "the decade of contemplation and stagnation." Although the emptiness Kabakov explores in this sketch is the same one treated in his essay "On Emptiness," here it has been lured into the picture and is therefore quite different. It is lucid, transparent, and is frequently called "whiteness." Kabakov identifies it as "the sun's energy, which has migrated into trees, and through them onto the paper, where it is still alive."[30] "The emptiness of the white page emerges here as an almost exact equivalent of silence, but not a silence of negation. Instead, it is the 'opposite'—plenitude, exceeding all that can be or has been 'uttered.'"[31] This silence, according to Kabakov, is the only true and unique reality, while everything that is inscribed on it in word and image represents only an ephemeral grid, placed in the universal energetic field, or a hive of mosquitoes dancing in the sun's rays. At this point, Kabakov prognosticates in a gnostic mode: "A time will come when all these representations will be washed aside and will melt away, the mosquitoes will fly away, and the white world will remain untouched, unperturbed and standing as before, all radiance."[32]

Thus Kabakov's attitude to emptiness is double-coded. On the one hand, emptiness is "a mighty, cloying, nauseating anti-energy," "which sucks off existence like a vampire" (from the essay "On Emptiness"[33]). On the other hand, emptiness is "an infinite space, emitting a benevolent shining light upon us" (from the preface to the album *Okno, Das Fenster, The Window*).[34]

In trying to establish the difference between these two interpretations, it becomes evident that "vampirelike" emptiness characterizes the world surrounding the artist, the one in which he lives and is obliged to share with his fellow citizens. By contrast, the "sun's" emptiness, which is identified with plenitude, manifests itself only in the artist's pictures, in the whiteness of the paper, shining through the letters and drawn lines. This is the whiteness the artist leaves intact on the final pages of his albums, as an eschatological perspective on his characters and the entire universe. The "white light/world [*svet*] remains unperturbed."

The preceding reading allows us to assume that the artist is not just confusing two qualities of emptiness or losing the thread of his interpretation of reality. Instead, we are justified in seeing the artist's transformation of one quality of emptiness into another as the overt or covert aim of his craft. By some inexplicable means, the accursed emptiness captured on paper is transformed into a radiating emptiness. It is as if the old witch, ridden to death by Khoma Brut in Gogol's *Vii,* were transformed into a dazzling beauty. It is then that the "iron grills" of colors and words, whose function it is to capture this emptiness, melt away of their own accord in the rays of its unsullied purity.

It becomes clear that this transformation of emptiness into plenitude has a mystical meaning and is close to gnostic teachings about "liberation." The body is a cage for the soul, the material world is a prison for the spiritual world, and the aim of existence is liberation from this prison and the attainment of *pleroma* (a gnostic term referring to an all-encompassing plenitude[35]) or, as Kabakov puts it, the attainment of a "limitless, bottomless space, a place from which light streams out."[36] This "heavenly" place and that hellish emptiness are separated by the positive entities of our earthly world, its words and colors. These perform a double role: by luring emptiness into a cage they transform it into plenitude. Words and colors speak about nothing so that this nothing may itself speak by means of words and colors, having itself become everything. Words and colors enfold emptiness in themselves only to let it unfold as a clean, shining sheet of paper. Only after being lured into the fold of words and colors can emptiness's radiating whiteness shake them off like weak colored shadows.

Such is Kabakov's double-sided metaphysics, which uses words and colors in order to discard them in the end. In the same way, apophatic theology rejects words and colors in order to point to that sphere beyond earthly limits, namely, to the Divine itself. This Divine, as perceived in apophatism, is simultaneously absolute darkness and absolute light. This is perhaps the theological answer to the riddle of Kabakov's two qualities of emptiness. When we look at *all,* we see *nothing.* Religious faith is the thin dividing line between plenitude and emptiness. For the artist, this faith is constituted by colors and words, positivities that separate *all* from *nothing.* Through the positivities of words and colors, the artist performs his ritual of faith. That is, he absorbs "something" into the painted canvas, transforming it from a shroud of death into a shroud of resurrection, through which the eternal *all* radiates.

This explains Kabakov's constant vacillation between these two qualities of emptiness, one representing his extreme pessimism in a universe of emptiness, the other the eschatological joy of the artist who manifests this emptiness on his canvas. Kabakov himself is partly aware of the theological nature of his artistic preoccupations. Reflecting on the double meaning of "whiteness" in his albums, Kabakov asks himself whether "this is simple nothing, empty surface" or "the infinite space of the light."[37] He comes to the conclusion that "visibility or invisibility," "the visibility of *all* or the visibility of *nothing* " is a profoundly metaphysical alternative. "This is not a new problem, it could also be formulated as the problem of 'looking without seeing' [or as that of 'looking at *all* and seeing *nothing* '—M. E.]. It is a problem contiguous with complex theological questions that we do not feel sufficiently competent to discuss here."[38] This religious meaning of emptiness remains present in the subtext of Kabakov's works, as their unconscious, which the artist indicates but cannot or does not wish to disclose by any other means except through his art.

11. The Critique of Pure Representation

In conclusion, let us return to the initial problem—the relationship of word and image in Kabakov's works. So far this relationship appeared to be symmetrical, as a relationship of two artistic media in the field of culture. However, in actual fact this relationship has its own temporal dynamics and is of a dual nature.

First of all, it is evident from his professional orientation, his training and status, that Kabakov is an artist rather than a writer. The starting point for his creative project is visual art. It is to this sphere that Kabakov brings to bear his gigantic captions, which sometimes take the place of the entire work of art itself. This is the sphere of the picture or album, not the book. In Kabakov's case, it is not the principles of painting that are brought to bear on literature, but the literary model that is adopted in painting. Consequently, the neo-lubok synthesis is not completely symmetrical. It includes the one-sided dynamic gesture of the active influence of literature on painting. This was the case, too, in Western conceptualism, which also emerged in the visual arts, signaling a break with pure representation and its transfer to the textual articulation of visual images. "This attitude," writes Sandro Sproccati, "implies that what is really important in the work is not so much its object-related physicality, its tangible production or the material fact of its presence, but rather the idea (concept, assertion and proposition) that lies behind the work, that precedes it, and that informs it."[39]

A similar shift can be observed in Kabakov's own artistic development. In the 1960s, he was still a painter in the ordinary sense of the word, groping for a personal style in the traditional genres of landscape, still-life, graphic drawings, book illustrations and so on. The 1970s saw the beginning of the period of albums. Here Kabakov painted illustrations to his own rather than to other authors' texts. Or, more precisely, he created total visual-textual works. True, the visual element still predominated in these works: the role of the texts, which appeared at the beginning and end of the album and only comprised a small portion of it, remained subsidiary, accompanying and commenting on a long series of single-page drawings. In the early 1980s, the focus shifted to stands, which contained a greater volume of texts, sometimes even displacing visual imagery altogether. This was the case, for instance, with the stand "The Guilty Woman" and numerous other graphic boards, time-tables, and dialogues. Sometimes the stands were entirely comprised of *ready-mades,* such as shovels, sticks, coat-hangers, and pots, which naturally increased the significance of the texts attached to these objects, as they commented on them and on their behalf.

By the mid-1980s, Kabakov's central genre was no longer the concrete work of art, which could be displayed, but the exhibition itself, the entire cultural milieu. An exhibition differs from a single display item in that it contains a massive amount of documentary and textual material: notices on walls, commentaries on pictures, biographies of artists, catalogues, books of reviews. The first imaginary exhibition created by Kabakov was entitled "A Fly with Wings." According to the artistic conception—but not the real-life intention—it was to have been mounted at the prestigious Pushkin Museum of Visual Arts in Moscow. The only visual component of this entire exhibition was the representation of a fly, with clearly visible joints, head, and feet, stylistically reminiscent of those found in a standard zoology textbook or popular medical encyclopedia. Another possible source for this work might have been the poster frequently seen in public dining halls and cafeterias: "Wash your hands before you eat." On each side of this small picture were displayed scores of pages of text, which contained the so-called exhibition material, consisting mainly of the reactions of imaginary viewers to what they had seen, that is to say, the above-mentioned fly. One museum visitor was indignant that such a trivial picture was thought worthy of being displayed in such a respectable museum; another recalled how flies had pestered him last summer at his dacha; a third was speculating, for the benefit of his female companion, on the possible allegorical meaning of the fly in light of contemporary social processes, and so on. In this way, the textual wings of the fly, extending over dozens of pages on both sides of the insect, exceeded by far its tiny visual body in volume and significance. The picture was transformed into a minute, slippery object of literary interpretation while the latter comprised the substance of this work of art.

The periods of Kabakov's artistic development have been sketched here only approximately and require more precise investigation.[40] However, the general trend of this development in the 1960s and through the 1980s is a movement from representation to text. Kabakov uses his original profession in order to explode it from inside and to "crucify" the image on the cross of the "word." Hence the question arises: can Kabakov be considered a painter at all?

Although no longer a painter, Kabakov can be called an artist in the same sense that Kant can be called a philosopher although he ceased being a metaphysician. The primary thrust of Kabakov's artistic activity can be called a *critique of pure representation*—in the Kantian sense of the term. For Kant, any thinkable essence of a thing can no longer be attritubed to the "thing-in-itself," since it is not "pure," not uncontaminated by the process of thought, but rather posited *a priori* by the structure of consciousness. For Kabakov, by analogy, representation is never "pure" since it is not divorced from thought, which it embodies and illustrates.

As is well known, the first paradigmatic perceptual shift of this kind—the transposition of a supposed primary entity to a secondary position—occurred in the field of astronomy, when it was established that the Earth moved around the Sun. This Copernican revolution, transposed by Kant to philosophy, is still in process, conquering ever new spheres of culture and arriving at that of visual art.

According to this new paradigm, every visual representation is nothing but an illustration of its own caption, of the verbally expressed thought of the artist. What appears to be pure representation, masquerading as a primary sensory perception and naively registering the forms of objects, is in fact a projection of thought, an illustration of the word bashfully hiding in the texture of being, which it nevertheless suffuses through and through. Human perception can neither produce nor see the "representation-in-itself" but only a correlation or projection of the word.

The question arises: how did the idea of pure representation come into culture? Did not all of proto-Renaissance and Renaissance painting arise in the margins of the pages of the Bible, as a gigantically multiplied illustration of the Word? But why does the Word need to be illustrated? Does the Book contain even a hint that the image is either desirable or even permissible? It does not. Instead, it is associated with sacrilege and idolatry. "Thou shalt not make unto thee any graven image, or any likeness of any thing that is in heaven above, or that is in the earth beneath, or that is in the water under the earth" (*Exodus*, 20:4). There can be no compromise between the Word, which is God, and its painted or clay representation, as long as we believe in the futility of the visible world and the eternity of the life-giving Word. Thus the early Christians believed that it was the Word that would bring the sword against the world, penetrating and destroying its visible outer form.

But the world endured and the Word, while taking deep roots in it, began to be reflected in images—at first in icons, and subsequently in pictures. The Word, which had become Flesh and Man, justified and sanctified the body of the world. This was the origin of the icon, which broke the taboo of the monotheistic prohibition on representation and at the same time confirmed that representation could be justified only as an image of the Word and an illustration of the Book. Gradually, with the restoration of the pantheism and cosmocentrism of the Ancients during the Renaissance, visual image was further and further removed from the Word, acquiring an illusory self-sufficiency and giving the impression of manifesting the truth of objects. However, objects manifested their first and final meaning only thanks to the Word, and painting—hiding the fact from itself—continued to exist as a direct or indirect illustration of the Word. The poor and the maimed became the objects of representation, their tatters portrayed in minute detail. However, the meaning of these representations, with their claims to realism and knowledge of the "things-in-themselves," was still attached to the Word about the poor, who were blessed, and about those who mourn and who will be comforted (St. Matthew, 5:3–4). The illustrative work continued, although progressively forgetting about the meaning it was illustrating. Incapable of restoring the essential Word, it reduced the Word to a *caption* under the picture. The painted image's sensory concreteness and capacity to strike or impress increased dramatically, which revived the pagan respect for the visible, self-sufficient and beautiful flesh of the world. Such was the progress of post-Renaissance painting. If in the icon the Word itself is incarnated, in the painting the flesh of the world achieves an inherent value that is (ultimately) beyond language. As a result, the *logos* was reduced to a small plate or label at the bottom of the picture, of interest only to the uneducated viewer or, conversely, the connoisseur; as for the "normal" viewer, he or she came to see the picture as a picture and not in order to read the "word" in it.

In the twentieth century, the artist has once again turned to the primordial meaning of the visual arts, which were destined to serve as exegesis and commentary on the Word and to make manifest its wisdom as revealed in Holy Scripture. Having affirmed the self-sufficiency of the visual principle, the Renaissance and modernity have drawn to a close, confirming Nikolai Berdiaev's well-known observation that the twentieth century will lead the world into a "new Middle Ages." The values of modernity, such as materialism, humanism, individualism and secularization, have run their course and are now exhausted. "The movement away from God will be reversed in a movement toward God." This will be a time when "God will once again become the centre of our entire life," and "knowledge, morality, art, government and the economy will once again become religious from the inside and freely, not coercively and from the outside."[41]

The "new Middle Ages" reemphasize the fact that the entire history of art—at least the history of Western art of the Christian era—was only an illustration of the Word. This means that the activity of an illustrator is more explicitly religious than the work of a painter engrossed in his own "pure" contemplation of the world. While the "true" artist might hide the word of his painting in colorful images, the illustrator bares the word that lies in the subtext of every sensory perception. From the vantage point of traditional aesthetics, the illustrator, compared to the easel painter and the sculptor, is considered an artist of the second rank, whose craft is an applied art. But from the religious point of view, the illustration provides a more profound revelation of the verbal meaning and conceptual source of art.

This explains why in the 1970s and 1980s, the illustrative, or "as if" illustrative activity of Kabakov had an inner correspondence with the upsurge in Russian religious consciousness, even if this correspondence was largely unconscious for the artist and even more so for his audience. It merely observed the artist's lack of fascination with "pure art," the appearance of things or the richness and subtlety of colors: Kabakov reduced all appearances to a concept, a word. In so doing he revealed to the spectators what could not be simply seen, but which had to be looked at with a "reading" rather than a "seeing" gaze.[42] This penetration of *logos* into the sphere of visual art was perceived as a religious paradox, as an anti-pagan gesture and an echo of the ancient monotheistic prohibition of idolatry. The visible world, dissolved within the pages of a book, became an illumination of sacred inscriptions.

Kabakov reminds us of the fact that word comes before image and hence predetermines the latter's purely illustrative status. Kabakov's role in contemporary culture thus corresponds to an astonishing degree to his long-time, openly professed official occupation: an artist-illustrator. In a narrow sense, Kabakov earned his living from the 1960s to the 1980s by illustrating children's stories and verses. In a wider—prophetic, not merely professional—sense, he uncovered the illustrative function of all pictorial art. With this he fulfilled his mission as an heir of the Book.[43] In Kabakov's works, the word reveals its non-illusory and non-representable meaning, shaking off the mantle of the image in what appears to be a premonition of the end of the visible universe.

Nevertheless, although reduced to a negligible part, to an atom of this new conceptualist cosmos, visuality continues to live on. It reappears in the images of a fly's wings or an ant's footprint. Or even as crumbs of garbage, so lyrically displayed in Kabakov's installations.[44] A broken pencil, a match, a bite of apple, a tram ticket, a post-office receipt, shaving cream, a catalogue of things to be taken on a journey: this materiality is not dead, because in order to be resurrected in a new body, a memory of the past has to be retained. Visuality thus retreats into the farthest corner of memory, echoing Pushkin's popular saying that "what will pass will become dear."

Through conceptualist exegesis and the textualization of image or object, Kabakov eventually arrives at the sacred uniqueness of this very object, which lies beyond language. That is why it is over there, beyond and after all its multiplying descriptions and interpretations.

Thus a trans-semiotic, trans-verbal sphere is posited and articulated through the persistent verbal renderings of the visual. This may explain why God created the world by word but did not limit it to verbality: in order to maintain the uniqueness, singularity of each thing as if it were an "image of God" non-reducible to any general concept or verbal abstraction. Thus conceptualism ultimately arrives at an effect opposite to its original intention: the aesthetic enjoyment of things and images in their minimality, as an indissoluble residue of visuality resistant to all textual interventions. In other words, after the image is made dead and obsolete in a conceptualist work, it is resurrected as a new quality, not as the "grand, luxurious visuality" of the modern and modernist art, but as the inescapable, super-determined, dispersed, fragmented visuality of the postmodern age.[45]

This perpetual leave-taking from visuality affects the viewer with a kind of nostalgic charm. Since Kabakov has already freed himself from this visuality, he can be called an illustrator. But inasmuch as he is still contemplating it with love, he can be called an artist.

1983, 1992

Figure 1 From Kabakov's album "The Window-Gazing Arkhipov" (one of the last pages: on the threshold of death)

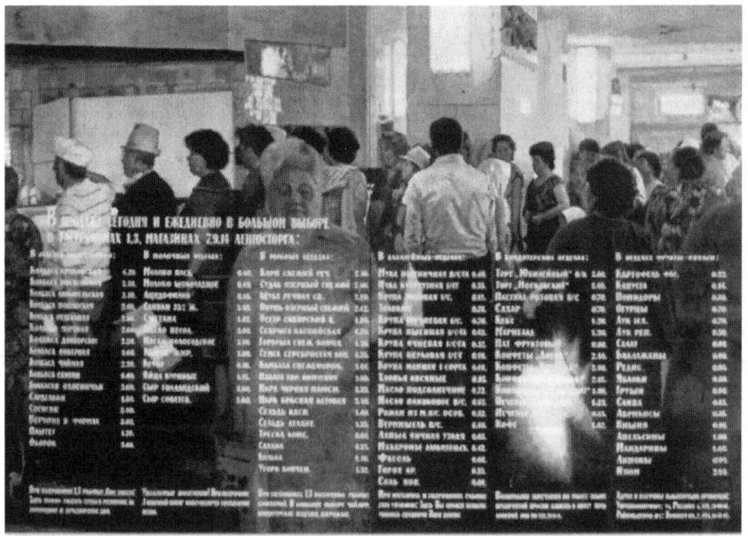

Figure 2 "Gastronom," 1981

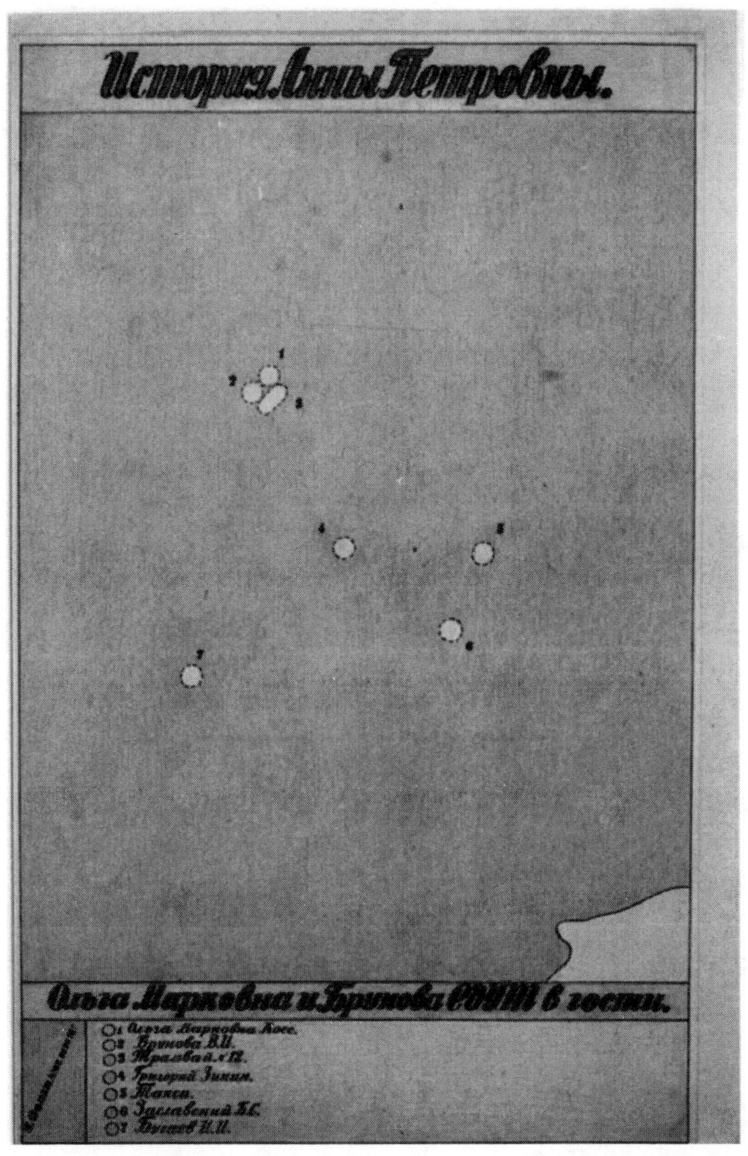

Figure 3 "Anna Petrovna's Dream," 1971

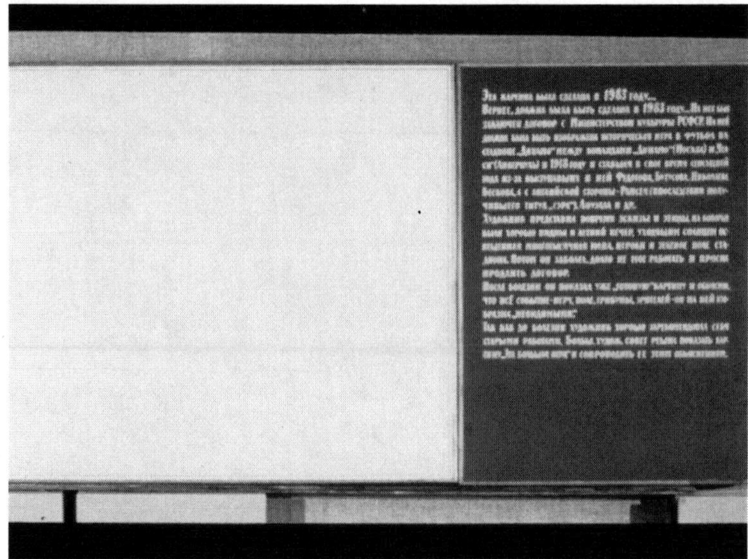

Figure 4 "At the Large Artistic Council," 1983

Figure 5 "Where Are They?," 1970/71

Figure 6 "Where Are They?," a series of eleven drawings, 1971

Notes

1. Ilya Kabakov was born in 1933 in Dnepropetrovsk. In 1957 he graduated from the Surikov Art School. Over the next thirty years be both illustrated children's books for Soviet publishing houses and became one of the first—together with Eduard Bulatov, Vitaly Komar and Alexander Melamid—to develop the principles of *sots-art* and conceptualism, not only practically, as an artist, but also as a theoretician and author of many essays on art and on the Moscow artistic scene of the 1970s/80s. Kabakov's creations have been exhibited in many Western galleries—Dina Vierny in Paris, Ronald Feldman in New York and others. Since the end of the 1980s, Kabakov has been living in Paris and New York.
2. Ilya Kabakov, *Okno. Das Fenster. The Window. Arkhipov Looking Through the Window.* Texts by Gean-Hubert Martin, Claudia Jolles. Benteli (pagination not given).
3. Kabakov himself noted this alternating and substituting of points of view. "Who are we going to be this time, spectator or character?… The situation 'spectator or character' is reversible and easily exchanged." Ilya Kabakov, Introduction to the Album *Okno. Das Fenster.*, "Has he stopped seeing or has he seen?"
4. Joseph Frank, "Spatial Form in Modern Literature," in his book *The Widening Gyre: Crisis and Mastery in Modern Literature* (New Brunswick, N.J., 1963), pp. 3–62.
5. Here are Kabakov's own thoughts on the subject: "In the Sixties, I started to depict the ordinary, banal object and saw in the banal and the commonplace great artistic possibilities—even their own metaphysics. The metaphysics of the commonplace is a very interesting pursuit, because metaphysics assumes a field of activity which is either lofty or earthly, either heaven or hell. The grey, the middling, the banal, it would seem, has no metaphysics. There is nothing to say about them: this is a pure zero, a pure grey, anonymity. And precisely this attracted me more and more …" *Novostroika. Culture in the Soviet Union Today.* The Institute of Contemporary Arts Document 8 (London, 1989): 46.
6. Quoted according to Norton Dodge and Alison Hilton, *New Art from the Soviet Union* (Washington, 1977): 44.
7. See "Avant-Garde Art and Religion," in Mikhail Epstein, *After the Future: The Paradoxes of Postmodernism and Contemporary Russian Culture*, trans. with Introduction by Anesa Miller-Pogacar (Amherst, Mass., 1995), pp. 62–66.
8. Acronym for the Leningrad State Trade Management.
9. Kabakov's stand (Russian *stend*), which was the center of his artistic attention in the early 1980s, should be distinguished from his later interest in installation, the construction of a three-dimensional environment, such as a room or apartment. A stand is a two-dimensional board, usually painted in white or brown and covered with texts and images. Sometimes a real object, such as a hammer or a spade, can be attached to it. Kabakov's stands are often parodic of those stands that were part of official propaganda and, like posters with slogans, could be seen everywhere in the Soviet Union: on the streets, in

buildings, administrative offices, industrial enterprises, educational institutions and so on.

10. An enigmatic acronym meaning something like a local housing office.
11. Another acronym for a housing maintenance office.
12. For example, the Latin poet Statius (c. 45–96) wrote a detailed ecphrasis of Domitian's equestrian statue in Silvae.
13. Lubok is "a popular print of a crude character with hand coloring; the text was usually carved from the same block or plate and printed below the illustration. Songs and other texts were printed in single sheets. Longer texts, such as tales, were printed on a series of sheets, usually on one side of the paper only and with an illustration on most or all of the papers, which were then loosely bound together into a booklet. /.../ [This] form of popular print illustration [was] introduced into Russia from the West early in the seventeenth century.... The subject matter was rapidly russianized.... Lubki have several diverse styles, depending on the subject: there are religious prints, some of which substituted for icons, as well as popular and folkloristic ones; there is also a large number of comic and satiric prints." William E. Harkins "Lubochnaia literatura, or 'chap' literature" and "Lubok," in *Handbook of Russian Literature*, ed. Victor Terras (New Haven and London, 1985), pp. 266, 267.
14. *The Lubok: Russian Folk Pictures* (Leningrad, 1984), illus. 28, 31.
15. Yu. M. Lotman, *Struktura khudozhestvennogo teksta* (Moscow, 1970).
16. Ibid., p. 351.
17. *The History of Art*, trans. from Italian by Geoffrey Culverwell and others (New York, 1989), p. 498.
18. On the pairing of slogan-poster and propaganda stand, as well as on the binarism of all official documents, see M. Epstein, "Plakat i stend," Almanakh *Zerkala*, vyp. 1 (Moscow, 1989): 307–10. This essay contains some of the impressions I gained from Kabakov's works and from conversations with the artist.
19. "From one point of view, one can treat this half culture negatively: as a mockery, a grotesque, the absurd. But it can also be understood as a positive development. You can view this half-culture as a cultural phenomenon and give it all the attributes of a culture—beauty, nobility, the capacity to dream." I. Kabakov, *Novostroika. Culture in the Soviet Union Today*, p. 46.
20. The revaluation of this theological idea took place in nineteenth century Russia in the form of socialist utopias, which endowed *sobornost'* with features of a national and domestic communality outside the church. As G. V. Florovsky remarks on the atmosphere of those times: "... in the enthusiasm for the ideals of the phalanster or the commune, it is not difficult to discern the unconscious and errant thirst for *sobornost'* ... " *Puti russkogo bogosloviia* (Paris, 1937), p. 295.
21. Kabakov [Album], Galerie Dina Vierny (Paris, 1985) [no pagination].
22. *Novostroika* [New Structures]. *Culture in the Soviet Union Today*, p. 47.
23. Ilya Kabakov, "Has he stopped seeing or has he seen?" Introduction to the Album *Window* [*Okno*].
24. Kabakov [Album], Galerie Dina Veierny (Paris, 1985).

25. Ilya Kabakov, "O pustote" (On Emptiness), in Ilya Kabakov, *Das Leben der Fliegen, The Life of the Flies, Zhizn' mukh* (Cologne, 1992), p. 233. This edition, with a preface by Boris Groys, contains Kabakov's texts in three languages: Russian, German, and English.
26. Ilya Kabakov, *Life of the Flies,* p. 232.
27. Ibid., p. 236.
28. Petr Iakovlevich Chaadaev (1794–1856) was Russia's first important thinker to express bitter disappointment at Russia's failure to contribute creatively to Western civilization. Compare his *Philosophical Letters and Apology of a Madman,* trans. and Introduction by Mary-Barbara Zeldin (Knoxville, Tenn., 1969).
29. Mikhail Kutuzov (1745–1813)—field marshal, the commander-in-chief of Russian army that defeated Napoleon's troops in the patriotic war of 1812 using the tactics of calculated retreat; a hero of Leo Tolstoy's novel *War and Peace.*
30. "The main thing is to turn the pages," [Manuscript] (Moscow, 1981), p. 1. Quoted according to the article by Claudia Jolles in Ilya Kabakov's album *Okno, Das Fenster, The Window.*
31. *The Seventies* [Manuscript] (Moscow, 1984), pg. 60.
32. Ibid., pp. 61–62.
33. Ilya Kabakov, *The Life of the Flies,* p. 84 and 232 [translation modified—SV-G].
34. Ilya Kabakov, Introduction to the Album *Okno, Das Fenster, The Window,* chapter on "Whiteness."
35. "A symbol of the manifesting Logos replete with all intelligences and potencies ...," G. A. S. Gaskell. *Dictionary of all Scriptures & Myths* (New York, Avenel, N.J., 1981), p. 582.
36. Ilya Kabakov, Introduction to the Album *Okno, Das Fenster, The Window,* chapter on "Whiteness."
37. Ibid.
38. Ilya Kabakov, Introduction to the Album *Okno, Das Fenster, The Window, op. cit.,* "Has he stopped seeing or has he seen?"
39. *The History of Art,* trans. from Italian by Geoffrey Culverwell and others (New York, 1989), p. 496. Among Western representatives of conceptualism, the (meta)artistic movement initiated in the mid-1960s by the American Joseph Kosuth (b. 1945), one can mention Robert Barry (b. 1936), Jan Dibbets (b. 1941), Lawrence Weiner (b. 1940), On Kawara (b. 1931), and Bernard Venet (b. 1941). On the history and theory of Western conceptualism, see Joseph Kosuth, *Art after Philosophy and After. Collected Writings, 1966–1990* (Cambridge, Mass. and London, 1991).
40. In the present chapter, we are not touching on Kabakov's last phase (from the late 1980s onward) which contains his work produced in the West, mostly in the three-dimensional genre of "total installation." See Kabakov's own account of his artistic experiments with this genre in Ilya Kabakov, *On the Total Installation* (the title and text in Russian, English and German) (Bonn, 1995).

41. Nikolai Berdiaev, *Novoe srednevekovie: razmyshleniia o sud'be Rossii i Evropy* [The New Middle Ages: Thoughts on the Destiny of Russia and Europe] (Moscow, 1990), pg. 25.
42. In fact, the word *chitat'* (to read), which has absorbed the root of *chtit'* (to honor, to revere), still retains the sacral meaning that was originally attached to both letters and the process of their understanding and interpretation. This underlying religious meaning of reading as reverence is absent (or at least never detected) in visual perception.
43. This is an allusion to the Jewish origins of Ilya Kabakov, which is one of the implicit factors of his artistic identity.
44. Here I am referring to Kabakov's works such as "The Ant" (1981), "Box with Garbage" (1981), "The Fly with Wings" (1982/83), "The Man Who Never Threw Anything Away" (1985–88), "The Life of the Flies" (1992), etc.
45. This postconceptualist aspect of the "word-image" relationship is treated at length in my article "Thing and Word: On the Lyrical Museum." Mikhail Epstein, *After the Future: The Paradoxes of Postmodernism and Contemporary Russian Culture*, trans. with Introduction by Anesa Miller-Pogacar (Amherst, Mass., 1995), pp. 253–279.

Chapter 22

THE PHILOSOPHICAL IMPLICATIONS OF RUSSIAN CONCEPTUALISM

Mikhail Epstein

In recent years the concept of postmodernism has often been deployed to explain the peculiarities of late Soviet and post-Soviet culture, such as the post-utopian mentality, a critical attitude toward traditional notions of reality, and ironic playfulness with regard to the sign systems of various ideologies.[1] In Russia, the literary and artistic movement most directly related to Western postmodernism became famous under the name "conceptualism." Initially, the name was borrowed from the Western artistic school founded in the late 1960s by Joseph Kosuth. Conceptual art from the very beginning was connected with philosophy and even claimed to be more genuinely philosophical than philosophy itself. "The twentieth century brought in a time which could be called 'the end of philosophy and the beginning of art.' … Art is itself philosophy made concrete."[2] Two lines of argument intersect in this statement. On the one hand, twentieth-century art is no more limited to the creation of material forms but starts to question the very nature of art and redefine it with each specific work. Art, therefore, becomes an articulation of the ideas about art. "'Conceptual Art' merely means a conceptual investigation of art."[3] On the other hand, analytical philosophy, as Kosuth proposes, has refuted any claims of philosophy to enunciate the truth, to make veritable propositions about the world. Therefore, philosophy has lost its privileged "scientific" status; in "postphilosophical" age, its function passes to art, which plays with signs and languages without any assumption of their credibility.

These two processes, the conceptualization of art and the aestheticization of philosophy, contribute together into their rapprochement and the redefinition of conceptual art as concrete philosophy. Instead of portraying a visible object, the conceptualist artist presents its verbal description, that is, a deliberately schematized generalization takes the place of a lifelike image. This device broke ground for metaphysical speculation about the nature of artistic reality as the mere projection of mental forms. Russian culture proved to be a fertile ground for the application of conceptualist theory, owing to the prevalence of ideological schemes and stereotypes throughout its history, especially during the Soviet period.

Another source of the term "conceptualism," less evident but perhaps more significant for the development of the movement in Russia, is the medieval philosophical school of the same name. Among the European scholastics of the thirteenth and fourteenth centuries, conceptualism functioned as a moderate version of nominalism, which asserted that all general ideas have their being not in reality itself but in the sphere of pure concepts. As such, this school was opposed to realism, which posited one continuum of physical and conceptual reality and insisted on ontological being of such universals as love, soul, goodness, etc. Strange as it may seem, an analogous confrontation of two intellectual trends occurred in the late Soviet period, with Marxism asserting the historical reality of such general ideas as "collectivism," "equality," "progress," and conceptualism arguing the purely nominative and mental basis of such ideological constructions. Like its medieval counterpart, conceptualism attempts to expose the realistic fallacy that attributes objective existence to general or abstract ideas. This was the hidden assumption of the Soviet system: it gave the status of absolute reality to its own ideological pronouncements. Virtually every facet of Soviet life was dictated by ideological presuppositions about the nature of social reality, and conceptualism attempted to expose the contingent nature of such concepts by unmasking them as constructions proceeding from the human mind or generated by linguistic practices.

The Russian version of conceptualism, which flourished in the 1970s and 1980s, established a theoretical distance toward the multiplicity of discourses that dominated Soviet culture. From the start, conceptualism was not a purely artistic movement, but relied heavily on a philosophical foundation. Conceptualist poetry and visual art are theoretically self-conscious, presuming a premeditated and ironic attitude toward the language of ideas. Conceptualism might be called a meta-ideological approach to arts, or a meta-aesthetic approach to ideology, since it strives to reflect upon the hidden ideological apriorisms of consciousness and to verbalize or visualize them. Since ideological stereotyping unconsciously preconditions our thinking, conceptualists propose to undermine this process of indoctrination by revealing it to consciousness. In a sense, conceptualism worked as a psychoanalytic instrument for deconstructing the repressive Soviet superego. If psychoanalysis involves curing neuroses by bringing repressed impulses to the light of individual consciousness, the conceptualist project was an "ideo-analysis" that aimed to cure the trauma of ideological obsessions by bringing them to the awareness of the collective subject.

Many Russian thinkers in the conceptualist trend are not philosophers in the conventional sense; rather they are the members of an artistic school, or its interpreters, or both. In this they are radically different from all the traditional schools of thought that relied solely upon linguistic discourse for the presentation of ideas. With its visual component, conceptualism overcomes the longstanding affiliation between philosophy and literature in Russia, and also contrasts with the Western bias for philosophy couched almost exclusively in oral or written discourse. This conventional bias went unquestioned for centuries, but with the advent of conceptualism we are finally prompted to wonder: why is philosophy obliged to be verbal? Why cannot it take visual or gestural form? The presupposition of conceptual art is, simply, that art may be practiced in the medium of conceptions, or mental projections; is not this precisely what philosophy is as well? Conceptual artists do not so much deal with visual forms per se, as with visualizations of concepts that constitute a kind of philosophical discourse translated into a system of objects and presented as works of art.

On the other hand, conceptual art problematizes not only the linguistic bias of philosophy but also the visual bias of the arts. The basis of conceptualism is a critique of *pure representation,* in the Kantian sense. For Kant, an intelligible essence does not belong to the thing-in-itself but is imposed on it through the a priori schemes of consciousness. Similarly, the visual element in art can be understood as only a projection of constructive imagination—an interpretation that regards the visual realm generally as an extension of a concept, while the concept itself can supplement or substitute for a picture or an image. This was done literally in the early works of Western conceptualism, where, for example, an encyclopedia article describing a chair was presented as an artistic object along with the chair itself and its reproduction in painting (Joseph Kosuth's *One and Three Chairs,* 1965, The Museum of Modern Art, New York). Traditionally, the visual component is privileged over the label, or verbal inscription, that accompanies and designates an autonomous work of art. In conceptual art, the textual component moves into the foreground; every visual work is conceived as an illustration of its label, of the artist's textual creativity. At the same time, a conceptual work is not merely an artistic illustration of a text, like in a book, where the visual is dependent on and subordinate to the literary narrative, and reproduces the plot; in conceptual art, a text itself functions as a visual work or interacts independently and creatively with a visual image. Moreover, a conceptualist does not even need to create a new artifact to label and sign, but can affix a title or signature to an existing real-world object, thereby transforming it into a concept. Thus Russian conceptualist artists Komar and Melamid "signed" an earthquake that occurred in Germany and sent a telegram to the chancellor notifying him that they were the authors of the event. This mode allows a conceptualist to create concepts out of anything whatsoever, making this artistic practice a bona fide philosophical activity, inasmuch as it carries out the conceptualization of the world.

Conceptualist thinking reveals the futile aggressiveness of the human mind, which imposes its own ideological schemes on a reality that is inaccessible as such, and yet is continually pursued via a process of representational substitutions and innumerable references without verifiable referents. In this view, any attempt at mental coherency is essentially madness, if we define the latter as the state of consciousness isolated from reality. From the conceptualist standpoint, traditional philosophy, as the most rigorously coherent way of thinking, is closest to madness, with its solipsistic fixations on absolute ideas. The only way to distinguish philosophy from madness is the self-irony of the philosopher; thus, in conceptualism, irony takes the place occupied by truth or verification in more ambitious philosophical systems, like German idealism or logical positivism. The method for relating philosophy to reality now involves not the positive correspondence or identification of thoughts and objects, but the revelation of an inexorable and irreducible disjunction between them, a gap bridged only by self-referential and therefore self-ironic conceptualizations. Irony becomes the only possible form of truth for conceptual philosophy, inasmuch as it lacks any criteria for verification but has innumerable criteria for philosophical self-falsification.

Conceptualism offers a radical challenge to totalitarian claims of absolute truth, to the kind of ideological madness that prescribes ideas for the interpretation and transformation of reality. Russian conceptualism may be considered an ironic imitation and inversion of the solipsistic activity of the collective supermind, which not only is imprisoned by its allegiance to absolute ideas but turns society itself into a prison or lunatic asylum. Conceptualism, as it emerged in the West, remained a narrowly artistic device and had a more limited scope, since its substitution of concept for object proceeded from the visual art's need for deeper self-reflection, without the implicit criticism of Western civilization as a whole. In Russia, conceptualism revealed much broader philosophical and critical potential, because it addressed an absolutely textualized and ideologized society and ironically reproduced the hidden patterns of this ideologization.

Conceptualist Vision of Socialist Realism: Andrei Sinyavsky

If a complete history of Russian conceptualism and postmodernism is ever written, then Andrei Siniavsky (born 1925) will definitely stand as one of its founders. Although Siniavsky himself does not use the term, generally preferring to disassociate himself from any established philosophical school, his writing has persistently taken a postmodern perspective, particularly as it tends to reinterpret classical models of socialist realism in the spirit of post-utopian sots-art, or "socialist art."[4] As one commentator puts it, "Sinyavsky is philosophic but not a philosopher, he is building no system, inventing no new vocabulary. This places him in the mainstream of the Russian tradition, in which literature and philosophy are not, as a rule, entirely differentiated."[5]

Siniavsky's book, *On Socialist Realism,* published in Paris in 1959, offers an original interpretation of this artistic method, challenging both the official Soviet valorization of socialist realism and its skeptical reception in the West. Siniavsky exposes the inner contradiction of the method, which attempts to join a teleological element (socialism) with a scientific one (realism). Socialist realism is logically inclined toward classicism as an aesthetic model, with its orientation toward sublime and idealistic norms of discourse. The realistic component, which is alien to socialism, introduces an involuntary element of parody into Soviet art. "It is impossible, without falling into parody, to produce a positive hero in the style of full socialist realism and yet make him into a psychological portrait. In this way, we will get neither psychology nor hero."[6] Siniavsky himself would prefer both hero and parody. He is not only sensitive enough to grasp the inherently parodic element in socialist realism, but he goes so far as to advise the self-conscious exploitation of parody as an enhancement of Soviet heroic art. He regrets that the eclectic mixture of realism and classicism that was officially promoted from the 1930s through the 1950s lacks the genuinely phantasmagoric proportions capable of transforming dull, didactic imitations of life into inspirational imitations of didacticism and teleology itself.

For example, Siniavsky proposes that Stalin's death, if presented as a religious event, could have generated parodic effects and become a theme of great art. "We could have announced on the radio that he did not die but had risen to heaven, from which he continued to watch us, in silence, no words emerging from beneath the mystic mustache. His relics would have cured men struck by paralysis or possessed by demons. And children, before going to bed, would have kneeled by the window and addressed their prayers to the cold and shining stars of the Celestial Kremlin."[7] Such a transformation of socialist realism into a religio-parodic form was accomplished more than twenty years later in the conceptualist works, or sots-art of Komar and Melamid. The titles of many of their paintings—such as "Stalin and the Muses" and "View of the Kremlin in a Romantic Landscape" (both from the series, "Nostalgic Socialist Realism," 1981–82)—suggest an implicit reference to Siniavsky's metasocialist project.

Instead of condemning socialist realism as false, demagogic, or simply bad art, as was routinely done at that time in the West, or praising its truthful reflection of life, as in the Soviet Union, Siniavsky eliminates the criterion of truth altogether, reinterpreting this canon as a system of interrelated signs that may be used for artistic purposes—not because they refer to some knowable reality, but precisely because they escape it. He was among the first to formulate the principle of parody and pastiche (conscious eclecticism) as a new source for contemporary art, and he opened the way for a highly innovative postmodern assimilation of socialist realism, which from the 1960s was generally considered a dead-end movement both in the West and in dissident circles within the USSR.

In later articles and in his book, *Soviet Civilization* (1988), Siniavsky continues his investigation of communism as a unique historical formation possessing its own unexplored, mystical depth. As compared with other researchers in this field, Siniavsky stresses the theatrical nature of the Soviet system, which was designed as a spectacle by the great directors Lenin and, especially, Stalin ("in his eyes he was the only actor-director on the stage of all Russia and all the world. In this sense, Stalin was a born artist"[8]).

Metaphysics of Emptiness and Garbage: Ilya Kabakov

Ilya Kabakov (born 1933) is one of the founding practitioners and chief proponents of Russian conceptualism. He is the author of many texts commenting on the contemporary situation in art and on general principles of conceptualist thinking.

Kabakov's thought is remarkable in that it focuses almost entirely on unique features of Soviet civilization and interprets them as general philosophical categories. The central category of his worldview might be called emptiness, or void, which he views as fundamental to Soviet reality. The qualities of "emptiness" and "vampirism" that Andrei Siniavsky identified in the national genius of Pushkin,[9] Kabakov ascribes to Russia itself, which he calls a "hole in space, in the world, in the fabric of being." Kabakov treats emptiness not merely as a lack of essential positive forms, a space waiting to be filled and organized; he presents the view that in Russia, unlike Western Europe, emptiness is a principle of destruction and disorganization which actively transforms all positive being into nonbeing. "By such ineradicable activeness, force and constancy, emptiness 'lives,' transforming being into its antithesis, destroying construction, mystifying reality, turning all into dust and emptiness.... Emptiness adheres to, merges with, sucks being. Its mighty, adhesive, nauseating antienergy is taken from the transfer into itself, which like vampirism, it gleans and extracts from the existence surrounding it."[10] If it is true that nature does not tolerate a vacuum, then in Russia the rule is inverted: a vacuum does not tolerate nature. One cannot interrogate emptiness for its causes and goals because its very nature is to annihilate such categories. "Why? What was the purpose? This question can be put only to the living, the intelligent, the natural, but not to emptiness. Emptiness is the other, antithetical side of any question."[11] Because such emptiness is active, nothing can be erected in its midst without immediately falling prey to a vampirism that drains its soul away. In Kabakov's view, this existence bordering on nonexistence is characteristic of the entirety of Soviet civilization, whose constructive endeavors are doomed by the very fact of their being founded in the metaphysical void.

In such an environment, all constructions implicitly contain their own undoing, giving rise to another important concept in Kabakov's thought, the "dump" or "garbage." Garbage is a metaphysical category, indicating the presence of nothingness within material things; it represents something that is simultaneously nothing. Moreover, every "something" is garbage-to-be. Although this fate is inevitable for every object, its historic manifestation is especially palpable in the Soviet Union. "I feel that man, living in our region, is simply suffocating in his own life among the garbage since there is nowhere to take it, nowhere to sweep it out—we have lost the border between garbage and non-garbage space. Everything is covered up, littered with garbage—our homes, streets, cities. We have no place to discard all this—it remains near us."[12] Here the problem of garbage disposal is metaphysical rather than logistical: it is not that there is no dump, but that no space can be found that is not a dump. There is no transcendental realm where the garbage might be disposed of (hell), or where a process of purification might originate (heaven).

For Kabakov, however, the meaning of garbage is ambivalent. It is not just the negative aspect of physical existence, but is the core of existence itself, since reality reveals its transitoriness in the form of garbage. As the material integrity of a thing deteriorates, its sentimental value progressively grows. An object that loses its functionality—becoming garbage—is preserved on the level of pure meanings, in memory. Thus garbage is intrinsically more ideal and spiritual than those brand-new things that serve us by their material utility. On behalf of one of his characters, "the man who never threw anything away," Kabakov writes: "Strange as it seems, I feel that it is precisely the garbage, that very dirt where important papers and simple scraps are mixed and unsorted, that comprises the genuine and only real fabric of my life, no matter how ridiculous and absurd it seems from the outside."[13] When things disclose their transitoriness and "nothingness," they also increase their value. Paradoxically, the dump is not only the cemetery for deceased things, but also the realm of their immortality, where they reveal their ultimate essence and meaning.

Many of Kabakov's exhibitions showcase items of garbage accompanied by elaborately descriptive labels that would seem more appropriate for objects of great esteem, like personal mementoes of celebrated historical figures. Kabakov's metaphysical dump is an inverted museum where the objects are of no great significance, as in conventional exhibitions, but rather the most miserable and negligible items from someone's personal life—such as a spent match, a shriveled apple core, an old receipt, or a pencil with a broken tip. A metaphysical tension arises from the relationship between the negligible materiality of these objects and their monumental verbal presentations.

The relationship between reality and language is a crucial point in Kabakov's philosophy that concentrates on the peculiar Russian logocentrism, the love for verbal expression that remains strikingly indifferent to the world of objects. "Language is a fundamental principle, an aspect of thought; the world of the dump plunges it into a new state where the word is separate from the thought, the title separate from the object; the text is separate from its meaning, the appellation is separate from that which it names; in general, every word is divorced from its signification."[14] Given that Russia is the zone of active emptiness, which imbues everything with nothingness, the activity of language is the only thing that remains real, or to use Jean Baudrillard's term, "hyperreal," since it creates an illusory reality of significations without signifieds. Kabakov explores the language of such classical Russian authors as Gogol, Dostoevsky, and Chekhov, identifying them as predecessors of typical Soviet intoxication with words, fantasmagoric verbosity inherent in ideocratic society. In the characteristic propensity of these classics for excessive, self-referential speech, Kabakov reveals a total loss of any object of communication. "But one must talk, speak out, speak again and again.... And therein lies the reason for the neurosis in our great literature, in the minds and nerves and memories of each one of us—

the neurosis of incessant talk, the preference for verbal self-realization, for the incessant, unflagging, raging sea of words."[15]

These comments may remind us of Mikhail Bakhtin's valorization of dialogic language, but Kabakov offers a much less sympathetic interpretation of the same phenomenon. For Bakhtin, the dialogic relationship is the only genuine mode of human existence: addressing the other through language. For Kabakov, this obsession with dialogue bears witness to the lack of any relationship between words and a corresponding reality. People are eager to immerse themselves in verbal communication because they seek to keep nothingness at bay with magical incantations. But the very abundance of their chatter betrays the presence of nothingness all around them and intensifies their verbal neurosis. Bakhtin admires the multireferentiality in the speech of Dostoevsky's characters, whose conversations play off of earlier conversations, themselves thickly imbedded with dialogic references. Kabakov sees this inclination for verbosity as a symptom of Russia's fear of emptiness and the implicit realization of its ubiquity. The speech of literary characters can only refer to other speech, because there is no reality beyond their words except for the void they try to drown out with their voices—a void that is only emphasized and augmented by the emptiness of their conversations.

Kabakov's analysis shows how Bakhtin's dialogical theory can be interpreted in a broader, conceptualist paradigm. For Bakhtin, to exist authentically means to communicate dialogically, which allows us to interpret Bakhtin himself as a utopian thinker seeking an ultimate transcendence of human loneliness, alienation, and objectification. Kabakov advances a postmodern perspective on this dialogical utopia, revealing the illusory character of a paradise of communication by showing that its language is only a self-referential miasma emanating from and covering over reality's emptiness. Bakhtin's attempt to overcome monological solipsism is characteristic of an existentialist gesture of flight from objectivity, which inevitably falls into the even more absurd solipsism of dialogue enclosed in itself. For monologic subjectivity, there still remains the world of external objects, whereas for dialogic intersubjectivity, which assimilates everything into the process of communication, there remains nothing real except for words and their meanings.

A large part of Kabakov's work is dedicated to theorizing the phenomenon of Soviet totalitarianism. Arguing that the "rupture between word and meaning creates an empty space in which lives and thrives something that can be termed 'total ideology,'"[16] he identifies a peculiar ontological/linguistic premise for the dictatorship of ideas in recent Russian history. When there is no reality to which language can refer, language itself runs the danger of substituting for reality. Like God creating the universe from nothing by the force of the Word, ideology has the power to create a reality out of language only because it proceeds from nothingness. "The word, which has been cut off from and thrown out of the nest which was its meaning, can now signify anything, depending on the direction of the ideological wind. In practice this means that a whole world of substituted meanings comes into existence."[17] Ideology itself, in Kabakov's terms, may be defined as the illusion of reality produced by language in the absence of reality as such. This accounts for the grandiose enterprises and construction projects of the Soviet era that proceeded not from an economic basis but from abstract concepts and ideological assumptions, which ultimately led to phantasmagoric and utterly ineffective results. From this standpoint, ideology is linguocracy, the capacity of language to produce and impose on others a pseudoreality that claims to be uniquely valid.

Strikingly, Kabakov defines conceptualism itself in nearly the same terms as he uses to describe ideology. First of all, he is careful to distinguish ideologically oriented Russian conceptualism from the aforementioned Western school of the same name, whose principle is "the idea instead of thing," or "one thing instead of another"; for example, the textual representation of a chair takes the place of its visual counterpart. The principle of Russian conceptualism might be phrased as "the idea instead of no thing," since the reality to which Western conceptual representations refer does not exist in Russia. Both principles operate by substitution, but while Western signs eventually refer back to reality, Russian signification borders only on emptiness. "This contiguity, closeness, touchingness, contact with nothing, emptiness, makes up, we feel, the basic peculiarity of 'Russian conceptualism.'"[18]

Conceptualism, then, shares with ideology a tendency to substitute signs or concepts for real substance. But the principal difference between them is that ideology claims its signs have real referents, while conceptualism reveals the emptiness of its own signs. Ideology conceals its own contingency, pretending to integrate signs with reality in such a way as to declare itself "true" and "all-embracing." Conceptualism exposes this "realistic fallacy," discloses the contingency of all concepts and refuses to ground itself in any reality. "Precisely because of its self-referentiality and the lack of windows or a way out to something else, it is like something that hangs in the air, a self-reliant thing, like a fantastic construction, connected to nothing, with its roots in nothing."[19] Conceptualism emerged organically in the Soviet milieu precisely because it is the underside of total ideology. The reality presented by Soviet ideology existed as an elaborate façade, a huge and expensive movie set, and conceptualism invites us to walk behind the scenes, to recognize the spectral and absurd side of this monumental construction. Whereas totalitarianism must found itself in a monistic metaphysics of ideas that become real, conceptualism offers a series of imaginary metaphysics, which in their interplay demonstrate the relativity of each and undermine any metaphysical pretensions.

The proliferation of metaphysic systems within conceptualism is conceived as a way to overcome the metaphysical dimension of discourse, not by the means of serious analytical criticism (as in Wittgenstein or Derrida), but through the self-ironic, self-parodic construction of systems that deliberately disclose their own contingency. Traditionally, metaphysics bases all of reality on some general presupposition, a concept so broad as to allow all phenomena to be deduced from it. The Idea in Plato's system, Absolute Spirit in Hegel, Matter and Economic Production in Marx, Will in Schopenhauer, Life in Nietzsche, Creative Impetus in Bergson, Being in Heidegger are examples of such grand philosophical constructions. But if we recognize, as conceptualism does, that all of these are merely concepts, that none has a privileged claim to the real, then any concept we might choose becomes equally efficient for the production of an imaginary metaphysics. Hence Kabakov intentionally chooses small and trivial objects as foundations for metaphysical discourse in order to suggest a conceptualist alternative to the grand schemes of traditional metaphysics.

One of Kabakov's most developed examples proceeds from the ordinary housefly, which acquires in his work the same status as, for instance, Hegel's Absolute Spirit. "The work presented here, the treatise 'The Fly with Wings' almost visually demonstrates the nature of all philosophical discourse—at its base may lie a simple, uncomplicated and even nonsensical object—an ordinary fly, for example. But yet the very quality of the discourse does not suffer in the least as a result of this. In this very way it is proven (and illustrated) that the idea of philosophizing and its goal consists not at all in the revelation of the original supposition (if this can turn out to be an ordinary fly), but rather in the very process of discourse, in the verbal frivolity itself, in the mutual suppositions of the beginnings and ends, in the flow of connections and representations of that very thing."[20] Besides demonstrating the contingency of metaphysical systems, Kabakov accomplishes two other closely related philosophical tasks. By contrasting the superficiality of the topic with the gravity of his chosen genre, Kabakov not only deconstructs the methodology of serious philosophy, but elevates the trivial to the status of a topic worthy of philosophical meditation. Instead of promoting abstract concepts, Kabakov argues the merits of so humble a creature as the housefly as a principle of explanation of such important spheres as economics, politics, arts, and civilization. The same device that allows him to deconstruct traditional philosophy also serves to construct a new range of philosophies that can assimilate the words and concepts of ordinary language in all its infinite richness. This pan-philosophical approach can also be applied to such concepts as chair or table or wall, identifying them as potential universals that may provide a more vivid elucidation of the world than such traditional concepts as Life or Being.

Although Kabakov selects concrete universals that are much narrower in scope than traditional abstract founding concepts, such as

Truth or Spirit, their specificity imparts an informational value that is lacking in the vagueness of more general terms. Thus Kabakov's metaphysics of the fly appear to be more informative than the traditional all-inclusive metaphysics of Life or Spirit. In his commentary on Kabakov's installation, "The Fly with Wings," which contains the treatise "The Fly as a Subject and Basis for Philosophical Discourse," Boris Groys, another conceptualist thinker, writes:

> Our culture contains a small stock of words that lack a clear, firmly defined meaning. These words are, in a way, linguistic jokers which, without meaning anything in particular, are thereby able to mean practically anything. Specifically, they include "being," "life," and "thought." These words mean simultaneously everything and nothing—and are equally applicable to anything at all. For this reason they have traditionally enjoyed great prestige in culture. Kabakov transforms the word "fly" into another of these joker-words which are potentially applicable to anything whatsoever.... In the ability of an ephemeral word bereft of a noble philosophical tradition to achieve the lofty status of the words which possess this tradition we may see a historic opportunity which is also open to the fly—the opportunity to construct a fly-paradise of its own, its own world of platonic, fly-essences.[21]

Thus Kabakov's multiple metaphysics presuppose the simultaneous double movement of a concept. An ordinary concept—like that of a fly—assumes metaphysical status, while metaphysical discourse is reduced to the genre of a speech game.

Kabakov's general project brings philosophy out of its narrow discursive domain into the realm of ordinary speech and artistic creation. By broadening the definition of philosophy, Kabakov, more than any other contemporary thinker, responds to the uniquely Russian mode of philosophizing, which is not so much abstract thinking about the world as it is a concrete implementation of concepts in everyday life. Kabakov demonstrates the absurdity of an existence that submits completely to ideological designs. Conceptualism simultaneously discloses the contingent character of concepts and the conceptual character of reality. Kabakov had a powerful influence on many Russian artists, critics, and thinkers of the 1970s and 1980s, who continue to develop conceptual models derived from the historical tradition of Russia. "Our local thinking, from the very beginning in fact, could have been called 'conceptualism.'"[22]

The Morality of Eclecticism: Vitaly Komar and Alexander Melamid

Vitaly Komar (born 1943) and Alexander Melamid (born 1945) are the founders of "sots-art" (1972), a style related through nostalgia and parody to the official canon of Soviet art. Komar and Melamid's own work is not limited to sots-art but proceeds from the diversity of ideological and mythological codes peculiar to both Russian and American "postcommunist" and "postmodern" societies. Like Ilya Kabakov, these artists supplement their visual work with programmatic discourse, proposing that certain ideas can function as self-sufficient works of art. What is it that distinguishes the idea-as-art from the idea as an element of ideological or philosophical system? Paradoxically, the art-idea is more quintessentially ideal than the idea imbedded in theoretical discourse, because it does not claim to transform reality as in ideology or to explain reality as in philosophy. Rather than weave itself into a tapestry of justification, clarification, argumentation, the art-idea presents itself purely as idea, idea as such. For the same reason, *conceptualism* establishes the concept as its basic unit, one that refers only to itself and not to external referent.

Komar and Melamid are sympathetic to Kierkegaard and Schlegel's discussions of self-irony as the moving force of philosophical wisdom and religious ascension. By taking such a position, a conceptualist may interpret even the most ostensibly serious philosophical and theological systems as implicitly ironical. Following the sots-artistic mode of reasoning, Komar and Melamid reinterpret in terms of ironic nostalgia not only the Soviet ideocracy, but what they consider to be the first monuments of communist thought, Plato's *Republic* and *Laws.* To the heated debate regarding the proto-totalitarian nature of Plato's idealism, Komar and Melamid bring an unexpected twist: was not Plato joking? Referring to the conclusion of *The Republic,* they write:

> The last thing that the story-teller hears as he is falling asleep is that one and the same person should be able to write both comedies and tragedies and that the person *who writes tragedies well will thus be a comedy-writer as well.* Plato's remark compels one to suspect that his ideal state is the first anti-utopia, a parody whose key has been lost in the darkness of the ages. One cannot help but sense a Socratic irony in the following contention of the "comedy-writers": "We are even the creators of the most beautiful tragedy, if not possibly the very best. For our entire state system offers a reproduction of the most beautiful and best life; we contend that this is precisely what is the most veritable tragedy." (*Laws,* 817B).[23]

Thus the entire conceptualist model extends itself to the very roots of those ideals and utopias that inspired the formation of subsequent Western civilization. It is a commonly held opinion that the Soviet implementations of Marxist ideology distorted the purity of the communist project, engendering a farcical realization of Marx's vision. But what if the farce preceded the vision? That is to say, what if the very concept of utopia, as promulgated by Plato, was originally conceived as a joke, as an anti-utopian fantasy? Then we could say that what became "utopia" is the distortion of a primordial parody, a kind of antiparody that approached in all seriousness what was meant to be taken as humor. Thus the Soviet implementation of Marx's vision might well be understood as the perfect realization of a misinterpretation—a joke that posterity failed to get. Komar and Melamid's theory reverses the entire retrospective of Western civilization and, though it probably cannot be validated, at least bears witness to the potential scope of ironic reversals inherent in the conceptualist way of thinking.

Notes

This research was supported from funds provided by the National Council for Soviet and East European Research (Washington, D.C.) and by an award from the Research Committee of Emory University (Atlanta), which, however, are not responsible for the contents of this article.

1. See, for example, "Symposium on Russian Postmodernism" (with Arkady Dragomoshchenko, Jerome McGann, Marjorie Perloff, Vitaly Chernetsky, et al.), *Postmodern Culture* 3, no. 2, (University of North Carolina, January 1993); "Russian Critical Theory and Postmodernism," forum, *Slavic and East European Journal* 39, no. 2 (1995); Mikhail Epstein, *After the Future: The Paradoxes of Postmodernism and Contemporary Russian Culture* (Amherst: Massachusetts University Press, 1995).
2. Joseph Kosuth, *Art after Philosophy and After: Collected Writings, 1966–1990* (Cambridge, MA: MIT Press, 1991), pp. 14, 52.
3. Ibid., p. 84.
4. This term was introduced by Vitaly Komar and Alexander Melamid, see section of this chapter.
5. Richard Lourie, *Letters to the Future: An Approach to Sinyavsky-Tertz* (Ithaca, NY, and London: Cornell University Press, 1975), p. 122.
6. Ibid., p. 90.
7. Ibid., p. 92.
8. Ibid., p. 98.
9. "Emptiness is the contents of Pushkin. Without emptiness he would have been incomplete." Progulki s Pushkinym, in, Abram Tertz (Andrei Siniavsky), *Sobranie sochinenii* v 2 tomakh. (Moscow: SP "Start," 1992), vol. 1, p. 373.
10. Ilya Kabakov, "On Emptiness," *Between Spring and Summer: Soviet Conceptual Art in the Era of Late Communism* (Tacoma, WA, and Boston, MA: Tacoma Art Museum and the Institute of Contemporary Art, 1990), p. 54.
11. Ibid., p. 54.
12. Ilya Kabakov, "The Man Who Never Threw Anything Away," *Ten Characters* (London: The Institute of Contemporary Arts, 1989), pp. 45–46.
13. Ibid., p. 44. Compare with Alexander Zinoviev's assessment of a dump: "Love your dump ..., since it is your house, and you have and will have no other house." *Zhivi* (Lausanne: L'Age d'Homme, 1989), p. 17.
14. Ilya Kabakov, "On the Subject of the Local Language," *Zhizn' mukh. Das Leben der Fliegen. Life of Flies,* p. 239.
15. "Epistemological Thirst," ibid., p. 242.
16. "On the Subject of the Local Language," ibid., p. 240.
17. Ibid.
18. "Conceptualism in Russia," ibid., p. 247.
19. Ibid., p. 249.
20. "The Fly as a Subject and Basis for Philosophical Discourse: Introduction," *Zhizn' mukh. Das Leben der Fliegen. Life of Flies.* p. 224.
21. Boris Groys, "We Shall Be Like Flies," ibid., pp. 212–13.
22. "Conceptualism in Russia," ibid., p. 249.
23. Vitaly Komar and Aleksandr Melamid, *Death Poems: Manifesto of Eclecticism* (New York: Galerie Barbara Farber, 1988), p. 111.

Part V

Postmodernism and Spirituality

Chapter 23

Post-Atheism

From Apophatic Theology to "Minimal Religion"

Mikhail Epstein

> We are turning demystification inside out: within the profane, we are discovering the sacred.
>
> *Mirca Eliade*

There are numerous philosophical investigations into the relationship between religion and art.[1] However, what interests me in the present chapter is not the eternal question traditionally broached, but the phenomenon of a new type of religious consciousness—or, more precisely, a religious unconscious—that is coming into existence in twentieth-century Russian culture. The term "religious unconscious" is applied here specifically to the state of Russian spirituality in the Soviet epoch and in particular to its latest phases when the official atheism is succeeded by various forms of post-atheist mentality.

What is commonly understood by the term "unconscious" is the sphere of primal drives and vital instincts, which the religious consciousness seeks to repress and eliminate. However, what was repressed and excluded during the Soviet epoch was precisely religious consciousness, which occupied the sphere of the unconscious in place of the baser instincts of hate, aggression, cruelty and destruction, ousted from it, transformed into consciousness, and promoted into ideological doctrine. This unique historical experiment, which reversed the relationship of these two spheres of the psyche and relegated religion to the sphere of the unconscious, requires radical theoretization to match the radical nature of the revolution that it represents. The West, too, has witnessed a similar process of relegating religion to the unconscious. However, as will be seen later, this process of secularization was much more moderate, and it has already received theoretical explanations from a theological point of view.[2]

In his late text, *Civilization and Its Discontents* (1929), Freud establishes a close connection between religious feeling and the unconscious. Both appear to share their origin in what Freud describes, alluding to a letter from his friend, Romain Rolland, as the "oceanic feeling." "It is … a feeling as of something limitless, unbounded—as it were, 'oceanic.'" According to Rolland, who is paraphrased by Freud, "[T]his feeling … is a purely subjective fact, not an article of faith; it brings with it no assurance of personal immortality, but it is the source of religious energy which is seized upon by the various Churches and religious systems, directed by them into particular channels, and doubtless also exhausted by them. One may … rightly call oneself religious on the ground of this oceanic feeling alone, even if one rejects every belief and every illusion."[3] Freud then goes on to explain the nature of this oceanic feeling by positing that there is no impenetrable barrier between the conscious Ego and the unconscious Id. The Ego is only the façade of the unconscious, an island, as it were, surrounded on all sides by an ocean. The same image recurs in C. G. Jung's writings, in his reflections on psychology and religion. "[T]he psyche … reaches so far beyond the boundaries of consciousness that the latter could easily be compared to an island in the ocean. Whereas the island is small and narrow, the ocean is immensely wide and deep and contains a life infinitely surpassing, in kind and degree, anything known on the island…."[4] Using this metaphor, it is possible to compare the atheization of Russian society in the Soviet epoch to the sinking of the ancient island of Atlantis, when all forms of conscious religiosity were not so much destroyed as banned into the depths of the unconscious, relegated to the bottom of that ocean from which they were once raised by the consciousness of many generations of religious believers.

A few remarks on the use of terminology in this investigation. The concept of "the unconscious" is not used in any strict psychoanalytic sense but rather as the notion of a general cultural paradigm, which can be pinpointed at various levels, including the psychological level, on a par with the historical, social, aesthetic, and theological. The unconscious is thus a sphere of either the psychic, the social or cultural life of the human subject, which lies beyond the boundary of his/her consciousness and is in a conflictual relationship with the individual's conscious attitudes. Thus the unconscious can be defined only in terms of the conscious—as its "other."

1. From Apophatic Theology to Atheism

Under the pressure of censorship—in both the social and psychoanalytic meaning of the term—the religious unconscious acquired new depth during the Soviet period. However, the repression of religious consciousness was not imposed from the outside alone, by an external force. This repression was rooted in the very heart of the religious and theological tradition dominant in Eastern Christianity and particularly in Russia. It is by no means an accident that the huge religious repressions and the rise of mass atheism took place within this cultural domain. This is because ever since the Byzantine period, Eastern Christianity has been home to the tradition of apophatic or negative theology.

According to the spiritual precepts of Pseudo-Dionysius Areopagite (writing around the fifth or beginning of the sixth century A.D.), God can neither be represented in images nor designated by any name, because He is more profound than any definition. God, or "the supreme Cause," "is neither knowledge nor truth. It is not kingship. It is not wisdom. It is neither one nor oneness, divinity nor goodness. Nor is it a spirit, in the sense in which we understand that term," wrote Pseudo-Dionysius, author of the *Areopagitica*, who rejected all the names for God without leaving us his own name.[5] "I pray we could come to this darkness so far above light! If only we lacked sight and knowledge so as to see, so as to know, unseeing and unknowing, that which lies beyond all vision and knowledge. For this would be really to see and to know: to praise the Transcendent One in a transcendent way, namely through the denial of all beings."[6] What we can conclude from this is that God has no place in consciousness, since the latter operates by the use of positive terms. To paraphrase Husserl, consciousness is always "consciousness of something," while God is not "something" and so escapes the definitions offered by consciousness. If our consciousness of God is false, that means that only by overcoming and negating consciousness can we reveal the truth about Him. Since consciousness is correlated with being, the aim is to reach non-being; and to do so, the aspirant must remain on the other side of consciousness. The locus of faith is thus transferred to the unconscious, and all positive sources of knowledge are extinguished and dispersed in its dark abysses.

Negative theology found expression above all in the Eastern branch of Christianity. According to Vladimir N. Lossky, an eminent Russian Orthodox theologian of the twentieth century, apophaticism "constitutes the fundamental characteristic of the whole theological tradition of the Eastern Church."[7]

The early eighteenth-century Russian icon, entitled "John the Evangelist in Silence," symbolizes this tradition. As is known, the Gospel of St. John is generally regarded as the most secretive, the most "mystagogic" of the Gospels and hence mystically connected with Orthodoxy. By the same system of symbolic correspondences, inherited from Church traditions, the Apostle Peter is connected with Catholicism, and St. Paul, by the freedom of his theological speculations, with Protestantism. To St. John is attributed not only the Fourth Gospel but the concluding chapter of the New Testament, Revelation. Hence the apocalyptic vision of the end of the world and the extinction of its visible and tangible forms also has a figurative connection with the Eastern theological tradition.

This icon depicts John the Evangelist,[8] using his right hand to hold open the beginning of his Gospel. We read: "In the beginning was the Word, and the Word was with God, and the Word was God.

The same was in the beginning with God. All things were made by him ..." John's left hand is raised to his lips, as if to make the sign of silence over the words themselves, sealing them with the mark of the inexpressible. At first glance, the meaning of these gestures might seem contradictory: the right hand reveals "the Word" while the left hand conceals it. But this is the very paradox of negative theology: it is because "the Word was God" that it must be enunciated in silence. All other words may be uttered: only this one mysterious Word must remain unuttered, through which everything came to be. In Eastern theology, this "rule of the left hand" was particularly respected. It barred the Word preached by the Gospel itself from the speaking mouth.

There have been many manifestations of apophaticism in Russian theology. The most fundamental was the suppression of theo-logy itself, the cutting off of *logos* or discourse on God. This Russian "anti-theology," with its fervent adherence to the principle of "inexpressibility," surpassed even Byzantine theology, which despite its advocacy of "wise silence," remained noisy and effusive. This perplexing self-erasure determines the particularity of Russian theology, in the sense that Georgy Florovsky defined it in his classic study *The Paths of Russian Theology*: "The history of Russian thought contains a good deal that is problematic and incomprehensible. The most important question is this: what is the meaning of Russia's ancient, enduring, and centuries-long intellectual silence?... Old Russian culture remained unformulated and mute. The Russian spirit received no creative literary and intellectual expression. The inexpressible and unexpressed quality of Old Russia's culture often appears unhealthy."[9]

Certainly, no one would deny that Russian theology produced numerous works in the fields of liturgy, dogmatics, and other disciplines, and that it experienced a particular upsurge in the second half of the nineteenth and early twentieth centuries. The point is in the fundamental attitude: in Russia, theology has never been regarded as a particularly important function of faith. Instead, the shortest path to God was either through the incessant repetition of the eight-word prayer to Jesus,[10] or via "inexpressible sighs." Even when, on occasion, Russian theology reclaimed its right to speak about God, it used as its inspiration the very tradition that denied the possibility of speaking about God. This is what happened in the period of Metropolitan Makarii (sixteenth century), when the theological foundations were laid for the culture of Muscovite Russia, and when for the first time perhaps, according to Florovsky, the attempt was made "to build culture as a system." Here, while taking a very selective attitude toward the Byzantine heritage, Muscovy betrayed its predilection for the works of the Areopagite: "Contemplative mysticism and asceticism—the best and most valuable part of Byzantine tradition—played no role in the conservative Muscovite synthesis.... However, the Athonite translation of *Areopagitica* did pass into Makarii's *Great Reading Compendium* or *Meneloges* [*Velikie chet'i minei*] and generally enjoyed an unexpectedly wide circulation and popularity (Ivan the Terrible greatly admired the *Areopagitica*)."[11]

It remains something of a mystery why Ivan the Terrible, whose reign was marked by alternating bouts of unbridled sinfulness and equally intense repentance, was so drawn to this work of negative theology. Perhaps there was a kind of correspondence between the apophatic paradox of knowing God through lack of knowing Him and the Russian Tzar's style of behavior, his mixture of extreme cruelty and fool-in-Christ (*iurodivyi*) humility: perhaps he found a confirmation of his superhuman calling in the very horror of his acts. According to this logic, if non-knowledge of God is the surest way to knowledge of God, then deviation from God's commandments is the way to God, a way to fulfill His unspoken will. Ivan the Terrible's piety was in itself a paradox: while filled with self-denial and repentance, it also drove him to commit new crimes or at the very least to be easily reconciled with them.[12]

It is useful to remember that negative theology developed in a Monophysite environment, which rejected the idea of Christ's human nature, accepting only his divine nature and hence attributing a certain virtuality, conditionality and illusoriness to his human incarnation. It is noteworthy that "the initial proclamation of the works of Pseudo-Dionysius Areopagite provoked discussions between the Orthodox and the Monophysites in Constantinople in 533 AD, during which the head of the Orthodox rejected their authenticity."[13] Later, however, these works became part of the canon of Orthodox patristic literature. It is also a fact that the ideas of negative theology played an important part in Western mystical heresies, mixing with Manichaeanism and Monophysitism—for example, the Cathars, Manichaeans and Anabaptists saw the elevation of the divine in the desecration of the human. Since matter constituted absolute evil, any method by which it could be eradicated—including lying, murder, betrayal, extreme asceticism or its opposite, reckless debauchery—was considered a good. Such an interpretation of "saintliness through blasphemy" is close to the religious philosophy of Ivan the Terrible, although whatever else he may be accused of, he remains innocent of deliberate sectarian deviations. However, while Monophysitism itself was always deemed heretical among the Orthodox, a certain element of "negative theology" became part of Orthodox religiosity.

We are not in a position to pursue all the lines of development of the apophatic theological tradition, but they very clearly lead us to the Russian nihilism of the nineteenth century and the Soviet atheism of the twentieth, in which negative theology becomes the negation of theism itself.[14] God is transposed beyond the region of knowledge as such, and all predicates of being attached to the notion of God are rejected. This dark and unhealthy side of apophaticism has been part of Russian theology through its entire history. According to Florovsky, "many believers acquired a dangerous habit of doing without any theology whatsoever, substituting it with whatever came their way—the Book of Rules, the *tipikon,* myths about ancient times, customs, or lyricism of spirit. What came into existence was a retrograde renunciation and avoidance of knowledge, a kind of theological aphasia, a surprising adogmatism and even agnosticism, for the sake of a self-deluding piety. This was the heresy of the new gnoseomachists.[15] … This gnoseomachy threatened the very health of spirituality."[16]

The anti-intellectual stance of Orthodoxy may account for the atheistic inclination of Russian thought. The opposition to knowledge of, and thought about, God—gnoseomachy—drove faith into the unconscious, clearing the way for the conscious cult of science, revolution, and social ideals. Theological "aphasia" and "agnosticism"—the malaise of word and knowledge—prepared the ground for atheism as a spiritual neurosis, a phenomenon of exiled religiosity. Superficially, it seemed that the nihilist negation of "everything," beginning with society, government, art, and morality, extended ultimately to the negation of "the holiest of holies." This is how the trend is described in a conversation between the "first nihilist" Bazarov and the gentleman Pavel Petrovich in Turgenev's *Fathers and Sons.* In reality, however, nihilism began with the "sacred," from which it spread to more peripheral areas, sanctified by religion. "There is no God" was the beginning of Russian youth's fascination with Buchner and Marx, with chemistry and revolution.

But where did this "there is no God" come from? Is its origin not in the ambivalence of apophatic theology itself, which by denying God any cognizable features plunges us into the depths of thoughtlessness-about-God and non-knowledge-of-God, ultimately leading to indifference toward or simple rejection of God?

According to Lossky, "[a]ll knowledge has as its object that which is. Now God is beyond all that exists. In order to approach Him it is necessary to deny all that is inferior to Him, that is to say, all that which is. (…) Proceeding by negations one ascends from the inferior degrees of being to the highest, by progressively setting aside all that can be known, in order to draw near to the Unknown in the darkness of absolute ignorance."[17] Nihilism is the ultimate and most extreme of such negations. Faith is plunged into the sphere of non-knowing about its own subject and about itself, while in atheism this non-knowing evolves into a militant ignorance and deliberate rejection of God.

It is in this sense that Soviet atheism can be regarded as the paradoxical development of apophatic theology, as its logical next step, leading to the erasure of its "theistic" and "theological" components. God is not only deprived of all His attributes, but of the predicate of existence itself. Godlessness and lack of faith become as it were the natural consequence of the apophatic negation of God and of the erasure of conscious faith. S. L. Frank noted this remarkable convergence of theology and atheism in the negation of the existence of

God himself. "If the word 'to exist' is to be understood in the sense of 'to be constituted in objective reality,' paradoxically the absence of faith and faith must converge in the negation of this predicate in its application to God.... The concept of atheism consists in the fact that in our immediate experience of objective reality, we do not encounter an object such as God.... This proposition as such is incontestable, and with regard to it faith is essentially concordant with non-faith."[18] The only difference is that in the first case the negation of God is but a step toward attaining God, while in the other it is the final point, at which reason stops and is petrified. That which serves to purify faith in apophatic theology becomes the negation of faith in atheism, and it is difficult to define logically where extreme apophaticism ends and nihilism and atheism begin. Clearly, God does not exist in the same way a visible object or perceptible phenomenon does. If this world exists, then God does not exist. If this tree exists, then God does not exist in this sense of "existence." In the final analysis, negative theology negates itself as theology, becoming atheism.

One might ask at this point why apophatic theology is most intimately, though not exclusively, connected with Eastern Christianity. Perhaps it is for the same reason that the Orient has been the cradle of religions embodying a negative infinity, represented through a "no"—Nirvana in Buddhism, Tao in Taoism. According to S. L. Frank, "negative theology is guided by the intuition that God's being as the primal source and primal foundation of being is super-logical and super-rational.... Consciousness here becomes immersed in a completely new, usually unknown dimension of being, receding into some sort of dark depths, which remove it endlessly from the ordinary 'earthly' world.... The practical sum total of this attitude is a limitless and excessive spiritual aloofness, which makes it in some respects similar to Hindu religiosity."[19]

Byzantium and Russia are thus close to the Orient in this respect but are not to be equated with it. Since apophatic theology still remains a Christian theology, it cannot deny the positive manifestation of God in the image of His Son, sent in flesh and blood to expiate the sins of man. But precisely because Christian revelation is essentially positive, and even iconic—that is, it is revealed in the fullness of the human personality of Christ—the development of negative theology in Christianity had to lead to atheism.

It is one thing when Shankara, the great Hindu thinker, attains Brahman through the negation of all its definitive traits: "Now there is no class of substance to which the Brahman belongs, no common genus. It cannot therefore be denoted by words which, like 'being' in the ordinary sense, signify a category of things. Nor can it be denoted by quality, for it is without qualities; nor yet by activity because it is without activity.... Therefore it cannot be defined by word or idea; as the Scripture says, it is the One 'before whom words recoil.'"[20] Or when Chuang-tsu, the great Taoist thinker, attains Tao through the negation of all positive characteristics in order to clarify the empty and formless nature of Tao itself: "The Tao cannot be heard; what can be heard is not It. The Tao cannot be seen; what can be seen is not It. The Tao cannot be expressed in words; what can be expressed in words is not It. Do we know the Formless which gives form to form? In the same way the Tao does not admit of being named."[21]

It is a different matter when a similar method is applied to the God of Christian theology; for this is a God who revealed himself, who descended to earth to assume human form, who died, was resurrected, and whose crucifixion wounds were physically touched by the apostle Thomas. Negative theology thus denies the positive attributes of a God whose very essence, according to Christian revelation, became visible and tangible in the figure of Christ:

> It is not soul or mind, nor does it possess imagination, conviction, speech, or understanding. Nor is it speech per se, understanding per se. It cannot be spoken of and it cannot be grasped by understanding. It is not number or order, greatness or smallness, equality or inequality, similarity or dissimilarity. It is not a substance, nor is it eternity or time.... It is not sonship or fatherhood and it is nothing known to us or to any other being. It falls neither within the predicate of nonbeing nor of being.[22]

Pseudo-Dionysius' formulations, so similar to those of Shankara and Chuang-tsu, acquire a different meaning in the context of "positive" religion. They dissolve its very core, the humanness of Christ, his "sonship," his existence in time, and his possession of speech. They potentially border on atheism.

In the Orient, the negative forms of knowledge of God do not lead to atheism. They remain forms of knowledge of God to the extent that their divine object is the absolute nothing, a pure and all-embracing emptiness. Nihilism is here not a denial of religion, but represents its profound essence and dignity. Within the Christian tradition, issuing from the fullness of the incarnation of God, the development of the negative moment in the knowledge of the divine is at first directed toward the cleansing of faith from idolatry and pagan superstitions. However, it ends by falling outside the framework of the knowledge of *God-Man*, and leads to atheism. *The negation of the positive attributes of Nothing is a religious extension into that Nothing. The negation of the positive attributes of God, who appeared in the flesh and who continues to nurture the faithful with his flesh, is already atheism.*[23]

However, this does not lead to the conclusion that atheism, in developing apophaticism to extremes, completely annihilates the religious principle. The paradox lies in the very fact that while apophaticism contained the seeds of atheism, atheism retains the seed of apophaticism. That is, atheism retains its own unconscious theology. *Apophaticism is a liminal phenomenon, through which faith crosses into atheism, while atheism itself reveals the unconscious of faith.* Radically expelled from consciousness, the religious descends into the depths of the unconscious, from whence it makes its presence felt by means of numerous clear or blurred signals, in the same manner that repressed sexuality, according to Freud, can "betray itself" through either criminal deviations, attacks of sadism and masochism, psychic illness, or the subtlest and loftiest artistic sublimations.

The atheistic society literally seethes with religious allusions, symbols, references, substitutions, and transformations. In part, this importunate neurosis of repressed religiosity is lived out by crude political actions: the creation of idols, the adulation of leaders and their images, and all sorts of state worship as well as regressions into forms of primitive tribal rituals. Nevertheless, the religious unconscious is expressed most strongly in the artistic works of an atheistic era. According to Freud, it was in fact artists who first discovered the unconscious; and *this primacy is retained even in those societies that ban and repress, not so much the libidinal drives, as higher religious aspirations.*

This religious unconscious is encoded with great finesse in both artistic works and the personalities of the artists themselves, and it takes a lot of careful critical activity to decode it. If it can be said that Leo Tolstoy and Fyodor Dostoesvky influenced their readers through the acuteness of their religious consciousness and by the force of their religious teaching, then in the atheistic period, the religious unconscious is often expressed by meaningful silence and the refusal to make any kind of confession or declaration of faith.

This skirting around religious topics is not a case of writers using coded, Aesopian language or allegory to express their religiosity. Although there are numerous illustrations of this kind of practice in Russian literature (for instance, Akhmatova's *Poem Without a Hero* and much of Pasternak's work), we have in mind here a fundamentally different phenomenon. It is *the unconscious revelation of religious intentions and not the conscious concealment of them.* Russian culture of the Soviet period offers unique material for the study of the psychology of the religious unconscious.[24]

2. Secularization and the "New Middle Ages"

Until now we have been emphasizing the specificity of Eastern apophaticism. Now we must incorporate it into the general perspective of the historical development of Christianity. Although apophaticism is innate to Eastern Christianity, there is no denying its long-standing influence on Western spirituality. Evidence of it can be seen in the works of several Western Christian mystics, such as Meister Eckhart, Nicholas of Cusa, and Jacob Boehme, all of whom glimpsed the "foundationless foundation" of God himself, His rootedenss in nothing. "Knowing unknowing," or "learned ignorance," is the name Nicholas of Cusa gave to the method for approaching Him.

It has already been pointed out that the ideas of "negative theology" had a place in the religious heresies of the West. However, it is secularization that best sums up the religious "convergence" of East and West whereby God becomes "nothing" on both sides of globe.

In this sense, atheism is a crude and violent form of secularization. Soviet [*sovetskaia*] culture thus represents the reverse side of secular [*svetskaia*] culture, hastily erecting its earthly gods in the absence of the heavenly God. The difference between secularization and atheism is not only in the choice of means: tolerance versus violence, gradual development versus haste, democracy versus totalitarianism. The difference lies in the fact that atheism, as a rule, transfers the energy of its negation into the affirmation of a new, earthly hierarchy, replacing the heavenly one. Godlike leaders make their appearance along with state forms of holy ritual, piety, and the "cult of personality." Secularization is slower to come to this process of transfer of faith and the replacement of its transcendental object. It does not use the new copper and bronze idols to try to cover up the gaping heavens. Rather it leaves the void empty, without substituting it with a quasi-faith, and through this facilitates the flooding of the unconscious with religious spirit.

If apophaticism itself is paradoxical, then atheism and secularization can be represented as two sides of one and the same paradox. Atheism is the possibility of quasi-faith, issuing from the negation of faith. Secularization is the possibility of faith, issuing from the absence of faith itself. God's place is not allocated to someone or something else, but in its emptiness is a reminder of the impossibility of seeing or perceiving Him palpably.

Of course, this sharp division between atheism and secularization understates the various shades of "unbelieving pseudo-faith" and "believing non-faith," widespread in both the Eastern and Western Christian world. However, what this division does provide is an explanation for the positive religious meaning of secularization, even if it consciously rejects religion, and the negative meaning of atheism, which consciously erects new idols.

In the preceding section we tried to explain how apophaticism can turn into atheism; in this section we shall try to see how secularization can facilitate a regeneration of faith and its purification from the idols of consciousness. The submergence of religion in the unconscious is interpreted, in a series of twentieth-century Western theological studies, as a means for religion's own salvation. In its act of self-consciousness, religion substitutes itself for God, becoming a form of ritualism and idolatry that worships only itself and its own earthly kingdom. Karl Barth stresses that it is precisely the unconscious nature of religion that can serve to assure its authenticity: it is what it is when it does not know what it is. "At the moment when religion becomes conscious of religion, when it becomes a psychologically and historically conceivable magnitude in the world, it falls away from its inner character, from its truth, to idols."[25]

Up to a point, secularization itself can be regarded as a phenomenon of modern religious apophaticism, of faith existing through the negation of faith. Such a repressed, unconscious religiosity can be observed in many works of art of the twentieth century. Unlike their Soviet counterparts, however, Western artists were not obliged to conceal this religiosity from their public. Rather, they tried to hide it from themselves.

Having consciously absorbed secular and even atheistic attitudes, both Soviet and Western artists found their own religiosity exiled to the unconscious. Thus instead of being expressed in the content of their works, it found expression in the formal aspects of their art. This is particularly true of the avant-garde artists—Duchamp and Malevich, Brecht and Mayakovsky, as well as the surrealists. For what could inspire the apocalyptic visions of the surrealists better than religious motifs? In his memoir, Salvador Dali mentions that any attempt to raise the subject of religion with André Breton, the leader of the surrealist movement, was met with absolute silence. He "refused to hear a word about religion," despite the fact that Dali did not wish to draw him into a discussion on traditional church doctrine, but a new religion, "which would be at once sadist, masochist, and paranoid."[26] All of Dali's efforts in this regard provoked nothing but a smile from Breton and a reference to the atheistic arguments of Feuerbach. This difference of opinion led to Dali's expulsion from the surrealist ranks and his later conversion to Catholicism.

The religious unconscious was not limited to the avant-garde. It also largely determined the work of authors such as Andrei Platonov and Osip Mandel'shtam, and even the works of theoreticians such as Mikhail Bakhtin and Alexei Losev. None of these artists and thinkers made any explicit comments on matters of faith in their mature works; indeed they conspicuously avoided them. Nevertheless, they built their artistic and intellectual worlds on the foundation of a "suspended," "sublated" or "ousted" religious experience and revelation. For example, Bakhtin's theory of the polyphonic novel is not ostensibly correlated with Dostoesvky's religious ideas. But it is perfectly clear that Dostoesvky's "polyphony" is internally connected with his understanding of Christian brotherhood and "the spirit of communality" [*sobornost'*], the problems of empathy and atonement, universal guilt and responsibility (the carrying of "each other's burdens"). Also in evidence is Bakhtin's indebtedness to the ideas of Martin Buber, who regards dialogue as the initial mode of communication between man and God, since only God is that primary and eternal "Thou," in whose presence man defines himself as "I." One might assume that Bakhtin did not dare use Soviet publications to declare openly the religious subtext of his ideas. However, he offered no direct testimony about his own religious convictions either in his numerous personal notes of the late period or in conversations with friends and followers. The explanation would seem to lie, rather, in the profound apophaticism that permeates all of twentieth-century culture, finding in Soviet atheism merely its most barbaric incarnation.

As Ludwig Wittgenstein remarked, "What one cannot speak about we must pass over in silence." Having concluded his *Tractatus Logico-Philosophicus* with this sentence, the thinker himself fell silent for the next twenty years. If in according with the apophatic principle, one cannot say anything about God, then He should not be spoken about at all. This would be in complete agreement with the Third Commandment: "Thou shalt not take the name of the Lord thy God in vain." This tendency to avoid the use of God's name, this refusal to engage in theological apologetics, declarative confessions of faith and religious instruction, is characteristic of twentieth-century spirituality. Hence the development of a critical attitude toward religion as distinct from faith, even among theologians themselves. For instance, Karl Barth writes: "... Religion forgets that she has a right to exist only when she continually does away with herself. Instead, she takes joy in her existence and considers herself indispensable."[27] Such a self-satisfied religion, seeking to triumph in the world, is inimical to the essence of faith, which is always "not of this world." Similarly, the self-denial of faith is testimony to its authenticity. Faith guards its unconscious core, its non-manifestation and even readily passes itself off as absence of faith.

Miguel de Unamuno (1864–1936) has a story about a priest who is endlessly devoted to his ministry and deserves the love of his parishioners. In the course of the action it is revealed that he is a non-believer and that he performs the rites only out of love for his neighbors, inflicting terrible suffering on himself through this duality. The hero of the story genuinely perceives himself as a godless man, whose piety is a masquerade. But for the author, the truth lies at an even deeper level. As the title "Saint Manuel the Good, Martyr" itself indicates, beyond his godlessness, of which Don Manuel is aware, there lies a genuine, unconscious saintliness, a readiness to serve and be martyred in the name of his fellow men, which means in the name of God. Thus the illusion of consciousness is uncovered twice. Don Manuel goes through a revelation about the illusion of faith and perceives his own lack of faith with horror. At the same time, the author reveals the illusion of non-faith, showing the reality of faith that lies behind it.[28]

This is not a mere literary device but a two-step historical process within European religiosity: in the first, religion loses its privileged position in consciousness; in the second, it reclaims it in the "underground" of the unconscious. The starting point for this process was the religiosity of the Middle Ages, which permeated the consciousness of European society. In the Renaissance, under this external cover of Christian civilization, irreligiosity grew as a historical force, ultimately resurfacing in the eighteenth century to determine the ideology of the French Enlightenment. In the nineteenth century, it took the form of conscious atheism in the writings of Feuerbach, Darwin, Marx, and Nietzsche. The re-evaluation of all values extended for approximately a century, between the appearance of Feuerbach's *The Essence of Christianity* in 1841 and Freud's *The Future of an Illusion* in 1927. Thus the Holy Trinity was reinterpreted as the representation of the human family (Feuerbach), while God as the adult projection of childhood dependence on an almighty father (Freud). The antithesis was drawn: religious consciousness gave way to antireligious or irreligious consciousness.

However, the movement of European religiosity did not end there. In the twentieth century religiosity has been increasingly revealed as the secrete, unconscious subtext of secular and atheistic movements. Nietzsche's anti-Christianity is revealed as an unconscious imitation of Christ, a *Mangodhood* complex (a reversal of Christ's Godmanhood).[29] In Marx's communistic teaching as well as in the revolutionary movement of the proletariat, which presented itself as the atheistic affirmation of the world of here-and-now, Messianic and eschatological motifs are conspicuous. The very beginnings of secularization and the rise of capitalism are seen as evolving out of the religious tendencies of Protestantism, which Max Weber's explored in his famous *The Protestant Ethics and the "Spirit" of Capitalism* (1905). The following remark by Georgy Florovsky is illuminating: "... people try to uncover in religious movements their social foundations. But were not, on the contrary, the socialist movements directed by a religious instinct, only one that was blind?!"[30] If the nineteenth century was busy seeking the socio-historical and bio-psychological origins of religion, the twentieth century has seen a gradual change in this attitude. The religious dimension is now perceived as that depth of the unconscious from which many irreligious or anti-religious movements of history have emerged. These include liberalism, communism, fascism, nationalism, the development of science and technology, the conquest of outer space, and so on. Secularization itself, according to the Protestant thinker Dietrich Bonhoeffer (1906–1945), is the form of humankind's new religious maturity, capable of independent acts of creation in the image and likeness of God.[31] The self-deceptive kind of godlessness that Don Manuel himself confesses to is confessed by the entire European civilization of the twentieth century. Its godlessness has turned out to be a superficial mask of faith, just as, conversely, the eighteenth and nineteenth centuries perceived religiosity as a mask of a deep skepticism and indifference to God.

Hence the appropriateness of the feeling, expressed by the Russian thinker Nikolai Berdiaev (1874–1948), that with the twentieth century, the world has entered "a new Middle Ages." The values of modern civilization—humanism, individualism, and secular culture—are already exhausted. Now is a time "when the movement away from God has ended and the movement toward God has begun," a time when "God should once again become the center of our entire life," while "knowledge, morality, art, government and the economy should become religious, but freely and from inside, not by compulsion and from outside."[32] At first glance it would seem that this prediction, made by Berdiaev in 1923, has not come true, just as the idea of a "universal theocracy," proposed by Vladimir Soloviev in the 1880s, did not. Discounting the scattered and ultimately insignificant fundamentalist movements, which appeared on the periphery of the political, cultural, and economic life of the twentieth century, it is impossible to discern any conscious movement toward theocentrism and even less toward theocracy in our time. Even less can one see the fulfillment of the Berdiaev's prophecy, which referred to Russian and European culture, in the sparks of Islamic fundamentalism that have flared up in Iran or Pakistan.

However, if we do not automatically equate the new "Middle Ages" with the old Middle Ages, and if we concede the shift of the religious vector into the sphere of the unconscious, then the picture of the twentieth century changes, acquiring a new spiritual depth. The "new medievalism" does not suspend the process of secularization but imparts a religious dimension to it. The essential point is that the religious dimension alienates itself from human consciousness in the course of secularization, assuming forms of the unconscious, which transcend the scope and level of human individuality. It was not only individual consciousness that freed itself from religiosity in the course of modernity. Religiosity itself freed itself from individual consciousness and now appears as something alienated, issuing from a non-individual unconscious. This is what Berdiaev probably had in mind when he spoke about the "end of humanism, individualism, formal liberalism of the culture of the Modern Age, and the beginnings of a new epoch of collective religiosity, in which ... everything which has remained in the subsoil and the unconscious of the new history, must come to the surface."[33] In the course of the modern age, extending from the Renaissance to the beginning of the twentieth century, the religious unconscious germinated, like a shadow cast by the gigantic effort of individual consciousness at self-liberation. Individuality has apparently achieved its ends; its "human rights" are recognized, at least formally, in almost the entire world. But to the extent that individuality freed itself from the shackles of religiosity, religiosity has freed itself from the constraints of individualism, emerging in trans-human and non-individual forms.

What should perhaps be the chief concern of the theology of the "new Middle Ages" is the *assimilation of the religious meaning of alienation*. Moreover, it should formulate the fundamental principles of a new dogmatics, issuing from the category of alienation. The old dogmatics had as its starting point the "appropriation" of God by the human subject. That is, it humanized God, who was conceived as an intimate being close to humans. This is where the concept of *kenosis* originated, meaning the expending of the godly nature in Christ in the process of His becoming a man and suffering an earthly fate. But the ascension of Christ, and more importantly, his two-thousand-year-long absence as a man amongst men, cannot fail to generate a demand for new concepts, at the basis of which lies the *alienation* of the Divine from the human.

This, then, is the religious meaning of the depopulated heavens: the Divine recedes into the distance, beyond the human. In its place arises a new religious sensibility, initially taken for atheism, which Sartre and Camus proclaimed to be the atheism of ultimate human liberation and despair. In actual fact, what we are facing is an extreme form of apophaticism, in which God appears as the radically Other, the Stranger, irrevocably distant from humans. Conversely, man feels alienated from God and, just as Camus portrayed him in his novel by the same name (*L'Etranger*), a stranger in relation to both God and world. This is not just the otherness of God in relation to humans, this is *the divinity of otherness* itself. Humanity feels this *divine otherness* in and around himself, as the resistance of his own creations and his creative force, which elude his domination. The new Middle Ages are cultivating the theology of alienation in new modes of the impersonal. One of its first variants is dialectical theology, which declares God's radical inaccessibility to humans: "He is not a thing among other things, but the *Wholly Other*, the infinite aggregate of all merely relative others."[34] This is the source of God's inaccessibility to thought: "The affirmation of God, man, and the world given in the New Testament is based exclusively upon the possibility of a new order absolutely beyond human thought; and therefore, as a prerequisite to that order, there must come a crisis that denies all human thought."[35]

The process of alienation in the Marxist-Existentialist tradition has as a rule been treated in a sociopsychological framework. Such a treatment, while correct, is not sufficient. It is a fact that society gives rise to structures that are heterogeneous to the human being, alienated from his individuality and incommensurate with his consciousness and intellect. In comparison to these structures—technological, communicational, political, and financial, all grown to a planetary scale—individual consciousness and individual beliefs are infinitesimally small. The twentieth century has in part rebelled against this form of alienation, striving to restore to the individual everything s/he created. Hence the revolutionary experiences of reverse "appropriations," the expropriation of the expropriators, which included God as the chief expropriator of human knowledge and power. But as a result of all these collectivist uprisings against alienation, new rigid structures, which are even further removed from the individual and the personal, have come to reinforce the total effect of alienation.

It would appear that this curse will have no end. The more Man[36] toils on Earth, the more prominently the Non-Human emerges in him: in governments and cities, technology and architecture, science and politics, poetry and painting. Man himself was engendered by the Non-Human, and now by an incomprehensible act the Non-Human is engendered by Man. Modernism and postmodernism have strengthened this feeling for the Non-Human, which issues from man himself but no more belongs to him than the Unconscious or the Other, forming his inaccessible roots. It was Paul Valéry who remarked that language was the most powerful tool of the Other, residing in ourselves. Later, the French psychoanalyst Jacques Lacan produced the formula that the unconscious *is* a language. If even the language with which we express our thoughts is a tool of the unconscious, a tool of the Other, speaking through us, then what can be said of technology or politics, which have always used man as a tool?

We thus come to the conclusion that the struggle against alienation is useless. Struggle only strengthens its power, encumbering humanity with new super-human structures, such as those produced by the revolutions of the twentieth century, paving the way for totalitarianism. But what is the meaning of this growing alienation? Perhaps it is time to realize that alienation is not just the guilt and curse of man, but a form of judgment about him, a form of his preparation for the encounter with God. The non-human, issuing from man: is this not the same Non-Human, from which man himself was fashioned? The only thing to do is to recognize the religious meaning of alienation and accept the belief that the Non-Human, transcending humans over the centuries, is nothing but the Divine itself. The It that created man is returning to pass judgment on him. To judge him by the measure of his own works, the non-human result of which is the premise of this unavertable judgment.

3. Theomorphism: The "Other" in Culture

There is an unbridgeable gap between our contemporaries and their creations. It is as if something alien interposes itself between creator and created, something unconscious and elusive. This form of the Other is the main revelation of contemporary culture arising not from a "beyond," but from its own self-alienating core. It is what is being enacted in contemporary culture, or, to be more precise, it is what is being enacted *with* it, since the latter is consciously demonstrating the unconscious character of its own creations by manifestly "mis-re-cognizing" them, underlining and playing up to their alienating effects. Everything that is said by postmodern writers and thinkers is placed between quotation marks. It is not they who are saying and writing it all; it is It speaking through them, the thinking and writing Other. The art of the twentieth century, especially postmodern art, is an art created on behalf of this Other. The author erases his signature since It speaks for him: Language or the Unconscious.

It is in this sense that one can speak of the "new Middle Ages," in which the human being is decentered in the world, ceding his centrality to the Other. The distinguishing feature of this Other, in contrast to the "old" medievalism, is its apophatic concealment. It cannot be illuminated for the individual consciousness and even less for the faith of the masses, it cannot become an object of religious perception, it cannot even take on the name of "God." Postmodernism insists on the alien origins and irreducibility of this Other, which cannot be mastered through history, science, or theology. Even the term "theocentrism" does not apply to it, not to mention "theocracy," since they positively designate God as a "center" or "power." It is fitting to speak only of the *theomorphism* of the new Middle Ages, since it alone imparts to all things and all created works the form of the Other, of the absent God, of the religious unconscious.

An example of ancient theomorphism is the mandala—an Oriental figurative symbol, whose unconscious religious substance was studied by C. G. Jung:

> Prejudiced by historical analogies, we would expect a deity to occupy the center of the mandala. The center is, however, empty.... We find no trace of a deity in the mandala, but, on the contrary, a mechanism. In the mandala there is not a trace of the Divinity.... Instead of God, we find a mechanism. The centre [of the mandala], as a rule, is emphasized. But what we find there is a symbol with a very different meaning. It is a star, the sun, a flower, a cross with equal sides, a precious stone, a cup filled with water or wine, a coiling snake, a man, but never God.[37]

Nonetheless, it is undeniable that "mandalas are expressions of a certain attitude which we cannot help calling 'religious.' Religion is a relationship to the highest or most powerful value, be it positive or negative."[38] In the theomorphic representation there is no trace of God, but the locus and form of his absence are precisely indicated as the "highest or most powerful value," even if this value is a negative one.

In this sense, theomorphism permeates the poetic works of Mandel'shtam and Pasternak. Images of deep winter, the squeaking sound of the frozen snow-crust, or, on the contrary, light snowfall, whirling snow-flakes are all theomorphic. They indicate the "Talmudic" mentality of Mandel'shtam (God as Law) and the Hasidic sensibility of Pasternak (God as Free Chance and Play). Though these two great Russian poets of the twentieth century never considered themselves representatives of Jewish spirituality, a religious orientation is revealed in the unconscious, theomorphic subtexts of their imagery. Pasternak's poetry may be understood as a manifestation of an Hasidic sensibility, with its emphasis on the transitional and miraculous, and its vision of the divine chaos of the universe, where spirituality flashes like sparks from the most ordinary things. In Mandel'shtam, whose work reflects a Talmudic mentality, the divine is evoked in terms of the weightiness and severity of the Law. Significantly, the poet identifies himself as a pupil studying the textbook of the Universe.[39] Theomorphism is also evident in the works of contemporary Russian poets such as the conceptualists and presentists, in whose works we find "a mechanism instead of God."[40]

A "mechanism instead of God" does not indicate a naive reification of God. On the contrary, it points to a subtle attempt to de-reify the whole conception of God. The fact is that the image of God can easily be taken for God himself. However, the image of a mechanism, which takes God's place, resists such an identification. This is where we find the greatest difference between pagan idolatry (polytheism) and contemporary theomorphism (post-theism). The pagan world identified God with an object. Theomorphism reveals and simultaneously conceals the Divine in the object and through this de-reifies the image of God himself. This explains why in contemporary theomorphic art, the objects selected for representation are so far removed from the Divine—trivia, toys, mechanisms, insects, natural phenomena with little aesthetic appeal, and "low" cultural phenomena. These objects seem to be the least appropriate to bear witness to God; rather, they indicate his presence through his absence, as in apophatic theology. In these objects we recognize the trace of God with surprise but, thanks to the irony that accompanies such inadequate representations, we are prevented from confusing these trivial objects with God himself.

Apophatic theology proceeds from the most probable to the least probable assertions and comparisons concerning God. As Pseudo-Dionysius Areopagite put it:

> … a manifestation through dissimilar shapes is more correctly applied to the invisible. So it is that scriptural writings, far from demeaning the ranks of heaven, actually pay them honor by describing them with dissimilar shapes so completely at variance with what they really are that we come to discover how those ranks, so far removed from us, transcend all materiality. /…/ Sometimes the images are of the lowliest kind, such as sweet-smelling ointment and corner stone. Sometimes the imagery is even derived from animals so that God is described as a lion or a panther, a leopard or a charging bear. /…/ So true negations and the unlike comparisons with their last echoes offer due homage to the divine things.[41]

The least adequate images are the most truthful since they bear witness to the impossibility of representing an authentic image of God. "Is it not closer to reality to say that God is life and goodness rather than that he is air or stone?"[42] Negative theology arranges its descriptions of God in a descending order of decreasing congruity, proceeding from images of grace, light, and beauty down to images of animals, mechanisms, and trivial things. Thus the irony of negativity progressively underlies the order of human assertions about God. In this sense, the entire history of Western religiosity can be understood as a transition from positivity to negativity, from affirmative to apophatic modes of theological reflection, increasingly advancing the least congruent images of God and eventually falling into silence about Him. Paganism was the most positive in its identification of God with visible objects of nature. Postmodernism embraces the pole of negativity, the extreme de-objectification of God.

Theomorphism in art also calls for the selection of objects that demonstrate the crisis of the "object" as such, its dissolution into formlessness and absence.[43] An object reaches its highest degree of alienation when it ceases to be an object, when it can no longer be contained in the hand or seen with the eye, when it disappears as an "object" of possession or perception. The object marks the trace of its own disappearance, fading from the visual field before our very eyes, visibly showing the degree of its invisibility. Such a de-reification of objects can also be understood as a sign of their increasing theomorphism. God himself, according to the conception of dialectical theology, is "an absolutely groundless source of the crisis of all objecthood …, the non-being of the world."[44] Since art is concerned with the representation of the world, to reveal the non-being of the world means to reveal its own non-being, to become anti-art.

The entire culture of the new Middle Ages is religious not in the sense that it has its own ready-made religious object, passed down through the generations. It is religious in the sense that it has no knowledge of its religious object, but is prepared to comply strictly with the rules of this un-knowing, clearly demarcating the figure of the Other, without smearing it with its own individualism and affectivity. Contemporary culture is religious in the sense that it is looking for nothing other than Otherness itself. The new Middle Ages are developing strict forms of non-knowledge of God; forms of non-feeling, non-cognition, non-ecstasy, non-illumination, non-grace. These forms are as strict as the positive forms of God-knowing and God-feeling (*bogomyslie i bogochuvstvie*) of the old Middle Ages. The new Middle Ages has taken an apophatic stance, not shirking even atheistic suppositions, provided they are theomorphic, that is, adhering to the form of God-as-Absence. The atheism of the nineteenth century, inherited by Soviet culture, was still infected with the pathos of militant humanism and collectivism. It assailed God with unseemly questions and demagoguery, which are unacceptable in polite society. God was asked to account for the injustices of this world, and to suffer and tremble before the mighty attacks of the revolutionary masses, storming the heavens. In this sense, Soviet atheism was still a product of the transitional period from humanism to the new Middle Ages. The Soviet period is thus reminiscent not so much of the old Middle Ages as of the barbarous times that preceded it, and which separated the Middle Ages from Antiquity—the period when the Classical gods had died but before the new forms of Christian civilization had taken hold. In this transitional state "between gods," humanity easily regressed into barbarism and bestiality.

By asserting that the new Middle Ages will differ from the "old" by its free acceptance of religion and a consciously creative experience of it, Berdiaev paid tribute to a form of humanism that he had earlier denounced: "The call to the new Middle Ages in our era is a call to a revolution of the spirit, to a new consciousness." All spheres of life "should become religious, in a free manner and from the inside, not through coercion and from the outside."[45] These words of Berdiaev carry faint echoes of the nineteenth century, which wanted to carry its humanism over into the new Middle Ages, transplanting its principles of freedom and voluntarism, reason and enlightenment. But the new Middle Ages—at least as it has come to be embodied in the twentieth century—is not distinguished from the "old" by the freedom of religious consciousness. Rather, its distinguishing feature is the profundity of the religious unconscious and its growing power over consciousness.

The very forms of God-Absence are no less strict, coercive, and alienating than the corresponding forms of God-Worship in the "old" Middle Ages. Conscious religiosity is just as vigorously expelled from contemporary culture as the protest against religious dogmas was quashed in the Middle Ages. God has no place in culture; He should not be anywhere—not as a name or a commandment, neither as a prohibition nor as an injunction. Any consciously religious element in a contemporary text is inevitably taken as dated or rhetorical, or simply as bad taste. The smallest allusion to a center, a hierarchy, to some privileged place in culture is perceived as a boring lapse, a breach of the rules of proper conduct. On the other hand, contemporary culture becomes very receptive the moment it is faced with God's Absence, with the presence of the Other, whether it be in the form of the unconscious, language, structure, play, or the sign (in the absence of a signified)—anything that an individual does not have at his command. Such an admission of his own lack of power is a credit to an individual, at least as long as he does not spoil it by struggling against and attempting to overcome this alienation. The best thing to do is to mutely agree with this alienation, accepting its relative truth. Contemporary culture thus sees itself as the locus of the Absent God lurking in the unconscious.

The new religiosity cannot assert anything about God, since He has not yet appeared—he is the God of the second coming, the God of the end. The "old" Middle Ages lived by the memory of the first coming, by the positive religion of revelation, manifested in the Old and New Testaments. Berdiaev correctly identified the "new Middle Ages" as a transitional phase between two epochs, "when the movement from God ends and the movement toward God begins." But the essential fact is that this movement is not a movement in reverse, it is not humankind's return to the same God it abandoned, or that God's return to the humankind He abandoned. If anything, it is an even farther withdrawal of God, a disappearance into an oblivion of the old God. It is a plunging of faith into the unconscious, from which one day a new religious consciousness may be born. This consciousness would be so new that it would not be turned toward the beginning but toward the end of time, to a God who will come to witness the end of the world and to judge the world. While God is still not here, His place remains empty in human consciousness and is taken up by different forms of the Other, such as language, nation, technology, and nature, which are theomorphic to the extent that God is the first and last Other. Through His Absence, God allows everything belonging to the Other to manifest itself in humans as their self-alienation. Thus alienated, a human being has the opportunity to anticipate how s/he will appear at the last judgment, before the face of the Other. Not only man's works but man himself will appear alienated from himself, when the time comes for him to be judged.

What follows from the above is that the concepts of "faith" and "image" should also be understood in their apophatic sense: faith embraces non-faith, while the artistic image encompasses the erasure and destruction of the image. Both *non-faith* and *non-image* find expression in Russian postmodern art. To write the particle *"non"* with a hyphen means to reveal a double meaning. *Non-faith* is not simply a negation of faith, but a negation that retains the original sense of the word, its vacant place, transferring faith from consciousness into the unconscious. The *non-image*, too, is approximately equivalent to the eschatological saying of Paul, that "the fashion of this world passeth away" (1 Corinthians, 7:31).[46] If this world is about to lose its form, then art must also attempt to represent the loss of the image. From graphic, tangible, representable visual images, art moves into the sphere of the *unrepresentable*. This is what the *faith-less* world and *image-less* art of the new Middle Ages looks like.

Although language has no words to substitute for "faith" and "image," the apophatic approach is essentially an attempt to overcome the limitations of language and to find the Other in language. "Faith and image" represent the theme of our reflection, while the result of this reflection can be expressed in all the grammatical permutations of these words, in their negation, their bracketing off in quotation marks, and their meaningful omission. Thus religion and art become part of a discussion at the outer limits of their meaning, encompassing both atheism and anti-art.

4. Angelism as a Postmodern Religion

In the current phase of the new Middle Ages, theomorphism has acquired certain features of *angelism*. The figure of the angel is a key image in postmodern spirituality. The angel represents the purest form of God-presence in the absence of God himself. The angel is a peculiar form of the Divine, alienated from both God and man, roaming in a mysterious expanse between sky and earth. Although it appeared that angels had left our world in the Renaissance, remaining only as a rhetorical figure in poetry and serving as a shibboleth for mystics, they have returned in the postmodern age.[47] They are a kind of exquisite machine for the production of alienated forms of spirit. These forms are distinct from both the theocentrism of the Middle Ages and from the anthropocentrism of modernity. In the religious tradition, the angel is a mediator between God and man.

In contemporary consciousness, the angel appears as the "other," the absolute "stranger," a pure mark of difference.

In recent times, a number of serious books and films have appeared, whose main heroes are angels. The most famous of these is the film *Wings of Desire,* directed by the German Wim Wenders,[48] in which angels descend to partake of earthly existence, mingling with human beings and even becoming human. Hugging them and peering into human eyes, the angels smile their lucid and sad smiles, in which ubiquitous understanding borders on complete non-understanding. The key here is that the angels have no specific message, they are not trying to teach human beings anything. The film ends with a scene in which an angel named Daniel, having become a man, stands in a circus arena, firmly holding a rope on which his beloved acrobat Marion is flying, turning and soaring. The masculine awakens in the angel, the angelic is revealed in the feminine. As he descends, she ascends.

These new angels cannot be segregated neatly into light and dark spirits. Unsure of their own mission, they enter tortuous relationships with human beings, unable themselves to make sense of them.

The question is: why do artistic works dealing with angels and their simultaneously alienated and participatory relation to earthly life elicit such mass interest? Why are they perceived as a revelation of the spiritual condition of our times?

In the Middle Ages, God stood in the center of the universe. In modernity, man came to occupy this spot. It is now clear that both theocentrism and anthropocentrism have negative aspects: the pyres of the Inquisition and the furnaces of Auschwitz. This is why it is now necessary to find an intermediary link in the spiritual hierarchy, one that is not so other-worldly as to deny the taste of earthly life, but not so worldly as to lose touch with a higher mode of existence. It is angels that occupy this intermediary zone. And this is why angels are at the center of the contemporary semi-religious consciousness.

One could suggest that the privileging of the world of angels in contemporary spirituality is in step with the development of the most "alienated" layer of culture, namely the "technosphere." Telephones, television sets, computers, airlines, and rockets are all angelesque. They represent the otherness of spirit in self-propelled physical bodies. The ultimate technologization and depersonalization of the social sphere reveals within itself theomorphic identities of "other spirits," called angels. Angelization is thus the newest phase of history, or rather of post-history, following industrialization, automation, atomization, and other radical technological accomplishments of the modern age. At the end of the twentieth century, we are witnessing not simply the "soulless" results of technological progress but also the mysterious and trans-human forms of its strange, alienated spirituality. What the modernist critics of Western civilization—Marxists, existentialists, humanists and psychoanalysts—regarded as alienation and dehumanization was, in fact, angelization, now revealed to the postmodern consciousness. Thus the modernist critique of a soulless civilization and its nostalgia for either archaic and elemental or classical and rational forms of culture is replaced by the postmodern admiration for the new, spiritually alienated angelesque forms of that civilization.

Following several decades of technological innovations, the supernatural and esoteric is making a come-back in the flesh of this world, as the sum-total of the world's estrangement from itself. Images separated from their originals, sounds divorced from speech, silver airplanes disappearing into clouds, are the hallmarks of our civilization on the eve of the twenty-first century. Were a medieval man to stray into this world, he would surely perceive it as the habitat of angels (whether dark or light ones is another issue). This angelesque sphere features super-human capacities realized in the form of automotive and self-propelled instruments. The world is covered with an invisible communications network. The telephone, with its ability to immediately transmit the sound of a voice from one end of the globe to the other, is reminiscent of those "voices" that come from who knows where, or from the vibrating waves of the air itself. Even the computer, on which I am at this moment writing these lines, and which is capable of storing them forever in its memory, is not merely a machine facilitating physical labor. It is an angelesque body, accomplishing for me, in my place, the work of my mind, and showing me its fruits by conjuring them up from the invisible radiant depths of the disk.

According to ancient belief, angels were servants of God, sitting at His throne, singing hosannas to him. In contemporary angelism, as a rule, there is not even a mention of the Creator. Contemporary angels are *messengers without a Message*, sovereign spiritual beings who do not relate to any single supernatural will or Supreme Being. They are spirits in and of themselves, manifesting the plurality of the transcendental worlds almost in the same manner in which multiculturalism demonstrates the plurality of the social worlds. One can thus say that angelism is multiculturalism, or rather multispiritualism of the supersensible realm.

The interest in angels is symptomatic of the contemporary state of culture, simultaneously wanting and not wanting to be religious. The anatomy of the angelesque is at the same time an anatomy of postmodern spirituality, which has escaped monotheistic religiosity but does not dare return to polytheism. The tortuous temptations of atheism and the tired insipidness of agnosticism having been overcome, postmodern religiosity has left behind both the belief in the Almighty and the disbelief in Him. What remains is communion with angels as pure spirits, representing a plurality of supersensible reasons and wills. Angelism is a sort of heavenly pluralism. It is the religion of postmodernity, which affirms the multiplicity of equally valid and self-valuable spiritual pathways in place of a single truth and a single ruling canon. If the traditional religious outlook subordinated the diversity of the earthly world to the single will of its Creator, and if agnosticism celebrated the diversity of the earthly world as opposed to the presumably unitary and authoritarian will beyond, the contemporary post-agnostic era has rediscovered the transcendental as the realm of pure difference.

Angelism is a new transcendental adventure of the Western spirit, seeking pluralism not only as an empirical phenomenon in its cultural and political life, but as the ultimate revelation of the diversity of spiritual worlds. One could ask: if the idea of pluralism is so crucial to the contemporary West, why does it not return to polytheism, which worships nature's elements in their diversity? The answer is because neopaganism, which is presently making tentative inroads into religious practices, knows the locus and origins of the gods, whereas angelism is profoundly and principally ignorant about them. The difference between gods and angels, despite the grammatical plural which they share, is that angels are transparent and lonely, while gods rule the earth with glee and fury. Paganism sacralizes the originary forces of nature and can act in concert with ecological and neo-fascist movements. But it scarcely touches the nerve of the new religiosity, born of the death of God and not of His transformation into Pan or a Naiad. Polytheism cannot bring true satisfaction to the contemporary mind that quests for a trace of the Divine rather than its fleshy presence. The sumptuously carnal gods of paganism can satisfy only desperate fringe-groups and those who have fallen outside their own times, living in dreams about an "archaic revolution"—that is, of a revolutionary return to the "Great Tradition."[49] To adulate the gods of fire or earth is a bookish project. The direction of neopaganism is thus backwards, into the world of children's book illustrations and the primal polytheism that has long since been thought through and discarded. Paganism does not look ahead, beyond monotheism and atheism.

Angelism, by contrast, is a *post-atheistic* and *post-agnostic* phase of religiosity. Angels are not gods, they are merely emissaries, who have forgotten who sent them, or who conceal that knowledge. This mission without a cause endows angels with a certain absent-mindedness and an alienated look. The contemporary individual recognizes himself in angels because he, too, has severed his connection with the ground of tradition and is flying in who-knows-what direction. Having left all points of orientation behind him, seeing the exhausted earth disappearing in industrial fumes, he has no sign-posts to direct forward, toward the fading outline of the One Creator. Is it possible, in such a situation of uncertainty, spiritual transparence, and loneliness, to worship the all-powerful gods, to celebrate the play of elemental forces?

Angels appeal to the contemporary religious sensibility because, unlike the gods of old, they wander bodiless at the limits of the earth. From time to time, at their own risk, they transgress these limits, with a feeling of guilt and under peril of punishment. Angelism overthrows the metaphysics of God's *presence.* It cleanses faith of the inevitable attributes of knowledge, religious certainty, and ontological authenticity. The origin of angels is unclear and can never be clarified, while God originates from Himself. Both the pagan gods and the God of monotheism are endowed with the fullness of a self-produced essence. Angels, by contrast, are representatives of some Other, which never manifests itself. An angel is a *trace* in the Derridean sense, a trace leading into a world beyond but not attesting or bearing witness to its reality. *Angelism is thus the consequence of a religious deconstruction of the other world, which leaves its "traces" or signifiers but does not reveal its signifieds. It sends messengers but does not reveal the Sender of the messages.* Angelism is thus testimony to a profound groundlessness of the world. Even the forces from beyond this world, which are called upon to explain and substantiate it, remain without "origins" or "divine nature" and are "secondary" and "mediating." Postmodernism thus languishes in this *infinite circle of representability*, a continuous annunciation without a Sender.

Rumors are passed on, but it is impossible to reveal their origin. Arising as rumors, they are by definition something "already" heard. Angels are these rumors from the world beyond, but no one knows who started them, or what they correspond to, or who is behind them. Angelism can also be expressed as the construction of faith in the subjunctive mood, following the demise of faith in the indicative and imperative moods, which stood for what was essentially true and what ought to be. The religious mind in this hypothetical modality thus moves along the thin line separating thesis and antithesis, faith and non-faith, avoiding taking sides and finding their synthesis impossible. This narrow line between them is the mark of a gentle difference, not sharp opposition. Difference, in turn, generates angels, which constitute the pluralist choice of the religious mind no longer prone to dogma and infallibility.

In the postmodern age, pure polytheism, monotheism, or agnosticism are impossible. All that remains possible is the *condition of possibility itself*, embodied in the phenomenon of *angels without God, messengers without a Message*, and vague metaphysical rumors instead of Revelation reaching us from the beyond.

5. Post-atheist Spirituality in Russia: Minimal Religion

The visual possibilities of angelism, with its magic plasticity of multidimensional bodies appearing out of nowhere and disappearing into nothing, have been welcomed by Western video culture, which has been courting these new religious tendencies with its commercial and technical talents. Angelism, as the brainchild of video culture and postmodernism, has not yet been transplanted to Russia. This is partly connected with the previously mentioned apophatic roots of Russian religiosity, which negates any form of bodily incarnation or manifestation of faith. The cult of angels would be as discordant with the traditions of Russian spirituality as sculptures are incompatible with the interior of Orthodox churches. The question we want to examine is how this apophatic tradition manifests itself in contemporary Russian religious life, before and after the demise of the atheistic State and its ideological apparatus.

Atheism, as has already been pointed out, was the crassest and most extreme manifestation of apophaticism. It negated not only the possibility of knowing God but the very existence of God. In practice, atheism took the form of the persecution of priests and the faithful, the closure of churches, and the eradication of all traces of religious culture.

This spiritual vacuum, created by Soviet atheism, gave rise, in the 1970s and 1980s, to a new type of religiosity. In an essay written in 1982 I called this post-atheist spirituality "poor," or "minimal" religion.[50] It took the form of "faith pure and simple," without clarifications or addenda, without any clear denominational characteristics. It manifested itself as an indivisible sense of God, outside historical, national, and confessional traditions. Thus *minimal religion became the next stage of apophaticism after it had crossed the line of atheism and reclaimed its religious content.* The atheistic negation of all religions gave rise to a "minimal" religiosity negating all positive distinctions among historical religions. Paradoxically, this "faith as such," "faith in general" was prepared by the atheist denial of all faiths.

A typical expression of such "minimal religiosity" can be found in the simple "credo" of a well-known contemporary Russian artist,

Garif Basyrov (born in 1944). Asked if he could be considered a faithful Muslim, Basyrov replied: "That's ridiculous. As any normal person I feel I am approaching something.... To use high-flown words, you can say I am on my way. But I am neither an expert in Islam, Buddhism, nor Christianity. All these rituals are not for me. One thing I do know for sure: God exists."[51]

For a minimal believer, God exists above and beyond all religions, thus nullifying their historical divisions. What is at issue here is the possibility of establishing a unitary religious consciousness through the experience of the negative void of the atheist world. This post-atheist spirituality is as historically unprecedented as the phenomenon of mass atheism that preceded and conditioned it.

The seven decades of Soviet atheism, whether one calls it "mass atheism," "scientific atheism," or "state atheism," was unquestionably a new phenomenon in world history.

Mass heresies were known before, but these did not change the core of a religious perception of the world. They did not suspend the belief in God, the Holy Scriptures, or the possibility of the soul's salvation. The German Anabaptists are a case in point.

In the past there have been periods of libertine thought, but these touched only the intellectual tip of the social iceberg without altering the religious mood of the masses. The French Enlightenment is a case in point.

Only in the Soviet Union did militant atheism penetrate into the masses. It created several generations of non-believers. Even if the majority were not antagonistic to religion, they became profoundly indifferent to it. Even if they themselves did not destroy churches and burn icons, neither did they pray or invoke the name of God; indeed they forgot about His very existence.

Could religion, which had been subjected to such a long period of persecutions and negations, be simply reborn in its earlier traditional forms? Or, on the contrary, could it be inferred that, since atheism was a historically new phenomenon, post-atheist spirituality, which superseded it, would have to be even more of a novelty?

* * *

What is taking place at present in post-atheist Russian society can be divided into three major tendencies.

One of these tendencies constitutes a "religious revival" proper. It is a return of Russian society to its pre-atheist beliefs. The traditional religions—Orthodoxy, Catholicism, Islam, Buddhism, Judaism—are regaining their status and influence in the spiritual, cultural, and even political life of Russia. Not surprisingly, these newly converted believers bring an emotional ardor and dogmatic ignorance to the life of their new Church. They are also bearers of a protective, romantic nationalism and messianism. However, in the end none of it goes beyond the confines of tradition: it merely fine-tunes the tradition to meet current needs.

Another tendency seeks to restore not the pre-revolutionary, but the archaic layers of religious traditions and can be characterized as neopaganism. As its adherents see it, Russia's salvation is not to be sought in a religion of the spirit, but in the ancient cult of nature. What is required is an immediate restoration of the pre-Christian Russian and Arian pantheon. More often than not, neopaganism is mixed with elegiac ecological sentiments, in which the pagan cult of nature is presented as the defender of nature against the encroachments of civilization. It is even more common to see Orthodox Christianity interpreted in the pagan spirit, as a special branch of Christianity, intimately connected to Russia's state and military apparatus and its God-bearing people. The advantage of Orthodoxy vis-à-vis other Christian confessions lies in its doubling as both a religion of the Heavenly Father and an ancient cult of Mother-Earth. Orthodoxy in this context appears as a militant form of patriotism, destined, from time immemorial, to defend Holy Russia from the "heresies" of Judaism, Catholicism, Freemasonry, and other "foreign contaminations." The new paganism also features the cultivation of magic, extra-sensory perception, parapsychology, spiritism and other similar beliefs, which go back to the earliest animistic and fetishistic practices.

Together with the return to traditional religion and the parallel immersion in pagan and Orthodox archaism, a third tendency can be observed in contemporary Russian religious life. To date, it has attracted the least attention because it tends to escape all forms of objectification. Its "minimality" almost precludes the formation of dogma or ritual and can be identified only as an internal impulse, a state of spirit, or a disposition of mind. This is what I call "poor" or "minimal" religion. For a Western observer, a more "recognizable" name for it would be religious modernism, universalism, or ecumenicism, even if these terms do not exactly correspond to the Russian phenomenon.

Imagine a young man from a typical Soviet family which, for two or three generations, was resolutely cut off from all religious traditions. Suddenly hearing a spiritual call in his soul, he cannot decide where to go in search of salvation. He tries the Orthodox Church, the Catholic Church, the Jewish Synagogue, Baptist and Lutheran services. He finds historically shaped traditions of faith everywhere. Yet he is eager to experience spirit as whole and indivisible. Looking for faith he finds only different denominations.

It is in this disparity between faith and beliefs that "minimal" religion emerges. It is a religion without an order of service, holy books, or specific rituals. It is notable that many more people are now abandoning atheism than joining specific denominations. These people can be characterized as "poor believers" who do not subscribe to any specific set of conventional religious practices. They belong to "religion" as such, without further definitions or qualifications. Their relationship to God is holistic, mirroring the wholeness and indivisibility of God Himself.

Thus the religious revival in post-communist Russia is not only a renaissance of traditional beliefs, which were widespread before the atheistic revolution: it is also the *naissance* of a qualitatively new, post-atheist kind of spirituality. In the soul of a "poor believer" there are no dogmatic or ritual preferences created by either a continuous historical tradition or long-standing family religious commitments. Just as the divisions among farmers' holdings were destroyed during collectivization, turning fertile land into wasteland, so the confessional divisions were also erased. This prepared the post-Soviet wasteland not only for a revival of old traditions, but also for a renewal of the religious consciousness as such, capable of transcending historically established boundaries.

In the prophet Isaiah we read: "There is a voice that cries: Prepare a road for the Lord through the wilderness, clear a highway across the desert for our God. Every valley shall be lifted up, every hill and mountain brought low: rugged places shall be made smooth and mountain-ranges be made a plain. Thus shall the glory of the Lord be revealed, and all mankind together shall see it: for the Lord himself hath spoken" (Isaiah, 40:3–5).

A question arises: was not this prophecy implemented, with uncanny precision, by Soviet atheism? Did not atheism actually prepare a road for "the glory of the Lord" by persecuting all beliefs, leveling all mountains and valleys, smoothing out different beliefs so that a trans-confessional spirituality could arise?

* * *

When I wrote the essay "Minimal Religion" in 1982, there was no way to substantiate my observations with sociological data. Now, with the development of democratic procedures in Russia, we have the instruments to statistically test the validity of these theoretical assumptions. A poll conducted in December 1995 by the Center for Sociological Research of Moscow State University, under the direction of S. V. Tumanov shows (from a sampling of 3,710 respondents) that 37.7 percent of the Russian population characterized itself as believers who do not observe religious rituals; only 12.8 percent of the respondents characterized themselves as observant believers. With regard to confessional self-determination, 12.8 percent of the religious population identified themselves as Christians in general (non-denominational), as compared with 71 percent Orthodox, 0.2 percent Catholics, and 0.7 percent Protestants. In addition, 2.7 percent of believers do not perceive any essential difference among denominations, and 2.5 percent have their own perception of God. Based on these statistics we can conclude that approximately 18 percent of the Russian religious population is non-denominational.[52]

Lyudmila Vorontsova and Sergei Filatov cite even more striking statistical data concerning what they call "just Christians" in contemporary Russia:

> The growth of religiosity and the increase in those who believe in God has not been accompanied by a growth in the popularity of Orthodoxy. Indeed, the years 1990–92 saw a sharp fall in its popularity. /…/ Orthodoxy's main competitor is not other religions, but the swiftly growing category of people with no denominational adherence: "just Christians." They grew two and a half times over the three years 1989–92 and in 1992 made up 52 percent of the population, while the number of Orthodox (of all jurisdictions) decreased. /…/ "Just Christians" are the neophytes who believe in God and have come to faith but are not prepared to enter the church unconditionally and to accept church disciplines…. The fact that the number of "just Christians" is growing at the expense of Orthodoxy testifies to the rebirth of Christianity not in the form of Orthodoxy as it was 70 years ago, but on a more modern, universal level.[53]

* * *

The phenomenon of "minimal religiosity" is illuminated by numerous works of Russian literature of the 1970s and 1980s. The literary protagonists of Andrei Bitov, Yuz Aleshkovsky, Yury Trifonov, Vasily Aksyonov, Bella Akhmadulina, and Venedikt Erofeev all crave a higher spirituality. To satisfy this craving, the heroes of this "new" Russian literature cannot turn to traditional forms of religiosity, because for several decades such forms had no common currency in Russian life. The new religiosity, which these fictional characters come to embody, is alienated from all objectified historical traditions.

The autobiographical protagonist of Bitov's story "Birds" [*Ptitsy*] is a typical "poor believer." Caught in a terrible thunder storm, which to him appears to presage the end of the world, he feels the need to pray to the Almighty, but his prayer comes out as "some sort of lowing prayer without words."[54] He is utterly shocked when, under the influence of his fear, he suddenly crosses himself quickly and correctly as he had never done before.

Another "poor believer" of Russian fiction of the 1970s is Venia Erofeev, the autobiographical protagonist of Venedikt Erofeev's novella *Moscow to the End of the Line (*Moskva-Petushki*)*.[55] Venia occasionally turns to God with the plea: "Oh, Lord, you see what I possess. But do I need all *this* ? Is *this* what my soul pines for?"[56] Venia's "Lord" exists outside all traditions and confessions. He has no temple in this world other than the littered train from which the hero's soul addresses itself to Him. The hero also has no church, no preconceived notion of religion, and no other method of proof of God's existence than the "hiccups" that overpower and release him with equal suddenness. "The Law is higher than all of us. Hiccups are higher than the Law.... We are trembling creatures while hiccuping is almighty. It is God's Right Hand, which is raised over us all.... *He* cannot be conceived by the mind, therefore *He* exists. So be perfect as your Heavenly Father is perfect."[57]

The "sixth" proof[58] of God's existence—proof by hiccups—may appear blasphemous or at the very least parodic in relation to canonical theological discourse. However, its main function is not comic or parodic. It acts, instead, as a revelation of the apophatic spirit of "poor" religiosity, which is on a par with the sacrilegious and eccentric behavior of the Russian fools-in-Christ, or "holy fools." The same logic of the negative knowledge of God applies here. Man knows God through things that man cannot control by his will or reason. Hiccups are an elementary example of such a thing: they are a sequence of unwilled bodily movements at unregulated temporal intervals. Using this negative logic, Erofeev can make the assertion, which appears to have come straight out of a treatise on apophatic theology: "*He* [God] cannot be conceived by reason, so consequently *He* is."

The transitional stage between (Marxist) atheism and (Christian) faith is admirably illustrated in Yuz Aleshkovsky's narrative *The Ring in the Case (Persten' v futliare)*, with the characteristic subtitle "A Christmas Novel." This didactic and grotesque narrative portrays the transformation into a "poor believer" of one Helio Revolverovich Serious, a die-hard atheist and "third-generation fighter against bourgeois prejudices," whose efforts to stamp out the belief in God have earned him a position in the upper ranks of the party hierarchy.

Shaken by the disintegration of his relationship with his beloved woman, and reduced to the breaking-point by the misery of his physical and spiritual existence, Helio suddenly experiences the need for prayer, not knowing to whom to address himself or about what to pray:

> "Perhaps I should have another try at praying to … but what can one pray about? That's the question.... About love?… It's too late.... About salvation?…"[59]

The numerous marks of omission are significant. They are a graphic embodiment of his impoverished religious feeling or, to be more specific, the apophatic nature of this religiosity, which cannot use images or words to describe the One, Who …

The hero then resorts to poetry and addresses Him with a line from Pasternak: "O Lord, how perfect are Thy works!"[60] However, he never specifies—neither for himself nor for the reader—whom he actually means when he says "Oh, Lord!" The phrase is pronounced almost like an interjection, a sigh—"Oh, Lord!" But in this case the universal character of the interjection does not signify indifference or automatism. On the contrary, it bears the stamp of a meaning attained through suffering and deeply felt experience. What would seem more natural for this seasoned atheist, erudite in the dialectic of "relativism" ("The Moslems picture him as Allah, while for the Christians he is simultaneously Father, Son and Holy Ghost, which shows that the assumptions of the different religions contradict one another, revealing their complete implausibility …"), than to ask himself: whom am I addressing, *which* God?

And that is precisely the point: twentieth-century atheism used the diversity and historicity of the world's religions and spiritual traditions as its most powerful argument against faith; that is, since there are so many religions, each with its own god, then there is no god. It was atheism that asked all those official, "passportlike" questions, trying to specify to which tradition or confession "god" might appertain: "date of birth," "nationality," "place of residence," and so on. It was a natural reaction on the part of post-atheist religiosity to erase this entire panoply of historical and national "essences" and to make a fresh start by setting up a pure, universal, "poor" and singular name, analagous to the interjection "Oh, God!" or "Oh, Lord!" lacking all specificity and without any determinants whatsoever. Atheism had used the diversity of religions to argue for the relativity of religion. Consequently, the demise of atheism signaled the return to the simplest, virtually empty and infinite form of monotheism and monofideism. If God is One, then faith must be one.

Sooner or later, a minimal believer usually joins a specific religious tradition, becoming an Orthodox Christian, a Baptist, or a Jew. But after having experienced this resonant space of the void, of the wilderness, of the "darkness upon the face of the deep," s/he preserves this new feeling of openness forever. It is there, in a wasteland of spirit, without any preparations, baptisms, and catechisms, that God suddenly grabs hold of him. In most places around the world, people are raised within a specific religious tradition and are brought to a church, a mosque, or a synagogue from childhood. In contemporary Russia, however, many people first experience the spirit in their hearts and then come to houses of worship. There are two different ways of conversion. One is a conversion to God through the church. This is the normal way of "conversion" in the world with established religious traditions. The other is a conversion to the church through God. This was the way of conversion in the times of Moses, Christ, and Luther. It is also the way of conversion in late atheist and post-atheist Russia.

One might speculate that this thrust toward religious reformation will dominate the spirit of twenty-first century Russia. The restoration of pre-atheist traditions is the focus of the current religious revival, but the atheistic past, the experience of the wilderness, cannot pass without a trace, and this trace of "the void" will manifest itself in a striving for a fullness of spirit, transcending the boundaries of historical denominations. Those people who have found God in the wilderness feel that the walls of the existing temples are too narrow for them and should be expanded.

Thus we have seen that three tendencies can be discerned in the misty dawn of Earth's first post-atheist society. One is traditionalism, which is housed in existing churches and subscribes to the existing religious subdivisions. A second is neopaganism, which is focused on archaic objects of worship such as the soil, blood, and national identity. The third is "poor" or "minimal" religion, which is free from historical divisions and seeks the unification of all religions in the gap between existing churches and the fullness of a future Epiphany.

It is significant that Russian religious thought of the early twentieth century, which now serves as a general reference point on all questions of Russian spirituality, furnishes models for all three tendencies. Traditionalism is connected with the figure of the priest Pavel Florensky. Its firm basis is in the philosophically interpreted Church canon and the heritage of the Church Fathers. The second, archaist, tendency is connected with the name of Vasily Rozanov. It is close to paganism and the primal cults of sun and earth, consecrating the universe of sex drives and fecundity. The third, modernist, tendency, inspired by Nikolai Berdiaev, issues from the apophatic conception of pure freedom, which posits itself as anterior to God and the act of creation. It presupposes an ecumenical unification of all religions in anticipation of the future Coming of God and the eschatological end of history.

* * *

While resisting and transcending totalitarianism, the post-atheist tendency of minimal religion nevertheless seeks to create a possibility for a new totality. Though the value of difference is not abandoned, post-atheist spirituality presupposes the value of something that is different from difference itself: some new, tentative, virtual, hypothetical, non-violent form of unity.

The very concept of spirituality seems strange and dated in the postmodern age, requiring theoretical revitalization. By de-emphasizing the category of "spirituality," postmodern theory demonstrates its own limitations and points to the need for a new, broader paradigm of thought. The Russian post-atheist experience is valuable not only because it can be related to certain postmodern theological speculations that undermine the representability of God,[61] but also because it leads beyond the conceptual framework of postmodernism by restoring the meaning of such an "obsolete" category as spirituality.

The notion of "Russian spirituality" evokes, for me, a distinct image, found in the first lines of the Book of Genesis: "The earth was without form and void, and darkness was upon the face of the deep; and the Spirit of God was moving over the face of the waters" (Genesis, 1:2). Essentially, Spirit is named and identified only at the very beginning of the creation of the world. In the subsequent acts of creation, God divides the world into light and darkness, separates water from dry land. But there is no mention of spirit, perhaps because spirit precedes all divisions, sweeps across all boundaries. And this is also true of the Russian mode of spirituality. It is as if this country were once again, through the destruction of all established religious forms and confessions, being thrown back into the atmosphere of the first day of creation. As Nikolai Berdiaev remarked, "[T]here is that in the Russian soul which corresponds to the immensity, the vagueness, the infinitude of the Russian land: spiritual geography corresponds with physical. In the Russian soul there is a sort of immensity, a vagueness, a predilection for the infinite, such as is suggested by the great plain of Russia."[62] Through division, new structures come into existence. But spirit is undivided and indivisible. It is both total and negative. It negates all forms because it moves in the void and in darkness, on "the earth without form."

Spirituality, as it emerges from the ruins of totalitarianism, recognizes the dignity of diverse ethnic and religious traditions but is not satisfied by any single one. Rather it seeks to establish a sacred space across the boundaries of cultures. Through such a phenomenon as minimal religion, Russian culture allows a glimpse of a new, post-postmodern perspective on spirituality, anticipated by its tragic experience of atheism, this "darkness upon the face of the deep."

In "classic" postmodernism, difference is opposed to unity—a unity whose totalitarian claims postmodernism rightly regards with suspicion. But in this rigid form, difference is confined to one dimension, ironically tending to foster relativistic *indifference* toward the various traditions and values. If all things and positions are simply different, there can be no deep mutual involvement among them, since any involvement presupposes at least the creation of a virtual unity. The question is: *what is different from difference itself?*

How can difference be what it is without incessant differentiation precisely from what it is? Multidimensional difference would be the process of *self-differentiation,* giving rise to new, non-violent, non-totalitarian totalities "different from difference," thereby proceeding not from a single will or power, but from the "zero point" or "border line" within diversity. Minimal religion can be regarded as one possible form of these new, non-totalitarian totalities.

Notes

1. The literature covering the problem of the relationship between religion and art is vast, since the aesthetic works of all the major Western thinkers ultimately converge on this problem. This is true of the works of Kant, Hegel, Schelling, Kierkegaard, Nietzsche, Vladimir Soloviev, George Santayana, Ernst Cassirer, Nikolai Berdiaev, Jacques Maritain, Hans Urs von Balthasar, Reinhold Niebuhr, Paul Tillich and many others.
2. For example, Harvey Cox, *The Secular City: A Celebration of Its Liberties and Invitation to Its Discipline* (New York, 1965).
3. *The Freud Reader,* ed. Peter Gay (New York, London, 1989), p. 723.
4. C. G. Jung, "Psychology and Religion," in his *Psychology and Religion: West and East,* 2d ed., trans. R. F. C. Hull (Princeton, 1969), p. 84.
5. Pseudo-Dionysius, "The Mystical Theology," in Pseudo-Dionysius, *The Complete Works,* trans. Colm Luibheid (New York, Mahwah, 1987), 141. The author "Areopagite" wrote in the name of Dionysius Areopagite, an Athenian of the 1st century A.D., converted to Christianity through the ministry of the Apostle Paul.
6. Pseudo-Dionysius, "The Mystical Theology," p. 138.
7. Vladimir Lossky, *The Mystical Theology of the Eastern Church* (Crestwood, N.Y., 1976), p. 26.
8. My observations are based on the reproduction, published by the Irkutsk section of the Soviet Cultural Foundation (VRIB, 1990).
9. Georgy Florovsky, *Ways of Russian Theology* (1937), in Georges Florovsky, *Collected Works* (Belmont, Mass., 1979), vol. 5, p. 1.
10. This is the so-called "Jesus prayer": "Gospodi Iisuse Khriste, syne Bozhii, pomiluj menia, greshnogo" [Lord Jesus Christ, the Son of God, have mercy on me, a sinner].
11. Georgy Florovsky, *Ways of Russian Theology,* p. 27.
12. Freud made an interesting remark on the ease with which repentance comes to the heroes of Dostoyevsky and (as Freud mistakenly thought) to the author himself, who "alternates sin with repentance." "… Repentance became a

technical device, clearing the way to further murders. Ivan the Terrible behaved in similar fashion; this accommodation with one's conscience is a typical Russian feature." Sigmund Freud, "Dostoevskii i ottseubiistvo" [Dostoyevsky and Parricide], *Ia i Ono. Trudy raznykh let* [The Ego and the Id: Works of Different Periods] (Tbilissi, 1991), vol. 1, p. 408. Perhaps the "accommodation with one's conscience" can be understood better if one assumes the following fiendish paradox: by committing sin and giving it externalized shape, I cleanse my soul from it, returning it to God.

13. S. S. Averintsev, "Pseudo-Dionysius Areopagite," in *Filosofskii entsiklopedicheskii slovar'* [Philosophical Encyclopaedic Dictionary], 2d ed. (Moscow, 1989), p. 525.
14. It is of considerable interest to note that Michel Foucault makes a similar paradigmatic connection between the development of what he calls "thought from outside" in Western culture of the early twentieth century and the tradition of "mystical thinking that has prowled the borders of Christianity since the texts of the Pseudo-Dionysus: perhaps it survived for a millennium or so in the various forms of negative theology." Michel Foucault, *Maurice Blanchot: The Thought From Outside,* trans. Brian Massumi (New York, 1987): 16 (Translator's note).
15. Gnoseomachy—struggle against knowledge (compare "theomachy"—struggle against God).
16. Georgy Florovsky, *Puti russkogo bogosloviia* (Paris, 1937), p. 503.
17. Vladimir Lossky, *The Mystical Theology of the Eastern Church,* p. 25.
18. S. L. Frank, *Real'nost' i chelovek: Metafizika chelovecheskogo bytia* [Reality and Man: The Metaphysics of Human Existence] (Paris, 1956), pp. 179, 180.
19. S. L. Frank, *Real'nost' i chelovek,* pp. 82–83.
20. Quoted according to Aldous Huxley, *The Perennial Philosophy* (New York, 1970), p. 24.
21. "The Writings of Kwang-cze" (book XXII), trans. James Legge, in *The Sacred Books of the East,* vol. 40, ed. F. Max Müller (Delhi, 1988), p. 69.
22. *Pseudo-Dionysius,* p. 141.
23. The paradoxes of this apophaticism are dealt with in my book *After the Future: The Paradoxes of Postmodernism and Contemporary Russian Culture* (Amherst, Mass., 1995), in the chapters "Avant-Garde Art and Religion" and "The Origins and Meaning of Russian Postmodernism." Russia's idiosyncratic religious intuition is such that it constantly needs to assimilate the positive, "Western" forms of culture in order to explode them from inside, demonstrating their illusoriness.
24. For specific analyses of the religious unconscious in the literary and artistic works of the Soviet era (Pasternak, Mandel'shtam, Venedikt Erofeev, Ilya Kabakov, the poetry of conceptualism and metarealism), see my book *Vera i obraz. Religioznoe bessoznatel'noe v russkoi kul'ture XX veka* [Faith and Image. The Religious Unconscious in Russian Culture of the Twentieth Century] (Tenafly, N.J., 1994). The present chapter is based on a revised version of the introduction to this book.

25. Karl Barth, "The Word of God and the Word of Man," in *Great Books of the Western World,* ed. Mortimer J. Adler et al., *Encyclopaedia Britannica,* vol. 55 (Chicago, 1990), p. 469.
26. Salvador Dali, *Diary of Genius* (New York, 1965), p. 12.
27. Karl Barth, "The Word of God," p. 469.
28. Similarly, in his story *Moskva-Petushki* (1969) [Moscow to the End of the Line], Venedikt Erofeev compares his hero's partiality to wine with the love of St. Theresa for the stigmata—the signs of Christ's passion and crucifixion on the body of the believer. The reverse sense of this comparison means that the "stout rosé" could be a covert form of martyr-like acceptance of the stigmata by Erofeev's hero. For more on this, see the chapter "Charms of Entropy and New Sentimentality" in this volume.
29. It is amazing that Salvador Dali, raised by his father in the spirit of pure Voltairian atheism, felt religiously inspired when he read Nietzsche for the first time: "... He had had the audacity to affirm: 'God is dead!' What? I had just learned that God did not exist, and now someone informed me that he had died.... Nietzsche, instead of driving me further into atheism, initiated me into the questions and doubts of pre-mystical inspiration, which was to reach its glorious culmination in 1951 when I drew up my *Manifesto.*" [He is here referring to the mystical *Manifesto* that marked Dali's acceptance of Catholic doctrine—ME]. Salvador Dali, *Diary of Genius,* p. 7. Indeed, the very idea of God's suffering and death, in the Nietzschean sense ("God is dead"), contains an unambiguous religious subtext, which is obvious both to Christians and pagans—the worshippers of the cult of Dionysus.
30. Georgy Florovsky, *Puti russkogo bogosloviia,* p. 295.
31. "We should not embellish the godlessness of the world, but we should see it in a new light. Now that the world has grown up, it is more godless, and perhaps for that very reason is closer to God than ever before." Dietrich Bonhoeffer, *Prisoner for God* (New York, 1959), p. 167. What is meant is that man's growing independence from God, and the disappearance of his "childlike" faith in an Almighty, caring presence, strengthens the image and likeness of God in man as a source of mature independence in the world. Only when the child stops "obeying" adults does he become mature. So, too, humanity in the twentieth century has entered its phase of maturity, of "Christianity without religion" or "religion without God."
32. Nikolai Berdiaev, *Novoe srednevekov'e. Razmyshleniia o sud'be Rossii i Evropy* (1924) [The New Middle Ages: Thoughts on the Destiny of Russia and Europe] (Moscow, 1990), p. 25.
33. Nikolai Berdiaev, *Novoe srednevekov'e,* p. 24.
34. Karl Barth, *The Word of God,* p. 471.
35. Ibid., p. 473.
36. The Russian noun *chelovek* refers to both "man" and "woman" in their collectivity as "human being." Here the translation "man" is intended as a gender-neutral term. [Editor]
37. C. G. Jung, "Psychology and Religion," p. 80.

38. Ibid., p. 81.
39. See the chapter "The Tsadik and the Talmudist: A Comparative Essay on Pasternak and Mandel'shtam" in Mikhail Epstein, *Vera i obraz. Religioznoe bessoznatel'noe v russkoi kul'ture XX veka* [Faith and Image. The Religious Unconscious in Russian Culture of the Twentieth Century] (Tenafly, N.J.: Hermitage Publishers, 1994), p. 117ff. English translation: "Judaic Spiritual Traditions in the Poetry of Pasternak and Mandel'shtam," in *Symposium. A Quarterly Journal in Modern Foreign Literatures*. Special Issue on Judaic Literature. *Identity and Distraction* (Winter 1998), vol. 53, No. 2.
40. See the chapters entitled "Avant-garde and Religion" and "As a Corpse I Lay in the Desert," in Mikhail Epstein, *Vera i obraz*, pp. 31–79 and 80–85.
41. Pseudo-Dionysius, *The Complete Works*, pp. 150, 152–153.
42. Ibid., p. 140.
43. See chapter 20 in this volume, "Emptiness as a Technique: Word and Image in Ilya Kabakov." Also in Michael Epstein, "Kabakov" (a fragment), in *Place Displacement Travel Exile, Five Fingers Review* (San Francisco), Special Issue no. 12 (1993): 127–134.
44. Karl Barth, *Der Romerbrief* (Munich, 1922), p. 57.
45. Nikolai Berdiaev, *Novoe srednevekov'e*, pp. 11, 25.
46. In the Russian translation of the New Testament, the word *obraz* is used, which means both "fashion" and "image" (*prokhodit obraz mira sego*).
47. Statistics indicate that about eight million Americans had encounters of one form or another with angels. In the 1990s, the study of angelism has gone beyond the confines of esotericism and has been absorbed into everyday culture. In 1995 and in English alone, more than three hundred books devoted to angels were published.

    I will cite some of the latest popular titles: Matthew Bunson, *Angels A to Z : A Who's Who of the Heavenly Host* (New York, 1996); Alma Daniel, *Ask Your Angels: A Practical Guide to Working with Angels to Enrich Your Life* (London, 1995); Billy Graham, *Angels* (Dallas, 1995); Peter Kreeft, *Angels and Demons: What Do We Really Know About Them?* (San Francisco, 1995); Jennifer Martin, *The Angels Speak: Secrets from the Other Side—Conversations Along the Path* (Sacramento, Cal., 1995); Robert F. Perkins, *Talking to Angels : A Life Spent in High Latitudes* (Boston, Mass., 1996); Michel Serres, *Angels, A Modern Myth* (Paris, 1995); Ambika Wauters, *The Angel Oracle: Working with the Angels for Guidance, Inspiration and Love* (New York, 1995).

    According to a leading NBC television program, broadcast in May 1994 and entitled *Angels—the Mysterious Messengers,* angels have never elicited as much interest at any other time in history.
48. The film was awarded the First Prize for directing at the 40th Cannes Film Festival (1987).
49. I refer, in particular, to René Guénon (1886–1951) and Julius Evola (1898–1974), founders of contemporary traditionalism as a metaphysical system; their views are associated with extreme right-wing politics.
50. See the section "Cultural Manifestos" in this volume.

51. Cited in Sergei Bardin, "Peizazh s sovietologom," in Garif Basyrov, *Grafika. Katalog vystavki* (Moscow, 1991), p. 31.
52. The results of the poll have been publicized on the Internet by the Russian National News Service (at http://www.nns.ru/elects/president/ank109.html and http://www.nns.ru/elects/president/voprosy/vopr2.html).
53. Lyudmila Vorontsova and Sergei Filatov, "Religiosity and Political Consciousness in Postsoviet Russia," *Religion, State and Society*, Keston Institute (England), vol. 22, No. 4 (1994): 401–402.
54. Andrei Bitov, "Ptitsy, ili Novye svedeniia o cheloveke" [Birds, or New Facts on Man] (1971, 1975), in Andrei Bitov, *Chelovek v peizazhe* (Moscow, 1985), p. 247.
55. For a detailed discussion of the Erofeev phenomenon, see chapter 23, "Charms of Entropy and New Sentimentality," in the present book.
56. Venedikt Erofeev, *Moskva-Petushki: Poema* (1969)[Moscow to the End of the Line: A Poem] (Moscow, 1990), p. 25.
57. Ibid., p. 55.
58. In his *Summa theologiae* Thomas Aquinas elaborated five logical proofs of God's existence, which were widely discussed in the subsequent religious-philosophical tradition.
59. Yuz Aleshkovsky, *Persten' v futliare. Rozhdestvenskii roman* [The Ring in the Case: A Christmas Novel], published in the journal *Zvezda* (St. Petersburg), No. 7 (1993): 44.
60. From the poem *V bol'nitse* [In Hospital] (1956). The title of Aleshkovsky's novel is also taken from this Pasternak poem, which ends with lines addressed by the dying hero to God: "You are holding me like an artifact and putting me away like a ring into a case." Boris Pasternak, *Sobranie sochinenii v 5 tomakh* (Moscow, 1989), vol. 2, p. 102.
61. See, for example, *Deconstruction and Theology*, ed. C. Raschke (New York, 1982); J. S. O'Leary, *Questioning Back: The Overcoming of Metaphysics in Christian Tradition* (Minneapolis, 1985); *Theology at the End of the Century: A Dialogue on the Postmodern* (Charlottesville, Va., 1990).
62. Nikolai Berdyaev, *The Russian Idea*, trans. R. M. French (Hudson, N.Y., 1992), p. 20.

Chapter 24

ONIONS AND CABBAGES

Paradigms of Contemporary Culture

Alexander Genis

During World War II, the psychoanalyst Carl Gustav Jung wrote that Germany's tragedy did not come as a surprise to him because he knew what Germans dreamed. We, by contrast, cannot claim to know what Russians dream, despite the opening of an Institute of Dreams and Virtual Reality,[1] in 1991 in Moscow, whose purpose was to collect and analyze the dreams of fellow Russians. Here we shall investigate the domains of art and aesthetics; and art, according to the same Jung, has the capacity to "grasp intuitively the transformations of the collective unconscious." A "tectonic" shift has occurred in the post-communist Russian psyche, revealing a new cultural paradigm and provoking a restratification of values, modes of perception, philosophical strategies, and metaphysical orientations. In trying to make sense of the changes that have taken place in Russian culture and life, we shall consider not only artists and writers, but viewers and readers as well; for the crowd of readers and spectators participates just as much in the formation of a time's "picture of the world" as the artists who produce that picture. It is the crowd that selects works of art which best reflect the views of the times. Thus the book shop also presents a portrait of the epoch.

Soviet Metaphysics

Communism is very much like language, in Ferdinand de Saussure's sense of the term. Like any language it consists of elements set out on two levels of meaning, which are like two floors of a building. The lower level—that of the signifier—is the color of the traffic light. The upper level—that of the signified—is the meaning with which the traffic light endows that color.

Communism was constructed from the end point—from the result end. Historical necessity deprived it of any free choice, without which a future is impossible. History was in essence already accomplished, fulfilled. Arbitrariness, caprice, and chance were mere pseudonyms for our ignorance, products of an incomplete knowledge or a lack of understanding of the cosmic edifice, in which everything was determined by the invincible forces of evolution. For the fatalist a natural death which is not predetermined is an inconceivable abstraction.

The cosmological "vanishing point" of communism was situated not in the past, and not in the future, but in the eternal. Since the *finale* was known in advance, history had a teleological character, while all existential collisions became plots insuring the inevitable resolution.[2] According to this world view, as in a good detective novel, nothing is superfluous. All roads—even the road back—lead to Rome. Given such a paradoxical geography, it was not clear which paths led to and which led away from the ultimate destination.

Communism was thus like a paranoid traffic-signal, obsessed by a persecution complex and hyperreal ideas. Whatever color flashed up on it, it always signified one and the same thing.

It is on this paranoid basis that Soviet metaphysics was erected, allowing the realization of a quotidian and ubiquitous transcendence of things and phenomena. Every step on "earth"—a plowed hectare of soil, or a driven nail, each act of truancy or a mistake at the typewriter, everything—was reflected in "heaven." Life was transformed into a total metaphor, which had no value without its sacred other, concealed in eternity.

This kind of perception of reality is close to that of the Middle Ages: "The notion of a heavenly hierarchy paralyzed the will of the people, obstructed their contact with the edifice of earthly society while leaving intact the heavenly one.... Man writhed in the fangs of the devil, was lost among the beating and palpitations of millions of wings on earth and in heaven, turning human life into a nightmare. The idea of reality was based not merely on the idea of an equivalent reality between heavenly and earthly spheres, but on the idea that together they formed a unity—a confused unity, enticing people into the snares of supernatural life."[3]

In the system of Soviet metaphysics, every word was endowed with a figurative meaning, every gesture was double-coded, every particular fact was incriminating proof. Life unfolded simultaneously in two mutually interdependent dimensions—the sacred and the profane. The eternal permeated the ephemeral, rendering it simultaneously futile and ritually significant. History metamorphosed into *historia sacra,* physics into metaphysics, prose into poetry, philosophy into theology, person into a fictional character, biography into plot, destiny into parable.

In the eschatological coordinates of communism, there was nothing that did not relate to the "End," that is, to the "vanishing point" which invested signs with meaning. Hence in the language of communism, there was only one signified, which had a myriad of signifiers.

In essence, the entire party system, which duplicated the managerial bureaucracy, was engaged in the realization of communist transcendence. It was a quest for the connecting links between any one signifier with the one and only signified. Millions of professional exegetes were involved in the process of reducing life to the common metaphysical denominator, transmuting the hidden into the manifest, the accidental into the logical, the temporal into the timeless, the profane into the sacred, chaos into order.

In the process, the signified itself ceased to have its own meaning. It became the ultimate, irreducible absolute, which had lost its signifying binarism. Since nothing definite could be said about it, it was perceived as a transcendental given, beyond the reach of earthly being and neither requiring nor tolerating any definition.

Certainly, at different times and in different circles, the "absolute" had its names: "communism," "communism with a human face," "truth," "the people," "democracy," "the motherland." What remained important was not the mutual incompatibility of all the various interpretations of the absolute, but the readiness of all of the interpretations to accommodate this absolute. The main thing was the faith in something incommensurate with the individual, something vastly larger than the individual, imparting meaning to words and actions, to life and history.

While communism remained a closed, totalitarian system, it provided both its friends and foes with a metaphysical justification for action, allowing or forcing everyone to take up a position for or against it.

The revelations of the injustices of the totalitarian system did not spell its doom. They merely increased its mythological potential, raising the number of signifiers while the signified remained the same: single, unique, and indescribable.

Empirical reality took shape only after it had been coordinated with the ideal, eternal reality, the parameters of which were prescribed by the ultimate end. As the young philosopher Ivan Dichev has said, "the official report functioned as a substitute for the past, the plan as a substitute for the future."[4] A fact acquired authenticity thanks to its symbiosis with its signified, when it manifested its hidden meaning, which is to say, when it became a metaphor.

Therein lay the essence of Soviet metaphysics: namely, its method of transforming being into metaphor. The only reality acknowledged as being true was the reality "described" in plans and reports, or in novels and poems.

The demiurgic aspirations of socialist realism were sustained by the same metaphysical essence. Socialist realism strove to "inscribe" the world and through this act of writing to substitute itself for it. Socialist realism's dream was to become like the map in one of Borges' stories; a map so complete and so accurate that in the end it substitutes itself for the country it was designed to represent.

Sots-realism, like its corresponding type of agricultural economy, recognized only extensive development. This is why it was engaged in a feverish and never-ending attempt to catch up with life, "writing down" or recording every new manifestation of it. Any "unrecorded" topic or theme was perceived as a rent in the very texture of being.

In this respect, the history of *glasnost* is instructive. Its successes were calculated according to how well the "naked" plots of empirical reality were covered over by a text. The quest for a thematic "virgin soil," which was in itself a particular form of real estate speculation, created a feeling of boom. The inauthenticity of this boom was quickly revealed when the numerous bestsellers of *perestroika,* all with enormous print-runs (such as Victor Astafeev's *The Sad Detective,* Valentin Rasputin's *Fire,* Chingiz Aitmatov's *The Execution Block* and Anatoly Rybakov's *The Children of the Arbat*), sank into the river of oblivion.

It was not the criticism of the Soviet regime that brought about the collapse of Soviet metaphysics: it was the suspension of its prescribed limits, its inability to function outside a closed system. This closed system was guaranteed through censorship. But it was not the concrete manifestations of censorship that mattered as much as the fact of the very existence of the prohibition. Taboos limit mythological space and create the necessary tension between "high" and "low," between immanent and transcendent reality.

No matter how full of holes the boundaries of censorship had become, Soviet metaphysics retained its capacity for self-propagation as long as the boundaries could still be transgressed. The already-mentioned Ivan Dichev thus posed the question, as early as 1990: "What would happen if we were to be told that it is permissible to write about anything? The reality that exists in the books of the most daring of writers would simply evaporate, the hierarchy of values would disintegrate, and mountains of pulp would hang loose in an existential void—which means that even the boldest are not really interested in having the taboos lifted."[5]

It is thus understandable that, propelled by the instinct of self-preservation, Soviet metaphysics endeavored either to ignore the fall of censorship, continuing to expose the fallen regime, or else was compelled to violate other taboos, such as sex, obscenities, violence, and bigotry. It is in this context—i.e., life in an "existential void"—that the ideological transformation and/or rebirth of many former dissidents can be explained.

Perestroika could be compared with the Reformation. The latter left the individual, as Jung said, alone "in a world bereft of symbols." The collapse of communism, leaving the Soviet world without its accumulated symbolic arsenal, led to a loss of its metaphysical paternity. From the depths of the axiological abyss now comes the cry: "In whose name?" This question is found, for instance, in an article by G. Pommerants entitled "From the Cup of Shame," in which the author suggests that the intelligentsia should devote itself to modeling a new universal signified for post-Soviet society. One of its variants would be "Russian culture."[6] This question presupposes that not being able to answer it means that life would not be worth living.

Having lost its signified, the language of communism died. Its signs became one-dimensional and lost their ability to express anything standing behind them. The traffic signal once again went haywire, but this time it was suffering from schizophrenia. In this schizophrenic system, the color red could at any given moment swap its meaning with the color green—which means that the relationship between signifier and signified had become arbitrary.

As an example of such a "schizophrenic" sign system, set up along a single level of signification, the father of modern structuralism, Claude Lévi-Strauss, singled out non-figurative painting. By the same token, one could say that post-Soviet society has migrated from a canvas of the socialist-realist painter Laktionov onto a canvas of Kandinsky.

In literature, such a "schizo-reality" is represented in the works of Vladimir Sorokin. Thus, one of his novels, entitled *The Norm,* deals in its entirety with the world of disintegrated signs. The first part of the novel consists of a series of monotonous sketches of Soviet life in all its banality. In each of these sketches there is a scene that portrays the ingestion of the mysterious "norm," which on closer inspection turns out to be human excrement. Inevitably, the reader falls back on an allegorical simile that is quite natural to

Soviet metaphysics, namely: if excrement is the signifier, and the Soviet regime, figuratively speaking, the signified, then the text consists of the commonplace scatological metaphor: "to survive here, you have to eat shit."

But it is at this point that Sorokin plays a trick on the reader. The metaphor is actualized in such a literal sense that it ceases to be a metaphor: the signifier is the norm, while the signified is the excrement. With the suspension of the subtext in Aesopian language, customary for Soviet literature, the metaphor has simply become a tautology. The subtextual or "actual" meaning thus vanishes from the text.

In other sections of this novel, the same hero, who has forfeited the meaning of a universal signified and been transformed into one among many signs, goes through new adventures. Sorokin insistently uses actualized metaphors, drawn from anthologies of Soviet verse, but here stripped of their figurative, symbolic meaning. For instance, in the chapter entitled "On the March," we have the following deconstruction of metaphor:

> —"At any time and through all the trials, whether we work in deserts or in the tropics, we are building the iron structures of atomic submarines and taking them down into the cruel world of the deep," Golovko, the foreman of the second detachment spoke out.
>
> The warrant officer Riukhov, who was drawing up a draft of the Manifesto of the Communist Party, raised his head:
>
> —"And the ships, storming the miles, are carrying, rocket like, such a charge, that their shock-worker force brooks no distances or obstacles."
>
> Golovko sat down beside him and pulled his [F. Engels's work] "Anti-during" from under his belt:
>
> —"And encircling the entire earth with our strategic orbit, we shall stand up for you, people of the workers planet."
>
> Riukhov turned the page:
>
> —"When the sky is barely visible for days on end and oxygen is scarce, we shall breathe our Native Land."
>
> In the evening, when in all the sectors the traditional sign was lit up: "ATTENTION! OXYGEN SHORTAGE!" the body of the submarine was concentrated on breathing their dear Native Land. Each man pressed the map of his own region to his mouth and was breathing,

> breathing, breathing. Golovko was breathing in the L'vov Region, Karpenko was breathing in the Zhitomir Region, Saiushev was breathing in the Moscow Region.... It was easiest of all for Manuev to breathe: he was born in Yakutsk.[7]

This quoted excerpt does not represent *sots-art* kitsch. Sorokin is not seeking comic effects alone. His texts are not intended as simple parodies of Soviet metaphysics but as investigations of it. He is studying its structure, the mechanisms by virtue of which it functions, testing the limits of its durability.

Another example of this kind of experimental investigation is to be found in a different segment of *The Norm,* written in the style of the Russian classics. In relation to the rest of the text, which is specifically Soviet in style, the "beautiful passage" resurrects the Chekhovian milieu, Turgenevian love, and Bunin's nostalgia. This "beautiful passage" therefore appears to play the role of authentic life, and to represent the normal, natural, and initial state of affairs, deviations from which have lead to the establishment of the nightmarish "norm." However, at this point Sorokin once again intervenes to destroy the illusion he initially created. Unexpectedly, without being in any way motivated, a coarse expletive, in Russian *mat,*[8] is introduced, ripping through the stylized classical text. The apparent whole of the universe of "true discourse" collapses like a punctured balloon in this way.

Consistent to the point of pedantry and inventive to the point of revulsion, Sorokin deconstructs the false signifieds, demonstrating the metaphysical emptiness that remains after the sign's collapse. This emptiness is rendered in the novel either by a page of lines filled with nothing but an endlessly repeated letter "a," or through pages simply left blank. Having guided the reader through the process of exhaustion of the metaphysical foundation of Soviet life, Sorokin leaves the reader alone with such an unbearable semantic emptiness that survival in it no longer seems possible.

The History of Reality

The French philosopher Jean Baudrillard writes that the evolution of the image passed through four stages. In the first stage, the image was akin to a mirror reflecting a surrounding reality. In the second, the image distorted this reality. In the third, the image *masked* the absence of reality. And finally, in the fourth stage, the image has become the *simulacrum*, a copy without an original, which exists in its own right, without any relationship to reality.[9]

The efficacy of this schema can be demonstrated on the material of Russian culture.

The "mirror stage" corresponds to the "honest" realism of the Russian classical canon of the nineteenth century. The image that distorts reality can be ascribed to the Russian avant-garde of Khlebnikov, Malevich or Meierkhold. The image that masks the absence of reality is documented in socialist realist art—an art of phantoms, such as the "socialist competitions" fought between cities or regions or factories for the labor prize and the trophy of the red flag. The art of the simulacrum is practiced by the *sots-artists* V. Komar and A. Melamid. An example of an image imitating non-extant originals is their painting "Stalin with the Muses."

At each stage of this development of the image, the image acquired a greater degree of importance while the importance of reality receded. If at first the image needed nature, in order to copy it, in the end the image dispensed with nature altogether: it "consumed" reality.

This preoccupation with the image as simulacrum is essential to Western pop art. Its brief is to investigate the life of the image severed from its prototype, living its own frighteningly independent life. Thus, in one of Andy Warhol's early works, "Little Peaches," it is not the fruit itself that is represented in the picture: it is the tin can that (presumably) carries them. The difference represented here is the crux of the entire trend: the difference shows that it is not the product that matters, but the packaging; not the essence, but the image.

Pop art brought about not so much an artistic revolution as a revolution in perception. This is indicated, paradoxically, by the historical mistake made by Khrushchev, who failed to notice his true enemy. At the very height of the pop art movement, at the beginning of the 1960s, Khrushchev attacked the harmless abstractionism of the sculptor Ernst Neizvestny and other young artists. But it was not the elitist experiments of the abstractionists that really posed a threat to Soviet metaphysics: it was the new pop art, which ultimately deconstructed its meaning. The lasting significance of pop art can be seen in the fact that, unlike abstract expressionism, which was preoccupied with the individual unconscious, pop art led to an art that explored the social unconscious. Looking anxiously at the world around him, the pop artist strove to understand the messages of a reality consisting of innumerable images of cosmonauts and cowboys, Lenins and Marilyn Monroes, Mao-Tse Tungs and Mickey Mouses.

The problems posed by pop art are in essence ecological. In the process of vanquishing the world around us, we cause not only virginal nature to disappear, but also virginal reality. The primary, fundamental, "raw" reality, not transformed by us, has become victim to the concerted manipulations of culture. A myriad of images, spread by means of mass communication, has polluted the environment, rendering it unusable in its pure form.

Human beings do not control a natural domain that is comparable to the artificial universe of culture. As Yury Lotman writes: "nature is the ideal model of its antipode, construed by culture."[10] Contemporary philosophy has a tendency to regard the world as "a collaboration between reality and social construction. No longer simply what is there, reality is subject to constant revision, deconstruction and reconstruction."[11]

Like the ecological crisis, the crisis of reality, called into being through the development of mass society and the means of mass communication, is a universal crisis. But in Russia this crisis has led to particularly radical change. In Russia, the lack of reality is felt more acutely than in the West. This is not only because the surrogate reality that substitutes for it is lower in quality; it is also because Soviet metaphysics always presented art with the task of portraying/representing an absolutely true, uncompromising, unique, and authentic reality, which Stalin exhorted writers to portray as "the truth." Moreover, it is this same belief in a single, genuine reality that underpins Solzhenitsyn's call to all Russians "not to live a lie."

The strategies of this "truth" differed, certainly. If the servile writers of socialist realism tempered their representation of "nature" with the Platonic idea of nature, the oppositional writers "debunked" that same idea, which they extrapolated from "nature." Both mathematical operations led to the same result: "nature" ceased to be itself and became a metaphor. Whatever the explicit content of such art—whether it be enlightened workers or repressions—its underlying meaning always stood for something else.

Attempts to break away from this model by introducing new themes led only to the model's expansion. Soviet art, swallowing up anti-Soviet art, swelled up as if treated with yeast, causing it to fill all of space. The only way out of this impasse was through another dimension: chaos.

Communism was obsessed with order. It saw itself as the force of regulated being, progressively carving an archipelago of order out of the sea of chaos.[12] Communism's cosmology was based on a teleological concept of the universe in which nothing elemental or accidental would remain by the time its "zero point" was reached. In his manifesto article *Proletarian Culture*, the young Andrei Platonov wrote:

> We view history as a path from the abstract to the concrete, from abstraction to reality, from metaphysics to physics, from chaos to organization.... We used to know only a world created in our mind.... We are stamping out our dreams and substituting them with reality.... If we were to remain in the world of childlike enchantment, playing with our feelings and imagination, if we were to engage endlessly in so-called artistic endeavors, we would all come to grief.[13]

Since the process of communist construction produced results diametrically opposed to those envisaged, Soviet metaphysics found itself engaged in an energetic cover-up of the widening abyss between theory and practice. The less order there was in life, the more order was demanded in art. This explains communism's growing intolerance of all forms of "unorganized" art—from the destruction of the avant-garde, begun with the infamous anti-Shostakovich article "Muddle Instead of Music," (*Pravda, 28* January 1936), to the intolerance of Khrushchev, who persecuted the abstractionists, and of Brezhnev, who "bulldozed" exhibitions.[14] It is no accident that of all the symbols of Soviet metaphysics, the most enduring was that of "order." While changing and adapting to current circumstances, it is still recognizable in calls for a "regulated market" and "a strong arm." Order, the last utopia of Soviet metaphysics, is opposed by chaos.

The discovery of "chaos" by the exact sciences, comparable in significance to that of the theory of evolution and quantum mechanics, has drawn the social sciences into its orbit of influence. A positive re-evaluation of chaos has given birth to a new picture of the world. In this new picture, in the words of Ilya Prigogine, the Nobel Prize winner for Chemistry in 1977, "order and disorder are not opposites but two things inseparable from one another."[15] Chaos is thus not the antagonist of order, but its partner.

In order to simulate the simplest situation of chaos, it is sufficient, scientists tell us, to attach one pendulum to another. The amplitude of the ordinary pendulum is described by elementary laws of mechanics, but the oscillation graph of the double pendulum is unpredictable.

In art, the creation of a "chaosphere"[16] requires introducing an element of the absurd into the text. This element fulfills the role of the second pendulum, becoming what could be called a generator of unpredictability.

The injection of non-sense into the text transposes the dialogue between text and reader into another language. This other language has similarities with the "rationally graspable and untranslatable" (Lévi-Strauss) language of music. It is precisely this kind of language that is used by rock culture.

In his investigation of the problem of the unpredictable, entitled *Kul'tura i vzryv* (Culture and Explosion), Yury Lotman wrote: "Art enlarges the realm of the unpredictable—the realm of information. Simultaneously, it creates a hypothetical world, experimenting with this space and proclaiming victory over it."[17] Art thus "opens up before the reader a world which is infinite, and a window onto the unpredictable, stretching to the far side of logic and experience." Such an art is capable of "transporting man" from a world of necessity "into a world of freedom." The most promising genre in which this love of freedom can unfold is the genre of science fiction. This is how Lotman describes the phenomenon: "The flux in the best of science fiction writing of the second half of the twentieth century carries us into a world that is so foreign to ordinary experience that any prognoses of technical progress sink in a sea of unpredictability."[18]

It is a fact that the phenomenally popular Strugatsky brothers have been among the few authors to survive the collapse of Soviet literature and the devastation of the Soviet book publishing trade. Would it not be true to say that their survival is due to the fact that they began their careful experiments with chaos already in the heyday of Soviet metaphysics?

Let us begin with a look at their best book, *The Snail on the Slope* (*Ulitka na sklone*). Written in 1965, it consists of two separate texts, which the authorities prevented from being published together. As the authors themselves explained, one part, entitled "The Forest," is the future; the other part, "The Administration," is the present. The idea of the story is that "the future never turns out to be either good or bad. It simply never turns out to be as we expect it."[19]

The separation of the present from the future destroys the causal connection, creating a "chaosphere" renowned for its inventiveness. A special role is played by textual devices for creating chaos, inserted into the text as generators of unpredictability. This is how such a textual chaos machine is set in motion:

> Kim dictated the numbers, while Perets punched them in, pressing the various functions of the calculating machine: multiplication, division, addition, subtraction, square root function. Everything was proceeding as usual.
>
> —"Twelve over ten," said Kim. "Multiply."
>
> —"One zero zero seven," Perets dictated mechanically and then he caught himself and said: "Listen, it's lying, isn't it? It should be one hundred and twenty."
>
> —"... I know, I know," said Kim impatiently. "One zero zero seven," he repeated.
>
> —"And now give me the square root of ten zero seven ..."
>
> —"In a minute," said Perets.[20]

It is obvious that a future extrapolated in the above manner will have nothing in common with the present. The "lying calculator" is the minefield hidden amidst the rigid determinism of Soviet metaphysics. It is not by chance that *The Snail on the Slope* could not be printed in the Soviet Union.

The role of chaos becomes even more explicit in the film *Stalker,* coproduced by the Strugatskys and Andrei Tarkovsky. A long series of rejected scenarios shows that what interested the director exclusively in the story "Roadside Picnic,"[21] which served as the prototype script, was the story's generator of unpredictability—the Zone. Tarkovsky discarded the entire science fiction paraphernalia of the story in order to ban the "logic" of metaphor, through which his film could have slid onto the rails of Soviet metaphysics. In *Stalker,* Tarkovsky thus translated the text of the Strugatskys from the language of allegory into the language of symbol.

The Zone in Tarkovsky's film is a "field of wonders" or Lotman's "realm of unpredictability." Here anything can happen because the Zone is not governed by laws, which we impute to nature.

If the universe of Soviet metaphysics is maximally anthropomorphized, that is, made into the image and likeness of man, Tarkovsky's Zone is totally alien to humans. That is why in the Zone the laws of man-made science do not operate.

Stalker is a film about the dialogue humans conduct with the "other." The language of Soviet metaphysics is unsuitable for this dialogue, because the interlocutors do not share the same signified. They can understand each other only in the language of experience. The mediator between the Zone and Man is Martyshka, the daughter of the Stalker, who carries on this dialogue directly. The Zone, which deprived her of her legs and hence of the means of free movement, gave her instead a telekinetic ability—the ability to move objects in space by the power of thought.

According to Boris Strugatsky, the main problem of working with Tarkovsky was in the disjunction between the cinematographic and literary visions of the world: "Words are literature, they make for a highly symbolic reality,… while cinema is … a completely real, one could even say brutally real world."[22] The "merciless" nature of cinema's realism emanates from, as Tarkovsky noted, its ability to freeze and "fix time, transforming it into a matrix of real time, which is preserved in metal containers for long durations, theoretically forever."[23]

Thus Tarkovsky's cinema deprives Soviet metaphysics of the source of its meanings—its eschatological "zero point."

The semiotician Vyacheslav Ivanov recalls a statement by the director during the filming of *The Mirror,* in which the main role was to have been played by Tarkovsky's mother:

> Out of the material, which in this ideal case comprises an entire life, from birth to death, the director selects and organizes those episodes that disclose the meaning of that life. Among contemporary directors, it was Pasolini who expressed an almost identical thought to Tarkovsky's fundamental conception of cinema. According to Pasolini, montage does the same with the film material as death does with life: it gives it meaning.[24]

Tarkovsky thus executes the process of Pygmalion, but in reverse. He tries to turn Galatea, a live human being—in this case his mother—into a work of art.

At first glance, such a practice would not seem alien to Soviet metaphysics, which demands that living heroes be transformed into artistic images. But the fundamental difference is that what was valued in the Soviet hero's prototype was not the individual but the typical. A human subject could become a fictional character only after having been generalized into a type: once transformed, for instance, from the real MAres'ev into a metaphoric MEres'ev.[25] A typical character in fiction is the very image of the "coordinated," "organized" personality, pulled out of the dark chaos of life and immersed in the lifeless world of art.

Tarkovsky needed a real human subject, not a typical one (in the same way that he needed a live cow for the filming of *Andrei Rublev*, a cow he allegedly burnt alive). This unrepeatable human subject, written with a small "h," was a unit in that alphabet whose language Tarkovsky used to converse with the "other."

This conception of life overflowing into art has been actively appropriated by Hollywood, where what is of greatest value is not fictitious scripts but actual human destinies. What is valued is the unrepeatability of the individual, whose living personality is a guarantee against the possible transformation of biography into the subject of fiction.

The logic of an artificial order kills the living thing, transforming it into an image. But in art, which operates with the "chaosphere" that each one of us carries within his- or herself, the living matter turned into an image does not forfeit its live potential. Looking at it through Baudrillard's model, one could say that the image reaches the fifth tier of evolution. Here the image enters a new, one could say mystical, relationship with reality. In search of realism, the image constructs a "hyperreality"—a form of art which does not imitate but produces reality.

Onions and Cabbages

Communism is the inverse of the religion of revelation. Its sinless Eden or classless Golden Age is not the initial but the final state of the world. However, this reorientation of the sacred "arrow of time" does not obviate the conception of a truth hidden under the rubble of darkness, unmitigated by the light of consciousness.

Soviet metaphysics in its entirety consists of an endless quest for true words and motifs, a perpetual act of unmasking. The maniacal suspiciousness of communism comes from a lack of trust in a life not informed by deliberate intention and adumbrated by a predetermined plan. Its inquisitorial spirit is directed at disclosing to the human being the true meaning of that being's destiny. Confession was thus considered the "queen of proof," since the criterion of guilt was hidden in the soul of the accused.

Despite all this, the procedure of spiritual interrogation does fit the old cultural paradigm. Within the parameters of the latter, the torture chamber can be seen as a version of Plato's cave, in which the quest for an authentic reality was carried out by the method of trial and error.

Soviet metaphysics shared with its cultural predecessors the notion of a reservoir of sense or meanings, constituting in its totality an ideal harmony. The recreation of this harmony was thought to be the aim of the artist. The artist did not create but *revealed* the truth existing in eternity. Mikhail Bulgakov's dialectics—"manuscripts don't burn" since only faded and inauthentic copies can burn—is a temporal version of an ineradicable invariant diluted throughout the universe. The creative act is the return of the temporal to the sphere of the eternal.

Such a system of beliefs could be called the "cabbage paradigm." Peeling off one leaf after another of false being, we reach the "core" of meaning. The movement of the spirit in this instance is centripetal. The vector of its movement is aimed at the depths of reality, toward its sacred core, which contains the central revelation of the entire cultural model. In relation to this sacred core, all other layers of reality are in principle superfluous; they only obstruct the penetration to the meaning-forming center.

A classic example of the cabbage paradigm is Tolstoy's story *The Death of Ivan Ilyich.* In it, Tolstoy exposes "normal" life, composed of career, family, and milieu, as inauthentic and without truth, a life spoiled by the hypocrisy of civilization. Only death opens man's eyes, forcing him to answer the most important, ultimate, and only question, from which there is no hiding behind the "screens" of culture:

> What was worst of all was that she distracted him, not so he would do anything but just so he would look straight in her eyes, look at her, and without doing anything, torture himself inexpressibly. In an effort to save himself from this condition, Ivan Ily'ich sought consolation, other screens, and these other screens for a brief time seemed to be saving him, but again, all of a sudden, they were not so much destroyed as shone though, as if she had penetrated everything and nothing could block her out.[26]

In this excerpt from Tolstoy's novella, we find the essence of the centripetal philosophy. If everything in life is a screen, why should one strive, why should one acquire a household, furniture, curtains—all of which destroys Ivan Ilyich? And where do all these curtains, all this "material" of life come from? Why work, accumulate, build, create? Why have culture, why have the cunningly constructed machine of civilization? "There is no purpose in it," is Tolstoy's answer, calling on the world to embrace simplicity as a principle of life. Having thus freed the human subject from the constraints of deceit, Tolstoy locates this subject in the unique "moment of truth," in which the authentic and natural reality, a reality "beyond the signifier," is no longer covered up by the life-saving "screens" of culture. This is the moment at which the human being finds himself face to face with death.

The same method of reaching an apophatic proximity to the sacred center was used by revolutionary art, although to a different purpose. The peeling off of leaves in search of the core was the structural formula of such famous avant-garde works as Mayakovsky's *A Cloud in Trousers* or Ilya Ehrenburg's *The Extraordinary Adventures of Julio Jurenito.*

Beginning with another of Ehrenburg's works, *The Thaw*, art begins to beat a path to the center, this time through the "leaves" of another culture. The liberal and oppositional literature of the 1960s, which "unmasked," and was published mainly in the journal *Novy mir* during the editorship of Alexander Tvardovsky, fit entirely into the "cabbage paradigm." The search for "truth" was the standard theme in all major works of this period. The word "truth" itself was a key word in both the literary and political struggle of the 1960s. Practically all major writers of the time described their path, in one form or another and with different aims, to a true socialism, unspoiled by Stalinism. The central thesis of the 1960s' doctrine was the purification of the foundation of the Soviet regime. This doctrine, in turn, played a crucial role in the ideology of perestroika, effectively ending only with the Gorbachev era.[27]

Here, in the 1990s, the metaphor of the cabbage is coming to the end of its paradigmatic significance. In its place we may draw on a new metaphor, signaling the emergence of a new cultural paradigm, born of the emptiness or *nothingness* that was perceived as fatal to the earlier paradigm.

Roland Barthes spoke of a pie without filling. We would like to supplement our image of the cabbage with the metaphor of the cored onion. In the paradigm of the onion, the emptiness at the center is not a cemetery but a source of meaning. This is the cosmic zero point, around which being germinates. This emptiness, which is both everything and nothing, is the focus of the world. The world is made possible only because of the emptiness at its center. It structures being, bestows form on things, and allows things to function.

It is this "creative emptiness" that is the basis of the canon of Lao-tse, the first philosopher of Chinese Taoism:

> Three scores of spokes converge in one wheel; the useful application of the wheel depends on the emptiness of the same. In moulding clay, a vessel is formed; its useful application depends on its emptiness. In cutting doors and windows, a house is built; the use of the house depends on this emptiness. For profit depends on availability, while useful application depends on emptiness.[28]

This seemingly exotic quotation is by no means arbitrary. The "onion paradigm" has much in common with the motifs of *Tao-te Ching.*[29] In fact, in the central monologue of *Stalker* there is a quotation from the seventy-sixth paragraph of Lao-tse's *Tao-te Ching* (The Way and Its Power):[30]

> When man is born, he is weak and supple; when he is dying, he is strong and rigid. When a tree is growing, it is tender and supple, but when it is dry and rigid, it is dying. Rigidity and stress are the companions of death; suppleness and weakness are the expression of the freshness of being.[31]

This litany on weakness is opposed to the willful impulse that determines the "cabbage paradigm." If the path to the sacred core is the path of destruction of the exterior, "inauthentic" layers of being, then the commandment of the *yurodivy*—of the blessed holy fool or the stalker, with his quiescent hopefulness—is completely in keeping with Lao-tse's teaching. For the stalker, the thought of destroying the existing world for the sake of a new one is completely alien, since the new itself is born out of the old. One must only refrain from obstructing its growth.

If in the "cabbage paradigm" chaos is on the outside while order is on the inside, in the "onion paradigm" chaos is the seed of the world, the "creative nothingness" of Prigogine, from which cosmos is born. The movement in the paradigm of chaos is thus not centripetal but centrifugal, directed outward. Consequently, meanings are not revealed, they are nurtured into growth, cultivated. For Tarkovsky, the value of weakness is in the fact that weakness is the hallmark, the sign of growth and the companion of change. In the "onion paradigm," vulnerability and even poverty of spirit are starting points, the essential prerequisites, the reserve of growth.

This dialectic of weakness has given rise to an entire pleiad of "meek" writers, among whom Venedikt Erofeev must be given patriarchal status. Erofeev's "weakness," represented by Vennya (Venichka), his angelic state of constant drunkenness, acts as the promise of a transformed world. In the poetic novel *Moscow Circles (Moskva-Petukhi)* alcoholism performs the function of the "generator of unpredictability." Getting drunk is the path to freedom, to becoming literally "not of this world." Here again, a parallel with Taoist writings forces itself on us: "A drunken man, who falls off a cart, even if he falls hard, will not be fatally injured. He has the same bones and body structure as others, but his injuries are different because his soul is whole. The drunk got into the cart unconsciously and fell out of it unconsciously."[32]

Vodka in Erofeev's poem-in-prose is the midwife of the new reality, going through its birth pangs in the soul of the hero. Every gulp makes the "rigid," ossified structures of the world grow a little younger, returning the world to a heterogeneity that is the opposite of the univocality or identity of signifier and signified. This heterogeneity is the protean amorphousness of chaos—a chaos that is pregnant with meaning, in which things and phenomena exist only *in potentio.*

The main structuring principle of Erofeev's poem-in-prose is the never-ending flow of free-indirect speech—a stream of consciousness free of the constraints of logic and causal connectedness. It is speech freed from the responsibility of meaning. The hero, Venichka, calls chance correspondences out of non-being, which are like unpredictable hiccups. Everything in this speech rhymes with everything else: a prayer rhymes with newspaper headlines, the names of boozers with the surnames of writers, poetic quotations with four-letter words. There is not a word uttered in the narrative that is *simply said.* Each line seethes with an incredible verbal power, engendered by the alcoholic state of the hero. The drunken hero dives headlong into this verbal "primal matter," admitting jokingly to the reader: "Like a phenomenon, I am endowed with a self-propagating *logos.*"

Venichka's *logos,* which is total knowledge and which includes analysis and intuition, reason and feeling, is self-propagating because Venichka sows words like seeds, from which meanings sprout. But the hero is only the sower. The readers are the reapers, who gather the harvest. Through the act of reading, the readers "realize" the poem, which otherwise exists only in the sphere of the potential.

Weakness as a cultural category is reflected in various ways in the works of very different writers on the contemporary Russian literary scene. Despite their diversity, however, all these works share a fundamental characteristic: that of a demonstrative infantilism, raised to the level of a conscious narrative point of view. It is this self-consciousness and demonstrativeness that distinguish it from the very specific "childishness" of socialist realism, which categorically refused to acknowledge it, sincerely believing itself to be a mature and "adult" art. On becoming a child, the writer of the "meek pleiade" escapes from a hopelessly closed adult world into an intermediate, adolescent state, where there is hope of growing up, acquiring meaning and growing a "metaphysical skin."

One of the most characteristic writers of this trend is Eduard Limonov, whose novels are confessions of a failure, blabberings of a child who has failed to grow up. The parameters of the poetics of Limonov's prose can be delimited by the following two excerpts, the first from *A Failure's Dairy,* the second from *This is Me, Edichka :* "Everyone I encountered had grown bigger than me"; and "I did not betray my dear ... childhood. All children are extremists. I, too, have remained an extremist, and have not become an adult."

The same category of weakness was used in a very different way by another Russian writer, Sergei Dovlatov. The secret of Dovlatov's enormous albeit posthumous success in Russia must be sought in the authorial persona of "Dovlatov," who is also the hero of Dovlatov's best works—*The Compromise (Kompromiss), The Reservation (Zapovednik), The Performance (Predstavlenie).* Both the writer Dovlatov and the fictional character "Dovlatov" consciously adopt a winning position: they describe a world that is abysmally imperfect, but they perceive it through the eyes of a fictional persona who is morally underdeveloped and imperfect to the same abysmal degree.

Dovlatov's hero is, in fact, not a hero at all. He is too weak to stand out from the degenerate world of vice, but too humane not to forgive the world—and himself—for its (his) sins. Dovlatov cannot teach the reader anything. He is neither better nor worse than the reader. But the reader, in turn, is grateful to the author who invites him to share in the sentiment of meekness, which is free from vanity.

In Dovlatov's notebooks, we find the following formula: "The narrator describes how people live. Prose writers describe how people should live. Prose writers describe the reason why people live."[33]

While Dovlatov took a most modest role for himself, his self-abasement was worse than pride. What it conceals is a secret rebellion against the literature of ideas, against the metaphysical subtext, against depth in general. Dovlatov was used to gliding on the surface of life, accepting life's manifestations with gratitude and a trust born of love. To be able to see everything, to be able to understand everything, to disagree about everything, not to try to change anything—this is a philosophy of life the Russian reader had not encountered before. That is perhaps why readers respond with such warm attachment to Dovlatov—he makes no demands on them. The most enchanting facet of Dovlatov is the unassuming nature of his revelations. The main thing he reveals is the fact that in a world that appears superfluous to itself, there is room only for a superfluous hero.

The theme of weakness is treated extensively by a genius of abjection: the capricious and hypersensitive Dmitry Galkovsky. The driving force of his enormous but only partly published novel, *The Endless Impasse (Beskonechnyi tupik)*,[34] is the feeling of fear of and animosity toward the "adult" world of the strong and the "real." His book is structured like an adolescent fantasy, driven by the narrator's desire for revenge against his detractors.

Viktor Pelevin, another representative of the new Russian literature, also takes up the theme of weakness. Pelevin re-evaluates power as weakness. In his novella, *Omon Ra,* Pelevin negates the fundamental antithesis of totalitarian society: the conflict between a weak individual and a strong state. In Pelevin's story, which is dedicated to the "heroes of the Soviet cosmos," there are no strong characters. The regime of a mighty "evil empire" has been reduced to the image of an impotent man, whose power is only simulated. This simulation is portrayed through comic details, such as a space-suit for the Moon expedition made from a sailor's pea-jacket and motorcycle goggles. Instead of a lunar module ("Lunohod"—the proud Soviet answer to the American Apollo), Pelevin's cosmonauts use a remodeled bicycle.

Pelevin does not use the demonstration of weakness for purposes of satirical portrayal or exposure of social ills: his aims are strictly metaphysical. Communism set out to transform consciousness. It is within the realm of the mind that communism's victories are achieved. These victories are theoretically possible as long as there remains even a single "pure soul" to colonize:

> As long as there is one soul in which our cause lives and achieves victory, this cause will not fail. For an entire universe will exist.... One pure and honest soul is enough for our country to emerge as the leader in the race for the cosmos. One such soul is enough to insure that the Red Flag will be unfurled on distant Moon, signaling the victory of socialism. But one such soul is necessary—even if only for one instant—because it is in this soul that the flag will be unfurled.[35]

Having exposed the weakness of the—as it were—almighty totalitarian regime, Pelevin tries to incorporate its heritage with new aims. In the "onion paradigm," a great deal of attention is paid to the communist experiment in the reclamation or colonization of the "space of the soul." This thesis is developed by Pelevin in the following manner:

> The Soviet world was so patently absurd and premeditatedly ugly that even a patient in a psychiatric clinic could not take it for an ultimate reality. This is how it happened that the inhabitants of Russia—and not necessarily its intelligentsia—automatically and without deliberate design or collusion, developed a superfluous, dysfunctional level of the psyche, which constituted an additional space of self-consciousness, one that is given to only a few in a normally developed society.
>
> The "sovok" (Soviet man) eked out his existence far removed from a normal life; instead, he was close to God, whose presence he failed to notice. Living on a rubbish-heap which was close to Eden, these "sovki" (the homo sovieticus) kept their newly opened spiritual eyes moist with "Caucasus" port.[36]

The metaphor of the "superfluous layer" of the psyche is of paradigmatic significance for the centrifugal cultural model, which does not seek out the hidden essence of the world, but constructs meanings in a special "superstructure" of reality, especially constructed for that purpose. In Russia, the collapse of communism freed this "additional layer" of the psyche, which the "onion paradigm" is hastening to appropriate.

Turning once again to the evidence of the book market, we find that it offers the missing components of the "onion paradigm": these are constituted by the currently popular works of two mystics, the Russian Peter Uspensky and the American Carlos Castaneda. Such taste can perhaps be explained by the fact that the teachings of these two writers intersect at a single point of departure—the point at which reality is viewed as interpretation.

In the introduction to his *Journey to Ixtlan,* Castaneda writes:

> Don Juan tried to convince me that the surrounding world was nothing more than a description of the world around me, which I perceived as the sole possible one because it had been foisted on me since infancy ...
>
> The main thing in Don Juan's magic is the awareness of our reality as one of the many possible descriptions of it.[37]

The same thought appears in the writings of Uspensky. His complex mystico-mathematical constructions are based on the idea that we perceive the world by imposing on it "the conditions of temporality and space:"

> Consequently, the world before we perceive it has no extension in space or existence in time. These are qualities we give it. Ideas of space and time arise in our mind ... space and time are categories of reason, that is, qualities we ascribe to the outside world. They are only landmarks, signs we place ourselves. They are graphs on which we plot the world.[38]

Consequently, if we change our conception of time and space, the nature of reality will also change. This is what Uspensky is leading up to when he calls on us to learn to perceive the "unbroken and continuous nature of reality."

This important preamble furnishes a radical conclusion to the culture of the "onion paradigm": reality is the consequence of the manipulation of time and space. The forms of perception of these, however, differ in various cultures and in different epochs. The models of time and space are discovered, developed, and invented by spiritual culture. Today this privilege is practically being usurped by art.

In the "cabbage paradigm," art was an instrument for cognizing reality, a reality that art itself was supposed to discover. In the "onion paradigm," art is a form of magic. It is a mechanism for the production of reality. We all live in the world invented by it.

Chronotope of a Mirage

The differences between the two paradigms stem from the difference in their relationship to space and time. In the cabbage paradigm, time played the main role. Communism, armed with the belief in the historical inevitability of evolution, believed that time was its ally. However, since in its eschatological model history had a beginning and an end, communism hurried to live out its time as quickly as possible. Since time was perceived as finite, it could run out just like the sands in an hourglass. The smaller the quantity of sand remaining in the top part of the hourglass, the quicker the end of history and the sooner the advent of eternity. The eternal race—*Time Forward* (the title of Valentin Kataev's paradigmatic socialist realist novel of 1932)—was motivated by the belief that any retardation—from a momentary stop to stagnation—was a betrayal of the future. Everyone wanted to speed up time—from Mayakovsky, promising to "ride to death the old mare of history," to Gorbachev, who began perestroika with a call for "acceleration." In order to make time march faster, it was made even more compact, packed into five-year plans.

If time was at a premium in the cabbage paradigm, there was a neutral feeling toward space. Space was semantically unmarked, homogeneous, and equivalent in each of its parts. The spirit of equality, which determined this attitude to space, was expressed not only in the words of the song "My address is not a house or a street, my address is the Soviet Union," but also in the title of a volume of Brodsky's poetry: *A Halt in the Wilderness.*

Space was the primary raw material, a storehouse destined for further processing, populated by things that would give it meaning. Space thus received no special treatment. On the contrary, space was that "wild" expanse of chaos and emptiness, eroding the dense, "enculturated" reality.

The first determining feature of the onion paradigm was a new attitude to time. Instead of an hourglass, the dominant symbol of this paradigm became the clock face with two hands. Linear time, running from past to future, gave way to cyclical time, in which the present is unceasingly produced. Since the end-point disappeared, the scale also changed; from a macrocosm, in which time was measured in historical epochs and economic formations, to a microcosm, measured in seconds. It became important not to live time, but to lengthen it by means of an ever finer segmentation of its structure. Pure duration gave way to "swelling" moments, growing on the tree of "today" like rings on a tree trunk.

In the onion paradigm, the attitude to space is similar to that of time: it too is structured, divided into increasingly smaller fragments. Instead of the image of a simple, spread out sheet, the new paradigm envisages a patchwork quilt. By isolating and domesticating one's own little "patch," a proliferation of borders is created.

In the cabbage paradigm, there was a single border—the state's. Fulfilling a universal function, this border determined the full range of meanings—from political to metaphysical. Elucidating the structuring of such "semiospheres," Lotman writes that "the evaluation of the inner or outer space is not a given. What is significant is the fact of the existence of the borders themselves."[39]

In the onion paradigm, the border changes its meaning. What is of importance is not only what is taking place on this or that side of the border; the border itself has a signifying value. The border is coeval with the very concept of *difference*—the border is the *limit*, which is being constantly crossed and re-crossed in an everchanging constellation of pure differences—national, regional, religious, political, cultural, artistic.

The greater the number of borders, the wider the frontier area. But this fragmentation of space does not lead to isolation; on the contrary, it brings about an intensification of contacts, since the essence of the border is that it must be crossed and re-crossed. The world thus draws closer to itself while at the same time operating on the principle of difference.

If *difference* was considered to be an obstacle on the road to a universal common aim according to the cabbage paradigm, in the onion paradigm difference becomes the object of and the basis for profound reflection. Everything of significance—that is, everything that can *signify,* have meaning, be perceived consciously—takes place on the borders between countries and peoples, between science and religion, art and life, nature and culture, man and woman, consciousness and the unconscious. That is to say, meaning is situated on the border between different realities.

Since reality according to the onion paradigm has an artificial origin, there is nothing to obstruct its "production" according to the elaborate schemes worked out in art. Consequently, there will be many realities produced and all of these will vie for supremacy, for influence, for the conquest of souls and for the occupation of those "empty levels" of the mind. In the era of mass communication, this struggle for supremacy will be carried out through the mass media. It is, in fact, going on already. It was not by accident that blood was spilled at the television headquarters in Bucharest, Vilnius, and Moscow during the political upheavals of the late 1980s and early 1990s. Wars are won not with rifles but with images, this at any rate since images have learned to create instead of to reflect reality.

Within the parameters of the cabbage paradigm, it is difficult to come to terms with this new, televised form of reality construction. In the old days it was assumed that television was a "window on the world" and that its function was thoroughly mimetic. Now the television image is as pliable as clay. One can fashion anything at all out of it and reality will follow obediently behind …

Who knows whether the twenty-first century will like living in a world in which reality is a plural noun, a world where mirages cannot be distinguished from reality, a world whose survival will depend on its ability to reinvent itself.

Notes

1. See "Son—semioticheskoe okno' [Dream as a Semiotic Window], *XXVI—e Vipperovskie chteniia* [XXVI-th Vipperovskie Readings] (Moscow, 1993).
2. *This type of consciousness can be called a quasi-religious consciousness.* An example of this type of consciousness can be seen in the following description: "The religious feeling consists in the perception that behind the manifestations of the visible world, man tries to divine the reality of another, higher order. The world appears as the arena of action of mysterious, deeply hidden, incredibly powerful forces." Dm. Bykov, *I'Personazhi v poiskakh avtora. K tipologii soviet-skoi religioznosti." Literaturnaia gazeta, 17 fevralia* (1993).
3. Zh. Le Gof, *Tsivilisatsia srednevekovogo zapada* (Moscow, 1920), p. 155.
4. I. Dichev, "Shest' razmyshlenii o postmodernizme, in *Poznanie v sotziokul'-turnom izmerenii* (Moscow, 1990), p. 36.
5. Ibid., p. 37.
6. G. Pomerants, "From the Cup of Shame," *Segodnia,* 15 April 1994.
7. V. Sorokin, *Norma* (Moscow, 1994), p. 239.
8. Coarse slang.
9. J. Baudrillard, *Simulations* (New York, 1983), p. 11.
10. Iu. Lotman, *Izbrannye stat'i v 3-kh tt,* vol. 1 (Tallinn, 1993), p. 9.
11. N. E. Hayles, "Complex Dynamics in Literature and Science," in *Chaos and Order* (Chicago, 1991), p. 14.
12. In her book *The Soviet Novel,* the American Slavist K. Clark speaks of the conflict between "spontaneity/stixijnost" and "consciousness/soznatellnost'" as basic to all socialist-realist art. K. Clark, *The Soviet Novel: History As Ritual,* 2d ed. (Chicago and London, 1985), pp. 15–24.
13. A. Platonov, *Proletarskaia poezia,* in *Sobranie sochinenii v 3-kh tt.* vol. 3 (Moscow, 1985), p. 523.
14. What is referred to here is a public exhibition at Izmailovsky Park in Moscow on 19 September 1974, which frenzied the authorities and led to such excesses as the calling of bulldozers to crush this open-air exhibition. See I. Golomshtok and A. Glezer, *Soviet Art in Exile* (New York, 1977).
15. I. Prigogine, "Pereotkrytie vremeni" [The Re-Discovery of Time], *Voprosy filosofii* 8 (1989): 9.
16. The term "chaosphere" has been proposed by J. Istvan Csicsery-Ronay in "Modeling the Chaosphere" in *Chaos and Order* (Chicago, 1991), pp. 244–263.
17. Yu. Lotman, *Kul'tura i vzryv* (Moscow, 1992), p. 189.
18. Ibid.
19. A. and B. Strugatsky, in "Prognoz: Beseda A. Bossart s brat'iami Strugatskimi," *Ogonek* 52 (1989): 20.
20. A. and B. Strugatsky, *Ulitka na sklone* (Frankfurt, 1972), p. 21. [We are not using the English translation by Alan Meyers, *The Snail on the Slope* (New York, 1980)].
21. In English: A. and B. Strugatsky, *Roadside Picnic—Tale of the Troika* (New York, 1976).

22. A. and B. Strugatsky, *Stsenarii* (Moscow, 1993), p. 345.
23. *Mir i fil'm, Andreiai Tarkovskogo. Razmyshleniia i issledovaniia* (Moscow, 1991), p. 200.
24. Vyacheslav Ivanov, *Vremia i veshchi*, p. 233.
25. Leo Tolstoy, *Sobranie sochinenii* v *14. tomakh,* vol. 10 (Moscow, 1952), p. 302.
26. Ibid.
27. See Petr Vail' and Alexander Genis, *Shestidesiatye: mir sovestkogo cheloveka* (Ann Arbor, Mich., 1989), pp. 139–155.
28. Lao-tse, *Tao-te Ching, Kniga puti i blagodati* [Classic of the Way of Power], chap. 11. Quoted after *Iz knig mudretsov. Proza drevnego Kitaia* (Moscow, 1987), p. 73.
29. *Tao-te Ching* is the only extant book of Lao-tse, the founder of Taoism, who lived in the sixth century B.C.
30. The best English translation is Arthur Waley, *The Way and Its Power* (1968).
31. *The Stalker.* Soundtrack of the film. Quoted from A. and B. Strugatsky *Stsenarii* (Moscow, 1993), p. 361.
32. Yang Chu (c. 400 B.C.E.), *The Book of Lieh-tzu.* Quoted from *Ateisty, materialisty, dialekteki drevnogo Kitaia* (Moscow, 1967), pp. 54–55.
33. S. Dovlatov, *Sobranie sochineniii v 3-kh tt,* vol. 3 (St. Petersburg, 1993).
34. Dmitry Galkovsky, *Beskonechnyi tupik, Novy mir,* no. 9, 11 (1992), also *Nash sovremennik,* no. 1–2 (1992).
35. V. Pelevin, *Omon Ra, Znamia,* no. 5 (1992): 62. Pelevin's collection of stories *Sinii fonar'* [The Blue Light], which received the small Booker Prize for 1993, has appeared in English in *Glas: New Russian Writing,* no. 4 (1993).
36. V. Pelevin, *Dzon Faulz i tragediia russkogo liberalizma', Nezavisimaia gazeta, 10* January 1993.
37. C. Castaneda [K. Kastaneda], *Puteshestvie v Ikstlan* (Riga, 1991), p. 4.
38. Peter Uspensky, *Tertium Organum,* reprint (St. Petersburg, 1992), p. 4 [Original edition: St. Petersburg, 1911].
39. Iu. Lotman, *Izbrannye stat'i v 3-kh tt.,* vol. 1 (Tallinn, 1993).

Chapter 25

CHARMS OF ENTROPY AND NEW SENTIMENTALITY

The Myth of Venedikt Erofeev

Mikhail Epstein

What is the end of a century? A calendar date, a historic landmark, a sum of accomplishments, the wisdom of experience? If we agree with Andrei Bely's penetrating pun, namely that "[T]he individual is the face of the century" (*chelovek—chelo veka*), then the end of the century is the image of the people who have brought it to its end, who personify this end. The face of the waning nineteenth century was seen in Friedrich Nietzsche and Vladimir Soloviev, who embodied the quintessence of their times and offered parting words and warnings to the coming century. Many ideas and judgements sum up the nineteenth century, but who can now remember them? What we remember are not so much the words of memorable individuals as the facial expression, the gestures, and intonations that marked their destiny.

While destroying old mythologies, history is constantly creating new myths to personify its fundamental ideas. There are great myths and small myths, universal myths and local myths, metropolitan and provincial ones. Yet even in the small myths the wholeness of the human character is such that not a single feature can be removed from this character without violating the overarching idea embodied in it. Such an embodied idea cannot be expressed abstractly, even if one were to try to do so in a hundred treatises, but can be observed in a contemporary, whom posterity rushes to include in "the category of young legends."[1]

In order to comprehend the fundamental idea structuring an epoch, we must look that epoch straight in the face. And we might well ask: whose face is it that holds our gaze at the close of the twentieth century? Who are the individuals, among the dead, who have fed its myths? For we shall say nothing about the living—their history is still ahead of them.

1. The Prerequisites of Myth Formation

According to contemporary scholarship, any myth represents an attempt to resolve contradictions, to mediate or reconcile extremes, to make ends meet.[2] There can be no longer any doubt that Venedikt Erofeev (1938—1990), author of the "prose poem" *Moscow to the End of the Line* (1969), has become just such a myth.[3] Indeed he is perhaps the last literary myth of the Soviet epoch, which itself came to a sudden end shortly after the death of the writer. The question we may ask in relation to this myth is: What riddle does Erofeeev solve? What extremes does he reconcile?

Russian literature abounds in myths, insofar as the social imagination is constituted almost exclusively by literature and its derivatives. The mythic significance of a writer, however, does not always correspond to his/her literary merit. Dostoevsky failed to become a myth, while Nadson became one, as well as Esenin. On the other hand, Pushkin did become one, while Griboyedov did not. What conditions are required for a writer to become a myth?

First of all, it is necessary for the writer to succeed in adopting a *persona*, preferably a lyrical one. Poets, as a rule, become myths because they create their own *persona*, in which fiction and reality fuse into one. Think of François Villon, Byron, Rimbaud, Blok. In this sense, *Moscow to the End of the Line* is not just a "long poem" or *poema*[4] (although it is actually a work of prose), but is a completely lyrical work, inasmuch as the author recreates his own personality in it. The real-life Venichka and the "Venichka" of the poem become the same person. This is already the beginning of the myth.

At the same time, it is necessary that the writer not embody himself completely in his work. The popular rumor-mill must have enough space in order to bring to the writer's works that which he could not or would not disclose about himself. If Venedikt's collected works had come to forty volumes instead of one skinny little volume, his commentators, archivists, and biographers would not have failed to appear. But popular imagination would have been stifled by all those volumes. There would not have been anything left to imagine, for the author would have said it all himself. For example, the myth of Leo Tolstoy is hampered by his own Collected Works, which total ninety volumes including rough drafts and variants. A myth does not like to lie, to evade the straight path of truth. It is only when facts are missing or when they contradict one another that myth gets down to business. Myth is very sensitive, even touchy: when it is shown a heap of materials, it says: "Well, then, believe the material!" It then turns away and becomes silent forever.

The best beginning for a myth is an untimely end, that is when witnesses to the mythmaker's life live long enough for their memories to grow dim, turning them into stories and then legends. Everything that was not resolved by the man, all his abruptly interrupted contradictions, are now resolved by the myth. Almost all Russian literary myths, from Pushkin to Vysotsky, are made up of people who "have departed without having finished loving, without having finished smoking their last cigarette."[5]

It is precisely this state of "not being finished" that allows a myth to take root, as if some idea, having failed to materialize in reality, glimmers instead as an eternal symbol. The writer becomes a myth because he did not live out his life, did not write himself out, did not express himself completely. Such at least is our perception of him. "Pushkin died in full bloom of his forces and, indisputably, carried away to his grave some great riddle. And now we are trying to solve this riddle without him."[6] That is why, side by side with Pushkin, we have the myth of Pushkin. All that was Pushkin but was not embodied in Pushkin himself now lives outside him. What could not be played out in an individual biography has been enacted in all of Russian culture since Pushkin's death. It is enacted through Lermontov and Dostoevsky, Akhmatova and Nabokov, through all of us. What could not achieve corporeality and manifest itself in its own time is condensed into a lasting symbol.

Within culture it is possible to differentiate between two kinds of entities: realized and potential ones. That which is realized becomes the history of culture. That which is not realized but has somehow declared its existence and taken shape at least embryonically becomes its myth. It is hard to say which of these entities predominates and is more important to culture. In Russian culture, with so much emphasis placed on history, the proportional importance of its myths is nevertheless very great. Myth is the recompense for a debt—for what has not been lived out. It is an apparition that leaves its premature grave in order to make its visitations on posterity.

In the case of myth it not a matter of physical age. The fifty-two years lived by Erofeev would have been quite enough for another writer to leave a monumental collection of works, including letters and textual commentary. But Erofeev could not and did not want to embody himself fully in his work. Instead, he destroyed himself, most probably, consciously. He was destroying himself as an author—and this was echoed by the dying protagonist in his fiction. He was also destroying himself as a *persona*—and this was echoed by the dying author. He ended the poem about himself with the words: "They plunged an awl right into my throat.... And since then I have not regained consciousness, and never shall."[7] If it were not for the ease with which Erofeev engaged in his own self-destruction, how would he have dared utter those prophetic words about himself: "... not regain consciousness ... never ..." ? And while he actually survived for twenty years after this end, Erofeev never regained full creative consciousness. Instead there were only momentary flashes which signaled the death throes of an artistic talent. With the last line of *Moscow to the End of the Line,* Erofeev killed the hero and himself. A writer wanting his work to continue would never have ended his story that way—out of superstitious horror.

The only thing that Erofeev might have failed to accomplish in his life was to destroy himself completely. He left behind a long poem, a drama, an essay—everything in the singular. But this was enough for a Erofeev myth to spring up. He remains not so much the author of his works as a character in them, about whom enough has been said to provoke interest, but not enough to satisfy it. Erofeev managed to say just enough about himself so as to remain forever unexpressed and unfinished. "Of course, Erofeev was more than his works" (Vladimir Muraviev); "... I think that [Venia] has realized himself well, if only one percent" (Aleksandr Leontovich); "Venia himself was more significant than his works" (Olga Sedakova).[8] It is precisely the way in which the creator exceeds his creation that forms the embryo of the myth. "He was more than the sum of what he did and produced."

This gap between the creator and his creation is filled by the creation of the myth. The artistic image of Venichka, created by Erofeev, is complemented by the mythological image of Erofeev himself, created by his friends, who themselves become minor heroes in this myth. Here they are, seated at an eternal feast around the hero of the "heroic-comic" poem: Venichka's jester is Tikhonov; Venichka's wise man is Sorokin; Venichka's "mad poetess" is Sedakova;[9] and so on.

2. The Myth of God's Fool

What is so unique about "Venichka" that a myth about him could enter the crush of our literary legends and occupy a special place among them? There is the myth of Sergei Esenin, the myth of Vladimir Vysotsky. There are less popular myths, for example, the one about Yury Olesha, drunkenly chasing his metaphors like pink elephants but nearly knocked down by a passing mouse. All of these myths mediate two extremes, which are highly characteristic for any "model" of the artist in the Soviet period: "talent—persecuted," "soul—smothered," "life—crippled."

Let us investigate the components of the "Venia myth." First, we see before us a hero, standing tall, flexible, stately, a magnet for all women. He allows them to worship at his shrine, he is surrounded by "priestesses" scattering flowers on the bed of his repose. Another mythopoeic characteristic of the hero concerned his relationship to alcohol: he drank but did not get drunk. In all his competitions with other experienced drunks, he emerged as victor. When they lay under the table in a sorry state, his eyes were as clear as glass.[10] Inner finesse, delicacy, neatness. And of course, a talented, intelligent, erudite man, who memorized hundreds of dates and lines of verse by heart, whose tongue was wittier than anyone else's and who was praised throughout the world for his prose poem.

At the same time, there was poverty and disorder, dismissal from all the universities where he had begun so brilliantly, work digging ditches and constructing cables, wandering, an inability to achieve anything in life, unrestrained drunkenness, no underwear, the loss of manuscripts and his passport, his insults at even his closest friends, throat cancer. And creative impotence: the epic poem that was written as a sort of amusement among his friends became his swan song.

These contradictions only emphasize our need for a myth as they can not be resolved by rational means. If talented, then why did he not write? If intelligent, why did he prefer the idea of "throwing himself down the bottle" to all other ideas? If he took pride in Russia, then why did she interest him so little and why could he not stand patriots? If he loved every kind of systematization, then why did he live in such a disorderly manner? If he was neat, then why did he become shabby? If he was gentle, then why did he act so crudely?

And then, between these extremes, the first draft of the myth creeps in: a holy fool. This outline is very attractive, proceeding from a common Russian affection for a type of holiness that does not rise above the world in white garments but flips head-over-heels down into the most indecent gutter, drowning in the charms of this earth. This is what Erofeev's closest friend, Vladimir Muraviev, writes: "Venichka had the sense that safe, everyday life was just a substitute for real life, and he destroyed it and in fact his destruction had a partly religious nuance."[11] It is for Christ's sake that a holy fool destroys his own life and puts that of others to the test.

Galina Erofeeva, Venedikt's widow (who committed suicide soon after his death), remarked that "there was always religion in him. One probably should not say it, but I think that he imitated Christ."[12] This does not contradict the comment by Muraviev: "… despite his religious potential, Venichka did not at all strive to live by Christian laws."[13] The point here is that what the holy fool does strive to live in is the spirit of Christian *lawlessness*, "making himself an obscenity."[14] Venichka had nowhere to lay his head, he slept "on a pile of garbage" and achieved the "paradox of the religious feat": mocking the feelings of both himself and those close to him, he produced in response a hail of ridicule and insults—all in perfect accord with the canons of Russian hagiography.[15] In figurative terms, he hurled stones at the houses of the virtuous and kissed the cornerstone of houses where "blasphemy" reigns,[16] exactly like Vasily the Blessed, the most celebrated of Russia's holy fools, in whose honor a cathedral was erected on Red Square. Although similarly blessed, Venichka however never made it to Red Square but was instead carried off somewhere to the side.[17] What we witness in him is the process of lumpen-ization of the Russian holy fool—from Vasily the Blessed to Erofeev.

Even Venia's amazing drunkenness is reminiscent of a saint's voluntary chains and fasts, from which he derives no joy. The taste of wine afforded him no pleasure, and the voluptuary's lip-smacking he found vulgar. In general, as Sedakova subtly notes, "one felt that his way of life was not one of trivial drunkenness, but some kind of service.… Torment and troubles were incomparably greater than satisfaction.… I have never met a more fierce enemy of any common "enjoyment" than Venichka. There was nothing viler for him than the thought of enjoying himself or seeking enjoyment."[18]

But this does not apply to Venia alone. It is common knowledge that in Russia, unlike, for example, in France or Georgia, people prefer "bitters," the better to consume their souls in incomprehensible sorrow and bitterness. Very few Russians like "sweets," and even if some crop up, such as the poets Briusov, Bal'mont or Severianin, there are no myths about them. Myths only form around those who drink from the bitter cup, without sweet abandon and ecstacy, who exacerbate their own and other people's heartaches. Like Esenin or Vysotsky.

What was the nature of the sorrow that Venia had so much of, but whose cause was never explained to anyone? He would hardly have appreciated the attempt by a recent memoirist to explain his sorrow as "the nightmare of the Communist era."[19] Instead, he would have considered such an explanation to be prophetic vulgarity from a future secondary-school class in Russian literature. It has already been argued that Eugene Onegin would not have been a superfluous man in the conditions of Soviet life, but rather an entirely productive member of society, a philologist or agronomist. A similar type of soul-saving argument is advanced in relation to Erofeev. Had he lived under a government of Constitutional Democrats or right-wing Socialist Revolutionaries, so the argument goes, Venia would have been able to overcome his personal sorrow, stop drinking vodka and come to sit judiciously on academic boards, sharing his considerable knowledge of meteorology and mushrooms. I doubt it, for the same sorrow as Erofeev's has hung over Russia in every kind of political weather in the past, and Russians have always coped with it by washing it down with vodka, followed by a snack or a chaser that is bitter, sour, or salty—but never sweet.

3. The Myth of the Hangover

Although the myth of "Venia" has gradually taken on definite form, it nevertheless shares many of the attributes of the myths of Esenin, Vysotsky, and even the unsuccessful myth of Nikolai Rubtsov.[20] All four burned themselves out, dissipated themselves, fell into darkness in order to behold the last saving light, as is recommended in Eastern "negative" theology, where God is represented as a "no"—as the negation of light, honor, cleanliness, dignity, wisdom and goodness, since all of these virtues have already been taken over by the Philistines and serve their abominable un-Christian prosperity in a Christian world. And only the holy fool makes his way to

God, casting off all propriety, as well as his outer and sometimes even his under garments.

But "Venichka" had something that did not fit the framework of the widely respected myths of "Seriozha" (Esenin) and "Volodia" (Vysotsky). If nothing else, there was his name, "Venichka," which he himself immortalized. Who else would have dared to present himself under such an affectionate diminutive in our cynical times, in a circle of drunks and brawlers—and then to pass for a hero among them? Later, another writer, following in Erofeev's footsteps, began to peddle a myth about himself by appropriating Erofeev's intonation: "It's me, Edichka."[21] But the first one to refer to himself with such meek pathos was "Venichka" Erofeev.

He did not like hyperbole at all, preferring litotes and diminutives. Moreover, the relationship of an author to words begins with his relationship to his own name, which in this case represented a bashful attempt to disarm others and to negate himself. And so Venia writes: "there were little birdies," "there were two little chaps," or he affixes the epithets "a tiny little red," "a little cold one" to his favorite beverage.[22] Although one might write off these litotes as drunken sentimentality, aimed at inspiring the same sort of worship for banquet glassware as for one's own children—"a little cup," "wa-wa," etc.—the fact remains that never before in Russian literature had revelry been expressed in such a sentimental, non-hyperbolic form.

The proverbial holy fool, including his poetic double, is often captured in the clichéd gesture of tearing the shirt from his chest to free his sincere, burning soul from all constrictions. By contrast, Venichka always held up his collar, out of embarrassment perhaps and so as not to bare his throat? "… Young and handsome, he always bashfully covered his throat, holding together the buttonless collar of his shirt."[23] "And if his top button came off, Venia would hold his collar with his hand so that it would not come open. This was his trademark gesture."[24] This is so unlike Seriozha (Esenin) and Volodia (Vysotsky; they would tear off their collars; they would drive their horses into a lather and tear the bridles off. In them was something of the jaunty spirit of revelry of the beginning of the twentieth century, the hysteria of the superhuman and the urgent desire to burn the candle at both ends in order to put out the light a little sooner. Only in his last years did Vysotsky start to recite: "Slow down, steeds, slow down." But his voice nevertheless broke into a back-breaking scream, as if with one hand he held the horses back and with the other lashed them forward.

But with Venichka one really gets an unambiguous sense of slowness. To be slow and to be incorrect was his credo. "Everything on earth should occur slowly and incorrectly so that a person would be unable to grow proud, so that man would be sad and confused."[25] When someone is convinced of his righteousness, he usually tries to set about things as quickly as possible: this is heroic success and youthful vitality. But in Venia there was not a trace of heroism, not even of that upside-down, decadent form that usually coexists historically with the kind of straightforward heroism whose aim is to teach. For Venichka, Maxim Gorky, whom he did not like, was just as alien as Igor Severianin, whom he did like. He was as far from the thrills of the summit as he was from the thrills of the abyss; as far also from Blok and Esenin, who divided themselves between heights and depths; far from righteous writers and rowdy singers. Any regularity perturbed him deeply. He ran from sobriety but did not fall into the opposite temptation, into the heroism of decadence—of rowdy chaos, of fiery intoxication. He drank but was not prone to drunken rage, or the exaltation of love-friendship or dangerous, hoarse courage. He drank more than his predecessors but he no longer got drunk. He was thus like a sober man, but one who is sober from the other end, not before drinking, but after it. Not a self-assured sober man, but one who has gone quiet, sad, and timid.

This sort of meekness was the kind he most appreciated in others, a meekness authentically known only to the drunk; or rather, the drunk who is gradually coming out of his drunken delirium.[26] Venia's state of glory was not the drinking binge, but the *hangover*, the delicate and over-scrupulous accounting for all previous binges, his own and others'. Any revelry going on around him, drunken ecstasies and the torn collar, thrilled him even less than the feats of Zoia Kosmodemianskaia.[27] In the dialectic of sobriety and drunkenness, the ultimate level is the hangover: the negation of negation.

Let us investigate the stages of this dialectic that inexorably leads from arrogance to meekness. Drinking is a means of driving out the demon of arrogance from a sober man who stands firmly on his own feet, who speaks clearly and deliberately, living as if he had complete mastery over his body and soul. But he need only take a drink and *voilà*: our good man will soon realize that things are not so obedient to him after all. Strut as he might with his worldly privileges; boast as he will about trampling the earth underfoot and mastering the meaning of things: gone is the arrogance of sobriety.

But what remains in reserve is the arrogance of drunkenness. Now the old friend does not care a damn, his lips are on fire with his own wit, his gaze burning from his own seductive powers: again the whole world spreads itself before him, but this time on an undulating road. He now feels light and confident precisely by virtue of not being in control.

After which the sobering-up begins and, "with disgust reciting the story of my life ..."[28] There is not a trace left of those earlier witticisms and fiery glances! Only drunken hiccups and winks exchanged with some plastered lassie. At first drinking knocked the arrogance out of the sober man, then sobriety knocked the arrogance out of the drunk, and finally, through the torments of shame, the third stage of this great synthesis is ushered in—the *hangover*. The sorrowful and wise hangover, simultaneously boring and illuminating. All a man can do at this stage is sigh, cooling himself by imbibing fresh air without polluting the air around him with his own breath. "... I sighed, sighed so deeply, that I almost dislocated everything I had."[29]

Such is this sly dialectic. Venia knocks out of himself, and out of those around him, first sober arrogance and then drunken arrogance.[30] He dislodges both types of arrogance, sober and drunken, finally arriving at the hangover, a state of extreme meekness. The one who suffers from a hangover is fastidious towards himself and consequently totally forgiving towards his neighbor. The one who suffers from a hangover offends no one; on the contrary, like a child he is offended by everyone. He is so weakened that he begins to display something virginal—a ticklishness and nervous sensitivity toward the slightest touch.

Venia, for example, was horribly touchy and feared tickling more than anything else. "I have a lot of ankles and armpits. I have them everywhere. An honest man must have a lot of ankles and armpits and must fear tickling."[31] Who before him in Russia was so ticklish, defending his honor laughing and kicking like a little girl? Not even Lermontov, Blok, or Gumilev, the most sublime of poets, was so ticklish. They created myths of the eternal feminine but had nothing of that kind of girlishness in them. Venia, afraid of the slightest touch, quivering and guffawing, was entirely virginal.[32] It is with this quality that he partakes of that "eternal-womanly" (*vechno-bab'ie*) quality of the Russian soul. Through him, however, "womanliness" ceases to be a quality of the mature woman and becomes, once again, a quality of the young maiden. From the point of view of a being consisting entirely of ankles and armpits, the entire world now seems rude in the light of this "womanly" softness and delicacy. What other man could be so fragile and so sensitive just because of a hangover?

> "Why are they all so rude? Huh? And why so in particular, so emphatically rude, just at such a time when it is impossible to be rude, when a man with a hangover has all his nerves exposed, when he is faint-hearted and timid? Why is it so?"[33]

It is strange: not only did Venia sense the rudeness of those around him, but those around him, even the most refined of them, such as the poet Olga Sedakova, sensed their own rudeness when they were in Venia's proximity. "… Next to him it was impossible not to sense one's own rudeness: the contrast was impressive."[34]

It must be said that neither of Venia's typical states, namely that of being "drunk or with a hangover," led to a loss of sobriety. Essentially, it was a single prolonged state, comprised of three stages: drinking, sobering up, suffering a hangover. "I, having tasted so much in this world that I have lost count and track—I am more sober than anyone in this world; sobriety just has a troubling effect on me …"[35] "Venia himself never got drunk. He did not permit himself to. He regarded the onset of dullheadedness, the drunken muttering and pestering as ill-mannered and boorish.… One of the virtues of our circle of friends was not getting drunk …"[36]

This is where the myth of Venichka truly begins—the myth about his *non-inebriety*, which must not be confused with simple, unconcerned sobriety. Sobriety is before, and *non-inebriety* occurs afterwards. Sobriety is self-righteous and didactic, while *non-inebriety* is meek and depressed. Sobriety can be under delusion and still get drunk on itself: non-inebriety can no longer get drunk on anything. And this is the highest state of the soul: when it has the fewest possible worldly ambitions and altogether very little animation (which comes from *anima*—"spirit," "breath") left in it—the state of faint-heartedness or lack of spirit [*malodushie* [37]]:

> Oh, if only the entire world, if everyone in the world were like me right now—timid and shy and unsure of everything: of himself, of the seriousness of his place under the heavens—how good it would be! No enthusiasts, no heroic feats, no obsessions!—a universal faint-heartedness. I would agree to live on earth for all eternity if they'd show me a little corner where there is not always room for a heroic feat. "Universal faint-heartedness"—this is really the salvation from all misfortunes, this is a panacea, the predicate of the greatest perfection![38]

Faint-heartedness is not as bad as it seems, and must not be confused with cowardliness. A coward is afraid for himself while one who is faint-hearted is afraid for everything on earth. His soul simply sinks to his boots when he touches a fragile vase or meets an intelligent person—as if he might somehow tear something, misplace something, injure something or someone. A faint-hearted person is delicate because more than anything else he fears offending someone. He does not have enough spirit to assume responsibility or to harbor a secret ambition.

4. Trans-Irony

At the center of the Venia myth is just this delicacy, an extremely rare and still little noticed attribute of Russian culture.[39] There is a lot of holiness and sin in it, much illumination and darkness, heights and depths, but little delicacy. Try to say that Tolstoy or Dostoevsky was delicate: it would sound funny applied to such prophetic giants.

Although there may have been some delicacy in them, it rarely came into view. As for the delicacy of a Chekhov or Timiriazev, of a doctor or a scholar, they simply could not have been other than delicate in the delicate circumstances of their time and profession.

But Venia's kind of delicacy, when he eats and drinks in the hallway of a train car because he feels shy in front of other passengers, is of a totally different kind. When he sighs bitterly over the vulgar "uncircumcised hearts,"[40] when he conceals from his drinking buddies his *sorties* prompted "by the call of nature," not daring to put into words his secret desires, Venichka is delicate in all respects—so delicate that he does not announce to his friends his intention to go to the bathroom. And even more delicately, he agrees to go to the bathroom only in order not to oppress them with his delicacy.[41]

Such delicacy in a person who by all indications ought not to and cannot be delicate, is something phenomenal and, at the same time, as Venia would say, something noumenal. This is a manifestation of a new kind of delicacy, turning Venia into the hero of an altogether indelicate milieu. If this delicacy had emanated from somewhere outside, from the realm of authority or high morality, it would be a simple object of ridicule. But here it emanates from the very heart of "plebeianism, of debauchery, and rebellion"—from Venichka himself, who is tasting both "A Komsomolka's Tear" and "Aunt Klava's Kiss," as well as other cocktails, some infused with shampoo, others with methyl alcohol, brake fluid, or something to prevent sweaty feet. Delicacy in such a creature is not a tribute to tradition or family, to upbringing or social norms. It cannot be obsolete. It cannot be edifying. It is other-worldly. "From my other-worldly point of view ..." as Venia used to say.[42]

Coming from Venia, even the words "infant," "angels," "sorrow" or "sigh," were not old-fashioned or pompous. He spoke often of "... immortal angels and dying children ..."[43] Who in the Soviet period would call his son an "infant," [*mladenets*][44] and his inner voices "angels"? Such words have not been in circulation since the time of the romantic and symbolist poets, such as Vasily Zhukovsky or Alexander Blok. These words reached Venia through a barrier of so much filth, verbal rot, and decay, that one involuntarily hears irony in them. Venia, however, does not use them ironically. To perceive irony in these pure words would be simply vulgar.

What would be more appropriate here is the word "counter-irony" (*protivoironiia*) as suggested by Erofeev's friend, the philologist Muraviev.[45] One might propose an even stronger term—"trans-irony"—indicating not just the opposition to irony, but rather a movement beyond irony, its sublation (to use Hegel's term). If irony inverts the sense of a straightforward, serious word, then trans-irony inverts the sense of irony itself, resurrecting seriousness—but now without its direct and monosemantic character. Trans-irony is not simply a denial of irony. Rather it is the metalevel of irony, which presupposes an irony toward irony itself and, therefore, a polysemantic play of literal and figurative meanings. Here, for example, is a dialogue between Venichka and the Lord:

> I took everything I had out of the suitcase and felt it: from a sandwich to the stout rosé at a ruble thirty-seven. Touched everything and began to languish. Again I touched it all—and I withered.... Lord, here you see what I possess. But do I really need *this* ? Is *this* really what my soul is longing for? This is what people have given me instead of what my soul is longing for! And if they'd given me *that*, would I really have needed *this*? Look, Lord, here: the stout rosé for a ruble thirty-seven ...
>
> And, all in blue flashes of lightning, the Lord answered me:
>
> "And what did Saint Theresa need stigmata for? She did not need them either, yet she desired them."
>
> "Yes, that's it!" I answered in delight. "Me too, me too—I desire it, but I do not need it in the least!"
>
> "Well, since it's desired, Venichka, go on and drink," I thought quietly, but was still slow to act. "Is the Lord going to say something more to me or not?"
>
> The Lord was silent.[46]

If one were so inclined, one could find a lot of irony in this passage. The stout rosé and the stigmata of Saint Theresa are so different that it would seem impossible to compare them without sinking into pathos. But at the same time: what exactly is being ridiculed? Where is the irony? In the stout rosé? That would be stupid. Saint Theresa? That would be even more stupid. It is as if the irony is implied, but only as a shade of trans-irony, as its expressive nuance. Trans-irony works with irony the same way that irony works with seriousness, lending it a different sense. The initially serious subtext can be read this way: "O, Saint Theresa! Ugh! Worthless Venichka!" Irony shifts the accents: everyone has his/her own pink spirits, one has stout rosé, another has stigmata. Trans-irony again shifts the accent: everyone has his/her own stigmata, one has holes in her hands and feet, another has stout rosé. It cannot be said that trans-irony restores the same level of seriousness as existed before the injection of irony. On the contrary, trans-irony immediately rejects both trivial seriousness and vulgar irony, establishing a new point of view—"God's point of view." What man does not need, he desires. Both holiness and drunkenness are located in this *gap* between need and desire. The greatest man is not too big for this gap, and the least worthy man is not too small for it.

Venia's entire style is made up of the kind of trans-irony that uses ready-made ironic clichés as its material. They have become just as ossified in social consciousness as have weighty, pathos-laden clichés. The two possible modes of receptions of the words "fatherland" or "Soviet power," for instance, have been frozen into clichéd gestures: either that of standing at attention or of sniggering behind one's hand. Venia, however, endows these words with a new intonation, which is neither serious nor ironic, but "otherworldly," so to speak, from beyond the grave:

> "Erofeev, as to the beloved Soviet government, to what extent did it fall in love with you when your fame became international?"
>
> "It decidedly paid no attention to me whatsoever. I love my government."
>
> "Why in particular do you love it?"
>
> "For everything."
>
> "Because it did not touch you and did not send you to prison?"
>
> "For that I especially love it. I am prepared to love my government for everything. [...]"
>
> "Where does this unrequited love of yours come from?"
>
> "In my opinion, it's requited, as far as I can see. I hope that it's requited, or else what's there for me to live for."[47]

This is an excerpt from an interview in *Kontinent,* which at the time was still being published in Paris. The interviewer tries in every way to get Venia "to kid," but Venia does not succumb to the temptation of cheap irony, any more than to the temptation of patriotic pride or pain. He answers the interviewer's absurd questions in the manner of souls at a spiritistic seance. His intonation is unassailably flat, disengaged. This precisely is trans-irony, which leaves just enough room for irony in order to signal its inappropriateness.

5. The Carnival Transcended

Trans-irony is a new quality of the Venia myth—and of the ritual performance associated with it. Any myth, scholars assert, is the verbal record and ideological justification of a certain rite.[48] In this sense the Venichka myth signifies a new rite of passage for the initiation of the young. Initiation is a dedication, a rite of entry into the social life and adulthood. Noble youths of the nineteenth century, leaving the cozy domestic realm and setting out on the path of masculine initiation, tried to be as coarse as possible. They swilled vodka and went visiting gypsy girls (think of Pierre Bezukhov in the first volume of *War and Peace*). Youths of the late Soviet period were also swilling vodka at a tender age. But they had no need to go visiting anywhere, everything was right next door in the dormitory: remember the way of life described by Venia and his friends![49]

Venichka's initiation began just where the initiation of the heroes of classic Russian literature left off, namely at the tavern-brothel, the dormitory-public house. While remaining within this familiar space, Venia however turned it inside-out, suddenly revealing the glimmering features of an aristocratic youth through the intoxicated and violent haze. It is almost as if we were going back to the sentimental era of Karamzin and Radishchev. Yes, ladies and gentlemen, reckless young people also know how to feel: "For if someone has an overscrupulous heart …"[50]

In those days, at the end of the 1960s and throughout the 1970s, the typical initiation of the young was called "Rabelaisation." It was based on Bakhtin's carnival theory and its association with the corporeal and comic depths of folk culture. All the orifices of the body had to be opened up to ingest and expel the flow of the universal circulation of matter. Drunkenness is only a small metaphor for the gushing excess with which Bakhtin, in his book-myth on Rabelais, associates such things as puking, spitting, sweating, snot, sneezing, gluttony, copulation, defecation, farting, and so on.[51]

All of this, however, Venia found terribly embarrassing. He was "unbelievably shy even in front of himself."[52] And he used to say that the person who deserves the most tenderness is "the one who pees in his pants in front of everyone."[53] What Venia did was turn the values, which had been turned upside down by a carnivalesque culture, the right way up again. The carnival appreciated this, as if it had not noticed that, around Venia, carnival ceased to be a carnival. Timidity that was expelled in a burst of obscenities is now extended to obscenity itself. "Tenderness toward the one who peed in his pants." Understandably, this is not the same as tenderness towards a sprig of lilac. It is tenderness that makes a detour around sentimentality, via the distance of carnival. However, this is no longer carnival either, but its afterlife. All former attributes, overturned by carnival, are now resurrected in a new, "noumenal" dimension. The tenderness and grief, weeping and timidity, loneliness and boredom are already transcendental, liberated from any attachment to their former objects.

Take, for example, sadness: what made Erofeev sad? He knew that every creature experiences post-coital sadness. This natural law was observed by Aristotle. But Venia, unlike Aristotle, "[was] constantly sad, before and after coitus."[54] Or, for example, a person usually feels animated when thoughts rush to his head whereas Venia would break out with the following confession: "Thoughts were pressing in my head, pressing so hard that I got depressed …"[55]

It is as if all the things for which people once had feelings had been torn away from Venia and placed at a distance of historic proportions. It is as if the necessary correspondence between feelings and objects had been abolished. Feelings are resurrected following the death of feelings, and the heart of man does not know to what to attach them. To what should grief be attached—to a child's tiny tear, as in Dostoevsky's *Brothers Karamazov*, or to "A Komsomolka's Tear,"

Venia's favorite cocktail? Venia, not wanting to miss the mark, grieves for everything simultaneously. Thus his sadness applies both to sad things and to things that are not sad at all, although his feeling is no less sad for it, perhaps now only otherworldly. It stands on the other side of former feelings, which have been dulled, cut off or torn out. What feelings are possible after the Holocaust, after the revolution, after Auschwitz and Kolyma: what kind of sadness is left? But then sadness opens "two enormous eyes" (O. Mandel'shtam) and searches for its object, about which it still knows nothing. Who said that there must be a strict correspondence between an object and a feeling, as in classicism? Even ordinary language does not manifest such a correspondence. Every sign, according to the founder of contemporary linguistics, Ferdinand de Saussure, is arbitrary, and any word can signify any object. Why then can sadness not refer to a happy object, and to a mundane object, and to a funny object, and to an entirely indifferent one? Is it not a sad thing if it is so indifferent? And is it not sad if it is so funny? Why can sorrow not refer to wine and merriment to stigmata? There is nothing carnivalesque here. It is simply another level of feelings. Meta-emotions.

Perhaps Venia himself did not notice this new post-carnivalesque transformation of his feelings—but Mikhail Bakhtin, who had an extraordinarily keen sense for everything carnivalesque, did. He was delighted by Erofeev's long poem, finding in it support for his theories of carnival and an expression of pure pantagruelism. In the poem, Venia is frequently occupied with rinsing his throat. Is this not reminiscent of Pantagruel, both in the proper and dictionary definition of his name? For the word "pantagruel," before being given to Rabelais' hero, was the name of a throat disease—the loss of one's voice as a result of heavy drinking (a drunkard's disease).[56] If only Bakhtin could have known to what degree the prophetic meaning of this name would be embodied in Erofeev's own destiny! The loss of voice towards the end, followed by several operations—which Erofeev survived—and finally death from cancer of the larynx. It was as if the essence of pantagruelism had been literally re-enacted down to the smallest detail of Erofeev's own life.

Nonetheless, despite being fatally doomed to the grotesque, Erofeev in a way escaped it. The phenomenon of Venichka, growing out of pantagruelism, outgrows it, contingent precisely on its literal and concrete embodiment. The carnival itself becomes an object of the carnivalesque, and with this it moves into the realm of a strange new seriousness.

It is significant that Bakhtin, delighted by the poem, did not approve of its denouement, because the hero appears to die "for real," and "entropy" seems to enter "carnival."[57] But what kind of seriousness can there be in carnival? What kind of entropy can there be in the midst of the carnivalesque splash of pent-up energies? Nevertheless, one can discern entropy and a fading of energy in Venia himself long before the end of the poem. Venia's shyness amidst carnivalesque revelry: is that not entropy? What has become poeticized is not debauchery: it is the "man with a hangover ... who is faint-hearted and quiet." And this poetics of "universal faint-heartedness" is, from the carnivalesque point of view, sheer entropy. The great Bakhtin sensed this, too, although he failed to appreciate its new value. He saw in Erofeev something kindred that was turning into something unfamiliar. He sensed that here carnival had ceased to be carnivalesque.[58]

The critic Andrei Zorin has remarked that, contrary to the laws of carnival, "elements of folk laughter in the end deceive the hero and expel him. Such an ending is foreshadowed from the beginning."[59] It is even more accurate to say that from beginning to end it is the author who deceives and expels the elements of folk culture. Insofar as the author and the hero are one, they do this together. The hero withdraws from the mob by escaping onto the platform of the train carriage. The author distances himself from the folk element [*narodnaia stikhiia*] by escaping into the space of artistic understatement (the litotes and diminutives). Together they alienate themselves from the masses through the name of "Venichka," as well as through flight into a private melancholy and a lyrical state of confusion and perplexity. Folk laughter [*smekh*], no less than folk diligence [*spekh*][60]—indeed the entire popular universe, filled with characters such as Vasily Terkin, Zoia Kosmodemianskaia and Aleksei Stakhanov—are equally alien to Venichka, who loves slowness and irregularity. As for his entropy: is it really such a bad thing?

6. The Charms of Entropy

For centuries the world has glorified energy or force in all its guises: from kinetic and potential energy to the energy of mind and body, the force of the collective and of the individual, the force of heroic feats and the force of humility, cosmic force and political force, creative force and moral force. Force (*energiia*) was glorified by Galileo and Goethe, Hegel and Tolstoy, Marx and Nietzsche, Faraday and Freud, Balzac and Darwin, Pushkin and Edison, Einstein and Sartre, Ford and Bakhtin. Perhaps because of its naturally lethargic state, Russia has especially prized force and energy, releasing it in explosions of heroism and revolution. And when revolution gave way to stagnation, it in turn sought to discharge itself in explosions of laughter and carnival. Force performed its great task in all parts of the world: it kept the planets turning, it split the atom, moved conveyors, produced the sexual and scientific/technical revolutions, turned heads and hearts, seduced young women and old men. Film stars, powerful minds, business sharks, bombshells, eastern gurus, and sports champions—all exuded energy and charm. Indeed energy was found to be seductive no matter what form it took, including decay and decadence.

And then suddenly Venia revealed the charms of entropy. In his hands, it acquired heart-warming traits: slowness and faint-heartedness. And in general terms, he was correct in so doing; for during his lifetime, in the second half of the twentieth century, there was no longer any reason to fear entropy. The case had been different at the end of the nineteenth century, when people suddenly began to fear it. This was because of the second law of thermodynamics, which threatened general entropy, a thermal end to the universe in which everything would come together, even out, forming one vast, identical and undifferentiated melange, neither cold not hot. And then the sun would go out, the earth would freeze. Such was the late-nineteenth-century vision of the end of the world.[61]

But after two world wars and countless revolutions, such fears became obsolete. It seemed that a force of unknown composition held the key to our universe, distending it with all kinds of cataclysms and insanities. Towards the end of the twentieth century humankind became wary of just this force, which it stumbled on, in its ignorance, thanks to nuclear physics. The shock of this discovery was so great that it nearly exploded the entire world. However, people were ashamed to admit that the very same force that was so attractive when paraded by a popular intellectual or political leader, by a writer or actor, was much less attractive when demonstrated at nuclear testing sites. Military men became the victims of social prejudice, fueled by the belief that the force in their hands was more dangerous than the force employed by energetic people who were actively engaged in seducing all of progressive humankind. Peaceful demonstrations focused on one type of force, not realizing that the world, held together by force, was dangerous as a whole, and that all forms of energy, passing into one another, were accelerating its end. Significantly, this end is pictured in the New Testament as the earth erupting in flames—and not in a flood or ice. The flood (of Noah's time) was just an experimental end, God's trial to bring out the righteous. The real end will come by fire:

> … by the word of God the heavens were of old, and the earth standing out of the water and in the water: Whereby the world that then was, being overflowed with water, perished: But the heavens and the earth, which are now, by the same word are kept in store, reserved unto fire against the day of judgment and perdition of ungodly men. […] … the heavens being on fire shall be dissolved, and the elements shall melt with fervent heat …[62]

Here the common word "fire" likely signifies energy, which has seethed and accumulated in humankind from time immemorial, only to erupt as the Last Judgment. Whether this end will come as revolution, carnival or both together is left unsaid. However, that the Last Judgment will be fiery, exploding with energy, is made clear.

Surprisingly, in a land abounding in all known forms of force and energy, a man appeared who stood out as a seductive example of faint-heartedness; a man who, to use Bakhtin's term (although to him, the theoretician of carnival, it was uninteresting), succeeded in making "entropy" interesting. Erofeev was able to convince countless readers that in an era of a superabundance of energy, there was special merit in injecting one's own little dose of entropy into it. A splash of entropy in the bonfire of energy. Faint-heartedness as a way of showing one's magnanimity.

Erofeev's whole being was dominated by entropy. Force never played in his facial features. A meager personal impression, received by the author of this mythographic study, can now be shared with the indulgent reader. I saw Venedikt Erofeev twice and on both occasions I was struck by the color of his face. The first time was in the mid-1970s—his face was brown. Not from the sun, not from a natural swarthiness, but earthy, as if he had been sleeping in an embrace with the land, although he had actually just gotten out of bed. When I saw him the second time, towards the end of the 1980s, his face was completely white. Not pale, but as if it were too brightly lit, or stained with chalk. On this occasion he was sitting in a lively literary café, at a party with poets and foreigners. And this is how his two faces remain in my memory: one—earthy, the other—chalky. The two colors of entropy. One could undoubtedly see the phenomenology of his life and the noumenosity of his death in these two faces, his peasant origins on the one hand and his artist's destiny on the other. But neither the energy of full-bloodedness or rude health played over his face—for this I can vouch. There was no fire in him.

That is why, though surrounded by a society of people who sat, stood or walked, Erofeev always preferred to recline. This was his means of slowing down. Perhaps, with time, Erofeev's slippers will become as famous as Oblomov's dressing-gown.[63] But Oblomov was stout and lazy, while Erofeev was thin and ascetic. His sluggishness was a product of work on himself. He pressed energy out of himself drop by drop. He did not give in to inertia, he created it. As God created the world out of nothing, so Erofeev created entropy out of his inborn energy. Oblomov remained a created character. Erofeev, on the other hand, authored himself.

Even food, which aroused the lazy Oblomov from his torpor, was a means of deceleration for Venia. Almost always hungry, he never rushed to satisfy his appetite. In reminiscences about him, there is remarkable agreement about Venia's dainty eating habits.

"And when he would sit down to eat, although during the war years there were shortages and food rations came in tiny portions, he always ate slowly, intelligently, and carefully, never betraying any sign of ravenousness" (Nina Frolova, Venia's sister). "… Venedikt very cautiously lifted the entire fried egg from the frying pan with a piece of bread. He was always very hungry, but expressed this timidly, ate without appearing voracious and manipulated a piece of bread with extreme delicacy" (Lidiia Liubchikova). "He was refined in all things. We lived together for fifteen years and I do not remember him once eating greedily" (Galina Erofeeva). "In general, I do not recall seeing jaw movement on his physiognomy, I do not remember him masticating—chewing was uncharacteristic of Venia" (Igor Avdiev).[64] Given these testimonies, how could one still look for a carnival glutton, when Erofeev failed even to show a chewing reflex?! Even less appropriate are the carnivalesque, clichéd images of the *gaping mouth* and *fat stomach*—the signs of volcanic eruptions of cosmic energy in the form of insatiable gluttony.[65]

With this in mind, one can argue that the historic force of the twentieth century was precisely generated by this chewing and swallowing instinct, which even the most revolutionary ideologies used in order to turn the world upside down. The face of this imperialistically-communistically-fascistically-cosmically-ideologically-atomico-energetic century is grotesque. "The grotesque face can be reduced, essentially, to the *gaping mouth*—everything else is simply a setting for *that mouth, for that yawning and devouring bodily cavity*."[66] Quick and fair distribution—this is how one might define the thrust and spirit of this most hungry and hurried of centuries in human history. After all its feats of sharing, its proper ending should have come about in the spirit of a Bakhtinian utopia, in a merry festival of general consumption. "Hunger rules the world"—this ancient truism has become the basis of modern ideology, while the quickest satisfaction of hunger has been transformed into a sacred obligation and the purpose of world history.[67]

For the founders of Marxism, whom Venia caustically studied out of duty and curiosity, "the physical self-production of the individual" was the mainspring of history. It constituted its primary fact, generating both the forces of production and the relationships of production as well as their conflicts, out of which grew social revolutions and the triumphs of the hungry over the sated. This would eventually lead to the triumph of satiety over hunger. The theory of carnival, in this sense, coalesces with and becomes the natural conclusion of the theory of revolution, according to which "the springs of social well-being and abundance will gush forth" (Karl Marx's definition of Communism), and the social body, celebrating its feast of excess in eating, sweating, defecating and copulating, will manifest itself as "growing, inexhaustible, indestructible, abundant and bearing the material principle of life …"[68]

Of course, there is no escaping from this basic material principle, which seizes one utterly and completely: "While the carnival is going on, there is no other life for anyone, except the life of the carnival. Out of it there is nowhere to go, for carnival does not know spatial boundaries. During the carnival, one can live only according to its laws, that is, according to the laws of carnivalesque *freedom.*"[69]

Only according to the laws of freedom—these words sound like they were engraved in stone, like a KGB command. But what of Venichka? For the first time in the history of the tempestuous carnival milieu, it is not rowdiness but ticklishness and timidity that acquire glory. It is the ability to use the words "angel" and "infant" not as a gag and without hysterical laughter. The collar, not unbuttoned, but very painstakingly held together. Not gluttony, but the cautious lifting of a fried egg with a piece of bread. Last but not least, a man who became a legend by managing, in a carnival atmosphere, to fart not even once in the course of a sorrow-laden life.

> —Here you have the very famous Venichka Erofeev himself. He is famous for a lot of things. But more than anything else, of course, for the fact that, in his entire life, he has never farted …
>
> —How's that!! Never once!!—ladies are amazed and examine me with eyes wide open.—Never once!!
>
> I begin to grow embarrassed, of course.[70]

Oh, the embarrassed suppresser of energies! We have never had such a myth here before.[71]

7. The New Sentimentality

Evidently, the "postmodern" era, which marks the twentieth century's fatigue with itself, is coming to an end. The century opened with a triumphant entry into a radiant future and is ending with parodying all the previous ages of humankind. Everything this century managed to swallow in an unprecedented intoxication of the mind with ideas, it now disgorges in the form of dreary self-repetitions and mocking citations. To paraphrase Erofeev, one might say that every century has its physical, spiritual, and mystical side; and our century is currently experiencing nausea from all sides,[72] especially in that one-sixth of the globe, which has suffered more severely than the other parts from this century's bingeing. Territories that had been swallowed up are being disgorged, along with pieces of nature that have been befouled and remnants of ideas of the founding fathers that have gone sour. Everything that had been so exciting and intoxicating now floods the site of the recent orgy with a cold mass of vomit.

The century is tired of itself—but fatigue generates new fatigue and so the century is becoming too lazy to project its fading images in the mirror of new parodies. A new kind of seriousness is growing, a seriousness that tests itself on laughter—and not laughing, tests its own courage—but does not dare. It is a very timid seriousness, one that resembles faint-heartedness, the fear of scaring something away and irreparably destroying something in ourselves and in the world without ourselves.

The myth of Erofeev reveals a new kind of sentimentality, or sentimentality at a new stage of development—one that includes carnival and parodic effects while simultaneously neutralizing and diffusing them. Is it not insanity to suggest that the twenty-first century could become the century of sentimentality? Is it possible that the twenty-first century will acquire a taste for thoughtfulness, quiet meditation and delicate melancholy in the same way as the twentieth century looked for inspiration in the age of the baroque, with its fantastic refinement, dramatic tension and overflowing force?

Is it possible that everything loud will begin to irritate us: explosions of anger, explosions of laughter? The rising of the masses, about which Ortega-y-Gasset prophesied, will come to an end and with it the aesthetics of revolution and carnival. People will begin to listen attentively to themselves and perhaps will even hear the voices of angels. They will once again wipe away the tears of innocent children with the edge of their handkerchief, but will not, with every child's tear, rise up against God to alter the world order. Berdiaev, as we know, tried to explain the Communist revolution as deriving from the heightened affectivity and sentimentality of the Russian people. "Russians used to become atheists out of pity and compassion, out of the inability to endure compassion."[73] The Russians, so it goes, are so sensitive to the suffering of others that they are ready to shatter the entire unjust world so as to be able to commiserate with the world's victims. Even Belinsky wrote about his raging love of humanity: "In order to give happiness to one half of humanity, I would be prepared to annihilate the other half with fire and sword." As Berdiaev remarked, "out of compassion, Belinsky is ready to preach tyranny and cruelty."[74]

Revolution, however, is not mature sentimentality, but rather, a miscarriage of sentimentality, a yearning to shed the excessive burden of feelings. Revolution represents an impatience with emotions, an inability to feel the full extent of one's own misery, and the desire to cut off and kill every emotion by finding an instantaneous, practical outlet for it.

In this sense, sentimentality is opposed to revolution. Sentimentality adores emotions since they edify the soul and are the aim of existence. Sentimentality, in the proper sense, means sensibility or sensitivity to everything pertaining to human feeling. But the sensibility of the twenty-first century will not be a straight-forward repetition of the sensitivity of the eighteenth century. It will not interpret the world in divisive terms of what is touching or horrible, adorable or repulsive. It will be capable of accommodating many contradictory feelings. It will restore to itself all that was torn away from sensitivity and directed against it by the nineteenth and twentieth centuries—nightmares, phantasms, catastrophes, revolutions. Everything that killed feelings will be reappropriated in order to make feelings keener. The new sensitivity will find a way of assimilating both the terrifying and the causal. It will smile upon both. But this smile will not be the same as parody: it will not be the alienation or suppression of emotions, but a mode of countering emotions with emotions. Sensitivity will be liberated from all accepted conventions, from the captivity in which it was still held by classicism, where feelings came under strict laws. It will become possible to feel everything and in every manner, to empathize with the sensuality of each and every object and to combine this empathy with the sense of every other object. Stern and Jean Paul will become the favorites of the twenty-first century. Using the legacy of the eighteenth century, it will value humor, the light garb of sentimentality, above all. And then—God knows—through Venedikt Erofeev, the continuity of the sentimental tradition, leading from the eighteenth to the twenty-first centuries, will be restored. And Venichka will suddenly find his place on the same shelf of the Russian library as poor Liza, who threw herself into the pond[74]—while he, the poor guy, cut himself on an awl. "I could have drowned myself in my own tears, but it didn't work out for me."[75]

In any case, the twenty-first century will probably make room for quite a few nooks in which heroic feats will have no place. Here the reader will sit quietly, bent over Venia's book, visited by flickering angels who will converse with him in Venia's language. And no matter what name is given to this mysterious century, it will surely be a century of timidity and delicacy, and of the sensitive hangover.

Notes

1. "… *Vrezaias' vnov' i vnov' s naskoku / V razriad predanii molodykh*"—Pasternak on Mayakovsky, in his poem *The Death of a Poet* (1930).
2. See, for instance, Claude Lévi-Strauss's theory of myth, according to which myth functions as a mediating term between fundamental binary oppositions, such as life and death, heaven and earth, laughter and tears and so on. "The purpose of myth is to provide a logical model capable of overcoming a contradiction…." Claude Lévi-Strauss, *Structural Anthropology*, trans. Claire Jacobson and Brook G. Schoepf (New York, 1963), p. 229.

3. One of the most important testimonies to this is the collection of materials *in memorium* under the general title "Several monologues about Venedikt Erofeev," in the journal *Teatr*, no. 9 (1991): 74–122.
4. "*Poema*," the Russian word for epic poem. However, in the romantic period, writers such as Gogol fashioned their own poemas-in-prose, *Dead Souls* being the most famous, and the one Erofeev certainly had in mind in calling his own short novel a *poema*. [Translator's note]
5. This was written by Nikolai Maiorvo, a poet of the war generation about his contemporaries who died young. Incidentally, what generation among us has not been a war generation? We have joined battle with autocracy and serfdom, with the peasantry and the intelligentsia, with the petty-bourgeoisie and the aristocracy, with literature and religion, with society and ourselves. Every generation has had its own war and its own victims, which means, its own myths. All of these deal with people who have not lived out their lives fully: Pushkin, Lermontov, Nadson, Blok, Gumilev, Esenin, Mayakovsky, Vysotsky, Brodsky. Some of these were great poets, others simply poetic natures. Their poetry was not so much in their verse as in their life, which was broken like the string of a guitar during the performance of a cruel romance.

   Perhaps the only exception among the myths of a "true poet who dies young" is Akhmatova (1889–1966), but she is mythologized as a special, feminine, maternal deity who died and rose again, having survived the Russian revolution and the great crises of the 1930s and 1940s.
6. Fyodor Dostoevsky, "Pushkin. An Essay," in *F. M. Dostoevsky ob iskusstve* (Moscow, 1973), p. 370.
7. Venedikt Erofeev, *Moskva-Petushki* (Moscow, 1990), p. 128. [Unless otherwise indicated, all translations are by Slobodanka Vladiv-Glover.]
8. See *Teatr* 9 (1991): 95, 97, 102.
9. Olga Sedakova (b. 1949) is a famous poet and essayist. See chapter 5 of this book.
10. Memoirs of Lidiia Liubchikova, *Teatr* 9 (1991): 80, 85.
11. See *Teatr* 9 (1991): 90.
12. Ibid., p. 88.
13. Ibid., p. 90.
14. As Georgy Fedotov writes, "… the affectation of immorality was not alien to the holy fool. The hagiographies of such men chastely cover this aspect of their feat with the stereotypical phrase 'making oneself an obscenity' [*pokhab sia tvoria*]. The life of a holy fool is one of constant vacillation between acts of moral salvation and acts of immoral mockery of them." Georgy Fedotov, *Saints of Ancient Rus'* (Moscow, 1990), pp. 200–201.
15. "… The holy fool affects insanity or immorality with the goal of attracting abuse from people." (G. Fedotov, p. 200). Compare this with the following remark by one of Erofeev's memoirists: "No, they never courted him, on the contrary, people loved to speak abusively and rudely to him. And he was often regarded as a buffoon.… He was constantly under attack and being offended in some way" (Muraviev, *Teatr*, p. 95).
16. From *The Life of Vasily the Blessed*. See Fedotov, p. 206. Compare with the following note on Erofeev: "Anything perfect or any aspiration to perfection he

suspected of inhumanity. 'Human' for him meant 'imperfect' ..." (Olga Sedakova, *Teatr*, p. 101).

17. From the beginning of the poem, Erofeev's hero is cast out onto the periphery of the ordered and sacred world; for him it is mystically impossible to be in the center. The poem starts with the following paragraph: "Everyone says: the Kremlin, the Kremlin. I hear about it from everyone but have never seen it myself. How many times already (a thousand), drunk or with a hangover, have I gone from North to South, from West to East, from one end to the other, right through systematically and haphazardly—and I never once saw the Kremlin." *Moskva-Petushki*, p. 15.
18. See *Teatr*, p. 98.
19. "The nightmare of the Communist era was the Sorrow which he experienced daily," *Teatr*, p. 102.
20. Nikolai Rubtsov (1936–71) was a leading representative of "village" poetry, with its aesthetization of "tranquillity" and "archaicism." His gloomy, unsociable temper and alcoholic excesses doomed him to live in obscurity, but after his tragic death (at the hands of his mistress), neo-Slavophile critics like Vadim Kozhinov proclaimed his poetry to be the embodiment of the Russian national character.
21. *It's Me, Edichka* is the title of a novel by Eduard Limonov. In fairness to Limonov, it should be pointed out that the Edichka myth has no connection with Venichka, but is rather a provincial, half-French, half-Dnepropetrovsk version of the myth of the superman, in which the shamelessness of the hero grows in proportion to his self-pity and his narcissistic enjoyment of himself, the One and Only. "When Erofeev read a piece of Limonov's prose, he said: 'I can't read this: I can't vomit'" (from the memoirs of Muraviev, *Teatr*, p. 95).
22. *Moskva-Petushki*, pp. 17, 45.
23. Compare Liubchikova, *Teatr*, p. 84.
24. Compare Avdiev, *Teatr*, p. 104. Or there is the following detail: "Even in the greatest heat when all the others had already taken their shirts off, he stayed in his jacket ..." (Liubchikova, *Teatr*, p. 104). "It is difficult to imagine Venia even in the most unbearable heat without his jacket ..." (Avdiev, *Teatr, p.* 104).
25. *Moskva-Petushki*, p. 16.
26. "It seems to me that I would not be mistaken if I said that he loved meekness above all else. Any display of meekness overwhelmed him" (Sedakova, *Teatr*, p. 99). In general women have described Venichka better in their memoirs than men. What men saw as the most important thing in Venia's life were carnival and his writing, though it was precisely these things—carnival and writing—from which, while paying tribute to them, Venia distanced himself inwardly. "A man carrying the idea of tenderness in him"—this expression, coined by his beloved Rozanov, is a fitting description of Venia's being, which women understood best. "The bitterest thing to recall is Venia's gentleness. It remained unclaimed" (Liubchikova, *Teatr, opt. cit.*, p. 83).
27. While telling of Venia's hatred of heroes and feats of courage, Olga Sedakova recalls that "the champion of this hatred became the unfortunate Zoia Kosmodemianskaia" (*Teatr*, p. 101). Zoia Kosmodemianskaia (1923–41) was a female partisan and heroine of World War II, executed by the Nazis. She

became a cult figure of Soviet propaganda.

28. Lines from Aleksandr Pushkin's poem *Recollection.*
29. Venedikt Erofeev, "Vasily Rozanov Through the Eyes of an Eccentric," Almanach, *Zerkala* (Moscow, 1989), p. 44.
30. Venia understood this dialectic perfectly, although in his own account the ultimate stage of synthesis was not entirely in keeping with Hegel: "Let's put it this way: if a quiet man drinks seven hundred and fifty grams, he will become rowdy and joyful. And if he adds seven hundred more? Will he be still rowdier and more joyful? No, he will become quiet again. If not looked at too closely, he will appear to have sobered up" (*Moskva-Petushki*, p. 50).
31. This is Venia's reasoning according to the memoirs of Igor Avdiev, *Teatr*, pp. 112–113. The following is Venia's own monologue: "No one in Russia is afraid of tickling, I am the only person in all of Russia who guffaws when he is tickled. I myself have tickled three women and ten men—not one of them responded with so much as a grimace or a laugh" (Venedikt Erofeev, "Vasily *Rozanov …,"* p. 40).
32. "Venia liked to laugh, and he laughed until he cried. He laughed like a girl, bending over in stitches, clasping his belly button with his elbows" (Igor Adviev, *Teatr*, p. 105).
33. *Moskva-Petushki*, p. 21.
34. *Teatr*, p. 99.
35. *Moskva-Petushki*, p. 122.
36. Avdiev, *Teatr*, p. 105.
37. Though this Russian word has a negative connotation in contemporary usage ("cowardice"), it echoes the first of Christ's blessings in his Sermon on the Mount: "Blessed are the poor in spirit …" (St. Matthew, 5:3).
38. *Moskva-Petushki*, p. 21.
39. Venia was aware of it and drew attention to it himself : "My delicacy does me great harm, it has spoiled my youth.… It is a sort of self-imposed limitation, a kind of prohibition imposed by shame.… I understand many of God's designs, but why he has endowed me with such chastity, I do not know to this day" *Moskva-Petushki, opt. cit.*, pp. 28, 30.
40. Sedakova, *Teatr*, p. 99.
41. "Since you've moved in, none of us have seen you heading for the bathroom even once. Okay, we are not talking about having to go for the big one! But you haven't even been out for a pee … not even a pee!… […] And so I got up and went. Not in order to relieve myself. In order to relieve them" *Moskva-Petushki*, pp. 29–30.
42. Sedakova, *Teatr*, p. 98.
43. *Moskva-Petushki, opt. cit.*, p. 43.
44. "Venedikt used to refer to his own child by the word 'infant'—and so this became a habit" (from the memoirs of Lidiia Liubchikova, *Teatr*, p. 81).
45. See Muraviev's playful introduction to *Moskva-Petushki.* Counter-irony here refers to something which was already used before Erofeev—by Kozma Prutkov, Alexei K. Tolstoy, Shchedrin in his late works, and Igor Severianin: "It is the same old Russian irony distorted into an all-Russian absurdity, as they say.… But

through this distortion, it completely forfeits its political coloring and the denunciatory power of the true believers" (*Moskva-Petushki*, p. 8). This definition is perhaps a little obscure, but the term is self-explanatory even without it.

46. *Moskva-Petushki*, p. 25.
47. Cited in *Teatr*, p. 95.
48. "... Sociologists and anthropologists who were interested in the interrelations between myth and ritual have considered them as mutually redundant.... They replicate each other; myth exists on the conceptual level and ritual on the level of action" (Claude Lévi-Strauss, *Structural Anthropology*, p. 232).
49. "So what's the story? Will Nina from room number 13 donate a fuck?" The humor here is based on a pun on the Russian "*Dai ebat*" meaning "give a fuck," but which as "Daian Eban" evokes the names of two popular Israeli politicians of the time (*Moskva-Petushki*, p. 33).
50. *Moskva-Petushki*, p. 30. "If someone had asked me in what century Venia would have been most comfortable, I would have said: at the end of the eighteenth century!... Venia felt such an affinity with Karamzin, Fonvizin and Derzhavin!" (Avdiev, *Teatr, p.* 115).
51. Mikhail Bakhtin, *Tvorchestvo Fransua Rable i narodnaia kul'tura srednevekov'ia i Renessansa.* (Moscow, 1965), pp. 344–346, 350, 389, and others.
52. Galina Erofeeva, *Teatr*, p. 89.
53. Sedakova, *Teatr*, p. 101.
54. Venedikt Erofeev, *"Vasily Rozanov ...,"* in *Zerkala*, p. 33.
55. *Moskva-Petushki*, p. 97.
56. M. Bakhtin, *Tvorchestvo Fransua Rable*, p. 352. "In sum, the common noun 'pantagruel,'" concludes Bakhtin, "is linked to the mouth, the throat, to drinking and to disease, which is to the entire grotesque set." Ibid.
57. This is the judgment of Andrei Zorin, in his article "A Landmark," in which he writes: "The poet, Oleg Chukhontsev, who was in contact with Mikhail Mikhailovich in the last years of his life, recounted to me how the eminent scholar read Erofeev's poem with delight and even compared it to *Dead Souls*. The ending of *Moskva-Petushki*, however, did not suit Bakhtin at all, for he saw 'entropy' in it" (*Teatr*, p. 121).
58. Venia's relationship to what was then considered the carnivalization of literature is evident in his appraisal of *The Master and Margarita*: "He did not take to Bulgakov at all, he hated *Master and Margarita* so much that he used to shake. Many wrote that there was a link between him and this book, but he himself used to say: '... I haven't even read *The Master*, I couldn't get past page fifteen!'" (Muraviev, *Teatr*, p. 93).
59. *Teatr*, p. 121.
60. *Spekh* means labor, feats and generally all forms of rushing. "Amid the noise and rushing of the folk ..." [*Sred' narodnogo shuma i spekha*] is the beginning of a poem by Osip Mandel'shtam (1937).
61. Here are merely some of the poetic images of the coming entropy, characteristic of the late nineteenth and early twentieth centuries: "I understood everything: the earth had long grown cold and extinct ..." (Afanasii Fet); "The world was deserted.... The Earth had grown cold...." (Ivan Bunin); "O, if you

knew, friends, the cold and darkness of the days to come" (Alexander Blok); "Everything will perish. It will come down to nothing. And the one who moves life, will burn out the last ray of light over the darkness of the planets" (Vladimir Mayakovsky).

62. The Second Epistle of Peter, 3: 5–7, 12.
63. About Erofeev's habit of reclining, see Liubchikova and Avdiev, *Teatr*, pp. 82, 85, 104. About his slippers, see Liubchikova, *Teatr*, pp. 80, 81. Venia went everywhere in slippers, though he, probably, did not have a robe. "… I don't wear a dressing gown even at home; but I wear slippers even outside …" *Moskva-Petushki*, p. 116.
64. See in *Teatr*, Frolova, p. 74; Liubchikova, p. 80; Erofeeva, p. 87; Avdiev, p. 104.
65. "Those parts of the body are accentuated where there is either an opening onto the outside world, or where the world enters the body, or where it protrudes from it, or where the body protrudes into the world, that is, the emphasis is on openings, protuberances, on all kinds of growths and warts: a gaping mouth, genitals, breasts, the phallus, a fat stomach, the nose" (M. M. Bakhtin, *Tvorchestvo Fransua Rable,…* pp. 31–32).
66. Ibid., p. 343.
67. "Base avarice has been the driving force of civilization from its beginnings to the present day; enrichment, and again nothing but enrichment, and a third time nothing but enrichment; the enrichment not of society as a whole, but of the single miserable individual—this was its only determining goal. If then in the depths of society, science continually developed and periods of the highest blossoming of art recurred, it is only because without this all the achievements of our age in the realm of the accumulation of riches would have been impossible" (F. Engels, "Proiskhozhdenie sem'i, chastnoi sobstvennosti i gosudarstva," in K. Marx and F. Engels, *Sochineniia,* 2d ed. [Moscow, 1961], vol. 21, p. 176). According to Engels's reasoning, greed was base so long as it served the interests of single individuals. But in the future, greed will work towards the well-being of the whole of society.
68. Mikhail Bakhtin, *Tvorchestvo Fransua Rable …,* p. 29.
69. Ibid., p. 10.
70. *Moskva-Petushki,* p. 30.
71. On 24 October 1998, on his sixtieth birthday, a monument to Erofeev was erected on the Kursky railway station in central Moscow from which he used to depart for Petushki, a little town where a monument to his beloved "a girl with a long plait" was erected on the same day. Venia has proved to be the first representative of late Soviet generations honored with a monument (even a double one) that confirms the mythological status of his personality.
72. Ibid., pp. 18–19.
73. Nikolai Berdiaev. *Istoki i smysl russkogo kommunizma* (Paris, 1955), p. 35.
74. Ibid., p. 34.
75. Liza is the heroine of Nikolai Karamzin's popular story "Poor Liza" (1792)—the masterpiece of Russian sentimentalism.
76. "Vasily Rozanov …," p. 32.

Conclusion

On the Place of Postmodernism in Postmodernity

Mikhail Epstein

1. Removing the Quotation Marks

Venedikt Erofeev is the first but certainly not the sole manifestation of the new sentimentality. At the end of the 1980s and particularly at the beginning of the 1990s, Erofeev's "sentimental aesthetics" became a major influence on Russian literature. Sergei Gandlevsky, one of the leading poets of his generation, has defined this trend as "a critical sentimentalism," holding the middle ground between two extremes, a lofty and detached metarealism that ignores contemporary life, and conceptualism, which is deliberately reductionist, ridiculing all stilted ideals and models of discourse. "Situated between two polar opposites, it [critical sentimentalism] borrows as needed from its more resolute neighbours, transforming their extremes in its own fashion: it diminishes the arrogance of the righteous poetry and curtails the excesses of the ironic poetry. Such a method of poetic perception of the world is more dramatic than the other two because its aesthetics is subject to minimal regulation; it has no ground except that of feeling, mind, and taste."[1] These principles define not only Gandlevsky's own poetry but the skeptical and sentimental "hangover poetics," which pulls the rug out from under not only the haughty sober person but the haughty drunk as well—a practice introduced into the latest Russian literature by Venedikt Erofeev.

It is significant that the conceptualist artists, who represent the most radical Russian version of postmodernism, have turned out to be most susceptible to the aesthetics of sentimentality. As early as the second half of the 1980s, Dmitry Prigov, the leader of the Moscow conceptualists, called for a change of direction toward a "new sincerity." Turning away from strict conceptualist schemas, which parodied models of Soviet ideology, the new movement was to strive for a lyrical assimilation of these dead layers of being and consciousness. This sincerity is *new* because it presupposes the death of the traditional sincerity, in which the inspired poet identified with his hero. However, at the same time, this *new sincerity* transcends the pointed alienation, the impersonalism, the quotedness proper to conceptualism. The new sincerity belongs to a post-quotation art, to a new, "shimmering aesthetics" (Dmitry Prigov's term), born of the mutual relation established between the voice of the author and the quoted material. "Taking the place of the conceptual, a shimmering relationship between the author and text has developed, in which it is very hard to define (not only for the reader but for the author, too) the degree of sincerity in the immersion into the text and the purity and distance of the withdrawal from it."[2] This "scintillating" aesthetics, reminiscent of the glimmering irony-as-seriousness present in the work of Erofeev ("trans-irony"), leads us into the sphere of "trans-lyricism," which is foreign to both modernism and postmodernism. This "post-postmodern" neo-sentimental aesthetics is defined not by the sincerity of the author or the quotedness of his style, but by the mutual interaction of the two. What is characteristic is the elusive border of their difference, which allows even the most sincere utterance to be perceived as a subtly quoted imitation, while a commonplace quotation may sound like a piercingly lyrical confession.

Here, for example, is the conceptualist Timur Kibirov, the most popular poet of the 1990s, addressing another famous conceptualist, Lev Rubinshtein, with the following words:

> I may be only a common wog,[3]
> you, forgive me, are a Jew!
> Why are we crying unseemly
> Over our Russia?

...
A vehicle stands on the bridge,
And the vehicle has no wheels.
Lev Semyonich! Be a man
Don't shirk tears!
...
In the dark turquoise sky
A quiet angel has flown by.
Have you managed to forget, Lyova,
What it is that he was singing?
...
Overshadowed by the foliage,
You and I do not seem big.
But we will be saved together
By Beauty, for Beauty's sake.
By Goodness and Truth, Lyova,
By the tears of Gethsemane,
By the crimson moistness of nuptials,
By the water turned to wine!
...
We are specks of evil dust,
But the soul is tepid-warm!
It is Easter, Lev Semyonych, Easter!
Lyova, unfurl your wings!
....
In God's Kingdom, oh Lyova,
In that Kingdom which cometh,
You incoherent Non-Christian,
I contest, we'll all come alive![4]

It would appear that conceptualism should exclude the serious usage of words such as "soul," "tear," "angel," "beauty," "truth," and "the Kingdom of Heaven" in their primary meaning. But here, at the very peak of conceptualism and, as it were, at the exit from it, suddenly these same words are being written again, some even with capital letters, which even the nineteenth century found overly pompous and old-fashioned. Having become haughty and stiff through centuries of traditional, official usage, these words have now been purified by being kept out of circulation. After going through a period of radical deadening and carnivalesque derision, they are now returning to a transcendental transparency and lightness, as if they were not of this world.

Some of the expressions in Kibirov's text—such as "we cry unseemly," "the soul is tepid-warm," "beauty will save us"[5]—are already conscious of their own banality and triteness. Nevertheless, they offer themselves as if they were both the first words ever encountered and the *last remaining* words, which essentially cannot be replaced by anything else. Any attempts to find substitutes for these words, in order to express the same meaning in a more original, subtle, or figurative manner would be perceived as an even more glaring banality and pretentiousness. The quotationality of these words is so obvious that they can no longer be reduced to irony but presuppose further lyrical assimilation. For conceptualism, quotationality is something that needs to be asserted over and over again. For postconceptualism, quotationality is the initial axiom, grounding all subsequent lyrical hypotheses. If conceptualism enacted the way in which the most important, lofty words had been turned into clichés, then the radical courage of postconceptualism is to be found in the way it takes up these same clichéd words and uses them in their literal meaning, which has by now split into two: into a "dead" meaning and a "born-again" meaning. Lyrical sincerity and sentimentality die out in these clichéd words, in order that death be trampled by death, so to speak.

This is the courage to which the poet exhorts his addressee: "Lev Semyonych! Be a man—do not shirk tears!" The courage of restraint is perceived as a form of cowardice, as fear in the face of banality: it gives way to the courage of impulsiveness, to the lyricism of banality. There is banality, there is the consciousness (*soznanie*) of this banality, there is the banality of this consciousness and there is, finally, the intentional consciousness (*soznatel'nost'*) of banality itself as a means of its transcendence. Kibirov sums it up as follows: "Don't run from banality, don't fight it face to face (that always produces the most tragicomic results). Attack from the rear; dig in where language, consciousness, and life have long been considered completely under the control of banality, where attack is least expected. (...) In this, it seems to me, is the purpose and duty of contemporary poetry."[6]

Kibirov's postconceptualism, with its "tepid soul," "quiet angel" and "the Kingdom of Heaven," is the next stage of development of Erofeev's trans-irony. It is the phase in which words, having been turned inside-out by carnival, reclaim their primary meaning: but this primary meaning is already detached, otherworldly, virtual. Trans-sentimentality is sentimentality after the death of sentimentality. It has passed through all the circles of carnival, irony and black humor, in order to become aware of its own banality, accepting it as an inevitability and as the source of a new lyricism.

It now becomes clear that all the "banal" concepts have not simply been undermined and replaced: they have gone through a profound metamorphosis and are now returning from another direction, under the sign of "trans." This applies not only to Erofeev's "trans-irony" and Prigov's "trans-lyricism." It also applies to something that could be called "trans-utopianism." This is the rebirth of utopia after its own death, after its subjection to postmodernism's severe skepticism, relativism, and its anti- or postutopian consciousness. Here is what several Moscow artists and art scholars of the postconceptual wave have said about the subject: "It is crucial that the problem of the universal be raised as a contemporary issue. I understand that it is a utopia. It is done completely consciously, yes, utopia is dead, so long live utopia. Utopia endows the individual with a more significant and a wider horizon" (Viktor Miziano). "The future of contemporary art is in the will to utopia, in the breakthrough into reality through a membrane of quotations, it is in sincerity and pathos" (Anatoly Osmolovsky).[7] The subject here is the resurrection of utopia after the death of utopia, no longer as a social project with claims to transforming the world, but as a new intensity of life experience and a broader horizon for the individual. Trans-utopianism, trans-pathos are projections of the same "lyrical" need, which transcended its own negation in postmodernism.

In considering the names that might possibly be used to designate the new era following postmodernism, one finds that the prefix "trans" stands out in a special way. The last third of the twentieth century developed under the sign of "post," which signaled the demise of such concepts of modernity as "truth" and "objectivity," "soul" and "subjectivity," "utopia" and "ideality," "primary origin" and "originality," "sincerity" and "sentimentality." All of these concepts are now being reborn in the form of "trans-subjectivity," "trans-idealism," "trans-utopianism," "trans-originality," "trans-lyricism," "trans-sentimentality," etc. This kind of lyricism, however, does not surge forth spontaneously from the soul; this idealism does not proudly soar above the material world; this utopianism is unlike the one at the beginning of the twentieth century, which aggressively sought to reconstruct the society. It is an "as if" lyricism, an "as if" idealism, an "as if" utopianism, aware of its own failures, insubstantiality, and secondariness. Nevertheless, these "trans" phenomena seek to come to self-expression in the form of repetition. Paradoxically as it may sound, it is precisely through repetition that they reclaim their primacy and authenticity. Tired gestures, which are no longer automatized, as in the poetics of postmodernism, are replete with their own lyricism. In repetition, in quotation, there is a naturalness, a simplicity, an inevitability that is lacking in a primary act, born of effort and with claims to revelation.

As a rule, the destiny of originality is to be turned into imitation and cliché, allowing the cliché itself to be perceived as a simple and unforced movement of the soul, a new sincerity. Over time, postmodernism itself may be perceived as an initial and inadequate reaction to this aesthetics of repetition, whose surprising emergence seemed to demand a full anaesthetization and automatization of feelings. Gradually, as repetition and citationality turn into habit, they will become the foundation for a new lyric poetry, whose journey has its beginning and not its end in ironic estrangement.

Umberto Eco has remarked that in the postmodern era even the language of feelings has lost its "innocence " and requires the use of quotation marks. The word "love" has been repeated so often that an educated person of our time is loathe to say simply to his beloved "I love you," without adding "I love you, as so-and-so has said …," quoting a poet or thinker of his own choice.[8] The "I love" in inverted commas represents a more differentiated feeling, more ironic, more indirectly seductive than a simple "I love"—a feeling that cannot be even expressed with a particular word but only with quotation marks. However, if these quotation marks were to be framed by another set of quotation marks, and these in turn by another, and yet another, then this increased complexity would not be echoed by the feeling. """"""I Love"""""" designates nothing but love for inverted commas. In fact, Eco's example already implies a doubling of quotation marks because the statement "I love you madly" is allegedly taken from Barbara Cartland, a prolific author of pulp fiction. In the mouth of a super-erudite and self-reflexive postmodern lover such a declaration: "As Barbara Cartland would put it, I love you madly," implies a double irony, as a quote from somebody who would have cited Barbara Cartland. This is how, along graded steps of reflexivity, in the absence of any support and repercussion of feelings, postmodernism's self-quoting art continued to move.

If at the early stage of postmodernism even the language of feelings was subjected to the use of quotation marks, then at present quotation marks have penetrated the word so deeply that, even without quotation marks, it bears the imprint of all its former usages. The word contains secondariness within itself, which is an imperative condition for the freshness of its repetition to be felt against the background of these former usages. When the word "I love" is uttered under these conditions, it means: yes, this is how Dante or Maupassant might have expressed it, but in the present case it is I who am saying it, and I have no other word with which to utter what is designated by it. Thus the trans-quotational word contains the presumption of guilt and an implicit act of apology—confessing its own citationality, the trans-quotational word at the same time underlines its absoluteness, its non-substitutability, its singularity. It is an affirmation of "I love," although the same "I love" might have been uttered by Pushkin, Tolstoy, and Mayakovsky. The postmodern utterance of "I love" was masked by citationality as a *loophole* for meaning, in which the subject of language could shield himself from its literal meaning and its responsible consequences. At the present time, citationality, by contrast, serves as a *trigger* of meaning: the repetition is underlined in order to cross out banality. The word consists of a double layer—the quoted and the trans-quotational, which is uttered for the first time, here and now, thus opening the way for a new polysemy.

While the polysemy of postmodernism consisted of a multiplicity of levels of reflection, play, and representation, of quotation marks being superimposed on quotation marks, the polysemy of the era of "trans" is of a higher order. It represents the movement of meaning in two directions at once: both the application and removal of quotation marks. The same word may sound like """""""I love"""""""" and I Love!!! Like """""""Kingdom of Heaven"""""""" and Kingdom of Heaven! The two dimensions of the text are inseparable: the *disquotation* issues from the depths of quotation marks, just as resurrection issues from the depths of death.

2. Postmodernism as the Beginning of Postmodernity

How can we define the place of postmodernism in the linear progression of world history? In the first place, we must distinguish between two heterogeneous terms that have been used to designate the "modern":

1. *Modernity* (or, in Russian terminology, *Novoe vremia* [New Times]) denotes a relatively long epoch of world history, beginning with the end of the Middle Ages and lasting approximately half a millennium, that is, beginning with the Renaissance and continuing until the middle of the twentieth century.
2. *Modernism* is a relatively short cultural period, coming at the end of the era of modernity and lasting approximately half a century, from the end of the nineteenth century until the 1950s and 1960s, depending on the version one follows.

Modernism does not merely end the era of modernity, it accentuates all its contradictions. In the first instance, it deepens the gulf between European individualism at its extreme limit of self-reflexivity and particularization, and the alienating, impersonal tendencies in culture and society (the development of mass society, totalitarian government, atomic and electronic technologies, the theoretical discovery of the unconscious and so on). Hence the theme of alienation, the unprecedented pessimism and the neo-mythologies of modernist art, in which individuality at its extreme limit is revealed as but a manifestation of the impersonal principles that are its antithesis. The explosion of these contradictions, accentuated by modernism, has taken humanity out of the domain of modernity as such, into the era commonly called postmodern.[9]

Just as the "modern" can be subdivided into two periods, a long one of modernity and a shorter one of modernism, so too may an analogous division be appropriate for the "postmodern." If not, it seems impossible to understand what the postmodern follows in the wake of—modernity or modernism. We are dealing here with two differently charged meanings of the prefix "post."

1. The "post" in "postmodernity," correlated with modernity, refers to a long epoch, at the beginning of which we find ourselves living today.
2. The "post" in "postmodernism," correlated with modernism, refers to the initial period of entry into that larger epoch of postmodernity.

If the two large eras—modernity and postmodernity—mirror each other, then it is logical that the end of the one and the beginning of the other will also mirror each other. In other words, *modernism is the concluding period of the epoch of modernity, while postmodernism is the first period of the epoch of postmodernity.*

This epoch of postmodernity, which had its inception in the very recent past, in the middle of the twentieth century, could last for several centuries. In this sense, it would mirror the epoch of modernity, which it has succeeded. Postmodernism, on the other hand, has so far lasted for but a short time, spanning only one or two generations. It may even be the case that postmodernism, like most such cultural complexes, will have an even shorter life span than the primary phenomenon against which it reacted, in this case modernism. Postmodernism, in fact, found things "ready-made": it arose after the problems and contradictions posed by modernism had been fully expressed. Its job was to solve them.

The fundamental thrust of postmodernism's solution was toward a new impersonalism, the use of the unconscious and superconscious, which are reminiscent of the medieval mentality. This was accompanied by fragmentariness, dispersion, eclecticism, irony with respect to the absolute (which appears under various names: "totality," "canon," "center," "logocentrism," "metaphysics," etc.). In other words, postmodernism works against two major postulates, that of the individual and the absolute, whose tortuous dividedness gave rise to the inexorably tragic sense of modernism, combining extreme optimism and extreme pessimism.

The man of modernity is embodied in Goethe's Faust, Dostoevsky's Raskolnikov and Nietzsche's Zarathustra. He aims for the absolute and tries to encompass it with his own personality. The collapse of this aspiration marked the end of the entire epoch of modernity. Modernism, with all its diverse philosophical and artistic schools —symbolism, expressionism, futurism, cubism, dadaism, suprematism, constructivism, surrealism, psychoanalysis—enacted the inability of the individual to encompass and subjugate the trans-individual, which assailed it from all sides, including from within itself. Diagnosing this condition could be expressed pessimistically, as in Kafka, or optimistically, as in Mayakovsky—as the terror of alienation or the ecstasy of collectivism. But in either case, it marked the end of modernity. Beyond it loomed the epoch of postmodernity, which Nikolai Berdiaev called a "new Middle Ages," by analogy with the premodern age. For Berdiaev, this signaled "the end of humanism, individualism, the formal liberalism of the culture of modernity."[10]

In its critique of modernity and all its accompanying categories, such as "subject" and "object," "individuality" and "reality," "author" and "history," postmodernism does indeed begin with a quasi-medieval, trans-personal, and anonymous perception of the world, even if it is not centered on God or the absolute but instead projected onto "alterity" as a measure of independently interactive factors. From this perspective, the principle of individuality is merely an illusory effect of impersonal mechanisms that act in and on us:

language, the unconscious, molecular, genetic, social and economic structures. The absolute is but an illusion of semiotic practices, a stylistic ploy, a projection of strivings for power that emanate from any discursive act and that begin with the inarticulate mumblings of the child demanding its mother's breast. The postmodern critique dethrones the absolute and the individual as two Western myths, formulated in the Middle Ages and modernity respectively. In keeping with this, there is a debunking both of the masks of individuality (authorship, originality, freedom) and of the absolute (the transcendental, truth, reality).

At this stage it is easy to suspend the contradictions and traumas that defined the modernist consciousness. A kind of medieval anonymity begins to dominate, but without the medieval faith in the absolute: instead there is a kind of game, but one in which the will of the players is unclear; all that is clear is the infinity of the toys of the game—signs, quotations, informational codes. According to Michel Foucault, postmodern writing "has merely transposed the empirical characteristics of an author to a transcendental anonymity. The extremely visible signs of the author's empirical activity are effaced to allow the play, in parallel or opposition, of religious and critical modes of characterization.... [T]he author has disappeared; God and man died a common death."[11] If modernism is a mixture of the agony of dying and the euphoria of hope, then postmodernism is the poetics of a successfully completed death and the play of posthumous masks (necropoetics). The tragedy of the division between the individual and the absolute, between the individual and society, and between consciousness and reality, becomes as impossible as the avant-garde utopia and ecstasy of overcoming that division. What kind of alienation is possible for a theory (postmodern) that does not accept anything as one's "own" and "originary"? There is nothing left to become alienated from. The cause of tragedy has thus disappeared, just as has the possibility of utopia. Quotationality instead of self-expression, simulation instead of truth, the play with signs instead of the reflection of reality, difference instead of contradiction: such is the post-individual, post-tragic, post-utopian world, fascinated by its own secondariness, its propensity to bring everything to completion, to use everything as material for the ultimate and infinite game.

Now is the time to remind ourselves of the radical finitude of even this ultimate of utopias called postmodernism. It is time to temporalize it, that is, to place it within the context of a history that ironically continues to advance. What will come after this "post" and what kind of regenerative meaning lies in the very gesture of inevitable repetition? What is the constructive meaning of deconstruction? What will be born from this feast of death and what will be resurrected from that which dies? It is these "proto" and "trans" phenomena—as signs of birth and resurrection—that will mark the long epoch of *postmodernity*, which is ahead and which comes *after* postmodernism.

Our current challenge is to demarcate two related historical concepts, Postmodernism and postmodernity, whose complex borders are being defined in our own time. Postmodernism, as we have seen, is part of a much larger historical formation, which we have called postmodernity. We have been able to account for only two or three initial decades of postmodernity (beginning with the 1960s or 1970s). We have taken stock not of postmodernity as a whole, but only of its initial, most declarative and critically minded stage: that of postmodernism. The concepts we have associated with the next stage of postmodernity coming *after postmodernism*—such as "shimmering aesthetics," "new sentimentality," "new utopianism," "subjunctive modality"—will, we trust, be helpful in understanding the long, many-century era that lies before us. What does all this mean: to live at the close of postmodernism but only at the threshold of postmodernity? What is postmodernity as far as it is irreducible to postmodernism? Living precisely in this smallest of intervals between postmodernism and some next stage of postmodernity we bear the responsibility for the meaning of this crucial moment.

Notes

1. Sergei Gandlevsky, "Absolution from Grief," in *Lichnoe delo No.— Literaturno-khudozhestvennyi al'manakh* [Personal Matter No.—A Literary and Artistic Almanach] (Moscow, 1991), p. 231.
2. Dmitry Prigov, "What More Is There to Say?", in *Third Wave: The New Russian Poetry,* ed. Kent Johnson and Stephen Ashby (Ann Arbor, Mich., 1992), p. 102.
3. "*Chechmek*"—"wog"—a colloquial, contemptuous or ironic name for a representative of the Eastern national minorities in Russia.
4. Timur Kibirov, "To Lev Rubinshtein" (1987–88), in Timur Kibirov, *Santimenty: Vosem' Knig* [Sentiments: Eight Books] (Belgorod, 1994), pp. 172, 179, 181. In the fifth stanza there is a reference to Biblical episodes: the miracle Christ performed at the wedding in Cana of transforming water into wine, and Christ's suffering before death in the garden of Gethsemane. It is significant that Kibirov's most comprehensive book of poetry is entitled *Sentiments,* and contains such "soul-touching" genres as the idyll, the elegy, and the epistle.
5. A purely conceptualist play on a literary cliché from Dostoevsky's *Idiot* ("beauty shall save the world") is given in Dmitry Prigov's poem *The Beautiful Oka Is Flowing …* (more on the latter in my book *Paradoksy novizny* [Paradoxes of Innovation], pp. 153–4). This poem is well known to Kibirov, who proceeds, in his postconceptualist manner, to take out of inverted commas the image which Prigov has placed in inverted commas. Thus the meaning of Dostoevsky's utterance is restored on the level of trans-irony.
6. *Third Way: The New Russian Poetry,*, p. 224.
7. *Kto est kto v sovremennom iskusstve Moskvy* [Who Is Who in Contemporary Moscow Art] (Moscow, 1993), without pagination. Viktor Miziano (b. 1957) is an art critic and curator of the Center of Contemporary Art in Moscow. He is the editor-in-chief of the *Khudozhestvennyi zhurnal* [Art Journal]. Anatoly Osmolovsky (b. 1969) is the leader of the anti-conceptualist movements of E.T.I. and the Revolutionary Rival Program NETSEZUDIK.
8. See Umberto Eco, Postscript to *The Name of the Rose* (New York, 1984).
9. Since all three correlative terms have exhausted their meaning in relation to the large historical epochs (antiquity, the Middle Ages, modernity), the introduction of the term "postmodernity" ("post-new" times) is a necessary if not entirely felicitous innovation. The alternative term—"newest times"—which was current in Soviet historiography, assumed a smoother transition between "modernity" ("the new times") and the "newest" times. It also differentiated the two epochs according to a simple degree of "newness" rather than in terms of a change of paradigm.
10. Nikolai Berdiaev, *Novoe srednevekov'e. Razmyshleniia o sud'be Rossii i Evropy* [The New Middle Ages: Reflections on the Destiny of Russia and Europe] (Moscow, 1990), p. 24.
11. Michel Foucault, "What Is an Author?", in *Critical Theory Since 1965*, ed. Hazard Adams and Leroy Searle (Tallahassee, Fla., 1990), p. 141.

Select Bibliography

Compiled by Mikhail Epstein and Slobodanka Vladiv-Glover

This list is not intended to be a full bibliography but rather a selective guide into the literature, art, and theory of Russian postmodernism.

Our thanks to Dr. June Pachuta Farris, bibliographer for Slavic, Eastern European, and Eurasian Studies at the University of Chicago Library, for assisting with the updated bibliography on Russian postmodernism.

Adamovich, Marina, and Inc. M. E. Sharpe. "Judith with the Head of Holofernes: Pseudoclassicism in Russian Literature during the 1990s." *Russian Studies In Literature* 38, no. 1 (December 1, 2001): pp. 85–99. *American Bibliography of Slavic and East European Studies,* EBSCO*host* (accessed September 2, 2014).

Alagova, Tamara S. *Tatyana Tolstaya in the Turmoil of Postmodernism.* N.p., 2000. [PhD dissertation]

Allen, Sharon Lubkemann. *EccentriCities: Writing in the margins of Modernism: St. Petersburg to Rio de Janeiro.* Manchester, UK: Manchester University Press, 2013. Durham Modern Languages Series; Variation: Durham Modern Languages Series.

Anufriev, Sergei, Leiderman, Iury, Peppershtein, Pavel. *Inspektion "Medhermeneutik." Auf sechs Büchern. Iz shesti knig.* Kunsthalle Düsseldorf, 1990. Parallel texts in Russian and German.

Aptekman, Marina. "Kabbalah, Judeo-Masonic Myth, and Post-Soviet Literary Discourse: From Political Tool to Virtual Parody." *Russian Review* 65, no. 4 (October 1, 2006): pp. 657–81. *American Bibliography of Slavic and East European Studies,* EBSCO*host* (accessed September 2, 2014).

Barker, Adele Marie. *Consuming Russia: Popular Culture, Sex, and Society since Gorbachev.* Durham, NC: Duke University Press, 2005.

Between Spring and Summer: Soviet Conceptual Art in the Era of Late Communism. Tacoma, WA, and Boston, MA: Tacoma Art Museum and The Institute of Contemporary Art, 1990. Includes contributions from Joseph Bakshtein, Ilya Kabakov, Dmitri Prigov, Alexander Rappaport, Mikhail Ryklin, Margarita Tupitsyn, Peter Wollen.

Bodin, Per-Arne, Stockholms universitet, and (Publisher). *Language, Canonization and Holy Foolishness: Studies in Postsoviet Russian Culture and the Orthodox Tradition.* Stockholm: Stockholm University, DotGain AB, 2009. Stockholm Slavic Studies, 38; Variation: Stockholm Slavic Studies, 38.

Burak, A. L. (Aleksandr L'vovich). *"The Other" in Translation: A Case for Comparative Translation Studies.* Bloomington, IN: Slavica, 2013.

Cheauré, Elisabeth, and Germany Deutsche Gesellschaft für Osteuropakunde. Fachgruppe Slawistik. Tagung. 10th: 1998: Berlin. *Kunstmarkt und Kanonbildung: Tendenzen in der russischen Kultur heute.* Berlin: Berlin Verlag A. Spitz, 2000. Osteuropaforschung, Bd. 42; Variation: Osteuropaforschung, Bd. 42.

Chernetsky, Vitaly. *Mapping Postcommunist Cultures: Russia and Ukraine in the Context of Globalization.* Montreal: McGill-Queen's University Press, 2007.

Chuprinin, Sergei, and Liv Bliss. "A Concept-Structured Life." *Russian Studies In Literature* 41, no. 4 (September 1, 2005): pp. 66–95. *American Bibliography of Slavic and East European Studies,* EBSCO*host* (accessed September 2, 2014).

Contemporary Russian Poetry: A Bilingual Anthology. Selected, with an introduction, translations, and notes by Gerald S. Smith. Bloomington & Indianapolis: Indiana University Press, 1993. Includes Dmitry Prigov, Aleksei Tsvetkov, Elena Shvarts, Ivan Zhdanov, Olga Sedakova, Aleksandr Eremenko, Aleksei Parshchikov, and others.

Cullum, Charles. "Rebels, Conspirators, and Parrots, Oh My! Lacanian Paranoia and Obsession in Three Postmodern Novels." *Critique: Studies in Contemporary Fiction* 52 no. 1 (2011): 1–16. *MLA International Bibliography,* EBSCO*host* (accessed September 2, 2014).

Czaplicka, John Ruble. *Cities after the Fall of Communism: Reshaping Cultural Landscapes and European Identity / Gelazis, Nida M.* Washington, DC: Woodrow Wilson Center Press; Baltimore: Johns Hopkins University Press, 2009.

Dobrenko, Evgeny. "Utopias of Return: Notes on (Post-)Soviet Culture and Its Frustrated (Post-)modernisation." *Studies in East European Thought* 63, no. 2 (June 2011): pp. 159–71. *Academic Search Complete,* EBSCO*host* (accessed September 2, 2014).

The End of the 20th Century, a special issue of *Slovo/Word,* no. 16 (New York, 1995). Includes contributions from Mikhail Epstein, Alexander Genis, Boris Paramonov, Petr Vail.

Endquote: Sots-Art Literature and Soviet Grand Style. Edited by Marina Balina, Nancy Condee, and Evgeny Dobrenko. Evanston, IL: Northwestern University Press, 2000.

Epstein, Mikhail. *Filosofiia vozmozhnogo.* S.–Peterburg, Aleteia, 2001

Epstein, Mikhail. *Ironia Ideala. Paradoksy russkoi literatury.* Moscow: Novoe literaturnoe obozrenie, 2015

Epstein, Mikhail. *Paradoksy novizny. O literaturnom razvitii XIX–XX vekov.* M.: Sovetskii pisatel', 1988.

Epstein, Mikhail. *Postmodern v Rossii. Literatura i teoriia.* M., izd. R. Elinina, 2000.

Epstein, Mikhail. *Postmodern v russkoi literature.* M.: Vysshaia shkola, 2005.

Epstein, Mikhail. *Religia posle ateizma: Novye vozmozhnosti teologii.* Moscow: AST-Press, 2013.

Epstein, Mikhail. *After the Future: The Paradoxes of Postmodernism and Contemporary Russian Culture.* Introduction and translation by Anesa Miller-Pogacar. Amherst: University of Massachusetts Press, 1995.

Epstein, Mikhail. *Cries in the New Wilderness: From the Files of the Moscow Institute of Atheism.* Translated and introduction by Eve Adler. Philadelphia: Paul Dry Books, 2002.

Epstein, Mikhail, Alexander Genis, and Slobodanka Vladiv-Glover. *Russian Postmodernism: New Perspectives on Post-Soviet Culture.* New York and Oxford: Berghahn Books, 1999.

Erjavec, Ales, ed. *Postmodernism and the Postsocialist Condition: Politicized Art under Late Socialism.* Berkeley: University of California Press, 2003.

Fadeicheva, Marianna A. "The Ideology and Discourse Practices of 'Us-ism' in Contemporary Russia." *Russian Social Science Review* 50, no. 5 (September 2009): p. 4. *MasterFILE Premier,* EBSCO*host* (accessed September 2, 2014).

Fadeicheva, Marianna A. "The Ideology and Discourse Practices of 'Us-ism' in Contemporary Russia." *Russian Politics & Law* 45, no. 3 (May 2007): pp. 62–73. *Academic Search Complete,* EBSCO*host* (accessed September 2, 2014).

Genis, Alexander. *Ivan Petrovich umer. Stat'i i rassledovaniia.* M., NLO, 1999.

Genis, Alexander. *Vavilonskaia bashnia. Iskusstvo nastoiashchego vremeni. Esse.* Moscow: Nezavisimaia gazeta, 1997.

Givens, John. "Russian Literature in the First Decade of the Twenty-First Century." *Russian Studies in Literature* 48, no. 1 (Winter 2011): pp. 3–7. *Academic Search Complete,* EBSCO*host* (accessed September 2, 2014).

Givens, John. "The Old and the New in Contemporary Russian Literature." *Russian Studies in Literature* 48, no. 4 (Fall 2012): pp. 3–6. *Academic Search Complete,* EBSCO*host* (accessed September 2, 2014).

Goricheva, Tatiana. *Pravoslavie i postmodernism.* Leningrad, izd. LGU, 1991.

Gresta, Eugenia. *Language as a Fact: The "New Poetry" of Nekrasov, Rubinshtein, Aizenberg, Tsvetkov.* N.p., 2001.

Groys, Boris. *The Total Art of Stalinism: Avant-Garde, Aesthetic Dictatorship, and Beyond.* Translated by Charles Rougle. Princeton, NJ: Princeton University Press, 1992.

Groys, Boris. *Utopiia i obmen.* Moscow: Znak, 1993.

Harrington, Alexandra Katherine, and University of Nottingham. *Reassessing the Poetry of Anna Akhmatova: From Modernism to Postmodernism.* Nottingham: University of Nottingham, 2002.

Ivanova, Natal'ia. "That Elusive Contemporaneity." *Russian Studies in Literature* 45, no. 3 (Summer 2009): pp. 30–52. *Academic Search Complete,* EBSCO*host* (accessed September 2, 2014).

Ivanova, Natal'ia. "The Life and Death of the Simulacrum in Russia." *Russian Studies in Literature* 38, no. 2 (Spring 2002): p. 41. *Academic Search Complete,* EBSCO*host* (accessed September 2, 2014).

Johnson, Emily D. "Twenty Years after the Collapse of the Soviet Union: Russian and East European Literature Today." *World Literature Today* no. 6 (2011): p. 32. *Literature Resource Center,* EBSCO*host* (accessed September 2, 2014).

Kabakov, Ilya. *On the "Total Installation."* Bonn: Cantz Verlag, 1995. Parallel texts in German, Russian, and English.

Kabakov, Ilya. *Installations 1983–1995.* Paris: Editions du Centre national Georges Pompidou, 1995.

Kabakov, Ilya. *Zhizn' mukh. Das Leben der Fliegen. Life of Flies.* Kolnischer Kunstverein. Edition Cantz, 1992. Texts in German, Russian, and English.

Kandinskaia, Natalia. *Postmoderne Groteske—groteske Postmoderne? Eine Analyse von vier Inszenierungen des Gegenwartstheaters.* Berlin: Lit, 2012. Resonanzen, Bd. 4; Variation: Resonanzen, Bd. 4.

Kangaspuro, Markku. *Russia: More Different than Most.* Helsinki: Kikimora, 2000. Series B, 16; Variation: Kikimora Publications; Series B, 16.

Kershaw, Baz. *Beyond Postmodernism / Ley, Graham.* Abingdon, Oxfordshire: Routledge, 2008. *Contemporary Theatre Review* 18, no. 3 (August 2008); Variation: Contemporary Theatre Review, v. 18, Pt. 3.

Kholmogorova O.V. *Sots-Art.* Moscow: Galart, 1994.

Kolesnikoff, Nina. *Russian Postmodernist Metafiction.* Bern and New York: Peter Lang, 2011.

Komar, Vitaly, and Alexander Melamid. *Death Poems: Manifesto of Eclecti-*

cism. New York: Galerie Barbara Farber, 1988. Texts in Russian and English.

Konets veka. Special Issue of the journalSlovo/Word. New York. 16, 1995. P. Vail, S. Volkov, A. Genis, B. Paramonov, M. Epstein.

Kulturpalast. Neue Moskauer Poesie & Aktionskunst, Herausgegeben und ins Deutsche übvertragen von Günter Hirt & Sascha Wonders. Wuppertal (Germany): S Press Tonbandverlag, 1984.

Kundrotas, Gintautas. "The Expression of Intonation in Lithuanian and Russian Postmodern Literature (J. Vanauskaite's Novel *The Castle of Sleeping Butterflies* and A. Sorokin's *Ball*). (English)." *Artistic Text: Understanding, Analysis, Interpretation / Meninis Tekstas* 6, no. 2 (February 2008): p. 193. *Publisher Provided Full Text Searching File,* EBSCO*host* (accessed September 2, 2014).

Kuritsyn, Viacheslav. *Kniga o russkom postmodernizme.* Sverdlovsk, 1991.

Kuritsyn, Viacheslav. *Russkii literaturnyi postmodernism.* M., OGI, 2000.

Laruelle, Marlène. *Russian Eurasianism: An Ideology of Empire.* Washington, DC: Woodrow Wilson Center Press; Baltimore: Johns Hopkins University Press, 2008.

Late Soviet Culture: From Perestroika to Novostroika. Edited by Thomas Lahusen. Translated by Gene Kuperman. Durham, NC, and London: Duke University Press, 1993.

Leving, Iurii. *Marketing Literature and Posthumous Legacies: The Symbolic Capital of Leonid Andreev and Vladimir Nabokov / White, Frederick H., 1970– ; Author.* Lanham, MD: Lexington Books, 2013.

Lipovetsky, Mark. *Russian Postmodernist Fiction: Dialogue with Chaos.* Edited by Eliot Borenstein. Armonk, NJ: M. E. Sharpe, 1999.

Lipovetsky, Mark. *Russkii postmodernizm. Ocherki istoricheskoi poetiki. Ekaterinburg: Ural'skii gosudarstvennyi pedagogicheskii universitet,* 1977.

Lipovetsky, Mark, Alexander Etkind, and Liv Bliss. "The Salamander's Return: The Soviet Catastrophe and the Post-Soviet Novel." *Russian Studies in Literature* 46, no. 4 (September 1, 2010): pp. 6–48. *American Bibliography of Slavic and East European Studies,* EBSCO*host* (accessed September 2, 2014).

Lipovetsky, Mark, and Birgit Beumers. "Reality Performance: Documentary Trends in Post-Soviet Russian Theatre." *Contemporary Theatre Review* 18, no. 3 (August 2008): pp. 293–306. *Humanities International Complete,* EBSCO*host* (accessed September 2, 2014).

MacFadyen, David. "Russian Post-modernism: New Perspectives on Post-Soviet Culture." *World Literature Today,* no. 1 (2001): *Literature Resource Center,* EBSCO*host* (accessed September 2, 2014).

Man'kovskaia N. B. "Parizh so zmeiami" (Vvedenie v estetiku postmodernizma). M.: IFRAN, 1995.

Moderne russische Poesie seit 1966, Eine Anthologie. Herausgegeben von Walter Thümler, Berlin: Oberbaum Verlag, 1990.

Modernizm i postmodernizm v russkoi literature i kul'ture. Edited by P. Pesonen, J. Heinonen, and G. V. Obatnin. *Slavica Helsingiensia 16.* Studia Russica Helsingiensia et Tartuensia V. Helsinki: Helsinki University Press, 1996.

Mozur, Joseph. "Viktor Pelevin: Post-Sovism, Buddhism, and Pulp Fiction." *World Literature Today* no. 2 (2002): p. 58. *Literature Resource Center,* EBSCO*host* (accessed September 2, 2014).

Nekanonicheskii klassik: Dmitrii Aleksandrovich Prigov, 1940–2007. Sbornik statei I materialov. Sost. Evgenii Dobrenko. M.: NLO, 2010.

The New Freedoms: Contemporary Russian and American Poetry: Poems, Essays, and Translations. Edited by Edward Foster and Vadim Mesyats. Hoboken, NJ: Stevens Institute of Technology, 1994. Among Russian poets and critics are N. Iskrenko, A. Dragomoshchenko, V. Kuritsyn, and M. Lipovetsky.

Noordenbos, Boris. "Ironic Imperialism: How Russian Patriots Are Reclaiming Postmodernism." *Studies in East European Thought* 63, no. 2 (June 2011): pp. 147–58. *Academic Search Complete,* EBSCO*host* (accessed September 2, 2014).

Novostroika. London: The Institute of Contemporary Arts Documents, 8. 1989. Interviews, critical essays, poems.

Oden, Thomas C. *Two Worlds: Notes on the Death of Modernity in America and Russia.* Downers Grove, IL: InterVarsity Press, 1992.

Olshanskaya, Natalia. "De-coding Intertextuality in Classic and Postmodern Russian Narratives." *Translation and Interpreting Studies: The Journal of the American Translation and Interpreting Studies Association* 6, no. 1 (March 2011): pp. 87–102.*Communication and Mass Media Complete,* EBSCO*host* (accessed September 2, 2014).

Ostashevsky, Eugene. "Dmitry Golynko's "Sashenka." *Gulf Coast: A Journal of Literature and Fine Arts* 20, no. 2 (Fall 2008): pp. 186–88. *Humanities International Complete,* EBSCO*host* (accessed September 2, 2014).

Ottovordemgentschenfelde, Natalia. *Jurodstvo: Eine Studie zur Phänomenologie und Typologie des Narren in Christo: Jurodivyj in der postmodernen russischen Kunst; Venedikt Erofeev Die Reise nach Petuski; Aktionismus Aleksandr Breners und Oleg Kuliks.* Frankfurt am Main [u.a.]: Lang, 2004. Print. Europäische Hochschulschriften; Reihe 18, Vergleichende Literaturwissenschaft, 111; Variation: Europäische Hochschulschriften; Reihe 18, Vergleichende Literaturwissenschaft, 111.

Parts, Lyudmila. *The Russian Twentieth-Century Short Story: A Critical Companion.* Brighton, MA: Academic Studies Press, 2010. Cultural

Revolutions: Russia in the Twentieth Century; Variation: Cultural Revolutions.

Poet-metarealisty: A. Eremenko. I. Zhdanov. A. Parshchikov. Moscow: MK-Periodika, 2002

Poety-kontseptualisty: D. A. Prigov. L. Rubishtein. T. Kibirov. Moscow: MK-Periodika, 2002.

Popovic, Dunja. "'Pravo na TRUP': Power, Discourse, and the Body in the Poetry of Nina Iskrenko." *Russian Review* 64, no. 4 (October 2005): pp. 628–41. *Academic Search Complete,* EBSCO*host* (accessed September 2, 2014).

Possamai, Donatella. *Che cos'è il postmodernismo russo? cinque percorsi interpretativi.* Padova: Il poligrafo, 2000. Saggi, 17; Variation: Saggi (Poligrafo (Firm), 17.

Postcommunism and the Body Politics. Edited by Ellen Berry. New York and London: New York University Press, 1995. Includes contributions by Mikhail Epstein, Masha Gessen, Helena Goscilo, Beth Holmgren, Harriet Murav et al.

Post-Soviet Art and Architecture. London and New York: Academy Editions (distributed in the United States by St. Martin's Press), 1994.

Postmodernisty o postkul'ture. Interv'iu s sovremennymi pisateliami i kritikami. Compl. introd. and ed. Serafima Roll. Moscow: LIA R. Elinina, 1996.

Postmodernizm. Entsiklopediia. Preface by Mozheiko M. A., Gritsanov A. A. Minsk: Interpressservis, 2001.

Rampton, Vanessa, and Muireann Maguire. "Russia on Edge: Centre and Periphery in Contemporary Russian Culture." *Studies in East European Thought* 63, no. 2 (June 1, 2011): pp. 87–94. *American Bibliography of Slavic and East European Studies,* EBSCO*host* (accessed September 2, 2014).

Ratcliff, Carter. *Komar and Melamid.* New York: Abbeville Press Publishers, 1988.

Re-entering the Sign: Articulating New Russian Culture. Edited by Ellen Berry and Anesa Miller-Pogacar. Ann Arbor: University of Michigan Press, 1995. Includes contributions from Mikhail Epstein, Viktor Erofeev, Georgy Gachev, Ilya Kabakov, Viacheslav Kuritsyn.

Russian Critical Theory and Postmodernism: The Theoretical Writings of Mikhail Epstein. Forum, *Slavic and East European Journal* 39, no. 3 (Fall 1995).

Ryklin, Mikhail. *Terrologiki.* Tartu-Moscow: Eidos (Ad Marginem series), 1992.

Skoropanova I. S. *Russkaia postmodernistskaia literatura.* 4 ed. Rev. M: Flinta: auka, 2002.

Slovar' terminov moskovskoi kontseptual'noi shkoly. Sost. Andrei Monastyrskii, Moscow: Ad Marginem, 1999.

Smith, Terry (Terry E.). *Contemporary Art: World Currents.* Upper Saddle River, NJ: Prentice Hall, 2011.

Sogrin, V. V. "Three Historical Subcultures in Post-Soviet Russia." *Russian Social Science Review* 55, no. 4 (July 2014): pp. 71. *MasterFILE Premier,* EBSCO*host* (accessed September 2, 2014).

Soulimani, Elvira (1976–) Auteur Nivière, Université de Nancy II, and Organisme de soutenance. *La prose russe contemporaine des années 1990 l'impact du postmodernisme sur la formation d'une écriture nouvelle.* S.l.: s.n., 2006.

Spieker, Sven. *Figures of Memory and Forgetting in Andrej Bitov's Prose: Postmodernism and the Quest for History.* Frankfurt am Main and New York: P. Lang, 1996.

Symposium on Russian Postmodernism (with Jerome McGann, Marjorie Perloff, Mikhail Epstein et al.). *Postmodern Culture* 3, no. 2 (University of North Carolina, January 1993).

Tekstura: Russian Essays on Visual Culture. Edited and translated by Alla Efimova and Lev Manovich, with preface by Stephen Bann. Chicago and London: Chicago University Press, 1993.

Terts Abram (Andrei Siniavsky). Chto takoe sotsialisticheskii realizm, in his book *Fantasticheskie povesti.* New York, 1967.

Third Wave: The New Russian Poetry. Edited by Kent Johnson and Stephen M. Ashby. Ann Arbor: University of Michigan Press, 1992. Includes theoretical introduction and afterword, poems and programmatic statements of twenty-one poets: V. Aristov, I. Kutik, A.Turkin, O. Sedakova, N. Kondakova, I. Zhdanov, P. Peppershtein, Yu. Arabov, V. Krivulin, and others.

Tulchinskii, G. L., and Stephen D. Shenfield. "The Word and Body of Postmodernism: From the Phenomenology of Irresponsibility to the Metaphysics of Freedom." *Russian Studies in Philosophy* 42, no. 3 (December 1, 2003): pp. 5–35. *American Bibliography of Slavic and East European Studies,* EBSCO*host* (accessed September 2, 2014).

Tupicyn, Viktor. *The Museological Unconscious: Communal (Post)modernism in Russia.* Cambridge, MA [u.a.]: MIT Press, 2009.

Tupitsyn Viktor. *Kommunal'nyi (post)modernizm: russkoe iskusstvo vtoroi poloviny XX veka.* M.: Ad Marginem, 1998.

Vaessens, Thomas, and editor. *Reconsidering the Postmodern: European Literature beyond Relativism / Dijk, Yra Van,; 1970– ; Editor.* Amsterdam: Amsterdam University Press, 2011.

Vassilieva, Ekaterina. *Das Motiv des Straflagers in der russischen Literatur der Postmoderne: Dovlatov, Sorokin, Makanin.* München: Sagner, 2014. Arbeiten und Texte zur Slavistik; Bd. 97; Variation: Arbeiten und Texte zur Slavistik, Bd. 97.

Vladiv-Glover, Slobodanka. "Excremental Poetics of Russian Postmodernism: The Phenomenon of Vladimir Sorokin," *Russian Modernism and Postmodernism.* Special Issue of *Soviet and Post-Soviet Review* 28, no. 3 (2001) [2002]: pp. 313–32.

Vladiv-Glover, Slobodanka. "A Genealogy of Post-Communist Ethics: Reappraisals of the Past and Future in Russian Postmodern Culture." AULLA Refereed Conference Proceedings (online): www.aulla.com.au/Proceedings%202007.html.

Vladiv-Glover, Slobodanka. "Popular Culture vs. Mass Culture: Tolstoy's *What Is Art?* As a Test for the Russian *detektiv.*" *Russian Modernism and Postmodernism.* Special Issue of *Soviet and Post-Soviet Review* 28, no. 3 (2001) [2002]: pp. 291–311.

Vladiv-Glover, Slobodanka. "Postmodernism in Eastern Europe after WWII: Yugoslav, Polish and Russian Literatures." *Australian Slavonic and East European Studies* 5, no. 2 (1991): pp. 123–44.

Vladiv-Glover, Slobodanka. "The Representation of the Object as Other in Modernism/Postmodernism: A Psychoanalytic Perspective." *Facta Universitatis Series in Philosophy, Sociology, Psychology and History* 10, no. 2, 2011, pp. 173–94.

Vladiv-Glover, Slobodanka. "The Russian Anti-Oedipus: Petrushevskaya's *Three Girls in Blue,*" *Australian Slavonic and East European Studies* 12, no. 2 (1998): 31–56.

Vladiv-Glover, Slobodanka. "Russian Postmodernism: A Cultural Diagnosis of Postmodern Russia." *Georgetown Journal of International Affairs* 8, no. 1 (Winter/Spring 2007): pp. 87–94).

Vladiv-Glover, Slobodanka. "Vladimir Sorokin's Post-Avant-Garde Prose and Kant's Analytic of the Sublime." In *Poetik der Metadiskursivitat: Zum postmodernen Prosa-, Film- und Dramenwerk Sorokins.* Edited by Dagmar Burkhart. "Die Welt der Slawen," Sammelbande-Sborniki, Band 6 (Munchen: Otto Sagner), pp. 21–35.

Vladiv-Glover, Slobodanka. "What Is Classical and Non-Classical Knowledge?" *Studies in East European Thought* (Springer), Special Issue on *Merab Mamardashvili* 58 (2006): pp. 205–38.

Vladiv-Glover, Slobodanka, ed. Post-Communist Popular Culture and the *detektiv* Novel Genre. Special Issue of *Soviet and Post-Soviet Review* 29, no. 3 (2002): pp. 221–311. Editor of Special Issue,

Vladiv-Glover, Slobodanka, ed. *Russian Modernism and Postmodernism.* Special Issue of *Soviet and Post-Soviet Review* 28, no. 3 (2001) [2002]: pp. 232–362. Guest editor of Special Issue.

Vladiv-Glover, Slobodanka M., ed. *Russian Postmodernism: New Perspectives on Post-Soviet Culture.* New York: Berghahn Books, 1999. 528 pp. With Mikhail Epstein and Alexander Genis.

Index of Names

Index of Subjects